Investigating the Social World

THE PINE FORGE PRESS SERIES IN RESEARCH METHODS AND STATISTICS

edited by Kathleen S. Crittenden

Through its unique modular format, this Series offers an unmatched flexibility and coherence for undergraduate methods and statistics teaching. The two "core" volumes, one in methods and one in statistics, address the primary concerns of undergraduate courses, but in less detail than found in existing texts. The smaller "satellite" volumes in the Series can either supplement these core books, giving instructors the emphasis and coverage best suited for their course and students, or be used in more advanced, specialized courses.

Investigating the Social World: The Process and Practice of Research, Second Edition, *by Russell K. Schutt*

Study Guide for Investigating the Social World: The Process and Practice of Research, Second Edition, *by Matthew Archibald and Russell K. Schutt*

A Guide to Field Research *by Carol A. Bailey*

Designing Surveys: A Guide to Decisions and Procedures *by Ronald Czaya and Johnny Blair*

Social Statistics for a Diverse Society *by Cnava Frankfort-Nachmias*

Regression: A Primer *by Paul Allison*

Experimental Design and the Analysis of Variance *by Robert Leik*

How Sampling Works *by Richard Maisel and Caroline Hodges Persell*

Forthcoming

Problem Solving in Crime and Criminal Justice Research *by Leslie Kennedy and David Forde*

Program Evaluation *by George McCall*

Other Pine Forge Press Titles of Related Interest

Adventures in Social Research: Data Analysis Using SPSS® for Windows® 95, Versions 7.5, 8.0, or Higher, *by Earl Babbie and Fred Halley*

Exploring Social Issues Using SPSS® for Windows® 95, Versions 7.5, 8.0, or Higher, *by John Boli, Joseph Healey, Earl Babbie, and Fred Halley*

Adventures in Criminal Justice Research: Data Analysis Using SPSS® for Windows® 95, Versions 7.5, 8.0, or Higher, *by George Dowdall, Kim Logio, Earl Babbie, and Fred Halley*

Investigating the Social World

THE PROCESS AND PRACTICE OF RESEARCH

Second Edition

Russell K. Schutt

University of Massachusetts, Boston

Pine Forge Press

Thousand Oaks, California ■ London ■ New Delhi

For information, address:

Pine Forge Press
A Sage Publications Company
2455 Teller Road
Thousand Oaks, California 91320
(805) 499-4224
e-mail: sales@pfp.sagepub.com

Sage Publications Ltd.
6 Bonhill Street
London EC2A 4PU
United Kingdom
http://www.sagepub.co.uk

Sage Publications India Pvt. Ltd.
M-32 Marker
Greater Kailash I
New Delhi 110 048 India

Production Manager: Windy Just
Production: Anne Draus, Scratchgravel Publishing Services
Manuscript Editor: Rebecca Smith
Interior Designer: Lisa Mirski Devenish
Illustrators: Thomas Linneman, Greg Draus
Typesetter: Scratchgravel Publishing Services
Cover Designer: Paula Shuhert and Graham Metcalfe

Printed in the United States of America

99 00 01 02 03 10 9 8 7 6 5 4 3 2

Library of Congress Cataloging-in-Publication Data
Schutt, Russell K.
    Investigating the social world : the process and practice of
research / by Russell K. Schutt. — 2nd ed.
        p.   cm. — (The Pine Forge Press series in research methods and
statistics)
    Includes bibliographical references and index.
    ISBN 0-7619-8561-1 (pbk. : acid-free paper)
    1. Social problems—Research. 2. Social sciences—Research. I.
Title. II. Series
HN29.S34   1999
361.1'072—ddc21   98-25312
                                                   CIP

About the Author

Russell K. Schutt, Ph.D., is Professor and Chair of Sociology at the University of Massachusetts, Boston. He is the co-author of *Organization in a Changing Environment, Responding to the Homeless: Policy and Practice* and numerous journal articles on organizations, law, homelessness, mental health, and teaching research methods. His research experience includes federally funded studies of housing options for severely mentally ill persons, surveys of homeless persons and service personnel, multimethod investigations of organizational change, and secondary analyses of juvenile justice decision making and craft union practices.

About the Publisher

Pine Forge Press is a new educational publisher, dedicated to publishing innovative books and software throughout the social sciences. On this and any other of our publications, we welcome your comments and suggestions.

Please call or write us at:

Pine Forge Press
A Sage Publications Company
2455 Teller Road
Newbury Park, CA 91320
(805) 499-4224
E-mail: sales@pfp.sagepub.com

Visit our World Wide Web site, your direct link to a multitude of on-line resources:

http://www.pineforge.com

to Julia Ellen Schutt

Brief Contents

Detailed Contents

Series Foreword

The Pine Forge Press Series in Research Methods and Statistics, consisting of core books in methods and statistics and a series of satellite volumes on specialized topics, allows instructors the flexibility to create a customized curriculum. Authors of volumes in the series are seasoned researchers and teachers as well as acknowledged experts in their fields. In addition to the core texts in research methods and statistics, the series offers more compact volumes focusing on sampling, field research methods, survey research, experimental design, and analysis of variance; books on regression and evaluation research are forthcoming.

In this second edition of *Investigating the Social World,* Russell K. Schutt provides a basic introduction to research methods. As in the first edition, his treatment is marked by his extensive and varied research experience, his conviction that sociological research must be applicable to real-world problems, and his belief that any serious research problem should be investigated by multiple methods. Principles and techniques are presented through examination of actual studies.

This second edition has been simplified and streamlined while retaining the real-world, contemporary research flavor. It features a new chapter on historical and comparative methods; improved treatment of causality; updated and expanded research illustrations; new appendices on searching the research literature, using the World Wide Web, and QSR NUD*IST in research; and new exercises using SPSS and the World Wide Web. The disk packaged with the volume contains interactive instructional exercises involving examples from crime and deviance, social inequalities, health and human services, and politics and social change. This text is comprehensive enough to stand alone as a methods text but streamlined enough to be used with selected satellite volumes.

Kathleen S. Crittenden
Series Editor

Preface

Imagine that you take a wrong turn and find your progress blocked by a gate like the one in the photo below. A sign informs you that no one can proceed unless granted access by a guard or by a resident of this "gated community." After you spend the extra time trying to find another route, you might well have some questions—for example, Why would people want to live in a gated community? Doesn't it somehow change social life for the people who live there? And how does it impact social life in the larger society?

Often we answer questions like these based on our previous experiences, deeply held beliefs, perhaps even prior college courses. Sometimes we ask friends for their opinions, or we just accept the opinions of a politician or a newspaper editor. Edward Blakely and Mary Gail Snyder (1997)

Photo by Gregory Draus

ALL VEHICLES
IN LEFT LANE
MUST STOP TO
BE IDENTIFIED
BEFORE
PROCEEDING

did much more to answer their questions about gated communities. They identified gated communities throughout the United States by searching computerized newspaper archives. They obtained statistical data on several gated communities. They held group discussions with gated community residents, and they interviewed local officials. In addition, they mailed a survey to community association board members. They investigated many gated communities, many aspects of gated communities, and they conducted their investigation from many angles.

Teaching and Learning Goals

If you are intrigued by the idea of pursuing answers to questions the way Blakely and Snyder did, you can understand the importance and the fun of investigating the social world. One purpose of this book is to introduce you to social science research methods like the ones Blakely and Snyder used and show how they improve on everyday methods of answering questions. Each chapter integrates instruction in research methods with investigation of interesting aspects of the social world: homelessness, domestic violence, substance abuse, crime, work organizations, stress, gender roles, democratization, and others.

Another purpose of this book is to give you the critical skills necessary to evaluate research. Just "doing research" is not enough. Just reading that some conclusions are "based on a research study" is not sufficient. For example, a newspaper reporter's story of a gated community outside Chicago quoted several individuals who lived and worked in the community and concluded that "people see their gate as a sensible civic improvement, not a symbolic betrayal of the social contract" (Grunwald, 1997:A8). But Blakely and Snyder studied many of these communities, not just one. They identified different types of gated communities and compared their current operations and histories. They reviewed the crime rates in several communities. They hired a facilitator to lead group discussions with residents of gated communities, public officials, realtors, and developers. They mailed a survey to governing boards of 7,000 community associations. Blakely and Snyder concluded in part that gated community residents believe that they are safer than residents of other local communities but that the crime rate actually changed little after gating.

Can we place more confidence in Blakely and Snyder's conclusions than we can in the reporter's story? Research studies that use a variety of methods and tap a variety of opinions are likely to yield more credible results than will casual inquiries with a narrower focus. However, even research studies have their strengths and weaknesses. So throughout this book, you will learn what questions to ask when critiquing a research study and how to evaluate the answers. You can begin to sharpen your critical teeth on the illustrative studies throughout the book.

Another goal of this book is to train you to actually do research. Substantive examples will help you see how methods are used in practice. Exercises at the end of each chapter give you ways to try different methods alone or in a group. A checklist for research proposals will chart a course for you when you plan more ambitious studies. But research methods cannot be learned by rote and applied mechanically. Thus you will learn what each major research technique adds to—and subtracts from—the utility of others and why multiple methods are often preferable. You will come to appreciate why the results of particular research studies must always be interpreted within the context of prior research and through the lens of social theory.

Organization of the Book

The way the book is organized reflects my beliefs in making research methods interesting, teaching students how to critique research, and viewing specific research techniques as parts of an integrated research strategy. The first two chapters introduce the why and how of research in general. Chapter 1 shows how research has helped us understand the problem of homelessness. Chapter 2 illustrates the basic stages of research with a series of experiments on the police response to domestic violence. The next three chapters discuss how to evaluate the way researchers design their measures, draw their samples, and justify their statements about causal connections.

Chapters 6, 7, 8, and 9 present the four most important methods of data collection: experiments, surveys, qualitative methods (including participant observation, intensive interviews, and focus groups), and historical and comparative research. The substantive studies in these chapters show how these methods have been used to improve our understanding of psychological well-being, political democratization, and social interactions at work, in nursing homes, and on school playgrounds.

Chapter 10 then examines studies that combine methods or that examine social processes within larger contexts. You will consider how to supplement survey research with qualitative data and with experimental features. You will see how much more can be learned when social researchers take account of social structure, results of multiple studies, and biological influences.

The last two chapters of the book focus on what to do with data after the data have been collected. Basic statistical methods are presented in Chapter 11, using for examples an analysis of voting patterns in the 1996 presidential election. Chapter 12 covers the development of research proposals and the reporting of research results.

Distinctive Features of the Second Edition

Innovations in approach, coverage, and organization are further expressed and highlighted by the following special features:

- *Examples of social research as it occurs in real-world settings.* Interesting studies of homelessness, domestic violence, crime, and other pressing social issues have been updated and extended from the first edition. They demonstrate that the exigencies of real life shape the application of research methods. This book also acknowledges the cross-pressures resulting from the conflicting requirements of different methods.

- *A unique "integration and review" chapter.* Chapter 10 shows how multiple methods and multiple studies can enrich our understanding of social processes and compensate for the weakness of particular methods. This special chapter also demonstrates how different steps in the research process, treated as discrete and separate topics in other textbooks, have a reciprocal relationship in real social research settings. It combines insights that were split in the first edition between two chapters.

- *Ethical concerns and ethical decision making.* Every step in the research process raises ethical concerns, so ethics should be treated in tandem with the study of specific methods. You will find ethics introduced in Chapter 2 and reviewed in the context of each method of data collection, data analysis, and reporting.

- *Supplementary books on important topics.* Procedural details often obscure important research concepts and principles. So, unlike other methods textbooks, this one does not try to provide detailed advice on every method. Instructors and students who would like more specific help will find in *The Pine Forge Press Series in Research Methods and Statistics* several supplementary books on such important topics as sampling, survey design, and field research.

- *Useful instructional software.* The enclosed disk has many new lessons designed to reinforce understanding of the key concepts presented in each of the first five chapters, including formulating research questions, identifying variables in hypotheses, specifying levels of measurement, determining units of analysis, and distinguishing longitudinal designs. You should spend enough time with these lessons to become very comfortable with the basic research concepts presented.

- *End-of-chapter exercises.* In addition to individual and group projects, each chapter includes exercises to give you experience in data analysis using SPSS®, the Statistical Package for the Social Sciences. End-of-chapter Web exercises will help you investigate interesting social questions through the Internet.

■ *Aids to effective study.* Lists of main points and key terms provide quick summaries at the end of each chapter. In addition, key terms are highlighted in boldface type when first introduced and defined in the text. Definitions for them are also found in the glossary/index at the end of the book. The instructor's manual includes more exercises that have been especially designed for collaborative group work in and outside of class.

Starting with SPSS

To carry out the SPSS exercises, you must already have SPSS on your computer or you must purchase the *Investigating the Social World* package that includes *SPSS Studentware®* on CD-ROM. The exercises use a subset of the 1996 General Social Survey dataset (included on the disk). This dataset includes many variables on topics such as work, family, gender roles, government institutions, race relations, and politics. Appendix E will get you up and running with SPSS for Windows—and you can then spend as much time as you like exploring characteristics and attitudes of Americans. Just start SPSS on your PC, open the GSS96b3 file (or one of the component subfiles if you're using *SPSS Studentware*), and begin with the first SPSS exercise in Chapter 1.

Acknowledgments

My gratitude and praise first to Steve Rutter, the president of Pine Forge Press. His familiarity with the social sciences and his commitment to their success has made it possible for this project to flourish. He is a scholar/ entrepreneur in the finest sense of both words and a great guy with whom to work. Also contributing vitally to success of the book project were the other exceptional members of the Pine Forge Press team—Paul O'Connell, Sherith Pankratz, Rebecca Smith, Windy Just, Pete Richardson, Jan Sather, and Jean Skeels—and, at Scratchgravel Publishing Services, Anne and Greg Draus.

Series editor Kathleen S. Crittenden helped again at every turn. Her careful readings and detailed comments helped to forestall many potential problems—just as they did when I studied statistics with her years ago. I also am indebted to the social scientists recruited by Steve Rutter to critique this edition, just as with the first. Their praise often sustained me, and their criticisms have surely saved me from unrealized confusions. First edition reviewers were:

Judith Stull, Temple University

Elizabeth Morrissey, Frostburg State University

DeeAnn Wenk, University of Oklahoma

Jack Dison, Arkansas State University

Greg Weiss, Roanoke College

Chandra Muller, University of Texas

Daniel S. Ward, Rice University

Lisa Callahan, Russell Sage College

Robbyn Wacker, University of Northern Colorado

Valerie Schwebach, Rice University

Herbert L. Costner, formerly of University of Washington

Sandra K. Gill, Gettysburg College

Scott Long, Indiana University

G. Nanjundappa, California State University, Fullerton

Barbara Keating, Mankato State University

Gary Goreham, North Dakota State University

Terry Besser, University of Kentucky

Josephine Ruggiero, Providence College

Catherine Berheide, Skidmore College

Bebe Lavin, Kent State University

Second edition reviewers were:

Matthew Archibald, University of Washington

Thomas Linneman, College of William & Mary

Gi-Wook Shin, University of California, Los Angeles

Gary Hytrek, University of California, Los Angeles

Ronald J. McAllister, Elizabethtown College

Janet Ruane, Montclair State University

Kelly Damphousse, Sam Houston State University
Manfred Kuechler, Hunter College (CUNY)
Nasrin Abdolali, Long Island University, C.W. Post
Michael R. Norris, University of Texas, El Paso
Andrew London, Kent State University
Karen Baird, SUNY, Purchase
Lin Huff-Corzine, University of Central Florida
Josephine A. Ruggiero, Providence College
Guang-zhen Wang, Russell Sage College
Debra S. Kelley, Longwood College
Keith Yanner, Central College
Howard Stine, University of Washington
Jay Hertzog, Valdosta State University
Virginia S. Fink, University of Colorado, Colorado Springs

Mary Ann Schwartz, Northeastern Illinois University
Lynda Ames, SUNY, Plattsburgh
Kristen Myers, Northern Illinois University
William J. Swart, The University of Kansas
Shernaaz M. Webster, University of Nevada, Reno
Kelly Moore, Barnard College, Columbia University
Ray Darville, Stephen F. Austin State University
Jana Everett, University of Colorado, Denver
Karin Wilkins, University of Texas, Austin
Jeffrey Prager, University of California, Los Angeles
Stephanie Luce, University of Wisconsin, Madison
Liesl Riddle, University of Texas, Austin

A special note of gratitude again to Herbert L. Costner, who contributed the insights of one of sociology's foremost methodologists. Mildred A. Schwartz's suggestions for the new chapter on historical and comparative methods helped greatly in refining my approach—renewing again my indebtedness to her, which was first incurred when she served as my dissertation advisor. My other former instructors and mentors in research methods and research projects each deserve a share of the praise that the first edition received: Donald Black, Kathleen S. Crittenden, William P. Bridges, Robert A. Dentler, George Farkas, Helen R. Miller, Albert J. Reiss, Jr., T. Paul Schultz, and Stanton Wheeler.

Other chapters and appendices benefited from special contributions by talented graduate students and faculty. Tom Linneman (now at William & Mary) deserves very special recognition. He revised most of the exhibits, contributed an excellent appendix on SPSS, and organized the graduate student team that expanded the disk exercises at the University of Washington. My thanks also to the other UW software team members—Mark Edwards, Lorella Palazzo, and Tim Wadsworth—and to Gary Hytrek and Gi-Wook Shin at UCLA for their good work. Matt Philbin designed the VisualBasic interface for the new software. Matthew Archibald, at the University of Washington, revised the student workbook and the instructor's manual. I also thank Judith Richlin-Klonsky for her assistance in revising the examples in Chapter 8, Sharlene Hesse-Biber for material to illustrate her qualitative analysis software, and Lyn Richards for the same type of illustrations and also for her appendix on QSR NU*DIST.

Several graduate students in Boston made important contributions. Heather Johnson at Northeastern University helped with text editing and developed most of the Web exercises. Chris Gillespie at the University of

Massachusetts, Boston, designed a number of the end-of-chapter SPSS exercises, and Ra'eda Al-Zubi processed many of the editorial changes in the text. Special thanks to Anne Foxx, who typed in many of the editorial changes and also kept our department running in her usual efficient style. The first edition benefited from the comments of Bob Dentler and students in his 1993–1994 graduate research methods class at the University of Massachusetts, Boston. I continue to be indebted to the many students I have had an opportunity to teach and mentor, at both the undergraduate and graduate levels. In many respects, this book could not have been so successful without the ongoing teaching experiences we have shared.

Since this text describes several collegial research studies and draws on several co-authored articles, I must also thank the social scientists and practitioners with whom I have been able to "learn by doing." There are far too many people in this group to credit each one properly, even though I have, with regret, deleted some of those mentioned in the first edition. These collaborators include: Hubert M. Blalock, Jr., James E. Blackwell, Brina Caplan, Herbert L. Costner, Neal Donovan, Kenneth Duckworth, Carol Fabyan, Mary L. Fennell, Floyd J. Fowler, Gerald R. Garrett, Stephen M. Goldfinger, Suzanne Gunston, Linda Jorgensen, Walter E. Penk, E. Sally Rogers, Larry J. Seidman, George S. Tolomiczenko, and Winston M. Turner. My knowledge of research methods and my understanding of the social world continue to benefit from my work with colleagues at the Massachusetts Mental Health Center, Department of Psychiatry, Harvard Medical School. I am grateful for the opportunities they have provided me, as I am to colleagues at the University of Massachusetts, Boston, with whom I have been working on research and teaching projects.

No scholarly book project can succeed without good library resources, and for these I continue to incur a profound debt to the Harvard University library staff and their extraordinary collection. I also have benefited from the resources maintained by the University of Massachusetts, Boston, librarians.

Again, most important, I thank my wife for her love and support and our daughter for all the joy she brings to our lives.

Russell K. Schutt
Lexington, Massachusetts

Investigating the Social World

1 Science, Society, and Social Research

■ ■ ■ ■ The winter of 1997 was not a good season for persons living on the street. In Boston, police found Jack Olson frozen to death on New Year's morning (Kahn, 1997). It had been 4 degrees Fahrenheit that New Year's Eve, and Mr. Olson had celebrated with an all-day vodka binge, followed by a night of drinking Listerine after the liquor stores closed. He had been panhandling and sleeping in shelters or on the streets. He had hoped to bring his two sons to Boston; he had gotten engaged to a woman two weeks previously; he had promised his fiancee that he would get sober. But on the morning of December 31 he started drinking and didn't stop.

Jack Olson was not the only homeless person to die on the streets of Boston that winter. But his death attracted more attention than most, perhaps because he had befriended so many others: "a beautiful person," his fiancee said. "He was a fun-loving, caring person if he was sober," a homeless friend recalled. Perhaps the attention had something to do with Mr. Olson's efforts to change. He had spent many weeks in detox, talked about finding a restaurant job, about making a home for himself and his sons. Perhaps it was because his death seemed so senseless: If only his friends had not left him curled up on a heating grate that night. Perhaps it was just an appealing human interest story for the holidays. In any case, Jack Olson's story soon disappeared from the newspapers. He had become, so to speak, just another statistic.

Does the Jack Olson story sound familiar? Such newspaper stories proliferate when the holiday season approaches, but what do they really tell us about homelessness? Why do people live on the streets? In the rest of this chapter, you will learn how the methods of social science research go beyond stories in the popular media to help us answer questions like these. By the chapter's end, you should know what is "scientific" in social science and appreciate how the methods of science can help us understand the problems of society.

■ ■ ■ ■ Reasoning About the Social World

The story of just one homeless person raises many questions. Take a few minutes to read each of the following questions and jot down your answers. Don't ruminate about the questions or worry about your responses: *This is not a test;* there are no "wrong" answers.

- How would you describe Jack Olson?
- Why do you think Jack Olson died?
- Was Jack Olson typical of the homeless population?
- In general, why do people become homeless?
- How have you learned about homelessness?

Now let's consider the possible answers to some of these questions. The information we have to describe Jack Olson is scant (Kahn, 1997). He had come to Boston from Arizona five years before he died, leaving a cook's job and a broken marriage. He wanted to make a new home for his two sons, but calls back to them in Arizona often ended in disappointment. He was a heavy drinker but also was being treated for manic-depressive illness, according to friends. A staff member of the church where Mr. Olson ate his free meals noted that "Jack had a hard life out there."

Do you have enough information now to understand why Jack Olson died? His fiancee sounded bitter about the possibility that people might have stepped over his body while on their way to New Year's celebrations: "Nobody should be allowed to go out and freeze to death." Should we attribute his death in part to a lack of concern by others? What about the apparent disappointments he suffered when he made calls to Arizona to talk to his sons? Was a feeling of failure in his role as a father a factor in his death? Was the cause of his death all "the sauce" he imbibed? "Alcohol is killing a lot of people out there," a social service worker noted. Or is inadequate treatment for mental illness the issue?

Now can you construct an adequate description of Jack Olson? Can you explain the reason for his death? Or do you feel you need to know more about Mr. Olson, about his friends and the family he grew up in? And how about his experiences with treatment for alcoholism and an apparent manic-depressive disorder? We've attempted to investigate just one person's experiences, and already our investigation is spawning more and more questions.

Questions and Answers About the Social World

When the questions concern not just one person but many people or general social processes, the possible questions and the alternative answers multiply. For example, consider the question of why people become homeless. Responses to a 1987 survey of Nashville residents, summarized in Exhibit 1.1, illustrate the diverse answers that people have (Lee, Jones, & Lewis, 1990). Compare these answers with the opinion you recorded earlier. Was your idea about the causes of homelessness one of the more popular ones?

We cannot avoid asking questions about the actions and attitudes of others. We all try to make sense of the social world, which is a very complex place, and to make sense of our position in it, which we have quite a personal stake in. In fact, the more that you begin to "think like a social scientist," the more questions will come to mind.

But why does each question have so many possible answers? Surely, our perspective plays a role. One person may see a homeless individual as a

Exhibit 1.1   **Popular Beliefs About Why People Become Homeless**

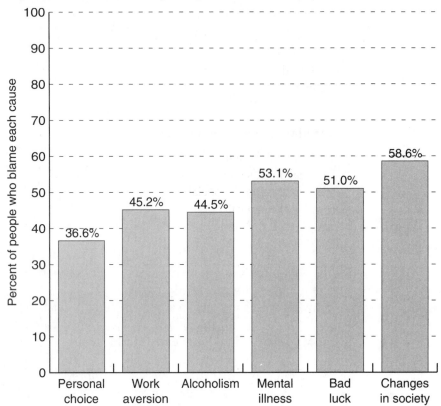

Source: Data from Lee, Jones, & Lewis, 1990:257.

victim of circumstance, and another person may see the same individual as a shiftless bum. When confronted with a homeless individual, one observer may stop to listen, another may recall a news story on street crime, and another may be reminded of her grandfather. Their different orientations will result in different answers to the questions prompted by the same individual or event.

Answers to questions about the social world also vary because what people have "seen" varies. The Nashville survey—by Barrett Lee, Sue Hinze Jones, and David Lewis (1990)—gives some idea of the basis for people's opinions about homelessness: Individuals who had less education and more conservative political beliefs were more likely than others to think that homelessness is a matter of personal choice. Personal contact also made a difference: People who had been panhandled by a homeless person were more likely to think that homelessness is a matter of personal choice.

But those who had had an informal conversation with a homeless person about something other than money were less likely to believe that homelessness is a matter of personal choice. Do these bases for opinions inspire your confidence? Is your opinion about why people become homeless based on direct experience, or is it based on what other people have said or written?

Everyday Errors in Reasoning

People give different answers to questions about the social world for yet another reason: It's simply too easy to make errors in logic, particularly when we are analyzing the social world in which we ourselves are conscious participants. We can call some of these "everyday errors" because they occur so frequently in the nonscientific, unreflective discourse about the social world that we hear on a daily basis.

My favorite example of everyday errors in reasoning comes from a letter to Ann Landers. The letter was written by someone who had just moved with her two cats from the city to a house in the country. In the city she had not let her cats outside and felt guilty about confining them. When they arrived in the country, she threw her back door open. Her two cats cautiously went to the door and looked outside for a while, then returned to the living room and lay down. Her conclusion was that people shouldn't feel guilty about keeping their cats indoors—that even when they have the chance, cats don't really want to play outside.

Do you see this person's errors in reasoning?

- *Overgeneralization.* She observed only two cats, both of which previously were confined indoors.
- *Selective observation or inaccurate observation.* She observed the cats at the outside door only once.
- *Illogical reasoning.* She assumed that others feel guilty about keeping their cats indoors and that cats are motivated by emotions.
- *Resistance to change.* She was quick to conclude that she had no need to change her approach to the cats.

You don't have to be a scientist or use sophisticated research techniques to avoid these four errors in reasoning. If you recognize these errors for what they are and make a conscious effort to avoid them, you can improve your own reasoning. In the process, you will also be implementing the admonishments of your parents (or minister, teacher, or other adviser) to not stereotype people; to avoid jumping to conclusions; to look at the big picture. These are the same errors that the methods of social science are designed to help us avoid.

Overgeneralization

Overgeneralization, an error in reasoning, occurs when we conclude that what we have observed or what we know to be true for some cases is true for all cases. We are always drawing conclusions about people and social processes from our own interactions with them but sometimes forget that our experiences are limited. The social (and natural) world is, after all, a complex place. We have the ability (and inclination) to interact with just a small fraction of the individuals who inhabit the social world, especially in a limited span of time.

Selective or Inaccurate Observation

We also have to avoid **selective observation**—choosing to look only at things that are in line with our preferences or beliefs. When we are inclined to criticize individuals or institutions, it is all too easy to notice their every failing. For example, if we are convinced in advance that all homeless persons are substance abusers, we can find many confirming instances. But what about homeless people like Debbie Allen, who ran away from a home she shared with an alcoholic father and psychotic mother; Charlotte Gentile, a teacher with a bachelor's degree living with two daughters in a shelter after losing her job; and Faith Brinton, who walked out of her rented home with her two daughters to escape an alcoholic and physically abusive husband and ended up in a shelter after her husband stopped paying child support? If we acknowledge only the instances that confirm our predispositions, we are victims of our own selective observation. Exhibit 1.2 depicts the difference between selective observation and overgeneralization.

Exhibit 1.2   **The Difference Between Overgeneralization and Selective Observation**

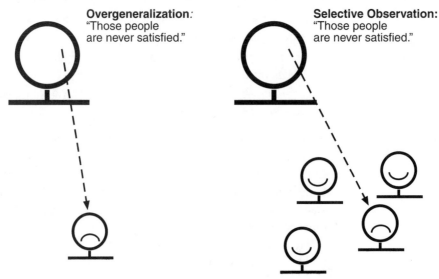

Recent research on cognitive functioning (how the brain works) helps to explain why our feelings so readily shape our perceptions (Seidman, 1997). Emotional responses to external stimuli travel a shorter circuit in the brain than reasoned responses do (see Exhibit 1.3). The result, according to some cognitive scientists, is that "what something reminds us of can be far more important than what it 'is'" (Goleman, 1995:294–295). Our emotions can influence us even before we begin to reason about what we have observed.

Our observations can also be simply inaccurate. If a woman says she is "hungry" and we think she said she is "hunted," we have made an **inaccurate observation.** If we think five persons are standing on a street corner when seven actually are, we have made an inaccurate observation.

Such errors occur often in casual conversation and in everyday observation of the world around us. In fact, our perceptions do not provide a direct window onto the world around us, for what we think we have sensed is not necessarily what we have seen (or heard, smelled, felt, or tasted). Even when our senses are functioning fully, our minds have to interpret what we have sensed (Humphrey, 1992). The optical illusion in Exhibit 1.4, which

Exhibit 1.3   **Anatomy of an Emotional Hijacking**

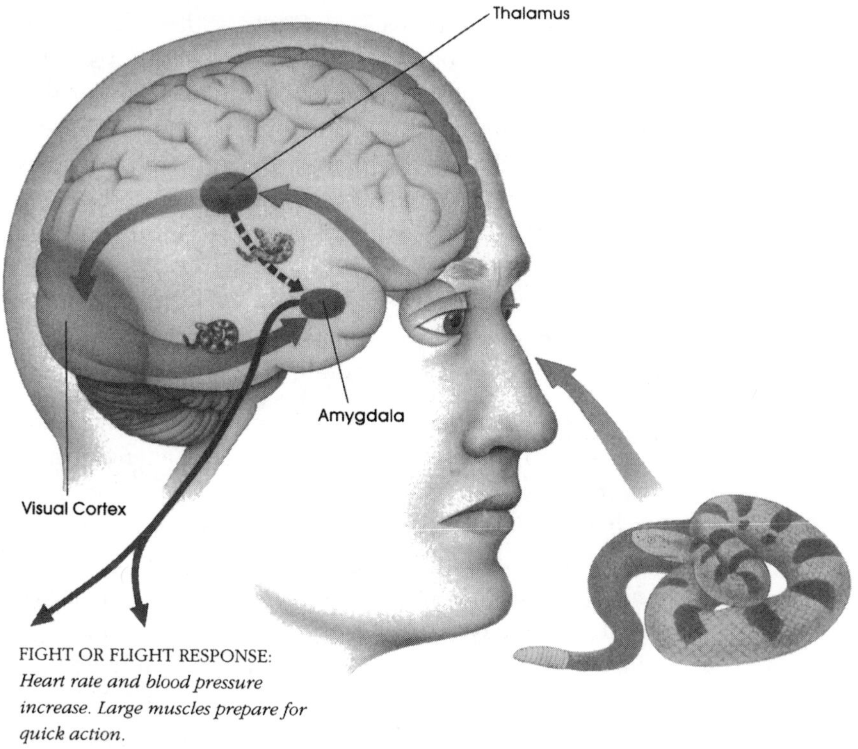

FIGHT OR FLIGHT RESPONSE: *Heart rate and blood pressure increase. Large muscles prepare for quick action.*

Source: Goleman, 1995:19.

Exhibit 1.4   **An Optical Illusion**

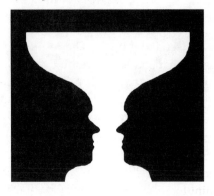

can be viewed as either two faces or a vase, should help you realize that perceptions involve interpretations. Different observers may perceive the same situation differently because they interpret it differently.

Illogical Reasoning

When we prematurely jump to conclusions or argue on the basis of invalid assumptions, we are using **illogical reasoning.** For example, it is not reasonable to propose that homeless individuals don't want to work if evidence indicates that the reason many are unemployed is a shortage of jobs or a tendency for the unemployed to have mental or physical disabilities. On the other hand, an unquestioned assumption that everyone who can work will work is also likely to be misplaced. Of course, logic that seems impeccable to one person can seem twisted to another—the problem usually is reasoning from different assumptions rather than just failing to "think straight."

Resistance to Change

Resistance to change, the reluctance to change our ideas in light of new information, may occur for several reasons:

■ *Ego-based commitments.* We all learn to greet with some skepticism the claims by leaders of companies, schools, agencies, and so on that people in their organization are happy, that revenues are growing, that services are being delivered in the best possible way. We know how tempting it is to make statements about the social world that conform to our own needs rather than to the observable facts. It can also be difficult to admit that we were wrong once we have staked out a position on an issue. For instance, we may want our experiences while volunteering in a shelter for homeless persons to confirm our political stance on homelessness and therefore resist changing our beliefs in response to new experiences.

■ *Excessive devotion to tradition.* Some degree of devotion to tradition is necessary for the predictable functioning of society. Social life can be richer and more meaningful if it is allowed to flow along the paths charted by those who have preceded us. But too much devotion to tradition can stifle adaptation to changing circumstances. When we distort our observations or alter our reasoning so that we can maintain beliefs that "were good enough for my grandfather, so they're good enough for me," we hinder our ability to accept new findings and develop new knowledge. The consequences can be deadly, as residents of Hamburg, Germany, might have realized in 1892 (Freedman, 1991). Until the last part of the 19th century, people believed that cholera, a potentially lethal disease, was due to minute, inanimate, airborne poison particles ("miasmas"). In 1850, English researcher John Snow demonstrated that cholera was, in fact, spread by contaminated water. When a cholera epidemic hit Hamburg in 1892, the authorities did what tradition deemed appropriate: digging up and carting away animal carcasses to prevent the generation of more miasmas. Despite their efforts, thousands died. New York City adopted a new approach based on Snow's discovery, which included boiling drinking water and disinfecting sewage. As a result, the death rate in New York City dropped to a tenth of what the death rate had been in a previous epidemic.

■ *Uncritical agreement with authority.* If we do not have the courage to evaluate critically the ideas of those in positions of authority, we will have little basis for complaint if they exercise their authority over us in ways we don't like. And if we do not allow new discoveries to call our beliefs into question, our understanding of the social world will remain limited. An extreme example of this problem was the refusal of leaders in formerly communist countries to acknowledge the decaying social and environmental fabric of their societies while they encouraged their followers to pay homage to the wisdom of Comrades Mao, Lenin, and Stalin. But we don't have to go so far afield to recognize that people often accept the beliefs of those in positions of authority without question.

Now take just a minute to reexamine the beliefs about homelessness that you recorded earlier. Did you grasp at a simple explanation even though reality is far more complex? Were your beliefs influenced by your own ego and feelings about your similarities to or differences from homeless persons? Are your beliefs perhaps based on stories you've heard about the "hobos" of an earlier era? Did you weigh carefully the opinions of political authorities or just accept or reject those opinions out of hand? Could knowledge of research methods help to improve your own understanding of the social world? Do you see some of the challenges faced by social science?

■ ■ ■ ■ **The Social Scientific Approach**

The **social science** approach to answering questions about the social world is designed to reduce greatly these potential sources of error in everyday reasoning. **Science** relies on logical and systematic methods to answer questions, and it does so in a way that allows others to inspect and evaluate its methods. In the realm of social research, these methods are not so unusual. After all, they involve asking questions, observing social groups, and counting people, which we often do in our everyday lives. However, social scientists develop, refine, apply, and report their understanding of the social world more systematically, or "scientifically," than Joanna Q. Public does:

■ Social science research methods can reduce the likelihood of overgeneralization by using systematic procedures for selecting individuals or groups to study that are representative of the individuals or groups to which we wish to generalize.

■ To avoid illogical reasoning, social researchers use explicit criteria for identifying causes and for determining whether these criteria are met in a particular instance.

■ Social science methods can reduce the risk of selective or inaccurate observation by requiring that we measure and sample phenomena systematically.

■ Because they require that we base our beliefs on evidence that can be examined and critiqued by others, scientific methods lessen the tendency to develop answers about the social world from ego-based commitments, excessive devotion to tradition, and/or unquestioning respect for authority.

> *Science* A set of logical, systematic, documented methods for investigating nature and natural processes; the knowledge produced by these investigations.
>
> *Social science* The use of scientific methods to investigate individuals, societies, and social processes; the knowledge produced by these investigations.

Motives for Social Research

Like you, social scientists read stories about individuals like Jack Olson, observe homeless persons in their everyday lives, and try to make sense of what they see. For most, that's the end of it. But for some social scientists, the problem of homelessness has become a major research focus. The motivations for selecting this particular research focus, as with any social science topic, can be any of the following or some combination:

■ *Policy motivations.* Many social service agencies and elected officials seek better descriptions of the homeless population so they can identify needs and allocate responsibility among agencies that could meet these needs. For example, federal agencies want to identify the scope of health problems among the homeless, and many state and local officials use social research to guide development of their social service budgets. Shelters for homeless persons often use research to learn more about the needs of their clientele. These policy guidance and program management needs have resulted in numerous research projects.

■ *Academic motivations.* The homeless population has been a logical focus for research on issues ranging from influences on physical health to consequences of poverty. For example, sociologists have long been concerned with the impact of different types and levels of social ties on individual behavior and attitudes. Homeless persons, cut off from community-based and other traditional social networks, provide an opportunity to study the effects of social isolation. For psychologists and psychiatrists, the homeless population provides a test case for evaluating the impact of residential and social instability on mental health. Those who study social policy also have sought to determine whether the "deinstitutionalization" of psychiatric patients in the 1960s and 1970s was actually a cause of homelessness in the 1980s and 1990s.

■ *Personal motivations.* Many of those who conduct research on homelessness feel that by doing so they can help to ameliorate the conditions that produce homelessness and thus reduce the suffering of homeless persons. Some social scientists first volunteered in shelters or soup kitchens and only later began to develop a research agenda based on their experiences. Community groups have sought help from social scientists to determine whether shelters for the homeless lower property values or influence the crime rate.

Social Research in Practice

Of course, homelessness did not first appear in the United States in the 1980s. Social historians have described homelessness as far back as colonial times, and the first survey of homeless persons was reported in 1899. But homeless persons became markedly more numerous and visible in the 1980s than they had been at any time since the Great Depression. Social scientists began studying contemporary homelessness in the early 1980s, amassing a substantial body of research findings that have refined knowledge about the problem and shaped social policy (Schutt & Garrett, 1992). These studies fall into the four categories of purposes for social scientific research:

- *Descriptive research.* Defining and describing social phenomena of interest is a part of almost any research investigation, but **descriptive research** was the primary focus of the early studies of homelessness. Some of the central questions were "Who is homeless?" and "What are the needs of homeless persons?" and "How many people are homeless?" Measurement (the topic of Chapter 3) and sampling (Chapter 4) are central concerns in descriptive research.

- *Exploratory research.* **Exploratory research** seeks to find out how people get along in the setting under question, what meanings they give to their actions, and what issues concern them. The goal is to learn "What is going on here?" and to investigate social phenomena without expectations. This purpose is associated with the use of methods that capture large amounts of relatively unstructured information. For example, researchers investigating homelessness in the 1980s were encountering a phenomenon with which they had no direct experience. Thus, an early goal was to find out what it was like to be homeless and how homeless persons made sense of their situation. Exploratory research like this frequently involves qualitative methods, which are the focus of Chapter 8.

- *Explanatory research.* Many consider explanation the premier goal of any science. **Explanatory research** seeks to identify causes and effects of social phenomena, to predict how one phenomenon will change or vary in response to variation in some other phenomenon. Homelessness researchers adopted explanation as a goal when they began to ask such questions as "Why do people become homeless?" and "Does the unemployment rate influence the frequency of homelessness?" Methods with which to identify causes and effects are the focus of Chapter 5.

- *Evaluation research.* Seeking to determine the effects of a social program or other type of intervention is a type of explanatory research, because it deals with cause and effect. However, **evaluation research** differs from other forms of explanatory research because evaluation research considers the implementation and effects of social policies and programs. These issues may not be relevant in other types of explanatory research. The problem of homelessness spawned many new government programs and, with them, evaluation research to assess the impact of these programs. Some of these studies are reviewed in Chapter 6, which covers experimental design.

I'll now summarize one study in each of these four areas to give you a feel for the projects motivated by these different concerns.

Description: Who Are the Homeless?

In the 1980s Dee Roth was chief of the Ohio Department of Mental Health's Office of Program Evaluation and Research. Her study of homelessness in Ohio, one of the most ambitious descriptive studies, was funded by the National Institute of Mental Health (Roth, Bean, Lust, & Saveanu, 1985). A general purpose of the study was to learn who the homeless are and how they relate to family, friends, and mental health agencies. (Appendix A summarizes the design of this study and the other studies discussed in detail in this book.)

Because homeless people do not have regular addresses or phone numbers, Roth could not simply select individuals from a list of currently occupied residences or phone numbers in use; instead, she designed a more complex study. The study's first element was a "key informant survey." Roth asked personnel in service agencies and shelters who worked with the homeless where homeless persons could be found in their local area and what the characteristics of these persons were. Then she surveyed state psychiatric hospital and community mental health agency staff and asked them to identify homeless persons who had used their facilities. Finally, her staff interviewed 979 homeless persons in 20 counties selected to represent urban, mixed, and rural areas throughout Ohio.

Responses in the key informant survey reinforce the importance of social scientific methods. These key informants were all employed in work with homeless persons, and yet their responses were not at all consistent. Their descriptions of the homeless population tended to focus only on the characteristics of homeless persons they interacted with in their own work, and almost none of the informants were able to estimate accurately the size of the homeless population in their county. Direct experience itself was an insufficient basis for developing a generalizable description.

Before I tell you the results of the survey of psychiatric hospitals and community mental health centers, let's try a little experiment. You probably have heard or read statements that give you an idea about the proportion of homeless persons served by such facilities. What is your guesstimate? Less than 10%, about one-third, more than half, or some other proportion? The answers: 7% of new hospital patients were homeless at the time they were admitted, and 4% of the discharged hospital patients were said by community mental health center staff to have become homeless at some time after they were discharged. Are you surprised or reassured?

Roth's homeless person survey revealed a diverse population not unlike that reported in other studies of the time. About 80% of the homeless were men, 66% were white, 50% were high school graduates (just over 10% had some college experience), only 10% were married, and almost 33% were veterans. Health problems were common. Almost one-third had been in a psychiatric hospital, and a similar proportion reported some psychiatric impairment; almost one-third reported physical health problems; one-fifth reported problem drinking.

Exploration: What Is It Like to Be Homeless?

By the mid-1980s, in spite of a spate of descriptive studies, sociologists David A. Snow and Leon Anderson (1987) felt that they still did not understand life on the streets and how people adapted to it. Snow and Anderson helped to close this research gap by conducting an exploratory field study of homeless persons in Austin, Texas. For one year, they (primarily Anderson) hung out with homeless persons, followed them through their daily routines, and asked them about their lives. Six homeless persons were studied more intensively with taped, in-depth life-history interviews. At the end of the year, Snow and Anderson had spent 405 hours in 24 different settings, from soup kitchens to hospitals, and had interacted, on average, three times each with 168 homeless persons.

One research focus was how homeless individuals try to justify to themselves their homelessness. This "identity work," Snow and Anderson found, took three different verbal forms, which are illustrated in the following quotes:

■ *Distancing.* " 'They have gotten used to living on the streets and are satisfied with it. But not me!' " (p. 1349).

■ *Embracement.* "His talk was peppered with references to himself as a tramp. He indicated, for example, that he had appeared on a television show in St. Louis as a tramp and that he had 'tramped' his way across the country" (p. 1355).

■ *Fictive storytelling.* " 'I'm going to catch a plane to Pittsburgh and tomorrow night I'll take a hot bath, have a dinner of linguini and red wine in my own restaurant . . . and have a woman hanging on my arm' " (p. 1362).

The prevalence of such identity talk suggested to Snow and Anderson that homeless persons share with the rest of the population a concern with their social standing. Before this study, social scientists had assumed that the homeless were preoccupied with basic survival. At the same time, Snow and Anderson caution us to avoid concluding that many homeless persons "want" to be homeless because they have embraced in their conversation the identity of being homeless; instead, Snow and Anderson point out, it is likely that the experience of being homeless causes people to adjust their identities.

Explanation: Why Do People Become Homeless?

Sociologist Peter H. Rossi secured funding from two private charitable foundations and the Illinois Department of Public Aid for a survey of homeless persons in Chicago in the fall and winter of 1986. His comparison of these persons with other extremely poor Chicagoans allowed him to address this explanatory research question: Why do people become homeless? Rossi's book on this research, *Down and Out in America: The Origins of Homelessness* (1989), has already become a classic.

Rossi surveyed a sample of homeless persons in shelters and all those he and his assistants could find on the streets. The street sample was something of a challenge. Rossi consulted with local experts to identify on which of Chicago's 19,400 blocks he would be most likely to find homeless persons at night. Then he drew samples of blocks from each of the three resulting categories: blocks with a high, medium, and low probability of having homeless persons at night. Finally, Rossi's interviewers visited these blocks on several nights between 1 a.m. and 6 a.m. and briefly interviewed people who seemed to be homeless.

After extensive analysis of the data, Rossi developed a straightforward explanation of homelessness: Homeless persons are extremely poor, and all extremely poor persons are vulnerable to being displaced because of the high cost of housing in urban areas. Those who are most vulnerable to losing their homes are individuals with problems of substance abuse or mental illness, which leave them unable to contribute to their own support. Extremely poor individuals who have these characteristics and are priced out of cheap lodging by urban renewal and rising housing prices often end up living with relatives or friends. However, the financial and emotional burdens created by this arrangement eventually strain social ties to the breaking point, and a portion of these persons therefore end up homeless.

Rossi made a series of recommendations to reduce homelessness based on his analysis of why people become homeless. Some examples: implement aggressive outreach programs to extend welfare coverage to the many eligible poor persons and families who do not now receive it; subsidize housing for younger unattached persons; stop the release of chronically mentally ill persons from hospitals until supportive living arrangements are arranged; and furnish support to families who subsidize their destitute, unattached members.

Evaluation: What Services Help the Homeless?

What should supportive housing of the type recommended by Rossi and others consist of? Psychiatrist Stephen M. Goldfinger, psychologist Barbara Dickey, social worker Sondra Hellman, and several other investigators (1997)—including psychologists Walter Penk and Larry Seidman, social worker Martha O'Bryan, and me—designed a study of homeless mentally ill persons in Boston to evaluate the effectiveness of different types of housing for this population. With funding from the National Institute of Mental Health, we recruited 118 mental health agency clients who were homeless and who were not judged to be a risk to themselves or others if they lived on their own.

We randomly assigned half of those who agreed to participate in the study to their own small efficiency apartments; the rest were assigned to one of eight group homes that were opened specifically for the study. We assigned people randomly to the two types of housing so we could be more confident that any differences found between the groups at the study's end had arisen after the subjects were assigned to the housing. We assigned case managers to all study participants in both housing types to ensure that medical and social services were provided.

The group homes were not the type of group living arrangements traditionally used by mental health authorities, with staffing around the clock and decision making firmly in the hands of the staff. Instead, the group homes were designed to assist residents to take control of their own affairs. Although the group homes began with full staffing, residents were encouraged to meet together to set rules for the household and eventually to terminate staff as they felt able to manage on their own. We termed this housing model "evolving consumer households."

Most study participants—80%, in fact—were still in their housing after one year in the study, and in most respects the two types of housing produced the same results. However, more of those living in the independent apartments left their housing at some point and returned to the streets or shelters. Paradoxically, though, those who were assigned to independent apartments were more satisfied with their housing (Schutt, Goldfinger, & Penk, 1997). Another difference, reported by the project's anthropologists, was the gradual emergence of collegial decision making in some of the group homes. And our neuropsychological tests identified an increase in mental flexibility among group home residents.

Strengths and Limitations of Social Research

These are only four of the dozens of large studies of homelessness since 1980, but they illustrate some of the questions social science research can address, several different methods social scientists can use, and ways social science research can inform public policy.

Notice how each of the four studies was designed to reduce the errors common in everyday reasoning:

■ The clear definition of the population of interest in each study and the selection of a broad, representative sample of that population in two studies (Roth's and Rossi's) increased the researchers' ability to draw conclusions without overgeneralizing findings to groups to which they did not apply.

- The use of surveys in which each respondent was asked the same set of questions reduced the risk of selective or inaccurate observation, as did careful and regular note-taking by the field researchers observing homeless persons on the streets of Austin and in the evolving consumer households in Boston.

- The risk of illogical reasoning was reduced by carefully describing each stage of the research, clearly presenting the findings, and carefully testing the basis for cause-and-effect conclusions.

- Resistance to change was reduced by designing an innovative type of housing and making an explicit commitment to evaluate it fairly.

Nevertheless, I would be less than honest if I implied that we enter the realm of beauty, truth, and light when we engage in social research or when we base our opinions only on the best available social research. Research always has some limitations and some flaws (as does any human endeavor), and our findings are always subject to differing interpretations. Social research permits us to see more, to observe with fewer distortions, and to describe more clearly to others what our opinions are based on, but it will not settle all arguments. Others will always have differing opinions, and some of those others will be social scientists who have conducted their own studies and drawn different conclusions. Are people encouraged to get off welfare by requirements that they get a job? Some research suggests that they are, other research finds no effect of work incentives, and one major study found positive but short-lived effects. More convincing answers must await better research, more thoughtful analysis, or wider agreement on the value of welfare and work.

But even in areas of research that are fraught with controversy, where social scientists differ in their interpretations of the evidence, the quest for new and more sophisticated research has value. What is most important for improving understanding of the social world is not the result of any particular study but the accumulation of evidence from different studies of related issues. By designing new studies that focus on the weak points or controversial conclusions of prior research, social scientists contribute to a body of findings that gradually expands our knowledge about the social world and resolves some of the disagreements about it.

Social researchers will always disagree somewhat because of their differing research opportunities, methodological approaches, and policy preferences. For example, much social science research indicates that low levels of social support increase the risk of psychological depression. But are these answers incorrect in some circumstances? One study of homeless persons suggested that social support was not associated with less depression, perhaps because of the extremely stressful circumstances homeless persons face (La Gory, Ritchey, & Mullis, 1990). But then another study using a different indicator found social support to be as beneficial for homeless persons as it is for others (Schutt, Meschede, & Rierdan, 1994). Additional studies using a variety of methods may resolve this discrepancy.

Whether you plan to conduct your own research projects, read others' research reports, or just think about and act in the social world, knowing about research methods has many benefits. This knowledge will give you greater confidence in your own opinions; improve your ability to evaluate others' opinions; and encourage you to refine your questions, answers, and methods of inquiry about the social world.

Of course, the methods of social science, as careful as they may be, cannot answer all questions about the social world. Should we do unto others what we would have them do unto us? That's a very important question about the social world, but we must turn to religion or philosophy with questions about values. Social research on the consequences of forgiveness or the sources of interpersonal conflict may help us understand and implement our values, but we can't pretend that good research will tell us which values should guide our lives.

■ ■ ■ ■ Validity: The Goal of Social Research

A scientist seeks to develop an accurate understanding of empirical reality, the reality we encounter firsthand, by conducting research that leads to valid knowledge about the world. And when is knowledge valid? We have reached the goal of **validity** when our statements or conclusions about empirical reality are correct. I look out my window and observe that it is raining—a valid observation, if my eyes and ears are to be trusted. I pick up the newspaper and read that Russian people have turned against political and economic reform. This conclusion is of questionable validity, based as it is on an interpretation of the meaning of votes cast by presumably only a portion of the Russian population. As you will see in Chapter 9, higher social status is associated with a greater probability of voting, a finding that seems valid for elections to government posts in the United States and possibly in Russia as well.

If validity sounds desirable to you, you're a good candidate for becoming a social scientist. If the goal of validity sounds a bit far-fetched—after all, how can we really be sure our understandings of empirical phenomena are correct when we can perceive the world only through the filter of our own senses?—you needn't worry. Such skepticism will help you to remember the tenuousness of all knowledge and will keep you properly skeptical about new discoveries.

Investigating the Social World is about validity more than anything else, about how to conduct research that leads to valid interpretations of the social world. I will refer to validity repeatedly, and I ask you to register it in your brain now as the central goal of social (and any other) science. The goal of social science is not to come up with conclusions that people will like or conclusions that suit our own personal preferences. The goal is to figure out how and why the social world—some aspect of it, that is—operates as it does.

We must be concerned with three aspects of validity: measurement validity, generalizability, and causal validity (also known as internal validity). Each of these three aspects of validity is essential: Conclusions based on invalid measures, invalid generalizations, or invalid causal inferences will themselves be invalid.

Imagine that we survey a sample of 250 Seattle residents and ask them two questions: "Do you have someone to depend on in times of need?" (the social support measure) and "During the past week, how often have you felt depressed?" (the depression measure). We then compare the frequency of depression between people with high and low levels of social support. We find that Seattle residents with less social support are more likely to say that they are depressed, and we conclude that the depression we found among some of Seattle's residents resulted, in part, from their lower level of social support.

But did our questions indeed tell us how depressed our respondents were and how high or low their level of social support was? If they did, we achieved measurement validity. Do our results hold true for the larger Seattle population to which our conclusion referred? If so, our conclusion would satisfy the criterion for generalizability. Did respondents' levels of depression tend to rise because of a reduction in their level of social support? If so, our conclusion is causally valid.

Measurement validity   Exists when a measure measures what we think it measures.

Generalizability   Exists when a conclusion holds true for the population, group, setting, or event that we say it does, given the conditions that we specify.

Causal validity (internal validity)   Exists when a conclusion that A leads to or results in B is correct.

The goal in social research is to achieve valid understandings of the social world by coming to conclusions that rest on valid measures and valid causal assertions and that are generalizable to the population of interest. Once we have learned how to develop studies that give us reasonably valid results and how to evaluate studies according to how well they meet this criterion, we will be well along on the road to becoming expert social researchers.

Measurement Validity

We can consider **measurement validity** the first concern in establishing the validity of research results, because without having measured what we think we measured, we really don't know what we're talking about. Measurement validity is the focus of Chapter 3.

To see how important measurement validity is, let's look at the case of the researchers who have found a high level of serious and persistent mental illness among homeless persons, based on interviews with samples of homeless persons at one point in time. The researchers have been charged with using invalid measures. Mental illness has typically been measured by individuals' responses to a series of questions that ask if they are feeling depressed, anxious, paranoid, and so on. Homeless persons more commonly say yes to these questions than do other persons, even other extremely poor persons who have homes.

But for these responses to be considered indicators of mental illness, the responses must indicate relatively enduring states of mind. Critics of these studies note that the living conditions of homeless persons are likely to make them feel depressed, anxious, and even paranoid. Feeling depressed may be a normal reaction to homelessness, not an indication of mental illness. Thus, the argument goes, typical survey questions may not provide valid measures of mental illness among the homeless. One careful research study suggests that this criticism is not correct, that homelessness is not in itself a cause of depression. Paul Koegel and M. Audrey Burnam (1992) found that the symptoms of depression most likely to result from the living conditions of some homeless people in Los Angeles, like having trouble with sleeping or concentrating, were not particularly more common among those studied than among those with homes.

Suffice it to say at this point that we must be very careful in designing our measures and in subsequently evaluating how well they have performed. We cannot just assume that measures are valid or invalid.

Generalizability

The **generalizability** of a study is the extent to which it can be used to inform us about persons, places, or events that were not studied. Generalizability is the focus of Chapter 4.

Although most American cities have many shelters for homeless persons and some homeless persons sleep on the streets to avoid shelters, many studies of "the homeless" are based on surveys of individuals found in just one shelter. When these studies are reported, the authors state that their results are based on homeless persons in one shelter. But then they go on to talk about "the homeless this" and "the homeless that," as if their study results represented all homeless persons in the city or even in the nation.

People may be especially quick to make this mistake in discussing studies of homeless persons because it's very difficult to track down homeless persons outside of shelters and because some shelter directors do not allow researchers to survey individuals at their shelters. Yet social researchers (and most everyone else, for that matter) are eager to draw conclusions about homeless persons in general. Generalizations make their work (and opinions) sound more important.

If every homeless person were like every other one, generalizations based on observations of one homeless person would be valid. But of course that's not the case. In fact, homeless persons who avoid shelters tend to be different from those who use shelters, and different types of shelters may attract different types of homeless persons. We are on solid ground if we question the generalizability of statements about homeless persons based on the results of a survey in just one shelter.

Generalizability has two aspects. **Sample generalizability** refers to the ability to generalize from a sample, or subset, of a larger population to that population itself. This is the most common meaning of generalizability. **Cross-population generalizability** refers to the ability to generalize from findings about one group or population or setting to other groups or populations or settings (see Exhibit 1.5). In this book I use the term **external validity** to refer only to cross-population generalizability, not to sample generalizability.

Sample generalizability Exists when a conclusion based on a sample, or subset, of a larger population holds true for that population.

Cross-population generalizability Exists when findings about one group or population or setting hold true for other groups or populations or settings (see Exhibit 1.5). Also called *external validity.*

Sample generalizability is a key concern in survey research. Political pollsters may study a sample of likely voters, for example, and then generalize their findings to the entire population of likely voters. No one would be interested in the results of political polls if they represented only the tiny sample that actually was surveyed rather than the entire population.

Cross-population generalizability occurs to the extent that the results of a study hold true for multiple populations; these populations may not all have been sampled, or they may be represented as subgroups within the

Exhibit 1.5   **Sample and Cross-Population Generalizability**

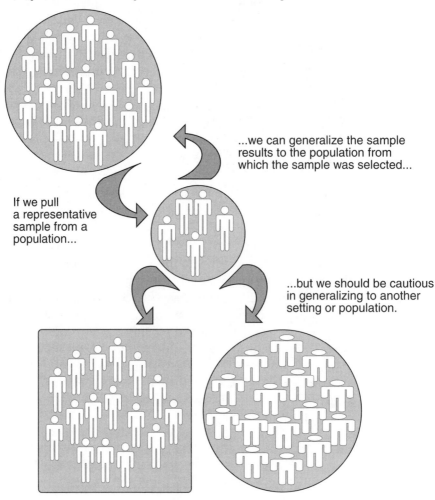

...we can generalize the sample results to the population from which the sample was selected...

If we pull a representative sample from a population...

...but we should be cautious in generalizing to another setting or population.

sample studied. Consider the debate over whether social support reduces psychological distress among homeless persons as it does among housed persons (Schutt et al., 1994). A study based on a sample of only homeless persons could not in itself resolve this debate. But in a heterogeneous sample of both homeless and housed persons, the effect of social support on distress among both groups could be tested.

Generalizability is a key concern in research design. We rarely have the resources to study the entire population that is of interest to us, so we have to select cases to study that will allow our findings to be generalized to the population of interest. We can never be sure that our propositions will hold under all conditions, so we should be cautious in generalizing to populations that we did not actually sample.

Causal Validity

Causal validity, also known as **internal validity,** refers to the truthfulness of an assertion that A causes B. It is the focus of Chapter 5.

Most research seeks to determine what causes what, so social scientists frequently must be concerned with causal validity. Imagine that we are searching for ways to improve high school programs. We start by searching for what seem to be particularly effective programs in area schools. We find a program at a local high school, Brookton Academy, that a lot of people have talked about, and we decide to compare the standardized achievement test scores of tenth graders in that school with those of tenth graders in another school, Hilltop School, that does not offer the special program. We find that students in the school with the special program have higher scores (see Exhibit 1.6), and we decide that the special program caused the

Exhibit 1.6 **Partial Evidence of Causality**

School	Program status	Post-program test scores
Brookton Academy	Mentoring program	85th percentile
Hilltop School	No mentoring program	65th percentile

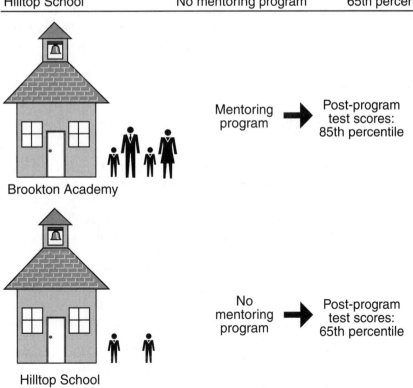

better scores. Are you confident about the causal validity of our conclusion? Probably not. Perhaps the students in the school with the special program performed better even before the special program began, even before they started school.

This is the sort of problem that randomized experiments like the Goldfinger et al. study of housing for the homeless are designed to resolve. By randomly assigning study participants to the two housing types, we made it very unlikely that persons who were older, substance abusers, lacking in social supports, and so on were disproportionately in one housing type rather than the other. We compared subjects in our housing groups in terms of hundreds of characteristics and found almost no differences at the start of the experiment.

On the other hand, causal conclusions also can be mistaken because of some factor that was not recognized during planning for the study, even in randomized experiments. Perhaps the school with the special program also had a better library, which is what led to the higher scores. If the independent apartments in the homeless housing study had been in neighborhoods with more drug pushers than the group homes had been in, residents in the independent apartments could have done more poorly for reasons quite apart from their housing type.

Establishing causal validity can be quite difficult. You will learn in more detail in subsequent chapters how experimental designs and statistics can help us evaluate causal propositions, but the solutions are neither easy nor perfect: We always have to consider critically the validity of causal statements that we hear or read.

Conclusion

I hope this first chapter has given you an idea of what to expect in the rest of the book. My aim is to introduce you to social research methods by describing what social scientists have learned about the social world as well as how they learned it. The substance of social science inevitably is more interesting than its methods, but the methods also become more interesting when they're not taught as isolated techniques. I have focused attention on research on homelessness in this chapter; in subsequent chapters, I will introduce research examples from other areas.

The theme of validity ties the book's chapters together. You must learn to ask of each research technique how it helps us come to more valid conclusions. Each technique must be evaluated in terms of its ability to help us with measurement validity, generalizability, and causal validity. You must ask a critical question of each research project you examine: How valid are its conclusions?

Chapter 2 continues to build the foundation for our study of social research by reviewing the types of problems that social scientists study, the role of theory, the major steps in the research process, and other sources of information that may be used in social research. I stress the importance of considering scientific standards in social research and review generally accepted ethical guidelines. Throughout the chapter, I use several studies of domestic violence to illustrate the research process.

Then I return to the subject of validity. Chapters 3, 4, and 5 discuss the three aspects of validity and the specific techniques used to maximize the validity of our measures, our generalizations, and our causal assertions. Research about the measurement of substance abuse, sampling of homeless persons, and the causes of violence is highlighted.

Chapters 6, 7, 8, and 9 introduce the four most important methods of data collection. Experimental studies, the subject of Chapter 6, are favored by many psychologists, social psychologists, and policy evaluation researchers. Survey research is the most common method of data collection in sociology, and I devote a lot of attention to the different types of survey in Chapter 7. Field research has long been the method of choice in anthropology, but it also has many adherents in sociology. Chapter 8 shows how field research techniques can uncover aspects of the social world that we are likely to miss in experiments and surveys. Comparative methods, the subject of Chapter 9, involve a collection of techniques that are used to study societies and groups in the past and to compare them to the present.

Plan to read Chapter 10 very carefully. I compare and contrast several different studies and point out some of the consequences of particular research strategies. I emphasize the value of integrating different methods of data collection and of examining variation in social phenomena across social contexts. I also examine several innovative approaches that take us to the boundaries of social science. By the end of the chapter, you should have a broader perspective on how much research methods have helped to improve understanding of the social world and how much remains to be done.

The last two chapters begin with an overview of the statistics that are needed to analyze most social research data. Chapter 11 is not a substitute for an entire course in statistics, but it gives you a good idea of how to use statistics in reporting the results of studies that you conduct and in interpreting the results of research reported by others. I present an extended example that will help you learn how to use particular statistics and illustrate the process of analyzing secondary data, data already collected by others. Chapter 12 focuses on the contents of research reports and the process of developing them. I give special attention to how to formulate research proposals and how to critique, or evaluate, reports of research that we encounter.

KEY TERMS

Causal validity
Cross-population generalizability
Descriptive research
Evaluation research
Explanatory research
Exploratory research
External validity
Generalizability
Illogical reasoning
Inaccurate observation

Internal validity
Measurement validity
Overgeneralization
Resistance to change
Sample generalizability
Science
Selective observation
Social science
Validity

HIGHLIGHTS

■ Social research cannot resolve value questions or provide answers that will convince everyone and remain settled for all time.

■ All empirically based methods of investigation are based on either direct experience or others' statements.

■ Four common errors in reasoning are overgeneralization, selective or inaccurate observation, illogical reasoning, and resistance to change. Illogical reasoning is due to the complexity of the social world, self-interestedness, and human subjectivity. Resistance to change may be due to unquestioning acceptance of tradition or of those in positions of authority or to self-interested resistance to admitting the need to change one's beliefs.

■ Social science is the use of logical, systematic, documented methods to investigate individuals, societies, and social processes, as well as the knowledge produced by these investigations.

■ Social research can be motivated by policy guidance and program management needs, academic concerns, and charitable impulses.

■ Social research can be descriptive, exploratory, explanatory, or evaluative—or some combination of these.

■ Valid knowledge is the central concern of scientific research. The three components of validity are measurement validity, generalizability (both from the sample to the population from which it was selected and from the sample to other populations), and causal (internal) validity.

EXERCISES

1. Select a social issue that interests you, like homelessness or crime. List at least four of your beliefs about this phenomenon. Try to identify the sources of each of these beliefs.

2. Review letters to the editor and opinion pieces in your local newspaper. Identify any errors in reasoning: overgeneralization, selective or inaccurate observation, illogical reasoning, or resistance to change.

3. Find a report of social science research in an article in a daily newspaper. What were the major findings? How much evidence is given about measurement validity, generalizability, and causal validity of the findings? What additional design features might have helped to improve the study's validity?

4. What topic would you focus on if you could design a social research project without any concern for costs? What are your motives for studying this topic?

5. Read the abstracts (initial summaries) of each article in a recent issue of a major social science journal. (Ask your instructor for some good journal titles.) On the basis of the abstract only, classify each research project represented in the articles as primarily descriptive, exploratory, explanatory, or evaluative. Note any indications that the research focused on other types of research questions.

6. Refer to the research topic you identified in Exercise 4. Develop four research questions related to that topic: descriptive, exploratory, explanatory, and evaluative. Be specific.

7. From the news, record statements of politicians or other leaders that concern some social phenomenon. Which statements do you think are likely to be in error? What evidence might improve the validity of these statements?

WEB EXERCISES

1. You have been asked to prepare a 5–10 minute class presentation on homelessness.

     Go to the National Coalition for the Homeless web site at

     http://nch.ari.net/

   to find information. Write up a brief outline for a 5–10 minute presentation including information on homelessness, statistics on homelessness, and so on.

2. After completing Exercise 1 above, you realize that your presentation includes some very depressing information about the homeless problem and you expect that your presentation will spark concern from your fellow students in the class. You want to get information regarding an organization dedicated to doing something about homelessness so that if anyone in the class asks what they can do to work against the homeless problem, you can give them some information.

     Go to

     http://www.pirg.org/nscahh

   Write up some information regarding the program, its goals, its projects, publications, and so on, as well as contact information for students who are interested in finding out more about the National Student Campaign Against Hunger and Homelessness.

SPSS EXERCISES

1. In the GSS96, the variable HOMELESS measures whether the respondent has contributed financially to the homeless.

    a. Create a bar chart of HOMELESS with the graph procedure.
       GRAPHS...
           BAR...
               Simple...Define...
                   % of cases
           Category Axis: HOMELESS
               [Be sure to select "Options" and indicate you want to leave
               out the missing values.]

    b. Write a research question for each of the types of social research (descriptive, exploratory, explanatory, evaluation) regarding the variable HOMELESS.

2. What could be the possible motives (policy, academic, personal) for conducting research associated with this variable? Explain.

2 The Process and Problems of Social Research

On July 4, 1997, the Pathfinder module landed on Mars after a six-month trip from Earth. Within a day, a little vehicle was exploring Martian rocks and soil. Cameras were transmitting live pictures back to Earth, where millions of people were tuned in through their computers to special World Wide Web sites set up for the occasion. Once again, science was transforming our image of the universe and helping us transcend our natural physical and mental limits, just as computers, brain-imaging devices, and nuclear power had done before. It is no exaggeration to say that the physical and natural sciences have forever altered human life and continue to do so. Although social science has nothing like this impact, it does influence the design of social programs, the course of elections, the composition of juries, the strategies of business—and most important, our understanding of the social world.

Consider the impact of research on domestic violence. It is a major problem in our society, with police responding to between 2 million and 8 million complaints of assault by a spouse or lover yearly (Sherman, 1992:6). In 1981, the Police Foundation and the Minneapolis Police Department began an experiment to determine whether arresting accused spouse abusers on the spot would deter repeat incidents. The study's results, which were widely publicized, indicated that arrest did have a deterrent effect. And so the percentage of urban police departments that made arrest the preferred response to complaints of domestic violence rose from 10% in 1984 to 90% in 1988 (Sherman, 1992:14). Six other cities then hosted studies like the Minneapolis experiment, but the results were not always so clear-cut as in the original study (Sherman, 1992; Sherman & Berk, 1984). The Minneapolis Domestic Violence Experiment, the studies modeled after it, and the related controversies provide many examples for a systematic overview of the social research process.

The first concern in social research, as in this chapter, is deciding what to study. Social theory plays a role, as a basis for formulating research questions and, later, understanding the larger implications of research results. The next step is to decide how to go about answering the research question. I use the Minneapolis experiment and its progeny to illustrate the three main research strategies: deductive, inductive, and descriptive. In all three, theory and data are linked. The chapter ends with scientific and ethical guidelines that should be adhered to no matter what the research strategy and shows how the Minneapolis experiment followed these guidelines. By the chapter's end, you should be ready to formulate a research question, design a general strategy for answering this question, and critique previous studies that addressed this question. You can think of Chapter 1 as having introduced the "why" of social research; Chapter 2 introduces the "how."

■ ■ ■ ■ Social Research Questions

How does a social researcher decide what to study? A **social research question** is a question about the social world that you seek to answer through the collection and analysis of firsthand, verifiable, empirical data. It is not a question about who did what to whom but a question about people in groups, about general social processes, about tendencies in community change. What distinguishes homeless persons from other poor persons? Does community policing reduce the crime rate? What influences the likelihood of spouse abuse? How do people react to social isolation? So many research questions are possible that it is more of a challenge to specify what does not qualify as a social research question than to specify what does.

But that doesn't mean it is easy to specify a research question. In fact, formulating a good research question can be surprisingly difficult. We can break the process into three stages: identifying one or more questions for study, refining the questions, and then evaluating the questions.

Identifying Social Research Questions

Social research questions may emerge from your own experience—from your "personal troubles," as C. Wright Mills (1959) put it. These could range from an awareness of the ways you benefited from being part of a religious community to the pain you suffer as a result of being a victim of crime to the realization that social relations in your new sorority are very different from those in your old college dorm. You may find yourself asking a question like "In what ways do people tend to benefit from church membership?" or "Does victimization change a person's trust in others?" or "How do initiation procedures influence group commitment?" Can you think of other possible research questions that flow from your own experiences in the social world?

Others' experiences are another fruitful source of research questions. Knowing a relative who was abused by a spouse, seeing a TV special about violence, or reading someone's autobiography can stimulate questions about general social processes. Can you draft a research question based on a relative's experiences, a TV show, or a book?

Other researchers may also pose interesting questions for you to study. Most research articles end with some suggestions for additional research that highlights unresolved issues. For example, Lawrence Sherman and Douglas Smith, with their colleagues, conclude an article on some of the replications of the Minneapolis experiment on police responses to spouse abuse by suggesting that "deterrence may be effective for a substantial segment of the offender population. . . . [H]owever, the underlying mechanisms remain obscure" (1992:706). A new study could focus on the mechanisms: why or under what conditions the arrest of offenders who are employed deters them from future criminal acts. Any issue of a journal in your field is likely to have comments that point toward unresolved issues.

The primary source of research questions for many social scientists is social theory. Some spend much of their careers conducting research intended to refine an answer to one central research question. For example, you may find rational choice theory to be a useful approach to understanding diverse forms of social behavior, because people do seem to you to make decisions on the basis of personal cost-benefit calculations. So you may ask whether rational choice theory can explain consumer behavior in stores and then whether it can explain homeless persons' interest in social services.

Finally, some research questions have very pragmatic sources. You may focus on a research question posed by someone else because it seems to be to your advantage to do so. Some social scientists conduct research on specific questions posed by a funding source in what is termed an RFP, a request for proposals. (Sometimes the acronym RFA is used, meaning request for applications.) Or you may learn that the social workers in the homeless shelter where you volunteer need help with a survey to learn about client needs, which becomes the basis for another research question.

Refining Social Research Questions

The problem is not so much coming up with interesting questions for research as it is focusing on a problem of manageable size. We are often interested in much more than we can reasonably investigate with limited time and resources. Researchers may worry about staking a research project (and thereby a grant or a grade) on a particular problem and so address several research questions at once, often in a jumbled fashion. It might also seem risky to focus on a research question that may lead to results discrepant with our own cherished assumptions about the social world. The prospective commitment of time and effort for some research questions may seem overwhelming, resulting in a certain degree of paralysis.

The best way to avoid these problems is to develop the research question one bit at a time. Don't keep hoping that the perfect research question will just spring forth from your pen. Instead, develop a list of possible research questions as you go along. At the appropriate time, you can look through this list for the research questions that appear more than once. Narrow your list to the most interesting, most workable candidates. Repeat this process as long as it helps to improve your research questions.

Evaluating Social Research Questions

In the third stage of selecting a research question, we evaluate the best candidate against the criteria for good social research questions: feasibility given the time and resources available, social importance, and scientific relevance (King, Keohane, & Verba, 1994).

The research question in the Minneapolis Domestic Violence Experiment—"Does prompt punishment deter spouse abuse?"—certainly meets the criteria of social importance and scientific relevance, but it would not be a feasible question for a student project. You might instead ask the question "Do people think punishment deters spouse abuse?" This is a question that you could study with an on-campus survey. Or perhaps you could work out an arrangement with a local shelter to study the question "What services do homeless people desire?" However, review of the literature might convince you that this question is not scientifically relevant because it has been studied enough.

Feasibility

We must be able to conduct any study within the time and given the resources we have. If time is short, questions that involve long-term change may not be feasible. Another issue is what people or groups we can expect to gain access to. Observing social interaction in corporate boardrooms may be taboo. Then we must consider whether we will have any additional resources, such as other researchers to collaborate with or research funds. Remember that there are severe limits on what one person can accomplish. On the other hand, we might work in an organization that collects data on employees, customers, or clients that are relevant to our research interests. We may be able to piggyback our research onto a larger research project. And are we prepared to handle large amounts of quantitative data? A computer and the skills to use it will be essential. Also take into account the constraints we face due to our schedules and other commitments.

The Minneapolis Domestic Violence Experiment shows how ambitious social research questions can be when a team of seasoned researchers secures the backing of influential groups. The project required hundreds of thousands of dollars, the collaboration of many social scientists and criminal justice personnel, and the volunteer efforts of 41 Minneapolis police officers. But many worthwhile research questions can be investigated with much more limited resources. You will read in subsequent chapters about studies that addressed important research questions with much more limited resources than the Minneapolis social scientists commanded.

Social Importance

Social research is not a simple undertaking, so we must focus on a substantive area that we feel is important, such as criminal justice, homelessness, interpersonal interaction, psychological distress, sex roles, sociology of the family, income inequality, mass media, and the like. We need to feel motivated to carry out the study; there is little point in trying to answer a question that doesn't interest us.

In addition, we should consider whether the research question is important to other people. Will an answer to the research question make a difference for society, for social relations? Again, the Minneapolis Domestic Violence Experiment is an exemplary case. But the social sciences are not wanting for important research questions. The April 1984 issue of the *American Sociological Review,* which contained the first academic article on the Minneapolis experiment, also included articles reporting research on elections, school tracking, discrimination, work commitment, school grades, organizational change, and homicide. All these articles addressed research questions about important social issues, and all raised new questions for additional research.

Scientific Relevance

Every research question should be grounded in the social science literature. Whether we formulate a research question because we have been stimulated by an academic article or because we want to investigate a current social problem, we must turn to the social science literature to find out what has already been learned about this question. (Appendix B explains how to find information about previous research, using both printed and computer-based resources.) It would be unreasonable to think of any social research question as being settled for all time. You can be sure that some prior study is relevant to almost any research question you can think of.

The Minneapolis experiment was built on a substantial body of contradictory theorizing about the impact of punishment on criminality (Sherman & Berk, 1984). Deterrence theory predicted that arrest would deter individuals from repeat offenses; labeling theory predicted that arrest would make repeat offenses more likely. The researchers found one prior experimental study of this issue, but it was conducted with juveniles. Studies among adults had not yielded consistent findings. Clearly, the Minneapolis researchers had good reason for another study. Prior research and theory also helped them develop the most effective research design.

■ ■ ■ ■   The Role of Social Theory

I have already pointed out that social theory can be a source of research questions. What deserves more attention at this point is the larger role of social theory in research. **Theories** help us make sense of many interrelated phenomena and predict behavior or attitudes that are likely to occur when certain conditions are met. Social scientists who connect their work to social theories can generate better ideas about what to look for in a study and develop conclusions with more implications for other research. Building and evaluating theory is therefore one of the most important objectives of social science.

Theory A logically interrelated set of propositions about empirical reality. *Examples of social theories:* structural functionalism, conflict theory, and symbolic interactionism.

For more than a hundred years, social scientists have been developing theories about social phenomena. Some of these theories reflect a substantial body of research and the thinking of many social scientists; others are formulated in the course of one investigation. A few have been widely accepted, at least for a time; others are the subject of vigorous controversy, with frequent changes and refinements in response to criticism and new research.

Most social research is guided by some theory, although the theory may be only partially developed in a particular study or may even be unrecognized by the researcher. When researchers are involved in conducting a research project or engrossed in writing a research report, they may easily lose sight of the larger picture. It is easy to focus on accumulating or clarifying particular findings rather than considering how the study's findings fit into a more general understanding of the social world.

We can use the studies of the police response to domestic assault to illustrate the value of theory for social research. Even in this very concrete and practical matter, we must draw on social theories to understand how people act and what should be done about those actions. Consider the three action options that police officers have when they confront a domestic assault suspect (Sherman & Berk, 1984:263). Fellow officers might urge forced separation to achieve short-term peace; police trainers might prefer mediation to resolve the underlying dispute; feminist groups might urge arrest to protect the victim. None of these recommendations is really a theory, but each suggests a different perspective on crime and legal sanctions. The traditional police perspective sees domestic violence as a family matter that should not be the object of formal legal action. The preference for mediation reflects the view that domestic violence involves a family crisis that can be solved with special counseling. The pro-arrest position views domestic violence as a crime as serious as that between strangers and favors arrest for its presumed deterrent effect.

You will encounter these different perspectives if you read much of the literature on domestic violence or even if you talk with your friends about

Exhibit 2.1   **Bases for Three Perspectives on Domestic Assault**

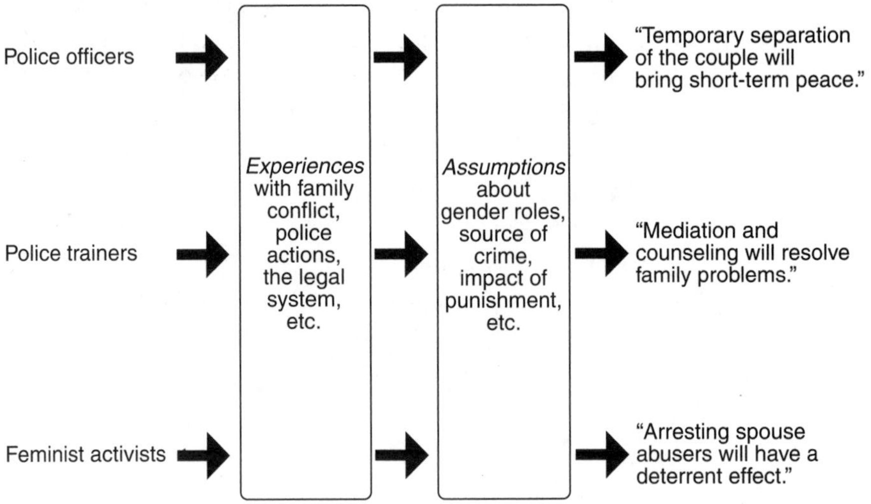

it. As Exhibit 2.1 shows, each perspective reflects different assumptions about gender roles, about the sources of crime, about the impact of punishment. In turn, these assumptions reflect different experiences with family conflict, police actions, and the legal system. What we believe about one crime and the appropriate response to it relates to a great many other ideas we have about the social world. Recognizing these relationships is a first step toward becoming a theoretically guided social researcher and a theoretically informed consumer of social research.

Remember, however, that social theories do not provide the answers to the questions we confront as we formulate topics for research. Instead, social theories suggest the areas on which we should focus and the propositions that we should consider for a test. For example, Sherman and Berk's (1984) domestic violence research was actually a test of predictions derived from two alternative theories of the impact of punishment on crime:

■ *Deterrence theory* expects punishment to deter crime in two ways. General deterrence occurs when people see that crime results in undesirable punishments, that "crime doesn't pay." The persons who are punished serve as examples of what awaits those who engage in proscribed acts. Specific deterrence occurs when persons who are punished decide not to commit another offense so they can avoid further punishment (Lempert & Sanders, 1986:86–87). Deterrence theory leads to the prediction that arresting spouse abusers will lessen their likelihood of reoffending.

■ *Labeling theory* distinguishes between primary deviance, the acts of individuals that lead to public sanction, and secondary deviance—the deviance that occurs in response to public sanction (Hagan, 1994:33). Arrest or some other public sanction for misdeeds labels the offender as deviant in the eyes of others. Once the offender is labeled, others will treat the offender as a deviant, and he or she is then more likely to act in a way that is consistent with the deviant label. Ironically, the act of punishment stimulates more of the very behavior that it was intended to eliminate. This theory suggests that persons arrested for domestic assault are more likely to reoffend than those who are not punished, which is the reverse of the deterrence theory prediction.

Theorizing about the logic behind punishment can also help us draw connections to more general theories about social processes. Deterrence theory reflects the assumptions of *rational choice theory,* which assumes that people's behavior is shaped by practical calculations: People break the law if the benefits of doing so exceed the costs. If crime is a "rational choice" for some people, then increasing the certainty or severity of punishment for crime should shift the cost-benefit balance away from criminal behavior. Labeling theory is rooted in *symbolic interactionism,* which focuses on the symbolic meanings that people give to behavior (Hagan, 1994:40). Instead of assuming that some forms of behavior are deviant in and of themselves (Scull, 1988:678), symbolic interactionists would view deviance as a consequence of the application of rules and sanctions to an "offender" (Becker, 1963:9). Exhibit 2.2 summarizes how these general theories relate to the question of whether or not to arrest spouse abusers.

Exhibit 2.2   **Two Social Theories and Their Predictions About the Effect of Arrest for Domestic Assault**

	Rational choice theory	**Symbolic interactionism**
Theoretical assumption	People's behavior is shaped by calculations of the costs and benefits of their actions.	People give symbolic meanings to objects, behaviors, and other people.
Criminological component	Deterrence theory: People break the law if the benefits of doing so outweigh the costs.	Labeling theory: People label offenders as deviant, promoting further deviance.
Prediction (effect of arrest for domestic assault)	Abusing spouse, having seen the costs of abuse (namely, arrest), decides not to abuse again.	Abusing spouse, having been labeled as "an abuser," abuses more often.

Does either deterrence theory or labeling theory make sense to you as an explanation for the impact of punishment? Do they seem consistent with your observations of social life? Over a decade after Sherman and Berk's study, Raymond Paternoster, Robert Brame, Ronet Bachman, and Lawrence Sherman (1997) decided to study punishment of spouse abuse from a different perspective. They turned to a social psychological theory called *procedural justice theory*, which explains law-abidingness as resulting from a sense of duty or morality. People obey the law from a sense of obligation that flows from seeing legal authorities as moral and legitimate. From this perspective, individuals who are arrested seem less likely to reoffend if they are treated fairly, irrespective of the outcome of their case, because fair treatment will enhance their view of legal authorities as moral and legitimate. Procedural justice theory expands our view of the punishment process by focusing attention on how police act rather than just on the legal decisions they make. Thus it gives us a sense of the larger importance of the research question.

Are you now less certain about the likely effect of arrest for spouse abuse? Will arrest decrease abuse because abusers do not wish to suffer from legal sanctions again? Will it increase abuse because abusers feel stigmatized by being arrested and thus are more likely to act like criminals? Or will arrest reduce abuse only if the abusers feel they have been treated fairly by the legal authorities? By suggesting such questions, social theory makes us much more sensitive to the possibilities and so helps us to design better research. Before, during, and after a research investigation, we need to keep thinking theoretically.

■ ■ ■ ■ Social Research Strategies

Social research is the effort to connect theory and empirical data, the evidence we find in the material world. As Exhibit 2.3 shows, theory and data have a two-way relationship. Research that begins with a theory implying that certain data should be found involves **deductive reasoning**, which moves from general ideas (theory) to specific reality (data). In contrast, **inductive reasoning** moves from the specific to the general.

Both deductive reasoning and inductive reasoning are essential to social science. We cannot test an idea fairly unless we use deductive reasoning, stating our expectations in advance and setting up a test in which our idea could be shown to be wrong. A theory that has not survived these kinds of tests can only be regarded as very tentative. Yet theories, no matter how cherished, cannot make useful predictions for every social situation or research problem that we seek to investigate. Moreover, we may find unexpected patterns in the data we collect, called **serendipitous findings** or

Exhibit 2.3   **The Links Between Theory and Data**

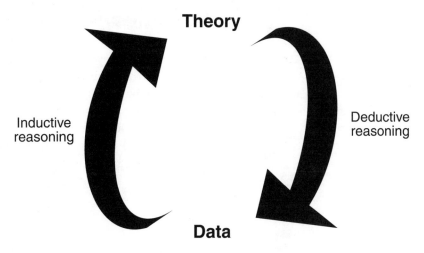

Ideas: What we think

Theory

Inductive
reasoning

Deductive
reasoning

Data

Reality: What we observe

anomalous findings. In either situation, we should reason inductively, making whatever theoretical sense we can of our unanticipated findings. Then, if the new findings seem sufficiently important, we can return to deductive reasoning and plan a new study to formally test our new ideas.

The Research Circle

This process of conducting research, moving from theory to data and back again, or from data to theory and back again, can be characterized as a **research circle.** Exhibit 2.4 depicts this circle. Note that it mirrors the relationship between theory and data shown in Exhibit 2.3 and that it comprises three main research strategies: deductive research, inductive research, and descriptive research.

Deductive Research

As Exhibit 2.4 shows, **deductive research** proceeds from theorizing to data collection and then back to theorizing. In essence, a specific expectation is deduced from a general premise and then tested.

Notice that a theory leads first to a **hypothesis,** which is a specific implication deduced from the more general theory. Researchers actually test a hypothesis, not the complete theory itself. A hypothesis proposes a relationship between two or more **variables,** characteristics or properties that can vary. Variation in one variable is proposed to predict, influence, or cause

Exhibit 2.4 **The Research Circle**

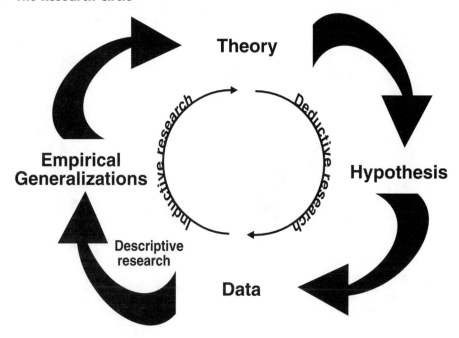

variation in the other variable. The proposed influence is the **independent variable;** its effect or consequence is the **dependent variable.** After the researchers formulate one or more hypotheses and develop research procedures, they collect data with which to test the hypothesis.

Hypothesis A tentative statement about empirical reality, involving a relationship between two or more variables.

Variable A characteristic or property that can vary (take on different values or attributes).

Independent variable A variable that is hypothesized to cause, or lead to, variation in another variable.

Dependent variable A variable that is hypothesized to vary depending on or under the influence of another variable.

Example of a hypothesis: The higher the poverty rate in a community, the higher the percentage of community residents who are homeless.
Example of an independent variable: poverty rate.
Example of a dependent variable: percentage of community residents who are homeless.

Exhibit 2.5 **Examples of Hypotheses**

Original Hypothesis	Independent Variable	Dependent Variable	IF-THEN Hypothesis
1. The higher the income, the greater the risk of tax fraud.	Income	Risk of tax fraud	IF income is higher, THEN the risk of tax fraud is greater.
2. The risk of property theft decreases as income increases.	Income	Risk of property theft	IF income is higher, THEN the risk of property theft is less.
3. If years of education decrease, income decreases.	Years of education	Income	IF years of education decrease, THEN income decreases.
4. Political conservatism increases with income.	Income	Political conservatism	IF income increases, THEN political conservatism increases.
5. Property crime is higher in urban areas than in suburban or rural areas.	Urbanization	Rate of property crime	IF areas are urban, THEN property crime is higher compared to crime in suburban or rural areas.

Hypotheses can be worded in several different ways, and identifying the independent and dependent variables is sometimes difficult. When in doubt, try to rephrase the hypothesis as an "if-then" statement: "*If* the independent variable increases (or decreases), *then* the dependent variable increases (or decreases)." Exhibit 2.5 presents several hypotheses with their independent and dependent variables and their "if-then" equivalents.

Exhibit 2.5 demonstrates another feature of hypotheses: **direction of association**. When researchers hypothesize that one variable increases as the other variable increases, the direction of association is positive (Hypotheses 1 and 4); when one variable decreases as the other variable decreases, the direction of association is also positive (Hypothesis 3). But when one variable increases as the other decreases, or vice versa, the direction of association is negative, or inverse (Hypothesis 2). Hypothesis 5 is a special case, in which the independent variable is categorical: It cannot be said to increase or decrease. In this case, the concept of direction of association does not apply, and the hypothesis simply states that one category of the independent variable is associated with higher values on the dependent variable.

The motives for deductive research include both explanation and evaluation (as described in Chapter 1). An example of explanatory deductive research is the Minneapolis Domestic Violence Experiment, in which Sherman and Berk (1984) sought to explain what sort of response by the authorities might keep a spouse abuser from repeating the offense. The researchers deduced from deterrence theory the expectation that arrest would deter domestic violence. They then collected data to test this expectation.

An example of evaluative deductive research is the Goldfinger housing study introduced in Chapter 1, in which my collaborators and I deduced from prior research and psychiatric literature the expectation that formerly homeless mentally ill individuals would be more likely to remain in group homes that they managed themselves than in independent apartments (Goldfinger et al., 1990). We then collected data to test this expectation. Even though we did not begin with an explicit theory, we did begin with ideas about social programs and seek to confirm them in reality.

In both explanatory and evaluative research, the statement of expectations for the findings and the design of the research to test these expectations strengthens the confidence we can place in the test. The deductive researcher shows her hand or states her expectations in advance and then designs a fair test of those expectations. Then, "the chips fall where they may"—in other words, the researcher accepts the resulting data as a more or less objective picture of reality.

Inductive Research

In contrast to deductive research, **inductive research** begins at the bottom of the research circle and then works upward (see Exhibit 2.4). The inductive researcher begins with specific data, which are then used to develop (induce) a general explanation (a theory) to account for the data. The patterns in the data are then summarized in one or more **empirical generalizations** that can be compared to the hypothesis. If the empirical generalizations are those stated in the hypothesis, then the theory from which the hypothesis was deduced is supported. If the empirical generalizations are inconsistent with the hypothesis, then the theory is not supported (Wallace, 1971:18).

The motive for inductive research is exploration. In Chapter 1, you read about an exploratory study of identity among the homeless, in which the researchers approached their data inductively (Snow & Anderson, 1987). The researchers interviewed homeless persons and then from their analysis of these data developed a theory about how homeless persons maintain their identities.

In strictly inductive research, the researcher already knows what he has found when he starts theorizing, or attempting to explain what accounts for these findings. The result can be new insights and provocative questions. But the adequacy of an explanation formulated after the fact is necessarily less certain than an explanation presented prior to the collection of data. Every phenomenon can always be explained in some way. Inductive explanations are thus more trustworthy if they are tested subsequently with deductive research.

Descriptive Research

You learned in Chapter 1 that description is one important motive for social research. Descriptive research can be considered a part of the research circle, even though such research does not involve connecting theory and data. As Exhibit 2.4 indicates, descriptive research starts with data and proceeds only to the stage of making empirical generalizations based on those data.

Valid description is important in its own right, but it is also critical in all research. Description of social phenomena can stimulate more ambitious deductive and inductive research. The Minneapolis Domestic Violence Experiment was motivated in part by a growing body of descriptive research indicating that spouse abuse is very common. You may recall from Chapter 1 that early research on homelessness was also primarily descriptive; by identifying the health problems and social backgrounds of homeless persons, this research helped to establish priorities for private charities and public agencies. Much important research for the government and public and private organizations is, like these homelessness studies, primarily descriptive: How many poor people live in this community? Is the health of the elderly improving? How frequently do convicted criminals return to crime? Simply put, good description of data is the cornerstone for the scientific research process and an essential component for understanding the social world.

Domestic Violence and the Research Circle

The Sherman and Berk study of domestic violence is a good example of how the research circle works. In an attempt to determine ways to prevent the recurrence of spouse abuse, the researchers repeatedly linked theory and data, developing both hypotheses and empirical generalizations.

Phase 1: Deductive Research

The first phase of Sherman and Berk's study was designed to test a hypothesis. According to deterrence theory, punishment will reduce recidivism, or the propensity to commit further crimes. From this theory, Sherman and Berk deduced a specific hypothesis: "Arrest for spouse abuse reduces the risk of repeat offenses." In this hypothesis, arrest is the independent variable, and variation in the risk of repeat offenses is the dependent variable (it is hypothesized to depend on arrest).

Of course, in another study arrest might be the dependent variable in relation to some other independent variable. For example, in the hypothesis "The greater the rate of layoffs in a community, the higher the frequency of arrest," the dependent variable is frequency of arrest. Only within the context of a hypothesis, or a relationship between variables, does it make sense to refer to one variable as dependent and the other as independent.

Sherman and Berk tested their hypothesis by setting up an experiment in which the police responded to complaints of spouse abuse in one of three ways, one of which was to arrest the offender. When the researchers examined their data (police records for the persons in their experiment), they found that of those arrested for assaulting their spouse, only 13% repeated the offense, compared to a 26% recidivism rate for those who were separated from their spouse by the police without any arrest. This pattern in the data, or empirical generalization, was consistent with the hypothesis that the researchers deduced from deterrence theory. The theory thus received support from the experiment (see Exhibit 2.6).

In designing their study, Sherman and Berk anticipated an important question: How valid was the connection they were trying to make between theory and data? The three dimensions of validity—measurement validity, generalizability, and causal validity—were at issue.

Determining whether spouses were assaulted after the initial police intervention was the key measurement concern. Official records of subsequent assaults by the suspect would provide one measure. But most spousal assaults are not reported to the police, and so research assistants also sought out the victims for interviews every two weeks during a six-month follow-up period. Although fewer than half the victims completed all the follow-up interviews, the availability of the self-report measure allowed the researchers to shed some light on the validity of the official data. In general,

Exhibit 2.6 The Research Circle: Minneapolis Domestic Violence Experiment

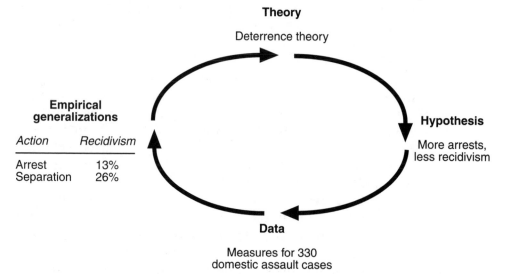

Source: Data from Sherman & Berk, 1984:267.

the two measures yielded comparable results, although some discrepancies troubled critics.

The generalizability of the study's results was the researchers' greatest concern. Minneapolis is no more a "typical" U.S. city than any other, and we cannot assume that police policies that are effective in Minneapolis will be equally effective in cities with very different political histories, criminal justice agencies, and population characteristics. Sherman and Berk (1984: 269) warned readers, "External validity will have to wait for replications"— that is, for repetitions of the study using the same research methods to answer the same research question.

Finally, Sherman and Berk's claims about the causal validity of their results rested primarily on the experimental design they used. The 330 domestic assault cases in the study were handled by the police in one of three ways: an arrest, an order that the offending spouse leave the house for eight hours, or some type of verbal advice by the police officers. The officers were not allowed to choose which "treatment" to apply (except in extreme cases, such as when severe injury had occurred or when the spouse had demanded that an arrest be made). Instead, the treatments were carried out by police in random order, according to the color of the next report form on a pad that had been prepared by the researchers.

By insisting on the random assignment of cases to treatments, the researchers tried to ensure that police officers would not arrest just the toughest spouses or the spouses who seemed most obnoxious or the spouses they encountered late in the day. In other words, the random assignment procedure made it unlikely that arrested spouse abusers would differ on average from the other spouse abusers except for the fact that they were arrested (although, because of chance factors, the possibility of other differences cannot be completely ruled out). The researchers' conclusion that arrest caused a lower incidence of repeat offenses therefore seems valid.

Phase 2: Deductive Research

Because of their doubts about the generalizability of their results, Sherman, Berk, and new collaborators began to journey around the research circle again, with funding from the National Institute of Justice for **replications** (repetitions) of the experiment in six more cities. These replications used the same basic research approach but with some improvements. The random assignment process was tightened up in most of the cities so that police officers would be less likely to replace the assigned treatment with a treatment of their own choice. In addition, data were collected about repeat violence against other victims as well as against the original complainant. Some of the replications also examined different aspects of the arrest process, to see whether professional counseling helped and whether the length of time spent in jail after arrest mattered at all.

By the time results were reported from five of the cities in the new study, a problem was apparent. In three of the cities—Omaha, Nebraska; Charlotte, North Carolina; and Milwaukee, Wisconsin—researchers were finding long-term increases in domestic violence incidents among arrestees. But in two—Colorado Springs, Colorado, and Dade County, Florida—the predicted deterrent effects seemed to be occurring (Sherman et al., 1992).

Sherman and his colleagues had now traversed the research circle twice in an attempt to answer the original research question, first in Minneapolis and then in six other cities. But rather than leading to more confidence in deterrence theory, the research results were calling it into question. Deterrence theory now seemed inadequate to explain empirical reality, at least as the researchers had measured this reality. So the researchers began to reanalyze the follow-up data from several cities to try to explain the discrepant results, thereby starting around the research circle once again (Berk, Campbell, Klap, & Western, 1992; Pate & Hamilton, 1992; Sherman et al., 1992).

Phase 3: Inductive Research

At this point, the researchers' approach became more inductive, and they began trying to make sense of the differing patterns in the data collected in the different cities. Could systematic differences in the samples or in the implementation of arrest policies explain the differing outcomes? Or was the problem an inadequacy in the theoretical basis of their research? Was deterrence theory really the best way to explain the patterns in the data they were collecting?

Sherman and his colleagues now turned to *control theory* (Toby, 1957), yet another broad explanation for social behavior. It predicts that having a "stake in conformity" (resulting from inclusion in social networks at work or in the community) decreases a person's likelihood of committing crimes. The implication is that people who are employed and married are more likely to be deterred by the threat of arrest than those without such stakes in conformity. And this is indeed what a reexamination of the data revealed: Individuals who were married and employed were deterred from repeat offenses by arrest, but individuals who were unmarried and unemployed were actually more likely to commit repeat offenses if they were arrested.

Now the researchers had traversed the research circle almost three times, a process perhaps better described as a spiral (see Exhibit 2.7). The first two times the researchers had traversed the research circle in a deductive, hypothesis-testing way. They started with theory and then deduced and tested hypotheses. The third time they traversed the research circle in a more inductive, exploratory way. They started with empirical generalizations from the data they had already obtained and then turned to a new theory to account for the unexpected patterns in the data. At this point they believed that deterrence theory makes correct predictions given certain con-

Exhibit 2.7 **The Research Spiral: Minneapolis Domestic Violence Experiment**

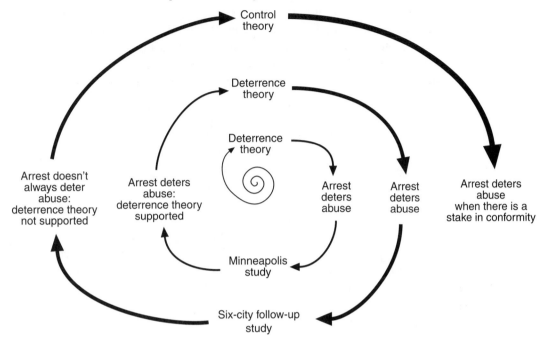

ditions and that another theory, control theory, may specify what these conditions are.

After two and one-half cycles through the research circle, the picture became more complex but also conceptually richer. The researchers came closer to understanding how to inhibit domestic violence. But they cautioned us that their initial question—the research problem—was still not completely answered. Employment status and marital status do not solely measure the strength of social attachments; they also are related to how much people earn and the social standing of victims in court. So maybe social ties are not really what make arrest an effective deterrent to domestic violence. The real deterrent may be cost-benefit calculations ("If I have a higher income, jail is more costly to me") or perceptions about the actions of authorities ("If I am a married woman, judges will treat my complaint more seriously"). More research was needed (Berk et al., 1992).

Phase 4: Deductive Research

In 1997, Paternoster, Sherman, and two other criminologists reexamined data from the Milwaukee Domestic Violence Experiment to test hypotheses derived from yet another theory. As explained earlier in this chapter, procedural justice theory predicts that people will comply with the law out of a sense of duty and obligation if they are treated fairly by legal authorities. In the Milwaukee sample, arrest had had a criminogenic effect: Those who were arrested were subsequently more likely to abuse their spouses than those who were simply warned. Paternoster and his colleagues thought that this effect might have been due to the way subjects were treated when they were arrested rather than simply to the fact that they were arrested. One of their hypotheses spells out the reasoning:

> Among those persons arrested for spouse assault, those who perceive themselves as being treated in a procedurally unfair manner will be more likely to commit acts of spouse assault in the future than those arrested persons who perceive themselves as being treated in a procedurally fair manner, net of other determinants of violence. (Paternoster, Brame, Bachman, & Sherman, 1997:173)

To carry out this study, Paternoster and his colleagues reexamined data collected earlier in Milwaukee, where the findings had seemed anomalous. However, this reanalysis of the data qualifies as deductive research, because the hypotheses were derived from theory and then tested with the data, rather than being induced by the data.

The procedural justice hypotheses were supported: Persons who were arrested in the Milwaukee experiment became more likely to reoffend only if they had been treated unfairly by the police. Otherwise, their rate of rearrest was similar to that for the persons who were not arrested. Thus another element was added to our understanding of the effects of the police response to domestic violence.

Clearly our understanding of effective responses to domestic violence will never truly be complete. Perhaps the actions of the police in Milwaukee had unique effects on those arrested; perhaps the lack of data on whether those who were not arrested felt they had been treated fairly distorted the picture. But research to date has greatly improved our understanding of this social problem. The future should yield an even better understanding, even though at times it may be hard to make sense out of conflicting findings from different studies. Science is an ongoing enterprise in which findings cumulate and eventually yield greater understanding or even radical revisions in our understanding. Social researchers don't need to worry about running out of work to do.

■ ■ ■ ■ Guidelines for Social Researchers

Any effort to understand the social world is plagued by pitfalls, including (as you learned in Chapter 1) such everyday errors in reasoning as overgeneralization, selective or inaccurate observation, illogical reasoning, and resistance to change. Social scientists cannot avoid these problems entirely, but they try to minimize their impact by adhering to certain guidelines.

The guidelines followed by social researchers fall into two categories: those that help keep research scientific and those that help keep research ethical. Both types of guidelines are essential for a field of inquiry that seeks empirical generalizations about human society. To point up their value, I'll use some examples from the domestic violence research.

Scientific Guidelines

The following nine guidelines are applicable to any type of scientific research, but they are particularly useful to social scientists and to those who read about social science. Adherence to these guidelines will reduce the temptation "to project on what is observed whatever [they] want the world to be for [their] own private purposes" (Hoover, 1980:131).

1. *Test ideas against empirical reality without becoming too personally invested in a particular outcome.* This "testing" approach is reflected in the research process and is implicit in the goal of validity. It contrasts markedly with our everyday methods of figuring things out, in which we typically just react to events as they happen, without much attention to whether we really are putting our ideas to a test. Empirical testing requires a neutral and open-minded approach: The scientist is personally disinterested in the outcome and is not swayed by the popularity or the social status of those who would prefer other outcomes.

2. *Plan and carry out investigations systematically.* Social researchers have little hope of conducting a careful test of their ideas if they do not think through in advance how they should go about the test and then proceed accordingly. But a systematic approach is not always easy. For example, Sherman and Berk needed to ensure that spouse abusers were assigned to be either arrested or not on a random basis rather than on the basis of the police officers' personal preferences. So the researchers devised an elaborate procedure using randomly sequenced report sheets in different colors. But the researchers found that police officers did not always follow this systematic procedure. Subsequently, in some replications of the study, the researchers ensured compliance with their research procedures by requiring police officers to call in to a central number to receive the experimentally determined treatment.

3. *Document all procedures, and disclose them publicly.* Social researchers who disclose the methods on which their conclusions rest allow others to evaluate for themselves the likely soundness of these conclusions. Such disclosure is a key feature of science. Again, Sherman and Berk (1984) provide a compelling example. In their research report, after describing the formal research plan, they describe at length the apparent "slippage" from this plan, which occurred primarily because some police officers avoided implementing the random assignment procedure.

4. *Clarify assumptions.* No investigation is complete unto itself; whatever the researcher's method, the research rests on some background assumptions. Research to determine whether arrest has a deterrent effect assumes that potential law violators think rationally, that they calculate potential costs and benefits prior to committing crimes. When a researcher conducts an election poll, the assumption is that people actually vote for the candidate they say they will vote for. When government unemployment statistics are used to describe the state of the economy, the assumption is that those statistics reflect actual fluctuations in unemployment. By definition, research assumptions are not tested, so we do not know for sure whether they are correct. In fact, researchers themselves do not always recognize the assumptions they are making. By taking the time to think about and to disclose their assumptions, researchers provide important information for those who seek to evaluate the validity of their conclusions.

5. *Specify the meaning of all terms.* Words often have multiple or unclear meanings. "Alienation," "depression," "cold," "crowded," and so on can mean different things to different people. Thus the terms used in scientific research must be defined explicitly and used consistently. For example, Sherman and Berk (1984) identified their focus as misdemeanor domestic assault, not just "wife beating." They specified that their work concerned those cases of spouse assault in which severe injury was not involved and both partners were present when police arrived.

6. *Maintain a skeptical stance toward current knowledge.* Scientists may feel very confident about interpretations of the social or natural world that have been supported by repeated investigations, but the results of any particular investigation must be examined critically. A general skepticism about current knowledge stimulates researchers to improve the validity of current research results and expand the frontier of knowledge. For example, in response to questions raised about the Sherman and Berk study, Lawrence Sherman and Ellen Cohn (1989) discussed 13 problems in the Minneapolis Domestic Violence Experiment in a published critique, weighing carefully the extent to which these problems might have affected its validity. This critique could then stimulate additional research designed to address the problematic aspects of the research.

7. *Replicate research, and accumulate knowledge.* No one study can be viewed as definitive in itself; usually at least some plausible threats to the validity of the conclusions exist. And no conclusion can be understood adequately apart from the larger body of knowledge to which the study is related. Scientific investigations may begin with a half-baked or off-the-wall idea, but a search of the literature for other relevant work must be

conducted in short order. The other side of the coin is that the results of scientific research must be published, to serve as a foundation for others who seek to replicate or extend the research. Sherman (1992) reported that when he and his colleagues decided to attempt some replications of their own experiment, they found that another research team was already planning to do so. The process of extending knowledge gained in the Minneapolis experiment had already begun.

8. *Maintain an interest in theory.* Theories organize the knowledge accumulated by numerous investigations into a coherent whole and serve as a guide to future inquiries. Even though much research is purely descriptive, such research can still serve as a basis for others to evaluate different theories. The Minneapolis Domestic Violence Experiment was devised initially as a test of the competing predictions of deterrence and labeling theory, but the researchers extended their attention to control theory to help them explain unanticipated findings. These theoretical connections make the research much more relevant to other criminologists working to understand different types of crime and social control.

9. *Search for regularities or patterns.* Science is concerned with classes rather than with individuals (except inasmuch as individuals are representatives of a class). Scientists assume that the natural world has some underlying order of relationships, that every event and individual is not so unique that general principles cannot be discerned (Grinnell, 1992:27–29). Individuals are not unimportant to social scientists; Sherman (1992:162–164), for example, described the abuse histories of two men to provide greater insight into why arrest could have different effects for different people. But the goal of elaborating individual cases is to understand social patterns that characterize many individuals.

These general guidelines are only ideals for social research. No particular investigation is going to follow every guideline exactly. Real investigations by social scientists do not always include much attention to theory, specific definitions of all terms, and so forth. But any study that strays far from these guidelines cannot be considered scientific.

Ethical Guidelines

Every scientific investigation, whether in the natural or social sciences, has an ethical dimension to it. First and foremost, the scientific concern with validity requires that scientists be honest and reveal their methods. (How can we otherwise determine if the requirement of honesty has been met?) Scientists also have to consider the uses to which their findings will be put. In addition, because social science is concerned with society and the human beings in that society, social researchers have some unique ethical concerns.

Honesty and Openness

Research distorted by political or personal pressures to find particular outcomes or to achieve the most marketable results is unlikely to be carried out in an honest and open fashion or to achieve valid results. For example, noted English biologist Sir Cyril Burt published fabricated evidence in 1961 that purported to show intelligence is determined primarily by heredity. In the 35 years before Burt's deliberate falsification was exposed, his study influenced much social science theory and research (and was in part responsible for Burt's knighthood) (Kamin, 1974). Efforts to evaluate the influence of inherited characteristics on people were considerably set back by this fraud.

Distinguishing between unintentional error and deliberate fraud can be very difficult. For example, a 1963 report of the United States Senate's Subcommittee on Problems of the Aged and Aging concluded that a study of elderly persons' health needs, publicized by the American Medical Association, was a "supposedly objective, scientific, academic study" but really a "pseudo-scientific half-effort" (Cain, 1967:78–79). The researchers were accused of having an upper-class bias in the design of their sample and of using some questions that underestimated elders' health needs. Yet the researchers were convinced they had adhered to scientific guidelines. It is not clear in this case, nor in many others, whether the research was designed to favor particular findings or to adapt to unavoidable constraints. Error, committed without any intent to defraud, is inevitable. Social scientists who do not do their best to minimize error skirt the boundaries of fraud, but the discovery of errors in a study should not in itself be taken as an indication of dishonesty.

Openness about research procedures and results goes hand in hand with honesty in research design. Openness is also essential if researchers are to learn from the work of others. In spite of this need for openness, some researchers may hesitate to disclose their procedures or results to prevent others from building on their ideas and taking some of the credit. You may have heard of the long legal battle between a U.S. researcher and a French researcher about how credit for discovering the AIDS virus should be allocated. Although such public disputes are unusual, concerns with priority of discovery are common. Scientists are like other people in their desire to be first. Enforcing standards of honesty and encouraging openness about research is the best solution for these problems.

The Uses of Science

Scientists must also consider the uses to which their research is put. Although many scientists believe that personal values should be left outside the laboratory, some argue that it is proper, even desirable, for scientists in their role as citizens to attempt to influence the way their research is used.

Concern over the uses of social science was the subject of a sharp debate among members of a task force on homelessness convened in 1986 by the National Academy of Sciences, which advises the government on science and health. The task force members wrote a lengthy report, as requested, on the dimensions of the problem and the state of scientific knowledge about homelessness. As expected by the academy, the report was written in a "bland, moderate style." But 10 of the 13 task force members insisted that an additional, impassioned declaration was needed:

> Contemporary American homelessness is an outrage, a national scandal. Its character requires a careful, sophisticated and dispassionate analysis—which this report provides—but its tragedy demands something more direct and human, less qualified and detached. We have tried to present the facts and figures of homelessness, but we were unable to capture the extent of our anger and dismay. (Altman et al., 1989:4)

The academy's president refused to include the supplementary statement in the final report because "the language was charged and polemical and emotional." Some social scientists would agree with the 10 dissident task force members, others with the academy's president (Schutt, 1989).

Sherman and Berk were also criticized by some social scientists because of their influence on social policy. In their case, the criticism was that they did not do enough to discourage changes in social policy due to their results. In fact, Sherman and Berk explicitly cautioned police departments not to adopt mandatory arrest policies based solely on their findings (Sherman, 1993). But because Sherman publicized the results of the research in the mass media, he was criticized by some social scientists for implicitly encouraging police departments to change their policies on the basis of preliminary evidence (the results of just one study in one city) (Binder & Meeker, 1993; Lempert, 1989). In part, the question was whether basing policy on partial information was preferable to waiting until the information was more complete. Sherman (1992:150–153) later pointed out that in the Omaha follow-up study, arrest warrants were very effective in reducing repeat offenses among spouse abusers who had already left the scene when police arrived at the time of the initial complaint. Absent offenders had not been included in the initial study; and because the Omaha finding was not publicized, it did not become known to police chiefs or battered women's groups. As a consequence, Sherman suggested, some domestic violence that might have been prevented was not prevented. How much publicity, and at what point in the research, is warranted?

Social scientists who conduct research on behalf of organizations and agencies may face additional difficulties. When an organization contracts with a researcher to evaluate a program, identify community needs, or explore product potential, usually the organization, not the researcher, controls the final report and the publicity it receives. If organizational leaders decide that particular research results are inconsistent with their funding requests, community image, or employee relations, they may refuse to release the results or require changes that the researcher deems unacceptable. In a situation like this, a researcher's desire to have findings used appropriately and reported fully can conflict with contractual obligations.

Researchers can often anticipate such dilemmas in advance and resolve them when the contract for research is negotiated—or decline a particular research opportunity altogether if acceptable terms cannot be worked out. But often these problems come up after a report has been drafted, when the researcher finds out that the report is unacceptable to a top-level administrator or executive whom the researcher does not even know. In addition, a researcher's need to have a job or to maintain particular personal relationships may make it difficult to act in what the researcher thinks is the most ethical manner. A way to minimize these possibilities is to acknowledge the source of research funding in reports and to scrutinize carefully those research reports funded by organizations or agencies having a stake in the outcome.

Research on People

In physics or chemistry, research subjects (objects and substances) may be treated to extreme conditions and then discarded when they are no longer useful. However, social (and medical) scientists must concern themselves with the way their human subjects are treated in the course of research. This "treatment" may involve manipulations in laboratory experiments, sensitive questions in survey research, observations in field studies, or analyses of personal data. Here I will review briefly current ethical standards for the treatment of human subjects—and dilemmas in their application. In the chapters on data collection, I will examine the specific ethical problems that may arise in the course of using particular research methods.

Contemporary standards for the treatment of human subjects are set by the federal government, by professional associations, by special university review boards, and in some cases by ethics committees in other organizations. Federal regulations require that the proposals of researchers seeking federal funds for research on human subjects be reviewed by an **institutional review board (IRB)** before they are submitted for federal review. IRBs at universities and other agencies in turn apply ethics standards set by government agencies, like the National Institutes of Health, and also may develop more specific guidelines of their own. The American Sociological Association (ASA) and other professional social science organizations have adopted ethics guidelines for practicing sociologists and review complaints of unethical practices when asked. I will use the ASA's code of ethics to illustrate some of the ethical standards (American Sociological Association, 1997).

The entire ASA code of ethics is available in print and is posted on the Web at http://www.asanet.org/ecoderev.html. But its standards concerning the treatment of human subjects are simple enough to state:

- Research should cause no harm to subjects.
- Participation in research should be voluntary, and therefore subjects must give their informed consent to participate in the research.
- Researchers should fully disclose their identity.
- Anonymity or confidentiality must be maintained for individual research participants unless it is voluntarily and explicitly waived.
- The benefits of a research project should outweigh any foreseeable risks.

As simple as these guidelines may seem, they are difficult to interpret in specific cases and harder yet to define in a way agreeable to all social scientists. For example, how should "no harm to subjects" be interpreted? Does it mean that subjects should not be at all harmed psychologically as well as physically? That they should feel no anxiety or distress whatever during the study or only after their involvement ends? Should the possibility of any harm, no matter how remote, deter research?

Consider the question of possible harm to the subjects of a well-known prison simulation study (Haney, Banks, & Zimbardo, 1973). The study was designed to investigate the impact of social position on behavior—specifically, the impact of being either a guard or a prisoner in a prison, a "total institution." The researchers selected 20 young men whom they judged to be the most stable and mature, and the least antisocial, of 75 applicants. The participants signed a contract agreeing to be either a guard or a prisoner in a simulated prison for two weeks, during which time they would be paid $15 daily and receive food, clothing, housing, and medical care. Some were randomly selected to be guards and were told to maintain order among the "prisoners," who were then incarcerated in a makeshift basement prison. Within the first two days, marked differences in behavior emerged between the two groups. The prisoners acted passive and disorganized, and the guards became verbally and physically aggressive (although physical abuse was not allowed) and arbitrary. Five "prisoners" were soon released for depression, uncontrollable crying, fits of rage, and in one case a psychosomatic rash; on the sixth day the researchers terminated the experiment. Through discussions in special postexperiment encounter sessions, feelings of stress among the participants who played the role of prisoner seemed to be relieved; follow-up during the next year indicated no lasting negative effects on the participants and some benefits in the form of greater insight.

Would you ban such experiments because of the potential for harm to subjects? Does the fact that the experiment yielded significant insights into the effect of a situation on human behavior—insights that could be used to improve prisons—make any difference (Reynolds, 1979:133–139)? Do you believe that this benefit outweighed the foreseeable risks?

The requirement of informed consent is also more difficult to define than it first appears. To be informed, consent must be given by persons who are competent to consent, have consented voluntarily, are fully informed about the research, and have comprehended what they have been told (Reynolds, 1979). Can prisoners give informed consent? Can children or even their guardians? Can students who are asked to participate in research by their professor? Can participants in covert experiments?

Fully informed consent may also reduce participation in research and, because signing consent forms prior to participation may change participants' responses, produce biased results (Larson, 1993:114). Experimental researchers whose research design requires some type of subject deception try to get around this problem by withholding some information before the experiment begins but then debriefing subjects at the end. In the **debriefing**, the researcher explains to the subject what happened in the experiment and why. However, even though debriefing can be viewed as a substitute in some cases for securing fully informed consent prior to the experiment, if the debriefed subjects disclose the nature of the experiment to other participants, subsequent results may still be contaminated (Adair, Dushenko, & Lindsay, 1985).

Well-intentioned researchers may also fail to foresee all the potential problems. In the prison simulation, all the participants signed consent forms, but how could they have been fully informed in advance? The researchers themselves did not realize that the study participants would experience so much stress so quickly, that some "prisoners" would have to be released for severe negative reactions within the first few days, or that even those who were not severely stressed would soon be begging to be released from the mock prison. If this risk was not foreseeable, was it acceptable for the researchers to presume in advance that the benefits would outweigh the risks?

Maintaining confidentiality is another key ethical obligation. However, this standard should be overridden if a health- or life-threatening situation arises and participants need to be alerted. Also, the standard of confidentiality does not apply to observation in public places and information available in public records.

The potential of withholding a beneficial treatment from some subjects is also cause for ethical concern. The Sherman and Berk experiment required the random assignment of subjects to treatment conditions and thus had the potential of causing harm to the victims of domestic violence whose batterers were not arrested. The justification for the study design, however, is quite persuasive: The researchers didn't know prior to the experiment which response to a domestic violence complaint would be most likely to deter future incidents (Sherman, 1992). The experiment provided clear evidence about the value of arrest, so it can be argued that the benefits outweighed the risks.

The evaluation of ethical issues in a research project should be based on a realistic assessment of the overall potential for harm to research subjects rather than an apparent inconsistency between any particular aspect of a research plan and a specific ethical guideline. For example, full disclosure of "what is really going on" in an experimental study is unnecessary if subjects are unlikely to be harmed. Nevertheless, researchers should make every effort to foresee all possible risks and to weigh the possible benefits of the research against these risks.

The extent to which ethical issues are a problem for researchers and their subjects varies dramatically with research design. Survey research, in particular, creates few ethical problems. In fact, researchers from Michigan's Institute for Survey Research interviewed a representative national sample of adults and found that 68% of those who had participated in a survey were somewhat or very interested in participating in another; the more times respondents had been interviewed, the more willing they were to participate again. Presumably they would have felt differently if they had been treated unethically (Reynolds, 1979:56–57). On the other hand, some experimental studies in the social sciences that have put people in uncomfortable or embarrassing situations have generated vociferous complaints and years of debate about ethics (Reynolds, 1979; Sjoberg, 1967).

Conclusion

Social researchers can find many questions to study, but not all questions are equally worthy. The ones that warrant the expense and effort of social research are feasible, socially important, and scientifically relevant.

The simplicity of the research circle presented in this chapter belies the complexity of the social research process. In the following chapters, I will focus on particular aspects of that process. Chapter 3 examines the interrelated processes of conceptualization and measurement, arguably the most important part of research. Measurement validity is the foundation for the other two aspects of validity. Chapter 4 reviews the meaning of generalizability and the sampling strategies that help us to achieve this goal. Chapter 5 introduces causal validity, the third aspect of validity, and illustrates different methods for achieving causal validity. The next four chapters then introduce different approaches to data collection—experiments, surveys, qualitative research, and comparative research—that help us, in different ways, to achieve validity.

As you encounter these specifics, don't lose sight of the basic guidelines that researchers need to follow to overcome the most common impediments to social research. Owning a large social science toolkit is no guarantee of making the right decisions about which tools to use and how to use them in the investigation of particular research problems. More important, our answers to research questions will never be complete or entirely certain. Thus, when we complete a research project, we should point out how the research could be extended and evaluate the confidence we have in our conclusions. Recall how the gradual elaboration of knowledge about homelessness and deterrence of domestic violence required sensitivity to research difficulties, careful weighing of the evidence, and identification of unanswered questions by several research teams.

Ethical issues also should be considered when evaluating research proposals and completed research studies. As the preceding examples show, ethical issues in social research are no less complex than the other issues that researchers confront. And it is inexcusable to jump into research on people without any attention to ethical considerations.

You are now forewarned about, and thus hopefully forearmed against, the difficulties that any scientists, but social scientists in particular, face in their work. I hope that you will return often to this chapter as you read the subsequent chapters, when you criticize the research literature, and when you design your own research projects. To be conscientious, thoughtful, and responsible—this is the mandate of every social scientist. If you formulate a feasible research problem, ask the right questions in advance, try to adhere to the research guidelines, and steer clear of the most common difficulties, you will be well along the road to fulfilling this mandate.

KEY TERMS

Anomalous finding
Debriefing
Deductive reasoning
Deductive research
Dependent variable
Direction of association
Empirical generalization
Hypothesis
Independent variable

Inductive reasoning
Inductive research
Institutional review board (IRB)
Replication
Research circle
Serendipitous finding
Social research question
Theory
Variable

HIGHLIGHTS

■ Research questions should be feasible (within the time and resources available), socially important, and scientifically relevant.

■ Building social theory is a major objective of social science research. Investigate relevant theories before starting social research projects, and draw out the theoretical implications of research findings.

■ The type of reasoning in most research can be described as primarily deductive or inductive. Research based on deductive reasoning proceeds from general ideas, deduces specific expectations from these ideas, and then tests the ideas with empirical data. Research based on inductive reasoning begins with specific data and then develops general ideas or theories to explain patterns in the data.

■ It may be possible to explain unanticipated research findings after the fact, but such explanations have less credibility than those that have been tested with data collected for the purpose of the study.

■ The scientific process can be represented as circular, with connections from theory, to hypotheses, to data, and to empirical generalizations. Research investigations may begin at different points along the research circle and traverse different portions of it. Deductive research begins at the point of theory; inductive research begins with data but ends with theory. Descriptive research begins with data and ends with empirical generalizations.

■ Replications of a study are essential to establish its generalizability in other situations. An ongoing line of research stemming from a particular research question should include a series of studies that, collectively, traverse the research circle multiple times.

■ Social scientists, like all scientists, should structure their research so that their own ideas can be proved wrong, should disclose their methods for others to critique, and should recognize the possibility of error. Nine specific guidelines are recommended here.

■ Scientific research should be conducted and reported in an honest and open fashion. Contemporary ethical standards also require that social research cause no harm to subjects, that participation be voluntary as expressed in informed consent, that researchers fully disclose their identity, that benefits to subjects outweigh any foreseeable risks, and that anonymity or confidentiality be maintained for participants unless it is voluntarily and explicitly waived.

EXERCISES

1. State a problem for research. If you have not already identified a problem for study, or if you need to evaluate whether your research problem is doable, a few suggestions should help to get the ball rolling and keep it on course.

   a. Jot down questions that have puzzled you in some area having to do with people and social relations, perhaps questions that have come to mind while reading textbooks or research articles or even while hearing news stories. Don't hesitate to jot down many questions, and don't bore your-self—try to identify questions that really interest you.

    b. Now take stock of your interests, your opportunities, and the work of others. Which of your research questions no longer seem feasible or interesting? What additional research questions come to mind? Pick out a question that is of interest and seems feasible and that your other coursework suggests has been the focus of some prior research or theorizing.

    c. Write out your research question in one sentence, and elaborate on it in one paragraph. List at least three reasons why it is a good research question for you to investigate. Then present your proposal to your classmates and instructor for discussion and feedback.

2. Search the literature on the topic you prepared in Exercise 1 or on some other topic, perhaps one you focused on in Chapter 1. Refer to Appendix B for guidance on conducting the search. Copy down at least 10 citations to articles or Web sites reporting research that seems highly relevant to your research question; then look up at least three of these articles or sites. Inspect the bibliographies of these three sources of information, and identify at least one more relevant article or Web site you could check.

    Write a brief description of each of the three sources you consulted, and evaluate its relevance to your research question. What additions or changes to your thoughts about the research question are suggested by the sources? How well did the authors summarize their work in their abstracts? What important points would you have missed if you had relied only on the abstracts?

3. Find an article or Web site that is cited in another source. Compare the cited source to what was said about it in the original article or site. Was the discussion of it accurate?

4. Research problems posed for explanatory studies must specify hypotheses and variables, which need to be stated properly and need to correctly imply any hypothesized causal relationship. Some lessons on the practice diskette distributed with your textbook will help you to learn the language of variables and hypotheses.

    To use these lessons, choose one of the four "Variables and Hypotheses" exercises from the opening menu. About 10 hypotheses are presented in the lesson. After reading each hypothesis, you must name the dependent and independent variables and state the direction (positive or negative) of the relationship between them. The program will evaluate your answers. If an answer is correct, the program will repeat it and go on to the next question. If you have made an error, the program will explain the error to you and give you another chance to respond. If your answer is unrecognizable, the program will instruct you to check your spelling and try again.

5. Classify five research projects you have read about, either in previous exercises or in other courses, as primarily inductive or deductive. Did you notice any inductive components in the primarily deductive projects? How much descriptive research was involved? Did the findings have any implications that you think should be investigated in a new study? What new hypotheses are implied by the findings?

6. Using the same research article you focused on in exercise 3, identify the stages of the research project corresponding to the points on the research circle. Did the research cover all four stages? Identify the theories and hypotheses underlying the study. What data were collected? What were the findings (empirical generalizations)?

7. Compare three studies concerning some social program or organizational policy. Several possibilities are research on Project Head Start, on the effects of welfare payments, on boot camps or other criminal justice policies, and on jury size. Would you characterize the findings as largely consistent or inconsistent? How would you explain discrepant findings?

8. Criticize the research in one of the articles you have reviewed for another exercise in terms of its adherence to each of the nine scientific guidelines for social research. Discuss the extent to which the study adhered to each guideline, and indicate what problem or problems might have occurred in the research as a result of deviation from the guidelines.

9. Pair up with one other student, and select one of the research articles you have reviewed for other exercises. Criticize the research in terms of its adherence to each of the nine scientific guidelines for social research, being generally negative but not unreasonable in your criticisms. The student with whom you are working should critique the article in the same way but from a generally positive standpoint, defending its adherence to the nine guidelines but without ignoring the study's weak points. Together, write a summary of the study's strong and weak points, or conduct a debate in class.

10. Evaluate one of the studies you found in Exercise 2 for its adherence to each of the ethics guidelines. How would you weigh the study's contribution to knowledge and social policy against its potential risks to human subjects?

WEB EXERCISES

1. Go to

    http://www.well.com/user/theory/

    By using the Web site and starting from the home page, explore The Common Theory Project. What is The Common Theory Project? What is its purpose? Click on the link to "What is the motivation for and purpose of the Project?" Click on "Belief One" and "Belief Two" to read about these ideas. What do you think of these beliefs? How do beliefs such as these play a role in, and influence, social science?

2. You've been assigned to write a paper on domestic violence and the law. To start, you would like to find out what the American Bar Association's stance is on the issue. Go to the American Bar Association Commission on Domestic Violence's Web site at

    http://www.abanet.org/domviol/mrdv/identify.html

    What is the American Bar Association's definition of domestic violence? How do they suggest one can identify a person as a victim of domestic violence? What do they identify as "basic warning signs"? Write your answers in a 1–2 page report.

SPSS EXERCISES

1. Browse the GSS96 variables dealing with gender roles by clicking on the "List Variables" button. These variables begin with FE...

   a. From these variables, write two research questions for inclusion in a student research paper that are feasible, given the GSS96 data, socially important, and scientifically relevant.

   b. Choose an FE... variable that you hypothesize to be associated with another variable in one of your research questions, and create a bar chart of that FE... variable.

2. You will now compare the distribution of your chosen FE... variable across the categories of another variable from the GSS96.

   a. Select all women and then request a bar chart of your chosen FE... variable. Then select all men and generate the bar chart again.
   DATA...
       SELECT CASES...
           If...SEX=2 (1 for men) [x unselected cases are filtered]

   b. Compare the distributions between the two bar charts and formulate a hypothesis as to the relationship between the two variables. Is there a relationship between SEX and your FE... variable?

   c. Now test your hypothesis (from Question #1) in the same way. What did you find out? What do you conclude?

3. Search the current literature in your library (or in another collection on-line from a home computer) and find an article that concerns your hypothesis. Do you think you should revise your hypothesis after searching the literature?

3 Conceptualization and Measurement

Concepts
Conceptualization in Practice
    Defining Substance Abuse
    Defining Alienation
    Defining Poverty
Concepts and Variables

Measurement Operations
Using Available Data
Constructing Questions
    Single Questions
    Question Sets
    Scales and Indexes
Making Observations
Using Indirect Measures
Combining Measurement Operations

Evaluation of Measures
Measurement Validity
    Face Validity
    Content Validity
    Criterion Validity
    Construct Validity
Reliability
    Test-Retest Reliability
    Interitem Reliability (Internal Consistency)
    Alternate-Forms Reliability
    Interobserver Reliability
Ways to Improve Reliability and Validity

Levels of Measurement
Nominal Level of Measurement

Substance abuse is a social problem of remarkable proportions. Alcohol is involved in about half of all fatal traffic crashes, and more than 1 million arrests are made annually for driving under the influence. As many as two-thirds of all persons arrested in urban areas test positive for drugs (Gruenewald, Treno, Taff, & Klitzner, 1997). College presidents rate alcohol abuse as the number-one campus problem (Wechsler, Davenport, Dowdall, Moeykens, & Castillo, 1994), and it is a factor in as many as two-thirds of on-campus sexual assaults (National Institute of Alcohol Abuse and Alcoholism [NIAA], 1995). All told, the annual costs of prevention and treatment for alcohol and drug abuse exceed $4 billion (Gruenewald et al., 1997).

Whether your goal is to learn how society works, to deliver useful services, or to design effective social policies, at some point you will probably need to read the research literature on substance abuse—perhaps even design your own study of it. Every time you begin to review or design relevant research, you will have to answer two questions: "What is meant by 'substance abuse' in this research?" (which concerns conceptualization) and "How was substance abuse measured?" (which concerns measurement). Both questions must be answered to evaluate the validity of substance abuse research. We cannot make sense of the results of a study until we know how the concepts were defined and measured. Nor are we ready to begin a research project until we have defined our concepts and constructed valid measures of them. Measurement validity is essential to successful research; in fact, without valid measures it is fruitless to attempt to achieve the other two aspects of validity, causal validity and generalizability.

In this chapter, I first address the issue of conceptualization, using substance abuse and related concepts as examples. I then focus on measurement, reviewing first how measures of substance abuse have been constructed using such operations as available data, questions, observations, and less direct and obtrusive measures. Then I tell you how to assess the validity and reliability of these measures. The final topic is the level of measurement reflected in different measures. By the chapter's end, you should have a good understanding of measurement, the first of the three legs on which a research project's validity rests.

■ ■ ■ ■ **Concepts**

A May 1997 *New York Times* article (Johnson, 1997) reported that five U.S. colleges were participating in a pilot program to ban alcohol in their fraternities. Moreover, the article claimed that "substance-free housing" would soon become the norm on U.S. campuses. Do you know just what the article means? Some of these **concepts**—"alcohol," "colleges," "campuses," and "pilot program"—are widely understood and commonly used. However, do we all have the same thing in mind when we hear these terms? For example, are junior colleges subsumed within the term "college"? Does the concept of "on campus" extend to fraternity houses that are not physically on college property? Does "substance-free housing" mean banning tobacco products as well as alcohol?

Concept A mental image that summarizes a set of similar observations, feelings, or ideas.

Conceptualization The process of specifying what we mean by a term. In deductive research, **conceptualization** helps to translate portions of an abstract theory into testable hypotheses involving specific variables. In inductive research, conceptualization is an important part of the process used to make sense of related observations.

Concepts like "substance-free housing" require an explicit definition before they are used in research because we cannot be certain that all readers will share the same definition. It is even more important to define concepts that are somewhat abstract or unfamiliar. When we refer to concepts like "poverty" or "social control" or "alienation," we cannot count on others knowing exactly what we mean.

Clarifying the meaning of such concepts does not benefit only those who are unfamiliar with them. Clarifying concepts is also important because the experts often disagree about their meaning or at least prefer different definitions. But we need not avoid using these concepts; we just have to specify clearly what we mean when we use them, and we must expect others to do the same.

Conceptualization in Practice

If we are to do an adequate job of conceptualizing, we must do more than just think up some definition, any definition, for our concepts. We may need to distinguish subconcepts, or dimensions, of the concept. We also should ask how the concept's definition fits within the theoretical framework guiding the research and what assumptions underlie this framework.

Defining Substance Abuse

What observations or images should we associate with the concept "substance abuse"? Someone leaning against a building with a liquor bottle, barely able to speak coherently? College students drinking heavily at a party? Someone in an Alcoholics Anonymous group drinking one beer? A 10-year-old boy drinking a small glass of wine in an alley? A 10-year-old boy drinking a small glass of wine at the dinner table in France? Do all these images share something in common that we should define as substance abuse for the purposes of a particular research study? Do some of them? Should we take into account cultural differences? Social situations? Physical tolerance for alcohol? Individual standards?

Many researchers now use the definition of substance abuse contained in the *Diagnostic and Statistical Manual, IV* (DSM-IV) of the American Psychiatric Association (Mueser et al., 1990:33): "repeated use of a substance to the extent that it interferes with adequate social, vocational, or self-care functioning." In contrast, substance dependence is defined as "development of tolerance to a substance such that the person requires larger dosages to achieve the same psychoactive effect, and the experience of withdrawal symptoms and craving after a period of abstinence from the substance." Note that these definitions rely on behavioral and biological criteria rather than social expectations or cultural norms.

We cannot judge the DSM-IV definition of substance abuse as "correct" or "incorrect." Each researcher has the right to conceptualize as he or she sees fit. However, we can say that the DSM-IV definition of substance abuse is useful, even good, in part because it has been very widely adopted. If we conceptualize substance abuse the same way that the DSM-IV does, many others will share our definition and understand what we are talking about. The definition of substance abuse has two other attractive features: It is stated in clear and precise language that should minimize differences in interpretation and maximize understanding; and it also can clearly be distinguished from the more specific concept of substance dependence.

One caution is in order. The definition of any one concept rests on a shared understanding of the terms used in the definition. So if our audience does not already have a shared understanding of terms like "adequate social functioning," "self-care functioning," and "repeated use," we must also define these terms before we are finished with the process of defining substance abuse.

Defining Alienation

Some concepts have multiple dimensions, bringing together several related concepts under a larger conceptual umbrella. One such concept is "alienation," defined by Robert Blauner as

> a general syndrome made up of a number of different objective conditions and subjective feeling-states which emerge from certain relationships between workers and the sociotechnical settings of employment. Alienation exists when workers are unable to control their immediate work processes [*powerlessness*], to develop a sense of purpose and function which connects their jobs to the overall organization of production [*meaninglessness*], to belong to integrated industrial communities [*isolation*], and when they fail to become involved in the activity of work as a mode of personal self-expression [*self-estrangement*]. (1964:15)

With this multidimensional conception of alienation, Blauner developed a much richer analysis of the consequences of technological change in industry than would have been possible if he had limited himself to a one-dimensional definition of alienation.

Defining Poverty

Decisions about how to define a concept reflect the theoretical framework that guides the researchers. For example, the concept "poverty" has always been somewhat controversial, because different notions of what poverty is shape estimates of how prevalent it is and what can be done about it.

Most of the statistics that you see in the newspaper about the poverty rate reflect a conception of poverty that was formalized by Mollie Orshansky of the Social Security Administration in 1965 and subsequently adopted by the federal government and many researchers (Putnam, 1977). She defined poverty in terms of what is called an *absolute* standard, based on the amount of money required to purchase an emergency diet that is estimated to be nutritionally adequate for about two months. The idea is that people are truly poor if they can barely purchase the food they need and other essential goods. This poverty standard is adjusted for household size and composition (number of children and adults), and the minimal amount needed for food is multiplied by three because a 1955 survey indicated that poor families spend about one-third of their incomes on food (Orshansky, 1977).

Some social scientists disagree with the absolute standard and have instead urged adoption of a *relative* poverty standard. They identify the poor as those in the lowest 5th or 10th of the income distribution or as those having some fraction of the average income. The idea behind this relative conception is that poverty should be defined in terms of what is normal in a given society at a particular time.

Some social scientists prefer yet another conception of poverty. With the *subjective* approach, poverty is defined as what people think would be the minimal income they need to make ends meet. Of course, many have argued that this approach is influenced too much by the different standards that people use to estimate what they "need" (Ruggles, 1990:20–23).

Which do you think is a more reasonable approach to defining poverty—an absolute standard, a relative standard, or a subjective standard? Our understanding of the concept of poverty is sharpened when we consider the theoretical ramifications of these alternative definitions.

Concepts and Variables

After we define the concepts in a theory, we can identify variables corresponding to the concepts and (if the concepts refer to variable phenomena) develop measurement procedures. This is an important step. Consider the concept of social control, which Donald Black defines as "all of the processes by which people define and respond to deviant behavior" (Black, 1984). What variables can represent this conceptualization of social control? Proportion of persons arrested in a community? Average length of sentences for crimes? Types of bystander reactions to public intoxication? Some combination of these?

Although we must proceed carefully to specify what we mean by a concept like social control, some concepts are represented well by the specific variables in the study and need not be defined so carefully. We may define binge drinking as heavy episodic drinking and measure it, as a variable, by asking people how many drinks they consumed in succession during some period (see Wechsler et al., 1994). That's pretty straightforward.

Be aware also that not every concept in a study is represented by a variable. For example, if the term "tolerance of drinking" is defined as the absence of rules against drinking in a fraternity, it brings to mind a phenomenon that varies across different fraternities at different colleges. But if we study social life at only those fraternities that prohibit drinking, tolerance of drinking would not be a variable: All the fraternities studied have the same level of tolerance, and thus tolerance of drinking is a constant and not a variable. Of course, the concept of tolerance of drinking would still be important for understanding social life in the "dry" fraternities.

■ ■ ■ ■ Measurement Operations

Once we have defined our concepts in the abstract—that is, after conceptualizing—and once we have specified the specific variables we want to measure, we must develop our measurement procedures. The goal is to devise **operations** that actually measure or indicate the concepts we intend to measure—in other words, to achieve measurement validity.

> *Operation* A procedure for identifying or indicating the value of cases on a variable.
>
> *Operationalization* The process of specifying the operations that will indicate the value of cases on a variable.

Exhibit 3.1 represents the **operationalization** process in three studies. The first researcher defines her concept, income, and chooses one variable—annual earnings—to represent it. This variable is then measured with responses to a single question, or **indicator**: "What was your total income from all sources in 1998?" The second researcher defines her concept, poverty, as having two aspects or dimensions, subjective poverty and absolute poverty. Subjective poverty is measured with responses to a survey question: "Do you consider yourself poor?" Absolute poverty is measured by comparing family income to the poverty threshold. The third researcher decides that her concept, social class, can be indicated with three measured variables: income, education, and occupational prestige. The values of these three variables for each case studied are then combined into a single indicator.

Exhibit 3.1 **Concepts, Variables, and Indicators**

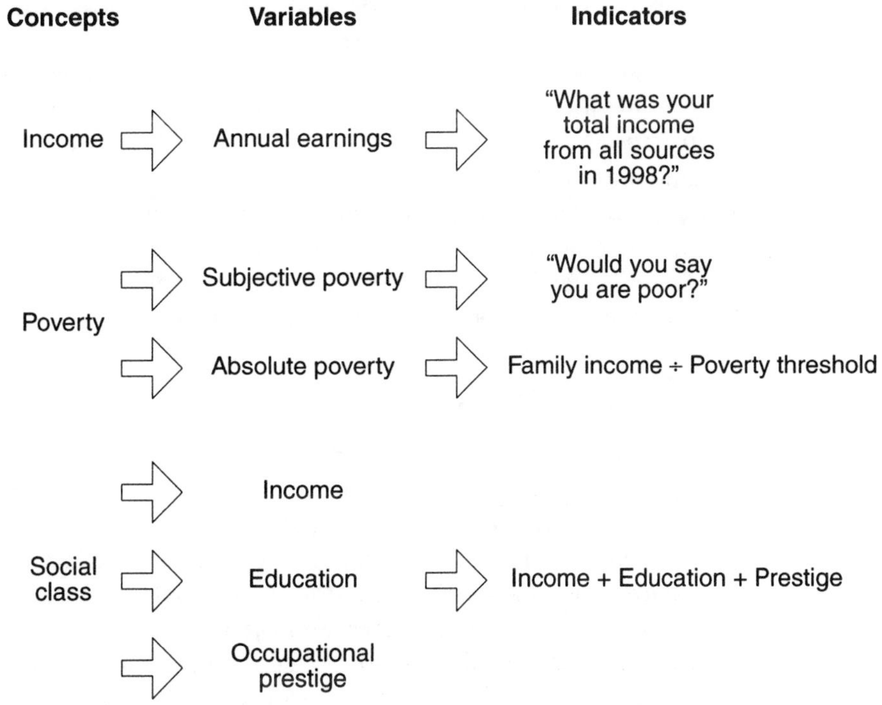

Concepts	Variables	Indicators
Income ⇨	Annual earnings ⇨	"What was your total income from all sources in 1998?"
Poverty ⇨	Subjective poverty ⇨	"Would you say you are poor?"
⇨	Absolute poverty ⇨	Family income ÷ Poverty threshold
Social class ⇨	Income	
⇨	Education ⇨	Income + Education + Prestige
⇨	Occupational prestige	

Good conceptualization and operationalization can prevent confusion later in the research process. For example, a researcher may find that substance abusers who join a self-help group are less likely to drink again than those who receive hospital-based substance abuse treatment. But what is it about these treatment alternatives that is associated with successful abstinence? Level of peer support? Beliefs about the causes of alcoholism? Financial investment in the treatment? If the researcher had considered such aspects of the concept of substance abuse treatment before collecting her data, she might have been able to measure different aspects of treatment and so figure out which, if any, were associated with differences in abstinence rates. Because she did not measure these variables, she will not contribute as much as she might have to our understanding of substance abuse treatment.

Social researchers have many options for operationalizing their concepts. Measures can be based on activities as diverse as asking people questions, reading judicial opinions, observing social interactions, coding words in books, checking census data tapes, enumerating the contents of trash receptacles, drawing urine and blood samples. Experimental researchers may operationalize a concept by manipulating its value: To operationalize the concept of exposure to anti-drinking messages, some subjects listen to a talk about binge drinking; others do not. I will focus here on the operations of using published data, asking questions, observing behavior, and using unobtrusive and indirect means of measuring people's behavior and attitudes. However, the particular measurement operations chosen for a study should be shaped by the research question.

Time and resource limitations also must be taken into account. For many sociohistorical questions (such as "How has the poverty rate varied since 1950?"), census data or other published counts must be used. On the other hand, a historical question about the types of social bonds among combat troops in 20th-century wars probably requires retrospective interviews with surviving veterans. The validity of the data is lessened by the unavailability of many veterans from World War I and by problems of recall, but direct observation of their behavior during the war is certainly not an option.

Using Available Data

Government reports are rich and readily accessible sources of social science data. Organizations ranging from nonprofit service groups to private businesses also compile a wealth of figures that may be available to some social scientists for some purposes. In addition, the data collected in many social science surveys are archived and made available for researchers who were not involved in the original survey project.

Before we assume that available data will be useful, we must consider how appropriate they are for our concepts of interest. We may conclude that some other measure would provide a better fit with a concept or that a particular concept simply cannot adequately be operationalized with the available data. For example, law-enforcement and health statistics provide several community-level indicators of substance abuse (Gruenewald et al., 1997). Statistics on arrests for the sale and possession of drugs, drunk driving arrests, and liquor law violations (such as sales to minors) can usually be obtained on an annual basis, and often quarterly, from local police departments or state crime information centers. Health-related indicators of substance abuse at the community level include single-vehicle fatal crashes, the rate of mortality due to alcohol or drug abuse, and the use of alcohol and drug treatment services.

Indicators like these cannot be compared across communities or the other units from which they were collected without reviewing carefully how they were constructed. The level of alcohol in the blood that is legally required to establish intoxication can vary among communities, creating the appearance of different rates of substance abuse even though drinking and driving practices may be identical. Enforcement practices can vary among police jurisdictions and over time.

We also cannot assume that available data are accurate, even when they appear to measure the concept in which we are interested and in a way that is consistent across communities. "Official" counts of homeless persons have been notoriously unreliable because of the difficulty of locating homeless persons on the streets, and government agencies have at times resorted to "guesstimates" by service providers. Even available data for such seemingly straightforward measures as counts of organizations can contain a surprising amount of error. For example, a 1990 national church directory reported 128 churches in a Midwest county; an intensive search in that county in 1992 located 172 churches (Hadaway, Marler, & Chaves, 1993: 744).

When legal standards, enforcement practices, and measurement procedures have been taken into account, comparisons among communities become more credible. However, such adjustments may be less necessary when the operationalization of a concept is relatively unambiguous, as with the homicide rate: Dead is dead. And when a central authority imposes a common data-collection standard, as with the FBI's Uniform Crime Reports, the odds that data will be comparable across communities also increase. Careful review of measurement operations is still important, since procedures for classifying a death as a homicide can vary between jurisdictions and over time. Sometimes refining the indicator can help. For example, the number of single-vehicle nighttime crashes, whether fatal or not, is a more specific indicator of the frequency of drinking and driving than just the number of single-vehicle fatal accidents (Gruenewald et al., 1997:40–41).

A wealth of data is available in survey datasets archived and made available to university researchers by the Interuniversity Consortium for Political and Social Research. One of its most popular survey datasets is the General Social Survey (GSS). The GSS is administered regularly to a sample of more than 1,500 Americans (annually until 1994, biennially since then). GSS questions vary from year to year, but an unchanging core of questions includes measures of political attitudes, occupation and income, social activities, substance abuse, and many other variables of interest to social scientists. However, when surveys are used in this way, after the fact, researchers must evaluate the survey questions as if they were developing questions for a new survey. Are the available measures sufficiently close to the measures needed that they can be used to answer the new research question?

Constructing Questions

Asking people questions is the most common operation for measuring social variables and probably the most versatile. Most concepts about individuals can be defined in such a way that measurement with one or more questions becomes an option. In this section I'll introduce some options for writing single questions, explain why single questions can be inadequate measures of some concepts, and then examine measurement approaches that rely on multiple questions to measure a concept.

Although in principle survey questions can be a straightforward and efficient means to measure individual characteristics, facts about events, level of knowledge, and opinions of any sort, in practice survey questions can result in misleading or inappropriate answers. All questions proposed for a survey must be screened carefully for their adherence to basic guidelines and then tested and revised until the researcher feels some confidence that they will be clear to the intended respondents (Fowler, 1995). Some variables may prove to be inappropriate for measurement with any type of question. We have to recognize that memories and perceptions of the events about which we might like to ask can be limited.

Specific guidelines for reviewing questions are presented in Chapter 7; here my focus is on the different types of survey questions.

Single Questions

Measuring variables with single questions is very popular. Public opinion polls based on answers to single questions are reported frequently in newspaper articles and TV newscasts: "Do you favor or oppose U.S. policy in . . . ?" "If you had to vote today, for which candidate would you vote?" Social science surveys also rely on single questions to measure many variables: "Overall, how satisfied are you with your job?" "How would you rate your current health?"

Single questions can be designed with or without explicit response choices. The question that follows is a **closed-ended question,** or **fixed-choice question,** because respondents are offered explicit responses to choose from. It has been selected from the Core Alcohol and Drug Survey distributed by the Core Institute, Southern Illinois University, for the FIPSE Core Analysis Grantee Group (Presley, Meilman, & Lyeria, 1994).

```
Compared to other campuses with which you are familiar, this
campus's use of alcohol is . . . (Mark one)
    Greater than other campuses
    Less than other campuses
    About the same as other campuses
```

Most surveys of a large number of people contain primarily fixed-choice questions, which are easy to process with computers and analyze with statistics. With fixed-choice questions, respondents are also more likely to answer the question that the researcher really wants them to answer. Including the response choices reduces ambiguity. However, fixed-response choices can obscure what people really think unless the choices are designed carefully to match the range of possible responses to the question.

Most important, response choices should be mutually exclusive and exhaustive, so that every respondent can find one and only one choice that applies to him or her (unless the question is of the "Check all that apply" format). To make response choices exhaustive, researchers may need to offer at least one option with room for ambiguity. For example, a questionnaire asking college students to indicate their school status should not use freshman, sophomore, junior, and senior as the only response choices. Most campuses also have students in a "special" category, and many have graduate students. So you might add "Other (please specify)" to the four fixed responses to this question. If respondents do not find a response option that corresponds to their answer to the question, they may skip the question entirely or choose a response option that does not indicate what they are really thinking.

Researchers who study small numbers of people often use **open-ended questions**—questions without explicit response choices, to which respondents write in their answers. The next question is an open-ended version of the earlier fixed-choice question:

```
How would you say alcohol use on this campus compares to that on other
campuses?
```

An open-ended format is preferable with questions for which the range of responses cannot adequately be anticipated—namely, questions that have not previously been used in surveys and questions that are asked of new groups. Open-ended questions can also lessen confusion about the meaning of responses involving complex concepts.

Mental illness, for example, is a complex concept that tends to have different meanings for different people. In a survey I conducted in homeless shelters, I asked staff whether they believed that people at the shelter had become homeless due to mental illness (Schutt, 1992). Forty-seven percent chose "Agree" or "Strongly agree" when given fixed-response choices. However, when these same staff members were interviewed in depth, with open-ended questions, it became clear that the meaning of these responses varied among staff. Some believed that mental illness caused homelessness by making people vulnerable in the face of bad luck and insufficient resources:

> Mental illness [is the cause]. Just watching them, my heart goes out to them. Whatever the circumstances were that were in their lives that led them to the streets and being homeless I see it as very sad. . . . Maybe the resources weren't there for them, or maybe they didn't have the capabilities to know when the resources were there. It is misfortune. (Schutt, 1992:7)

Other staff believed that mental illness caused people to reject housing opportunities:

> I believe because of their mental illness that's why they are homeless. So for them to say I would rather live on the street than live in a house and have to pay rent, I mean that to me indicates that they are mentally ill. (Schutt, 1992:7)

Just like fixed-choice questions, open-ended questions should be reviewed carefully for clarity before they are used. For example, if respondents are just asked "When did you move to Boston?" they might respond with a wide range of answers: "In 1944." "After I had my first child." "When I was 10." "20 years ago." Such answers would be very hard to compile. A careful review should identify potential ambiguity. To avoid it, rephrase the question to guide the answer in a certain direction, such as "In what year did you move to Boston?" Or provide explicit response choices (Center for Survey Research, 1987).

Question Sets

Writing single questions that yield usable answers is always a challenge, whether the response format is fixed-choice or open-ended. Simple though they may seem, single questions are prone to problems due to **idiosyncratic variation,** which occurs when individuals' responses vary because of their reactions to particular words or ideas in the question. Differences in respondents' backgrounds, knowledge, and beliefs almost guarantee that they will understand the same question differently. If some respondents do not know some of the words in a question, we will not know what their answers mean—if they answer at all. If a question is too complex, respondents may focus on different parts of the question. If prior experiences or culturally based orientations lead different groups to interpret questions differently, answers will not have a consistent meaning.

In some cases the effect of idiosyncratic variation can be dramatic. For example, when people were asked in a survey whether they would "forbid" public speeches against democracy, 54% agreed. When the question was whether they would "not allow" public speeches against democracy, 75% agreed (Turner & Martin, 1984:ch. 5). Respondents are less likely to respond affirmatively to the question "Did you see *a* broken headlight?" than they are to the question "Did you see *the* broken headlight?" (Turner & Martin, 1984:ch. 9).

If just one question is used to measure a variable, the researcher may not realize that respondents had trouble with a particular word or phrase in the question. One solution is to phrase questions more carefully; the guidelines in Chapter 7 for writing clear questions should help to reduce idiosyncratic variation due to different interpretations of questions. But the best option is to devise multiple rather than single questions to measure concepts.

For example, Henry Wechsler and associates (1994) studied binge drinking in a large survey of college students. They operationalized binge drinking in terms of both the quantity of alcohol consumed in one episode and the recency of that episode, and they specified different quantities of alcohol for rating men and women as binge drinkers. The result was a set of four questions to assess binge drinking, measuring gender, recency of last drink, and quantity consumed. The quantity question had two versions, one for men and one for women: "Think back over the last two weeks. How many times have you had five or more drinks in a row?" (for men) or "four or more drinks in a row" (for women).

Scales and Indexes

When several questions are used to measure one concept, the responses may be combined by taking the sum or average of responses. A composite measure based on this type of sum or average is termed an **index** or **scale.** The idea is that idiosyncratic variation in response to particular questions will average out, so that the main influence on the combined measure will be the concept that all the questions focus on. In addition, the index can be considered a more complete measure of the concept than can any one of the component questions.

Creating an index is not just a matter of writing a few questions that seem to focus on a concept. Questions that seem to you to measure a common concept might seem to respondents to concern several different issues. The only way to know that a given set of questions does, in fact, form an index is to administer the questions to people like those you plan to study. If a common concept is being measured, people's responses to the different questions should display some consistency. Special statistics called **reliability measures** help researchers decide whether responses are consistent.

Exhibit 3.2   **Example of an Index: Short Form of the Center for Epidemiologic Studies Depression Index (CES-D)**

At any time during the past week . . . (Circle one response on each line)	Never	Some of the time	Most of the time
a. Was your appetite so poor that you did not feel like eating?	1	2	3
b. Did you feel so tired and worn out that you could not enjoy anything?	1	2	3
c. Did you feel depressed?	1	2	3
d. Did you feel unhappy about the way your life is going?	1	2	3
e. Did you feel discouraged and worried about your future?	1	2	3
f. Did you feel lonely?	1	2	3

Source: Radloff, 1977.

Because of the popularity of survey research, indexes already have been developed to measure many concepts, and some of these indexes have proved to be reliable in a range of studies. It usually is much better to use such an index to measure a concept than it is to try to devise questions to form a new index. Use of a preexisting index both simplifies the work involved in designing a study and facilitates comparison of findings to those obtained in previous studies.

The questions in Exhibit 3.2 are a short form of an index used to measure the concept of depression, the Center for Epidemiologic Studies Depression Index (CES-D). Many researchers in different studies have found that these questions form a reliable index. Note that each question concerns a symptom of depression. People may have idiosyncratic reasons for having a particular symptom without being depressed; for example, persons who have been suffering a physical ailment may say that they have a poor appetite. But by combining the answers to questions about several symptoms, the index score reduces the impact of this idiosyncratic variation.

Another example is an index used to measure student perceptions of tolerance for substance abuse on college campuses (Core Institute, 1994), an excerpt from which is shown in Exhibit 3.3. Alone, no one of these questions would be sufficient to capture the overall tolerance of substance abuse on campus. The totality of a person's responses to these questions is likely to provide a more accurate indication of tolerance for substance abuse than would a single, general question, such as "Do students on this campus feel that drinking or using drugs is OK?"

Exhibit 3.3 **Example of an Index: Excerpt from the Index
of Student Tolerance of Substance Abuse**

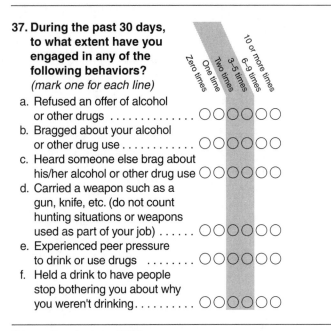

Source: Core Institute, 1994.

The advantages of using indexes rather than single questions to measure important concepts are very clear, and so surveys often include sets of multiple-item questions. However, four cautions are in order:

■ *Our presupposition that each component question is indeed measuring the same concept may be mistaken.* Although we may include multiple questions in a survey in order to measure one concept, we may find that answers to the questions are not related to one another and so the index cannot be created. Alternatively, we may find that answers to just a few of the questions are not related to the answers given to most of the others. We may therefore decide to discard these particular questions before computing the average that makes up the index.

■ *Combining responses to specific questions can obscure important differences in meaning among the questions.* My research on the impact of AIDS prevention education in shelters for the homeless provides an example. In this research, I asked a series of questions to ascertain respondents' knowledge about HIV risk factors and about methods of preventing exposure to those risk factors. I then combined these responses into an overall knowledge index. I was somewhat surprised to find that the knowledge index scores were no higher in a shelter with an AIDS education program than in a shelter without such a program. However, further analysis showed that respondents in the shelter with an AIDS education program were more knowledgeable than the other respondents about the specific ways of preventing AIDS, which were in fact the primary focus of the program. Combining responses to these questions with the others about general knowledge of HIV risk factors obscured an important finding (Schutt, Gunston, & O'Brien, 1992).

■ *The questions in an index may cluster together in subsets.* All the questions may be measuring the intended concept, but we may conclude that this concept actually has several different aspects. A **multidimensional index** has then been obtained. This conclusion can in turn help us to refine our understanding of the original concept. For example, my colleagues and I included in a survey of homeless mentally ill persons a set of questions to measure their residential preferences (Schutt, Goldfinger, & Penk, 1992). When we designed these questions, we sought to measure the continuum of sentiment ranging from a desire to remain in a shelter, to a desire to live in a group home, to a desire to live in an independent apartment. Our questions ranged from several about whether people wanted to live with others or by themselves to whether they wanted to have staff in their residence. But statistical analysis indicated that the questions actually formed three subsets, corresponding to three dimensions of residential preference: desire for stable housing, desire for living in a group home with other people, and desire to have staff in the home (see Exhibit 3.4). Identification of these three dimensions gave us a better understanding of the concept of residential preference.

An index may be designed explicitly to measure multiple conceptual dimensions. But often the same dimensions do not reappear in a subsequent study. The researcher must then try to figure out why: Does the new population studied view issues differently than prior populations surveyed with the index? Were the dimensions found in previous research really just chance associations among the questions making up the larger index? Have sentiments changed since the earlier studies when the multidimensional index was developed? Only after an index has been used in several studies can we begin to have confidence in the answers to the questions it is based on.

■ *Sometimes particular questions are counted, or weighted, more than others in the calculation of the index.* Some questions may be more central to the concept being measured than others and so may be given greater weight in the index score. It is difficult to justify this approach without extensive testing, but some well-established indexes do involve differential weighting.

Exhibit 3.4 **Residential Preference Index: Examples of Components**

Desire to Leave Questions

Would you like to move into permanent housing some time next year, or would you rather stay here [a shelter]?

LIKE TO MOVE	1
IT DEPENDS	2
RATHER STAY HERE	3

How important is it to you to have a place of your own? Would you say it is . . .

EXTREMELY IMPORTANT	1
VERY IMPORTANT	2
SOMEWHAT IMPORTANT	3
NOT IMPORTANT	4

Group Preference Questions

Would you rather share a house with four or five other folks from here instead of getting your own apartment?

LIKE THE IDEA A LOT	1
LIKE THE IDEA SOMEWHAT	2
DON'T REALLY CARE, NOT SURE	3
DISLIKE THE IDEA SOMEWHAT	4
DISLIKE THE IDEA A LOT	5

If you could move into some regular housing, would you want to keep in touch with any of the other residents here?

LIKE THE IDEA A LOT	1
LIKE THE IDEA SOMEWHAT	2
DON'T REALLY CARE, NOT SURE	3
DISLIKE THE IDEA SOMEWHAT	4
DISLIKE THE IDEA A LOT	5

Staff Preference Questions

If you moved out of here to a regular house, would you want staff to live there?

LIKE THE IDEA A LOT	1
LIKE THE IDEA SOMEWHAT	2
DON'T REALLY CARE, NOT SURE	3
DISLIKE THE IDEA SOMEWHAT	4
DISLIKE THE IDEA A LOT	5

Even if you didn't want it, would it be OK if staff did live there?

LIKE THE IDEA A LOT	1
LIKE THE IDEA SOMEWHAT	2
DON'T REALLY CARE, NOT SURE	3
DISLIKE THE IDEA SOMEWHAT	4
DISLIKE THE IDEA A LOT	5

Source: Schutt, Goldfinger, & Penk, 1992.

Making Observations

Observations can be used to measure characteristics of individuals, events, and places. The observations may be the primary form of measurement in a study, or they may supplement measures obtained through questioning.

Direct observations can be used as indicators of some concepts. For example, Albert Reiss (1971) studied police interaction with the public by riding in police squad cars, observing police-citizen interactions and recording their characteristics on a form. Notations on the form indicated such variables as how many police-citizen contacts occurred, who initiated the contacts, how compliant citizens were with police directives, and whether police expressed hostility toward the citizens.

Using a different approach, psychologists Dore Butler and Florence Geis (1990) studied unconscious biases and stereotypes that they thought might hinder the advancement of women and minorities in work organizations. In one experiment, discussion groups of male and female students were observed from behind one-way mirrors as group leaders presented identical talks in each group. The observers (who were not told what the study was about) rated the number of frowns, furrowed brows, smiles, and nods of approval as the group leaders spoke. (The leaders themselves did not know what the study was about.) Group participants made disapproving expressions, such as frowns, more often when the group leader was a woman than when the leader was a man. To make matters worse, the more women talked, the less attention they were given. Butler and Geis concluded that there was indeed a basis for unconscious discrimination in these social patterns.

Observations may also supplement data collected in an interview study. This approach was used in a study of homeless persons participating in the Center for Mental Health Services' ACCESS program (Access to Community Care and Effective Services and Supports). After a 47-question interview, interviewers were asked to record observations that would help to indicate whether the respondent was suffering from a major mental illness. For example, the interviewers indicated, on a scale from 0 to 4, the degree to which the homeless participants appeared to be responding during the interview to voices or noises that others couldn't hear or to other private experiences (U.S. Department of Health and Human Services, 1995).

Many interviews contain at least a few observational questions. Clinical studies often request a "global," or holistic, interviewer rating of clients, based on observations and responses to questions throughout the interview. One such instrument is called the Global Assessment of Functioning Scale.

Direct observation is often the method of choice for measuring behavior in natural settings, as long as it is possible to make the requisite observations. Direct observation avoids the problems of poor recall and self-serving distortions that can occur with answers to survey questions. It also allows measurement in a context that is more natural than an interview. But observations can be distorted too. Observers do not see or hear everything, and everything they do see is filtered by their own senses and perspectives. Moreover, in some situations the presence of an observer may cause people to act differently than they would otherwise (Emerson, 1983). I will discuss these issues in more depth in Chapter 8, but it is important to begin to consider them whenever you read about observational measures.

Using Indirect Measures

When we have reason to be skeptical of potential respondents' answers to questions, when we cannot observe the phenomena of interest directly, and when there are no sources of available data, we can use **unobtrusive measures,** which allow us to collect data about individuals or groups without their direct knowledge or participation (Webb, Campbell, Schwartz, & Sechrest, 1966). However, the opportunities for using unobtrusive measures are few, and the information they can provide is often limited to crude counts or estimates.

The physical traces of past behavior are one type of unobtrusive measure. To measure the prevalence of drinking in college dorms or fraternity houses, we might count the number of empty bottles of alcoholic beverages in the surrounding dumpsters. Student interest in the college courses they are taking might be measured by counting the number of times that books left on reserve as optional reading are checked out or the number of class handouts left in trash barrels outside a lecture hall.

You can probably see the difficulties that might be created by such techniques. It also should be apparent that much care must be taken to develop an indicator that is useful for comparative purposes. For instance, you might calculate the ratio of the bottles in the dumpsters to the number of residents in the dorm and adjust for the time since the last trash collection. Counts of usage of books on reserve will only be useful if you take into account how many copies of the books are on reserve for the course, how many students are enrolled in the course, and whether reserve reading is required.

Content analysis, another type of indirect measurement, studies representations of the research topic in such media forms as news articles, TV shows, and radio talk shows. An investigation of the drinking climate on campuses might include a count of the amount of space devoted to ads for alcoholic beverages in a sample of issues of the student newspaper. Campus publications also might be coded to indicate the number of times that statements discouraging substance abuse appear. Content analysis techniques also can be applied to legal opinions, historical documents (see Chapter 9), and novels, songs, or other cultural productions. With this tool, you could measure the severity of punishments for crimes involving substance abuse, the degree of approval of drinking expressed in TV shows or songs, or the number of mentions of substance abuse in legislative sessions.

Combining Measurement Operations

Using available data, asking questions, making observations, and using indirect measures are interrelated measurement tools, each of which may include or be supplemented by the others. From people's answers to survey questions, the U.S. Bureau of the Census develops widely consulted census reports on people, firms, and geographic units in the United States. Data from employee surveys may be supplemented by information available in company records. Interviewers may record observations about those whom they question. Researchers may use insights gleaned from questioning participants to make sense of the social interaction they have observed. Unobtrusive indicators could be used to evaluate the honesty of survey responses.

The choice of a particular measurement method is often determined by available resources and opportunities, but measurement validity is enhanced if this choice also takes into account the particular concept or concepts to be measured. Responses to such questions as "How socially engaged were you at the party?" or "How many days did you use sick leave last year?" are unlikely to provide information as valid as direct observation or company records. On the other hand, observations at social gatherings may not answer our questions about why some people do not participate; we may just have to ask people. Or if no agency is recording the frequency of job loss in a community, we may have to ask direct questions.

Questioning can be a particularly poor approach for measuring behaviors that are very socially desirable, such as voting or attending church; or that are socially stigmatized or illegal, such as alcohol or drug abuse. The tendency of people to answer questions in socially approved ways was demonstrated in a study of church attendance in the United States (Hadaway et al., 1993). More than 40% of adult Americans say in surveys that they attend church weekly—a percentage much higher than in Canada, Australia, or Europe. However, a comparison of observed church attendance with self-reported attendance suggested that the actual rate of church attendance was much lower (see Exhibit 3.5). Always consider the possibility of measurement error when only one type of operation has been used. Of course, it is much easier to recognize this possibility than it is to determine the extent of error resulting from a particular measurement procedure. See the February 1998 issue of the *American Sociological Review* for a fascinating exchange of views and evidence on the subject of measuring church attendance.

Exhibit 3.5 **The Inadequacy of Self-Reports Regarding Socially Desirable Behavior: Observed versus Self-Reported Church Attendance**

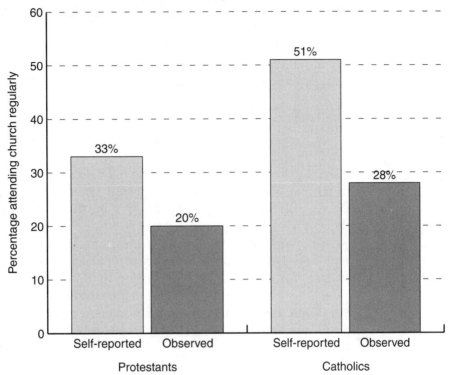

Source: Data from Hadaway et al., 1993:744–746.

■ ■ ■ ■ Evaluation of Measures

This issue of measurement error is very important. Do the operations developed to measure our concepts actually do so—are they valid? If we have weighed our measurement options, carefully constructed our questions and observational procedures, and carefully selected from the available data indicators, we should be on the right track. But we cannot have much confidence in a measure until we have empirically evaluated its validity.

Measurement Validity

The extent to which measures indicate what they are intended to measure can be assessed with one or more of four basic approaches: face validation, content validation, criterion validation, and construct validation. Whatever the approach to validation, no one measure is going to be valid for all times and places. For example, the validity of self-report measures of substance abuse varies with such factors as whether the respondents are sober or intoxicated at the time of the interview, whether the measure refers to recent or lifetime abuse, and whether the respondents see their responses as affecting their chances at receiving housing, treatment, or some other desired outcome (Babor, Stephens, & Marlatt, 1987). In addition, persons with severe mental illness are, in general, less likely to respond accurately (Corse, Hirschinger, & Zanis, 1995). These types of possibilities should always be considered when evaluating measurement validity.

Face Validity

Researchers apply the term **face validity** to the confidence gained from careful inspection of a concept to see if it is appropriate "on its face." For example, measuring people's favorite color seems unlikely on its face to tell us much about their alcohol consumption patterns. A measure with greater face validity would be a count of how many drinks they had consumed in the past week.

Although every measure should be inspected in this way, face validation in itself does not provide very convincing evidence of measurement validity. The question "How much beer or wine did you have to drink last week?" may look valid on its face as a measure of frequency of drinking, but people who drink heavily tend to underreport the amount they drink. So the question would be an invalid measure in a study that includes heavy drinkers.

Content Validity

Content validity establishes that the measure covers the full range of the concept's meaning. To determine that range of meaning, the researcher may solicit the opinions of experts and review literature that identifies the different aspects of the concept.

An example of a measure that covers a wide range of meaning is the Michigan Alcoholism Screening Test (MAST). The MAST includes 24 questions representing the following subscales: recognition of alcohol problems by self and others; legal, social, and work problems; help seeking; marital and family difficulties; liver pathology (Skinner & Sheu, 1982). Many experts familiar with the direct consequences of substance abuse agree that these dimensions capture the full range of possibilities. Thus the MAST is believed to be valid from the standpoint of content validity.

Criterion Validity

When people drink an alcoholic beverage, the alcohol is absorbed into their blood and then gradually metabolized (broken down into other chemicals) in their liver (NIAAA, 1997). The alcohol that remains in their blood at any point, unmetabolized, impairs both thinking and behavior (NIAAA, 1994). As more alcohol is ingested, cognitive and behavioral consequences multiply. These biological processes can be identified with direct measures of alcohol concentration in the blood, urine, or breath. Questions about drinking behavior, on the other hand, can be viewed as attempts to measure indirectly what biochemical tests measure directly.

Criterion validity is established when the scores obtained on one measure can be accurately compared to those obtained with a more direct or already validated measure of the same phenomenon (the criterion). A measure of blood-alcohol concentration or a urine test could serve as the criterion for validating a self-report measure of drinking, as long as the questions we ask about drinking refer to the same period. Observations of substance use by friends or relatives could also, in some circumstances, serve as a criterion for validating self-report substance use measures.

Criterion validation studies of substance abuse measures have yielded inconsistent results. Self-reports of drug use agreed with urinalysis results for about 85% of the drug users who volunteered for a health study in several cities (Weatherby et al., 1994). On the other hand, the posttreatment drinking behavior self-reported by 100 male alcoholics was substantially less than the drinking behavior observed by the alcoholics' friends or relatives (Watson, Tilleskjor, Hoodecheck-Schow, Pucel, & Jacobs, 1984). Such inconsistent findings can occur because of differences in the adequacy of a measure across settings and populations. We cannot assume that a measure that was validated in one study is also valid in another setting or with a different population.

The criterion that researchers select can itself be measured either while or after measuring the variable that is to be validated. **Predictive validity** is the ability of a measure to predict scores on a criterion measured in the future. For example, a store might administer a test of sales ability to new sales personnel and then validate the measures by comparing these test scores with the subsequent sales performance of the new personnel, the criterion. **Concurrent validity** exists when a measure yields scores that are closely related to scores on a criterion measured at the same time. The store might validate its test of sales ability by administering it to sales personnel who are already employed and then comparing their test scores to their sales performance. Or a measure of walking speed based on mental counting might be validated concurrently with a stop watch.

An attempt at criterion validation is well worth the effort because it greatly increases confidence that the measure is measuring what was intended. However, often no other variable might reasonably be considered a criterion for feelings or beliefs or other subjective states. If we were interested in measuring alienation as Blauner (1964) defined it, what direct indicator of meaninglessness or self-estrangement could serve as a criterion? Even with variables for which a reasonable criterion exists, the researcher may not be able to gain access to the criterion—as would be the case with a tax return or employer document as a criterion for self-reported income.

Construct Validity

Measurement validity can also be established by showing that a measure is related to a variety of other measures as specified in a theory. This validation approach, known as **construct validity,** is commonly used in social research when no clear criterion exists for validation purposes. For example, in one study of the validity of the Addiction Severity Index (ASI), A. Thomas McLellan and his associates (1985) compared subject scores on the ASI to a number of indicators that they felt from prior research should be related to substance abuse: medical problems, employment problems, legal problems, family problems, psychiatric problems. They could not use a criterion validation approach because they did not have a more direct measure of abuse, such as laboratory test scores or observer reports. However, their extensive research on the subject had given them confidence that these sorts of problems were all related to substance abuse, and thus their measures seemed to be valid from the standpoint of construct validity. Indeed, the researchers found that individuals with higher ASI ratings tended to have more problems in each of these areas, giving us more confidence in the ASI's validity as a measure.

A somewhat different approach to construct validation is termed **discriminant validity**. In this approach, scores on the measure to be validated are compared to scores on another measure of the same variable and to scores on variables that measure different but related concepts. Discriminant validity is achieved if the measure to be validated is related most strongly to its comparison measure and less so to the measures of other concepts. McLellan et al. (1985) found that the ASI passed this test, too: The ASI's measures of alcohol and drug problems were related more strongly to other measures of alcohol and drug problems than they were to measures of legal problems, family problems, medical problems, and the like.

The distinction between criterion and construct validation is not always clear. Opinions can differ about whether a particular indicator is indeed a criterion for the concept that is to be measured. For example, if you need to validate a question-based measure of sales ability for applicants to a sales position, few would object to using actual sales performance as a criterion. But what if you want to validate a question-based measure of the amount of social support that people receive from their friends? Should you just ask people about the social support they have received? Could friends' reports of the amount of support they provided serve as a criterion? Are verbal accounts of the amount of support provided adequate? What about observations of social support that people receive? Even if you could observe people in the act of counseling or otherwise supporting their friends, can an observer be sure that the interaction is indeed supportive? There isn't really a criterion here, just related concepts that could be used in a construct validation strategy. Even biochemical measures of substance abuse are questionable as criteria for validating self-reported substance use. Urine test results can be altered by ingesting certain substances, and blood tests vary in their sensitivity to the presence of drugs over a particular period.

What both construct and criterion validation have in common is the comparison of scores on one measure to scores on other measures that are predicted to be related. It is not so important that researchers agree that a particular comparison measure is a criterion rather than a related construct. But it is very important to think critically about the quality of the comparison measure and whether it actually represents a different view of the same phenomenon. For example, it is only a weak indication of measurement validity to find that scores on a new self-report measure of alcohol use are associated with scores on a previously used self-report measure of alcohol use.

Reliability

Reliability means that a measurement procedure yields consistent scores when the phenomenon being measured is not changing (or that the measured scores change in direct correspondence to actual changes in the phenomenon). If a measure is reliable, it is affected less by random error, or chance variation, than if it is unreliable. Reliability is a prerequisite for measurement validity: We cannot really measure a phenomenon if the measure we are using gives inconsistent results.

There are four possible indications of unreliability. For example, a test of your knowledge of research methods would be unreliable if every time you took it you received a different score even though your knowledge of research methods had not changed in the interim, not even as a result of taking the test more than once. Similarly, an index composed of questions to measure knowledge of research methods would be unreliable if respondents' answers to each question were totally independent of their answers to the others. A measure also would be unreliable if slightly different versions of it resulted in markedly different responses. Finally, an assessment of the level of conflict in social groups would be unreliable if ratings of the level of conflict by two observers were not related to each other.

Test-Retest Reliability

When researchers measure a phenomenon that does not change between two points separated by an interval of time, the degree to which the two measurements yield identical values is the **test-retest reliability** of the measure. If you take a test of your math ability and then retake the test two months later, the test is performing reliably if you receive a similar score both times—presuming that nothing happened during the two months to change your math ability. Of course, if events between the test and the retest have changed the variable being measured, then the difference between the test and retest scores should reflect that change.

When ratings by an observer are being assessed at two or more points in time, rather than ratings by the subjects themselves, test-retest reliability is termed **intraobserver reliability** or **intrarater reliability**.

One example of how test-retest reliability may be assessed is a study by Linda Sobell and her associates (1988) of alcohol abusers' past drinking behavior (using the Lifetime Drinking History questionnaire) and life changes (using the Recent Life Changes questionnaire). All 69 subjects in the study were patients in an addiction treatment program. They had not been drinking prior to the interview (determined by a breath test). The two questionnaires were administered by different interviewers about two or three weeks apart, both times asking the subjects to recall events eight years prior to the interviews. Reliability was high: 92% of the subjects reported the same life events both times and at least 81% of the subjects were classified consistently at both interviews as having had an alcohol problem or not. When asked about their inconsistent answers, subjects reported that in the earlier interview they had simply dated an event incorrectly, misunderstood the question, evaluated the importance of an event differently, or forgotten an event. Answers to past drinking questions were less reliable when they were very specific, apparently because the questions exceeded subjects' capacities to remember accurately.

Interitem Reliability (Internal Consistency)

When researchers use multiple items to measure a single concept, they are concerned with **interitem reliability** (or internal consistency). For example, if we are to have confidence that a set of questions (like those in Exhibit 3.2) reliably measures depression, the answers to the questions should be highly associated with one another. The stronger the association among the individual items, and the more items that are included, the higher the reliability of the index.

Alternate-Forms Reliability

Researchers are testing **alternate-forms reliability** when they compare subjects' answers to slightly different versions of survey questions (Litwin, 1995:13–21). A researcher may reverse the order of the response choices in an index or modify the question wording in minor ways and then readminister that index to subjects. If the two set of responses are not too different, alternate-forms reliability is established.

A related test of reliability is the **split-halves reliability** approach. A survey sample is divided in two by flipping a coin or using some other random assignment method. These two halves of the sample are then administered the two forms of the questions. If the responses of the two halves of the sample are about the same, the measure's reliability is established.

Interobserver Reliability

When researchers use more than one observer to rate the same persons, events, or places, **interobserver reliability** is their goal. If observers are using the same instrument to rate the same thing, their ratings should be very similar. If they are similar, we can have much more confidence that the ratings reflect the phenomenon being assessed rather than the orientations of the observers.

Assessing interobserver reliability is most important when the rating task is complex. Consider a commonly used measure of mental health, the Global Assessment of Functioning Scale (GAFS), a bit of which is shown in Exhibit 3.6. The rating task seems straightforward, with clear descriptions of the subject characteristics that are supposed to lead to high or low GAFS scores. But in fact the judgments that the rater must make while using this scale are very complex. They are affected by a wide range of subject characteristics, attitudes, and behaviors as well as by the rater's reactions. As a result, interobserver agreement is often low on the GAFS, unless the raters are trained carefully.

Ways to Improve Reliability and Validity

We must always assess the reliability of a measure if we hope to then be able to establish its validity. In fact, because it usually is easier to assess reliability than validity, you will see more evaluations of measurement reliability in research reports than evaluations of measurement validity.

Remember that a reliable measure is not necessarily a valid measure, as Exhibit 3.7 illustrates. This discrepancy is a common flaw of self-report measures of substance abuse. The multiple questions in self-report indexes of substance abuse are answered by most respondents in a consistent way, so the indexes are reliable. However, a number of respondents will not admit to drinking, even though they drink a lot. Their answers to the questions are consistent, but they are consistently misleading. As a result, some indexes based on self-report are reliable but invalid. Such indexes are not useful and should be improved or discarded. Unfortunately, many measures are judged to be worthwhile on the basis only of a reliability test.

The reliability and validity of measures in any study must be tested after the fact to assess the quality of the information obtained. But then, if it turns out that a measure cannot be considered reliable and valid, little can be done to save the study. Hence it is supremely important to select in the first place measures that are likely to be reliable and valid. In studies that use interviewers or observers, careful training is often essential in order to achieve a consistent approach. In most cases, however, the best strategy is to use measures that have been used before and whose reliability and validity have

Exhibit 3.6 **The Challenge of Interobserver Reliability: Excerpt from the Global Assessment of Functioning Scale (GAFS)**

Consider psychological, social, and occupational functioning on a hypothetical continuum of mental health–illness. Do not include impairment in functioning due to physical (or environmental) limitations

Code   (Note: Use intermediate codes when appropriate, e.g. 45, 68, 72.)

100
91   **Superior functioning in a wide range of activities, life's problems never seem to get out of hand, is sought by others because of his or her many positive qualities. No symptoms.**

90
81   **Absent or minimal symptoms** (e.g., mild anxiety before an exam) **good functioning in all areas, interested and involved in a wide range of activities, socially effective, generally satisfied with life, no more than everyday problems or concerns** (e.g., an occasional argument with family members).

80
71   **If symptoms are present, they are transient and expectable reactions to psychosocial stressors** (e.g., difficulty concentrating after family argument); **no more than slight impairment in social, occupational, or school functioning** (e.g., temporarily falling behind in schoolwork).

70
61   **Some mild symptoms** (e.g., depressive mood and mild insomnia) **OR some difficulty in social, occupational, or school functioning** (e.g., occasional truancy or theft within the household), **but generally functioning pretty well, has some meaningful interpersonal relationships.**

60
51   **Moderate symptoms** (e.g., flat affect and circumstantial speech, occasional panic attacks) **OR moderate difficulty in social, occupational, or school functioning** (e.g., few friends, conflicts with peers or co-workers).

50
41   **Serious symptoms** (e.g., suicidal ideation, severe obsessional rituals, frequent shoplifting) **OR any serious impairment in social, occupational, or school functioning** (e.g., no friends, unable to keep a job).

40
31   **Some impairment in reality testing or communication** (e.g., speech is at times illogical, obscure, or irrelevant) **OR major impairment in several areas, such as work or school, family relations, judgment, thinking, or mood** (e.g., depressed man avoids friends, neglects family, and is unable to work, child frequently beats up younger children, is defiant at home, and is failing at school).

30
21   **Behavior is considerably influenced by delusions or hallucinations OR serious impairment in communication or judgment** (e.g., sometimes incoherent, acts grossly inappropriately, suicidal preoccupation) **OR inability to function in almost all areas** (e.g., stays in bed all day, no job, home, or friends).

20
11   **Some danger of hurting self or others** (e.g., suicide attempts without clear expectation of death, frequently violent, manic excitement) **OR occasionally fails to maintain minimal personal hygiene** (e.g., smears feces) **OR gross impairment in communication** (e.g., largely incoherent or mute).

10
1   **Persistent danger of severely hurting self or others** (e.g., recurrent violence) **OR persistent inability to maintain minimal personal hygiene OR serious suicidal act with clear expectation of death.**

0   Inadequate information.

Source: American Psychiatric Association, 1994.

Exhibit 3.7 **The Difference Between Reliability and Validity: Drinking Behavior**

Measure: "How much do you drink?"

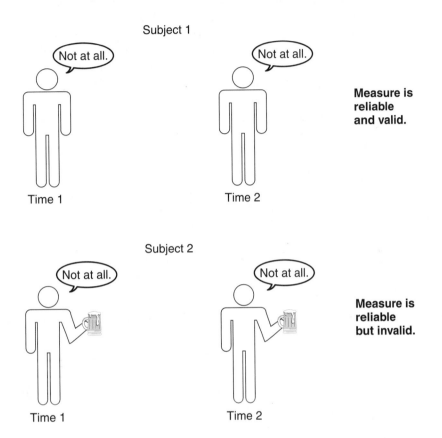

Subject 1

Not at all.

Not at all.

Measure is reliable and valid.

Time 1

Time 2

Subject 2

Not at all.

Not at all.

Measure is reliable but invalid.

Time 1

Time 2

been established in other contexts. But the selection of "tried and true" measures still does not absolve researchers from the responsibility of testing the reliability and validity of the measure in their own studies.

When the population studied or the measurement context differs from that in previous research, instrument reliability and validity may be affected. So the researchers must take pains with the design of their study. For example, test-retest reliability has proved to be better for several standard measures used to assess substance use among a new population, among homeless persons, when the interview was conducted in a protected setting, and when the measures focused on factual information and referred to a recent time interval (Drake, McHugo, & Biesanz, 1995). Subjects who were younger, female, recently homeless, and less severely afflicted with psychiatric problems were also more likely to give reliable answers.

It may be possible to improve the reliability and validity of measures in a study that already has been conducted if multiple measures were used. For example, in our study of housing for homeless mentally ill persons, funded by the National Institute of Mental Health, we assessed substance abuse with several different sets of direct questions as well as with reports from subjects' case managers and others (Goldfinger et al., 1996). We found that the observational reports were often inconsistent with self-reports and that different self-report measures were not always in agreement—hence were unreliable. A more reliable measure was initial reports of lifetime substance abuse problems, which identified all those who subsequently abused substances during the project. We concluded that the lifetime measure was a valid way to identify persons at risk for substance abuse problems. No single measure was adequate to identify substance abusers at a particular point in time during the project. Instead, we constructed a composite of observer and self-report measures that seemed to be a valid indicator of substance abuse over six-month periods.

If the research focuses on previously unmeasured concepts, new measures will have to be devised. Researchers can use one of three strategies to improve the likelihood that these new measures will be reliable and valid (Fowler, 1995):

- *Engage potential respondents in group discussions about the questions to be included in the survey.* This strategy allows researchers to check for consistent understanding of terms and to hear the range of events or experiences that people will report.

- *Conduct cognitive interviews.* Ask people test questions, then probe with follow-up questions about how they understood the question and what their answer meant.

- *Audiotape test interviews during the pretest phase of a survey.* The researchers then review these audiotapes and systematically code them to identify problems in question wording or delivery.

Although these strategies have been developed for refining survey questions, they can also be used to refine observational procedures to improve reliability and validity.

Levels of Measurement

When we know a variable's level of measurement, we can better understand how cases vary on that variable and so understand more fully what we have measured. Level of measurement also has important implications for the type of statistics that can be used with the variable, as you will learn in Chapter 11. There are four **levels of measurement:** nominal, ordinal, interval, and ratio. Exhibit 3.8 depicts the differences among these four levels.

> *Level of measurement* The complexity of the mathematical means that can be used to express the relationship between a variable's values. The nominal level of measurement, which is qualitative, has no mathematical interpretation; the quantitative levels of measurement—ordinal, interval, and ratio—are progressively more complex mathematically.

Exhibit 3.8   **Levels of Measurement**

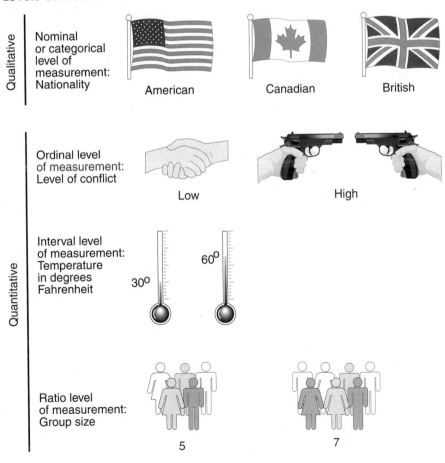

Nominal Level of Measurement

The **nominal level of measurement** (also called the categorical or qualitative level) identifies variables whose values have no mathematical interpretation; they vary in kind or quality but not in amount. In fact, it is conventional to refer to the values of nominal variables as attributes instead of values. Gender is one example. The variable "gender" has two attributes (or categories or qualities): male and female. We might indicate male with the value 1 and female with the value 2, but these numbers do not tell us anything about the difference between male and female except that they are different. Female is not one unit more of "gender" than male, nor is it twice as much "gender." Ethnicity, occupation, religious affiliation, and region of the country are also measured at the nominal level. A person may be Spanish or Portuguese, but one ethnic group does not represent more ethnicity than another—just a different ethnicity. A person may be a doctor or a truck driver, but one does not represent three units more occupation than the other.

Although the attributes of categorical variables do not have a mathematical meaning, they must be assigned to cases with great care. The attributes we use to measure, or categorize, cases must be mutually exclusive and exhaustive:

■ A variable's attributes or values are **mutually exclusive** if every case can have only one attribute.

■ A variable's attributes or values are **exhaustive** when every case can be classified into one of the categories.

When a variable's attributes are mutually exclusive and exhaustive, every case corresponds to one, and only one, attribute. Imagine the challenge of coming up with an exhaustive set of attributes when a large sample is being studied.

Ordinal Level of Measurement

The first of the three quantitative levels is the **ordinal level of measurement**. At this level, the numbers assigned to cases specify only the order of the cases, permitting "greater than" and "less than" distinctions. The Core Alcohol and Drug Survey (Core Institute, 1994) measures substance abuse with a series of questions that permit ordinal distinctions (see Exhibit 3.9).

The properties of variables measured at the ordinal level are illustrated in Exhibit 3.8 by the contrast between the level of conflict in two groups. The first group, symbolized by two people shaking hands, has a low level of conflict. The second group, symbolized by two persons pointing guns at each other, has a high level of conflict. To measure conflict, we would put

Exhibit 3.9　**Example of Ordinal Measures: Core Alcohol and Drug Survey**

17. Within the last <u>year</u> about how often have you used...
(mark one for each line)

Columns: Did not use / Once/year / 6 times/year / Once/month / Twice/month / Once/week / 3 times/week / 5 times/week / Every day

a. Tobacco (smoke, chew, snuff) . .
b. Alcohol (beer, wine, liquor) . . . .
c. Marijuana (pot, hash, hash oil)
d. Cocaine (crack, rock, freebase)
e. Amphetamines (diet pills, speed)
f. Sedatives (downers, ludes) . . . .
g. Hallucinogens (LSD, PCP) . . . .
h. Opiates (heroin, smack, horse). .
i. Inhalants (glue, solvents, gas). .
j. Designer drugs (ecstasy, MDMA)
k. Steroids . . . .
l. Other illegal drugs . . . .

Source: Core Institute, 1994.

the groups "in order" by assigning the number 1 to the low-conflict group and the number 2 to the high-conflict group. The numbers thus indicate only the relative position or order of the cases. Although "low level of conflict" is represented by the number 1, it is not one less unit of conflict than "high level of conflict," which is represented by the number 2.

As with nominal variables, the different values of a variable measured at the ordinal level must be mutually exclusive and exhaustive. They must cover the range of observed values and allow each case to be assigned no more than one value.

Interval Level of Measurement

The numbers indicating the values of a variable at the **interval level of measurement** represent fixed measurement units but have no absolute, or fixed, zero point. This level of measurement is represented in Exhibit 3.8 by the difference between two Fahrenheit temperatures. Although 60 degrees is 30 degrees hotter than 30 degrees, 60 in this case is not twice as hot as 30. Why not? Because "heat" does not begin at 0 degrees on the Fahrenheit scale.

An interval-level measure is created by a scale that has fixed measurement units but no absolute, or fixed, zero point. The numbers can therefore

Exhibit 3.10   **Example of Interval-Level Measures: Core Alcohol and Drug Survey**

26. How do you think your close friends feel (or would feel) about you...
(mark one for each line)

Columns: Don't disapprove / Disapprove / Strongly disapprove

a. Trying marijuana once or twice .... ○ ○ ○
b. Smoking marijuana occasionally .... ○ ○ ○
c. Smoking marijuana regularly .... ○ ○ ○
d. Trying cocaine once or twice .... ○ ○ ○
e. Taking cocaine regularly .... ○ ○ ○
f. Trying LSD once or twice .... ○ ○ ○
g. Taking LSD regularly .... ○ ○ ○
h. Trying amphetamines once or twice .... ○ ○ ○
i. Taking amphetamines regularly............. ○ ○ ○
j. Taking one or two drinks of an alcoholic beverage (beer, wine, liquor) nearly every day .... ○ ○ ○
k. Taking four or five drinks nearly every day..... ○ ○ ○
l. Having five or more drinks in one sitting ...... ○ ○ ○
m. Taking steroids for body building or improved athletic performance .... ○ ○ ○

Source: Core Institute, 1994.

be added and subtracted, but ratios are not meaningful. Again, the values must be mutually exclusive and exhaustive.

Social scientists often treat indexes that were created by combining responses to a series of variables measured at the ordinal level as interval-level measures. An index of this sort could be created with responses to the Core Institute's questions about friends' disapproval of substance use (see Exhibit 3.10). The survey has 13 questions on the topic, each of which has the same three response choices. If "Don't disapprove" is valued at 1, "Disapprove" is valued at 2, and "Strongly disapprove" is valued at 3, the summed index of disapproval would range from 12 to 36. Or the responses could be averaged to retain the original 1–3 range. The average could then be treated as a fixed unit of measurement. So a score of 20 could be treated as if it were four more units than a score of 16.

Ratio Level of Measurement

The numbers indicating the values of a variable at the **ratio level of measurement** represent fixed measuring units and an absolute zero point (zero means absolutely no amount of whatever the variable indicates). On a ratio scale, 10 is two points higher than 8 and is also two times greater than 5. "Ratio" numbers can be added and subtracted, and because the numbers begin at an absolute zero point, they can be multiplied and divided (so ratios can be formed between the numbers). For example, people's ages can be represented by values ranging from 0 years (or some fraction of a year) to 120 or more. A person who is 30 years old is 15 years older than someone who is 15 years old ($30 - 15 = 15$) and is twice as old as that person ($30/15 = 2$). Of course, the numbers also are mutually exclusive and exhaustive, so that every case can be assigned one and only one value.

Exhibit 3.8 displays an example of a variable measured at the ratio level. The number of people in the first group is 5, and the number in the second group is 7. The ratio of the two groups' sizes is then 1.4, a number that mirrors the relationship between the sizes of the groups. Note that there does not actually have to be any "group" with a size of 0; what is important is that the numbering scheme begins at an absolute zero—in this case, the absence of any people.

The Case of Dichotomies

Dichotomies, variables having only two values, are a special case from the standpoint of levels of measurement. The values or attributes of a variable such as gender clearly vary in kind or quality, not in amount. Thus the variable is categorical—measured at the nominal level. Yet we can think of the variable in a slightly different way, as indicating the presence of the attribute "female" (or "male") or not. Viewed in this way, there is an inherent order: A female has more of the attribute (it is present) than a male (the attribute is not present).

That is not all. Because only one contrast between the values of any two cases is possible, the concept of fixed units of measurement does not really apply. Whatever the "distance" between the attributes "female" and "not-female," that is the unit of measurement. So you can even think of a dichotomy as an interval-level measurement.

Comparison of Levels of Measurement

Exhibit 3.11 summarizes the types of comparisons that can be made with different levels of measurement, as well as the mathematical operations that are legitimate. All four levels of measurement allow researchers to assign different values to different cases. All three quantitative measures allow researchers to rank cases in order.

Researchers choose levels of measurement in the process of operationalizing the variables; the level of measurement is not inherent in the

Exhibit 3.11 **Properties of Measurement Levels**

Examples of comparison statements	Appropriate math operations	Relevant level of measurement			
		Nominal	Ordinal	Interval	Ratio
A is equal to (not equal to) B	$= (\neq)$	✓	✓	✓	✓
A is greater than (less than) B	$> (<)$		✓	✓	✓
A is three more than (less than) B	$+ (-)$			✓	✓
A is twice (half) as large as B	$\times (/)$				✓

variable itself. Many variables can be measured at different levels, with different procedures. For example, the Core Alcohol and Drug Survey (Core Institute, 1994) identifies binge drinking by asking students, "Think back over the last two weeks. How many times have you had five or more drinks at a sitting?" You might be ready to classify this as a ratio-level measure. However, this is a closed-ended question, and students are asked to indicate their answer by checking "None," "Once," "Twice," "3 to 5 times," "6 to 9 times," or "10 or more times." Use of these categories makes the level of measurement ordinal. The distance between any two cases cannot be clearly determined. A student with a response in the "6 to 9 times" category could have binged just one more time than a student who responded "3 to 5 times." You just can't tell.

The more information available, the more ways we have to compare cases. We also have more possibilities for statistical analysis with quantitative than with qualitative variables. Thus, it often is a good idea to try to measure variables at the highest level of measurement possible, if doing so does not distort the meaning of the concept that is to be measured. Measure age in years, if possible, rather than in categories—unless your goal is to compare teenagers to young adults and so you need only an ordinal distinction.

Be aware, however, that other considerations may preclude measurement at a high level. For example, many people are very reluctant to report their exact incomes, even in anonymous questionnaires. So asking respondents to report their income in categories (such as under $10,000, $10,000–19,999, $20,000–29,999) will result in more responses, and thus more valid data, than asking respondents for their income in dollars.

■ ■ ■ ■ **Conclusion**

Remember always that measurement validity is a necessary foundation for social research. Gathering data without careful conceptualization or conscientious efforts to operationalize key concepts often is a wasted effort.

The difficulties of achieving valid measurement vary with the concept being operationalized and the circumstances of the particular study. The examples in this chapter of difficulties in achieving valid measures of substance abuse should sensitize you to the need for caution. But don't let these difficulties discourage you: Substance abuse is a relatively difficult concept to operationalize because it involves behavior that is socially stigmatized and often illegal. Most other concepts in social research present fewer difficulties. But even substance abuse can be measured adequately with the proper research design.

Planning ahead is the key to achieving valid measurement in your own research; careful evaluation is the key to sound decisions about the validity of measures in others' research. Statistical tests can help to determine whether a given measure is valid after data have been collected, but if it appears after the fact that a measure is invalid, little can be done to correct the situation. If you cannot tell how key concepts were operationalized when you read a research report, don't trust the findings. And if a researcher does not indicate the results of tests used to establish the reliability and validity of key measures, remain skeptical.

KEY TERMS

Alternate-forms reliability
Closed-ended question
Concept
Conceptualization
Concurrent validity
Construct validity
Content analysis
Content validity
Criterion validity
Dichotomy
Discriminant validity
Exhaustive attributes
Face validity
Fixed-choice question
Idiosyncratic variation
Index
Indicator
Interitem reliability
Interobserver reliability

Interval level of measurement
Intrarater (or intraobserver) reliability
Level of measurement
Multidimensional index
Mutually exclusive attributes
Nominal level of measurement
Open-ended question
Operation
Operationalization
Ordinal level of measurement
Predictive validity
Ratio level of measurement
Reliability
Reliability measure
Scale
Split-halves reliability
Test-retest reliability
Unobtrusive measure

HIGHLIGHTS

∎ Conceptualization plays a critical role in research. In deductive research, conceptualization guides the operationalization of specific variables; in inductive research, it guides efforts to make sense of related observations.

■ Concepts may refer to either constant or variable phenomena. Concepts that refer to variable phenomena may be very similar to the actual variables used in a study, or they may be much more abstract.

■ Concepts are operationalized in research by one or more indicators, or measures, which may derive from observation, self-report, available records or statistics, books and other written documents, clinical indicators, discarded materials, or some combination.

■ Single-question measures may be closed-ended, with fixed-response choices; open-ended; or partially closed, with fixed-response choices and an option to write another response.

■ Question sets may be used to operationalize a concept.

■ Indexes or scales measure a concept by combining answers to several questions and so reduce idiosyncratic variation. Four questions should be explored with every intended index: Does each question actually measure the same concept? Does combining items in an index obscure important relationships between individual questions and other variables? Is the index multidimensional? Is differential weighting used in the calculation of the index scores?

■ The validity of measures should always be tested. There are four basic approaches: face validation, content validation, criterion validation (either predictive or concurrent), and construct validation. Criterion validation provides the strongest evidence of measurement validity, but there often is no criterion to use in validating social science measures.

■ Measurement reliability is a prerequisite for measurement validity, although reliable measures are not necessarily valid. Reliability can be assessed through a test-retest procedure, in terms of interitem consistency, through a comparison of responses to alternate forms of the test, or in terms of consistency among observers.

■ Level of measurement indicates the type of information obtained about a variable and the type of statistics that can be used to describe its variation. The four levels of measurement can be ordered by complexity of the mathematical operations they permit: nominal (least complex), ordinal, interval, ratio (most complex). The measurement level of a variable is determined by how the variable is operationalized. Dichotomies, a special case, may be treated as nominal or as ordinal or interval levels of measurement.

EXERCISES

1. Are important concepts in social research always defined clearly? Are they defined consistently? Search the literature for six research articles that focus on

"substance abuse," "alienation," "poverty," or some other concept suggested by your instructor. Is the concept defined clearly in each article? How similar are the definitions? Write up what you have found in a short report.

2. What are some of the research questions you could attempt to answer with available statistical data? Visit your library, and ask for an introduction to the government documents collection. Inspect the volumes from the U.S. Bureau of the Census that report population characteristics by city and state. List 10 questions you could explore with such data.

3. Now it's time to try your hand at operationalization. Formulate a few fixed-choice questions to measure variables pertaining to the concepts you researched for Exercise 1, such as perceptions of the level of substance abuse in your community or expectations about future job security. Arrange to interview one or two other students with the questions you have developed. Ask one fixed-choice question at a time, record your interviewee's answer, and then probe for additional comments and clarifications. Your goal is to discover what respondents take to be the meaning of the concept you used in the question and what additional issues shape their response to it.

   When you have finished all the interviews, analyze your experience: Did the interviewees interpret the fixed-choice questions and response choices as you intended? Did you learn more about the concepts you were working on? Should your conceptual definition be refined? Should the questions be rewritten, or would more fixed-choice questions be necessary to capture adequately the variation among respondents?

4. Now try index construction. You might begin with some of the questions you wrote for Exercise 2. Try to write about four or five fixed-choice questions that each measure the same concept. Write each question so it has the same response choices. Now conduct a literature search to identify an index that another researcher used to measure your concept or a similar concept. Compare your index to the published index. Which seems preferable to you? Why?

5. Develop a plan for evaluating the validity of a measure. Your instructor will give you a copy of a questionnaire actually used in a study. Pick out one question, and define the concept that you believe it is intended to measure. Then develop a construct validation strategy involving other measures in the questionnaire that you think should be related to the question of interest—if it measures what you think it measures.

6. One quick and easy way to check your understanding of levels of measurement is with a short quiz on the practice diskette. Select one of the "Levels of Measurement" options from the main menu. Then read the review information at the start of the lesson. You will then be presented with about 10 variables and response choices and asked to identify the level of measurement for each one. If you make a mistake, the program will give a brief explanation about that level of measurement.

7. The questions in Exhibit 3.12 are selected from my survey of shelter staff (Schutt & Fennell, 1992). First, identify the level of measurement for each question. Then, rewrite each question so that it measures the same variable but at a different level. For example, you might change a question that measures age at the

Exhibit 3.12 **Selected Shelter Staff Survey Questions**

1. What is your current job title?

2. What is your current employment status?
   Paid, full time   1
   Paid, part time (less than 30 hours per week)   2

3. When did you start your current position? _____ / _____ / _____
                                                Month   Day   Year

4. In the past month, how often did you help guests deal with each of the
   following types of problems? (*Circle one response on each line.*)
   Very often --- Never

	Very often						Never
Job training/placement	1	2	3	4	5	6	7
Lack of food or bed	1	2	3	4	5	6	7
Drinking problems	1	2	3	4	5	6	7

5. How likely is it that you will leave this shelter within the next year?
   Very likely   1
   Moderately   2
   Not very likely   3
   Not likely at all   4

6. What is the highest grade in school you have completed at this time?
   First through eighth grade   1
   Some high school   2
   High school diploma   3
   Some college   4
   College degree   5
   Some graduate work   6
   Graduate degree   7

7. Are you a veteran?
   Yes   1
   No   2

Source: Schutt, 1988.

ratio level, in years, to one that measures age at the ordinal level, in categories. Or you might change a variable measured at the ordinal level to one measured at the ratio level. For the categorical variables, those measured at the nominal level, try to identify at least two underlying quantitative dimensions of variation, and write questions to measure variation along these dimensions. For example, you might change a question asking which of several factors the respondent thinks is responsible for homelessness to a series of questions that ask how important each factor is in generating homelessness.

What are the advantages and disadvantages of phrasing each question at one level of measurement rather than another? Do you see any limitations on the types of questions for which levels of measurement can be changed?

WEB EXERCISES

1. How would you define "alcoholism"? Write a brief definition. Based on this conceptualization, describe a method of measurement that would be valid for a study of alcoholism (alcoholism as you define it). Now go to the Center of Alcohol Studies (CAS) homepage at :

    http://www.rci.rutgers.edu/~cas2/

    Choose "Related Links"
    Choose "Other Related Internet Links"
    Choose "National Council on Alcohol and Drug Dependence"
    Choose "Definition of Alcoholism"

    What is the definition of alcoholism used by the National Council on Alcohol and Drug Dependence (NCADD)? How is "alcoholism" conceptualized? Based on this conceptualization, give an example of one method that would be a valid measurement in a study of alcoholism.

    Now look at some of the other related links accessible from the CAS and NCADD Web sites. What are some of the different conceptualizations of alcoholism that you find? How does the chosen conceptualization affect one's choice of methods of measurement?

2. You've been asked to do a study of the organizational needs of your college. The data you gather will be used to help create policy that will direct progress and improvement of the school. Go to the Organizational Universe System homepage at:

    http://ous.usa.net

    Choose "Freebies"
    Choose "Sensing With Focus Groups"
    Read Sensing With Focus Groups and use it to help you create a plan to pursue your study using focus groups as a method of data collection. Customize the questions, guidelines, etc., that Sensing With Focus Groups recommends in order to meet the needs of your research project.

    How have you conceptualized the issues you want to address in the study? How will the study measure and "get a sense" of the needs of your college community?

3. Use the Web to find information regarding alcohol consumption by people under age 21. Report on your findings. How is "alcohol consumption" conceptualized and measured in the various sources you find? List your sources and the Web sites where they are found.

    Hint: Try searching for the words *alcohol* and *consumption* and *age*.

SPSS EXERCISES

1. View the variable information for the variables ASKDRINK, ASKDRUGS, and SOCBAR.

    UTILITIES...
    VARIABLES...
    ASKDRINK

ASKDRUGS

SOCBAR

At which levels (nominal/categorical, ordinal, interval, ratio) are each of these variables measured?

2. ASKDRINK and ASKDRUGS are part of an index involving the following question: Before giving an individual SECRET or TOP SECRET clearance, the government should have the right to ask him or her detailed, personal questions in the following areas:

	Definitely	Probably	Probably	Definitely	DON'T KNOW
a. Financial and credit history	1	2	3	4	8
b. Criminal arrests and convictions	1	2	3	4	8
c. Illegal drug use	1	2	3	4	8

Now answer the following questions:

a. What is the concept being measured by this index?

b. Do you agree that each of these variables belong in the index? Explain.

c. What additional variables would you like to see measured by this index?

4 Sampling

Sample Planning
Define Sample Components and the Population
Evaluate Generalizability
Assess the Diversity of the Population
Consider a Census

Sampling Methods
Probability Sampling Methods
  Simple Random Sampling
  Systematic Random Sampling
  Stratified Random Sampling
  Cluster Sampling
Nonprobability Sampling Methods
  Availability Sampling
  Quota Sampling
  Purposive Sampling
  Snowball Sampling
Lessons About Sample Quality

Sampling Distributions
Estimating Sampling Error
Determining Sample Size

Conclusion

KEY TERMS
HIGHLIGHTS
EXERCISES
WEB EXERCISES
SPSS EXERCISES

■ ■ ■ ■ A common technique in journalism is to put a "human face" on a story. For instance, a reporter for *The New York Times* went to an emergency assistance unit near Yankee Stadium to ask homeless mothers about new welfare policies that require recipients to work. One woman with three children suggested, "If you work a minimum wage job, that's nothing. . . . Think about paying rent, with a family." In contrast, another mother with three children remarked, "It's important to do it for my kids, to set an example."

A story about deportations of homeless persons in Moscow focused on the case of one 47-year-old Russian laborer temporarily imprisoned in Social Rehabilitation Center No. 2. He complained that in the town to which he would have to return, "I have no job, no family, no home" (Swarns, 1996:A1).

These are interesting comments in effective articles, but we do not know whether they represent the opinions of most homeless persons in the United States and Russia, of most homeless persons in New York City and Moscow, of only persons found in the emergency assistance unit near Yankee Stadium and in Social Rehabilitation Center No. 2—or of just a few people in these locations who caught the eye of these specific reporters. In other words, we don't know how generalizable these comments are, and if we don't have confidence in their generalizability, their validity is suspect. Because we have no idea whether these opinions are widely shared or quite unique, we cannot really judge what they tell us about the social world.

In this chapter, I first review the rationale for using sampling in social research and consider two alternatives to sampling. The topic then turns to specific sampling methods and when they are most appropriate, using examples from efforts to study the population of homeless persons. I introduce the concept of sampling distribution and explain how it helps in estimating our degree of confidence in statistical generalizations. By the chapter's end, you should understand which questions you need to ask to evaluate the generalizability of a study as well as what choices you need to make when designing a sampling strategy.

■ ■ ■ ■ **Sample Planning**

You have encountered the problem of generalizability in each of the studies you have read about in this book. For example, Dee Roth, J. Bean, N. Lust, and T. Saveanu (1985) generalized their sample-based description of homeless persons to the population of homeless persons in Ohio; Peter Rossi (1989) generalized his conclusions about homelessness from a Chicago sample to the United States; and Lawrence Sherman and Richard Berk (1984) and others tried to determine the generalizability of findings from their study of domestic violence in Minneapolis. Whether we, like these other researchers, are designing a sampling strategy or are evaluating the generalizability of someone else's findings, we have to understand how and why researchers decide to sample. Sampling is very common in social research, but sometimes it isn't necessary.

Define Sample Components and the Population

Let's say that we are designing a study of a topic that involves a lot of people (or other entities)—the **elements** in our study. We don't have the time or resources to study the entire **population**, all the elements in which we are interested, and so we resolve to study a **sample**, a subset of this population.

We may collect our data directly from the elements in our sample. Some studies are not so simple, however. The entities we can easily reach to gather information are not the same as the entities about whom we really want information. So we may collect information about the elements from another set of entities, which are called the **sampling units**. For example, if we interview mothers to learn about their families, the families are the elements and the mothers are the sampling units. If we survey department chairpersons to learn about college departments, the departments are the elements and the chairpersons are the sampling units.

In a study in which individual people are sampled and are the focus of the study—a "single-stage" sample—the sampling units are the same as the elements. However, if a sample is selected in two or more stages, the units selected at each stage—let's say, groups and individuals within the groups—are sampling units, but it may be that only one of the sampling units is the study's elements (see Exhibit 4.1). For example, a researcher might sample families for a survey about spending practices and then interview one parent (a sample) in each sampled family to obtain the information. The families are the *primary* sampling units (and are the elements in the study), and the parents are *secondary* sampling units (but they are not elements, since they provide information about the family).

One key issue with selecting or evaluating sample components is understanding exactly what population they represent. In a survey of "adult Americans," the general population may reasonably be construed as all residents of the United States who are at least 21 years old. But always be alert to ways in which the population may have been narrowed by the sample selection procedures. Perhaps only English-speaking adult residents of the continental United States were actually sampled. The population for a study is the aggregation of elements that we actually focus on and sample from, not some larger aggregation that we really wish we could have studied.

Some populations, such as the homeless, are not identified by a simple criterion such as a geographic boundary or an organizational membership.

Exhibit 4.1   **Sample Components in a Two-Stage Study**

Sample of schools

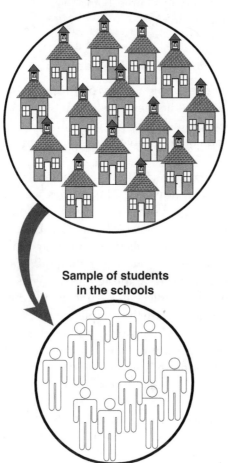

Schools are the elements and
the primary sampling unit.

**Sample of students
in the schools**

Students are the secondary sampling
units; they provide information
about the schools.

Clear definition of such a population is difficult but quite necessary. Anyone should be able to determine just what population was actually studied.
However, studies of homeless persons in the early 1980s "did not propose
definitions, did not use screening questions to be sure that the people they
interviewed were indeed homeless, and did not make major efforts to cover
the universe of homeless people." (Perhaps just homeless persons in one
shelter were studied.) The result was "a collection of studies that could not
be compared" (Burt, 1996:15). Several studies of homeless persons in urban
areas addressed the problem by employing a more explicit definition of the
population: People are homeless if they have no home or permanent place
to stay of their own (renting or owning) and no regular arrangement to stay
at someone else's place (Burt, 1996).

Even this more explicit definition still leaves some questions unanswered: What is a "regular arrangement"? How permanent does a "permanent place" have to be? In a study of homeless persons in Chicago, Michael Sosin, Paul Colson, and Susan Grossman (1988) answered these questions in their definition of the population of interest:

> We define the homeless as: those current[ly] residing for at least one day but for less than fourteen with a friend or relative, not paying rent, and not sure that the length of stay will surpass fourteen days; those currently residing in a shelter, whether overnight or transitional; those currently without normal, acceptable shelter arrangements and thus sleeping on the street, in doorways, in abandoned buildings, in cars, in subway or bus stations, in alleys, and so forth; those residing in a treatment center for the indigent who have lived at the facility for less than 90 days and who claim that they have no place to go, when released. (p. 22)

This definition reflects accurately Sosin et al.'s concept of homelessness and allows researchers in other locations or at other times to develop procedures for studying a comparable population. The more complete and explicit the definition of the population from which a sample was selected, the more precise our generalizations can be.

Evaluate Generalizability

Once we have defined clearly the population from which we will sample, we need to determine the scope of the generalizations we will seek to make from our sample. Do you recall from Chapter 1 two different meanings of generalizability?

- *Can the findings from a sample of the population be generalized to the population from which the sample was selected?* Did Roth's findings apply to Ohio, Rossi's to Chicago, Sherman and Berk's to Minneapolis? This type of generalizability was defined as *sample generalizability* in Chapter 1.

- *Can the findings from a study of one population be generalized to another, somewhat different population?* Are homeless people in Ohio or Chicago similar to those in other states? In other countries? Were spouse abusers in Minneapolis like those in other cities, states, or countries? Are findings from a laboratory study involving college students similar to what would have been found if employed adults had been studied in their places of employment? This type of generalizability was defined as *cross-population generalizability* in Chapter 1.

This chapter focuses attention primarily on the problem of sample generalizability: Can findings from a sample be generalized to the population from which the sample was drawn? This is really the most basic question to ask about a sample, and social research methods provide many tools with which to address it.

Sample generalizability depends on sample quality, which is determined by the amount of **sampling error,** the difference between the characteristics of a sample and the characteristics of the population from which it was selected. The larger the sampling error, the less representative the sample—and thus the less generalizable the findings. To assess sample quality when you are planning or evaluating a study, ask yourself these questions:

■ From what population were the cases selected?

■ What method was used to select cases from this population?

■ Do the cases that were studied represent, in the aggregate, the population from which they were selected?

> *Sampling error* Any difference between the characteristics of a sample and the characteristics of the population from which it was drawn. The larger the sampling error, the less representative the sample.

But researchers often project their theories onto groups or populations much larger than, or simply different from, those they have actually studied. The population to which generalizations are made in this way can be termed the **target population,** a set of elements larger than or different from the population that was sampled and to which the researcher would like to generalize any study findings. When we generalize findings to target populations, we must be somewhat speculative. We must carefully consider the validity of claims that the findings can be applied to other groups, geographic areas, cultures, or times.

Because the validity of cross-population generalizations cannot be tested empirically, except by conducting more research in other settings, I will not focus much attention on this problem here. But I'll return to the problem of cross-population generalizability in Chapter 6, which addresses experimental research, and in Chapter 10, which discusses combining the results of studies that have been conducted in different settings.

Assess the Diversity of the Population

Sampling is unnecessary if all the units in the population are identical. Physicists don't need to select a representative sample of atomic particles to learn about basic physical processes. They can study a single atomic particle, because it is identical to every other particle of its type. Similarly, biologists don't need to sample a particular type of plant to determine whether a given chemical has toxic effects on it. The idea is, "If you've seen one, you've seen 'em all."

What about people? Certainly all people are not identical (nor are other animals in many respects). Nonetheless, if we are studying physical or psychological processes that are the same among all people, sampling is not needed to achieve generalizable findings. Psychologists and social psychologists often conduct experiments on college students to learn about processes that they think are identical across individuals. They believe that most people would have the same reactions as the college students if they experienced the same experimental conditions. Field researchers who observe group processes in a small community sometimes make the same assumption.

There is a potential problem with this assumption, however: There's no way to know for sure if the processes being studied are identical across all people. In fact, experiments can give different results depending on the type of people who are studied or the conditions for the experiment. Stanley Milgram's (1965) classic experiments on obedience to authority, among the most replicated (repeated) experiments in the history of social psychological research, illustrate this point very well. The Milgram experiments tested the willingness of male volunteers in New Haven, Connecticut, to comply with the instructions of an authority figure to give "electric shocks" to someone else, even when these shocks seemed to harm the person receiving them. In most cases the volunteers complied. Milgram concluded that people are very obedient to authority.

Were these results generalizable to all men, to men in the United States, or to men in New Haven? Similar results were obtained in many replications of the Milgram experiments—when the experimental conditions and subjects were similar to those studied by Milgram. Other studies showed that some groups were less likely to react so obediently. Given certain conditions, such as another "subject" in the room who refused to administer the shocks, subjects were likely to resist authority.

So what do the experimental results tell us about how people will react to an authoritarian movement in the real world, when conditions are not so carefully controlled? In the real social world, people may be less likely to react obediently as well. Other individuals may argue against obedience to a particular leader's commands or people may see on TV the consequences of their actions. But alternatively, people may be even more obedient to authority than the experimental subjects, as they get swept up in mobs or are captivated by ideological fervor. Milgram's research gives us insight into human behavior, but there's no guarantee that what he found with particular groups in particular conditions can be generalized to the larger population (or to any particular population) in different settings.

Generalizing the results of experiments and of participant observation is risky, because such research often studies a small number of people who don't represent any particular population. Researchers may put aside concerns about generalizability when they observe the social dynamics of specific clubs, college dorms, and the like or in a controlled experiment when they test the effect of, say, a violent movie on feelings for others. But we will have to be cautious about generalizing the results of such studies.

The larger point is that social scientists rarely can skirt the problem of demonstrating the generalizability of their findings. If a small sample has been studied in an experiment or field research project, the study should be replicated in different settings or, preferably, with a **representative sample** of the population to which generalizations are sought (see Exhibit 4.2). The social world and the people in it are just too diverse to be considered "identical units." Social psychological experiments and small field studies have produced good social science, but they need to be replicated in other settings, with other subjects, to claim any generalizability. Even when we believe that we have uncovered basic social processes in a laboratory experiment or field observation, we should be very concerned with seeking confirmation in other samples and in other research.

> *Representative sample* A sample that "looks like" the population from which it was selected in all respects that are potentially relevant to the study. The distribution of characteristics among the elements of a representative sample is the same as the distribution of those characteristics among the total population. In an unrepresentative sample, some characteristics are overrepresented or underrepresented.

Consider a Census

In some circumstances, it may be feasible to skirt the issue of generalizability by conducting a **census**—studying the entire population of interest—rather than drawing a sample. This is what the federal government tries to do every 10 years with the U.S. Census. Censuses also include studies of all the employees (or students) in small organizations, studies comparing all 50 states, and studies of the entire population of a particular type of organization in some area. However, in all of these instances, except for the U.S. Census, the population that is studied is relatively small.

The reason that social scientists don't often attempt to collect data from all the members of some large population is simply that doing so would be too expensive and time-consuming (and they can do almost as well with a sample). Some social scientists do conduct research with data from the U.S.

Exhibit 4.2 **Representative and Unrepresentative Samples**

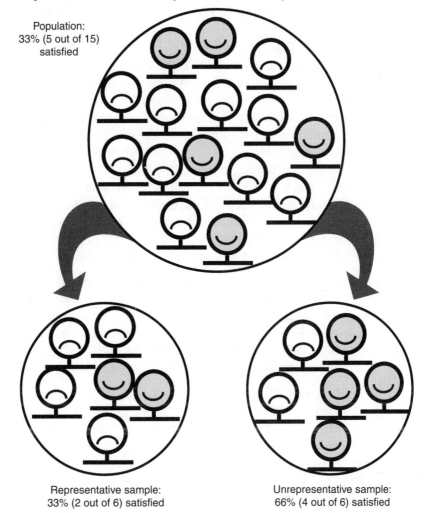

Population:
33% (5 out of 15)
satisfied

Representative sample:
33% (2 out of 6) satisfied

Unrepresentative sample:
66% (4 out of 6) satisfied

Census, but it's the government that collects the data and your tax dollars
that pay for the effort. For the 1990 census, the Bureau of the Census needed
more than 300,000 employees just to follow up on the households that did
not return their census form in the mail (Navarro, 1990). The entire 1990
census effort cost $2.6 billion (Holmes, 1994).

Even if the population of interest for a survey is a small town of 20,000
or students in a university of 10,000, researchers will have to sample. The
costs of surveying "just" thousands of individuals exceed by far the budgets for most research projects. In fact, even the U.S. Bureau of the Census
cannot afford to have everyone answer all the questions that should be

covered in the census. So it draws a sample. Every household must complete a short version of the census (it had 14 questions in 1990), and a sample consisting of one in six households must complete a long form (with 45 additional questions).

Another costly fact is that it is hard to get people to complete a survey. Federal law requires all citizens to complete their census questionnaire, but other researchers have no such compulsion to rely on. So most researchers must make multiple efforts to increase the rate of response to their survey. The smaller numbers of potential subjects typical of samples can increase the resources for better follow-up procedures. (I will give more attention to the problem of nonresponse in Chapter 7.)

And now it's time to admit that even the U.S. Bureau of the Census, with all its resources, is failing to count all the nation's households. Congress' General Accounting Office estimates that almost 10 million people were not included in the 1990 census and 4.4 million were counted twice (Holmes, 1994). Difficulties with the 1990 census included

> too many doors to knock on, and too many people living without doors, [and] a rate of noncooperation that exceeded the estimates of even the most severe critics. . . . Those overcounted . . . tend to be wealthier and more rural than those undercounted. In poor urban neighborhoods, field workers are often afraid to enter tenements and housing projects. (Gleick, 1990:22–23, 26)

Because of these problems, many statisticians recommend that the U.S. Census survey a large sample of Americans rather than the complete population, and the Bureau of the Census has tested the feasibility of focusing follow-up efforts on a sample of those who do not return their census form in the mail nor respond to phone interview attempts or door-to-door visits (Holmes, 1994). The basic idea is to invest more resources in increasing the rate of response of a representative sample of persons who do not respond easily, rather than spreading even the government's substantial resources thinly over the total respondent pool (Stout, 1997a). These statisticians believe it is "Better to hound 1 in 10 than 10 in 10" (Holmes, 1996:A18). Some argue that the U.S. Constitution requires a complete census but a well-designed sample may still be preferable (Stout, 1997b:31).

One final caution about census studies: Be sure you know exactly what population has been studied. James Wright and Eleanor Weber (1987) undertook a massive study of homeless persons as part of the national Health Care for the Homeless program (HCH). Teams including doctors, nurses, and social workers filled out a contact form each time they delivered services to homeless persons in a variety of sites in 19 cities. After about a year, the resulting HCH database included information about 34,035 clients obtained on 90,961 contact forms. This database is a complete census of persons receiving care from HCH clinics. But the program operated in only 19 large U.S. cities, only 18 of the cities provided usable data, and the number of HCH clients appeared to include only between one-quarter and one-third of the total homeless population in these cities (Wright & Weber, 1987:22–24, 34–35). Thus the study was a census of the population of HCH clients in 18 cities, not at all a census of the entire homeless population in the nation. We might think it likely that the HCH population is similar to the general homeless population, but we won't know until we figure out how well the HCH population represents all those who are homeless.

Sampling Methods

We can now study more systematically the features of samples that make it more or less likely that they will represent the population from which they are selected. The most important distinction that needs to be made about samples is whether they are based on a probability or a nonprobability sampling method. Sampling methods that allow us to know in advance how likely it is that any element of a population will be selected for the sample are termed **probability sampling methods**. Sampling methods that do not let us know the likelihood in advance are termed **nonprobability sampling methods**.

Probability sampling methods rely on a random, or chance, selection procedure, which is in principle the same as flipping a coin to decide which of two people "wins" and which one "loses." Heads and tails are equally likely to turn up in a coin toss, so both persons have an equal chance to win. That chance, their **probability of selection**, is 1 out of 2, or .5.

> *Probability of selection* The likelihood that an element will be selected from the population for inclusion in the sample. In a census of all the elements of a population, the probability that any particular element will be selected is 1.0. If half the elements in the population are sampled on the basis of chance (say, by tossing a coin), the probability of selection for each element is one-half, or .5. As the size of the sample as a proportion of the population decreases, so does the probability of selection.

Flipping a coin is a fair way to select one of two people because the selection process harbors no systematic bias. You might win or lose the coin toss, but you know that the outcome was due simply to chance, not to bias. For the same reason, a roll of a six-sided die is a fair way to choose one of six possible outcomes (the odds of selection are 1 out of 6, or .17). Dealing out a hand after shuffling a deck of cards is a fair way to allocate sets of cards in a card game (the odds of each person getting a particular outcome, such as a full house or a flush, are the same). Similarly, state lotteries use a random process to select winning numbers. Thus the odds of winning a lottery, the probability of selection, are known, even though they are very much smaller (perhaps 1 out of 1 million) than the odds of winning a coin toss.

There is a natural tendency to confuse the concept of **random sampling**, in which cases are selected only on the basis of chance, with a haphazard method of sampling. On first impression, "leaving things up to chance" seems to imply not exerting any control over the sampling method. But to ensure that nothing but chance influences the selection of cases, the researcher must proceed very methodically, leaving nothing to chance except the selection of the cases themselves. The researcher must follow carefully controlled procedures if a purely random process is to occur. In fact, when reading about sampling methods, do not assume that a random sample was obtained just because the researcher used a random selection method at some point in the sampling process. Look for these two particular problems: selecting elements from an incomplete list of the total population and failing to obtain an adequate response rate.

If the **sampling frame** (the list from which the elements of the population were selected) is incomplete, a sample selected randomly from that list will not really be a random sample of the population. You should always consider the adequacy of the sampling frame. Even for a simple population like a university's student body, the registrar's list is likely to be at least a bit out of date at any given time. For example, some students will have dropped out, but their status will not yet be officially recorded. Although you may judge the amount of error introduced in this particular situation to be negligible, the problems are greatly compounded for a larger population. The sampling frame for a city, state, or nation is always likely to be incomplete because of constant migration into and out of the area. Even unavoidable omissions from the sampling frame can bias a sample against particular groups within the population.

A very inclusive sampling frame may still yield systematic bias if many sample members cannot be contacted or refuse to participate. Nonresponse is a major hazard in survey research because nonrespondents are likely to differ systematically from those who take the time to participate. You should not assume that findings from a randomly selected sample will be generalizable to the population from which the sample was selected if the rate of nonresponse is considerable (certainly not if it is much above 30%).

Probability Sampling Methods

Probability sampling methods are those in which the probability of selection is known and is not zero (so there is some chance of selecting each element). These methods randomly select elements and therefore have no sys-

tematic bias; nothing but chance determines which elements are included in the sample. This feature of probability samples makes them much more desirable than nonprobability samples when the goal is to generalize to a larger population.

Even though a random sample has no systematic bias, it will certainly have some sampling error due to chance. The probability of selecting a head is .5 in a single toss of a coin and in 20, 30, and however many tosses of a coin you like. But it is perfectly possible to toss a coin twice and get a head both times. The random "sample" of the two sides of the coin is selected in an unbiased fashion, but it still is unrepresentative. Imagine selecting randomly a sample of 10 people from a population comprising 50 men and 50 women. Just by chance, can't you imagine finding that these 10 people include 7 women and only 3 men? Fortunately, we can determine mathematically the likely degree of sampling error in an estimate based on a random sample (as you'll see later in this chapter)—assuming that the sample's randomness has not been destroyed by a high rate of nonresponse or by poor control over the selection process.

In general, both the size of the sample and the homogeneity (sameness) of the population affect the degree of error due to chance; the proportion of the population that the sample represents does not. To elaborate:

■ *The larger the sample, the more confidence we can have in the sample's representativeness.* If we randomly pick 5 people to represent the entire population of our city, our sample is unlikely to be very representative of the entire population in terms of age, gender, race, attitudes, and so on. But if we randomly pick 100 people, the odds of having a representative sample are much better; with a random sample of 1,000, the odds become very good indeed.

■ *The more homogeneous the population, the more confidence we can have in the representativeness of a sample of any particular size.* Let's say we plan to draw samples of 50 from each of two communities to estimate mean family income. One community is very diverse, with family incomes varying from $12,000 to $85,000. In the other, more homogeneous community, family incomes are concentrated in a narrow range, from $41,000 to $64,000. The estimated mean family income based on the sample from the homogeneous community is more likely to be representative than is the estimate based on the sample from the more heterogeneous community. With less variation to represent, fewer cases are needed to represent the homogeneous community.

■ *The fraction of the total population that a sample contains does not affect the sample's representativeness, unless that fraction is large.* We can regard any sampling fraction under 2% with about the same degree of confidence (Sudman, 1976: 184). In fact, sample representativeness is not likely to increase much until the sampling fraction is quite a bit higher. Other things being equal, a sample of 1,000 from a population of 1 million (with a sampling fraction of 0.001, or 0.1%) is much better than a sample of 100 from a population of 10,000 (although the sampling fraction is 0.01, or 1%, which is 10 times higher). The size of the samples is what makes representativeness more likely, not the proportion of the whole that the sample represents.

Polls to predict presidential election outcomes illustrate both the value of random sampling and the problems that it cannot overcome. In most presidential elections, pollsters have predicted accurately the outcomes of the actual vote by using random sampling and, these days, phone interviewing to learn whom likely voters intend to vote for. Exhibit 4.3 shows how close these sample-based predictions have been in the last 10 contests. The big exception was the 1980 election, when a third-party candidate had an unpredicted effect. Otherwise, the small discrepancies between the votes predicted through random sampling and the actual votes can be attributed to random error.

But election polls have produced some major errors in prediction. The reasons for these errors illustrate some of the ways in which unintentional systematic bias can influence sample results. In 1936, a *Literary Digest* poll predicted that Alfred M. Landon would defeat President Franklin Delano Roosevelt in a landslide, but instead Roosevelt took 63% of the popular vote. The problem? The *Digest* mailed out 10 million mock ballots to people listed

Exhibit 4.3   **Election Outcomes: Predicted[1] and Actual**

Winner/Year	Polls	Result
Kennedy (1960)	49%	50%
Johnson (1964)	64%	61%
Nixon (1968)[2]	44%	43%
Nixon (1972)	59%	61%
Carter (1976)	49%	50%
Reagan (1980)[2]	42%	51%
Reagan (1984)	57%	59%
Bush (1988)	50%	53%
Clinton (1992)[2]	41%	43%[3]
Clinton (1996)[2]	52%[4]	46%[5]

[1]Polls one week prior to election
[2]There was also a third-party candidate.
[3]Outcome from *Academic American Encyclopedia*, on-line version.
[4]Source of 1996 poll data: Gallup poll (http://www.gallup.com/poll/data/96prelec.html).
[5]Outcome from Mediacity.com Web pages E6, 8/30/97.
Source: 1960–1992 data, Gallup poll (Loth, 1992).

in telephone directories, automobile registration records, voter lists, and so on. But in 1936, the middle of the Great Depression, only relatively wealthy people had phones and cars, and they were more likely to be Republican. Furthermore, only 2,376,523 completed ballots were returned, and a response rate of only 24% leaves much room for error. Of course, this poll was not designed as a random sample, so the appearance of systematic bias is not surprising. Gallup was able to predict the 1936 election results accurately with a randomly selected sample of just 3,000 (Bainbridge, 1989:43–44).

In 1948, pollsters mistakenly predicted that Thomas E. Dewey would beat Harry S. Truman, based on the random sampling method that George Gallup had used successfully since 1934. The problem? Pollsters stopped collecting data several weeks before the election, and in those weeks many people changed their minds (Kenney, 1987). So the sample was systematically biased by underrepresenting shifts in voter sentiment just before the election.

The year 1980 was the only year in the preceding 32 that pollsters had the wrong prediction in the week prior to the election. With Jimmy Carter ahead of Ronald Reagan in the polls by 45% to 42%, Gallup predicted a race too close to call. The outcome: Reagan 51%, Carter 42%. The problem? A large bloc of undecided voters, an unusually late debate with a strong performance by Reagan, and the failure of many pollsters to call back voters whom interviewers had failed to reach on the first try (these harder-to-reach voters were more likely to be Republican-leaning) (Dolnick, 1984; Loth, 1992). In this case, the sample was systematically biased against voters who were harder to reach and those who were influenced by the final presidential debate. The presence in the sample of many undecided voters was apparently an accurate representation of sentiment in the general population, so the problem would not be considered "sample bias"; but it did make measuring voting preferences all the more difficult.

Because they do not disproportionately exclude or include particular groups within the population, random samples that are successfully implemented avoid systematic bias. Random error can still be considerable, however, and different types of random samples vary in their ability to minimize it. The four most common methods for drawing random samples are simple random sampling, systematic random sampling, stratified random sampling, and cluster sampling.

Simple Random Sampling

Simple random sampling requires some procedure that generates numbers or otherwise identifies cases strictly on the basis of chance. As you know, flipping a coin and rolling a die both can be used to identify cases strictly on the basis of chance, but these procedures are not very efficient tools for drawing a sample. A **random number table,** like the one in Appendix F, simplifies the process considerably. The researcher numbers all the elements in the sampling frame and then uses a systematic procedure for picking corresponding numbers from the random number table. (Exercise 2 explains the process step by step.) Alternatively, a researcher may use a lottery procedure. Each case number is written on a small card, and then the cards are mixed up and the sample selected from the cards.

When a large sample must be generated, these procedures are very cumbersome. Fortunately, a computer program can easily generate a random sample of any size. The researcher must first number all the elements to be sampled (the sampling frame) and then run the computer program to generate a random selection of the numbers within the desired range. The elements represented by these numbers are the sample.

Organizations that conduct phone surveys often draw random samples with another automated procedure, called **random digit dialing**. A machine dials random numbers within the phone prefixes corresponding to the area in which the survey is to be conducted. Random digit dialing is particularly useful when a sampling frame is not available. The researcher simply replaces any inappropriate numbers (those that are no longer in service or that are for businesses, for example) with the next randomly generated phone number.

The probability of selection in a true simple random sample is equal for each element. If a sample of 500 is selected from a population of 17,000 (that is, a sampling frame of 17,000), then the probability of selection for each element is 500/17,000, or .03. Every element has an equal chance of being selected, just like the odds in a toss of a coin (1/2) or a roll of a die (1/6). Thus simple random sampling is an "equal probability of selection method," or EPSEM.

Simple random sampling can be done either with or without replacement sampling. In **replacement sampling**, each element is returned to the sampling frame after it is selected so that it may be sampled again. In sampling without replacement, each element selected for the sample is then excluded from the sampling frame. In practice it makes no difference whether sampled elements are replaced after selection, as long as the population is large and the sample is to contain only a small fraction of the population.

In a study involving simple random sampling, Bruce Link and his associates (1996) used random digit dialing to contact adult household members in the continental United States for an investigation of public attitudes and beliefs about homeless people. Sixty-three percent of the potential interviewees responded. The sample actually obtained was not exactly comparable to the population sampled: Compared to U.S. Census figures, the sample overrepresented women, people ages 25 to 54, married people, and those with more than a high school education; it underrepresented Latinos.

How does this sample strike you? Let's assess sample quality using the questions posed earlier in the chapter:

■ *From what population were the cases selected?* There is a clearly defined population: the adult residents of the continental United States (who live in households with phones).

■ *What method was used to select cases from this population?* The case selection method is a random selection procedure and there are no systematic biases in the sampling.

■ *Do the cases that were studied represent, in the aggregate, the population from which they were selected?* The findings are very likely to represent the population sampled, because there were no biases in the sampling and a very large number of cases was selected. However, 37% of those selected for interviews could not be contacted or chose not to respond. This rate of nonresponse seems to create a small bias in the sample for several characteristics.

We also must consider the issue of cross-population generalizability: Do findings from this sample have implications for any larger group beyond the population from which the sample was selected? Because a representative sample of the entire U.S. adult population was drawn, this question has to do with cross-national generalizations. Link and his colleagues don't make any such generalizations. There's no telling what might occur in other countries with different histories of homelessness and different social policies.

Systematic Random Sampling

Systematic random sampling is a variant of simple random sampling. The first element is selected randomly from a list or from sequential files, and then every *n*th element is selected. This is a convenient method for drawing a random sample when the population elements are arranged sequentially. It is particularly efficient when the elements are not actually printed (that is, there is no sampling frame) but instead are represented by folders in filing cabinets. For example, at a homeless shelter in Boston, a colleague and I drew a systematic random sample of intake records (Garrett & Schutt, 1990).

Systematic random sampling requires three steps:

1. The total number of cases in the population is divided by the number of cases required for the sample. This division yields the **sampling interval**, the number of cases from one sampled case to another. If 50 cases are to be selected out of 1,000, the sampling interval is 20; every 20th case is selected.

2. A number from 1 to 20 (or whatever the sampling interval is) is selected randomly. This number identifies the first case to be sampled, counting from the first case on the list or in the files.

3. After the first case is selected, every *n*th case is selected for the sample, where *n* is the sampling interval. If the sampling interval is not a whole number, the size of the sampling interval is varied systematically to yield the proper number of cases for the sample. For example, if the sampling interval is 30.5, the sampling interval alternates between 30 and 31.

In almost all sampling situations, systematic random sampling yields what is essentially a simple random sample. The exception is a situation in which the sequence of elements is affected by **periodicity**—that is, the sequence varies in some regular, periodic pattern. For example, the houses in a new development with the same number of houses on each block (eight, for example) may be listed by block, starting with the house in the northwest corner of each block and continuing clockwise. If the sampling interval is 8, the same as the periodic pattern, all the cases selected will be in the same position (see Exhibit 4.4). But in reality, periodicity and the sampling interval are rarely the same.

Exhibit 4.4 **The Effect of Periodicity on Systematic Random Sampling**

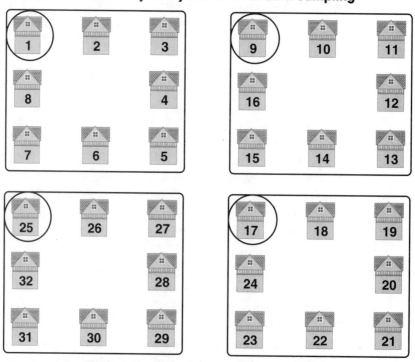

If the sampling interval is 8 for a study in this neighborhood, every element of the sample will be a house on the northwest corner—and thus the sample will be biased.

Stratified Random Sampling

Although all probability sampling methods use random sampling, some add additional steps to the sampling process in order to make sampling more efficient or easier. One sample is more efficient than another when it is easier to obtain without sacrificing confidence that the sample statistics are representative of the population. Samples are easier to collect when they require less time, money, or prior information.

Stratified random sampling uses information known about the total population prior to sampling to make the sampling process more efficient. First, all elements in the population (that is, in the sampling frame) are distinguished according to their value on some relevant characteristic. That characteristic forms the sampling strata. Next, elements are sampled randomly from within these strata. For example, race may be the basis for distinguishing individuals in some population of interest. Within each racial category, individuals are then sampled randomly.

Why is this method more efficient than drawing a simple random sample? Imagine that you plan to draw a sample of 500 from an ethnically diverse neighborhood. The neighborhood population is 15% black, 10% Hispanic, 5% Asian, and 70% white. If you drew a simple random sample, you might end up with disproportionate numbers of each group. But if you created sampling strata based on race and ethnicity, you could randomly select cases from each stratum: 75 blacks (15% of the sample), 50 Hispanics (10%), 25 Asians (5%), and 350 whites (70%). By using **proportionate stratified sampling,** you would eliminate any possibility of error in the sample's distribution of ethnicity. Each stratum would be represented exactly in proportion to its size in the population from which the sample was drawn (see Exhibit 4.5).

In **disproportionate stratified sampling**, the proportion of each stratum that is included in the sample is intentionally varied from what it is in the population. In the case of the sample stratified by ethnicity, you might select equal numbers of cases from each racial or ethnic group: 125 blacks (25% of the sample), 125 Hispanics (25%), 125 Asians (25%), and 125 whites (25%). In this type of sample, the probability of selection of every case is known but unequal between strata. You know what the proportions are in the population, and so you can easily adjust your combined sample statistics to reflect these true proportions. For instance, if you want to combine the ethnic groups and estimate the average income of the total population, you would have to "weight" each case in the sample. The weight is a number you multiply by the value of each case based on the stratum it is in. For example, you would multiply the incomes of all blacks in the sample by 0.6 (75/125), the incomes of all Hispanics by 0.4 (50/125), and so on. Weighting in this way reduces the influence of the oversampled strata and increases the influence of the undersampled strata to just what they would have been if pure probability sampling had been used.

Exhibit 4.5   **Stratified Random Sampling**

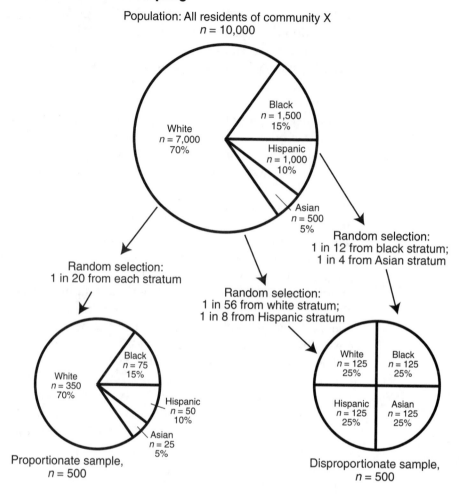

Population: All residents of community X
n = 10,000

White
n = 7,000
70%

Black
n = 1,500
15%

Hispanic
n = 1,000
10%

Asian
n = 500
5%

Random selection:
1 in 20 from each stratum

Random selection:
1 in 56 from white stratum;
1 in 8 from Hispanic stratum

Random selection:
1 in 12 from black stratum;
1 in 4 from Asian stratum

White
n = 350
70%

Black
n = 75
15%

Hispanic
n = 50
10%

Asian
n = 25
5%

Proportionate sample,
n = 500

White
n = 125
25%

Black
n = 125
25%

Hispanic
n = 125
25%

Asian
n = 125
25%

Disproportionate sample,
n = 500

Why would anyone select a sample that is so unrepresentative in the
first place? The most common reason is to ensure that cases from smaller
strata are included in the sample in sufficient numbers to allow separate
statistical estimates and to facilitate comparisons between strata. Remember that one of the determinants of sample quality is sample size. The same
is true for subgroups within samples. If a key concern in a research project
is to describe and compare the incomes of people from different racial and
ethnic groups, then it is important that the researchers base the mean income of each group on enough cases to be a valid representation. If few
members of a particular minority group are in the population, they need to
be oversampled. Such disproportionate sampling may also result in a more
efficient sampling design if the costs of data collection differ markedly between strata or if the variability (heterogeneity) of the strata differs.

Cluster Sampling

Stratified sampling requires more information than usual prior to sampling (about the size of strata in the population); cluster sampling, on the other hand, requires less prior information. Specifically, **cluster sampling** can be useful when a sampling frame is not available, as often is the case for large populations spread out across a wide geographic area or among many different organizations.

A **cluster** is a naturally occurring, mixed aggregate of elements of the population, with each element appearing in one and only one cluster. Schools could serve as clusters for sampling students, blocks could serve as clusters for sampling city residents, counties could serve as clusters for sampling the general population, and businesses could serve as clusters for sampling employees.

Drawing a cluster sample is at least a two-stage procedure. First, the researcher draws a random sample of clusters. A list of clusters should be much easier to obtain than a list of all the individuals in each cluster in the population. Next, the researcher draws a random sample of elements within each selected cluster. Because only a fraction of the total clusters are involved, obtaining the sampling frame at this stage should be much easier.

In a cluster sample of city residents, for example, blocks could be the first-stage clusters. A research assistant could walk around each selected block and record the addresses of all occupied dwelling units. Or in a cluster sample of students, a researcher could contact the schools selected in the first stage and make arrangements with the registrar to obtain lists of students at each school. Cluster samples often involve multiple stages (see Exhibit 4.6).

How many clusters and how many individuals within clusters should be selected? As a general rule, cases in the sample will be closer to the true population value if the researcher maximizes the number of clusters selected and minimizes the number of individuals within each cluster. Unfortunately, this strategy also maximizes the cost of the sample. The more clusters selected, the higher the travel costs. It also is important to take into account the homogeneity of the individuals within clusters—the more homogeneous the clusters, the fewer cases needed per cluster.

Cluster sampling is a very popular method among survey researchers, but it has one drawback: Sampling error is greater in a cluster sample than in a simple random sample. This error increases as the number of clusters decreases, and it decreases as the homogeneity of cases per cluster increases.

Many professionally designed surveys use multistage cluster samples or even combinations of cluster and stratified probability sampling methods. For example, Rossi (1989) drew a disproportionate stratified cluster sample of shelter users for his Chicago study (see Exhibit 4.7). The shelter sample was stratified by size, with smaller shelters having a smaller likelihood of selection than larger shelters. In fact, the larger shelters were all selected;

Exhibit 4.6 **Cluster Sampling**

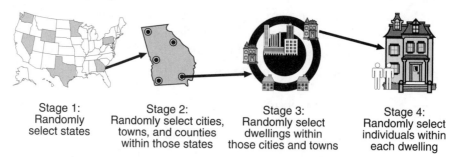

Stage 1:	Stage 2:	Stage 3:	Stage 4:
Randomly select states	Randomly select cities, towns, and counties within those states	Randomly select dwellings within those cities and towns	Randomly select individuals within each dwelling

they had a probability of selection of 1.0. Within the selected shelters, shelter users were then sampled using a systematic random selection procedure (except in the small shelters, in which all persons were interviewed). Homeless persons living on the streets were also sampled randomly. In the first stage, city blocks were classified in strata based on the likely concentration of homeless persons (estimated by several knowledgeable groups). Blocks were then picked randomly within these strata and, on the survey night between 1 A.M. and 6 A.M., teams of interviewers screened each person found

Exhibit 4.7 **Chicago Shelter Universe and Shelter Samples, Fall and Winter Surveys**

	Fall	Winter
A. Shelter Universe and Samples		
Eligible shelters in universe	28	45
Universe bed capacities	1,573	2,001
Shelters drawn in sample	22	27

B. Details of Winter Shelter Sample

Shelter Size Classification	Number in Universe	Number in Sample	Occupant Sampling Ratio
Large (37 or more beds)	17	17	0.25
Medium (18–33 beds)	12	6	0.50
Small (under 18 beds)	16	4	1.00

Note: Shelters were drawn with probabilities proportionate to size, with residents sampled disproportionately within shelters to form a self-weighting sample. Sampling ratios for the phase two sample are given in panel B.
Source: Rossi, 1989:225.

outside on that block for her or his homeless status. Persons identified as homeless were then interviewed (and given $5 for their time). The rate of response for two different samples (fall and winter) in the shelters and on the streets was between 73% and 83%.

How would we evaluate the Chicago homeless sample, using the sample evaluation questions?

- *From what population were the cases selected?* The population was clearly defined for each cluster.

- *What method was used to select cases from this population?* The random selection method was carefully described.

- *Do the cases that were studied represent, in the aggregate, the population from which they were selected?* The unbiased selection procedures make us reasonably confident in the representativeness of the sample, although we know little about the nonrespondents and therefore may justifiably worry that some types of homeless persons were missed.

Cross-population generalization seems to be reasonable with this sample, since it seems likely that the findings reflect general processes involving homeless persons. Rossi clearly thought so, because his book's title referred to homelessness in America, not just in Chicago.

Nonprobability Sampling Methods

Four nonprobability sampling methods are used with some frequency: availability sampling, quota sampling, purposive sampling, and snowball sampling. Because they do not use a random selection procedure, we cannot expect a sample selected with any of these methods to yield a representative sample. Nonetheless, these methods may be useful when random sampling is not possible, with a research question that does not concern a large population, or for a preliminary, exploratory study.

Availability Sampling

Elements are selected for **availability sampling** because they're available or easy to find. Thus this sampling method is also known as a haphazard, accidental, or convenience sample. News reporters often use person-on-the-street interviews—availability samples—to inject color into a news story and show what ordinary people think. You already have encountered availability samples in the example of homeless persons like Jack Olson (Chapter 1) and in the journalistic examples at the start of this chapter.

An availability sample is often appropriate in social research—for example, when a field researcher is exploring a new setting and trying to get some sense of prevailing attitudes or when a survey researcher conducts a preliminary test of a new set of questions. And there are many ways to select elements for an availability sample: standing on street corners and talking to whoever walks by; asking questions of employees who come to pick up their paychecks at a personnel office and who have time to talk to a researcher; surveying merchants who happen to be at work when the researcher is looking for subjects. I have occasionally had my methods students learn about survey research by interviewing students who happen to be using the school cafeteria. A participant observation study of a group may require no more sophisticated approach. When Philippe Bourgois, Mark Lettiere, and James Quesada (1997) studied homeless heroin addicts in San Francisco, they immersed themselves in a community of addicts living in a public park. These addicts became the availability sample.

But now I'd like you to answer each of the sample evaluation questions (page 121) with person-in-the-street interviews of the homeless in mind. If your answers are something like "The population was unknown," "The method for selecting cases was haphazard," and "The cases studied do not represent the population," you're right! There is no clearly definable population from which the respondents were drawn, and no systematic technique was used to select the respondents. There certainly is not much likelihood that the interviewees represent the distribution of sentiment among homeless persons in the Boston area or of welfare mothers or of impoverished rural migrants to Moscow or of whatever we imagine the relevant population is. But perhaps person-in-the-street comments to news reporters do suggest something about what homeless persons think. Or maybe they don't; we can't really be sure.

But let's give reporters their due: If they just want to have a few quotes to make their story more appealing, nothing is wrong with their sampling method. However, their approach gives us no basis for thinking that we have an overview of community sentiment. The people who happen to be available in any situation are unlikely to be just like those who are unavailable. We shouldn't kid ourselves into thinking that what we learn can be generalized with any confidence to a larger population of concern.

Availability sampling often masquerades as a more rigorous form of research. Popular magazines periodically survey their readers by printing a questionnaire for readers to fill out and mail in. A follow-up article then appears in the magazine under a title like "What You Think About Intimacy in Marriage." If the magazine's circulation is large, a large sample can be achieved in this way. The problem is that usually only a tiny fraction of readers return the questionnaire, and these respondents are probably unlike other readers who did not have the interest or time to participate. So the survey is based on an availability sample. Even though the follow-up article may be interesting, we have no basis for thinking that the results describe the readership as a whole—much less the population at large.

Quota Sampling

Quota sampling is intended to overcome the most obvious flaw of avail-ability sampling—that the sample will just consist of whoever or whatever is available, without any concern for its similarity to the population of inter-est. The distinguishing feature of a quota sample is that quotas are set to en-sure that the sample represents certain characteristics in proportion to their prevalence in the population.

Suppose that you wish to sample adult residents of a town in a study of support for a tax increase to improve the town's schools. You know from the town's annual report what the proportions of town residents are in terms of gender, race, age, and number of children. You think that each of these char-acteristics might influence support for new school taxes, so you want to be sure that the sample includes men, women, whites, blacks, Hispanics, Asians, older people, younger people, big families, small families, and child-less families in proportion to their numbers in the town population.

This is where quotas come in. Let's say that 48% of the town's adult resi-dents are men and 52% are women; that 60% are white, 15% are black, 10% are Hispanic, and 15% are Asian. These percentages and the percentages cor-responding to the other characteristics become the quotas for the sample. If you plan to include a total of 500 residents in your sample, 240 must be men (48% of 500), 260 must be women, 300 must be white, and so on. You may even set more refined quotas, such as certain numbers of white women, white men, and Asian men.

With the quota list in hand, you (or your research staff) can now go out into the community looking for the right number of people in each quota category. You may go door to door, go bar to bar, or just stand on a street corner until you have surveyed 240 men, 260 women, and so on.

Some features of quota sampling may appear in what are primarily availability sampling strategies. For instance, Doug Timmer, Stanley Eitzen, and Kathryn Talley (1993:7) interviewed homeless persons in several cities and other locations for their book on the sources of homelessness. Persons who were available were interviewed, but the researchers paid some atten-tion to generating a diverse sample. They interviewed 20 homeless men who lived on the streets without shelter and 20 mothers who were found in family shelters. About half of those the researchers selected in the street sample were black, and about half were white. Although the researchers did not use quotas to try to match the distribution of characteristics among the total homeless population, their informal quotas helped to ensure some diversity in key characteristics.

Even when we know that a quota sample is representative of the particu-lar characteristics for which quotas have been set, we have no way of know-ing if the sample is representative in terms of any other characteristics. In

Exhibit 4.8 **Quota Sampling**

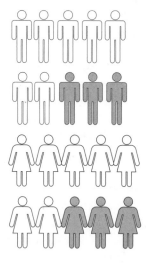

Population
50% male, 50% female
70% white, 30% black

Quota sample
50% male, 50% female

Representative of gender distribution
in population, not representative of
race distribution.

Exhibit 4.8, for example, quotas have been set for gender only. Under the circumstances, it's no surprise that the sample is representative of the population only in terms of gender, not in terms of race. Interviewers are only human; they may avoid potential respondents with menacing dogs in the front yard, or they could seek out respondents who are physically attractive or who look like they'd be easy to interview. Realistically, researchers can set quotas for only a small fraction of the characteristics relevant to a study, so a quota sample is really not so much better than an availability sample (although following careful, consistent procedures for selecting cases within the quota limits always helps).

This last point leads me to another limitation of quota sampling: You must know the characteristics of the entire sample to set the right quotas. In most cases researchers know what the population looks like in terms of no more than a few of the characteristics relevant to their concerns. And in some cases they have no such information on the entire population. If you're now feeling skeptical of quota sampling, you've gotten the drift of my remarks.

Purposive Sampling

In **purposive sampling,** each sample element is selected for a purpose, usually because of the unique position of the sample elements. Purposive sampling may involve studying the entire population of some limited group (directors of shelters for homeless adults) or a subset of a population (mid-level managers with a reputation for efficiency). Or a purposive sample may be a "key informant survey," which targets individuals who are particularly knowledgeable about the issues under investigation.

Herbert Rubin and Irene Rubin (1995:66) suggest three guidelines for selecting informants when designing any purposive sampling strategy. Informants should be

- "Knowledgeable about the cultural arena or situation or experience being studied."
- "Willing to talk."
- "Represent[ative of] the range of points of view."

In addition, Rubin and Rubin suggest continuing to select interviewees until you can pass two tests:

- *Completeness.* "What you hear provides an overall sense of the meaning of a concept, theme, or process" (p. 72).
- *Saturation.* "You gain confidence that you are learning little that is new from subsequent interview[s]" (p. 73).

Adhering to these guidelines will help to ensure that a purposive sample adequately represents the setting or issues studied.

Of course, purposive sampling does not produce a sample that represents some larger population, but it can be exactly what is needed in a case study of an organization, community, or some other clearly defined and relatively limited group. In an intensive organizational case study, a purposive sample of organizational leaders might be complemented with a probability sample of organizational members. Before designing her probability samples of hospital patients and homeless persons, Dee Roth (1990:146 – 147) interviewed a purposive sample of 164 key informants from organizations that had contact with homeless people in each county she studied.

Snowball Sampling

For **snowball sampling**, you identify one member of the population and speak to him or her, then ask that person to identify others in the population and speak to them, then ask them to identify others, and so on. The sample thus "snowballs" in size. This technique is useful for hard-to-reach or hard-to-identify, interconnected populations (at least some members of the population know each other), such as drug dealers, prostitutes, practicing criminals, participants in Alcoholics Anonymous groups, gang leaders, and informal organizational leaders. It also may be used for charting the relationships among members of some group (a sociometric study), for exploring the population of interest prior to developing a formal sampling plan, and for developing what becomes a census of informal leaders of small organizations or communities. However, researchers using snowball sampling normally cannot be confident that their sample represents the total population of interest, so generalizations must be tentative.

Rob Rosenthal (1994) used snowball sampling to study homeless persons living in Santa Barbara, California:

> I began this process by attending a meeting of homeless people I had heard about through my housing advocate contacts. . . . One homeless woman . . . invited me to . . . where she promised to introduce me around. Thus a process of snowballing began. I gained entree to a group through people I knew, came to know others, and through them gained entree to new circles. (pp. 178, 180)

One problem with this technique is that the initial contacts may shape the entire sample and foreclose access to some members of the population of interest:

> Sat around with [my contact] at the Tree. Other people come by, are friendly, but some regulars, especially the tougher men, don't sit with her. Am I making a mistake by tying myself too closely to her? She lectures them a lot. (Rosenthal, 1994:181)

More systematic versions of snowball sampling can reduce this potential for bias. The most sophisticated, termed "respondent-driven sampling," gives financial incentives to respondents to recruit peers (Heckathorn, 1997). Limitations on the number of incentives that any one respondent can receive increase the sample's diversity. Targeted incentives can steer the sample to include specific subgroups. When the sampling is repeated through several waves, with new respondents bringing in more peers, the composition of the sample converges on a more representative mix of characteristics. Exhibit 4.9 shows how the sample spreads out through successive recruitment waves to an increasingly diverse pool (Heckathorn, 1997:178).

Lessons About Sample Quality

Some lessons are implicit in my evaluations of the samples in this chapter:

■ We can't evaluate the quality of a sample if we don't know what population it is supposed to represent. If the population is unspecified because the researchers were never clear about just what population they were trying to sample, then we can safely conclude that the sample itself is no good.

■ We can't evaluate the quality of a sample if we don't know just how cases in the sample were selected from the population. If the method

Exhibit 4.9   **Respondent-Driven Sampling**

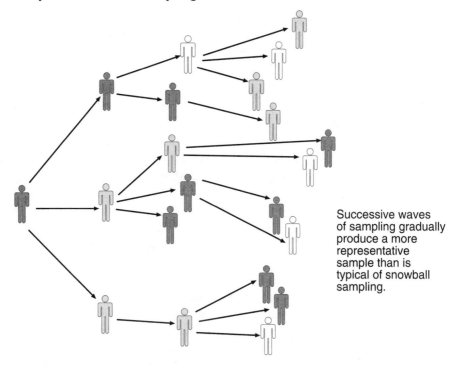

Successive waves
of sampling gradually
produce a more
representative
sample than is
typical of snowball
sampling.

Instructions to respondents:
"We'll pay you $5 each for up to three names, but only one of those names
can be somebody from your own town. The others have to be from somewhere else."

was specified, we then need to know whether cases were selected in a
systematic fashion and on the basis of chance. In any case, we know that
a haphazard method of sampling (as in person-on-the-street interviews)
undermines generalizability.

■ Sample quality is determined by the sample actually obtained, not just
by the sampling method itself. If many of the people selected for our
sample are **nonrespondents** or people (or other entities) who do not
participate in the study although they have been selected for the sample,
the quality of our sample is undermined—even if we chose the sample
in the best possible way.

■ We need to be aware that even researchers who obtain very good
samples may talk about the implications of their findings for some
group that is larger than or just different from the population they actually sampled. For example, findings from a representative sample of students in one university often are discussed as if they tell us about university students in general. And maybe they do; we just don't know.

■ ■ ■ ■ **Sampling Distributions**

A well-designed probability sample is one that is likely to be representative of the population from which it was selected. But as you've seen, random samples still are subject to sampling error due just to chance. To deal with that problem, social researchers take into account the properties of a **sampling distribution,** *a hypothetical distribution of a statistic across all the random samples that could be drawn from a population.* Any single random sample can be thought of as just one of an infinite number of random samples that, in theory, could have been selected from the population. If we had the finances of Gatsby and the patience of Job and were able actually to draw an infinite number of samples, and we calculated the same type of statistic for each of these samples, we would then have a sampling distribution. Understanding sampling distributions is the foundation for understanding how statisticians can estimate sampling error.

What does a sampling distribution look like? Because a sampling distribution is based on some statistic calculated for different samples, we need to choose a statistic. Let's focus on the arithmetic average, or mean. I will explain the calculation of the mean in Chapter 11, but you may already be familiar with it: You add up the values of all the cases and divide by the total number of cases. Let's say you draw a random sample of 500 families and find that their average (mean) family income is $36,239. Imagine that you then draw another random sample. That sample's mean family income might be $31,302. Imagine marking these two means on graph paper and then drawing more random samples and marking their means on the graph. The resulting graph would be a sampling distribution of the mean.

Exhibit 4.10 demonstrates what happened when I did something very similar to what I have just described—not with an infinite number of samples and not from a large population but through the same process using the 1996 General Social Survey (GSS) sample as if it were a population. First, I drew 49 different random samples, each consisting of 30 cases, from the 1996 GSS. (The standard notation for the number of cases in each sample is $n = 30$.) Then I calculated for each random sample the approximate mean family income (approximate because the GSS does not ask for actual income in dollars). I then graphed the means of the 49 samples. Each column in Exhibit 4.10 shows how many samples had a particular family income. The mean for the "population" (the total sample) is $40,043, and you can see that the sampling distribution centers around this value. However, although many of the sample means are close to the "population" mean, some are quite far from it. If you had calculated the mean from only one sample, it could have been anywhere in this sampling distribution. But that one mean is unlikely to have been far from the population mean—that is, unlikely to have been close to either end (or "tail") of the distribution.

Exhibit 4.10 **Partial Sampling Distribution: Mean Family Income**

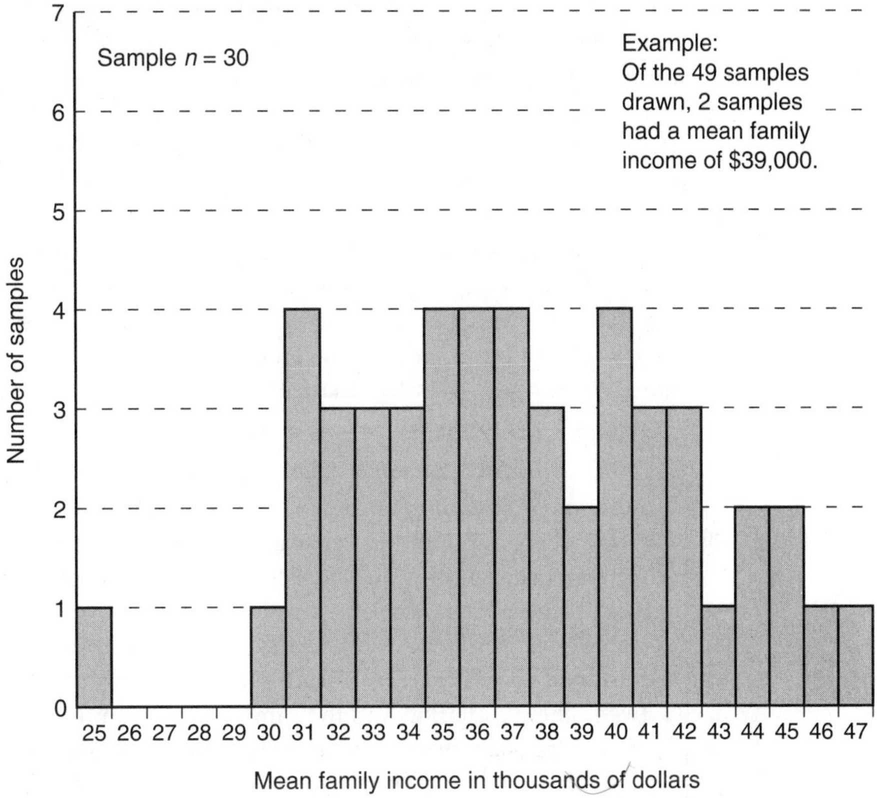

Source: Data from General Social Survey, 1996.

Estimating Sampling Error

We don't actually observe sampling distributions in real research; researchers just draw the best sample they can and then are stuck with the results—one sample, not a distribution of samples. A sampling distribution is a theoretical distribution. However, we can use the properties of sampling distributions to calculate the amount of sampling error that was likely with the random sample used in a study. The tool for calculating sampling error is called **inferential statistics.**

Inferential statistics A mathematical tool for estimating how likely it is that a statistical result based on data from a random sample is representative of the population from which the sample is assumed to have been selected.

Sampling distributions for many statistics, including the mean, have a "normal" shape. A graph of a **normal distribution** looks like a bell, with one "hump" in the middle, centered around the population mean, and the number of cases tapering off on both sides of the mean. Note that a normal distribution is symmetric: If you folded it in half at its center (at the population mean), the two halves would match perfectly. This shape is produced by random sampling error. The value of the statistic varies from sample to sample because of chance, so higher and lower values are equally likely.

The partial sampling distribution in Exhibit 4.10 does not have a completely normal shape because it involves only a small number of samples (49), each of which has only 30 cases. Exhibit 4.11 shows what the sampling distribution of family incomes would look like if it formed a perfectly normal distribution—if, rather than 49 random samples, I had selected thousands of random samples.

Systematic sampling error Overrepresentation or underrepresentation of some population characteristic in a sample due to the method used to select the sample. A sample shaped by **systematic sampling error** is a biased sample.

Random sampling error (chance sampling error) Differences between the population and the sample that are due only to chance factors (random error), not to systematic sampling error. **Random sampling error** may or may not result in an unrepresentative sample. The magnitude of sampling error due to chance factors can be estimated statistically.

The properties of a sampling distribution facilitate the process of statistical inference. In the sampling distribution, the most frequent value of the **sample statistic** or the statistic (such as the mean) computed from sample data, is identical to the **population parameter**—the statistic computed for the entire population. In other words, we can have a lot of confidence that the value at the peak of the bell curve represents the norm for the entire population. A population parameter also may be termed the **true value** for the statistic in that population. A sample statistic is an estimate of a population parameter.

In a normal distribution, a predictable proportion of cases also falls within certain ranges. Inferential statistics takes advantage of this feature and allow researchers to estimate how likely it is that, given a particular sample, the true population value will be within some range of the statistic. For example, a statistician might conclude from a sample of 30 families that we can be 95% confident that the true mean family income in the total

Exhibit 4.11   **Normal Sampling Distribution: Mean Family Income**

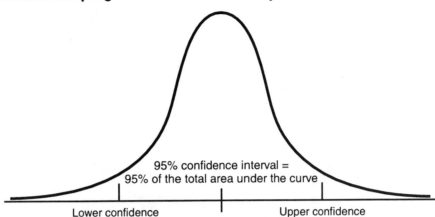

95% confidence interval =
95% of the total area under the curve

Lower confidence
limit = $38,922

Upper confidence
limit = $41,164

Mean family income = $40,043

population is between $38,922 and $41,164. The interval from $38,922 to $41,164 would then be called the "95% **confidence interval** for the mean." The upper ($41,164) and lower ($38,922) bounds of this interval are termed the **confidence limits**. Exhibit 4.11 marks such confidence limits, indicating the range that encompasses 95% of the area under the normal curve; 95% of all samples would fall within this range.

Although all normal distributions have these same basic features, they differ in the extent to which they cluster around the mean. A sampling distribution is more compact when it is based on larger samples. Stated another way, we can be more confident in estimates based on larger random samples because we know that a larger sample creates a more compact sampling distribution. Compare the two "sampling distributions" of mean family income in Exhibit 4.12. Both depict the results for about 50 samples. However, in one study each sample comprised 100 families, and in the other study each sample comprised only 5 families. Clearly, the larger samples result in a sampling distribution that is much more tightly clustered around the mean than is the case with the smaller samples. The 95% confidence interval for mean family income for the entire GSS sample of 2,561 cases (the ones that had valid values of family income) was $38,922 to $41,164—an interval only about $2,242 wide. But the 95% confidence interval for the mean family income in one GSS subsample of 100 cases was much wider, with limits of $35,238 and $47,960. And for a subsample of only 5 cases, the 95% confidence interval was very broad: $13,191 to $74,809. Such small samples often result in statistics that actually give us very little useful information about the population.

Exhibit 4.12   **The Effect of Sample Size on Sampling Distributions**

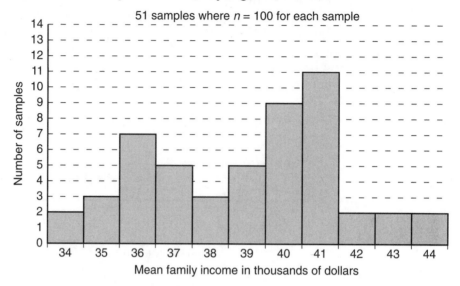

51 samples where *n* = 100 for each sample

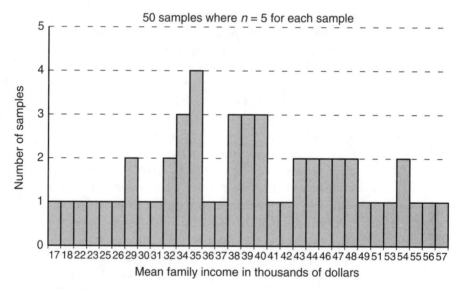

50 samples where *n* = 5 for each sample

Source: General Social Survey, 1996.

Other confidence intervals, such as the 99% confidence interval, can be reported. As a matter of convention, statisticians use only the 95%, 99%, and 99.9% confidence limits to determine the range of values that contain the true value. These conventional limits reflect the conservatism inherent in classical statistical inference: Don't make an inferential statement unless you are very confident (at least 95% confident) that it is correct.

The less precise an estimate of a particular statistic from a particular sample, the more confident we can be—and the wider the confidence interval. The 95% confidence interval for the entire GSS sample is $38,922 to $41,164 (a width of $2,242); the 99% confidence interval is $38,567 to $41,519 (a width of $2,952).

I have not explained how to calculate confidence intervals, which is a subject better left to a statistics course. But you should now have a sense of how researchers make inferences from a random sample to a population.

Determining Sample Size

Now that you know that more confidence can be placed in the generalizability of statistics from larger samples, you may be eager to work with random samples that are as large as possible. Unfortunately, researchers often cannot afford to sample a very large number of cases. They therefore try to determine during the design phase of their study how large a sample they must have to achieve their purposes. They have to consider the degree of confidence desired, the homogeneity of the population, the complexity of the analysis they plan, and the expected strength of the relationships they will measure:

■ The less sampling error desired, the larger the sample size must be.

■ Samples of more homogeneous populations can be smaller than samples of more diverse populations. Stratified sampling uses prior information on the population to create more homogeneous population strata from which the sample can be selected, so it can be smaller than if simple random sampling were used.

■ If the only analysis planned for a survey sample is to describe the population in terms of a few variables, a smaller sample is required than if a more complex analysis involving sample subgroups is planned.

■ When the researchers will be testing hypotheses and expect to find very strong relationships among the variables, they will need a smaller sample to detect these relationships than if they expect weaker relationships.

Researchers can make more precise estimates of the sample size required through a method termed "statistical power analysis" (Kraemer & Thiemann, 1987). Statistical power analysis requires a good advance estimate of the strength of the hypothesized relationship in the population. In addition, the math is complicated, so it helps to have some background in mathematics or to be able to consult a statistician. For these reasons, many researchers do not conduct formal power analyses when deciding how many cases to sample.

You can obtain some general guidance about sample sizes from the current practices of social scientists. For professional studies of the national population in which only a simple description is desired, professional social science studies typically have used a sample size of between 1,000 and 1,500, with up to 2,500 being included if detailed analyses are planned. Studies of local or regional populations often sample only a few hundred people, in part because these studies lack sufficient funding to draw larger samples. Of course, the sampling error in these smaller studies is considerably larger than in a typical national study (Sudman, 1976:87).

■ ■ ■ ■ Conclusion

Sampling is a powerful tool for social science research. Probability sampling methods allow a researcher to use the laws of chance, or probability, to draw samples from which population parameters can be estimated with a high degree of confidence. A sample of just 1,000 or 1,500 individuals can be used to estimate reliably the characteristics of the population of a nation comprising millions of individuals.

But researchers do not come by representative samples easily. Well-designed samples require careful planning, some advance knowledge about the population to be sampled, and adherence to systematic selection procedures—all so that the selection procedures are not biased. And even after the sample data are collected, the researcher's ability to generalize from the sample findings to the population is not completely certain. The best that he or she can do is to perform additional calculations that state the degree of confidence that can be placed in the sample statistic.

The alternatives to random, or probability-based, sampling methods are almost always much less palatable, even though they typically are much cheaper. Without a method of selecting cases likely to represent the population in which the researcher is interested, research findings will have to be carefully qualified. Unrepresentative samples may help researchers understand which aspects of a social phenomenon are important, but questions about the generalizability of this understanding are left unanswered.

Social scientists often seek to generalize their conclusions from the population that they studied to some larger target population. The validity of generalizations of this type is necessarily uncertain, for having a representative sample of a particular population does not at all ensure that what we find will hold true in other populations. Nonetheless, as you will see in Chapter 10, the cumulation of findings from studies based on local or otherwise unrepresentative populations can provide important information about broader populations.

KEY TERMS

Availability sampling
Census
Cluster
Cluster sampling
Confidence interval
Confidence limits
Disproportionate stratified sampling
Element of a population
Inferential statistics
Nonprobability sampling method
Nonrespondent
Normal distribution
Periodicity
Population
Population parameter
Probability of selection
Probability sampling method
Proportionate stratified sampling
Purposive sampling
Quota sampling
Random digit dialing

Random number table
Random sampling
Random sampling error
Replacement sampling
Representative sample
Sample
Sample statistic
Sampling distribution
Sampling error
Sampling frame
Sampling interval
Sampling unit
Simple random sampling
Snowball sampling
Stratified random sampling
Systematic bias
Systematic random sampling
Systematic sampling error
Target population
True value of a statistic

HIGHLIGHTS

- Sampling theory focuses on the generalizability of descriptive findings to the population from which the sample was drawn. It also considers whether statements can be generalized from one population to another.

- Sampling is unnecessary when the elements that would be sampled are identical, but the complexity of the social world makes it difficult to argue very often that different elements are identical. Conducting a complete census of a population also eliminates the need for sampling, but the resources required for a complete census of a large population are usually prohibitive.

- Nonresponse undermines sample quality: It is the obtained sample, not the desired sample, that determines sample quality.

- Probability sampling methods rely on a random selection procedure to ensure no systematic bias in the selection of elements. In a probability sample, the odds of selecting elements are known, and the method of selection is carefully controlled.

- A sampling frame (a list of elements in the population) is required in most probability sampling methods. The adequacy of the sampling frame is an important determinant of sample quality.

■ Simple random sampling and systematic random sampling are equivalent probability sampling methods in most situations. However, systematic random sampling is inappropriate for sampling from lists of elements that have a regular, periodic structure.

■ Stratified random sampling uses prior information about a population to make sampling more efficient. Stratified sampling may be either proportionate or disproportionate. Disproportionate stratified sampling is useful when a research question focuses on a stratum or on strata that make up a small proportion of the population.

■ Cluster sampling is less efficient than simple random sampling but is useful when a sampling frame is unavailable. It is also useful for large populations spread out across a wide area or among many organizations.

■ Nonprobability sampling methods can be useful when random sampling is not possible, when a research question does not concern a larger population, and when a preliminary exploratory study is appropriate. However, the representativeness of nonprobability samples cannot be determined.

■ The likely degree of error in an estimate of a population characteristic based on a probability sample decreases with the size of the sample and the homogeneity of the population from which the sample was selected. Sampling error is not affected by the proportion of the population that is sampled, except when that proportion is large. The degree of sampling error affecting a sample statistic can be estimated from the characteristics of the sample and knowledge of the properties of sampling distributions.

EXERCISES

1. Locate one or more newspaper articles reporting the results of an opinion poll. What information does the article provide on the sample that was selected? What additional information do you need to determine whether the sample was a representative one?

2. Select a random sample using the table of random numbers in Appendix F. Compute a statistic based on your sample, and compare it to the corresponding figure for the entire population. Here's how to proceed:
   a. First select a very small population for which you have a reasonably complete sampling frame. One possibility would be the list of asking prices for houses advertised in your local paper. Another would be the listing of some characteristic of states in a U.S. Census Bureau publication, such as average income or population size.
   b. The next step is to create your sampling frame, a numbered list of all the elements in the population. If you are using a complete listing of all elements, as from a U.S. Census Bureau publication, the sampling frame is the same as

the list. Just number the elements (states). If your population is composed of housing ads in the local paper, your sampling frame will be those ads that contain a housing price. Identify these ads, and then number them sequentially, starting with 1.

c. Decide on a method of picking numbers out of the random number table in Appendix F, such as taking every number in each row, row by row (or you may move down or diagonally across the columns). Use only the first (or last) digit in each number if you need to select 1 to 9 cases or only the first (or last) two digits if you want fewer than 100 cases.

d. Pick a starting location in the random number table. It's important to pick a starting point in an unbiased way, perhaps by closing your eyes and then pointing to some part of the page.

e. Record the numbers you encounter as you move from the starting location in the direction you decided on in advance, until you have recorded as many random numbers as the number of cases you need in the sample. If you are selecting states, 10 might be a good number. Ignore numbers that are too large (or small) for the range of numbers used to identify the elements in the population. Discard duplicate numbers.

f. Calculate the average value in your sample for some variable that was measured—for example, population size in a sample of states or housing price for the housing ads. Calculate the average by adding up the values of all the elements in the sample and dividing by the number of elements in the sample.

g. Go back to the sampling frame and calculate this same average for all the elements in the list. How close is the sample average to the population average?

3. Shere Hite's popular book *Women and Love* (1987) is a good example of the claims that are often made based on an availability sample. In this case, however, the sample didn't necessarily appear to be an availability sample because it consisted of so many people. Hite distributed 100,000 questionnaires to church groups and many other organizations and received back 4.5%; 4,500 women took the time to answer some or all of her 127 essay questions regarding love and sex. Is Hite's sample likely to represent American women in general? Why or why not? You might take a look at the book's empirical generalizations and consider whether they are justified.

4. Draw a snowball sample of people who are involved in bungee jumping or some other uncommon sport that does not involve teams. Ask friends and relatives to locate a first contact, and then call or visit this person and ask for names of others. Stop when you have identified a sample of 10. Review the problems you encountered, and consider how you would proceed if you had to draw a larger sample.

5. In professional journals, select five articles that describe research using a sample drawn from some population. Identify the type of sample used in each study, and note any strong and weak points in how the sample was actually drawn. Did the researchers have a problem due to nonresponse? Considering the sample, how confident are you in the validity of generalizations about the

population based on the sample? Do you need any additional information to evaluate the sample? Do you think a different sampling strategy would have been preferable? What larger population were the findings generalized to? Do you think these generalizations were warranted? Why or why not?

WEB EXERCISES

1. Search the Web for five sources of information on the living conditions of the homeless. Briefly describe your sources and list the Web sites where they can be found. How do these sources of information differ in their approach to collecting information? What statistics do they present? Do they report the sampling method used in the studies from which they obtained these statistics? What sampling methods were used? Evaluate the sampling methods in terms of representativeness and generalizability. How would you improve on the sampling methods to increase the representativeness and generalizability of the data? If no sampling methods are mentioned, propose one that would have been appropriate to obtain the statistics.

    Hint: If you are having trouble locating sites, try starting from a large scholarly Internet resource and using it to link to more specific sites. Just one example of such a resource can be found at **http://lib-www.ucr.edu** (this is the URL for INFOMINE—Scholarly Internet Resource Collections).

2. What can you learn about sampling on the Web? Conduct a search on "sampling" and "population" and select a few of these sites. List a few new points that you learn about sampling.

SPSS EXERCISES

1. The variable HOMELESS measures whether an individual has contributed money to the homeless. Create a frequency distribution for this variable from the GSS96 sample.

2. Now select random samples of the GSS96 respondents and compare them with the original output from Exercise 1.
    a. Select a random sample containing approximately 20 of the respondents.
       DATA…
          SELECT CASES…
             Random sample of cases…
                Approx. 5% of all cases
    b. Request a frequency distribution for the variable HOMELESS and record the VALID PERCENT of this sample who answered yes.
    c. Select a random sample containing 1% of the respondents.
    d. Create a frequency distribution of this sample for the variable HOMELESS and record the VALID PERCENT of this sample who answered yes.
    e. Repeat steps a–d 10 times.

3. Plot the results of 2b & 2d on separate sheets of graph paper.
    a. To make the graphs, mark the vertical axis off in equal intervals from 0 to 5.

Mark the horizontal axis off in equal intervals of 10 from 0 to 100. You will indicate on the horizontal axis the percentage in each sample who said yes.

b. Make an X to indicate this percentage for each sample. If two samples have the same percentage, place the corresponding X's on top of each other. The X for each sample should be 1 unit high on the vertical axis.

c. Make a mark to indicate on the horizontal axis the percentage of the total sample who answered yes (from Exercise 1).

d. You now have two sampling distributions, one for percentages from 10 samples of size 20 and one from 10 samples of size 5.

e. By how much do the percentages obtained from the samples in each distribution tend to differ from the percentage based on the total sample?

f. How do these sampling distributions differ from each other?

5 Causation and Research Design

Meanings of Causation
Nomothetic Causes
Idiographic Causes
Synthetic Causal Explanations

Criteria for Causal Explanation
Association
Time Order
Nonspuriousness
Mechanism
Context

Research Designs to Determine Causality
Nomothetic Research Designs
  Experimental Research
  Nonexperimental Research
  Comparison of Experimental and Nonexperimental Designs
Idiographic Research Designs
  Explanation in Field Research
  Event-Structure Analysis
Combined Research Designs

Research Designs to Determine Time Order
Cross-Sectional Designs
Longitudinal Designs
  Repeated Cross-Sectional Designs
  Fixed-Sample Panel Designs
  Event-Based Designs

Units of Analysis and Errors in Causal Reasoning
Individual and Group Units of Analysis
The Ecological Fallacy and Reductionism

Conclusion

KEY TERMS
HIGHLIGHTS
EXERCISES
WEB EXERCISES
SPSS EXERCISES

■ ■ ■ ■ We've actually had some good news about crime and violence in recent years: "Longest Decline in 25 Years Seen by F.B.I." (Butterfield, 1997); "New York Crime Rate Plummets to Levels Not Seen in 30 Years" (Krauss, 1996); "Gun Violence May Be Subsiding" (Butterfield, 1996b); "After 10 Years, Juvenile Crime Begins to Drop" (Butterfield, 1996a). Is this news too good to be true? If it is true will the trend last? Who should get the credit for this heartening trend? To answer these questions we need to investigate the causes of crime.

There are many causal candidates, according to the news articles. Geoffrey Canada, president of Harlem's Rheedlen Centers for Children and Families, states in one article that changing attitudes toward violence among young people has been key (Butterfield, 1996a). Frank A. Camino, a Manhattan realtor, feels safer because of a decline in the crack-cocaine market (Krauss, 1996). Attorney General Janet Reno highlights law-enforcement strategies (Butterfield, 1996a). Sarah Brady points to the Brady bill's requirement of a waiting period to buy a hand gun (Butterfield, 1996b). Chicago detective Sergeant Tom Keane stresses tougher prison sentences (Butterfield, 1996a), and Cleveland's Sergeant Kaminski suggests the decline in bars and hence in barroom brawls (Butterfield, 1996a). Boston Police Commissioner Paul Evans (Radin, 1997:B7) touts the benefits of community policing strategies but cautions that "anyone who comes into a city like this and looks for one central cause just doesn't get it."

Identifying causes—figuring out why things happen—is the goal of most social science research, as well as a critical interest of newspaper reporters, government officials, and ordinary citizens (Larson & Garrett, 1996:222-251). Unfortunately, valid explanations of the causes of social phenomena do not come easily. Research must be designed carefully if we are to draw causal conclusions. And even researchers who proceed with care often encounter obstacles to achieving causal validity.

This chapter considers the ways causation has been defined and the criteria proposed for achieving causally valid explanations. I review three general types of research design for identifying causal effects and then focus on the ways research can be designed to identify whether the cause truly precedes the effect, one of the critical issues involved in achieving causal validity. You will also learn how to identify the units of analysis in a research design so causal conclusions can be stated in terms of the appropriate units. By the end of the chapter, you should have a good grasp of the meaning of causation and be able to ask the right questions to determine whether causal inferences are likely to be valid. And perhaps you will have another answer or two about the causes of crime and violence.

■ ■ ■ ■ Meanings of Causation

In the movie *Money Train*, two men spray the inside of a subway token booth with a flammable liquid, blowing up the toll booth and killing the collector (Grimes, 1995). In 1995, while the movie was still showing in theaters, a similar incident actually occurred in a New York City subway. The toll collector was hospitalized with widespread third-degree burns. The media violence, it was soon alleged, had caused the crime.

How would you evaluate this claim? What evidence do we need to develop a valid conclusion about a hypothesized causal effect? First we must distinguish two different causal questions that are suggested by the toll booth crime. The more general research question is, Does media violence result in actual violence? We also might ask a much more specific question: Did this particular movie scene lead a particular person in New York City to commit this particular crime? Exhibit 5.1 depicts the difference between the more general nomothetic type of question and the more specific, idiographic type.

Nomothetic Causes

Most social scientists think of a cause as an explanation for some characteristics, attitudes, or behaviors of groups or types of individuals or other entities (such as families, organizations, or cities) or for events. For example, a sociologist may seek to determine whether the experience of abuse during childhood leads people to commit crimes as adults. The question is not whether a particular experience of abuse caused a particular individual to commit crimes but whether this relationship between childhood abuse and crime tends to hold for many individuals—that is, whether it is true on average.

A causal explanation involving a relationship between an independent variable and a dependent variable (between childhood abuse and likelihood of committing crimes, for example) is termed a **nomothetic causal explanation.** Such an explanation identifies common influences on a number of cases or events; it exemplifies "logico-scientific reasoning," abstracting

Exhibit 5.1   **Idiographic and Nomothetic Research Foci**

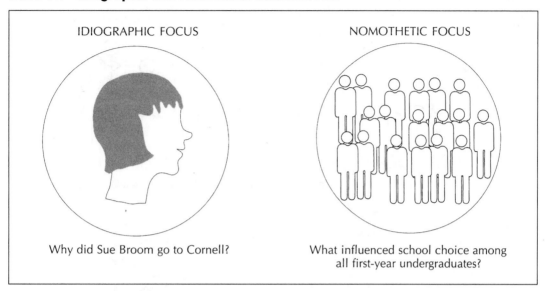

IDIOGRAPHIC FOCUS

NOMOTHETIC FOCUS

Why did Sue Broom go to Cornell?

What influenced school choice among all first-year undergraduates?

from concrete events to find general patterns (Richardson, 1995). It also can be termed a variable-oriented explanation because it involves relationships between variables: Did variation in the independent variable (exposure to media violence) cause variation in the dependent variable (likelihood of committing violent crimes)?

In this perspective, researchers who claim a causal effect have concluded that the value of cases on the dependent variable differs from what their value would have been in the absence of variation in the independent variable. For instance, likelihood of committing violent crimes was higher for individuals who were abused as children than it would have been if these same individuals had not been abused as children. Likelihood of committing violent crimes was higher for individuals exposed to media violence than it would have been if these same individuals had not been exposed to media violence. The situation as it would have been in the absence of variation in the independent variable is termed the **counterfactual** (see Exhibit 5.2).

Of course, the fundamental difficulty with this perspective is that we never really know what would have happened at the same time to the same people (or groups, cities, and so on) if the independent variable had not varied—because it did. We can't rerun real-life scenarios (King, Keohane, & Verba, 1994). However, we could observe the aggressiveness of people's behavior before and after they were exposed to media violence. But this comparison involves an earlier time period, when by definition the people and their circumstances were not exactly the same.

Exhibit 5.2   **The Counterfactual in Causal Research**

Independent variable:

Dependent variable:

Actual situation:
People who watch violence on TV are more likely to commit violent acts.

Independent variable:

Dependent variable:

Counterfactual situation:
The same people watch nonviolent TV shows at the same time, in the same circumstances. They are not more likely to commit violent acts.

But we do not need to give up hope! Far from it. We can design research to create conditions that are very comparable indeed, so that we can confidently assert our conclusions **ceteris paribus**—other things being equal. We can examine the impact on the dependent variable of variation in the independent variable alone, even though we will not be able to compare the same people at the same time in exactly the same circumstances except for the variation in the independent variable. And by knowing the ideal standard of comparability, we can improve our research designs and strengthen our causal conclusions even when we cannot come so close to living up to the meaning of *ceteris paribus*.

Idiographic Causes

The other meaning of the term *cause* is one that we have in mind very often in everyday speech. This is the **idiographic causal explanation**: the concrete, individual sequence of events, thoughts, or actions that resulted in a particular outcome for a particular individual or that led to a particular event (Hage & Meeker, 1988). An idiographic explanation also may be termed an individualist, a historicist, or a case-oriented explanation.

A causal explanation that is idiographic includes statements of initial conditions and then relates a series of events at different times that led to the outcome, or causal effect. This narrative, or story, is the critical element in an idiographic explanation, which may therefore be classified as narrative reasoning (Richardson, 1995:200–201). Idiographic explanations focus on particular social actors, in particular social places, at particular social times (Abbott, 1992). Idiographic explanations are also typically very concerned with context, with understanding the particular outcome as part of a larger set of interrelated circumstances. Idiographic explanations thus can be termed holistic.

Idiographic explanation is deterministic, focusing on what caused a particular event to occur or what caused a particular case to change. As in nomothetic explanations, idiographic causal explanations can involve counterfactuals, by trying to identify what would have happened *if* a different circumstance had occurred. But unlike nomothetic explanations, the notion of a probabilistic relationship, an average effect, does not really apply. A deterministic cause has an effect in every case under consideration.

Idiographic reasoning could be used to explain why the subway criminals blew up the toll collector's booth. Perhaps they were abused by their parents as children and learned aggressive styles of behaving. Then they began to socialize with others who were aggressive and lacked self-control. They got in trouble at school, weren't able to secure good jobs, and concluded they couldn't achieve success through legitimate pursuits. They saw a movie that showed how to get money by robbing toll collectors, which got them thinking. I could go on, but I think you get the point.

Causal effect (nomothetic perspective)   The finding that change in one variable leads to change in another variable, *ceteris paribus* (other things being equal).

Causal effect (idiographic perspective)   The finding that a series of events following an initial set of conditions leads in a progressive manner to a particular event or outcome.

Example of a nomothetic causal explanation: Individuals arrested for domestic assault tend to commit fewer subsequent assaults than similar individuals who are accused in the same circumstances but not arrested.

> *Example of an idiographic causal explanation*: An individual is neglected by her parents but has a supportive grandparent. She comes to distrust others, has trouble in school, is unable to keep a job, and eventually becomes homeless. She subsequently develops a supportive relationship with a shelter case manager, who helps her find a job and regain her housing (based on K. Hirsch, 1989).

Synthetic Causal Explanations

Nomothetic explanations are favored by survey researchers and those who use experimental research. Indeed, many such researchers consider nomothetic explanations the only legitimate meaning of the word *cause*. The idiographic concept of cause is more often used by anthropologists and sociologists who seek to explain how customs, groups, or societies develop; by historians, who seek to explain historical events, such as why World War I began; and by historical and comparative sociologists and political scientists, who may explain the growth of institutions, ideologies, or other group phenomena as sequences of events within a society or may compare major events among a small number of societies.

Despite the clear lines drawn between them, both types of causal explanation may be used in a particular investigation, resulting in what is sometimes called a **synthetic causal explanation**. For example, I once attempted to explain why a public employee union changed over time from a participatory democratic structure to a more bureaucratic form of organization (Schutt, 1986; see also Lipset, Trow, & Coleman, 1956). My explanation combined a historical account of the union's development (an idiographic explanation) with the results of surveys that showed that union members in expanding occupations were less likely than union members in stagnant or shrinking occupations to support a participatory democratic structure (a nomothetic explanation). A comparative method for identifying the causes of historical events or processes that combines nomothetic and idiographic causal explanation is examined in more detail in Chapter 9.

■ ■ ■ ■ Criteria for Causal Explanation

Can you imagine a friend saying, after reading about the *Money Train* incident, "See, media violence causes people to commit crimes"? I know that you yourself, after reading Chapter 1, wouldn't be so quick to jump to such a conclusion: Don't overgeneralize, you would remind yourself. When your friend insists, "But I recall that type of thing happening before," you might even suspect selective observation (see Chapter 1). However, as social scientists who want to have some confidence in the validity of our causal statements, we must meet a higher standard.

Specifically, we need to consider five criteria for deciding whether a causal connection exists—that is, for developing internally valid statements about causal relationships. The first three of these criteria—empirical association, appropriate time order, and nonspuriousness—are widely accepted as the bases for identifying a nomothetic causal effect. They are also important in idiographic explanation. The other two criteria—identifying a causal mechanism and specifying the context in which the effect occurs—are the primary focus of most approaches to idiographic causal explanation. However, evidence that meets these latter two criteria can also considerably strengthen nomothetic causal explanations.

Brad Bushman's (1995) experiment on media violence and aggression illustrates well the five criteria for establishing causal relationships. Bushman's study focused in part on this specific research question: Do individuals who view a violent videotape act more aggressively than individuals who view a nonviolent videotape?

Undergraduate psychology students were recruited to watch a 15-minute videotape in a special room (one student at a time). Half the students watched a movie excerpt that was violent (from *Karate Kid III),* and half watched a nonviolent movie excerpt (from *Gorillas in the Mist*). After viewing the videotape, the students were told that they were to compete with another student, in a different room, on a reaction-time task. When the students saw a light cue, they were to react by trying to click a computer mouse faster than their opponents. On a computer screen, the students set a level of noise (radio static) that their opponents would hear when the opponents reacted more slowly. The students themselves heard this same type of noise when they reacted more slowly than their opponents, at the intensity level supposedly set by their opponents.

Each student in the study participated in 25 trials, or competitions, with the unseen opponent. Their aggressiveness was operationalized as the intensity of noise that they set for their opponents over the course of the 25 trials. The louder the noise level they set, the more aggressively they were considered to be behaving toward their opponents. The question that we will focus on first is whether students who watched the violent video behaved more aggressively than those who watched the nonviolent video.

Association

The results of Bushman's experiment are represented in Exhibit 5.3. The average intensity of noise administered to the opponent was indeed higher for students who watched the violent videotape than for those who watched the nonviolent videotape. But is Bushman justified in concluding from

Exhibit 5.3   **Association: Noise Intensity for Two Groups in an Experiment**

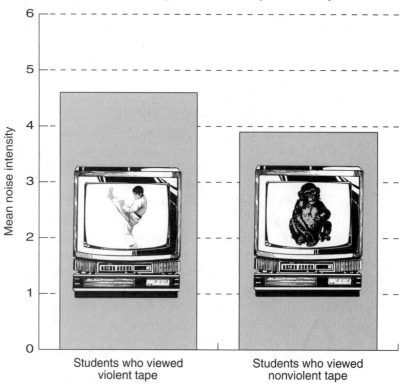

Source: Adapted from Bushman, 1995.

these results that viewing a violent videotape increased aggressive behavior in his subjects? Would this conclusion have any greater claim to causal validity than the statement that "your friend" made in response to the *Money Train* incident? Perhaps it would.

If for no other reason, we can have greater confidence in Bushman's conclusion because he did not observe just one student who watched a violent video and then acted aggressively. That would be the parallel to the one incident like the *Money Train* situation. Instead, Bushman observed a number of students, some of whom watched a violent video and some of whom did not. So his conclusion is based on finding an **association** between the independent variable (viewing of a violent videotape) and the dependent variable (likelihood of aggressive behavior). This is what Exhibit 5.3 shows.

An empirical (or observed) association between the independent and dependent variables is the first criterion researchers use for identifying a causal effect. For example, Klaus Miczek and his associates (1994:389) concluded that alcohol plays an important role in violent crime because, compared to other drugs, "Alcohol stands out as the drug that is most consistently and seriously linked to [associated with] many types of aggressive and violent behavior." On the other hand, Rita Simon and Sandra Baxter (1989:192–193) found no association in their study. They tested the hypothesis that the propensity of the women in a country to commit violent crimes declines as the level of women's labor force participation and education increase. In a sample of 31 countries, the researchers found no association between female crime and labor force participation or education, so they rejected their hypothesis.

Time Order

Association is a necessary criterion for establishing a causal effect, but it is not sufficient. Suppose you find in a survey that most people who have committed violent crimes have also watched the movie *Money Train* and that most people who have not committed violent crimes have not watched the movie. You have found an association between watching the movie and committing violent crimes. But imagine you learn that the movie was released after the crimes were committed. Watching the movie could not possibly have led to the crimes. Perhaps the criminals watched the movie because their commission of violent crimes made them interested in violent movies.

This discussion points up the importance of the criterion of **time order**. To conclude that causation was involved, we must see that cases were exposed to variation in the independent variable before variation in the dependent variable. Bushman's experiment satisfied this criterion because he controlled the variation in the independent variable: All the students saw the videotape excerpts (which varied in violent content) before their level of aggressiveness was measured.

Nonspuriousness

Even when research establishes that two variables are associated and that variation in the independent variable preceded variation in the dependent variable, we cannot be sure we have identified a causal relationship between the two variables. Have you heard the old adage "Correlation does not prove causation"? It is meant to remind us that an association between two variables might be caused by something else. If we measure children's shoe sizes and their academic knowledge, for example, we will find a positive association. However, the association results from the fact that older children have larger feet as well as more academic knowledge. Shoe size does not cause knowledge or vice versa.

Before we conclude that variation in an independent variable caused variation in a dependent variable, we must have reason to believe that the relationship is nonspurious. **Nonspuriousness** is a relationship between two variables that is not due to variation in a third variable. When this third variable, termed an **extraneous variable**, causes the variation, it is said to have created a **spurious relationship** between the independent and dependent variables. We need to design our research so that we can see what happens to the dependent variable when only the independent variable varies.

So the fact that someone blew up a toll booth after seeing the movie *Money Train* might be related to the fact that he was feeling enraged against society and so went to see a violent movie (see Exhibit 5.4). But seeing the violent movie itself in no way led the person to commit the crime.

Does Bushman's claim of a causal effect rest on any stronger ground? To evaluate nonspuriousness, you need to know about one more feature of his experiment. He assigned students to watch either the violent video or the nonviolent video randomly—that is, by the toss of a coin. Because he used random assignment, the characteristics and attitudes that students already possessed when they were recruited for the experiment could not influence which of the two videos they watched. As a result, the students' characteristics and attitudes could not explain why one group reacted differently than the other after watching the videos. In fact, because Bushman used 296 students in his experiment, it is highly unlikely that the group that watched the violent video and the group that watched the nonviolent video differed

Exhibit 5.4 **A Spurious Relationship**

Spurious relationship

The extraneous variable creates the spurious relationship

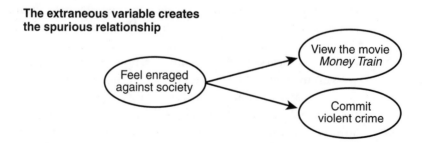

in any relevant way at the outset even on the basis of chance. This experimental research design meets the criterion of nonspuriousness. Bushman's conclusion that viewing video violence caused aggressive behavior thus rests on firm ground indeed.

Many social scientists believe that the case for a nomothetic causal effect need go no further. Causal (internal) validity is achieved by meeting the criteria of association, time order, and nonspuriousness.

Mechanism

Confidence in a conclusion that two variables have a causal connection will be strengthened, however, if a **mechanism**—some discernible means of creating a connection—can be identified (Cook & Campbell, 1979:35; Marini & Singer, 1988). Many social scientists (and scientists in other fields) argue that no nomothetic causal explanation is adequate until a causal mechanism is identified.

Bushman did not empirically identify a causal mechanism in his experiment, but he did suggest a possible causal mechanism for the effect of watching violent videos. Before I can explain that causal mechanism, I have to tell you about yet one more aspect of his research. He wasn't just interested in whether viewing violent films results in aggressive behavior. Actually, his primary hypothesis was that individuals who are predisposed to aggression at the outset will be more influenced by a violent film than individuals who are not aggressive at the outset. And that is what happened: Individuals who were predisposed to aggression became more aggressive after watching Bushman's violent video, but individuals who were not predisposed to aggression did not become more aggressive.

After the experiment, Bushman (1995) proposed a causal mechanism to explain why aggressive individuals became even more aggressive after watching the film:

> . . . high trait aggressive individuals [people predisposed to aggression] are more susceptible to the effects of violent media than are low trait aggressive individuals because they possess a relatively large network of aggressive associations that can be activated by violent cues. Habitual exposure to television violence might be partially responsible. (p. 959)

Note that this explanation relies more on speculation than on the actual empirical evidence from this particular experiment. Nonetheless, by proposing a reasonable causal mechanism that "connects" the variation in the independent and dependent variables, Bushman strengthens the argument for the causal validity of his conclusions.

It is often possible to go beyond speculation by designing research to test one or more possible causal mechanisms. Perhaps Bushman will design a new study to measure directly the size of individuals' "network of aggressive associations" that he posits are part of the mechanism by which video violence influences aggressive behavior.

Context

No cause has its effect apart from some larger **context** involving other variables. A cause is really one among a set of interrelated factors required for the effect (Hage & Meeker, 1988; Papineau, 1978). You could say that we do not fully understand the causal effect of media violence on behavioral aggression unless we have identified the related conditions. As we have just seen, Bushman (1995) proposed at the outset of his research a condition for the effect of media violence on aggression: media violence would increase aggression only among individuals who are already predisposed to aggression.

Identification of the context in which a causal effect occurs is not itself a criterion for a valid causal conclusion. Some of the contextual factors may not turn out to be causes of the effect being investigated. The question for researchers is, How many contexts should we check out? In a classic study of children's aggressive behavior in response to media violence, Albert Bandura, Dorothea Ross, and Sheila Ross (1963) checked several contextual factors. They found that effects varied with the children's gender and with the gender of the opponent toward whom they acted aggressively but not with whether they saw a real (acted) or filmed violent incident. For example, children reacted more aggressively after observing men committing violent acts than after observing women committing these same acts. But Bandura and his colleagues did not address the role of violence within the children's families or the role of participation in sports or many other factors that could be involved in children's responses to media violence. Bandura et al. strengthened their conclusions by focusing on a few likely contextual factors.

Specifying the context for a causal effect helps us to understand that effect, but it is a process that can never really be complete. We can always ask what else might be important: The country in which the study is conducted? The age of the study participants? What we need to do is to review carefully the results of prior research and the implications of relevant theory to determine what contextual factors are likely to be important in a causal relationship. Our confidence in causal conclusions should be stronger when we know these factors were taken into account.

Research Designs to Determine Causality

The criteria for establishing causal effects are met to different degree different ways by different research designs. In this section I will expla how four types of research design approach the five causal criteria. The first two research designs—experimental research and nonexperimental research—are suited to nomothetic causal explanation. The other two designs—explanation in field research and event-structure analysis—are more suited to idiographic explanation. Each of these sections should increase your understanding of the methods of data collection introduced in Chapter 1 and presented at length in Chapters 6 through 9. At this point I will only introduce the basic features of the different research designs. Some of the many different versions of these designs will be covered in Chapters 6 through 9. I will also emphasize here the value of combining research designs (a focus of Chapter 10).

Nomothetic Research Designs

When researchers seek causal explanations based on analysis of how a group of subjects react to some experience or treatment, they frequently use an experimental research design. They manipulate the independent variable in at least two groups of subjects and observe what happens to the dependent variable. When such manipulation is not possible or desirable, however, they turn to nonexperimental research design. Although they are still concerned with causality, still focus on groups rather than individuals, and still analyze independent and dependent variables, they observe rather than manipulate. This difference has implications for validity that you should understand whether you are doing research yourself or evaluating someone else's research.

Experimental Research

Bushman's (1995) study of the effect of media violence is a good example of the **experimental approach** to establishing a causal effect (which is explored further in Chapter 6). Here I will use Bushman's study to point up how each of the elements of an experimental design helps to identify the causal effect:

- An experiment has two or more groups that vary in terms of their value on the independent variable. One group receives some "treatment," such as watching the violent videotape. This group is termed the "experimental group." The group that does not receive the treatment is termed the "comparison group." As you have already learned,

behavioral aggression increased in Bushman's experimental group—
those who watched the violent videotape—but not in the comparison
group. He found an association between watching the violent video
and behaving aggressively.

In an experiment, the researcher introduces variation in the independent
variable and then measures the dependent variable. The students in
Bushman's study watched one of the two videotapes before their aggressiveness was measured. So the research design ensured that variation in the cause occurred before its hypothesized effect.

■ The main advantage of experimental designs is that they reduce the risk
of spurious effects. **Randomization** is the basic technique: As Exhibit 5.5
shows, cases are assigned randomly, as by the toss of a coin, to either the
experimental group or the comparison group. As a result of such **random assignment**, no other difference would be expected at the outset of
the experiment; the groups would differ only in terms of the independent variable. Even randomly assigned groups may differ because of
chance, of course, but we can estimate with statistics just how likely this
variation is and take it into account in our conclusions. If, in fact, the
groups do not differ in terms of any characteristic other than their value
on the independent variable, any association found between the independent and dependent variables cannot be spurious because of preexisting differences.

These defining features of experimental design permit experiments to meet
the three basic criteria for identifying nomothetic causes: association, time
order, and nonspuriousness.

Experimental researchers do not always try to identify a causal mechanism, leaving the way in which a treatment had (or didn't have) an effect as

Exhibit 5.5   **Random Assignment to One of Two Groups**

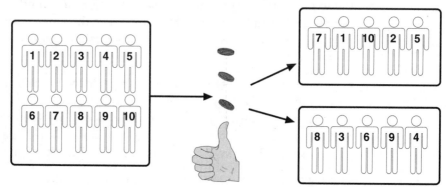

a "black box." However, it is preferable to consider explicitly the causal mechanism in an experiment because identification of some of the variables intervening between the treatment and its presumed effect can greatly increase understanding of why the treatment did or didn't work (Costner, 1989). As you saw earlier, Bushman speculated about the causal mechanism involved in the effects he identified. An alternative is to ask the subjects after the experiment to report on what they felt or thought during the experiment.

Yet another approach is to conduct further experiments to identify causal mechanisms. In their study of deterrence of spouse abuse (introduced in Chapter 2), Lawrence Sherman and Richard Berk (1984) designed follow-up experiments to test or control for several causal mechanisms that they wondered about after their first experiment: Did recidivism decrease for those who were arrested for spouse abuse because of the exemplary work of the arresting officers? Did recidivism increase for arrestees as time passed? Was recidivism lower for the arrestees only because the comparison condition (warning abusers and separating them from the spouses they had abused) was poorly implemented? Investigating these possible causal mechanisms was a critical element in Sherman and Berk's eventual explanation of how arrest influences recidivism.

Experimental researchers also do not always try to identify the context influencing the causal relationships they observe. However, they can try to identify contextual factors by repeating the experiment in other settings, with other subjects, or with different versions of the experimental treatment. In his experimental design, Bushman (1995) included tests for the importance of several contextual factors.

Nonexperimental Research

The **nonexperimental approach** to establishing causality (sometimes called the descriptive or observational approach) involves studying naturally occurring variation in the dependent and independent variables, without any intervention by the researchers (or anyone else). Instead, the researchers equate cases prior to exposure to the independent variable. Survey research (the subject of Chapter 7) is the primary type of nomothetic nonexperimental research design.

William Bailey (1990) used a nonexperimental approach to investigate the association between the monthly homicide rate in the United States from 1976 to 1987 (the dependent variable) and the amount of TV publicity given to public executions of murderers during this period (the independent variable). Because the homicide rate did not vary in relation to publicity, Bailey concluded that publicity about capital punishment does not cause variation in the homicide rate. Numerous other studies have failed to find a deterrent effect for publicity about capital punishment, so the notion that capital punishment deters homicide appears to be on very weak ground.

Nonexperimental research designs can be either cross-sectional or longitudinal. In a **cross-sectional research design**, all data are collected at one point in time. Thus identifying the time order of effects can be an insurmountable problem with such a design. In a **longitudinal research design**, however, data are collected at two or more points in time, and so identification of the time order of effects can be quite straightforward. I will review different types of longitudinal designs later in this chapter. At this point I want to emphasize the problem of identifying causal effects in cross-sectional research. If we are not sure about the time order, we cannot be sure of the causal order.

For example, Robert Sampson (1987) studied urban black violence, with the specific hypothesis that higher rates of black family disruption (the percentage of female-headed black households with children) result in more violence. He found that family disruption is associated with higher rates of black male violence (he also found similar relationships among whites). Does this finding establish that family disruption causes violence among urban black males? Or, as Sampson asks, does violent crime lead to family disruption, because women are unlikely to marry or remain married to men who are incarcerated? Because Sampson collected his data on family disruption and violence at the same point in time, this alternative time order cannot definitively be ruled out.

Another concern with nonexperimental research is meeting the criterion of nonspuriousness. In nonexperimental research, unlike experimental research, cases cannot be assigned randomly to receive one or another value of the independent variable, so it is hard to determine whether variation in the dependent variable is due to variation in the independent variable or to something else altogether. Consider the relationship Sampson found between family disruption and the homicide rate. The two variables may have been correlated, but they may have had no causal relationship whatsoever. Perhaps an extraneous variable, joblessness, led to both family disruption and greater likelihood of violence (see Exhibit 5.6). If joblessness is what results in the association between the two other variables, then the apparent causal relationship between family disruption and the homicide rate is spurious; they are merely correlated.

To reduce the risk of spuriousness, nonexperimental researchers use the technique of **statistical control**. Exhibit 5.7 represents the important concept of statistical control with a hypothetical study of the relationship between attending a "boot camp" in prison (a highly regimented, discipline-focused rehabilitation program) and the likelihood of committing crimes after prison (the recidivism rate). In Exhibit 5.7, the data for all prisoners show that prisoners who attended boot camp were less likely to return to committing crimes after they left prison. However, as the more detailed data show, more female prisoners attended boot camp than male prisoners, and so gender may play a significant role in recidivism. The researchers decided

Exhibit 5.6 **Extraneous Variables in Nonexperimental Research: Family Disruption and the Homicide Rate (Sampson)**

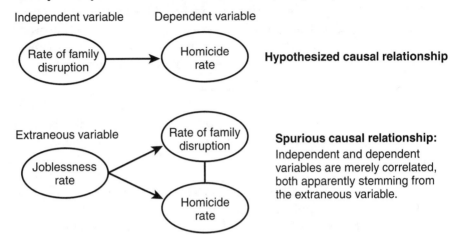

Independent variable   Dependent variable

Rate of family disruption → Homicide rate   **Hypothesized causal relationship**

Extraneous variable

Joblessness rate → Rate of family disruption / Homicide rate

Spurious causal relationship: Independent and dependent variables are merely correlated, both apparently stemming from the extraneous variable.

Exhibit 5.7 **The Use of Statistical Control to Reduce Spuriousness**

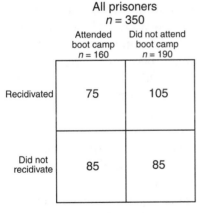

All prisoners
n = 350

	Attended boot camp *n* = 160	Did not attend boot camp *n* = 190
Recidivated	75	105
Did not recidivate	85	85

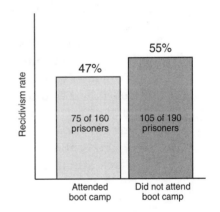

Recidivism rate

47% — 75 of 160 prisoners — Attended boot camp

55% — 105 of 190 prisoners — Did not attend boot camp

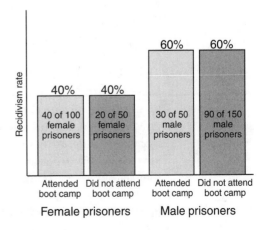

Female prisoners
n = 150

Male prisoners
n = 200

	Attended boot camp *n* = 100	Did not attend boot camp *n* = 50	Attended boot camp *n* = 50	Did not attend boot camp *n* = 150
Recidivated	40	20	30	90
Did not recidivate	60	30	20	60

Recidivism rate

40% — 40 of 100 female prisoners — Attended boot camp

40% — 20 of 50 female prisoners — Did not attend boot camp

60% — 30 of 50 male prisoners — Attended boot camp

60% — 90 of 150 male prisoners — Did not attend boot camp

Female prisoners   Male prisoners

to reduce the risk of spuriousness by using statistical control methods: They examined the association between attending boot camp and postprison criminality separately for men and for women. It appears now that attending boot camp did not reduce recidivism. It just appeared to do so because women both were more likely to attend boot camp and are less likely to commit crimes after prison, whether they attended boot camp or not.

> *Statistical control* A technique used in nonexperimental research to reduce the risk of spuriousness. One variable is held constant so the relationship between two or more other variables can be assessed without the influence of variation in the control variable.
>
> *Example*: Sampson (1987) found that the relationship between rates of family disruption and violent crimes held true for cities with similar levels of joblessness (the control variable). So the rate of joblessness could not have caused the association between family disruption and violent crime.

Similarly, Sampson (1987) statistically controlled for variation in joblessness when he tested for a relationship between rates of family disruption and violence. In effect, he compared family disruption and rates of violence for cities with similar levels of joblessness. Because the relationship between family disruption and violence still held after joblessness was controlled, our confidence that the hypothesized association was not spurious—that it was not due to the extraneous influence of joblessness—is strengthened considerably.

Our confidence in causal conclusions based on nonexperimental research also increases with identification of a causal mechanism. Such mechanisms, which are termed **intervening variables** in nonexperimental research, help us to understand how variation in the independent variable results in variation in the dependent variable. For example, Robert Sampson and John Laub (1990) found that people who were delinquent as juveniles were more likely to commit crimes as adults. They also found, as Exhibit 5.8 shows, that juvenile delinquency was followed in later years by lower levels of job stability, career aspirations, and marital attachment; these in turn were associated with higher rates of adult criminality. The identification of causal mechanisms in this research was particularly important because it also indicated how juvenile delinquents might be prevented from becoming adult criminals: Juvenile delinquents who achieve stable jobs, develop career aspirations, and become committed to a spouse are then less likely to commit crimes.

Of course, identification of one (or two or three) intervening variables does not end the possibilities for clarifying the causal mechanisms. You

Exhibit 5.8   **Intervening Variables in Nonexperimental Research:
Juvenile Delinquency and Adult Criminality (Sampson & Laub)**

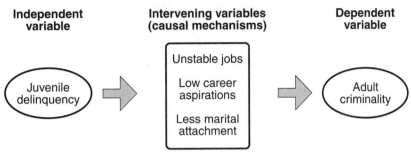

might ask why juvenile delinquency tends to result in lower career aspirations or why career aspirations influence adult criminality. You could then conduct research to identify the mechanisms that link, for example, juvenile delinquency and career aspirations. (Perhaps schoolteachers tell delinquents that they will never get ahead, so the juveniles' aspirations decline. Or perhaps delinquents decide that committing crimes is more fun than working in a regular job.) This process could go on and on. The point is that identification of a mechanism through which the independent variable influences the dependent variable increases our confidence in the conclusion that a causal connection does indeed exist.

When you think about the role of variables in causal relationships, don't confuse variables that cause spurious relationships with those that intervene in causal relationships—even though both are "third variables" that do not appear in the initial hypothesis. In Exhibit 5.6 the extraneous variable, joblessness, creates a spurious relationship. By contrast, in Exhibit 5.8, the three intervening variables are part of the process that links the independent variable and the dependent variable; intervening variables help to explain the relationship between the independent variable (juvenile delinquency) and the dependent variable (adult criminality).

Nonexperimental research is well suited to exploring the context in which causal effects occur. Administering surveys in many different settings and to different types of individuals is usually much easier than administering experiments in different ways.

Comparison of Experimental and Nonexperimental Designs

Given the differences in their approaches to establishing causality, how similar are the results of experimental and nonexperimental hypothesis tests? Not enough attention has been given to answering this question, but the existing evidence is not very encouraging. For example, an experimental study found that youth earnings increased as a result of participation in a supported work program, but nonexperimental studies tended to show a decrease in earnings due to program participation. In general, the extent of the differences in results depended on which specific comparison group was selected and which variables were statistically controlled (Fraker & Maynard, 1987; LaLonde, 1986). Unfortunately, a nonexperimental researcher usually has no way of knowing exactly which variables to control to meet the criterion of nonspuriousness or which comparison group to select to most closely approximate the results that would have been obtained with an experimental design.

The difficulty of establishing nonspuriousness does not rule out the use of nonexperimental data to evaluate causal hypotheses. In fact, when enough nonexperimental data are collected to allow tests of multiple implications of the same causal hypothesis, the results can be very convincing (Freedman, 1991).

In any case, nonexperimental tests of causal hypotheses will continue to be popular because practical and ethical problems in randomly assigning people to different conditions preclude the test of many important hypotheses with an experimental design. Just remember to consider carefully possible sources of spuriousness and other problems when evaluating causal claims based on individual nonexperimental studies. Conclusions about causal effects based on nonexperimental studies are more likely to be valid if the comparison group was very similar to the group that received the treatment of interest or if many potentially important variables were statistically controlled.

Idiographic Research Designs

There are several different approaches to what can be considered idiographic causal explanations, but they all revolve around a narrative of events and processes that indicates a chain of causes and effects. A description of two of these approaches should give you some ideas about how to develop and criticize idiographic causal explanations. We will first examine a field researcher's explanation of crime in an urban community and then a narrative explanation of a historical event.

Explanation in Field Research

When field researchers seek to develop causal explanations, they often take an idiographic approach. The rich detail about events and processes that field research generates (see Chapter 8) can be the basis for a convincing idiographic, narrative account of why things happened as they did.

Elijah Anderson's (1990) field research in a poor urban community produced a narrative account of how drug addiction often resulted in a downward slide into residential instability and crime:

When addicts deplete their resources, they may go to those closest to them, drawing them into their schemes. . . . [T]he family may put up with the person for a while. They provide money if they can. . . . They come to realize that the person is on drugs. . . . Slowly the reality sets in more and more completely, and the family becomes drained of both financial and emotional resources. . . . Close relatives lose faith and begin to see the person as untrustworthy and weak. Eventually the addict begins to "mess up" in a variety of ways, taking furniture from the house [and] anything of value. . . . Relatives and friends begin to see the person . . . as "out there" in the streets. . . . One deviant act leads to another. (Anderson, 1990:86–87)

A well-constructed narrative, like Anderson's, pays close attention to time order (what happens when) and to causal mechanisms (just how particular events lead to other events). It leaves the reader with a feeling for why things happened as they did.

However, it is difficult to make a convincing case that one particular causal narrative should be chosen over an alternative narrative. We face two problems: First, it may not be clear when particular events begin or end, which makes it difficult to decide how the parts of a narrative go together. Second, any event can be a part of several different causal narratives at once, and the determination of which events act as causes in particular narratives may be quite ambiguous (Abbott, 1992). Do economic frustrations in the family result in young people getting involved with drugs, or is it the other way around? Does low self-esteem result in vulnerability to the appeals of drug dealers, or does a chance drug encounter precipitate a slide in self-esteem? Because of these ambiguities, any narrative or historicist interpretation can only be regarded as tentative.

Event-Structure Analysis

More structured methods of idiographic causal analysis attempt to lessen some of these problems. For instance, Larry Griffin (1993) used event-structure analysis to explain a lynching in 1930s Mississippi. **Event-structure analysis** is a systematic method for showing the underlying structure of action in a chronology of events. The lynching that Griffin analyzed occurred after David Harris, an African-American who sold moonshine from his home, was accused of killing a white tenant farmer. After the killing was reported, the local deputy was called, and a citizen search party was formed. The deputy did not intervene as the search party trailed Harris and then captured and killed him. Meanwhile, Harris's friends killed another African-American who had revealed Harris's hiding place. This series of events is outlined in Exhibit 5.9.

Exhibit 5.9 **Event-Structure Analysis: Lynching Incident in the 1930s (Griffin)**

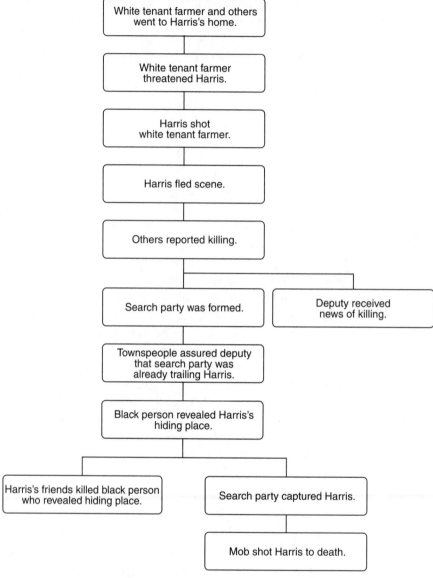

Source: Adapted from Griffin, 1993:1110.

Which among the numerous events occurring between the time that the tenant farmer confronted Harris and the time that the mob killed Harris had a causal influence on that outcome? To identify causal links, Griffin identified plausible counterfactual possibilities—events that might have occurred but did not—and considered whether the outcome might have been changed if a counterfactual had occurred instead of a particular event. For example:

> If, contrary to what actually happened, the deputy had attempted to stop the mob, might the lynching have been averted? . . . Given what happened in comparable cases and the Bolivar County deputy's clear knowledge of the existence of the mob and of its early activities, his forceful intervention to prevent the lynching thus appears an objective possibility. (Griffin, 1993: 1112)

So, Griffin concluded, nonintervention by the deputy had a causal influence on the lynching.

Combined Research Designs

One of the most satisfying ways to identify causal relations is to combine approaches, a technique described in more detail in Chapter 9. For example, Seymour Martin Lipset and his colleagues (1956) combined nomothetic and idiographic approaches to explain the preservation of a democratic form of government by the International Typographical Union (ITU) while so many other unions were becoming undemocratic. They traced the history of the ITU over a century and also surveyed union members at one point in time. The historical and descriptive analyses, presented in different chapters of their book, *Union Democracy*, complement each other and thus increase our confidence in the causal explanation the researchers developed (see Schutt, 1986).

Lipset et al.'s historical, idiographic analysis reveals that the union was formed from preexisting independent unions and that a two-party system emerged in 1911 after a period of factional conflict. These events created a dynamic process of political conflict. This democratic competition was passed down from generation to generation of ITU members. Specific historical events reinforced ideological cleavages between the two parties, thus helping to maintain electoral competition.

The nomothetic causal analysis in *Union Democracy* relies on a membership survey conducted at one point in time. Analysis of the survey data shows how the characteristics and attitudes of individuals and the features of their workplaces were associated with the propensity to participate in political affairs and with the closeness of votes in union elections. This nomothetic causal explanation complemented the idiographic explanation of why democratic practices survived for so long in the union.

Timothy Wickham-Crowley's (1992) study of Latin American guerrilla movements was very different but also combined elements of nomothetic and idiographic causal explanation. He hypothesized that revolutions succeed in Latin America when three conditions are met: peasant support, adequate military power by the guerrilla movement, and a weak political regime that tends to push diverse opposition elements into alliance with one another. Wickham-Crowley then used idiographic analysis to review the history of the guerrilla movements in Latin America, comparing the situation in each country in terms of the three hypothesized causes, and used nomothetic methods to analyze changes over time in both the causal factors and in the strength of the guerrilla movements (see also Ragin, 1987).

■ ■ ■ ■ **Research Designs to Determine Time Order**

Earlier I mentioned that nonexperimental research designs include one-shot, cross-sectional surveys as well as longitudinal designs, in which data are collected repeatedly for many years. In this section I will review the key features of cross-sectional designs and the major types of longitudinal research design. In the process, you will learn more about the causal criterion of time order and the features of research designs that help us to meet this criterion.

Cross-Sectional Designs

A cross-sectional research design is one in which all data are collected at one point in time. With a cross-sectional design, a researcher can easily determine whether two variables are associated. Sampson's (1987) study of the association among male joblessness, family disruption, and violence is a good example. However, it can be difficult, and sometimes impossible, to determine time order with cross-sectional data. If you need to know whether variation in the independent variable occurred prior to variation in the dependent variable, you usually need to measure the independent variable at some time before you measure the dependent variable.

In four circumstances, cross-sectional data can reasonably be used to infer the time order of effects. In these circumstances, the data provide measures of variables in earlier periods. In effect, they are longitudinal, in the sense that they can be ordered in time (Campbell, 1992).

■ *The independent variable is fixed at some point prior to the variation in the dependent variable.* So-called demographic variables that are determined at birth—such as sex, race, and age—are fixed in this way. So are variables like education and marital status, if we know when the value of cases on these variables was established and if we know that the value of cases on the dependent variable was set some time later. For example, say we hypothesize that education influences the type of job individuals have. If we know that respondents completed their education before taking their current jobs, we would satisfy the time order requirement even if we were to measure education at the same time we measure type of job. However, if some respondents possibly went back to school as a benefit of their current job, the time order requirement would not be satisfied.

∎ *We believe that respondents can give us reliable reports of what happened to them or what they thought at some earlier point in time.* Julie Horney, D. Wayne Osgood, & Ineke Haen Marshall (1995) provide an interesting example of the use of such retrospective data. The researchers wanted to identify how criminal activity varies in response to changes in life circumstances. They interviewed 658 newly convicted male offenders sentenced to a Nebraska state prison. In a 45- to 90-minute interview, they recorded each inmate's report of his life circumstances and of his criminal activities for the preceding two to three years. They then found that criminal involvement was related strongly to adverse changes in life circumstances, such as marital separation or drug use. Retrospective data are often inadequate for measuring variation in past psychological states or behaviors, however, because what we recall about our feelings or actions in the past is likely to be influenced by what we feel in the present. For example, retrospective reports by both adult alcoholics and their parents appear to greatly overestimate the frequency of childhood problems (Vaillant, 1995). People cannot report reliably the frequency and timing of many past events, from hospitalization to hours worked. However, retrospective data tends to be reliable when it concerns major, persistent experiences in the past, such as what type of school someone went to or how a person's family was structured (Campbell, 1992).

∎ *Our measures are based on records that contain information on cases in earlier periods.* Government, agency, and organizational records are an excellent source of time-ordered data after the fact. However, sloppy record keeping and changes in data-collection policies can lead to inconsistencies, which must be taken into account. Another weakness of such archival data is that they usually contain measures of only a fraction of the variables that we think are important.

∎ *We know that cases were equivalent on the dependent variable prior to the treatment.* For example, we may hypothesize that a training program (independent variable) improves the English-speaking abilities (dependent variable) of a group of recent immigrants. If we know that none of the immigrants could speak English prior to enrolling in the training program, we can be confident that any subsequent variation in their ability to speak English did not precede exposure to the training program. This is one way that traditional experiments establish time order: Two or more equivalent groups are formed prior to exposing one of them to some treatment.

Longitudinal Designs

Except in the special cases just noted (which can themselves be considered types of longitudinal design), it is risky to draw conclusions about causality on the basis of cross-sectional data. In longitudinal research, in contrast, data are collected that can be ordered in time. By measuring the value of cases on an independent variable and a dependent variable at each of these different times, the researcher can determine whether variation in the independent variable precedes variation in the dependent variable.

Many versions of longitudinal design exist (Campbell, 1992). In some longitudinal designs, the same sample (or panel) is followed over time; in other designs, sample members are rotated or completely replaced. The population from which the sample is selected may be defined broadly, as when a longitudinal survey of the general population is conducted. Or the population may be defined narrowly, as when members of a specific age group are sampled at multiple points in time. The frequency of follow-up measurement can vary, ranging from a before-after design with just one follow-up to studies in which various indicators are measured every month for many years.

Certainly it is more difficult to collect data at two or more points in time than at one time. Quite frequently researchers simply cannot, or are unwilling to, delay completion of a study for even one year in order to collect follow-up data. But think of the many research questions that really should involve a much longer follow-up period: What is the impact of job training on subsequent employment? How effective is a school-based program in improving parenting skills? Under what conditions do traumatic experiences in childhood result in mental illness? It is safe to say that we will never have enough longitudinal data to answer many important research questions. The value of longitudinal data is so great that every effort should be made to develop longitudinal research designs when they are appropriate for the research question asked. The following discussion of three types of longitudinal design will give you a sense of the possibilities.

Repeated cross-sectional design A type of longitudinal study in which data are collected at two or more points in time from different samples of the same population.

Fixed-sample panel design A type of longitudinal study in which data are collected from the same individuals—the panel—at two or more points in time. In another type of panel design, panel members who leave are replaced with other persons.

Event-based design A type of longitudinal study in which data are collected at two or more points in time from individuals in a population defined by a common starting point or event (a cohort).

Examples of cohorts: College class of 1997, people who graduated from high school in the 1980s, General Motors employees who started work between 1990 and the year 2000, people who were born in the late 1940s or the 1950s (the "baby boom generation").

Repeated Cross-Sectional Designs

Repeated cross-sectional studies, also known as **trend studies**, have become fixtures of the political arena around election time. Particularly in presidential election years, we have all become accustomed to reading weekly, even daily, reports on the percentage of the population that supports each candidate. Similar polls are conducted to track sentiment on many other social issues. For example, a 1993 poll reported that 52% of adult Americans supported a ban on the possession of handguns, compared to 41% in a similar poll conducted in 1991. According to pollster Louis Harris, this increase indicated a "sea change" in public attitudes (Barringer, 1993). Another researcher said, "It shows that people are responding to their experience [of an increase in handgun-related killings]" (Barringer, 1993:1).

Repeated cross-sectional surveys are conducted as follows:

1. A sample is drawn from a population at time 1, and data are collected from the sample.
2. As time passes, some people leave the population and others enter it.
3. At time 2 a different sample is drawn from this population.

These features make the repeated cross-sectional design appropriate when the goal is to determine whether a population has changed over time. Has racial tolerance increased among Americans in the past 20 years? Are employers more likely to pay maternity benefits today than they were in the 1950s? These questions concern changes in the population as a whole, not changes in individuals within the population. We want to know whether racial tolerance increased in society, not whether this change was due to migration that brought more racially tolerant people into the country or to individual U.S. citizens becoming more tolerant. We are asking whether employers overall are more likely to pay maternity benefits today than they were yesterday, not whether any such increase was due to recalcitrant employers going out of business or to individual employers changing their maternity benefits. When we do need to know whether individuals in the population changed, we must turn to a panel design.

Fixed-Sample Panel Designs

Panel designs allow identification of changes in individuals, groups, or whatever we are studying. This is the process for conducting fixed-sample panel studies:

1. A sample (called a panel) is drawn from a population at time 1, and data are collected from the sample.

2. As time passes, some panel members become unavailable for follow-up, and the population changes.

3. At time 2, data are collected from the same people as at time 1 (the panel)—except for those people who cannot be located.

Because a panel design follows the same individuals, it is better than a repeated cross-sectional design for testing causal hypotheses. For example, Sampson and Laub (1990) used a fixed-sample panel design to investigate the effect of childhood deviance on adult crime. They studied a sample of white males in Boston when the subjects were between 10 and 17 years old and then followed up when the subjects were in their adult years. Data were collected from multiple sources, including the subjects themselves and criminal justice records. Sampson and Laub (1990:614) found that children who had been committed to a correctional school for persistent delinquency were much more likely to commit crimes as adults: 61% were arrested between the ages of 25 and 32, compared to 14% of those who had not been in correctional schools as juveniles. In this study, juvenile delinquency unquestionably occurred before adult criminality. If the researchers had used a cross-sectional design to study the past of adults, the juvenile delinquency measure may have been biased by memory lapses, by self-serving recollections about behavior as juveniles, or by loss of agency records.

If you now wonder why every longitudinal study isn't designed as a panel study, you've understood the advantages of panel designs. However, remember that this design does not in itself establish causality. Variation in both the independent variable and the dependent variables is due to some other variable, even to earlier variation in what is considered the dependent variable. In the example in Exhibit 5.10 there is a hypothesized association between delinquency in the 11th grade and grades obtained in the 12th grade (the dependent variable). The time order is clear. However, both variables are consequences of grades obtained in the 7th grade. The apparent effect of 11th-grade delinquency on 12th-grade grades is spurious because of variation in the "dependent" variable (grades) at an earlier time.

Panel designs are also a challenge to implement successfully, and often are not even attempted, because of two major difficulties:

Exhibit 5.10 **Causality in Panel Studies**

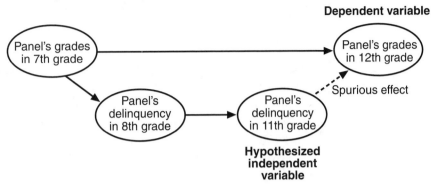

Although delinquency in the 11th grade and grades in the 12th grade are clearly associated and the time order is clear, causality cannot be determined. In reality, grades in the 7th grade also play a role.

- *Expense and attrition.* It can be difficult, and very expensive, to keep track of individuals over a long period, and inevitably the proportion of panel members who can be located for follow-up will decline over time. Panel studies often lose more than one-quarter of their members through attrition (D. Miller, 1991:170). However, subject attrition can be reduced substantially if sufficient staff can be used to keep track of panel members. In their panel study, Sampson and Laub (1990) lost only 12% of the juveniles in the original sample (8% if you do not count those who had died). The consequences of a high rate of subject attrition are that the follow-up sample may no longer be representative of the population from which it was drawn and may no longer provide a sound basis for estimating change. Subjects who were lost to follow-up may have been those who changed the most, or the least, over time. It does help to compare the baseline characteristics of those who are interviewed at follow-up with characteristics of those lost to follow-up. If these two groups of panel members are not very different, it is less likely that changes had anything to do with characteristics of the missing panel members.
- *Subject fatigue.* Panel members may grow weary of repeated interviews and drop out of the study, or they may become so used to answering the standard questions in the survey that they start giving stock answers rather than actually thinking about their current feelings or actions (Campbell, 1992). This is called the problem of **subject fatigue**. Fortunately, subjects do not often seem to become fatigued in this way. For example, at the end of an 18-month-long housing study in Boston, only 3

or 4 individuals (out of 93 who could still be located) refused to participate in the fourth and final round of interviews—even though the interviews took a total of about five hours to complete (Schutt, Goldfinger, &
Penk, 1997).

Because panel studies are so useful, social researchers have developed
increasingly effective techniques for keeping track of individuals and over-
coming subject fatigue. But when resources do not permit use of these techniques to maintain an adequate panel, repeated cross-sectional designs can
usually be employed at a cost not a great deal higher than that of a one-
time-only cross-sectional study. The payoff in explanatory power should be
well worth the cost.

Event-Based Designs

An event-based design, often called a **cohort study**, is like the repeated
cross-sectional design but with one important exception: The follow-up
samples (at one or more times) are selected not from the whole population
but from the same **cohort,** or from people who all have experienced a similar event. A cohort consists of individuals or groups with a common starting point. Examples include:

■ Birth cohorts—those who share a common period of birth (those born in
the 1940s, 1950s, 1960s, and so on)

■ Seniority cohorts—those who have worked at the same place for about 5
years, about 10 years, and so on

■ School cohorts—freshmen, sophomores, juniors, seniors

An event-based design can be a type of repeated cross-sectional design
or a type of panel design. In an event-based repeated cross-sectional design,
separate samples are drawn from the same cohort at two or more different
times. In an event-based panel design, the same individuals from the same
cohort are studied at two or more different times.

We can see the value of event-based research in a comparison of two
studies that estimated the impact of public and private schooling on high
school students' achievement test scores. In a cross-sectional study, James
Coleman, Thomas Hoffer, and Sally Kilgore (1982) compared standardized
achievement test scores of high school sophomores and seniors in public,
Catholic, and other private schools. They found that test scores were higher
in the private high schools (both Catholic and other) than in the public high
schools. But was this difference a causal effect of private schooling? Perhaps
the parents of higher-performing children were choosing to send them to
private rather than to public schools. In other words, the higher achievement levels of private-sector students might have been in place before they

started high school and not have developed as a consequence of their high school education.

The researchers tried to reduce the impact of this problem by statistically controlling for a range of family background variables: family income, parents' education, race, number of siblings, number of rooms in the home, number of parents present, mother working, and other indicators of a family orientation to education. But some critics pointed out that even with all these controls for family background, the cross-sectional study did not ensure that the students had been comparable in achievement when they started high school.

So James Coleman and Thomas Hoffer (1987) went back to the high schools and studied the test scores of the former sophomores two years later, when they were seniors; in other words, the researchers used an event-based panel design. This time they found that the verbal and math achievement test scores of the Catholic school students had increased more over the two years than was the case for the public school students; it was not clear whether the scores of the other private school students had increased. Irrespective of students' initial achievement test scores, the Catholic schools seemed to "do more" for their students than did the public schools. This finding continued to be true even when dropouts were studied too. The researchers' causal conclusion rested on much stronger ground because they used an event-based design.

■ ■ ■ ■ **Units of Analysis and Errors in Causal Reasoning**

Regardless of the research design, we can easily come to invalid conclusions about causal influences if we do not know what **units of analysis** the measures in our study refer to—that is, the level of social life on which the research question is focused, such as individuals, groups, towns, or nations.

Individual and Group Units of Analysis

In most sociological and psychological studies, the units of analysis are individuals. The researcher may collect survey data from individuals, analyze the data, and then report on, say, how many individuals felt socially isolated and whether substance abuse by individuals was related to their feelings of social isolation. Data are collected from individuals, and the focus of analysis is on the individual.

The units of analysis may instead be groups of some sort, such as families, schools, work organizations, towns, states, or countries. For example, a researcher may collect data from town and police records on the number of accidents in which a driver was intoxicated and the presence or absence of a server liability law in the town (these laws make those who serve liquor liable for accidents caused by those to whom they served liquor). The researcher can then analyze the relationship between server liability laws and the frequency of accidents due to drunk driving (perhaps also taking into account town population). Because the data describe the town, towns are the units of analysis.

In some studies, groups are the units of analysis but data are collected from individuals. For example, Robert Sampson, Stephen W. Raudenbush, and Felton Earls (1997) studied influences on violent crime in Chicago neighborhoods. Collective efficacy was one variable they hypothesized as an influence on the neighborhood crime rate. This variable was a characteristic of the neighborhood—the extent to which residents were likely to help other residents and were trusted by other residents. However, they measured this variable in a survey of individuals. The responses of individual residents about their perceptions of their neighbors' helpfulness and trustworthiness were averaged together to create a collective efficacy score for each neighborhood. It was this neighborhood measure of collective efficacy that was used to explain variation in the rate of violent crime between neighborhoods. The data were collected from individuals and were about individuals, but they were combined (aggregated) so as to describe neighborhoods. The units of analysis were thus groups (neighborhoods).

In a study like Sampson's, we can distinguish the concept of units of analysis from the **units of observation**. Data were collected from individuals, the units of observation, and then the data were aggregated and analyzed at the group level. In some studies, the units of observation and the units of analysis are the same. The important point is to know. A conclusion that "crime increases with joblessness" could imply either that individuals who lose their jobs are more likely to commit a crime or that a community with a high unemployment rate is likely to have a high crime rate—or both. Whether we are drawing conclusions from data or interpreting others' conclusions, we have to be clear about which relationship is being referred to.

We also have to know the units of analysis to interpret statistics appropriately. Measures of association tend to be stronger for group-level than for individual-level data because measurement errors at the individual level tend to cancel out at the group level (Bridges & Weis, 1989:29–31).

The Ecological Fallacy and Reductionism

Researchers should make sure that their causal conclusions reflect the units of analysis in their study. Conclusions about processes at the individual level should be based on individual-level data; conclusions about group-level processes should be based on data collected about groups. In most

Exhibit 5.11   **Errors in Causal Conclusions**

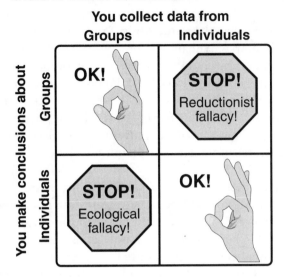

cases, violation of this rule creates one more reason to suspect the validity of the causal conclusions.

A researcher who draws conclusions about individual-level processes from group-level data is making what is termed an **ecological fallacy** (see Exhibit 5.11). The conclusions may or may not be correct, but we must recognize that group-level data do not describe individual-level processes. For example, a researcher may examine factory records and find that the higher the percentage of unskilled workers in factories, the higher the rate of employee sabotage in those factories. But the researcher would commit an ecological fallacy if she then concluded that individual unskilled factory workers are more likely to engage in sabotage. This conclusion is about an individual-level causal process (the relationship between the occupation and criminal propensities of individuals), even though the data describe groups (factories). It could actually be that white-collar workers are the ones more likely to commit sabotage, perhaps because in factories with more unskilled workers the white-collar workers feel they won't be suspected.

Bear in mind that conclusions about individual processes based on group-level data are not necessarily wrong. We just don't know for sure. Say that we find communities with higher average incomes have lower crime rates. The only thing special about these communities may be that they have more individuals with higher incomes, who tend to commit fewer crimes. Even though we collected data at the group level and analyzed them at the group level, they reflect a causal process at the individual level (Sampson & Lauritsen, 1994:80–83).

When data about individuals are used to make inferences about group-level processes, a problem occurs that can be thought of as the mirror image of the ecological fallacy: the **reductionist fallacy**, or **reductionism** (see Exhibit 5.11). For example, William Wilson (1987:58) notes that we can be misled into concluding from individual-level data that race has a causal effect on violence. However, community-level data reveal that almost 40% of poor blacks lived in extremely poor areas in 1980, compared to only 7% of poor whites. The concentration of African-Americans in poverty areas, not the race or other characteristics of the individuals in these areas, may be the cause of higher rates of violence. Explaining violence in this case requires community-level data.

The fact that errors in causal reasoning can be made should not deter you from conducting research with aggregate data nor make you unduly critical of researchers who make inferences about individuals on the basis of aggregate data. When considered broadly, many research questions point to relationships that could be manifested in many ways and on many levels. Sampson's (1987) study of urban violence is a case in point. His analysis involved only aggregate data about cities, and he explained his research approach as in part a response to the failure of other researchers to examine this problem at the structural, aggregate level. Moreover, Sampson argued that the rates of joblessness and family disruption in communities influence community social processes, not just the behavior of the specific individuals who are unemployed or who grew up without two parents. Yet Sampson suggests that the experience of joblessness and poverty is what tends to reduce the propensity of individual men to marry and that the experience of growing up in a home without two parents in turn increases the propensity of individual juveniles to commit crimes. These conclusions about the behavior of individuals seem consistent with the patterns Sampson found in his aggregate, city-level data; so it seems unlikely that he is committing an ecological fallacy when he proposes them.

The solution is to know what the units of analysis and units of observation were in a study and to take these into account in weighing the credibility of the researcher's conclusions. The goal is not to reject out of hand conclusions that refer to a level of analysis different from what was actually studied. Instead, the goal is to consider the likelihood that an ecological fallacy or a reductionist fallacy has been made when estimating the causal validity of the conclusions.

■ ■ ■ ■ Conclusion

Causation and the means for achieving causally valid conclusions in research is the last of the three legs on which the validity of research rests. In this chapter, you have learned about the two main meanings of causation (nomothetic and idiographic) and about the five criteria used to evaluate the extent to which particular research designs may achieve causally valid findings. You have been exposed to the problem of spuriousness and the ways that randomization and statistical control deal with it. You have also learned how to establish the time order of effects in nonexperimental research and how to come to causal conclusions that are appropriate to the research design.

I should reemphasize that the results of any particular study are part of an always changing body of empirical knowledge about social reality. Thus our understandings of causal relationships are always partial. Researchers always wonder whether they have omitted some relevant variables from their controls or whether their experimental results would differ if the experiment were conducted in another setting or whether they overlooked a critical historical event. But by using consistent definitions of terms and maintaining clear standards for establishing the validity of research results—and by expecting the same of others who do research—social researchers can contribute to a growing body of knowledge that can reliably guide social policy and social understanding.

When you read the results of a social scientific study, you should now be able to evaluate critically the validity of the study's findings. If you plan to engage in social research, you should now be able to plan an approach that will lead to valid findings. And with a good understanding of the three dimensions of validity (measurement validity, generalizability, and causal validity) under your belt, you are ready to focus on the four major methods of data collection used by social scientists. Each of these methods tends to use a somewhat different approach to achieving validity.

KEY TERMS

Association
Causal effect (idiographic perspective)
Causal effect (nomothetic perspective)
Ceteris paribus
Cohort
Cohort study
Context
Counterfactual
Cross-sectional research design
Ecological fallacy
Event-based design
Event-structure analysis
Experimental approach
Extraneous variable

Fixed-sample panel design
Idiographic causal explanation
Intervening variable
Longitudinal research design
Mechanism
Nomothetic causal explanation
Nonexperimental approach
Nonspuriousness
Random assignment
Randomization
Reductionist fallacy (reductionism)
Repeated cross-sectional design
Spurious relationship
Statistical control

Subject fatigue
Synthetic causal explanation
Time order

Trend study
Units of analysis
Units of observation

HIGHLIGHTS

■ Causation can be defined in either nomothetic or idiographic terms. No-mothetic causal explanations deal with effects on average. Idiographic causal explanations deal with the sequence of events that led to a particular outcome.

■ The concept of nomothetic causal explanation relies on a comparison. The value of cases on the dependent variable is measured after they have been exposed to variation in an independent variable. This measurement is compared to what the value of cases on the dependent variable would have been if they had not been exposed to the variation in the independent variable (the counterfactual). The validity of nomothetic causal conclusions rests on how closely the comparison group comes to the ideal counterfactual.

■ From a nomothetic perspective three criteria are generally viewed as necessary for identifying a causal relationship: association between the variables, proper time order, and nonspuriousness of the association. In addition, the basis for concluding that a causal relation exists is strengthened by identification of a causal mechanism and the context.

■ Association between two variables is in itself insufficient evidence of a causal relationship. This point is commonly made with the expression "Correlation does not prove causation."

■ Experiments use random assignment to make comparison groups as similar as possible at the outset of an experiment in order to reduce the risk of spurious effects due to extraneous variables.

■ Nonexperimental designs use statistical controls to reduce the risk of spuriousness. A variable is controlled when it is held constant so that the association between the independent and dependent variables can be assessed without being influenced by the control variable.

■ Ethical and practical constraints often preclude the use of experimental designs.

■ Idiographic causal explanations can be difficult to identify because the starting and ending points of particular events and the determination of which events act as causes in particular sequences may be ambiguous.

■ Causal explanations can combine nomothetic and idiographic approaches, resulting in a more complete explanation of historical or other ongoing processes.

■ Longitudinal designs are usually preferable to cross-sectional designs for establishing the time order of effects. Longitudinal designs vary in terms of whether the same persons are measured at different times, how the population of interest is defined, and how frequently follow-up measurements are taken. Fixed-sample panel designs provide the strongest test for the time order of effects, but they can be difficult to carry out successfully because of their expense and subject attrition and fatigue.

■ We do not fully understand the variables in a study until we know what units of analysis, what level of social life, they refer to.

■ Invalid conclusions about causality may occur when relationships between variables measured at the group level are assumed to apply at the individual level (the ecological fallacy) and when relationships between variables measured at the level of individuals are assumed to apply at the group level (the reductionist fallacy). Nonetheless, many research questions point to relationships at multiple levels and may profitably be answered by studying different units of analysis.

EXERCISES

1. Review articles in several newspapers, copying down all causal assertions. These might range from assertions that the stock market declined because of uncertainty in the Middle East to explanations about why a murder was committed or why test scores are declining in U.S. schools. Inspect the articles carefully, noting all evidence used to support the causal assertions. Are the explanations nomothetic or idiographic or a combination of both? Which criteria for establishing causality in a nomothetic framework are met? How satisfactory are the idiographic explanations? What other potentially important influences on the reported outcome have been overlooked?

2. Select several research articles in professional journals that assert, or imply, that they have identified a causal relationship between two or more variables. Are each of the criteria for establishing the existence of a causal relationship met? Find a study in which subjects were assigned randomly to experimental and comparison groups to reduce the risk of spurious influences on the supposedly causal relationship. How convinced are you by the study?

    Find a survey study that makes causal assertions based on the relationships, or correlations, among variables. What variables have been statistically controlled? List other variables that might be influencing the relationship but that have not been controlled. How convinced are you by the study?

3. Find an idiographic causal explanation for why a historical event (such as a war) occurred or why a person ended up doing something notable (like achieving high office or committing a heinous crime). You might use a history book or a biography as your source. Identify the major influences mentioned in the causal process. Convert this explanation to a nomothetic one by restating the major influences as variables that could affect many people. Propose a study to test the hypotheses involved in this nomothetic explanation.

4. Search *Sociological Abstracts* or another index to the social science literature for several articles on studies using any type of longitudinal design. You will be searching for article titles that use words like *longitudinal, panel, trend, over time.* How successful were the researchers in carrying out the design? What steps did the researchers who used a panel design take to minimize panel attrition? How convinced are you by those using repeated cross-sectional designs that they have identified a process of change in individuals? Did any researchers use retrospective questions? How did they defend the validity of these measures?

5. The practice diskette contains lessons on units of analysis and the related problems of the ecological fallacy and reductionism. Choose the Units of Analysis lesson from the main menu. It describes several research projects and asks you to identify the units of analysis in each. Then it presents several conclusions for particular studies and asks you to determine whether an error has been made.

6. Propose a hypothesis involving variables that could be measured with individuals as the units of analysis. How might this hypothesis be restated so as to involve groups as the units of analysis? Would you expect the hypothesis to be supported at both levels? Why or why not? Repeat the exercise, this time starting with a different hypothesis involving groups as the units of analysis and then restating it so as to involve individuals as the units of analysis.

WEB EXERCISES

1. Go to SocioRealm at

   http://www.geocities.com/~sociorealm/welcome5.htm

   Choose "Criminology."

   From the links supplied, find information regarding a subject of your choosing related to crime and/or violence (for example, youth violence, corporate crime, rape, etc.). Report on the prevalence and/or extent of the phenomenon you have identified. By using this same site, report on one theory that gives an explanation for the phenomenon you have identified (choose, for example, "Explanations of Criminal Behavior" for ideas). Is the explanation you have given causal or nomothetic? Explain. Come up with an idea for a research design that would test the link you have theorized between the phenomenon you have identified and the cause you have suggested.

2. Go to Crime Stoppers International's (CSI) Web site at

   http://www.c-s-i.org/

   Explore CSI's Web pages. How is CSI "fighting crime"? What does CSI's approach assume about the cause of crime? Do you think CSI's approach to "fighting crime" is based on valid conclusions about causality? Explain.

3. Search the Web for sites that report on crime and/or violence (such as Web sites of popular newspapers, magazines, or other sources). What types of explanations do they give for the crime/violence they report? What are the assumptions being made? Do you think the causal explanations are valid? Explain. Be sure to note URL's for the sites you use.

SPSS EXERCISES

1. Using SPSS it is possible to explore relationships between variables from the GSS96. We will test the hypothesis that the higher the income, the more likely people are to spend time doing volunteer work.

   a. To make the association between the two variables more easily identifiable we will use a recoded version of family income with fewer categories: INCOM91Z. The GSS96 asked a series of questions about volunteer work with a variety of organizations. We can create an index variable from these questions to indicate whether a respondent has done volunteer work in any way. This variable is named VOL2.

   b. Generate a cross-tabulation of VOL2 by INCOM91Z. Select column percents and compare the percent volunteering for anything at each income level. Describe the association between the two variables. Was our hypothesis supported? Explain.

2. Now that we have established an association between INCOM91Z and VOL2 we must determine whether or not the association is spurious.

   a. Generate a cross-tabulation of VOL2 by INCOM91Z by DEGREE. Describe the association between volunteering and income for each category of DEGREE.

   b. Does DEGREE appear to create a spurious relationship between VOL2 and income? Explain.

6 Experiments

KEY TERMS
HIGHLIGHTS
EXERCISES
WEB EXERCISES
SPSS EXERCISES

■ ■ ■ ■ How does the organization of work influence attitudes and behavior? The influence of the workplace has been a central concern of sociologists since the discipline's origins in the 19th century. In the late 1800s, Emile Durkheim (1964) theorized about the impact of the division of labor on social solidarity, Max Weber (1947) identified the attitudes appropriate for employment in rational bureaucratic organizations, and Karl Marx (1967) speculated on the effects of workers' separation from the means of production. In the late 20th century, researchers from all the social science disciplines have accumulated a substantial body of research based on investigations in many different types of work organizations. Experimental research, the subject of this chapter, has been used to test some very specific but quite important hypotheses about the impact of work and work-related training.

In Chapter 5, Brad Bushman's (1995) research about the impact of media violence provides a good example of how experiments are used to test causal hypotheses. You have also seen the value of experimental research in the study of housing for homeless persons described in Chapter 1 and in the research on domestic violence in Chapter 2. This chapter examines experimental methodology in more detail: You will learn to distinguish the different types of experimental design (which include true experiments, quasi-experiments, and evaluation research), to evaluate the utility of particular designs for reaching causally valid conclusions, and to consider ethical problems in experimentation.

■ ■ ■ ■ **True Experiments**

True experiments must have at least three things:

- Two comparison groups (in the simplest case, an experimental and a control group)
- Variation in the independent variable before assessment of change in the dependent variable
- Random assignment to the two (or more) comparison groups

The combination of these features permits us to have much greater confidence in the validity of causal conclusions than is possible in other research designs. Our confidence in the validity of an experiment's findings is further enhanced by

- Identification of the causal mechanism
- Control over the context of an experiment

You will learn more about each of these key features of experimental design as you review three different experimental studies about work and its impact. I will use simple diagrams to help describe and compare the experiments' designs. These diagrams also show at a glance just how well suited any experiment is to identifying causal relations, by indicating whether it has a comparison group, a pretest and a posttest, and randomization.

Experimental and Comparison Groups

True experiments must have at least one **experimental group**—subjects who receive some treatment—and at least one **comparison group**—subjects to whom the experimental group can be compared. The comparison group differs from the experimental group in terms of one or more independent variables, whose effects are being tested. In other words, the difference between the experimental and comparison groups is determined by variation in the independent variable.

Experimental group In an experiment, the group of subjects that receives the treatment or experimental manipulation.

Comparison group The group of subjects that is exposed to a different treatment than the experimental group (or that has a different value on the independent variable).

Control group A comparison group that receives no treatment instead of a different treatment.

In many experiments the independent variable indicates the presence or absence of something, such as receiving a treatment program or not receiving it. In these experiments the comparison group, consisting of the subjects who do not receive the treatment, is termed a **control group.**

An experiment can have more than one experimental group if the goal is to test several versions of the **treatment** (the independent variable) or several combinations of different treatments. An experiment also may have more than one comparison group, as when outcome scores for the treatment group need to be compared to more than one comparison group.

An example of the importance of having experimental and comparison groups is provided by Richard Price, Michelle Van Ryn, and Amiram Vinokur (1992). The researchers hypothesized that a job-search program to help newly unemployed persons could reduce the risk of depression among this group. The researchers tested this hypothesis with a sample of unemployed persons who volunteered for job-search help at Michigan Employment Security Commission offices. The unemployed volunteers were randomly assigned either to participate in eight three-hour group seminars over a two-week period (the treatment) or to receive self-help information on job search in the mail (the comparison condition). The primary outcome measure was an index of depression symptoms (see Exhibit 6.1). The researchers found fewer depression symptoms among the subjects who had participated in the group seminars. Price et al. (1992:165), speculating about the causal mechanism underlying the long-term beneficial effects of the job-search seminars, noted that those in the seminars were more likely to obtain jobs, which would naturally decrease their risk of depression.

The Price et al. study is also a good example of why the comparison group in an experiment often is not a true control group. Remember, a control group receives no intervention whatsoever. Compared to conducting a job-search seminar for the experimental group, mailing job-search information to the comparison group seems like no intervention. But the mailing was important for two reasons. First, it was probably ethically necessary to provide all study participants with some additional help. Second, the plan to mail the materials allowed the researchers to recruit subjects with the promise that they would receive something for their participation.

Price et al. could not carefully control conditions, because the experimental treatment required subjects to attend a series of training sessions over two weeks; between sessions, many other events at home and in the community could have influenced the subjects' levels of depression. However, the training sessions as a whole were the experimental treatment, so the researchers had little concern that something other than the treatment

Exhibit 6.1 **Experimental and Comparison Groups: Job-Search Help and Depression (Price et al., 1992)**

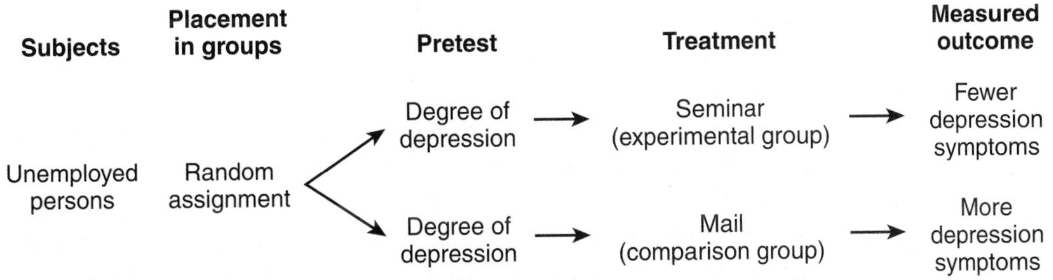

would happen during the sessions to affect the results. And because the subjects were randomly assigned to the groups, their home and community environments during the treatment period should have been the same, on average. So even though the conditions for all the subjects were not literally controlled during the experiment, the nature of the treatment and the random composition of the groups make it unlikely that any bias occurred as a result.

Pretest and Posttest Measures

All true experiments have a **posttest**—that is, measurement of the outcome in both groups after the experimental group has received the treatment. In fact, we might say that any hypothesis-testing research involves a posttest: The dependent variable is measured after the independent variable has had its effect, if any. Many true experiments also have **pretests** which measure the dependent variable prior to the experimental intervention. A pretest is exactly the same as the posttest, just administered at a different time. Strictly speaking, a true experiment does not require a pretest. When researchers use random assignment, the groups' initial scores on the dependent variable and on all other variables are very likely to be similar. Any difference in outcome between the experimental and comparison groups is therefore likely to be due to the intervention (or to other processes occurring during the experiment), and the likelihood of a difference just on the basis of chance can be calculated.

But, in fact, having pretest scores can be advantageous. They provide a direct measure of how much the experimental and comparison groups changed over time. They allow the researcher to verify that randomization was successful (that chance factors did not lead to an initial difference between the groups). In addition, by identifying subjects' initial scores on the dependent variable, a pretest provides a more complete picture of the conditions in which the intervention had (or didn't have) an effect (Mohr, 1992:46–48).

An experiment may have multiple posttests and perhaps even multiple pretests. Multiple posttests can identify just when the treatment has its effect and for how long. They are particularly important for treatments delivered over time (Rossi & Freeman, 1989:289–290).

Randomization

Randomization, or random assignment, is what makes the comparison group in a true experiment such a powerful tool for identifying the effects of the treatment. A randomized comparison group can provide a good estimate of the counterfactual—the outcome that would have occurred if the subjects who were exposed to the treatment actually had not been exposed but otherwise had had the same experiences (Mohr, 1992:3; Rossi & Freeman, 1989:229). If the comparison group differed from the experimental group in any way besides not receiving the treatment (or receiving a different treatment), a researcher would not be able to determine for sure what the unique effects of the treatment were.

Assigning subjects randomly to the experimental and comparison groups ensures that systematic bias does not affect the assignment of subjects to groups. But of course random assignment cannot guarantee that the groups are perfectly identical at the start of the experiment. Randomization removes bias from the assignment process—but only by relying on chance, which itself can result in some intergroup differences. Fortunately, researchers can use statistical methods to determine the odds of ending up with groups that differ very much on the basis of chance, and these odds are low even for groups of moderate size. The larger the group the less likely it is that even modest differences will occur on the basis of chance and the more possible it becomes to draw conclusions about causal effects from relatively small differences in the outcome.

Note that the random assignment of subjects to experimental and comparison groups is not the same as random sampling of individuals from some larger population (see Exhibit 6.2). In fact, random assignment (randomization) does not help at all to ensure that the research subjects are representative of some larger population; instead, representativeness is the goal of random sampling. What random assignment does—create two (or more) equivalent groups—is useful for ensuring internal validity, not generalizability.

But random assignment does share with random sampling the use of a chance selection method. In random assignment, a random procedure is used to determine into which group each subject is placed; in random sampling, a random procedure is used to determine which cases are selected for the sample. The random procedure—tossing a coin, using a random number table, or generating random numbers with a computer—can be basically the same in both random assignment and random sampling.

Because they both select cases on the basis of chance, random assignment and random sampling can use the mathematics of probability to estimate the odds of obtaining a given result solely on the basis of chance. A report of an experimental outcome will often include a probabilistic statement, such as "The likelihood of obtaining an outcome difference this large between the experimental and comparison groups on the basis of chance or random assignment is less than 5 out of 100" (or just $p < .05$). This type of probabilistic statement is similar to those that can be made about the likelihood of a sample statistic representing a population, although the language is somewhat different. For example, a researcher might say of an

Exhibit 6.2 **Random Sampling versus Random Assignment**

Random sampling (a tool for ensuring generalizability):
Individuals are randomly selected from a population to participate in a study.

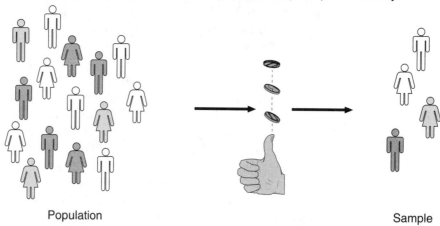

Population   Sample

Random assignment, or randomization (a tool for ensuring internal validity):
Individuals who are to participate in a study are randomly divided into an
experimental group and a comparison group.

Experimental group

Study participants   Comparison group

association between variables in a nonexperimental study using a random
sample, "The likelihood of finding an association this large between the independent and dependent variables on the basis of chance (or random sampling), when there was no association in the population from which the
sample was drawn, is less than 5 out of 100."

Matching is another procedure sometimes used to equate experimental
and comparison groups, but by itself it is a poor substitute for randomization. Matching of individuals in a treatment group with those in a compari-

Exhibit 6.3   **Experimental Design Combining Matching and Random Assignment**

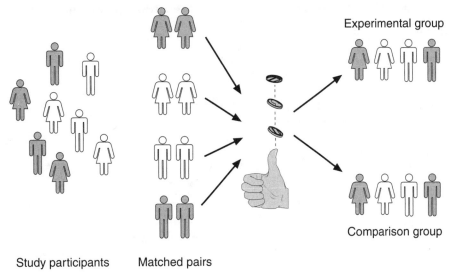

Study participants   Matched pairs   Experimental group   Comparison group

son group might involve pairing persons on the basis of similarity of gender, age, year in school, or some other characteristic. The basic problem is that, as a practical matter, individuals can be matched on only a few characteristics; unmatched differences between the experimental and comparison groups may still influence outcomes. However, matching combined with randomization can reduce the possibility of differences due to chance. For example, if individuals are matched in terms of gender and age and then the members of each matched pair are assigned randomly to the experimental and comparison groups, the possibility of differences due to chance in the gender and age composition of the groups is eliminated (see Exhibit 6.3). Matching is also used in some quasi-experimental designs when randomization is not possible, as you will see later.

Robert Drake, Gregory McHugo, Deborah Becker, William Anthony, and Robin Clark (1996) used a variant of the classic **randomized comparative change design**, also termed the **pretest-posttest control group design**, to test the value of two different approaches to providing employment services for people diagnosed with severe mental disorders. Their experimental design is depicted in Exhibit 6.4. (The diagram at the top is a standard form of notation for the design of true experiments.) One approach, Group Skills Training (GST), emphasizes preemployment skills training and uses separate agencies to provide vocational and mental health services. The other approach, Individual Placement and Support (IPS), provides vocational and mental health services in a single program and places people directly into jobs without preemployment skills training. The researchers

Exhibit 6.4 **Randomized Comparative Change Design: Employment Services for People with Severe Mental Disorders (Drake et al., 1996)**

Experimental group:	R	O_1	X	O_2	O_3	O_4	
Comparison group:	R	O_1		O_2	O_3	O_4	

Key: R = Random assignment
       O = Observation (employment status at pretest or posttest)
       X = Experimental treatment

	O_1	X	O_2	O_3	O_4
Experimental group	Pretest	Preemployment skills training	Posttest at 6 months	Posttest at 12 months	Posttest at 18 months
Comparison group	Pretest		Posttest at 6 months	Posttest at 12 months	Posttest at 18 months

hypothesized that GST participants would be more likely to obtain jobs during the 18-month study period than would IPS participants. Cases were assigned randomly to the two groups, and then:

1. Both groups received a pretest.
2. One group received the experimental intervention, and the other did not.
3. Both groups received three posttests, at 6, 12, and 18 months.
4. Contrary to the researchers' hypothesis, the IPS participants were twice as likely to obtain a competitive job as the GST participants. The IPS participants also worked more hours and earned more total wages. Although this was not the outcome Drake et al. had anticipated, it was valuable information for policy makers and program planners.

Identification of the Causal Mechanism

The distinguishing features of true experiments—experimental and comparison groups, pretests and posttests, and randomization—do not help researchers identify the mechanisms by which treatments have their effects. In fact, this question of causal mechanism often is not addressed in experimental research. The hypothesis test itself does not require any analysis of mechanism, and if the experiment was conducted under carefully controlled conditions during a limited span of time, the causal effect (if any) may seem to be quite direct. But attention to causal mechanisms can augment experimental findings.

Indeed, causal mechanisms have been an increasing concern in medical research. Identifying the way in which specific drugs have biochemical effects can lead to the development of more effective drugs with fewer unwanted side effects.

In the social sciences as well, researchers often focus attention on the mechanism by which a social program has its effect (Mohr, 1992:25–27; Scriven, 1972). Their goal is to measure the intermediate steps in the chain by which the program leads to the change that is the program's primary focus. But even in social research in the laboratory, the causal mechanism can become a focus of investigation as researchers try to refine their understanding of why the independent variable has an effect.

Diane Liang, Richard Moreland, and Linda Argote (1995) tried to identify the causal mechanism when they tested the effect of group training compared to individual training for a work task. Their design, summarized in Exhibit 6.5, is similar to the design of Price et al.'s experiment on the relationship between job-search help and depression (see Exhibit 6.1), except for the absence of a pretest. The research question posed by Liang et al. stemmed from their interest in the concept of "transactive memory." According to an earlier theorist (Wegner, 1986, as cited in Liang et al., 1995: 385), "Shared experiences often lead groups of people to encode, store, and retrieve relevant information together." The result is a transactive memory system, "a combination of the knowledge possessed by particular group members and an awareness of who knows what." One of the researchers' hypotheses was that groups whose members are trained together rather than alone will recall more about how to perform a task.

Exhibit 6.5 **Randomized Comparative Posttest Design: Group Training for a Work Task (Liang et al., 1995)**

Experimental group: R   X   O

Comparison group: R   O

Key: R = Random assignment
O = Observation (pretest or posttest)
X = Experimental treatment

	X	**O**
Experimental group	Group training	Posttest: Radio assembly
Comparison group		Posttest: Radio assembly

The experiment was conducted with undergraduate business students at Carnegie Mellon University. In a laboratory, participants were asked to assemble the AM portion of an AM/FM radio. The student subjects were told that they would be trained for this task and then expected to complete it in a group. Half the students were then randomly assigned to group training and half to individual training. The training sessions lasted about an hour. One week later, the students were placed in small groups (three subjects of the same sex) and asked to assemble the radios. Students who had been trained in a group worked with that group to assemble the radios. All students were told that those in the best work group would receive a $20 bonus. As hypothesized, groups whose members were trained together remembered more about how to assemble the radio than groups whose members were trained alone. They also made fewer errors in assembling the radios.

To help identify the causal mechanism involved in the group work, Liang et al. videotaped all work groups and then scored the tapes for evidence of transactive memory: coordination of tasks, trust in one another's knowledge, and specialization of group members in remembering distinct aspects of radio assembly. Other group processes that did not reflect transactive memory were also scored, such as strength of group identification and task motivation. As predicted, the work groups that had been trained as a group showed more evidence of transactive memory systems. The superior performance of these groups was not explained by the other group processes.

Control over Conditions

A prerequisite for meeting each of the other criteria for identifying causal relations is maintaining control over the conditions to which subjects are exposed after they are assigned to the experimental and comparison groups. If these conditions begin to differ, the variation between the experimental and comparison groups will not be that which was intended. Even a subsequent difference in the distribution of cases on the dependent variable will not provide clear evidence of the effect of the independent variable. Such unintended variation is often not much of a problem in laboratory experiments, where the researcher has almost complete control over the conditions (and can ensure that these conditions are nearly identical for both groups). But control over conditions can become a very big concern for experiments, like Drake and his colleagues' study of employment services for the mentally disordered, that are conducted in the field—in real-world settings.

Summary: Causality in True Experiments

The three studies reviewed here were true experiments because each had at least one experimental and one comparison group to which subjects were randomly assigned. They also compared variation in the dependent variable after variation in the independent variable, although they differed in number of pretests and posttests. Liang et al. did not have a pretest in their study of group versus individual training for a work task; Drake et al. had multiple posttests in their study of employment services for the mentally disturbed. The studies also differed in the extent to which the researchers maintained control over conditions and investigated causal mechanisms. Liang et al.'s laboratory experiment allowed conditions to be carefully controlled, and they investigated systematically the causal processes involved. Price et al. could not control conditions in their study of job-search programs for the newly unemployed, but they used subjects selected randomly from different environments. Control over conditions, investigation of the causal mechanism, and pretesting are not defining features of true experiments, but they are nonetheless important components to evaluate in any experimental design.

Let's examine how well true experiments meet the criteria for identifying a nomothetic cause that were identified in Chapter 5:

■ *Association between the hypothesized independent and dependent variables.* As you have seen, experiments can provide unambiguous evidence of association by means of experimental and comparison groups.

■ *Time order of effects of one variable on the others.* Unquestionably arrest for spouse abuse preceded recidivism in the Lawrence Sherman and Richard Berk (1984) study (described in Chapter 2) and the job loss seminars in the Price et al. study preceded the differential rates of depression between the experimental and comparison groups. In experiments with a pretest, time order can be established by comparing posttest to pretest scores. In experiments with random assignment of subjects to the experimental and comparison groups, time order can be established by comparison of posttest scores only.

■ *Nonspurious relationships between variables.* Nonspuriousness is difficult to establish—some would say impossible—in nonexperimental designs. The random assignment of subjects to experimental and comparison groups is what makes true experiments such powerful designs for testing causal hypotheses. Randomization controls for the host of possible extraneous influences that can create misleading, spurious relationships in both experimental and nonexperimental data. If we determine that a design has used randomization successfully, we can be much more confident in the resulting causal conclusions.

- *Mechanism that creates the causal effect.* The features of a true experiment do not in themselves allow identification of causal mechanisms; as a result there can be some ambiguity about how the independent variable influenced the dependent variable and the resulting causal conclusions.

- *Context in which change occurs.* Control over conditions is more feasible in many experimental designs than it is in nonexperimental designs, but it is often difficult to control conditions in field experiments. Later in this chapter, you will see how the lack of control over experimental conditions can threaten internal validity.

■ ■ ■ ■ Quasi-Experiments

Often, testing a hypothesis with a true experimental design is not feasible with the desired subjects and in the desired setting. Such a test may be too costly or take too long to carry out, it may be inappropriate for the particular research problem, or it may presume ability to manipulate an intervention that already has occurred. To overcome these problems, yet still benefit from the logic of the experimental method, researchers may instead use designs that retain several components of experimental design but differ in important details.

Usually the best alternative to an experimental design, as far as maximizing internal validity is concerned, is a quasi-experimental design. Although the term is not defined consistently by all experts, we can consider a **quasi-experimental design** to be one in which the comparison group is predetermined to be comparable to the treatment group in critical ways, such as being eligible for the same services or being in the same school cohort (Rossi & Freeman, 1989: 313). These research designs are "quasi" experimental because subjects are not randomly assigned to the comparison and experimental groups, and we therefore cannot be as confident in their causal conclusions as we can be with experimental designs.

I will discuss here the two major types of quasi-experimental designs (others can be found in Cook & Campbell, 1979; Mohr, 1992):

- *Nonequivalent control group designs.* **Nonequivalent control group designs** have experimental and comparison groups that are designated before the treatment occurs and are not created by random assignment.

- *Before-and-after designs.* A **before-and-after design** has a pretest and posttest but no comparison group. In other words, the subjects exposed to the treatment serve, at an earlier time, as their own controls.

Exhibit 6.6 diagrams these two types of quasi-experiment. I will also discuss in this section one type of design that is similar to the nonequivalent

Exhibit 6.6 **Quasi-Experimental Designs**

Nonequivalent control group design:
Police enforcement of seat-belt laws (Watson, 1986)

Experimental group: O_1 X O_2
Comparison group: O_1 O_2

	O_1	X	O_2
Experimental community	Pretest: Percentage using seat belts	Police enforcement of seat-belt law	Posttest: Percentage using seat belts
Comparison community	Pretest: Percentage using seat belts		Posttest: Percentage using seat belts

Before-and-after design:
Soap-opera suicide and actual suicide (Phillips, 1982)

Experimental group: O_1 X O_2

O_1	X	O_2
Pretest: Suicide rate	Soap-opera suicide	Posttest: Suicide rate

Ex post facto control group design:
Self-managing work teams (Cohen & Ledford, 1994)

Experimental group O_1 X O_2
Comparison group O_1 O_2

	O_1	X	O_2
Experimental group	Pretest: Measures of satisfaction and productivity	Self-managing work team	Posttest: Measures of satisfaction and productivity
Comparison group	Pretest: Measures of satisfaction and productivity		Posttest: Measures of satisfaction and productivity

Key: R = Random assignment
      O = Observation (pretest or posttest)
      X = Experimental treatment

control group design, and often confused with it, but that does not meet as well the criteria for quasi-experimental designs.

• *Ex post facto control group designs*. Like nonequivalent control group designs, this design has experimental and comparison groups that are not created by random assignment. But unlike the groups in non-equivalent control group designs, the groups in ex post facto designs are designated after the treatment has occurred.

Nonequivalent Control Group Designs

In this type of quasi-experimental design, a comparison group is selected to be as comparable as possible to the treatment group. Two selection methods can be used:

■ *Individual matching*. Individual cases in the treatment group are matched with similar individuals in the comparison group. A Mexican-American male about 20 who is assigned to the treatment group may be matched with another Mexican-American male about 20 who is assigned to the comparison group. The problem with this method is determining in advance which variables should be used for matching. It is also unlikely that a match can actually be found for all cases. However, in some situations matching can create a comparison group that is very similar to the experimental group. For example, some studies of the effect of Head Start, the government program that prepares disadvantaged toddlers for school, used participants' siblings to make up the comparison group. They were like the experimental group of Head Start participants in many ways.

■ *Aggregate matching*. In most situations when random assignment is not possible, the second method of matching makes more sense: identifying a comparison group that matches the treatment group in the aggregate rather than trying to match individual cases. Matching in the aggregate means finding a group that has similar distributions on key variables: the same average age, the same percentage female, and so on. For this design to be considered even quasi-experimental, however, individuals may not choose which group to join or where to seek services; in other words, they themselves cannot opt for or against the experimental treatment.

Roy Watson's (1986) study of the deterrent effect of police action on violations of a seat-belt law illustrates a quasi-experimental nonequivalent control group design. This study used aggregate matching and a pretest. It was conducted in British Columbia, Canada, where a mandatory seat-belt law had been enacted but had not elicited high rates of compliance. Watson selected two communities of comparable size where police enforcement of the seat-belt law was low. The units of analysis in the study were drivers; seat-belt usage was the dependent variable.

In a pretest, Watson measured seat-belt usage in both communities. Then, in the experimental community, he instituted a media campaign to increase seat-belt usage, followed by increased police enforcement of the seat-belt law. A posttest followed both the media campaign and the increased police enforcement. In the comparison community, one posttest was conducted at about the same time as a final posttest in the experimental community. Because the two communities were physically distant and in different media markets, it seems unlikely that the experiment in one community would have affected the other community while the study was in progress. As Exhibit 6.7 shows, the experimental program had a marked effect on seat-belt use.

Before-and-After Designs

The common feature of before-and-after designs is the absence of a comparison group: All cases are exposed to the experimental treatment. The basis for comparison is instead provided by the pretreatment measures in the experimental group. These designs are thus useful for studies of interventions that are experienced by virtually every case in some population, such as total coverage programs like Social Security or single-organization studies of the effect of a new management strategy.

The simplest type of before-and-after design is the fixed-sample panel design. As you may recall from Chapter 5, a panel design involves only one pretest and one posttest. It does not itself qualify as a quasi-experimental design because comparing subjects to themselves at just one earlier point in time does not provide an adequate comparison group. Many influences other than the experimental treatment may affect a subject following the pretest—basic life experiences for a young subject, for instance.

David P. Phillips's (1982) study of the effect of TV soap-opera suicides on the number of actual suicides in the United States illustrates a more powerful **multiple group before-after design.** In this design, several before-after comparisons are made involving the same variables but different groups. Phillips identified 13 soap-opera suicides in 1977 and then recorded the U.S. suicide rate in the weeks prior to and following each TV story. In effect, the researcher had 13 different before-after studies, one for each suicide story. In 12 of these 13 comparisons, deaths due to suicide increased from the week before each soap-opera suicide to the week after (see Exhibit 6.8). Phillips also found similar increases in motor-vehicle deaths and crashes during the same period, some portion of which reflects covert suicide attempts.

Exhibit 6.7   **Driver Use of Seat Belts in Two Communities (Watson, 1986)**

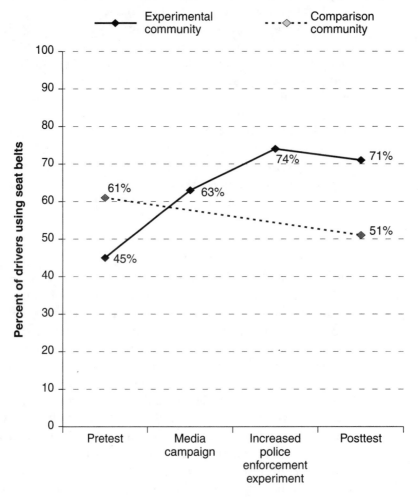

Source: Data from Watson, 1986:298.

Another type of before-and-after design involves multiple pretest and posttest observations of the same group. Most methodologists distinguish between **repeated measures panel designs,** which include several pretest and posttest observations, and **time series designs,** which include many (preferably 30 or more) such observations in both pretest and posttest periods. Repeated measures panel designs are stronger than simple before-and-after panel designs because they allow the researcher to study the process by which an intervention or treatment has an impact over time.

Exhibit 6.8 **Real Suicides and Soap-Opera Suicides (Phillips, 1982)**

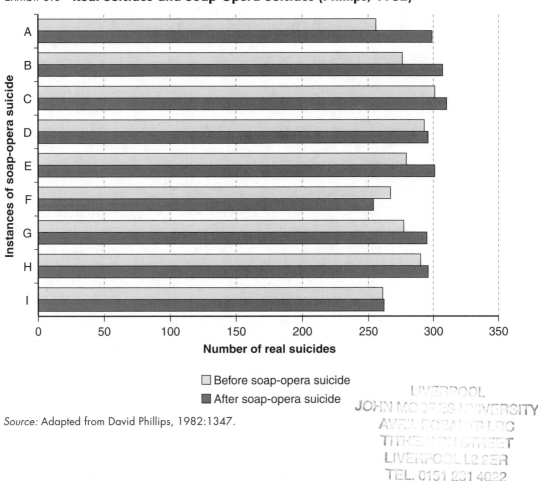

Before soap-opera suicide
After soap-opera suicide

Source: Adapted from David Phillips, 1982:1347.

Time series designs are particularly useful for studies of the impact of new laws or social programs that affect everyone and that are readily assessed by some ongoing measurement. For example, we might use a time series design to study the impact of a new seat-belt law on the severity of injuries in automobile accidents, using a monthly state government report on insurance claims. Special statistics are required to analyze time series data, but the basic idea is to identify a trend in the dependent variable up to the date of the intervention or event whose effect is being studied and then to project the trend into the postintervention period. This projected trend is then compared to the actual trend of the dependent variable after the intervention. A substantial disparity between the actual and projected trend is evidence that the intervention or event had an impact (Rossi & Freeman, 1989:260–261, 358–363).

Ex Post Facto Control Group Designs

A design in which the treatment and comparison groups are designated after the treatment is administered is termed an **ex post facto** (after the fact) **control group design.** This design should perhaps be considered a non-experimental rather than a quasi-experimental design because the comparison group may not be comparable to the treatment group. The problem is that if the treatment takes any time at all, people with particular characteristics may select themselves for the treatment or avoid it. However, carefully designed ex post facto studies can result in comparisons between the treatment and control groups that give us almost as much confidence in the validity of their causal conclusions as we can have in the causal conclusions from a quasi-experimental design (Rossi & Freeman, 1989:343–344).

Susan Cohen and Gerald Ledford's (1994) study of the effectiveness of self-managing teams used a well-constructed ex post facto design. They studied a telecommunication company with some work teams that were self-managing and some that were traditionally managed (meaning that a manager was responsible for the team's decisions). Work groups were identified as self-managing if managers and employees agreed that the employees worked as a team, were responsible for making a product or providing a service, and had discretion over key work decisions. Each work group with these characteristics was matched with a traditionally managed work group that produced the same product or service.

Cohen and Ledford found the self-reported quality of work life to be higher in the self-managing groups than in the traditionally managed groups. Job performance also seemed higher in the self-managing groups in clerical and craft functions but not in small business offices. A special review of operations in the small business offices revealed that their work did not lend itself to a team approach. This finding helped to specify the context in which the hypothesized cause would have its effect.

What distinguishes this study design from a quasi-experimental design is the fact that the teams themselves and their managers had some influence on how they were managed. As the researchers noted, "If the groups which were already high performers were the ones selected to be self-managing teams, then the findings could be due to a selection bias rather than any effects of self-management" (Cohen & Ledford, 1994:34). Thus, preexisting characteristics of employees, managers, or their team composition might have influenced which "treatment" they received, as well as the outcomes achieved. However, the work histories and demographic characteristics of the two groups were similar, and the members of each group rated one another as similarly proficient. In addition, the dropout rate during the study did not differ between the groups so much as to affect the outcome measures. These additional tests give us more confidence that indeed the difference in management style between the two groups, and not their makeup,

But in field experiments, what has been planned as a random assignment process may deteriorate when it is delegated to front-line program staff. This problem occurred in the Sherman and Berk domestic violence experiment in Minneapolis. Police officers sometimes violated the random assignment plan because they thought the circumstances warranted arresting a suspect who had been randomly assigned to receive just a warning. In several of the follow-up studies, the researchers maintained closer control over the assignment process so that randomization could be maintained.

Even when random assignment works as planned, the groups can become different over time because of **differential attrition,** or what can be thought of as "deselection." That is, the groups become different because subjects are more likely to drop out of one of the groups for various reasons. This is not a likely problem in a laboratory experiment that occurs in one session. But some laboratory experiments occur over time—for instance, Liang et al.'s experiment on group training required subjects to return for a second session after one week—and so differential attrition can become a problem. Subjects who experience the experimental condition may become more motivated than comparison subjects to continue in the experiment.

Differential attrition is quite common in field experiments that evaluate the impact of social programs (Cook & Campbell, 1979:359–366). Subjects who receive some advantageous program benefit are more likely to stay in the experiment (making themselves available for measurement in the posttest); subjects who are not receiving program benefits are more likely to drop out. Another possibility is that individuals who are more in need of a program, such as severe alcoholics in a detoxification study, are more likely to drop out (Rossi & Freeman, 1989:236).

In evaluation research that involves monitoring program impact over an extended period, the possibility of differential attrition can be very high. When the treatment group is receiving some service or benefit that the control group is not, individuals in the control group will be more likely to drop out of the study altogether. A study of the benefits of a health-insurance program actually had to abandon tracking its control group because subjects weren't cooperating (Hunt, 1985:274–275).

The Price et al. unemployment study managed to retain 80% to 90% of the subjects in both the experimental and comparison groups at each follow-up, so it would seem not to have had a problem with differential attrition (see Exhibit 6.1). However, it in fact had a major problem with attrition before the treatment even began. To actually receive the experimental intervention, those assigned to the job-search seminar had to make the effort to attend. Only 308 of the 606 respondents randomly assigned to the job-search seminar actually appeared for a seminar, making it likely that the subjects in the experimental group were quite different from those assigned to the comparison group. To compensate for this likely bias, the researchers adopted a conservative strategy: Their outcome analysis was based on comparing all the subjects initially assigned to the experimental condition with all the subjects assigned to the control condition (although 10% to 20% did not return their questionnaires in either group and so could not be included in the outcome analysis). The findings regarding the effect of participation in the job-search seminar therefore seem particularly strong.

When subjects are not assigned randomly to treatment and comparison groups, as in nonequivalent control group designs, the threat of selection bias is very great. Even if the researcher selects a comparison group that matches the treatment group on important variables, there is no guarantee that the groups were similar initially in terms of the dependent variable or in terms of some other characteristic that ultimately influences posttest scores. However, a pretest helps the researchers to determine and control for selection bias. Because most variables that might influence outcome scores will also have influenced scores on the pretest, statistically controlling for the pretest scores also serves to control for unmeasured variables that influenced the pretest scores.

Endogenous Change

The type of problem subsumed under the label **endogenous change** occurs when natural developments in the subjects, independent of the experimental treatment itself, account for some or all of the observed change between pretest and posttest. Endogenous change includes these three specific threats to internal validity:

■ *Testing.* Taking the pretest can in itself influence posttest scores. Subjects may learn something or be sensitized to an issue by the pretest and as a result, respond differently the next time they are asked the same questions, on the posttest.

■ *Maturation.* Changes in outcome scores during experiments that involve a lengthy treatment period may be due to maturation. Subjects may age, or gain experience in school or grow in knowledge all as part of a natural maturational experience and thus respond differently on the posttest than on the pretest.

■ *Regression.* People experience cyclical or episodic changes that result in different posttest scores, a phenomenon known as a **regression effect**. Subjects who are chosen for a study because they received very low scores on a test may show improvement in the posttest, on average, simply because some of the low scorers were having a bad day. On the other hand, individuals selected for an experiment because they are suffering from tooth decay will not show improvement in the posttest because a decaying tooth is not likely to improve in the natural course of things. It is hard in many cases to know whether a phenomenon is subject to naturally occurring fluctuations, so the possibility of regression effects should be considered whenever subjects are selected because of their extremely high or low values on the outcome variable (Mohr, 1992:56, 71–79).

Testing, maturation, and regression effects are generally not a problem in true experiments. Both the experimental group and the comparison group take the pretest, so even if this experience itself leads to a change in posttest scores, the comparison between the experimental and comparison groups will not be affected. Of course, in experiments with no pretest, testing effects are not a problem. Similarly, both the experimental and comparison groups are equally subject to maturation and regression, since they are the same at the outset (unless chance factors led to a difference). These endogenous changes may affect outcome scores for both groups, but both groups should be equally affected, and so estimates of treatment effects should not be biased.

Endogenous change is a major problem with before-and-after designs, however. In panel designs with a single pretest and a single posttest, any change may be due to testing, maturation, or regression. But a study that is completed within a short time may have little concern with maturation effects, and use of a diverse subject group will reassure those concerned about regression effects. Unfortunately, the possibility of endogenous change accounting for pretest-posttest change cannot be eliminated with before-and-after designs. Repeated measures panel studies and time series designs are better because they allow the researcher to trace the pattern of change or stability in the dependent variable up to and after the treatment. Ongoing effects of maturation and regression can thus be identified and taken into account.

External Events

History, or **external events** during the experiment (things that happen outside the experiment), could change subjects' outcome scores. Examples are newsworthy events that have to do with the focus of an experiment and major disasters to which subjects are exposed. This problem is often referred to as a **history effect**—history during the experiment, that is.

Causal conclusions can be invalid in true experiments because of the influence of external events, but not every experiment is affected by them. An experiment's specific features must be considered carefully to evaluate the possibility of problems due to external events. For example, in an experiment in which subjects go to a particular location for the treatment and the control group subjects do not, something in that location unrelated to the treatment could influence the experimental subjects. Experimental and comparison group subjects in the Drake et al. study of supported work received services from different agencies for the duration of the study, so external events that happened to the subjects in one group might not have happened to those in the other group. In this way external events are a major concern in evaluation studies that compare programs in different cities or states (Hunt, 1985:276–277).

The more carefully controlled the conditions for experimental and comparison groups, the less likely external events are to invalidate the causal conclusions of an experiment. External events seldom affect laboratory experiments like the Liang et al. group training study. External events are also unlikely to make the experimental and comparison groups incomparable when the subjects are selected from a larger population and do not go somewhere special for the experiment, as was the case in the Sherman and Berk domestic violence study; the experimental and comparison groups within any city should have experienced similar external events in the period after the treatment (arrest) was administered and before the end of the follow-up period. The Price et al. unemployment study assigned subjects to the experimental and comparison groups randomly from the available population of volunteers; the only risk of different external events for the two groups was something unplanned that might have occurred only with the treatment group participants when they came in for treatment.

As in true experiments, in nonequivalent control group designs, using a comparison group can minimize the effect of external events if the two groups are exposed to the same environment during the experiment. For example, the relatively constant level of seat-belt use in the comparison community in the Watson study suggests that a national series of TV announcements to encourage compliance is not what resulted in the changes in seat-belt use observed in the experimental community (Watson, 1986:294).

Before-and-after designs are much less prone to problems of external events, and become quasi-experimental when the researchers make multiple before-after comparisons or when they apply multiple pretest and posttest measures to the same group in successive time intervals. If multiple before-after comparisons yield comparable results, the observed pretest-posttest change is less likely to be due to unique external events that would have affected only some of the comparisons. For example, Phillips's use of multiple before-after comparisons makes it much less likely that the observed increases in actual suicides following soap-opera suicides were due to either particular historical events or cyclical fluctuations.

Contamination

Contamination occurs in an experiment when the comparison group is in some way affected by, or affects, the treatment group. This problem basically arises from failure to control adequately the conditions of the experiment. When comparison group members are aware that they are being denied some advantage, they may as a result increase their efforts to compensate, creating a problem termed **compensatory rivalry**, or the **John**

Henry effect (Cook & Campbell, 1979:55). On the other hand, comparison group members may become demoralized if they feel that they have been left out of some valuable treatment and may perform worse than they would have outside the experiment. The treatment may seem, in comparison, to have had a more beneficial effect than it actually did. Both compensatory rivalry and demoralization thus distort the impact of the experimental treatment. Similar problems could occur if members of the experimental group become aware of the control group and feel differently as a result.

Although the components of a true experiment guard against internal invalidity due to history and selection, the threat of contamination is always present. Careful inspection of the research design can determine whether contamination is likely to be a problem in a particular experiment. If the experiment is conducted in a laboratory, if members of the experimental group and the comparison group have no contact while the study is in progress, and if the treatment is relatively brief, contamination is not likely to be a problem. To the degree that these conditions are not met, the likelihood of contamination will increase.

Contamination could have been a problem in the Liang et al. group training study because students in the different conditions could have interacted during the week between the training session and the posttest. However, contamination would only have been a problem in the Sherman and Berk domestic violence study if those whom the police included in the study knew of one another, or in the Drake et al. employment services study if participants in the different programs interacted with each other. The potential for contamination was probably greater in the field-based unemployment training study by Price et al., because all participants used the same unemployment offices.

The threat of contamination is not necessarily any different in a quasi-experimental design than it is in a true experiment. Some nonequivalent control group designs minimize the threat of contamination by using a comparison group whose members will have no contact with the treatment group or awareness of the treatment. For example, Watson chose for his seat-belt compliance study two communities that were far enough apart to be in different media markets.

Treatment Misidentification

Treatment misidentification occurs when the treatment itself is not what causes the outcome but rather some intervening process that the researcher has not identified and is not aware of. This term can also refer to unknown concomitants or consequences of being in the control group that have to do with the experimental manipulation. In either case, the subjects experience something other than, or in addition to, what the researchers believed they will experience. Treatment misidentification has at least three sources:

■ *Expectancies of experimental staff.* Change among experimental subjects may be due to the positive **expectancies of the experimental staff** who are delivering the treatment rather than due to the treatment itself. This type of treatment misidentification can occur even in randomized experiments. Even well-trained staff may convey their enthusiasm for an experimental program to the subjects in subtle ways. Such positive staff expectations thus create a **self-fulfilling prophecy.** Because social programs are delivered by human beings, such expectancy effects can be very difficult to control in field experiments. However, in experiments on the effects of treatments like medical drugs, **double-blind procedures** can be used: Staff delivering the treatments do not know which subjects are getting the treatment and which are receiving a placebo, something that looks like the treatment but has no effect.

■ *Placebo effect.* Treatment misidentification may occur when subjects receive a treatment that they consider likely to be beneficial and improve because of that expectation rather than because of the treatment itself. In medical research, where the placebo is often a chemically inert substance that looks like the experimental drug but actually has no effect, research indicates that the **placebo effect** itself produces positive health effects in two-thirds of patients suffering from relatively mild medical problems (Goleman, 1993a:C3). Placebo effects can also occur in social science research. The only way to reduce this threat to internal validity is to treat the comparison group with something similar.

■ *Hawthorne effect.* Members of the treatment group may change in terms of the dependent variable because their participation in the study makes them feel special. This problem could occur when treatment group members compare their situation to that of members of the control group, who are not receiving the treatment, in which case it would be a type of contamination effect. But experimental group members could feel special simply because they are in the experiment. The **Hawthorne effect** is named after a famous productivity experiment at the Hawthorne electric plant outside Chicago. Workers were moved to a special room for a study of the effects of lighting intensity and other work conditions on their productivity. After this move, the workers began to increase their output no matter what change was made in their working conditions, even when the conditions became worse. The researchers concluded that the workers felt they should work harder because they were part of a special experiment. By the time the study was over, the researchers had become convinced that it was social interaction among workers, not physical arrangements, that largely determined their output. Most management historians believe that the human relations school of management began with this insight (although many have since disputed the interpretation that "feeling special" was the causal mechanism resulting in improved productivity).

To avoid treatment misidentification, field researchers are increasingly using process analysis. Process analysis is also a necessary component of evaluation studies, when researchers need to very confident that the effects they observe are due to the policy or program change they are studying (Hunt, 1985:272–274). In a **process analysis**, periodic measures are taken throughout the experiment to assess whether the treatment is being delivered as planned. In the Goldfinger et al. housing study (introduced in Chapter 1), for example, our treatment group subjects actually resided in eight different group homes. We had to monitor the operation of these homes to determine that they were each being run according to the principles underlying the "evolving consumer household" model that we had proposed to test. Drake et al. also collected process data, to monitor the implementation of the two employment service models they tested. One site did a poorer job of implementing the Individual Placement and Support model than the other site, but overall the required differences between the experimental conditions were achieved. Similarly, Cohen and Ledford measured carefully the characteristics of work groups to confirm that those they had been told were self-managing actually functioned in this way.

Generalizability

The need for generalizable findings can be thought of as the Achilles heel of the true experimental design. The design components that are essential for a true experiment and that minimize the threats to causal validity make it more difficult to achieve sample generalizability—being able to apply the findings to some clearly defined larger population. In contrast, cross-population generalizability is no more or less achievable with experiments than with other research designs. As you learned in Chapter 1, the extent to which treatment effects can be generalized across subgroups and to other populations and settings is termed external validity.

Sample Generalizability

Subjects who can be recruited for a laboratory experiment, randomly assigned to a group, and kept under carefully controlled conditions for the study's duration are unlikely to be a representative sample of any large population of interest to social scientists. Can they be expected to react to the experimental treatment in the same way as members of the larger population? The more artificial the experimental arrangements, the greater the problem (Campbell & Stanley, 1966:20–21).

It is not only the characteristics of the subjects themselves that determine the generalizability of the experimental results. The generalizability of the treatment and of the setting for the experiment also must be considered (Cook & Campbell, 1979:73–74).

Generalizability can be a particular concern in evaluation research, because the findings may result in policy changes that affect people throughout the nation. Rarely can the entire nation be sampled for subjects in an experimental evaluation of a social program, however. The need to repeatedly contact subjects and to monitor program implementation makes it prohibitively expensive for even the federal government to fund such research in more than a few states.

But a researcher can take steps both before and after an experiment to increase a study's generalizability. Field experiments are likely to yield findings that are more generalizable to broader populations than are laboratory experiments, for which subjects must volunteer. Sherman and Berk's experimental study of arrest and domestic violence and Watson's quasi-experimental study of seat-belt use were both conducted with people and police engaged in their normal activities in real communities, greatly increasing our confidence in the studies' generalizability.

In a few field experiments, participants can be selected randomly from the population of interest, and thus the researchers can achieve results generalizable to that population. For example, some studies of the effects of income supports on the work behavior of poor persons have randomly sampled persons within particular states before randomly assigning them to experimental and comparison groups. The Sherman and Berk arrest study did not use random selection, but because it was to include all actual domestic assault cases processed by police in two Minneapolis precincts during a certain period, the resulting sample of cases should have been representative of at least these two precincts.

But in most experiments, neither random selection from the population nor selection of the entire population is possible. Potential subjects must make a conscious decision to participate—thus probably resulting in an unrepresentative pool of volunteers. Or the experiment must be conducted in a limited setting, perhaps a particular organization, and thus may not apply to other settings. Even in the Sherman and Berk study, many police officers did not actually participate, so the attempt to include all domestic assault cases meeting study criteria did not succeed; the study's results thus may not have been generalizable even to the two precincts studied.

When random selection is not feasible, the researchers may be able to increase generalizability by selecting several sites for conducting the experiment that offer marked contrasts in key variables of the population. The follow-up studies to Sherman and Berk's work, for example, were conducted in cities that differed from Minneapolis, the original site, in social class and ethnic composition. As a result, although the findings are not statistically generalizable to a larger population, they do give some indication of the study's general applicability (Cook & Campbell, 1979:76–77).

External Validity

> **External validity** The applicability of a treatment effect (or non-effect) across subgroups within an experiment or other study and across different populations or times or settings.
>
> *Example:* Sherman and Berk (1984) found that arrest reduced repeat offenses for employed subjects but not for unemployed subjects. The effect of arrest thus varied with employment status, so a conclusion that arrest deters recidivism would not be exernally valid.

Researchers are often interested in determining whether treatment effects identified in an experiment hold true for subgroups of subjects. Of course, determining that a relationship between the treatment and the outcome variable holds true for certain subgroups does not establish that the relationship also holds true for these subgroups in the larger population, but it suggests that the relationship might be externally valid.

Imagine a field experiment in which subjects were randomly sampled from the population of interest but in which the treatment effect occurred only for some subgroups. The finding about the overall treatment effect would be generalizable to the population but would not apply to all groups within the population. In this instance, the external validity of the conclusions would be equivalent to their cross-population generalizability.

We have already seen examples of how the existence of treatment effects in particular subgroups of experimental subjects can establish both the external validity of the findings and their cross-population generalizability. For example, Price et al. found that intensive job-search assistance reduced depression among individuals who were at high risk for it because of other psychosocial characteristics; however, the intervention did not influence the rate of depression among individuals at low risk for depression. This is an important interaction effect that limits the generalizability of the findings, even if Price et al.'s sample was representative of the population of unemployed persons.

Such analyses may not be possible in an experiment that suffers significant attrition of subjects. Individuals who did not show up for the Price et al. job-search workshops may have differed from those who did show up in ways that were related to their responsiveness to the workshops. To avoid serious challenge to the internal validity of their results, Price et al. included in their analysis outcomes for those who did not attend the workshops. But we still don't know whether those who chose not to attend would have reacted as favorably as those who did attend. The best researchers can do to evaluate such possibilities is to try to measure subjects' characteristics before the attrition occurs and then test for differences between those who quit and those who remain in the study.

Cross-population generalizability may also be hampered by problems with differential rates of selection across study sites. An experimental study of the effect of hormone-replacement therapy for postmenopausal women has had difficulty recruiting the 27,500 women needed from 40 health centers nationwide (Knox, 1997). In the Boston area, with its many hospitals and universities, recruitment has been especially difficult because many women have already made up their minds about the value of hormone replacement and therefore are unwilling to have their therapy determined by random assignment. If this recruitment problem is not overcome, the study results may not be generalizable to women who are very informed about health issues.

As an example of the way external validity in experiments supports generalizability, consider P. Christopher Earley's (1994) study of the effect of individual and group training on workers from different cultures. By design, the study included a systematic evaluation of the external validity of the findings. In one component of the investigation, managers from Hong Kong, the People's Republic of China, and the United States were recruited from training seminars for a laboratory study of the value of group training. Participants were assigned randomly to either individual or group training. The researchers believed that a "worker from an individualistic culture strives to improve work performance because of the recognition he or she may receive, whereas a worker from a collectivistic culture seeks improvement because of the gains his or her group may receive" (Earley, 1994:89). Thus they expected that the group training would be more effective in the countries with a more collectivistic culture (Hong Kong and China) and the individual training would be more effective in the United States.

As Exhibit 6.9 shows, the experiment provided some support for this cultural hypothesis. In addition, no matter what the cultural setting, workers who were themselves more collectivistic in their work orientation improved more with group training than with individual training. So the impact of the type of training varied with both the culture and the individual. By testing in this way for the external validity of the relationship between the training and the outcomes, Earley gives us a much richer understanding of the work process than was possible in a single-culture study like Liang et al.'s study of work groups among college students in the United States. Ultimately, however, the external validity of experimental results will increase

Exhibit 6.9 **External Validity in Experiments: Group Training and Culture (Earley, 1994)**

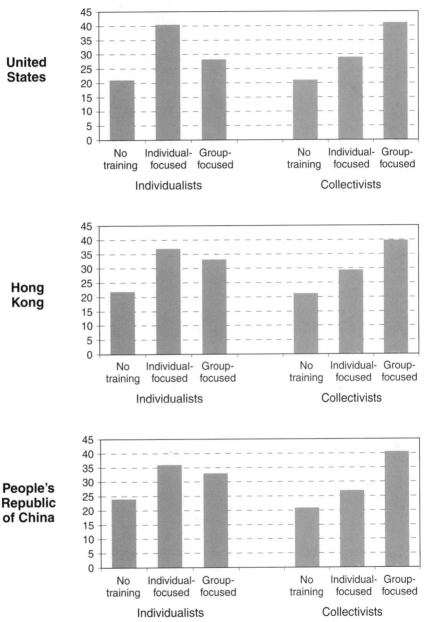

with the success of replications taking place at different times and places and using different forms of the treatment. As indicated by the replications of the Sherman and Berk study of arrest for domestic violence, the result may be a more complex, nuanced understanding of the hypothesized effect.

Interaction of Testing and Treatment

A variant on the problem of external validity occurs when the experimental treatment has an effect only when particular conditions created by the experiment occur. One such problem occurs when the treatment has an effect only if subjects have had the pretest. The pretest sensitizes the subjects to some issue, so that when they are exposed to the treatment, they react in a way they would not have reacted if they had not taken the pretest. In other words, testing and treatment interact to produce the outcome. For example, answering questions in a pretest about racial prejudice may sensitize subjects so that when they are exposed to the experimental treatment, seeing a film about prejudice, their attitudes are different than they would have been. In this situation, the treatment truly had an effect, but it would not have had an effect if it were repeated without the sensitizing pretest.

Researchers sometimes deliberately take advantage of the interaction of testing and treatment to increase external validity. One design for doing so randomly assigns subjects to at least two experimental groups and at least two comparison groups, with one experimental group and one comparison group having a pretest and the others not having a pretest (see Exhibit 6.10). If testing and treatment do interact, the difference in outcome scores between the experimental and comparison groups will be different for subjects who took the pretest compared to those who did not.

■ ■ ■ ■ Ethical Issues in Experimental Research

Social science experiments often involve subject deception. Primarily because of this feature, some experiments have prompted contentious debates about research ethics. Experimental evaluations of social programs also

Exhibit 6.10 **Solomon 4-Group Design Testing the Interaction of Pretesting and Treatment**

Experimental group: R O_1 X O_2

Comparison group: R O_1 O_2

Experimental group: R   X O_2

Comparison group: R O_2

Key: R = Random assignment
O = Observation (pretest or posttest)
X = Experimental treatment

pose ethical dilemmas because they require researchers to withhold possibly beneficial treatment from some of the subjects, selected on the basis of chance. In this section, I will weigh the ethical problems posed by experimental research.

Deception

Deception occurs when subjects are misled about research procedures to determine how they would react to the treatment if they were not research subjects. Deception is a critical component of many social experiments, in part because of the difficulty of simulating real-world stresses and dilemmas in a laboratory setting. Elliot Aronson and Judson Mills (1959), for example, wanted to learn how severity of initiation influences liking for real social groups. But they could not practically design a field experiment on initiation. Their alternative, which relied on a tape-recorded discussion staged by the researcher, was of course deceptive. In many experiments, if subjects understood what was really happening to them the results would be worthless.

Although the American Sociological Association's *Code of Ethics* does not discuss experimentation explicitly, one of its principles highlights the ethical dilemma posed by deceptive research:

> The process of conducting sociological research must not expose
> respondents to substantial risk of personal harm. Informed consent
> must be obtained when the risks of research are greater than the risks of
> everyday life. (1989:3)

Does "informed consent" mean that subjects must be told just what they will be experiencing and why? When are the "risks of research" greater than those of everyday life?

Aronson and Mills's study of severity of initiation (at an all-women's college in the 1950s) is a good example of experimental research that does not pose greater-than-everyday risks to subjects. The students who were randomly assigned to the "severe initiation" experimental condition had to read a list of embarrassing words. I think it's fair to say that even in the 1950s, reading a list of potentially embarrassing words in a laboratory setting and listening to a taped discussion are unlikely to increase the risks to which students are exposed in their everyday lives. Moreover, the researchers informed subjects that they would be expected to talk about sex and could decline to participate in the experiment if this requirement would bother them. None dropped out.

To further ensure that no psychological harm was caused, Aronson and Mills explained the true nature of the experiment to subjects after the experiment. The subjects' reactions were typical:

None of the Ss expressed any resentment or annoyance at having been misled. In fact, the majority were intrigued by the experiment, and several returned at the end of the academic quarter to ascertain the result. (1959:179)

Except for those who are opposed to any degree of deception whatsoever in research (and there are some), the minimal deception in the Aronson and Mills experiment, coupled with the lack of any ascertainable risk to subjects, would meet most standards of ethical research.

Some social science laboratory experiments have involved much more deception and an apparently greater risk of harm to subjects. Needless to say, they have stimulated more questions about research ethics. Stanley Milgram's (1965) landmark experiments on obedience to authority raise most of the relevant issues. Milgram's research was stimulated by the success with which Germany's Nazi regime in the 1930s and 1940s enlisted the participation of ordinary citizens in unconscionable acts of terror and genocide. Milgram set out to identify through laboratory experiments the conditions under which ordinary citizens would resist authority figures' instructions to inflict pain on others.

Men recruited through newspaper ads in New Haven and Bridgeport, Connecticut, came to an experimental room. There they met another supposed volunteer and were told they were to participate in a study of the learning process. The subject then was designated to play the role of the teacher by a rigged "random" procedure, which left the other volunteer, who was actually a confederate of the researcher, to play the role of the student. The rest, as they say, is history. The supposed student went into another room for the rest of the experiment. The experimenter then instructed the teacher-subject to help the student memorize words by administering an electric shock (with a phony machine) every time the student failed to remember the correct word, increasing the voltage level for each successive shock. The researcher patiently encouraged the subject to continue the shocks even when they went beyond points on the machine dial marked clearly "Extreme Intensity Shock" and "Danger: Severe Shock."

Much to the surprise of Milgram and others, the great majority of subjects administered shocks beyond the danger level, even though the actors who were being shocked begged the subjects to stop, complained about a heart condition, and/or banged on the wall in feigned pain. The teacher-subjects were not oblivious to the pain they were supposedly causing: They trembled, groaned, broke into nervous laughter, and generally did not seem to want to go on. But in most cases they did go on.

Other variants of Milgram's basic experiment found that subjects' willingness to administer the shocks declined when the student was in the same room, when a nonauthoritative figure gave the instructions, or when another volunteer was present who protested against administering the shocks.

The research was a success: Milgram had identified at least some of the conditions in which ordinary people would resist authority. But was the research ethical? Thorough **debriefing** of each participant was used to lessen the probability of harm to subjects: Participants completed a questionnaire after the experiment; Milgram informed them about the experiments' purposes and methods and evaluated their reactions to the experiment. Participants were then interviewed after one year. No evidence of lingering trauma was uncovered, and almost all participants said they strongly supported the research.

Paul Reynolds (1979:130–133) makes several additional points:

■ The knowledge resulting from these experiments could be of substantial benefit to the general public if it were used to reduce conflict in organizations and to encourage individuals to question authority. On the other hand, there was some risk that organizational leaders might use the knowledge to manipulate members.

■ The research had no direct major benefits to participants while clearly producing much stress for individuals during the experiment and possibly some self-doubt afterward. However, the follow-up interviews indicated that research subjects had interpreted the experiment so as to avoid a harmful level of self-blame.

■ The research subjects were not a disadvantaged group, and their rights and welfare were taken adequately into account through careful monitoring of the experiment (it was stopped for subjects in extreme stress), full debriefing, and follow-up interviews.

Overall, Reynolds suggests, the costs of the research were minor relative to its benefits:

> The effects for the individuals cannot be considered benign: they suffered extreme stress. . . . But participants appeared to have received no lasting negative effects. . . . The value of the project can be judged only on the basis of its contribution to knowledge and possible contributions to the improvement of society. (1979:132–133)

Nevertheless, such an experiment is unlikely to be permitted today by an institutional review board adhering to current federal ethical guidelines. Given the potential for psychological harm beyond the risks of everyday living, current guidelines would require that informed consent be obtained from the subjects. Informed consent, in turn, would seem to require that subjects be told that another human being was not going to be harmed in the experiment. And since the experimental design required deceiving subjects about this precise point, informed consent could not have been carried out. Clearly, the need to adhere to ethical standards can conflict with the investigation of important social issues.

Selective Distribution of Benefits

Field experiments conducted to evaluate social programs also can involve issues of informed consent (Hunt, 1985:275–276). One ethical issue that is somewhat unique to field experiments is the **distribution of benefits**: How much are subjects harmed by the way benefits are distributed as part of the experiment? For example, Sherman and Berk's experiment, and its successors, required police to make arrests in domestic violence cases largely on the basis of a random process. When arrests were not made did the subjects' abused spouses suffer? Price et al. randomly assigned unemployed individuals who had volunteered for job-search help to an intensive program. Were the unemployed volunteers assigned to the comparison group at a big disadvantage?

Is it ethical to give some potentially advantageous or disadvantageous treatment to people on a random basis? Random distribution of benefits is justified when the researchers do not know whether some treatment actually is beneficial or not—and, of course, it is the goal of the experiment to find out. Chance is as reasonable a basis for distributing the treatment as any other. Also, if insufficient resources are available to fully fund a benefit for every eligible person, distribution of the benefit on the basis of chance to equally needy persons is ethically defensible.

The extent to which participation was voluntary varied in the field studies discussed in this chapter. Potential participants in the Price et al. study signed a detailed consent form in which they agreed to participate in a study involving random assignment to one of two types of job-search help, but researchers only accepted into the study persons who expressed equal preference for the job-search seminar and the mailed job materials (for those in the comparison condition).

Thus Price et al. avoided the problem of not acceding to subjects' preferences. It therefore doesn't seem at all unethical that the researchers gave treatment to only some of the subjects. As it turned out, subjects did benefit from the experimental treatment (the workshops). Now that the study has been conducted, government bodies will have a basis for expecting that tax dollars spent on job-search workshops for the unemployed will have a beneficial impact. If this knowledge results in more such programs, the benefit of the experiment will have been very considerable indeed.

Unlike Price et al.'s subjects, individuals who were the subjects of domestic violence complaints in the Sherman and Berk study had no choice about being arrested or receiving a warning, nor were they aware that they were in a research study.

Perhaps it seems unreasonable to let a random procedure determine how police resolve cases of domestic violence. And indeed it would be unreasonable if this procedure were a regular police practice. The Sherman and Berk experiment and its successors do pass ethical muster, however, when seen for what they were: a way of learning how to increase the effectiveness of police responses to this all-too-common crime. The initial Sherman and Berk findings encouraged police departments to make many more arrests for these crimes, and the follow-up studies resulted in a better understanding of when arrests are not likely to be effective. The implications of this research may be complex and difficult to implement, but the research provides a much stronger factual basis for policy development.

■ ■ ■ ■ ■ Conclusion

True experiments play two critical roles in social science research. First, they are the best research design for testing nomothetic causal hypotheses. Even when conditions preclude use of a true experimental design, many research designs can be improved by adding some experimental components. Second, true experiments also provide a comparison point for evaluating the ability of other research designs to achieve causally valid results.

In spite of their obvious strengths, true experiments are used infrequently to study many of the research problems that interest social scientists. There are three basic reasons: The experiments required to test many important hypotheses require far more resources than most social scientists have access to; most of the research problems of interest to social scientists simply are not amenable to experimental designs, for reasons ranging from ethical considerations to the limited possibilities for randomly assigning people to different conditions in the real world; and finally, the requirements of experimental design usually preclude large-scale studies and so limit generalizability to a degree that is unacceptable to many social scientists.

And just because it is possible to test a hypothesis with an experiment, it may not always be desirable to do so. When a social program is first being developed and its elements are in flux, it is not a good idea to begin a large evaluation study that cannot possibly succeed unless the program design remains constant. Researchers should wait until the program design stabilizes somewhat. It also does not make sense for evaluation researchers to test the impact of programs that cannot actually be implemented or that are unlikely to be implemented in the real world because of financial or political problems (Rossi & Freeman, 1989:304–307).

Even laboratory experiments are inadvisable when they do not test the real hypothesis of interest but test instead a limited version amenable to laboratory manipulation. The intersecting complexity of societies, social relationships, and social beings—of people and the groups to which they belong—is so great that it often defies reduction to the simplicity of a laboratory or restriction to the requirements of experimental design. Yet the virtues of experimental designs mean that they should always be considered when explanatory research is planned.

KEY TERMS

Before-and-after design
Comparison group
Compensatory rivalry
Contamination
Control group
Debriefing
Differential attrition
Distribution of benefits
Double-blind procedure
Endogenous change
Ex post facto control group design
Expectancies of experimental staff
Experimental group
External event
Evaluation research
Hawthorne effect
History effect
John Henry effect
Matching

Multiple group before-after design
Nonequivalent control group design
Placebo effect
Posttest
Pretest
Pretest-posttest control group design
Process analysis
Quasi-experimental design
Randomized comparative change
   design
Regression effects
Repeated measures panel design
Selection bias
Self-fulfilling prophecy
Time series design
Treatment
Treatment misidentification
True experiment

HIGHLIGHTS

■ The independent variable in an experiment is represented by a treatment or other intervention. Experiments have a comparison group that represents what subjects are like on the dependent variable without the treatment. In true experiments, subjects are assigned randomly to comparison groups.

■ Experimental research designs have three essential components: use of at least two groups of subjects for comparison, measurement of the change that occurs as a result of the experimental treatment, and use of random assignment. In addition, experiments may include identification of a causal mechanism and control over experimental conditions.

■ Random assignment of subjects to experimental and comparison groups eliminates systematic bias in group assignment. The odds of a difference between the experimental and comparison groups on the basis of chance can be calculated. It becomes very small for experiments with at least 30 subjects per group.

- Random assignment and random sampling both rely on a chance selection procedure, but their purposes differ. Random assignment involves placing predesignated subjects into two or more groups on the basis of chance; random sampling involves selecting subjects out of a larger population on the basis of chance. Matching of cases in the experimental and comparison groups is a poor substitute for randomization because identifying in advance all important variables on which to make the match is not possible. However, matching can improve the comparability of groups when it is used to supplement randomization.

- Causal conclusions derived from experiments can be invalid because of selection bias, endogenous change, the effects of external events, cross-group contamination, or treatment misidentification. In true experiments, randomization should eliminate selection bias and bias due to endogenous change. External events, cross-group contamination, and treatment misidentification can threaten the validity of causal conclusions in both true experiments and quasi-experiments.

- Process analysis can be used in experiments to identify how the treatment had (or didn't have) its effect—a matter of particular concern in field experiments. Treatment misidentification is less likely when process analysis is used.

- The generalizability of experimental results declines if the study conditions are artificial and the experimental subjects are unique. Field experiments are likely to produce more generalizable results than experiments conducted in the laboratory.

- Causal conclusions can be considered externally valid if they apply to all the subgroups in a study. When causal conclusions do not apply to all the subgroups, they are not generalizable to corresponding subgroups in the population—and thus they are not externally valid. Causal conclusions can also be considered externally invalid when they occur only under the experimental conditions.

- Subject deception is common in laboratory experiments and poses unique ethical issues. Researchers must weigh the potential harm to subjects and debrief subjects who have been deceived. In field experiments, a common ethical problem is selective distribution of benefits. Random assignment may be the fairest way of allocating treatment when treatment openings are insufficient for all eligible individuals and when the efficacy of the treatment is unknown.

EXERCISES

1. Read the original article reporting one of the experiments described in this chapter. Critique the article using as your guide the article review questions presented in Appendix C. Focus on the extent to which experimental conditions

were controlled and the causal mechanism was identified. Did inadequate control over conditions or inadequate identification of the causal mechanism make you feel uncertain about the causal conclusions?

2. Arrange with an instructor in a large class to conduct a multiple pretest-posttest study of the impact of watching a regularly scheduled class movie. Design a 10-question questionnaire to measure knowledge about the topics in the film. Administer this questionnaire shortly before and shortly after the film is shown and then again one week afterward. After scoring the knowledge tests, describe the immediate and long-term impact of the movie.

3. Design a laboratory experiment to determine whether watching a violent movie leads to more violent attitudes or actions. Describe how your design incorporates the five components of experiments. Evaluate how well your design meets the criteria for identifying a nomothetic cause.

4. Select a true experiment, perhaps from the *Journal of Experimental and Social Psychology* or the *Journal of Personality and Social Psychology* or from sources suggested in class. Diagram the experiment using the exhibits in this chapter as a model. Discuss the extent to which experimental conditions were controlled and the causal mechanism was identified. How confident can you be in the causal conclusions from the study, based on review of the threats to internal validity discussed in this chapter: selection bias, endogenous change, external events, contamination, and treatment misidentification? How generalizable do you think the study's results are to the population from which cases were selected? To specific subgroups in the study? How thoroughly do the researchers discuss these issues?

5. Repeat Exercise 4 with a quasi-experiment.

6. Critique the ethics of one of the experiments presented in this chapter. What specific rules do you think should guide researchers' decisions about subject deception and the selective distribution of benefits?

7. Volunteer for an experiment! Contact the psychology department, and ask about opportunities for participating in laboratory experiments. Discuss the experience with your classmates.

WEB EXERCISES

1. Go to Sociosite at

   http://www.pscw.uva.nl/sociosite

   Choose "Subject Areas."
   Choose a sociological subject area you are interested in.
   Find an example of research that has been done using experimental methods in this subject. Explain the experiment. Choose at least five of the "Key Terms" listed at the end of this chapter that are relevant to and incorporated in the research experiment you have located on the Web. Explain how each of the five key terms you have chosen plays a role in the research example you have found on the Web.

2. Design an experiment that involves the impact of Internet usage on human behavior. State your hypothesis and describe your experimental research design for testing the hypothesis.

3. Search the Web for examples of social science research that involve experiments using control groups and experimental groups. Find at least three examples, describe the experimental research design of each, and state the Web site at which each is located.

   Hint: Search for clusters of key words such as *social science, research, experiment, experimental design, experimental group, control group,* etc.

SPSS EXERCISES

Do the features of work influence attitudes about the work experience? We can test some hypothetical answers to this question with the GSS96 dataset, although not within the context of an experimental design.

1. Describe the feelings of working Americans about their jobs and economic rewards, based on their responses to questions about balancing work and family demands, their satisfaction with their finances, and their job satisfaction. Generate the frequencies as follows:

   STATISTICS
       SUMMARIZE
           FREQUENCIES balwkfam, satfin, satjob

2. Do these feelings vary with work features?
   a. Pose at least three hypotheses in which one of the work feelings variables is the dependent variable and the following three variables are the independent variables: earnings, number of employees in the workplace, and employment status (working full time as compared to part time or not working). Now test these hypotheses by comparing average scores on the attitudinal variables between categories of the independent variables:

      STATISTICS
          COMPARE MEANS
              MEANS
                  Dependent List: satfin, satjob, balwkfam
                  Independent List: rinc91d, local2, wrk2

   b. Which hypotheses appear to be supported? (Remember to review the distributions of the dependent variables [Q1a] to remind yourself what a higher average score indicates on each variable).

   c. If you already have had a statistics course, you will want to know whether the differences in mean values between the categories of the independent variables is statistically significant. You can test this with the t-test procedure, also available in the STATISTICS menu.

   d. Do you wonder whether the differences you have identified occur for particular subgroups of employees? You can examine the differences for particular subgroups with the MEANS procedure by repeating the menu commands you used in 2a for one comparison (choose one dependent variable and one independent variable), and then selecting

NESTED
Independent List: SEX

This procedure will show you the means of SATJOB for men and women who work for small and large firms. You can examine the effect of other variables by substituting their variable names for SEX.

3. Design a laboratory experiment to test one relationship that you have identified. You will need to think of a way to vary the values of the independent variable in a laboratory situation. (For example, you might set up work groups that differ in size.)

7   Survey Research

Survey Research in the Social Sciences
Attractive Features of Survey Research
  Versatility
  Efficiency
  Generalizability
The Omnibus Survey
A Cautionary Note

Questionnaire Development and Assessment
Maintain Consistent Focus
Build on Existing Instruments
Write Clear and Meaningful Questions
  Avoid Confusing Phrasing
  Minimize the Risk of Bias
  Avoid Making Disagreement Disagreeable
  Minimize Fence-Sitting and Floating
Refine and Test Questions
Add Interpretive Questions
Organize the Questionnaire Logically
Write a Persuasive Introduction or Cover Letter

Survey Designs
Mailed, Self-Administered Surveys
Group-Administered Surveys
Surveys by Telephone
  Reaching Sample Units
  Maximizing Response to Phone Surveys
In-Person Interviews
  Balancing Rapport and Control
  Maximizing Response to Interviews
A Comparison of Survey Designs

Ethical Issues in Survey Research
Confidentiality
Disclosure
Conclusion

The intersection between work and family life has changed considerably during the 20th century. For much of the industrial period, separation of work and family activities and a gender-based division of responsibilities were the norm. But we have seen in recent decades a dramatic increase in the proportion of two-income families, many more single-parent/single-earner families, more telecommuting and other work-at-home arrangements, and some changes in the household division of labor. Social scientists who seek to understand these changes in the social structure have had plenty to keep themselves busy.

Ohio State sociology professor Catherine Ross (1990) wanted to know how these changes shape people's sense of control and, in turn, how their sense of control affects feelings of depression, anxiety, and distress. To answer these questions, she proposed to the National Science Foundation a survey of adult Americans. In this chapter I will use her successful project to illustrate some key features of survey research, after an initial review of the reasons for using survey methods. I explain the major steps in questionnaire design and then consider the features of four types of survey, highlighting the unique problems attending each one and suggesting some possible solutions. I discuss ethics issues in the final section. By the chapter's end, you should be well on your way to becoming an informed consumer of survey reports and a knowledgeable developer of survey designs—as well as a more informed student of the relationships among work, family, and well-being.

Survey Research in the Social Sciences

Survey research involves the collection of information from a sample of individuals through their responses to questions. Ross turned to survey research for her study of social structure and well-being because it is an efficient method for systematically collecting data from a broad spectrum of individuals and social settings. As you probably have observed, a great many social scientists—as well as newspaper editors, political pundits, and marketing gurus—make the same methodological choice. In fact, surveys have become such a vital part of our society's social fabric that we cannot assess much of what we read in the newspaper or see on TV without having some understanding of this method of data collection (Converse, 1984).

Modern survey research methods were developed in the early and middle years of the 20th century (Lazarsfeld & Oberschall, 1965; Oberschall, 1972). Beginning in the 1920s, psychologists used surveys to test the abilities of students, employees, and army recruits. For their part, sociologists conducted a few ambitious attitude surveys of the general population, such as Emory S. Bogardus's study of race relations, which had a sample of 1,725 respondents (Converse, 1984). Industrial psychologists began to rely on surveys to study employee morale and other attitudes. Psychologist Paul F. Lazarsfeld studied consumers' reactions to particular products before moving into sociology and becoming one of the discipline's leading survey proponents (Converse, 1984).

Political needs also stimulated the growth of survey research. Professional polling became a regular fixture after the 1936 presidential election: Professional polling firms correctly predicted that President Franklin Delano Roosevelt would win reelection, but the poorly designed *Literary Digest* poll led to an infamous forecast that challenger Alfred M. Landon would win (see Chapter 4). The U.S. Bureau of the Census began to supplement its 10-year census with more frequent surveys of population samples to monitor income and other economic variables. Government-funded sociologists used surveys to measure popular support for military intervention in the years leading up to World War II and then surveyed soldiers during the war about their morale and other concerns (Converse, 1984).

Since the early days of survey research, professional survey organizations have provided a base of support for social science researchers affiliated with universities. The development of electronic computers also aided the growth of survey research, allowing great increases in the speed and accuracy with which data could be processed and reported. Surveys soon became the most popular research method in sociology. Around 1950, just under a quarter of sociology journal articles used survey data; by about 1965, the proportion had risen to 55%. As Exhibit 7.1 shows, a similar transformation occurred in economics and social psychology, although in these disciplines survey research remained somewhat less popular than other research methods; in social psychology, experiments continued to be the most common method (Presser, 1985).

Exhibit 7.1 **Growth in the Popularity of Survey Research**

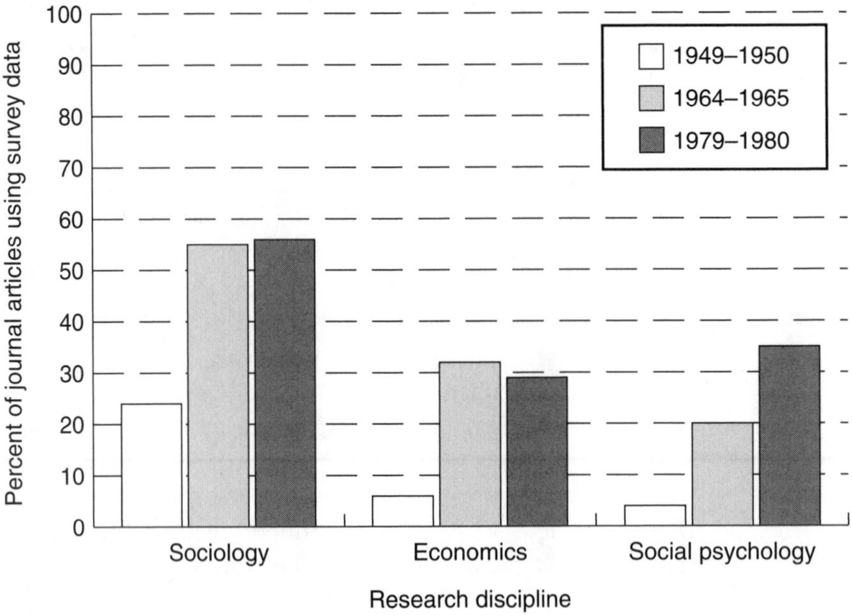

Source: Data from Presser, 1985:96.

Attractive Features of Survey Research

Regardless of its scope, survey research owes its continuing popularity to three features: versatility, efficiency, and generalizability.

Versatility

First and foremost is the versatility of survey methods. Although a survey is not the ideal method for testing all hypotheses or learning about every social process, a well-designed survey can enhance our understanding of just about any social issue. Ross's survey covered a range of topics about work and health, and there is hardly any other topic of interest to social scientists that has not been studied at some time with survey methods. Politicians campaigning for election use surveys, as do businesses marketing a product, governments assessing community needs, agencies monitoring program effectiveness, and lawyers seeking to buttress claims of discrimination or select favorable juries.

Efficiency

Surveys also are popular because data can be collected from many people at relatively low cost and, depending on the survey design, relatively quickly.

Catherine Ross contracted with the University of Illinois Survey Research Laboratory for her 1990 telephone survey of 2,000 adult Americans. SRL estimated that the survey would incur direct costs of $60,823—only $30.41 per respondent—and take five to six months to complete. Large mailed surveys cost even less, about $10 to $15 per potential respondent, although the costs can increase greatly when intensive follow-up efforts are made. Surveys of the general population using personal interviews are much more expensive, with costs ranging from about $100 per potential respondent for studies in a limited geographical area to $300 or more when lengthy travel or repeat visits are needed to connect with respondents (Floyd J. Fowler, personal communication, January 7, 1998, Center for Survey Research, University of Massachusetts–Boston; see also Dillman, 1982; Groves & Kahn, 1979). As you would expect, phone surveys are the quickest survey method, which accounts for their popularity in political polling.

Surveys also are efficient because many variables can be measured without substantially increasing the time or cost. Mailed questionnaires can include up to 10 pages of questions before respondents begin to balk (and before more postage must be added). In-person interviews can be much longer, taking more than an hour; for example, the 1991 General Social Survey included 196 questions, many with multiple parts, and was 75 pages long. The upper limit for phone surveys seems to be about 45 minutes.

Of course, these efficiencies can be attained only in a place with reliable communications infrastructure (Labaw, 1980:xiii–xiv). A reliable postal service, which is required for mail surveys, has generally been available in the United States—although residents of the Bronx, New York, have recently complained that delivery of local first-class mail often takes two weeks or more, almost ruling out mail surveys (Purdy, 1994). Phone surveys can be effective in the United States because 95% of households have phones (Czaja & Blair, 1995).

Also important to efficiency are the many survey organizations that provide the trained staff and the proper equipment for conducting high-quality surveys.

Generalizability

Survey methods lend themselves to probability sampling from large populations. Thus survey research is very appealing when sample generalizability is a central research goal. In fact, survey research is often the only means available for developing a representative picture of the attitudes and characteristics of a large population.

Surveys also are the method of choice when cross-population generalizability is a key concern, because they allow a range of social contexts and subgroups to be sampled. The consistency of relationships can then be examined across the various subgroups.

The Omnibus Survey

Most surveys are directed at a specific research question. In contrast, an **omnibus survey** covers a range of topics of interest to different social scientists. It has multiple sponsors or is designed to generate data useful to a broad segment of the social science community rather than to answer a particular research question.

One of sociology's most successful omnibus surveys is the General Social Survey (GSS) of the National Opinion Research Center at the University of Chicago. After taking a teaching position at Dartmouth College, James A. Davis, who had worked at the National Opinion Research Center for 10 years, was dismayed to discover how difficult it was for faculty in small schools to obtain worthwhile survey data. Starting in 1972, the National Science Foundation agreed to fund the GSS as an annual, publicly available national survey on topics of general interest to sociologists. In 1992 the GSS changed to a biennial schedule.

Today, the GSS is administered as a 90-minute interview to a probability sample of almost 3,000 Americans. It includes more than 500 questions about background characteristics and opinions, with an emphasis on social stratification, race relations, family issues, social control, and morale. It explores political views, work experiences, social ties, news sources, and views on law, health, and religion. Questions and topic areas are chosen by a board of overseers drawn from the ranks of sociology's best survey researchers.

The core of the GSS is a set of questions asked in each survey. Other questions are repeated only every other time, and some questions are added in single- or multiyear supplements paid for by special grants. Since 1988, most of the questions have been asked in each survey, but many of them have been asked of only a randomly selected subset of respondents. This **split-ballot design** allows the inclusion of more questions without increasing the survey's cost. The split-ballot design also allows experiments on the effect of question wording: Different forms of the same question are included in the split-ballot subsets.

What is most remarkable about the GSS is its availability. The survey datasets are distributed at cost to any interested individual (only $95 for a single year's dataset), and most universities obtain the GSS each year. The data are then available to faculty and students free of charge. By 1992, over 2,800 articles, scholarly papers, books, and dissertations had used GSS data. Many instructors use GSS data in methods, statistics, and other courses (Davis & Smith, 1992; National Opinion Research Center, 1992).

Other survey datasets are made available for use by scholars through the Inter-University Consortium for Political and Social Research (more de-

Exhibit 7.2   **The Sharing of Data (Ross, 1990)**

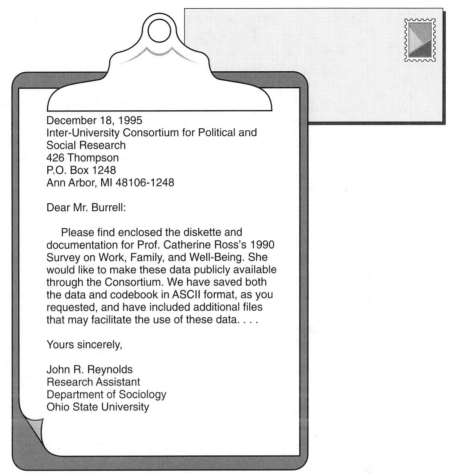

December 18, 1995
Inter-University Consortium for Political and
Social Research
426 Thompson
P.O. Box 1248
Ann Arbor, MI 48106-1248

Dear Mr. Burrell:

Please find enclosed the diskette and
documentation for Prof. Catherine Ross's 1990
Survey on Work, Family, and Well-Being. She
would like to make these data publicly available
through the Consortium. We have saved both
the data and codebook in ASCII format, as you
requested, and have included additional files
that may facilitate the use of these data. . . .

Yours sincerely,

John R. Reynolds
Research Assistant
Department of Sociology
Ohio State University

tails about this are in Chapter 9). For example, Ross made her 1990 survey dataset available in this way (see Exhibit 7.2).

In addition to singing the praises of the GSS, I must point out the deficiency of the omnibus approach: the limited depth that can be achieved in any one substantive area. In some years the GSS gets around this problem by going into greater depth in a particular area. For example, the 1991 GSS included many questions about work experiences and related attitudes. For many research questions, the GSS provides more than enough information. But the best way to get survey data about a particular topic is still the survey developed around that topic alone.

A Cautionary Note

It might be said that surveys are too easy to conduct. Organizations and individuals often decide that a survey would help to solve some important problem because it seems so easy to prepare a form with some questions and send it out. But without careful attention to sampling, measurement, and overall survey design, the effort is likely to be a flop. Such flops are too common for comfort, and the responsible survey researcher must take the time to design surveys properly and to convince sponsoring organizations that this time is worth the effort (Turner & Martin, 1984:68).

The fact that today most presidential election polls accurately predict the outcome shows how well surveys can gauge popular sentiment. But when the reality that is measured is such a complex moving target as in election campaigns, we need to proceed with caution. For example, in the 1988 race between George Bush and Michael Dukakis, 14 national voter preference polls were conducted in August alone (70 between May and October). One August poll showed Dukakis ahead of Bush by 19 percentage points, one showed Bush ahead of Dukakis by 5 points, and the rest of the polls varied widely between these two extremes. (Bush actually won by 3 points.)

Andrew Kohut (1988), president of the Gallup polling organization, has identified many of the reasons for the discrepancies in such election polls:

■ Different questions may be used in different surveys to measure preferences.

■ Question order varies from poll to poll. Support for a more liberal candidate may increase, for example, if the question about whom the voter will choose is preceded by questions asking about an unpopular policy associated with a conservative government.

■ Call-back procedures differ. Some pollsters stress quick results and sacrifice follow-up calls to locate nonrespondents. They therefore miss many potential voters.

■ Polling organizations differ in their means of predicting who will not vote and who does not really have a preference and in their policies about including these persons in the poll.

■ Respondents' lack of knowledge about a candidate and confusion about the political issues being debated may lead to very unreliable polling results—particularly early in a political campaign season, when opinions are less well formed.

■ Candidates may derive very temporary benefits from their party's nominating convention or from other major national events. Polls conducted just after such events may give a misleading impression of a candidate's strength.

■ Sampling error can produce different findings just on the basis of chance. Although we can determine the degree of confidence that can be placed in a sample estimate, we have no way of knowing for sure whether the result of a particular survey based on a random sample is far off the mark because of sampling error.

The general conclusion: Differences in how questions are asked, how the sample is drawn, and when the poll is conducted can result in what appear to be inconsistent results. Thus informed consumers of election polls focus on trends over time and averages across different polls rather than on the results of a particular poll. Nonelection surveys tend to be less sensitive to these problems, but public sentiment about social issues from welfare reform to international politics may change so rapidly that these potential difficulties can never be ignored.

■ ■ ■ ■   ## Questionnaire Development and Assessment

The **questionnaire** (or **interview schedule,** as it's often called in interview-based studies) is the central feature of the survey process. Without a well-designed questionnaire tailored to the study's purposes, survey researchers have little hope of achieving their research goals.

Questionnaire   The survey instrument containing the questions in a self-administered survey.

Interview schedule   The survey instrument containing the questions asked by the interviewer in an in-person or phone survey.

The way a questionnaire should be designed varies with the specific survey method used and with other particulars of a survey project. There can be no precise formula for a well-designed questionnaire. Nonetheless, some key principles should guide the design of any questionnaire, and some systematic procedures should be considered for refining it. The questionnaire developed for Ross's (1990) study of the psychological effects of changes in household structure illustrates some of the following principles and procedures.

Maintain Consistent Focus

A survey (with the exception of an omnibus survey) should be guided by a clear conception of the research problem under investigation and the population to be sampled. Does the study seek to describe some phenomenon in detail, to explain some behavior, or to explore some type of social relationship? Until the research objective is formulated clearly, survey design cannot begin. Throughout the process of questionnaire design, this objective should be the primary basis for making decisions about what to include and exclude, what to emphasize or treat in a cursory fashion. Moreover, the questionnaire should be viewed as an integrated whole, in which each section and every question serves a clear purpose related to the study's objective and is a complement to other sections or questions.

In her "final summary report," Ross (1989) stated her objective clearly: "to develop and test a theory that links women's and men's objective position at home and in the labor force to their subjective sense of control over life, and in turn to emotional and physical well-being." She then included only questions relevant to these objectives: "I will develop a questionnaire with instruments to measure conditions of work and home, sociodemographic characteristics such as employment and marital status, socioeconomic status, and age; the sense of control; and depression, anxiety, anger, and other psychological outcomes." The first question in her interview asked about the respondent's employment status and was followed immediately by questions about work tasks and reactions to work. Although her 20-page questionnaire contained a total of 63 questions, each one related to the issues that her respondents were told the study was about.

Surveys often include too many irrelevant questions and fail to include questions that, the researchers realize later, are crucial. One way to ensure that possibly relevant questions are asked is to use questions suggested by prior research, theory, or experience or by experts (including participants) who are knowledgeable about the setting under investigation. Of course, not even the best researcher can anticipate every question that hindsight will suggest would have been worthwhile nor those that are worthless. Researchers tend to try to avoid "missing something" by erring on the side of extraneous questions (Labaw, 1980:40).

Build on Existing Instruments

If another researcher already has designed a set of questions to measure a key concept in your study, that existing set of questions can be termed a **survey instrument**, and evidence from previous surveys indicates that these questions provide a good measure of the concept, then by all means use that instrument. Resources like Delbert Miller's (1991) *Handbook of Research Design and Social Measurement* can give you many ideas about existing instruments; your literature review at the start of a research project should be an even better source. Catherine Ross drew many of her measures from an extensive body of prior research (including her own). She measured feelings of distress with the well-established Center for Epidemiological Studies' Depression scale (see Chapter 3), self-esteem with a measure developed by Morris Rosenberg (1965), and learned helplessness with Martin Seligman's (1975) scale.

But there is a trade-off here. Questions used previously may not concern quite the right concept or may not be appropriate in some ways to your population. Ross (1990:8) even used the need to develop new measures for the study of work and family issues as a selling point in her research proposal: "Part of the proposed project will be to refine, modify, and develop measures, in addition to reviewing literature on already developed measures." Together with John Mirowsky (Mirowsky & Ross, 1991), she developed a new measure of the sense of control, the central concept in her 1990 survey. So even though using a previously designed and well-regarded instrument may reassure other social scientists, it may not really be appropriate for your own specific survey. A good rule of thumb is to use a previously designed instrument if it measures the concept of concern to you and if you have no clear reason for thinking it is inappropriate with your survey population. You can always solicit the opinions of other researchers before making a final decision.

Write Clear and Meaningful Questions

All hope for achieving measurement validity is lost unless survey questions are clear and convey the intended meaning to respondents. You may be thinking that you ask people questions all the time and have no trouble understanding the answers you receive; maybe it doesn't seem that writing clear and meaningful questions would be difficult. But consider just a few of the differences between everyday conversations and standardized surveys:

■ Survey questions must be asked of many people, not just one.

■ The same survey question must be used with each person, not tailored to the specifics of a given conversation.

■ Survey questions must be understood in the same way by people who differ in many ways.

■ You will not be able to rephrase a survey question if someone doesn't understand it.

■ Survey respondents don't know you and so can't be expected to catch the nuances of expression that your friends are used to.

These features make a survey very different from natural conversation and make question writing a challenging and important task for survey researchers.

Question writing for a particular survey might begin with a brainstorming session or a review of previous surveys. Then whatever questions are being considered must be systematically evaluated and refined. Even a survey instrument that has already been used extensively and evaluated positively must be put to the test. Questions that were clear and meaningful to one population may not be so to another. Nor can you assume that a question used in a previously published study was carefully evaluated.

The way questions are worded can have a great effect on the way they are answered—and hence the results of the survey.

Avoid Confusing Phrasing

Good grammar is a basic requirement for clear questions. Clearly and simply phrased questions are most likely to have the same meaning for different respondents. So be brief and to the point.

In addition, avoid vagueness: Questions about thoughts and feelings will be more reliable if they refer to specific times or events (Turner & Martin, 1984:300). Usually a question like "On how many days did you read the newspaper in the last week?" produces more reliable answers than one like "How often do you read the newspaper? (frequently, sometimes, never)." In her survey, Ross (1990) sensibly asked the question "Do you currently smoke 7 or more cigarettes a week?" rather than "Do you smoke?" And don't make unreasonable demands of your respondents' memories. One survey asked, "During the past 12 months, about how many times did you see or talk to a medical doctor?" According to their written health records, respondents forgot 60% of their doctor visits (Goleman, 1993b:C11). So limit questions about specific past experiences to, at most, the past month, unless your focus is on major events that are unlikely to have been forgotten.

A sure way to muddy the meaning of a question is to use double negatives: "Do you disagree that there should not be a tax increase?" Respondents have a hard time figuring out which response matches their sentiments. Such errors can easily be avoided with minor wording changes, but even experienced survey researchers can make this mistake unintentionally, perhaps while trying to avoid some other wording problem. For instance, in a survey commissioned by the American Jewish Committee, the Roper polling organization wrote a question about the Holocaust that was carefully worded to be neutral and value-free: "Does it seem possible or does it seem impossible to you that the Nazi extermination of the Jews never happened?" Among a representative sample of adult Americans, 22% answered it was possible the extermination never happened (Kifner, 1994:A12). Many Jewish leaders and politicians were stunned, wondering how one in five Americans could be so misinformed. But a careful reading of the question reveals how confusing it is: Choosing "possible," the seemingly positive response, means that you don't believe the Holocaust happened. In fact, the Gallup organization then rephrased the question to avoid the double negative, giving a brief definition of the Holocaust and then asking, "Do you doubt that the Holocaust actually happened or not?" Only 9% responded that they doubted it happened. When a wider range of response choices was given, only 2.9% said that the Holocaust "definitely" or "probably" did not happen.

So-called **double-barreled questions** are also guaranteed to produce uninterpretable results because they actually ask two questions but allow only one answer. For example, during the Watergate scandal, Gallup poll results indicated that, when the question was "Do you think President Nixon should be impeached and compelled to leave the presidency, or not?" only about a third of Americans supported impeaching President Richard M. Nixon. But when the Gallup organization changed the question to ask respondents if they "think there is enough evidence of possible wrongdoing in the case of President Nixon to bring him to trial before the Senate, or not," over half answered yes. Apparently the first, "double-barreled" version of the question confused support for impeaching Nixon—putting him on trial before the Senate—with concluding that he was guilty before he had had a chance to defend himself (Kagay & Elder, 1992:E5).

It is also important to identify clearly what kind of information each question is to obtain. Some questions focus on attitudes, or what people say they want or how they feel. Some questions focus on beliefs, or what people think is true. Some questions focus on behavior, or what people do. And some questions focus on attributes, or what people are like or have experienced (Dillman, 1978:79–118; Gordon, 1992). Rarely can a single question effectively address more than one of these dimensions at a time.

Whichever type of information a question is designed to obtain, be sure it is asked of only the respondents who may have that information. If you include a question about job satisfaction in a survey of the general population, first ask respondents whether they have a job. These **filter questions** create **skip patterns.** For example, respondents who answer no to one question are directed to skip ahead to another question, but respondents who answer yes go on to the **contingent question.** Skip patterns should be indicated clearly with arrows or other marks in the questionnaire as demonstrated in Exhibit 7.3.

Minimize the Risk of Bias

Specific words in survey questions should not trigger biases, unless that is the researcher's conscious intent. Biased or loaded words and phrases tend to produce misleading answers. For example, a 1974 survey found that 18% of respondents supported sending U.S. troops "if a situation like Vietnam were to develop in another part of the world." But when the question was reworded to mention sending troops to "stop a communist takeover"—"communist takeover" being a loaded phrase—favorable responses rose to 33% (Schuman & Presser, 1981:285).

Responses can also be biased when response alternatives do not reflect the full range of sentiment on an issue. When people pick a response choice,

Exhibit 7.3 **Filter Questions and Skip Patterns**

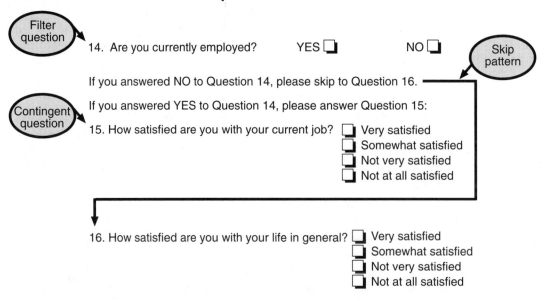

they seem to be influenced by where they are placing themselves relative to the other response choices. For example, the Detroit Area Study (Turner & Martin, 1984:252) asked the following question: "People feel differently about making changes in the way our country is run. In order to keep America great, which of these statements do you think is best?" When the only response choices were "We should be very cautious of making changes" and "We should be free to make changes," only 37% said that we should be free to make changes. However, when a response choice was added that suggested we should "constantly" make changes, 24% picked that response and another 32% chose the "free to make changes" response, for a total of 56% who seemed open to making changes in the way our country is run (Turner & Martin 1984:252).

To minimize biased responses, researchers may test reactions to the phrasing of a question. When Ross (1990) was seeking to determine respondents' interests in household work rather than formal employment, she took special care to phrase her questions in a balanced, unbiased way. For example, she asked: "If you could choose, would you rather do the kind of work people do on jobs or the kind of work that is done around the house?" Her response options were "Jobs," "House," "Both," "Neither," "Don't care," and "Don't know." She could easily have biased the distribution of responses to this question by referring to housework as "the kind of work that women traditionally have done around the house." The explicit gender-typing would probably have made men less likely to choose housework as their preference. Note that, if Ross's purpose had been to find out how men respond to explicitly gender-linked roles, this wording would have been appropriate. Bias can only be defined in terms of the concept that the question is designed to measure.

Avoid Making Disagreement Disagreeable

People often tend to "agree" with a statement just to avoid seeming disagreeable. Questions and response choices should be phrased to reduce this tendency, with the goal of making each response option seem as socially approved, as "agreeable," as every other. You can see the impact of this human tendency in a 1974 Michigan Survey Research Center survey that asked who was to blame for crime and lawlessness in the United States. When one question stated that individuals were more to blame than social conditions, 60% of the respondents agreed. But when the question was rephrased so respondents were asked, in a balanced fashion, whether individuals or social conditions were more to blame, only 46% chose individuals.

You may also gain a more realistic assessment of respondents' sentiment by adding to a question a counterargument in favor of one side to balance an argument in favor of the other side. Thus, you should ask in an employee survey whether employees should be required to join the union or be able to make their own decision about joining rather than just asking whether employees should be required to join the union. In one survey, 10% more respondents said they favored mandatory union membership when the counterargument was left out than when it was included. It is reassuring to know, however, that this approach does not change the distribution of answers to questions about which people have very strong beliefs (Schuman & Presser, 1981:186).

Minimize Fence-Sitting and Floating

Two related problems in question writing also stem from people's desire to choose an acceptable answer. There is no uniformly correct solution to these problems; researchers have to weigh the alternatives in light of the concept to be measured and whatever they know about the respondents.

Fence-sitters, people who see themselves as being neutral, may skew the results if you force them to choose between opposites. In most cases, about 10% to 20% of such respondents—those who do not have strong feelings on an issue—will choose an explicit middle, neutral alternative (Schuman & Presser,1981:161–178). Adding an explicit neutral response option is appropriate when you want to find out who is a fence-sitter.

Even more people can be termed **floaters**: respondents who choose a substantive answer when they really don't know. A third of the public will provide an opinion on a proposed law that they know nothing about if they are asked for their opinion in a closed-ended survey question that does not

Exhibit 7.4   **The Effect of Floaters on Public Opinion Polls**

Responses to "Are government leaders smart?"

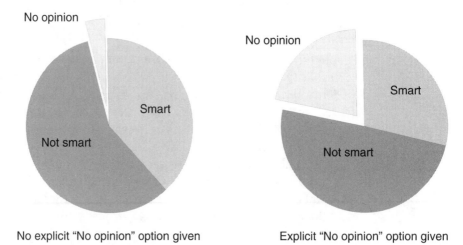

No explicit "No opinion" option given   Explicit "No opinion" option given

Source: Data from Schuman & Presser, 1981:121.

include "Don't know" as an explicit response choice. However, 90% of these persons will select the "Don't know" response if they are explicitly given that option. On average, offering an explicit response option increases the "Don't know" responses by about a fifth (Schuman & Presser, 1981:113–160).

Exhibit 7.4 depicts the results of one study that tested the effect of giving respondents an explicit "No opinion" option to the question "Are government leaders smart?" Notice how many more people chose "No opinion" when they were given that choice than when their only explicit options were "Smart" and "Not smart."

The "Don't know" option has been a bone of contention for political pollsters. The debate heated up after the 1992 election, in which come-from-behind candidate Bill Clinton raced past President George Bush after the Democratic convention, but then appeared to be losing his lead just before the election. David W. Moore, director of the University of New Hampshire's Survey Center, argued in a *New York Times* article that the last-minute changes showed that the "Undecided" category was being undercounted. Only 10% of the voters were classified as undecided by the major pollsters, but Moore reminded readers that "there are many undecided voters who play our polling game—who specify a candidate they might choose 'if the election were held today' but who have no commitment to that candidate beyond the time of the interview" (Moore, 1992:E15).

The accepted solution is to use **forced-choice questions**, without a "Don't know" option. Just after President Clinton's victory, Frank Newport, editor in chief of the Gallup poll, defended pollsters' efforts to get all prospective voters to declare a preferred candidate:

> It would not be very instructive for pollsters . . . to allow large numbers of voters to claim they are undecided all through the election season. We would miss the dynamics of change, we would be unable to tell how well candidates were doing in response to events, and publicly released polls would be out of synchronization with private, campaign polls. (Newport, 1992:A28)

Because there are so many floaters in the typical survey sample, the decision to include an explicit "Don't know" option for a question is important. This decision is particularly important with surveys of less-educated populations because "Don't know" responses are offered more often by those with less education—except for questions that are really impossible to decipher, to which more educated persons are likely to say they don't know (Schuman & Presser, 1981:113–146). Unfortunately, the inclusion of an explicit "Don't know" response choice leads some people who do have a preference to take the easy way out and choose "Don't know."

Including an open-ended question in which respondents are asked to discuss their opinions (or reasons for having no opinion) can at least shed some light on why some persons choose "Don't know" in response to a particular question (Smith, 1984). And researchers who use in-person or telephone interviews (rather than self-administered questionnaires) may get around the dilemma somewhat by reading the response choices without a middle or "Don't know" alternative but recording a noncommittal response if it is offered. Ross's (1990) questionnaire for her survey on the changing U.S. household included the following example:

```
If you could choose, would you rather do the kind of
work people do on jobs or the kind of work that is done
around the house?
Jobs ........................................... 1
House .......................................... 2
BOTH ........................................... 3
NEITHER ........................................ 4
DON'T CARE ..................................... 5
DON'T KNOW ..................................... 8
```

Refine and Test Questions

Adhering to the preceding question-writing guidelines will go a long way toward producing a useful questionnaire. However, simply asking what appear to you to be clear questions does not ensure that people have a consistent understanding of what you are asking. You need some external feedback—the more of it the better.

One important form of feedback results from simply discussing the questionnaire content with others. Persons who should be consulted include other researchers, key figures in the locale or organization to be surveyed (such as elected representatives, company presidents, and community leaders), and some individuals from the population to be sampled. Run your list of variables and specific questions by such figures whenever you have a chance. Reviewing the relevant literature to find results obtained with similar surveys and comparable questions is also an important step to take, if you haven't already conducted such a review before writing your questions.

Another increasingly popular form of feedback comes from guided discussions among potential respondents, called focus groups, to check for consistent understanding of terms and to identify the range of events or experiences about which people will be asked to report. By listening and observing the focus group discussions, researchers can validate their assumptions about what level of vocabulary is appropriate and what people are going to be reporting (Fowler, 1995).

Professional survey researchers have also developed a technique for evaluating questions called the **cognitive interview** (Fowler, 1995). Although the specifics vary, the basic approach is to ask people test questions, then probe with follow-up questions to learn how they understood the question and what their answers mean.

No questionnaire should be considered ready for use until it has been pretested. Try answering the questionnaire yourself, and then revise it. Try it out on some colleagues or other friends, and then revise it. Then select a small sample of individuals from the population you are studying or one very similar to it, and try out the questionnaire on them. Audiotape the test interviews for later review, or include in the pretest version of a written questionnaire some space for individuals to add comments on each key question.

Review the distribution of responses to each question, listen to the audiotapes, or read all the comments, and then code what you heard or read to identify problems in question wording or delivery. Revise any questions that respondents do not seem to interpret as you had intended or that are not working well for other reasons. By design, Ross's survey of U.S. households included systematic pretesting, as Johnny Blair noted in a letter to Ross summarizing the procedure to be used:

> Before being used for data collection, the survey questionnaire will be given a pretest consisting of 30 interviews conducted in Illinois. The pretest will be used to evaluate the adequacy of the questionnaire, to try out systematically all the various procedures in the main survey, to

establish and evaluate codes for questionnaire responses, and to gauge the length of the interview. Only upon the basis of the diagnostic information obtained in the pretest interviews will the fully refined version of the survey questionnaire be prepared, ready for administration in the full-scale survey. (Personal communication, April 10, 1989)

Add Interpretive Questions

A survey researcher can also try to understand what respondents mean by their responses after the fact—that is, by including additional questions in the survey itself. Adding such **interpretive questions** after key survey questions is always a good idea, but it is of utmost importance when the questions in a survey have not been pretested.

An example from a study of people with motor-vehicle driving violations illustrates the importance of interpretive questions:

> When asked whether their emotional state affected their driving at all, respondents would reply that their emotions had very little effect on their driving habits. Then, when asked to describe the circumstances surrounding their last traffic violation, respondents typically replied, "I was mad at my girlfriend," or "I had a quarrel with my wife," or "We had a family quarrel," or "I was angry with my boss." (Labaw, 1980:71)

Were these respondents lying in response to the first question? Probably not. More likely, they simply didn't interpret their own behavior in terms of general concepts like "emotional state." But their responses to the first question were likely to be misinterpreted without the further detail provided by answers to the second.

Consider five issues when you develop interpretive questions—or when you review survey results and need to consider what the answers tell you:

- *What do the respondents know?* Answers to many questions about current events and government policies are almost uninterpretable without also learning what the respondents know. In studies like Ross's, however, which focused on personal experiences and feelings, questions assessing knowledge are not so necessary.

- *What relevant experiences do the respondents have?* Such experiences undoubtedly color the responses. For example, the meaning of opinions about crime and punishment may be quite different for those who have been crime victims themselves and those who have not been. Ross had to begin her survey with a question about the respondent's current employment status, which determined whether many of the work-related questions would be relevant. Similarly, her questions about child care were preceded by questions to determine whether the respondent had children.

■ *How consistent are the respondents' attitudes, and do they express some larger perspective or ideology?* An employee who seeks more wages because she believes that all employer profits result from exploitation is expressing a different sentiment from one who seeks more wages because she really wants a more expensive car with which to impress her neighbors.

■ *Are respondents' actions consistent with their expressed attitudes?* We probably should interpret differently the meaning of expressed support for gender equality from married men who help with household chores and those who do not. Questions about behavior may also provide a better way to assess orientations than questions about attitudes. Labaw (1980: 100) points out that "the respondent's actual purchase of life insurance is a more accurate representation of what he believes about his life insurance needs than anything he might say in response to a direct question" about whether it is important to carry life insurance. In her study, Ross eschewed attitudinal questions about household roles altogether, instead focusing on behaviors—in such questions as "What percentage [of the housework] do you do?" and "Who makes decisions in your household?"

■ *How strongly are the attitudes held?* The attitudes of those with stronger beliefs are more likely to be translated into action than attitudes that are held less strongly. Just knowing the level of popular support for, say, abortion rights or gun control thus fails to capture the likelihood of people to march or petition their representatives on behalf of the cause; we also need to know what proportion of supporters feel strongly (Schuman & Presser, 1981:ch.9). Thus, rather than just asking if respondents favored or opposed their spouse having a job, Ross (1990) used the following question and response choices to measure attitude strength in her telephone survey:

```
How do you feel about your (spouse/partner) having a
job? (Are you/Would you be). . .
    Strongly in favor, ..........................1
    Somewhat in favor, .........................2
    Somewhat opposed, or .......................3
    Strongly opposed? ..........................4
    MIXED ......................................5
    DOES NOT CARE/UP TO HIM/HER ................6
```

Organize the Questionnaire Logically

Once the basic topics and specific variables for a questionnaire have been identified, they can be sorted into categories (which may become separate sections), and listed in tentative order. Ross's (1990) questionnaire contained the following four sections: sociodemographic questions, social-psychological questions, questions about health and well-being, and questions about work and employment.

Throughout the question-writing process, the grouping of variables in sections and the ordering of questions within sections need to be adjusted. These adjustments will in turn require changes in the specific questions, in an iterative process that leads to an increasingly polished, coherent questionnaire.

Question order is important because it can influence the meaning attached to specific questions. A book edited by Charles Turner and Elizabeth Martin (1984) provides a good example to illustrate this point. Responses in the 1973 General Social Survey to a question about general happiness appeared to indicate a sharp increase from the preceding year (about 7 percentage points). But this increase occurred only for respondents who were married (their general happiness increased by 10%). As it turned out, this change did not reflect an increase in the happiness of married persons at all but instead a change in the placement of the happiness question in the questionnaire. In 1973, the GSS included a question about marital happiness just before the general happiness question; in 1972 it had not. Apparently the marital happiness question put married respondents in a good frame of mind when they answered the next question on general happiness.

A similar phenomenon has been observed with questions about abortion. When a sample of the general public was asked, "Do you think it should be possible for a pregnant woman to obtain a legal abortion if she is married and does not want any more children?" 58% said yes. However, when this abortion question was preceded by one asking whether the respondent would allow abortion of a defective fetus, only 40% said yes to the more permissive question. Clearly the first question altered respondents' frame of reference, perhaps by making abortion simply to avoid having more children seem frivolous compared to the problem of having a defective fetus (Turner & Martin, 1984:135).

Both these examples illustrate the potential impact of question order on the answers given. This potential is greatest when two or more questions concern the same issue or closely related issues, as in the example of the two questions about abortion, so that asking one question affects reactions to the next question. The impact of question order also tends to be greater for general, summary-type questions, as with the general happiness example (Schuman & Presser, 1981:23–77).

There is no real "cure" for this potential problem, although the problem may at least be identified if the question order is reversed on a subset of the questionnaires (the so-called split-ballot technique). What is most important is to be aware of the potential for problems due to question order and to evaluate carefully the likelihood of their occurrence in any particular questionnaire. Those who report survey results should mention, at least in a footnote, the order in which key questions were asked when more than one such question was used (Labaw, 1980).

Questionnaires should conform to several other organizational guidelines as well:

- Major topic divisions within the questionnaire should be organized in separate sections, each of which is introduced with a brief statement.

- Instructions should be used liberally to minimize respondent confusion. Instructions should explain how each type of question is to be answered (such as by circling a number or writing a response)—in a neutral way that isn't likely to influence responses. This type of instruction is particularly important with groups of questions having standard answers laid out in what is called a "matrix format," with the same set of response choices next to each question, because many respondents do not realize that they should circle one response on each line. Instructions also should route respondents through skip patterns.

- Instructions may also be used to clarify for respondents why some information is included in the questionnaire (such as the implicit instruction to skip a set-off box of lines that are "For coding purposes only").

- The questionnaire should look attractive and easy to complete. There should be substantial open space; resist the temptation to cram as many questions as possible onto one page. Response choices should be printed in a different format and location from the questions (such as in all capital letters down the middle of the page).

- Response choices should be designated by numbers to facilitate coding and data entry after the questionnaire is completed.

Exhibit 7.5 contains portions of the questionnaire Ross used in her phone survey of contemporary families. This page illustrates three of the features that I have just reviewed: numeric designation of response choices, clear instructions, and an attractive, open layout. Since this is a questionnaire read over the phone, rather than a self-administered questionnaire, there was no need for more explicit instructions about the matrix question (Question 49) or for a more distinctive format for the response choices (Questions 45 and 48).

Write a Persuasive Introduction or Cover Letter

The **cover letter** for a mailed questionnaire and the introductory statement read by interviewers are critical to the survey's success. The initial statement to respondents sets the tone for the entire questionnaire. A carefully prepared cover letter or initial statement should increase the response rate and

Exhibit 7.5 A Page from Ross's Interview Schedule

45. In the past 12 months about how many times have you gone on a diet
    to lose weight?   v94

    Never 0
    Once 1
    Twice 2
    Three times or more 3
    Always on a diet 4

46. What is your height without shoes on?   v95

    _____ ft.   _____ in.

47. What is your weight without clothing?   v96

    _____ lbs.

48a. Do you currently smoke 7 or more cigarettes a week?   v97

    Yes .... 1 --> (SKIP TO Q.49)
    No 2

48b. Have you <u>ever</u> smoked 7 or more cigarettes a week?   v98

    Yes 1
    No 2

49. How much difficulty do you have . . .

	No diffi-culty,	Some diffi-culty, or	A great deal of diffi-culty?	
a. Going up and down stairs? Would you say ..	1	2	3	v99
b. Kneeling or stooping?	1	2	3	v100
c. Lifting or carrying objects less than 10 pounds, like a bag of groceries?	1	2	3	v101
d. Using your hands or fingers?	1	2	3	v102
e. Seeing, even with glasses?	1	2	3	v103
f. Hearing?	1	2	3	v104
g. Walking?	1	2	3	v105

Source: Ross, 1990.

result in more honest and complete answers to the survey questions; a poorly prepared cover letter or initial statement can have the reverse effects. The cover letter or introductory statement must be

■ *Credible.* The letter should establish that the research is being conducted by a researcher or organization that the respondent is likely to accept as a credible, unbiased authority. Research conducted by government agencies, university personnel, and recognized research organizations (like Gallup or RAND) is usually credible in this sense. On the other hand, a questionnaire from an animal rights group on the topic of animal rights will probably be viewed as biased.

■ *Personalized.* The cover letter should include a personalized salutation (not just "Dear Student," for example), close with the researcher's signature, and refer to the respondent in the second person ("Your participation . . .").

■ *Interesting.* The statement should interest the respondent in the contents of the questionnaire. Never make the mistake of assuming that what is of interest to you will also interest your respondents. Try to put yourself in their shoes before composing the statement, and then test your appeal with a variety of potential respondents.

■ *Responsible.* Reassure the respondent that the information you obtain will be treated confidentially, and include a phone number to call if the respondent has any questions or would like a summary of the final report. Point out that the respondent's participation is completely voluntary (Dillman, 1978:165–172).

Exhibit 7.6 is an example of a cover letter for a questionnaire.

Survey Designs

The four basic survey designs are the mailed survey, group-administered survey, phone survey, and in-person interview. Each survey has some unique advantages and disadvantages:

■ *Setting.* Most surveys are conducted in settings where only one respondent completes the survey at a time; most mailed questionnaires and phone interviews are intended for completion by only one respondent. The same is usually true of in-person interviews, although sometimes researchers interview several family members at once. On the other hand, a variant of the standard survey is a questionnaire distributed simultaneously to a group of respondents, who complete the survey while the researcher (or assistant) waits. Students in classrooms are typically the

Exhibit 7.6 **Sample Questionnaire Cover Letter**

University of Massachusetts at Boston
Department of Sociology
(617) 287-6250
May 24, 1998

Jane Doe
AIDS Coordinator
Shattuck Shelter

Dear Jane:

   AIDS is an increasing concern for homeless people and for homeless
shelters. The enclosed survey is about the AIDS problem and related issues
confronting shelters. It is sponsored by the Life Lines AIDS Prevention
Project for the Homeless—a program of the U.S. Centers for Disease Control
and the Massachusetts Department of Public Health.

   As an AIDS coordinator/shelter director, you have learned about
homeless persons' problems and about implementing programs in response to
those problems. The Life Lines Project needs to learn from your
experience. Your answers to the questions in the enclosed survey will
improve substantially the base of information for improving AIDS
prevention programs.

   Questions in the survey focus on AIDS prevention activities and on
related aspects of shelter operations. It should take about 30 minutes to
answer all the questions.

   Every shelter AIDS Coordinator (or shelter director) in Massachusetts
is being asked to complete the survey. And every response is vital to the
success of the survey: the survey report must represent the full range of
experiences.

   You may be assured of complete confidentiality. No one outside of the
university will have access to the questionnaire you return. (The ID
number on the survey will permit us to check with nonrespondents to see if
they need a replacement survey or other information.) All information
presented in the report to Life Lines will be in aggregate form, with the
exception of a list of the number, gender, and family status of each
shelter's guests.

   Please mail the survey back to us by Friday, March 5—and feel free to
call if you have any questions.

   Thank you for your assistance.

   Yours sincerely,

Russell K. Schutt   *Stephanie Howard*
Russell K. Schutt, Ph.D.   Stephanie Howard
Project Director   Project Assistant

group involved, although this type of group distribution also occurs in surveys of employees and of members of voluntary groups.

■ *Manner of administration.* The four survey designs also differ in the manner in which the questionnaire is administered. Mailed and group surveys are completed by the respondents themselves. During phone and in-person interviews, however, the researcher or a staff person asks the questions and records the respondent's answers.

■ *Questionnaire structure.* Survey designs also differ in the extent to which the content and order of questions are structured in advance by the researcher. Most mailed, group, and phone surveys are highly structured, fixing in advance the content and order of questions and response choices. Some of these types of surveys, particularly mailed surveys, may include some open-ended questions (respondents write in their answers rather than checking off one of several response choices). In contrast, although in-person interviews are often highly structured, they may include many questions without fixed response choices. In fact, the least structured interviews may proceed from an interview guide rather than a fixed set of questions. The interviewer may vary questions according to the respondent's answers so as to cover each of the topics in the interview guide and clarify answers as much as possible.

Exhibit 7.7 summarizes the typical features of the four different survey designs. The rest of this section focuses on the unique advantages and disadvantages of each design.

Mailed, Self-Administered Surveys

A **mailed survey** is conducted by mailing a questionnaire to respondents, who then administer the survey themselves. The central concern is maximizing the response rate. The final response rate is unlikely to be much above 80% and almost surely will be below 70% unless procedures to maximize the response rate are followed to the letter. A response rate below 60%

Exhibit 7.7 **Typical Features of the Four Survey Designs**

Design	Setting	Manner of administration	Questionnaire structure
Mailed survey	Individual	Self	Mostly structured
Group survey	Group	Self	Mostly structured
Phone survey	Individual	Professional	Structured
In-person interview	Individual	Professional	Structured or unstructured

is a disaster, and even a 70% response rate is not much more than minimally acceptable. It is hard to justify the representativeness of the sample if more than a third failed to respond.

Some ways to maximize the response rate (Fowler, 1988:99–106; Mangione, 1995:79–82; D. C. Miller, 1991:144) include:

- Make the questionnaire attractive, with plenty of white space.
- Use contingent questions and skip patterns infrequently. When they are necessary, guide respondents visually through the pattern.
- Make individual questions clear and understandable to all the respondents. No interviewers will be on hand to clarify the meaning of the questions or to probe for additional details.
- Use no more than a few open-ended questions, because respondents are likely to be put off by the idea of having to write out answers.
- Include a personalized and professional cover letter. Using an altruistic appeal (informing respondents that their response will do some good) seems to produce a response rate 7% higher than indicating that respondents will receive something for their participation.
- Have a credible research sponsor. According to one investigation, a sponsor known to respondents may increase their rate of response by as much as 17%. The next most credible sponsors are state headquarters of an organization and then other people in a similar field. Publishing firms, college professors or students, and private associations elicit the lowest response rates.
- Write an identifying number on the questionnaire so you can determine who nonrespondents are.
- A small incentive can help. Even a coupon or ticket worth $1 can be enough to increase the response rate.
- Include a stamped, self-addressed return envelope with the questionnaire.

Most important, use follow-up mailings to encourage initial nonrespondents to return a completed questionnaire. Don Dillman (1978) recommends a standard procedure for follow-up mailings:

1. Send a reminder postcard, thanking respondents and reminding nonrespondents, to all sample members two weeks after the initial mailing.

2. Send a replacement questionnaire with a new cover letter only to nonrespondents about three or four weeks after the initial mailing.

3. Send another replacement questionnaire with a new cover letter eight weeks after the initial mailing—by certified mail if possible (it's pretty expensive). If enough time and resources are available for telephone contacts or in-person visits for interviews, they will also help.

If Dillman's procedures are followed, and the guidelines for cover letters and questionnaire design also are adhered to, the response rate is almost certain to approach 70%. One review of studies using Dillman's method to survey the general population indicates that the average response to a first mailing will be about 24%; the response rate will rise to 42% after the postcard follow-up, to 50% after the first replacement questionnaire, and to 72% after a second replacement questionnaire is sent by certified mail (Dillman, Christenson, Carpenter, & Brooks, 1974).

The response rate may be higher with particular populations surveyed on topics of interest to them, and it may be lower with surveys of populations that do not have much interest in the topic. When a survey has many nonrespondents, getting some ideas about who they are, by comparing late respondents to early respondents, can help to determine the likelihood of bias due to the low rate of response. If those who returned their questionnaires at an early stage are more educated or more interested in the topic of the questionnaire, the sample may be biased; if the respondents are not more educated or more interested than nonrespondents, the sample will be more credible.

Related to the threat of nonresponse in mailed surveys is the hazard of incomplete response. Some respondents may skip some questions or just stop answering questions at some point in the questionnaire. But fortunately, this problem does not occur often with well-designed questionnaires. Potential respondents who have decided to participate in the survey usually complete it. But there are many exceptions to this observation, since questions that are poorly written, too complex, or about sensitive personal issues simply turn off some respondents. The revision or elimination of such questions during the design phase should minimize the problem.

Group-Administered Surveys

A **group-administered survey** is completed by individual respondents assembled in a group. The response rate is not usually a major concern in surveys that are distributed and collected in a group setting because most group members will participate. The real difficulty with this method is that it is seldom feasible, for it requires what might be called a captive audience. With the exception of students, employees, members of the armed forces, and some institutionalized populations, most populations cannot be sampled in such a setting.

Ross and a colleague, John Mirowsky, took advantage of the availability of students to test a new measure of "sense of control" that they had developed for the study on changes in U.S. household structure (Mirowsky & Ross, 1991:134). Here is a brief description of the test:

The student subjects were enrolled in an introductory sociology course during fall 1988. The section was not taught by the authors, and neither the textbook nor prior lectures mentioned locus of control. The students read the instructions and questions and recorded answers on a standard machine-readable "bubble form" of the type used routinely in examinations. They were assured of the confidentiality of their answers and instructed not to identify themselves on the answer sheet. . . . Because of inadequate, incomplete responses, the answers of 18 students were removed, resulting in a sample of $N_s = 225$.

One issue of special concern with group-administered surveys is the possibility that respondents will feel coerced to participate and as a result will be less likely to answer questions honestly. Also, because administering a survey in this way requires approval of the powers that be—and this sponsorship is made quite obvious by the fact that the survey is conducted on the organization's premises—respondents may infer that the researcher is not at all independent of the sponsor. No complete solution to this problem exists, but it helps to make an introductory statement emphasizing the researcher's independence and giving participants a chance to ask questions about the survey. The sponsor should also understand the need to keep a low profile and to allow the researcher both control over the data and autonomy in report writing.

Surveys by Telephone

In a **phone survey,** interviewers question respondents over the phone and then record respondents' answers. Phone interviewing has become a very popular method of conducting surveys in the United States because almost all families have phones. But two matters may undermine the validity of a phone survey: not reaching the proper sampling units and not getting enough complete responses to make the results generalizable.

Reaching Sample Units

Today, drawing a random sample is easier than ever because of random digit dialing (Lavrakas, 1987). A machine calls random phone numbers within designated exchanges, whether or not the numbers are published. When the machine reaches an inappropriate household (such as a business in a survey directed to the general population), the phone number is simply replaced with another.

The University of Illinois Survey Research Laboratory used the following procedures to draw a sample for Ross's study of social structure and well-being:

The universe for this study will be all persons 18–65 years of age, in the coterminous United States. A national probability sample designed to yield 2,000 interviews will be generated by the random-digit-dialing technique developed by J. Waksberg. The Waksberg method involves a two-stage sample design in which primary sampling units (PSUs) are selected with probabilities proportionate to size at the first stage and a specified cluster size at the second stage. To achieve 2,000 interviews, approximately 8,400 telephone numbers will be sampled. In order to avoid any potential bias in the sex or age distributions of the sample that might result from simply interviewing the persons who answer the telephone, a further sampling stage is required. For each selected household, one person will be chosen from all adults 18–65 years of age in that household in such a way that each adult has an equal probability of being selected for an interview. (J. E. Blair, personal communication to C. E. Ross, April 10, 1989)

However households are contacted, the interviewers must ask a series of questions at the start of the survey to ensure that they are speaking to the appropriate member of the household. Exhibit 7.8 displays a phone interview schedule, the instrument containing the questions asked by the interviewer. This example shows how appropriate and inappropriate households can be distinguished in a phone survey, so that the interviewer is guided to the correct respondent.

Maximizing Response to Phone Surveys

Three issues require special attention in phone surveys. First, because people often are not home, multiple call-backs will be needed for many sample members. The failure to call people back was one of the reasons for the discrepancy between poll predictions and actual votes in the 1988 presidential race between George Bush and Michael Dukakis. Kohut (1988) found that if pollsters in one Gallup poll had stopped attempting to contact unavailable respondents after one call, a 6-percentage-point margin for Bush would have been replaced by a 2-point margin for Dukakis. Those with more money and education are more likely to be away from home, and such persons are also more likely to vote Republican.

Phone surveys also must cope with difficulties due to the impersonal nature of phone contact. Visual aids cannot be used, so the interviewer must be able to convey verbally all information about response choices and skip patterns. With phone surveys, then, instructions to the interviewer must clarify how to ask each question, and response choices must be short. The Survey Research Laboratory developed the instructions shown in Exhibit 7.9 (page 262) to clarify procedures for asking and coding a series of questions that Ross used to measure symptoms of stress within households.

Exhibit 7.8   **Phone Interview Procedures for Respondent Designation**

PATH COMMUNITY SURVEY   Metro Social Services
CALL RECORD (CR)   Nashville-Davidson County, TN
                                   October 1987

Respondent Household (RH)

_____

Case No. [SEE TOP OF   *Call* Outcome Codes
_____ INTERVIEW FORM]
                                  CI = Completed interview
Date Precontact Letter   PC = Partially completed
Mailed   RI = Refused interview
                                  II = Impossible: language,
                                       etc.
_____   BN = Business number
                                  OC = Number outside county
                                  NA = No answer
[TRY REACHING RH ON FIVE   BS = Busy signal
DIFFERENT DAYS BEFORE   LD = Line disconnected
CLOSING OUT CR]   WN = Wrong number
                                  UL = Unlisted number
                                  ML = Message left on machine
                                  NC = Number changed
                                  CB = Call back [WRITE DATE]
                                       Date:
                                       Time:
                                       R's First Name:

Call Record: Day/Date   Call No.   Time   Call
Outcome

_____

_____

_____   Case No.

Introduction

A. Hello, is this the (*R's last name*) residence?

   *[IF NOT, SAY: The number I was calling *is* (*R's phone
   no.*) and it was for the (*R's first and last name*)
   residence. IF WRONG NUMBER, CODE OUTCOME IN CR AND
   TERMINATE WITH: I'm sorry to have bothered you. Goodbye.]

---

continued on next page

Exhibit 7.8   **Phone Interview Procedures for Respondent Designation *(continued)***

B. My name is _____. I'm calling for Metro Social
   Services and the Tennessee Department of Human Services.
   We're conducting a study to find out how local residents
   feel about the issue of homelessness in our community.
   Your household has been randomly selected to help us with
   this important task.

C. I don't know if you've seen it yet, but a letter about
   the study was mailed to your home several days ago. Just
   to verify our records, your home is located in Davidson
   County, isn't it?

   *[IF NOT, ASK: What county are you in? WRITE COUNTY ON RH
   LABEL, CODE OUTCOME IN CR, AND TERMINATE WITH: I'm sorry
   but only Davidson County residents are eligible for the
   study. Thanks anyway. Goodbye.]

D. **We need to interview men in some households and women in
   others so that our results will represent all adults in
   the county. According to our selection method, I need to
   interview the . . .**

   DESIGNATED R: youngest / oldest / man / woman

   **presently living in your household who is at least 18
   years of age. May I please speak with him/her?**

   *[IF PERSON ON PHONE, GO TO E.]

   *[IF NO SUCH PERSON, ASK: As a substitute, then, may I
   please speak with the . . .
   SUBSTITUTE R: youngest / oldest / man / woman in your
   household who is at least 18? IF PERSON ON PHONE, GO TO
   E.
   IF NOT AVAILABLE, MAKE ARRANGEMENTS TO CALL BACK AND
   WRITE DATE, TIME, AND R'S FIRST NAME IN CR. CLOSE WITH:
   Please tell (*R's first name*) that I will be calling back
   on (*date and time*). Thank you.]

   *[IF DIFFERENT PERSON COMES TO PHONE, REPEAT B AND ADD:
   You are the adult who's been randomly chosen in your
   household. GO TO E.]

   *[IF NOT AVAILABLE, MAKE ARRANGEMENTS . . . (see above)]

E. **The questions I'd like to ask you are easy to answer and
   should take only about 15 minutes. Everything you tell me
   will be kept strictly confidential. If you have any
   questions about the study, I'll be happy to answer them
   now or later. Okay?**

continued on next page

Exhibit 7.8   **Phone Interview Procedures for Respondent Designation (continued)**

```
Time interview started:

Person actually interviewed:

    1  Designated R
    2  Substitute R

I'll be using the word "homeless" to mean not having a
permanent address or place to live. Please think about all
types of people who fit that description as we go through
the interview.

Here's the first question.

1. Right now, how important is homelessness as a public
   issue in Nashville? Would you say it's . . . [READ 0-2]

    0    Not too important        8    DK
    1    Somewhat important, or   9    NR
    2    Very important?
```

Source: Metro Social Services, Nashville-Davidson County, TN, 1987. *PATH Community Survey.*

In addition, interviewers must be prepared for distractions as the respondent is interrupted by other household members. Sprinkling interesting questions throughout the questionnaire may help to maintain respondent interest. In general, rapport between the interviewer and the respondent is likely to be lower with phone surveys than with in-person interviews, and so respondents may tire and refuse to answer all the questions (D. C. Miller, 1991:166).

Careful interviewer training is essential for phone surveys. This is how one polling organization describes its training:

> In preparation for data collection, survey interviewers are required to attend a two-part training session. The first part covers general interviewing procedures and techniques as related to the proposed survey. The second entails in-depth training and practice for the survey. This training includes instructions on relevant subject matter, a question-by-question review of the survey instrument and various forms of role-playing and practice interviewing with supervisors and other interviewers. (J. E. Blair, personal communication to C. E. Ross, April 10, 1989)

Exhibit 7.9 **Sample Interviewer Instructions (Ross, 1990)**

Question:
41. On how many of the past 7 days have you . . .

                                                          Number of days

    a. Worried a lot about little things? ...   _____

    b. Felt tense or anxious? . . . .   _____

Instructions for interviewers:
Q41 For the series of "On how many of the past 7 days,"
make sure <u>the</u> <u>respondent</u> gives the numerical answer. If he/
she responds with a vague answer like "not too often" or
"just a few times," ask <u>again</u> "On how many of the past 7
days would you say?" Do <u>NOT</u> lead the respondent with a
number (e.g., "would that be 2 or 3?"). If R says "all of
them," verify that the answer is "7."

Question:
45. In the past 12 months about how many times have you
    gone on a diet to lose weight?

    Never   0

    Once   1

    Twice   2

    Three times or more   3

    Always on a diet   4

Instructions for interviewers:
Q45 Notice that this question ends with a question mark.
That means that you are <u>not</u> to read the answer categories.
Rather, wait for R to respond and circle the appropriate
number.

Procedures can be standardized more effectively, quality control maintained, and processing speed maximized when phone interviewers are assisted by computers:

> The interviewing will be conducted using "CATI" (Computer-Assisted Telephone Interviewing). . . . The questionnaire is "programmed" into the computer, along with relevant skip patterns throughout the instrument. Only legal entries are allowed. The system incorporates the tasks of interviewing, data entry, and some data cleaning. (J. E. Blair, personal communication to C. E. Ross, April 10, 1989)

Phone surveying is the method of choice for relatively short surveys of the general population. Response rates in phone surveys tend to be very high—often above 80%—because few individuals will hang up on a polite caller or refuse to stop answering questions (at least within the first 30 minutes or so). Ross achieved a response rate of 82% over a three-month period at the end of 1990, resulting in a final sample for her study of 2,031 Americans.

In-Person Interviews

What is unique to the **in-person interview**, compared to the other survey designs, is the face-to-face social interaction between interviewer and respondent. If money is no object, in-person interviewing is often the best survey design.

In-person interviewing has several advantages: Response rates are higher than with any other survey design, when potential respondents are approached by a courteous interviewer; questionnaires can be much longer than with mailed or phone surveys; the questionnaire can be complex, with both open-ended and closed-ended questions and frequent branching patterns; the order in which questions are read and answered can be controlled by the interviewer; the physical and social circumstances of the interview can be monitored; respondents' interpretations of questions can be probed and clarified.

But researchers must be alert to some special hazards due to the presence of an interviewer. Respondents should experience the interview process as a personalized interaction with an interviewer who is very interested in the respondent's experiences and opinions. At the same time, however, every respondent should have the same interview experience—asked the same questions in the same way by the same type of person, who reacts similarly to the answers. Therein lies the researcher's challenge—to plan an interview process that will be personal and engaging and yet consistent and nonreactive (and to hire interviewers who can carry out this plan). Without a personalized approach, the rate of response will be lower and answers will be less thoughtful—and potentially less valid. Without a consistent approach, information obtained from different respondents will not be comparable—less reliable and less valid.

Balancing Rapport and Control

Adherence to some basic guidelines for interacting with respondents can help interviewers to maintain an appropriate balance between personalization and standardization:

■ Project a professional image in the interview, that of someone who is sympathetic to the respondent but nonetheless has a job to do.

■ Establish rapport at the outset by explaining what the interview is about and how it will work and by reading the consent form. Ask the respondent if he or she has any questions or concerns, and respond to these honestly and fully. Emphasize that all the respondent says is confidential.

■ During the interview, ask questions from a distance that is close but not intimate. Stay focused on the respondent, and make sure that your posture conveys interest. Maintain eye contact, respond with appropriate facial expressions, and speak in a conversational tone of voice.

■ Be sure to maintain a consistent approach; deliver each question as written and in the same tone of voice. Listen empathetically, but avoid self-expression or loaded reactions.

■ Repeat questions if the respondent is confused. Use nondirective probes—such as "Can you tell me more about that?"—for open-ended questions.

As with phone interviewing, computers can be used to increase control of the in-person interview. In a computer-assisted personal interviewing (CAPI) project, interviewers carry a laptop computer that is programmed to display the interview questions and to process the responses that the interviewer types in, as well as to check that these responses fall within allowed ranges. Interviewers seem to like CAPI, and the data obtained are of at least as good quality as with a noncomputerized interview (Shepherd, Hill, Bristor, & Montalvan, 1996).

The presence of an interviewer may make it more difficult for respondents to give honest answers to questions about sensitive personal matters. For this reason, interviewers may hand respondents a separate self-administered questionnaire containing the more sensitive questions. After answering these questions, the respondent then seals the separate questionnaire in an envelope so that the interviewer does not know the answers. When this approach was used for the GSS questions about sexual activity, about 21% of men and 13% of women who were married or had been married admitted to having cheated on a spouse ("Survey on Adultery," 1993: A20). You may have heard reports of much higher rates of marital infidelity, but these were from studies using unrepresentative samples.

Although in-person interview procedures are typically designed with the expectation that the interview will involve only the interviewer and the respondent, one or more other household members are often within earshot. In a mental health survey in Los Angeles, for example, almost half the interviews were conducted in the presence of another person (Pollner & Adams, 1994). It is reasonable to worry that this third-party presence will influence responses about sensitive subjects—even more so because the likelihood of a third party being present may correspond with other subject characteristics. For example, in the Los Angeles survey, another person was present in 36% of the interviews with Anglos, in 47% of the interviews with

African-Americans, and in 59% of the interviews with Hispanics. However, there is no consistent evidence that respondents change their answers because of the presence of another person. Analysis of this problem with the Los Angeles study found very little difference in reports of mental illness symptoms between respondents who were alone and those who were in the presence of others.

Maximizing Response to Interviews

Even if the right balance has been struck between maintaining control over interviews and achieving good rapport with respondents, in-person interviews can still have a problem. Because of the difficulty of catching all the members of a sample, response rates may suffer. Exhibit 7.10 displays the breakdown of nonrespondents to the 1990 General Social Survey. Of the total original sample of 2,165, only 86% (1,857) were determined to be valid selections of dwelling units with potentially eligible respondents. Among these potentially eligible respondents, the response rate was 74%. The GSS is a well-designed survey using carefully trained and supervised interviewers, so this response rate indicates the difficulty of securing respondents from a sample of the general population even when everything is done "by the book."

Exhibit 7.10 **Reasons for Nonresponse in Personal Interviews (1990 General Social Survey)**

Of 1,857 units in the sample . . .

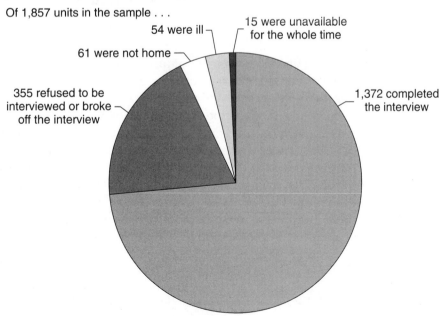

54 were ill

15 were unavailable for the whole time

61 were not home

355 refused to be interviewed or broke off the interview

1,372 completed the interview

Source: Data from Davis & Smith, 1992:54.

Several factors affect the response rate in interview studies. People with less education participate somewhat less in surveys of political issues (perhaps because they are less aware of current political issues). High-income persons tend to participate less in surveys about income and economic behavior (perhaps because they are suspicious about why others want to know about their situation). Response rates tend to be lower in central cities, in part because of difficulties in finding people at home and gaining access to high-rise apartments and in part because of interviewer reluctance to visit some areas at night, when people are more likely to be home (Fowler, 1988:45–60).

Unusual strains and disillusionment in a society can also undermine the general credibility of research efforts and the ability of interviewers to achieve an acceptable response rate. Consider the experience of many interviewers in the recent census conducted by Russia's post-Communist government:

> Svetlana A. Berikova had just come home when she heard the knock on the door. "Who?" she barked. . . . "What do you want from me?"
>
> Gently, as she had already done many times, Marina V. Kondrashova, who is 19, explained that she was a census-taker sent by the government to ask some important questions about how Mrs. Berikova and her family were making their way in the new Russia.
>
> "Census! Census?" Mrs. Berikova, 62, shouted incredulously, launching into a furious rant about the recent death of her husband, the "pathetic, useless" pension that forces her to keep working, and the pervasive crime that fills her every day with dread. "My entire life is shattered. They have taken everything. And you're here to take a census?" (Specter, 1994:A4)

At a time of extreme social turmoil, it may not be possible even in interview studies to raise the rate of response to an acceptable level. But in more ordinary times, repeated follow-up attempts will usually increase the response rate considerably, both by locating persons who are initially not at home and by encouraging all but the most adamant refusers to participate.

An advance letter may help to orient sample members positively toward the interview. In the letter and during all direct contacts with potential respondents, the project's purposes should be described accurately. Respondents must be reassured that the project is important and that the survey does not threaten respondents in any way. Emphasizing the researcher's commitment to confidentiality is always an important aspect of this reassurance (Fowler, 1988:52–53).

A Comparison of Survey Designs

Which survey design should be used when? Group-administered surveys are similar in most respects to mailed surveys, except that they require the unusual circumstance of having access to the sample in a group setting. We therefore don't need to consider this survey design by itself; what applies to mailed surveys applies to group-administered survey designs, with the exception of sampling issues. Thus, we can focus our comparison on the three survey designs that involve the use of a questionnaire with individuals sampled from a larger population: mailed surveys, phone surveys, and in-person surveys. Exhibit 7.11 summarizes their strong and weak points.

Exhibit 7.11   **Advantages and Disadvantages of Three Survey Designs**

Characteristics of design	In-person survey	Mail survey	Phone survey
Representative sample			
Opportunity for inclusion is known			
For completely listed populations	High	High	High
For incompletely listed populations	High	Medium	Medium
Selection within sampling units is controlled (e.g., specific family members must respond)	High	Medium	High
Respondents are likely to be located	Medium	High	High
If samples are heterogeneous	High	Medium	High
If samples are homogeneous and specialized	High	High	High
Questionnaire construction and question design			
Allowable length of questionnaire	High	Medium	Medium
Ability to include			
Complex questions	High	Medium	Low
Open questions	High	Low	High
Screening questions	High	Low	High
Tedious, boring questions	High	Low	High
Ability to control question sequence	High	Low	High
Ability to ensure questionnaire completion	High	Medium	High
Distortion of answers			
Odds of avoiding social desirability bias	Low	High	Medium
Odds of avoiding interviewer distortion	Low	High	Medium
Odds of avoiding contamination by others	Medium	Medium	High
Administrative goals			
Odds of meeting personnel requirements	Low	High	High
Odds of implementing quickly	Low	Low	High
Odds of keeping costs low	Low	High	Medium

Source: Adapted from Dillman, 1978:74–75. *Mail and Telephone Surveys: The Total Design Method.* Copyright © 1978 Don A. Dillman. Reprinted by permission of John Wiley & Sons, Inc.

The most important consideration in comparing the advantages and disadvantages of the three methods is the likely response rate they will generate. Because of the great weakness of mailed surveys in this respect, they must be considered the least preferred survey design from a sampling standpoint. However, researchers may still prefer a mailed survey when they have to reach a widely dispersed population and don't have enough financial resources to hire and train an interview staff or to contract with a survey organization that already has an interview staff available in many locations.

Contracting with an established survey research organization for a phone survey is often the best alternative to a mailed survey. The persistent follow-up attempts that are necessary to secure an adequate response rate are much easier over the phone than in person. But the process is not simple:

> Working phone numbers in the sample are called up to 10 times at different times of the day and on different days of the week before the number is recorded as a noncontact. To facilitate contact with households and individuals, telephoning is done in the evening during the week, and during the day over weekends. A final disposition is obtained and recorded for each sample telephone number, i.e., whether an interview, refusal, noncontact, nonworking number, or other disposition. "Control" reports are issued weekly showing progress of the work through various stages of data collection. (J. E. Blair, personal communication to C. E. Ross, April 10, 1989)

In-person surveys are clearly preferable in terms of the possible length and complexity of the questionnaire itself, as well as the researcher's ability to monitor conditions while the questionnaire is being completed. Mailed surveys often are preferable for asking sensitive questions, although this problem can be lessened in an interview by giving respondents a separate sheet to fill out on their own. Although interviewers may themselves distort results, either by changing the wording of questions or failing to record answers properly, this problem can be lessened by careful training, monitoring, and tape-recording the answers.

A phone survey limits the length and complexity of the questionnaire but offers the possibility of very carefully monitoring interviewers (Dillman, 1978; Fowler, 1988:61–73):

> Supervisors in [one organization's] Telephone Centers work closely with the interviewers, monitor their work, and maintain records of their performance in relation to the time schedule, the quality of their work, and help detect and correct any mistakes in completed interviews prior to data reduction and processing. (J. E. Blair, personal communication to C. E. Ross, April 10, 1989)

These various points about the different survey designs lead to two general conclusions. First, in-person interviews are the strongest design and generally preferable when sufficient resources and a trained interview staff are available; telephone surveys have many of the advantages of in-person interviews at much less cost. Second, a decision about the best survey design for any particular study must take into account the unique features and goals of the study.

■ ■ ■ ■ Ethical Issues in Survey Research

Survey research usually poses fewer ethical dilemmas than do experimental or field research designs. Potential respondents to a survey can easily decline to participate, and the methods of data collection are quite obvious. Only in group-administered survey designs might the respondents be, in effect, a captive audience (probably of students or employees), and so they require special attention to ensure that participation is truly voluntary. (Those who do not wish to participate may be told they can just hand in a blank form.)

Confidentiality

Do any of the questions have the potential to embarrass respondents or otherwise subject them to adverse consequences? If the answer to this question is no—and it often is in surveys about general social issues—other ethical problems are unlikely. But if the questionnaire includes questions about attitudes or behaviors that are socially stigmatized or generally considered to be private or questions about actions that are illegal, the researcher must proceed carefully and ensure that respondents' rights are protected.

The first step to take with potentially troublesome questions is to consider omitting or modifying them. Researchers often include some questions in surveys just out of curiosity or out of a suspicion that the questions might prove to be important. If sensitive questions fall into this category, they probably should be omitted. There is no point in asking "Have you ever been convicted of a felony?" if the answers are unlikely to ever be used in the analysis of survey results.

Many surveys do include some essential questions that might in some way prove damaging to the subjects if their answers were disclosed. To prevent any possibility of harm to subjects due to disclosure of such information, it is critical to preserve subject **confidentiality**. Nobody but research personnel should have access to information that could be used to link respondents to their responses, and even that access should be limited to what is necessary for specific research purposes. Only numbers should be used to identify respondents on their questionnaires, and the researcher should keep the names that correspond to these numbers in a safe, private location, unavailable to staff and others who might otherwise come across them. Follow-up mailings or contact attempts that require linking the ID numbers with names and addresses should be carried out by trustworthy assistants under close supervision.

Not many surveys can provide true **anonymity**, so that no identifying information is ever recorded to link respondents with their responses. The main problem with anonymous surveys is that they preclude follow-up attempts to encourage participation by initial nonrespondents, and they prevent panel designs, which measure change through repeated surveys of the same individuals. In-person surveys rarely can be anonymous because an interviewer must in almost all cases know the name and address of the interviewee. However, phone surveys that are meant only to sample opinion at one point in time, as in political polls, can safely be completely anonymous. When no future follow-up is desired, group-administered surveys also can be anonymous. To provide anonymity in a mail survey, the researcher should omit identifying codes from the questionnaire but could include a self-addressed, stamped postcard so the respondent can notify the researcher that the questionnaire has been returned without creating any linkage to the questionnaire itself (Mangione, 1995:69).

Any survey could allow anonymous responses to a subset of particularly sensitive questions. A tear-off sheet containing these questions and a separate return envelope, without any identifying information, could be included with a mailed survey. In an in-person interview, this special section could be left with the respondent to be completed later and returned by mail. Of course, a response obtained in this way cannot be linked with the response of the same subject to the same question in some later follow-up survey. But if it decreases the nonresponse rate, this method can provide more valid results for the initial survey.

Disclosure

Another critical ethical focus in a survey research project is the cover letter included with a mailed survey or the introductory statement read in in-person, phone, and group interviews. The cover letter or introductory statement must explain clearly the nature and purposes of the survey and inform respondents that their participation is voluntary. Cover letters or introductory statements for surveys of populations (like clients, employees, and students) to which the researcher gains access through an organization or school also require the assurance that a decision not to participate will not affect services, benefits, or grades.

The cover letter or introductory statement also must disclose the researcher's affiliation and the project's sponsors. The purposes of the survey should be briefly described. A contact number for those who wish to ask questions or register complaints also should be included.

If the survey could possibly have any harmful effects, these should be disclosed fully in the cover letter or introductory statement; steps taken by the researcher to reduce such effects (such as procedures for maintaining confidentiality) should also be mentioned. Potential benefits may be mentioned as well, particularly any possible direct benefits to the respondents, such as a monetary reward for participation or an opportunity to give feedback to the government. More general, intangible survey benefits, such as contributing to knowledge about an issue, may be mentioned but should not be overemphasized.

Many researchers promise a copy of a survey report to interested respondents. They include in the cover letter a phone number or address for the respondent to contact for the report and then make sure that requests for reports are honored.

■ ■ ■ ■ **Conclusion**

Survey research is an exceptionally efficient and productive method for investigating a wide array of social research questions. In six months, Catherine Ross's survey produced a unique, comprehensive dataset on work, family, and health issues. These data allowed Ross and her coauthors to investigate the relations among sex stratification, health lifestyle, and perceived health (Ross & Bird, 1994); between education and health (Ross & Wu, 1995); between physical impairment and income (Mirowsky & Hu, 1996); among gender, parenthood, and anger (Ross & Van Willigen, 1996); and among age, the sense of control, and health (Mirowsky, 1995; Mirowsky & Ross, 1992; Ross & Wu, 1996). As a result, we know much more about how social structure influences health, what might be done to mitigate the negative health consequences of aging and low income, and where social theories of health need to be improved.

In addition to the potential benefits for social science, considerations of time and expense frequently make a survey the preferred data-collection method. One or more of the four survey designs reviewed in this chapter can be applied to almost any research question. It is no wonder that surveys have become the most popular research method in sociology and that they frequently inform discussion and planning about important social and political questions.

The relative ease of conducting at least some types of survey research leads many people to imagine that no particular training or systematic procedures are required. Nothing could be further from the truth. But as a result of this widespread misconception, you will encounter a great many nearly worthless survey results. You must be prepared to examine carefully the procedures used in any survey before accepting its findings as credible. And if you decide to conduct a survey, you must be prepared to invest the time and effort required to follow proper procedures.

KEY TERMS

Anonymity
Cognitive interview
Confidentiality
Contingent question
Cover letter
Double-barreled question
Fence sitter
Filter question
Floater
Forced-choice question
Group-administered survey

In-person interview
Interpretive question
Interview schedule
Mailed survey
Omnibus survey
Phone survey
Questionnaire
Skip pattern
Split-ballot design
Survey instrument
Survey research

HIGHLIGHTS

■ Surveys are the most popular form of social research because of their versatility, efficiency, and generalizability. Many survey datasets, like the General Social Survey, are available for social scientists to use in teaching and research.

■ Surveys can fail to produce useful results because of problems in sampling, measurement, and overall survey design. Political polling can produce inconsistent results because of rapid changes in popular sentiment.

■ A survey questionnaire or interview schedule should be designed as an integrated whole, with each question and section serving some clear purpose and complementing the others.

■ Questions must be worded carefully to avoid confusing respondents or encouraging a less-than-honest response. Inclusion of "Don't know" choices and neutral responses may help, but the presence of such options also affects the distribution of answers. Open-ended questions can be used to determine the meaning that respondents' attach to their answers. Answers to any survey questions may be affected by the questions that precede them in a questionnaire or interview schedule.

■ Every questionnaire and interview schedule should be pretested on a small sample that is like the sample to be surveyed.

■ The cover letter for a mailed questionnaire and the introductory statement for an interview should be credible, personalized, interesting, and responsible.

■ Response rates in mailed surveys are typically well below 70% unless multiple mailings are made to nonrespondents and the questionnaire and cover letter are attractive, interesting, and carefully planned. Response rates for group-administered surveys are usually much higher.

■ Phone interviews using random digit dialing allow fast turnaround and efficient sampling. Multiple call-backs may be required, but once they are contacted, most people can be interviewed by phone for 30 to 45 minutes.

■ In-person interviews have several advantages over other types of surveys: They allow longer and more complex interview schedules, monitoring of the conditions when the questions are answered, probing for respondents' understanding of the questions, and high response rates.

■ Most survey research poses few ethical problems because respondents are able to decline to participate—an option that should be stated clearly in the cover letter or introductory statement. Special care must be taken when questionnaires are administered in group settings (to "captive audiences") and when sensitive personal questions are to be asked; subject confidentiality should always be preserved.

EXERCISES

1. Read the original article reporting one of the surveys described in this book (check Appendix A or the text of the chapters for ideas). Critique the article using the questions presented in Appendix C as your guide, but focus particular attention on sampling, measurement, and survey design.

2. *Responding to the Homeless: Policy and Practice* (Schutt & Garrett, 1992) includes in an appendix an interview schedule for case managers at homeless shelters. Check the book out of your library and critique the form. What are the key concepts in the instrument? Which measures do you think are strong? Weak? Point out the key features of the interview schedule, including sections, response formats, skip patterns, and routing instructions. Do you think the order of the sections and of the questions within sections makes sense? Why or why not? What do you think might be the advantages and disadvantages of having shelter case managers administer this instrument?

3. Each of the following questions was used in a survey that I received at some time in the past. Evaluate each question and its response choices using the guidelines for question writing presented in this chapter. What errors do you find? Try to rewrite each question to avoid such errors and improve question wording.

   a. The first question in an Info World (computer publication) "product evaluation survey":

   ```
   How interested are you in PostScript Level 2 printers?
   _____ Very  _____ Somewhat  _____ Not at all
   ```

b. From a Greenpeace "National Marine Mammal Survey":

```
Do you support Greenpeace's nonviolent, direct action to
intercept whaling ships, tuna fleets and other commercial
fishermen in order to stop their wanton destruction of
thousands of magnificent marine mammals?
_____ Yes    _____ No    _____ Undecided
```

c. From a U.S. Department of Education survey of college faculty:

```
How satisfied or dissatisfied are you with each of the follow-
ing aspects of your instructional duties at this institution?
```

	Very Dissat.	Somewhat Dissat.	Somewhat Satisf.	Very Satisf.
a. The authority I have to make decisions about what courses I teach.	1	2	3	4
b. Time available for working with students as advisor, mentor . . .	1	2	3	4

d. From a survey about affordable housing in a Massachusetts community:

```
Higher than single-family density is acceptable in order to
make housing affordable.
```

Strongly Agree	Agree	Undecided	Disagree	Strongly Disagree
1	2	3	4	5

e. From a survey of faculty experience with ethical problems in research:

```
Are you reasonably familiar with the codes of ethics of any of
the following professional associations?
```

	Very Familiar	Familiar	Not too Familiar
American Sociological Association	1	2	0
Society for the Study of Social Problems	1	2	0
American Society of Criminology	1	2	0

```
If you are familiar with any of the above codes of ethics, to
what extent do you agree with them?
```

Strongly Agree	Agree	No Opinion	Disagree	Strongly Disagree

```
Some researchers have avoided using a professional code of
ethics as a guide for the following reason. Which responses,
if any, best describe your reasons for not using all or any of
the parts of the codes?
```

	Yes	No
1. Vagueness	1	0
2. Political pressures	1	0
3. Codes protect only individuals, not groups	1	0

f. From a survey of faculty perceptions:

> Of the students you have observed while teaching college
> courses, please indicate the percentage who significantly
> improve their performance in the following areas.
> Reading   ____%
> Organization____%
> Abstraction ____%

g. From a University of Massachusetts–Boston student survey:

> A person has a responsibility to stop a friend or relative
> from driving when drunk.
> Strongly Agree __ Agree __ Disagree __ Strongly Disagree __
>
> Even if I wanted to, I would probably not be able to stop most
> people from driving drunk.
> Strongly Agree __ Agree __ Disagree __ Strongly Disagree __

4. Consider how you could design a split-ballot experiment to determine the effect of phrasing a question or its response choices in different ways. Check recent issues of the local newspaper for a question used in a survey of attitudes about some social policy or political position. Propose some hypothesis about how the wording of the question or its response choices might have influenced the answers people gave and devise an alternative that differs only in this respect. Distribute these questionnaires to a large class (after your instructor makes the necessary arrangements) to test your hypothesis.

5. Write five to six questions for a one-page questionnaire on some issue of concern to students. You might focus on career goals and plans, political preferences, or satisfaction with the university. Include some questions to measure characteristics (such as social-class background or year in school) that might help to explain the attitudes. Make all but one of your questions closed-ended.

6. Conduct a preliminary pretest of the questionnaire you wrote for Exercise 5 by interviewing two students. Follow up the closed-ended questions with open-ended questions that ask the students what they meant by each response or what came to mind when they were asked each question. Take account of these answers when you revise your questions.

7. Polish up the organization and layout of the questionnaire you wrote for Exercise 5. Write a cover letter that presumes that the survey will be administered to students in a class at your school. Submit the questionnaire and cover letter to your instructor for comment and evaluation.

8. I received in my university mailbox some years ago a two-page questionnaire that began with the following "cover letter" at the top of the first page:

> *Faculty Questionnaire*
> This survey seeks information on faculty perception of the
> learning process and student performance in their undergraduate
> careers. Surveys have been distributed in nine universities in
> the Northeast, through random deposit in mailboxes of selected
> departments. This survey is being conducted by graduate students

affiliated with the School of Education and the Sociology
Department. We greatly appreciate your time and effort in helping
us with our study.

Critique this cover letter, and then draft a more persuasive one.

9. *Down and Out in America,* by Peter Rossi (1989), includes in an appendix an annotated bibliography of survey-based studies of homeless and extremely poor populations. Critique the survey designs based on Rossi's descriptions. Which designs seemed likely to produce more generalizable results? Comment on sample generalizability and cross-population generalizability. Propose a plan to survey either homeless persons or those who provide services to homeless persons in some city in your state. How would you draw a sample? How would you approach potential respondents? What survey design do you think would have the greatest chance of success?

10. In Chapter 6, review the description of the experiment by Richard Price, Michelle Van Ryn, and Amiram Vinokur (1992). Propose a survey design that would test the same hypothesis but with a sample from a larger population. Your survey design can be longitudinal but should remain experimental, not quasi-experimental. Compare your survey design to the original experimental design. What are the advantages and disadvantages of your survey design in terms of causal validity? Generalizability? Measurement validity?

WEB EXERCISES

1. Go to the Centre for Applied Social Surveys Web site at

 http://www.scpr.ac.uk/cass

 Choose "Question Bank"
 Choose "Start a Search"
 Choose "Key Word Search: Question Bank"
 Search the Question Bank for survey questions related to race and/or ethnicity and/or class. Explore the various sets of survey questions the Question Bank gives you access to. Find 10 questions that you think are well designed and explain why you think so for each. Find 10 questions that you think are poorly designed and explain why you think so for each.

 You may find you need to install the Adobe Acrobat Reader to do this. If so, just follow the on-line instructions.

2. Go to The Question Factory at

 http://www.erols.com/bainbri/qf.htm

 Choose "A Brief Explanation" to find out about The Question Factory.
 How does The Question Factory work? What is the survey design? How does The Question Factory incorporate "open-ended" and "fixed-choice" questions into its surveys? Compare and contrast the information gathered from open-ended questions and fixed-choice questions. Choose one subject from the list of "Results of Earlier Surveys." Briefly describe the survey and the survey results.

3. Search the Web for electronic journal articles that report on research that uses surveys to collect information regarding race or class. Find at least five articles and briefly describe each.

Hint: Many academic and scholarly journals post their articles on the Web. Most of the popular journals have Web sites devoted to on-line electronic versions of their publications. You can find multiple links to such journals at many of the general social science Web sites. A possible place to start is at Humanities Hub at

http://www.gu.edu.au/gwis/hub/hub.home.html

SPSS EXERCISES

How do the features of work and home life, and the balance between them, affect health and emotional health? Several questions in the GSS96 allow us to address this question.

1. Generate cross-tabulations to show the relationship among several health-related variables and work status, role as supervisor at work, income level, and the balance between work and family life:

STATISTICS
    CROSSTABS
        ACROSS wrk2, wksup, rinc91d balwk2
        DOWN health2, rush2, happy2
            STATISTICS column percents

(If you have had a statistics course, you will also want to request the CHI-SQUARE statistic for each of the above tables.)

Describe the relationships you have found in the tables, noting the difference in the distribution of the dependent (row) variables between the two categories of each of the independent (column) variables.

2. Do these relationships vary for men and women? Add the variable SEX as a CONTROL variable in your cross-tabulation request. Describe your results, indicating whether each relationship occurs for both men and women in the sample.

3. What else do you think needs to be taken into account in order to understand these relationships? For example, should you take into account the marital status of the respondents? Why or why not?

8 Qualitative Methods: Observing, Participating, Listening

EXERCISES
WEB EXERCISES
SPSS EXERCISES

"You have to look into a patient's eyes as much as you can, and learn to get the signals from there." This suggestion was made by a nurse explaining to future nursing home assistants how they were to deal with a dying patient. One of those future assistants, Timothy Diamond (1992:17), was also a sociologist intent on studying work in nursing homes. For us, the statement he recorded has a dual purpose: It exemplifies qualitative methods, in which sociologists learn by observing as they participate in a natural setting; it also reminds us that some features of the social world (dare I say many?) are ill suited to investigation with experiments or surveys.

In this chapter you will learn how qualitative methods were used to illuminate the inside of a nursing home and the attitudes and actions of its staff (Diamond, 1992). You will observe schoolchildren on a playground as they define the behavior appropriate for boys and for girls (Thorne, 1993). Throughout the chapter, you will learn, from a variety of other examples, that some of our greatest insights into social processes can result from what appear to be very ordinary activities: observing, participating, listening, and talking.

But you will also learn that qualitative research is much more than just doing what comes naturally in social situations. Qualitative researchers must observe keenly, sensitively plan their participation, take notes systematically, question respondents strategically, and prepare to spend more time and invest more of their whole selves than often occurs with experiments or surveys. Moreover, if we are to have any confidence in the validity of a qualitative study's conclusions, each element of its design must be reviewed as carefully as we would review the elements of an experiment or survey.

The chapter begins with an overview of the major features of qualitative research, as reflected in Diamond's (1992) study of nursing homes. The next section discusses the various approaches to participant observation research, which is the most distinctive qualitative method, and reviews the stages of research using participant observation. I then review in some detail the issues involved in intensive interviewing before briefly explaining focus groups, an increasingly popular qualitative method. The last two sections cover issues that are of concern in any type of qualitative research project: analyzing the data collected and making ethical decisions. By the chapter's end, you should appreciate the hard work required to translate "doing what comes naturally" into systematic research, be able to recognize strong and weak points in qualitative studies, and be ready to do some of it yourself.

Fundamentals of Qualitative Methods

Qualitative techniques can often be used to enrich experiments and surveys. **Qualitative methods** also refer to several distinctive research designs: participant observation, intensive interviewing, and focus groups. Participant observation and intensive interviewing are often used in the same project; focus groups combine some elements of these two approaches into a unique data-collection strategy.

> *Participant observation* A qualitative method for gathering data that involves developing a sustained relationship with people while they go about their normal activities.
>
> *Intensive interviewing* A qualitative method that involves open-ended relatively unstructured questioning in which the interviewer seeks in-depth information on the interviewee's feelings, experiences, and perceptions (Lofland & Lofland, 1984:12).
>
> *Focus groups* A qualitative method that involves unstructured group interviews in which the focus group leader actively encourages discussion among participants on the topics of interest.

Although these three qualitative designs differ in many respects, they share several features that distinguish them from experimental and survey research designs (Denzin & Lincoln, 1994; Maxwell, 1996; Wolcott, 1995):

■ *Collection primarily of qualitative rather than quantitative data.* Any research design may collect both qualitative and quantitative data, but qualitative methods emphasize observations about natural behavior and artifacts that capture social life as it is experienced by the participants rather than in categories predetermined by the researcher.

■ *Exploratory research questions, with a commitment to inductive reasoning.* Qualitative researchers typically begin their projects seeking not to test preformulated hypotheses but to discover what people think and how they act, and why, in some social setting. Only after many observations do qualitative researchers try to develop general principles to account for their observations.

∎ *A focus on previously unstudied processes and unanticipated phenomena.* Previously unstudied attitudes and actions can't adequately be understood with a structured set of questions or within a highly controlled experiment. So qualitative methods have their greatest appeal when we need to explore new issues, investigate hard-to-study groups, or determine the meaning people give to their lives and actions. Diamond (1992:4) asked, "What was life like inside, day in and day out? Who lived in nursing homes, and what did they do there?"

∎ *An orientation to social context, to the interconnections between social phenomena rather than to their discrete features.* The context of concern may be a program or organization, a "case," or a broader social context. For example:

> In this book I begin not with individuals, although they certainly appear in the account, but with *group life*—with social relations, the organization and meanings of social situations, the collective practices through which children and adults create and recreate gender in their daily interactions. . . . [C]hildren's collective activities should weigh more fully in our overall understanding of gender and social life. (Thorne, 1993:4)

∎ *A focus on human subjectivity, on the meanings that participants attach to events and that people give to their lives:* "Through life stories, people 'account for their lives.'. . . [T]he themes people create are the means by which they interpret and evaluate their life experiences and attempt to integrate these experiences to form a self-concept" (Kaufman, 1986: 24–25).

∎ *Use of idiographic rather than nomothetic causal explanation.* With its focus on particular actors and situations and the processes that connect them, qualitative research tends to identify causes as particular events embedded within an unfolding, interconnected action sequence (Maxwell, 1996:20–21). The language of variables and hypotheses appears only rarely in the qualitative literature.

∎ *Reflexive research design, in which the design develops as the research progresses:*

> Each component of the design may need to be reconsidered or modified in response to new developments or to changes in some other component. . . . The activities of collecting and analyzing data, developing and modifying theory, elaborating or refocusing the research questions, and identifying and eliminating validity threats are usually all going on more or less simultaneously, each influencing all of the others. (Maxwell, 1996:2–3)

- *Sensitivity to the subjective role of the researcher.* Little pretense is made of achieving an objective perspective on social phenomena.

> I felt closer to the girls not only through memories of my own past, but also because I knew more about their gender-typed interactions. I had once played games like jump rope and statue buyer, but I had never ridden a skateboard and had barely tried sports like basketball and soccer. . . . Were my moments of remembering, the times when I felt like a ten-year-old girl, a source of distortion or insight? (Thorne, 1993:26)

We can see all these elements emerge in the development of qualitative methods. They also appear in Diamond's (1992) nursing home study.

Origins of Qualitative Research

Anthropologists and sociologists laid the foundation for modern qualitative methods while doing **field research** in the early decades of the twentieth century. Dissatisfied with studies of native peoples that relied on second-hand accounts and inspection of artifacts, anthropologists Franz Boas and Bronislaw Malinowski went to live in or near the communities they studied. Boas visited Native American villages in the American Northwest; Malinowski lived among New Guinea natives. Neither truly participated in the ongoing social life of those they studied (Boas collected artifacts and original texts, and Malinowski reputedly lived as something of a noble among the natives he studied), but both helped to establish the value of intimate familiarity with the community of interest and thus laid the basis for modern anthropology (Emerson, 1983:2–5).

Many of sociology's field research pioneers were former social workers and reformers. Some brought their missionary concern with the spread of civic virtue among new immigrants to the Department of Sociology and Anthropology at the University of Chicago. Their successors continued to focus on sources of community cohesion and urban strain but came to view the city as a social science "laboratory" rather than as a focus for reform. They adopted the fieldwork methods of anthropology to studying the "natural areas" of the city and the social life of small towns (Vidich & Lyman, 1994). By the 1930s, 1940s, and 1950s, qualitative researchers were emphasizing the value of direct participation in community life and sharing in subjects' perceptions and interpretations of events (Emerson, 1983:6–13).

Case Study: Making Gray Gold

You can get a better feel for qualitative methods by reading the following excerpts from Timothy Diamond's book about nursing homes, *Making Gray Gold* (Diamond, 1992), and reasoning inductively from his observations. See if you can induce from these particulars some of the general features of field research. Ask yourself, What was the research question? How were the issues of generalizability, measurement, and causation approached? How did social factors influence the research?

Let's begin near the beginning of Diamond's account:

> First I went to school for six months in 1982, two evenings a week and all day Saturdays, to obtain the certificate the state required [to work in a nursing home]. Then, after weeks of searching for jobs, I worked in three different nursing homes in Chicago for periods of three to four months each. (Diamond, 1992:5)

As this excerpt indicates, Diamond's research involved becoming a participant in the social setting that was the object of his study. Note how long Diamond spent gathering data: more than a year of full-time work.

Diamond also describes for us the development of his research questions. A medical sociologist, his curiosity about health care for older people was piqued when he happened to become acquainted with Ina Williams and Aileen Crawford in a coffee shop across the street from the nursing home where they worked as assistants. He began to wonder,

> How does the work of caretaking become defined and get reproduced day in and day out as a business?. . . How, in other words, does the everyday world of Ina and Aileen and their co-workers, and that of the people they tend, get turned into a system in which gray can be written about in financial journals as producing gold, a classic metaphor for money? What is the process of making gray gold? (Diamond, 1992:5)

With these exploratory research questions in mind, Diamond explains why he chose participant observation as his research method:

> I wanted to collect stories and to experience situations like those Ina and Aileen had begun to describe. I decided that . . . I would go inside to experience the work myself. (Diamond, 1992:5)

The choice of participant observation precluded random sampling of cases, but Diamond did not ignore the need to generalize his findings. He went to considerable lengths to include three nursing homes that would represent a range of care-giving arrangements:

> These [nursing] homes were situated in widely different neighborhoods of the city. In one of them residents paid for their own care, often with initial help from Medicare. In the other two, most of the residents were supported by Medicaid. . . . In the course of writing, I visited many homes across the United States to validate my observations and to update them in instances where regulatory changes had been instituted. (Diamond, 1992:6)

The data in Diamond's study were notes on the activities of the people as he observed and interacted with them. He did not use structured questionnaires and other formal data-collection instruments. So his data are primarily qualitative rather than quantitative.

As for his method, it was inductive. First he gathered data. Then, as data collection continued, Diamond figured out how to interpret the data, how to make sense of the social situations he was studying. His analytic categories ultimately came not from social theory but from the categories by which people themselves described one another and made sense of their social world. These categories seem to have broad applicability, suggesting the generalizability of the researcher's findings. For instance, one of the teachers Diamond encountered while earning his certificate passed along a unique way of making sense of the caregiver's role in a nursing home:

> The tensions generated by the introductory lecture and . . . ideas of career professionalism were reflected in our conversations as we waited for the second class to get under way. Yet within the next half hour they seemed to dissolve. Mrs. Bonderoid, our teacher, saw to that. A registered nurse and nurse practitioner, an African American woman of about fifty, she must have understood a lot about classroom jitters and about who was sitting in front of her as well. "What this is going to take," she instructed, "is a lot of mother's wit." "Mother's wit," she said, not "mother wit," which connotes native intelligence irrespective of gender. She was talking about maternal feelings and skills. (Diamond, 1992:17)

Diamond did develop general conclusions about social life from his research. In the nursing home, he argues,

> there were two kinds of narratives on caregiving: one formal, written, and shared by the professionals and administrators; another submerged, unwritten, and shared by the people who lived and worked on the floors. (Diamond, 1992:215)

To summarize, Diamond's research began with an exploratory question (to find out what was going on) and proceeded inductively throughout, developing general concepts to make sense of specific observations. Although Diamond, a white man, was something of an outsider in a setting dominated by women of color, he was able to share many participants' experiences and perspectives. His in-depth descriptions and idiographic connections of sequences of events enabled him to construct plausible explanations about what seemed to be a typical group. He thus successfully used field research to explore human experiences in depth, carefully analyzing the social contexts in which they occur.

■ ■ ■ ■ Participant Observation

Diamond carried out his study through **participant observation,** termed "fieldwork" in anthropology. It is a method in which natural social processes are studied as they happen (in "the field" rather than in the laboratory) and left relatively undisturbed. It is the seminal field research method, a means for seeing the social world as the research subjects see it, in its totality, and for understanding subjects' interpretations of that world (Wolcott, 1995:66). By observing people and interacting with them in the course of their normal activities, participant observers seek to avoid the artificiality of experimental designs and the unnatural structured questioning of survey research (Koegel, 1987:8).

The term *participant observer* actually represents a continuum of roles (see Exhibit 8.1), ranging from being a complete observer, who does not

Exhibit 8.1 **The Observational Continuum**

To study a political activist group...

You could take the role of complete observer:

You could take the role of participant and observer:

You could take the role of covert participant:

participate in group activities and is publicly defined as a researcher, to being a covert participant, who acts just like other group members and does not disclose his or her research role. Many field researchers develop a role between these extremes, publicly acknowledging being a researcher but nonetheless participating in group activities. In some settings, it also is possible to observe covertly, without acknowledging being a researcher or participating.

Choosing a Role

The first concern of all participant observers is to decide what balance to strike between observing and participating and whether to reveal their role as a researcher. These decisions must take into account the specifics of the social situation being studied, the researcher's own background and personality, the larger sociopolitical context, and ethical concerns. Which balance of participating and observing is most appropriate also changes during most projects, often many times. And the researcher's ability to maintain either a covert or an overt role will many times be challenged.

Complete Observation

Barrie Thorne (1993) had little choice but to adopt the role of a complete observer when, as an adult, she began to observe children's social interaction in school playgrounds. In **complete observation**, researchers try to see things as they happen, without disrupting the participants:

> I like to think of myself as having hung out in classrooms, lunchrooms, playgrounds, relating to kids in a friendly and sometimes helpful fashion, treating them, in my analysis and writing, with respect. But, like all field workers, I was also a spectator, even a voyeur, passing though their lives and sharing few real stakes with those they studied. Several kids asked me if I was a spy, and, in a way, I was, especially when I went in search of activities and meanings they created when not in the company of adults. . . . [I]n the very act of documenting their autonomy, I undermined it, for my gaze remained, at its core and its ultimate knowing purpose, that of a more powerful adult. (Thorne, 1993:27)

So the researcher's very presence as an observer alters the social situation being observed. It is not "natural" in most social situations for an observer to be present, one who will record at some point her or his observations for research and publication purposes. The observer thus sees what individuals do when they are being observed, which is not necessarily what they would have done had an observer not been present. This is the problem of **reactive effects,** as Thorne notes:

> On the playground, the kids sometimes treated me as an adult with formal authority. Calling "Yard duty, yard duty," or "Teach-er!" they ran up with requests for intervention—"Make Ralph give me back my ball"; "Burt threw the rope onto the roof." I responded by saying, "I'm not a yard duty," and usually by refusing to intervene, telling those who asked for help that they would have to find someone who was a yard duty, or handle the situation by themselves. (Thorne, 1993:17)

The extent to which reactive effects are a problem varies with the situation. In social settings involving many people, in which observing while standing or sitting does not attract attention, the complete observer is unlikely to have much effect on social processes. For example, I observed the delegate meetings of a public-employee union for about four years, sitting like most delegates and taking notes like many others (Schutt, 1986). I came to know many of the participants, but in a large room with about 40 other people, my presence seemed to have had no impact on the meetings.

On the other hand, when the social setting involves few people and observing is unlike the usual activities in the setting, or when the observer differs in obvious respects from the participants, the complete observer is more likely to have an impact:

> My greater size; my access to special relations with the principal, teachers, and aides; and my sheer status as an adult in an institution that draws sharp generational divisions and marks them with differences in power and authority, posed complicated obstacles to learning from kids. (Thorne, 1993:16)

Even the clearest distinction of the researcher's role cannot prevent the emergence of pressures to become more of a participant:

> I could usually rely on playground aides to be on the lookout and to handle scenes of physical injury. It was harder for me to stay detached when kids hurt one another's feelings and I sometimes tried to soothe these situations. For example, . . . Sherry asked, "Why did your mother leave you?" Jessica replied, "She wanted to marry a guy, but they had a fight and she didn't." Almost simultaneously, Nancy spoke up. "She left because she didn't love you." Jessica blushed and I resonated with her stung feelings. Feeling quite maternal, I tried to comfort Jessica by putting my arm around her and saying, "I'm sure it was hard for your mother to leave." (Thorne, 1993:20)

Participation and Observation

Most field researchers adopt a role that involves some active participation in the setting. Usually they inform at least some group members of their research interests, but then they participate in enough group activities to develop rapport with members and to gain a direct sense of what group members experience. This is not an easy balancing act, but

> the key to participant observation as a fieldwork strategy is to take seriously the challenge it poses to participate more, and to play the role of the aloof observer less. Do not think of yourself as someone who needs to wear a white lab coat and carry a clipboard to learn about how humans go about their everyday lives. (Wolcott, 1995:100)

Richard Fenno (1978) provides a good example of the rapport-building function of participation in his study of relationships between members of the U.S. House of Representatives and their constituents:

> Once, for example, I arrived in a district in time to make a Friday night event, only to find the congressman had been unable to leave Washington. . . . I sat down beside someone [at campaign headquarters] and started stamping and sealing a huge stack of envelopes. An hour or two later, someone asked me to help with a telephone poll, which I did. (Fenno, 1978:267)

As a result of his contribution, Fenno was shown the confidential poll results and invited to a campaign strategy meeting the next day.

Participating and observing has two clear ethical advantages as well. Because group members know the researcher's real role in the group, they can choose to keep some information or attitudes hidden. By the same token, the researcher can decline to participate in unethical or dangerous activities without fear of exposing his or her identity.

Most field researchers who opt for disclosure get the feeling that, after they have become known and at least somewhat trusted figures in the group, their presence does not have any palpable effect on members' actions. The major influences on individual actions and attitudes are past experiences, personality, group structure, and so on, so the argument goes, and these continue to exert their influence even when an outside observer is present. The participant observer can presumably be ethical about identity disclosure and still observe the natural social world. Of course, the argument is less persuasive when the behavior to be observed is illegal or stigmatized, so that participants have reason to fear the consequences of disclosure to any outsider.

In practice it can be difficult to maintain a fully open research role even in a setting without these special characteristics.

> During and after the fieldwork the first question many people asked was "Did you tell them?". . . I had initially hoped to disclose at every phase of the project my dual objective of working as a nursing assistant and writing about these experiences. In some instances it was possible to disclose this dual purpose, in others it was not. I told many nursing

assistants and people who lived in the homes that I was both working and investigating. I told some of my nursing supervisors and some administrators. . . . The short answer is that as the study proceeded it was forced increasingly to become a piece of undercover research. (Diamond, 1992:7–8)

Even when researchers maintain a public identity as researchers, ethical dilemmas arising from participation in group activities do not go away. In fact, researchers may have to "prove themselves" to group members by joining in some of their questionable activities. For example, police officers gave John Van Maanen (1982) a nonstandard and technically prohibited pistol to carry on police patrols. Harold Pepinsky (1980) witnessed police harassment of a citizen but did not intervene when the citizen was arrested. Trying to strengthen his ties with a local political figure in his study of a poor Boston community he called Cornerville, William Foote Whyte (1955) illegally voted multiple times in a local election.

Experienced participant observers try to lessen some of the problems of identity disclosure by evaluating both their effect on others in the setting and the effect of others on the observers, writing about these effects throughout the time they are in the field and while they analyze their data. They also are sure while in the field to preserve some physical space and regular time when they can concentrate on their research and schedule occasional meetings with other researchers to review the fieldwork. Participant observers modify their role as circumstances seem to require, perhaps not always disclosing their research role at casual social gatherings or group outings but being sure to inform new members of it.

Covert Participation

To lessen the potential for reactive effects and to gain entry to otherwise inaccessible settings, some field researchers have adopted the role of covert participant, keeping their research secret and trying their best to act like other participants in a social setting or group. **Covert participation** is also known as **complete participation.** Laud Humphreys (1970) served as a "watch queen" so that he could learn about men engaging in homosexual acts in a public restroom. Randall Alfred (1976) joined a group of Satanists to investigate group members and their interaction. Erving Goffman (1961) worked as a state hospital assistant while studying the treatment of psychiatric patients.

Although the role of covert participant lessens some of the reactive effects encountered by the complete observer, covert participants confront other problems:

■ *Covert participants cannot take notes openly or use any obvious recording devices.* They must write up notes based solely on memory and must do so at times when it is natural for them to be away from group members.

■ *Covert participants cannot ask questions that will arouse suspicion.* Thus they often have trouble clarifying the meaning of other participants' attitudes or actions.

■ *The role of covert participant is difficult to play successfully, because covert participants will not know how regular participants would act in every situation in which the researchers find themselves.* Regular participants have entered the situation from social backgrounds and goals different from the researchers'. Researchers' spontaneous reactions to every event are unlikely to be consistent with those of the regular participants. Suspicion that researchers are not "one of us" may then have reactive effects, obviating the value of complete participation (Erikson, 1967). In his study of the Satanists, for example, Alfred pretended to be a regular group participant until he completed his research, at which time he informed the group leader of his covert role. Rather than act surprised, the leader told Alfred that he had long considered Alfred to be "strange," not like the others—and we will never know for sure how Alfred's observations were affected. Even Diamond, though an acknowledged researcher in the nursing home, found that simply disclosing the fact that he did not work another job to make ends meet set him apart from other nursing assistants:

> "There's one thing I learned when I came to the States," [said a Haitian nursing assistant]. "Here you can't make it on just one job." She tilted her head, looked at me curiously, then asked, "You know, Tim, there's just one thing I don't understand about you. How do you make it on just one job?" (Diamond, 1992:47–48)

■ *Covert participants need to keep up the act at all times while in the setting under study.* Researchers may experience enormous psychological strain, particularly in situations where they are expected to choose sides in intragroup conflict or to participate in criminal or other acts. Of course, some covert observers may become so wrapped up in the role they are playing that they adopt not just the mannerisms but also the perspectives and goals of the regular participants—they "go native." At this point, they abandon research goals and cease to evaluate critically what they are observing.

Ethical issues have been at the forefront of debate over the strategy of covert participation. Kai Erikson (1967) argues that covert participation is by its very nature unethical and should not be allowed except in public settings. Covert researchers cannot anticipate the unintended consequences of their actions for research subjects, Erikson points out. If others suspect the researcher's identity or if the researcher contributes to, or impedes, group action, these consequences can be adverse. In addition, other social scientists are harmed when covert research is disclosed—either during the research or upon its publication—because distrust of social scientists increases and access to research opportunities may decrease.

But a total ban on covert participation would "kill many a project stone dead" (Punch, 1994:90). Studies of unusual religious or sexual practices and of institutional malpractice would rarely be possible. "The crux of the matter is that some deception, passive or active, enables you to get at data not obtainable by other means" (Punch, 1994:91). Therefore, some field researchers argue that covert participation is legitimate in some settings. If the researcher maintains the confidentiality of others, keeps commitments to others, and does not directly lie to others, some degree of deception may be justified in exchange for the knowledge gained (Punch, 1994:90).

Entering the Field

Entering the field, the setting under investigation, is a critical stage in a participant observation project because it can shape many subsequent experiences. Some background work is necessary before entering the field—at least enough to develop a clear understanding of what the research questions are likely to be and to review one's personal stance toward the people and problems likely to be encountered. With participant observation, researchers must also learn in advance how participants dress and what their typical activities are, so as to avoid being caught completely unprepared.

For his study, Diamond tried to enter a nursing home twice, first without finding out about necessary qualifications:

> My first job interview. . . . The administrator of the home had agreed to see me on [the recommendation of two current assistants]. [T]he administrator . . . probed suspiciously, "Now why would a white guy want to work for these kinds of wages?" . . . He continued without pause, "Besides, I couldn't hire you if I wanted to. You're not certified." That, he quickly concluded, was the end of our interview, and he showed me to the door. (Diamond, 1992:8–9)

After taking a course and receiving his certificate, Diamond was able to enter the role of nursing assistant as others did, with one qualification:

> Ms. North, who conducted the interviews, oriented each of us to the program. . . . It was a rushed interview because the waiting room was filled, largely with women of color in their twenties and thirties, and Ms. North seemed anxious to enroll her next candidate. "Do you have any questions?" she asked while closing my file.
>
> I had many questions, but time for just one. "I'm a little uncomfortable being the only man and one of the few white people signing up. Will I be out of place?" (Diamond, 1992:14–15)

Many field researchers avoid systematic study and extensive reading about a setting for fear that it will bias their first impressions, but entering without any sense of the social norms can lead to disaster. Whyte came close to such disaster when he despaired of making any social contacts in Cornerville and decided to try an unconventional entry approach (unconventional for a field researcher, that is). In *Street Corner Society*, the account of his study, Whyte describes what happened when he went to a hotel bar in search of women to talk with:

> I looked around me again and now noticed a threesome: one man and two women. It occurred to me that here was a maldistribution of females which I might be able to rectify. I approached the group and opened with something like this: "Pardon me. Would you mind if I joined you?" There was a moment of silence while the man stared at me. He then offered to throw me downstairs. I assured him that this would not be necessary and demonstrated as much by walking right out of there without any assistance. (Whyte, 1955:289)

The entry gambit that finally worked for Whyte was to rely on a local community leader for introductions. Such a person may become an informant throughout the project, and most participant observers make a point of developing at least one trusted informant in a group under study. A helpful social worker at the local settlement house introduced Whyte to "Doc," who agreed to help:

> Well, any nights you want to see anything, I'll take you around. I can take you to the joints—gambling joints—I can take you around to the street corners. Just remember that you're my friend. That's all they need to know [so they won't bother you]. (Whyte, 1955:291)

Thorne had to begin her study of schoolchildren through the adults in charge:

> I entered the field through adult gatekeepers. A friend introduced me to Miss Bailey, the fourth-fifth-grade Oceanside teacher, and she, in turn, agreed to let me observe in her classroom, as did Mr. Welch, the school principal, who asked only that I not "disrupt" and that I report back my findings. My more formal entry into Ashton School, via the district Title IX office, seemed to make the Ashton principal a little nervous. But Mrs. Smith, the kindergarten teacher, and Mrs. Johnson, the second-grade teacher, seemed at ease when I was in their classrooms, and I had ample latitude to define my presence to the students of both schools. (Thorne, 1993:16)

When participant observing involves public figures who are used to reporters and researchers, a more direct approach may secure entry into the field. Fenno approached most of the members of Congress he would study with a "cold turkey" letter:

> Dear Representative ———,
> I am writing to ask if you might be willing to let me travel around with you when you are in your district for a three- or four-day period sometime this spring. I am a professor of political science at the University of Rochester and am writing a book on the relations between congressmen and their constituencies. I'm trying to learn about the subject by accompanying a dozen or so House members as they work in their districts. (Fenno, 1978:257)

Fenno received only two refusals. He attributed the willingness of his subjects to be observed and questioned in this way to a variety of reasons, including their interest in a change in the daily routine, their commitment to making themselves available, a desire for more publicity, the flattery of scholarly attention, and interest in helping to teach others about politics. Other groups have other motivations, but in every case some consideration of these potential motives in advance should help smooth entry into the field.

In short, field researchers must be very sensitive to the impression they make and the ties they establish when entering the field. This stage lays the groundwork for collecting data from people who have different perspectives and for developing relationships that the researcher can use to surmount the problems in data collection that inevitably arise in the field.

Developing and Maintaining Relationships

Researchers must be careful to manage their relationships in the research setting so they can continue to observe and interview diverse members of the social setting throughout the long period typical of participant observation (Maxwell, 1996:66). Every action the researcher takes can develop or undermine this relationship:

> Although a note-taking adult cannot pass as even an older elementary student, I tried in other ways to lessen the social distance between me and the kids. I avoided positions of authority and rarely intervened in a managerial way, and I went through the days with or near the kids rather than along the paths of teachers and aides. Like others who have done participant-observation with children, I felt a little elated when kids violated rules in my presence, like swearing or openly blowing bubble gum where these acts were forbidden, or swapping stories about recent acts of shoplifting. These incidents reassured me that I had shed at least some of the trappings of adult authority and gained access to kids' more private worlds. (Thorne, 1993:18–19)

Maintaining trust is the cornerstone to successful research engagement, as indicated by the following example of a failure in Van Maanen's police research:

> Following a family beef call in what was tagged the Little Africa section of town, I once got into what I regarded as a soft but nonetheless heated debate with the officer I was working with that evening on the merits of residential desegregation. My more or less liberal leanings on the matter were bothersome to this officer, who later reported my disturbing thoughts to his friends in the squad. Before long, I was an anathema to this friendship clique and labeled by them undesirable. Members of this group refused to work with me again. (Van Maanen, 1982:110)

So Van Maanen failed to maintain a research (or personal) relationship with this group. Do you think he should have kept his opinions about residential desegregation to himself? How honest should field researchers be about their feelings? Should they "go along to get along"?

Whyte used what in retrospect was a sophisticated two-part strategy to develop and maintain relationships with the Cornerville street-corner men. The first part of Whyte's strategy was to maintain good relations with Doc and, through Doc, to stay on good terms with the others. The less obvious part of Whyte's strategy was a consequence of his decision to move into Cornerville, a move he decided was necessary to really understand and be accepted in the community. The room he rented in a local family's home became his base of operations. In some respects, this family became an important dimension of Whyte's immersion in the community: He tried to learn Italian by speaking with family members, and they conversed late at night as if Whyte were a real family member. But Whyte recognized that he needed a place to unwind after his days of constant alertness in the field, so he made a conscious decision not to include the family as an object of study. Living in this family's home became a means for Whyte to maintain standing as a community insider without becoming totally immersed in the demands of research (Whyte, 1955:294–297).

Experienced participant observers have developed some sound advice for others seeking to maintain relationships in the field (Whyte, 1955:300–306; Wolcott, 1995:91–95):

■ Develop a plausible (and honest) explanation for yourself and your study.

■ Maintain the support of key individuals in groups or organizations under study.

■ Don't be too aggressive in questioning others (for example, don't violate implicit norms that preclude discussion of illegal activity with outsiders). Being a researcher requires that you not simultaneously try to be the guardian of law and order.

■ Ask very sensitive questions only of informants with whom your relationship is good.

■ Don't fake your social similarity with your subjects. Taking a friendly interest in them should be an adequate basis for developing trust.

■ Avoid giving or receiving monetary or other tangible gifts but without violating norms of reciprocity. Living with other people, taking others' time for conversations, going out for a social evening all create expectations and incur social obligations, and you can't be an active participant without occasionally helping others. But you will lose your ability to function as a researcher if you come to be seen as someone who gives away money or other favors. Such small forms of assistance as an occasional ride to the store or advice on applying to college may strike the right balance.

■ Be prepared for special difficulties and tensions if multiple groups are involved. It is hard to avoid taking sides or being used in situations of intergroup conflict.

Sampling People and Events

Decisions to study one setting or several and to pay attention to some people and events rather than others will shape field researchers' ability to generalize about what they have found as well as the confidence that others can place in the results of their study. Limiting a particular study to a single setting allows a more intensive portrait of actors and activities in that setting but also makes generalization of the findings questionable.

We may be reassured by information indicating that a "typical" case was selected for study or that the case selected was appropriate in some way for the research question. We also must keep in mind that many of the most insightful participant observation studies were conducted in only one setting and draw their credibility precisely from the researcher's thorough understanding of that setting. Nonetheless, studying more than one case or setting almost always strengthens the causal conclusions and makes the findings more generalizable (King, Koehane, & Verba, 1994).

To make his conclusions more generalizable, Diamond (1992:5) worked in three different Chicago nursing homes "in widely different neighborhoods" and with different fractions of residents supported by Medicaid. He then "visited many homes across the United States to validate my observations." Thorne (1993:6–7) observed in a public elementary school in California for eight months and then, four years later, for three months in a public elementary school in Michigan:

> The demographics of the Oceanside and Ashton schools were remark-
> ably similar. Each had around four hundred students who were from
> various "white" ethnicities; between 12 and 14 percent were Chicano or
> Latino; around 5 percent were African-American. In the California
> school there were a few Filipino-American and Japanese-American
> students, and one child with parents from India, and in the Michigan
> school there were a scattering of Native American students. (Thorne,
> 1993:7)

In both studies, the researchers' ability to draw from different settings in developing conclusions gives us greater confidence in their studies' generalizability. Still, the two schools that Thorne studied represented little more than a convenience sample of schools—the schools that were available to her for study when she was ready to study them. Diamond's selection of nursing homes seems somewhat more purposively determined to ensure the representation of different types of homes (see also Maxwell, 1996:69–73).

A more systematic approach to sampling in participant observation studies has been termed **theoretical sampling** (Glaser & Strauss, 1967). When field researchers discover in an investigation that particular processes seem to be important, implying that certain comparisons should be made or that similar instances should be checked, the researchers then choose new settings or individuals to study as well, as diagrammed in Exhibit 8.2 (Ragin, 1994:98–101). Fenno's strategy for selecting members of Congress to observe in their home districts exemplifies this type of approach:

> Whom should I observe? . . . If I had been certain about what types of
> representatives and what types of districts to sample, I would already
> have had answers to a lot of the questions raised in this book. My
> procedure was slowly to build up the size of the group being observed
> and constantly to monitor its composition to see what commonly
> recognized types of members or districts I might be neglecting. Then I
> would move to remedy any imagined deficiencies. I spent a lot of time
> trying to figure out a priori what types of members or districts might
> pose serious tests for, or exceptions to, whatever generalizations
> seemed to be emerging—with the intent of bringing such members or
> districts into the group. At one point, I noticed there were too many
> lawyers; the next two people I chose were nonlawyers. (Fenno,
> 1978:253)

You already learned in Chapter 4 about nonprobability sampling methods, which can also be used to develop a more representative range of opinions and events in a field setting. For instance, purposive sampling, of which theoretical sampling is a type, can be used to identify opinion leaders and representatives of different roles. With snowball sampling, field re-

Exhibit 8.2   **Theoretical Sampling**

Original cases interviewed in a study of cocaine users:

Realization: Some cocaine users are businesspeople.
Add businesspeople to sample:

Realization: Sample is low on women.
Add women to sample:

Realization: Some female cocaine users are mothers of young children.
Add mothers to sample:

searchers learn from participants about who represents different subgroups in a setting. Quota sampling also may be employed to ensure the representation of particular categories of participants. Using some type of intentional sampling strategy within a particular setting can allow tests of some hypotheses that would otherwise have to wait until comparative data could be collected from several settings (King, Keohane, & Verba, 1994).

When field studies do not require ongoing, intensive involvement by researchers in the setting, the **experience sampling method (ESM)** can be used. The experiences, thoughts, and feelings of a number of people are sampled randomly as they go about their daily activities. Participants in an ESM study carry an electronic pager and fill out reports when they are beeped. For example, 107 adults carried pagers in Robert Kubey's (1990) ESM study of television habits and family quality of life. Participants' reports indicated that heavy TV viewers were less active during non-TV family activities, although heavy TV viewers also spent more time with their families and felt as positively toward other family members as did those who watched less TV. Although ESM is a powerful tool for field research, it is still limited by the need to recruit people to carry pagers. Ultimately, the generalizability of ESM findings relies on the representativeness, and reliability, of the persons who cooperate in the research.

Taking Notes

Written notes are the primary means of recording participant observation data (Emerson, Fretz, & Shaw, 1995). Of course, "written" no longer means handwritten; many field researchers jot down partial notes while observing and then retreat to their computer to write up more complete notes on a daily basis. The computerized text can then be inspected and organized after it is printed out, or it can be marked up and organized for analysis using one of several computer programs designed especially for the task.

It is almost always a mistake to try to take comprehensive notes while engaged in the field—the process of writing extensively is just too disruptive. The usual procedure (see Exhibit 8.3) is to jot down brief notes about highlights of the observation period. These brief notes can then serve as memory joggers when writing the actual **field notes** at a later session. With the aid of the brief notes and some practice, researchers usually remember a great deal of what happened, as long as the comprehensive field notes are written within the next 24 hours—that night or upon arising the next day.

The following excerpts shed light on the note-taking processes that Diamond and Thorne used while in the field. Taking notes was more of a challenge for Diamond because many people in the setting did not know that he was a researcher:

> While I was getting to know nursing assistants and residents and experiencing aspects of their daily routines, I would surreptitiously take notes on scraps of paper, in the bathroom or otherwise out of sight, jotting down what someone had said or done. (Diamond, 1992:6–7)

Thorne was able to take notes openly:

> I went through the school days with a small spiral notebook in hand, jotting descriptions that I later expanded into field notes When I was at the margins of a scene, I took notes on the spot. When I was more fully involved, sitting and talking with kids at a cafeteria table or playing a game of jump rope, I held observations in my memory and recorded them later. (Thorne, 1993:17)

Usually writing up notes takes as long as making the observations. Field notes must be as complete, detailed, and true to what was observed and

Exhibit 8.3 **The Note-Taking Process**

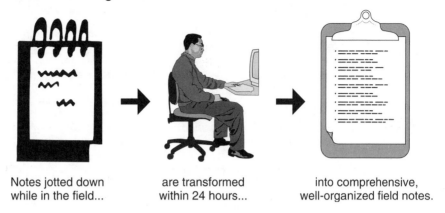

Notes jotted down while in the field... are transformed within 24 hours... into comprehensive, well-organized field notes.

heard as possible. Quotes should be clearly distinguished from the researcher's observations and phrased in the local vernacular; pauses and interruptions should be indicated. The surrounding context should receive as much attention as possible, and a map of the setting always should be included, with indications of where individuals were at different times.

Careful note-taking yields a big payoff. On page after page, field notes will suggest new concepts, causal connections, and theoretical propositions. Social processes and settings can be described in rich detail, with ample illustrations. Exhibit 8.4, for example, contains field notes recorded by Norma Ware, an anthropologist studying living arrangements for homeless mentally ill persons (see the discussion of Goldfinger, Schutt, et al., 1997, in Chapter 1). The notes contain observations of the setting, the questions the anthropologist asked and the answers she received, and her analytic thoughts about one of the residents. What can be learned from just this one page of field notes? The mood of the house at this time is evident, with joking, casual conversation, and close friendships. "Dick" remarks on problems with household financial management, and at the same time we learn a bit about his own activities and personality (a regular worker who appears to like systematic plans). We see how a few questions and a private conversation elicit information about the transition from the shelter to the house, as well as about household operations. The field notes also provide the foundation for a more complete picture of one resident, describing "Jim's" relationships with others, his personal history, his interests and personality, and his orientation to the future. We can see analytic concepts emerge in the notes, such as the concept of "pulling himself together" and of some house members working as a "team." You can imagine how researchers can go on to develop a theoretical framework for understanding the setting and a set of concepts and questions to inform subsequent observations.

Exhibit 8.4 **Field Notes from an ECH***

I arrive around 4:30 P.M. and walk into a conversation between Jim and somebody else as to what color jeans he should buy. There is quite a lot of joking going on between Jim and Susan. I go out to the kitchen and find Dick about to take his dinner out to the picnic table to eat (his idea?) so I go ask if I can join him. He says yes. In the course of the conversation, I find out that he works 3 days a week in the "prevoc" program at the local day program, Food Services branch, for which he gets $10 per week. Does he think the living situation will work out? Yes. All they need is a plan for things like when somebody buys something and then everybody else uses it. Like he bought a gallon of milk and it was gone in two days, because everyone was using it for their coffee. I ask if he's gone back to the shelter to visit and he says "No. I was glad to get out of there." He came to [the ECH] from [a shelter] through homeless outreach [a Department of Mental Health program]. Had been at [the shelter] since January. Affirms that [the ECH] is a better place to live than the shelter. Why? Because you have your own room and privacy and stuff. How have people been getting along with each other? He says, "Fine."

I return to the living room and sit down on the couch with Jim and Susan. Susan teases Jim and he jokes back. Susan is eating a T.V. dinner with M and M's for dessert. There is joking about working off the calories from the M and M's by doing sit-up's, which she proceeds to demonstrate. This leads to a conversation about exercise during which Jim declares his intention to get back into exercise by doing sports, like basketball.

Jim seems to have his mind on pulling himself together, which he characterizes as "getting my old self back." When I ask him what he's been doing since I saw him last, he says, "Working on my appearance." And in fact, he has had a haircut, a shave, and washed his clothes. When I ask him what his old self was like, he says, "you mean before I lost everything?" I learn that he used to work two jobs, had "a family" and was into "religion." This seems to have been when he was quite young, around eighteen. He tells me he was on the street for 7-8 years, from 1978-1985, drinking the whole time. I ask him whether he thinks living at [the ECH] will help him to get his "old self back" and he says that it will "help motivate me." I observe that he seems pretty motivated already. He says yes, "but this will motivate me more."

Jim has a warm personality, likes to joke and laugh. He also speaks up--in meetings he is among the first to say what he thinks and he talks among the most. His "team" relationship with Bill is also important to him--"me and Bill, we work together."

*Evolving Consumer Household (see Chapter 1).
Source: Norma Ware, Ph.D., Department of Social Medicine, Harvard Medical School, unpublished ethnographic notes, 1991.

Complete field notes must provide even more than a record of what was observed or heard. Notes also should include descriptions of the methodology: where researchers were standing while observing, how they chose people for conversation or observation, what counts of people or events they made and why. Sprinkled throughout the notes also should be a record of the researchers' feelings and thoughts while observing: when they were disgusted by some statement or act, when they felt threatened or intimidated, why their attention shifted from one group to another. Notes like these provide a foundation for later review of the likelihood of bias or of inattention to some salient features of the situation.

Managing the Personal Dimensions

Our overview of participant observation would not be complete without considering its personal dimensions. Because field researchers become a part of the social situation they are studying, they cannot help but be affected on a personal, emotional level. At the same time, those being studied react to researchers not just as researchers but as personal acquaintances—and often as friends, sometimes as personal rivals. Managing and learning from this personal side of field research is an important part of any project.

The impact of personal issues varies with the depth of researchers' involvement in the setting. The more involved researchers are in multiple aspects of the ongoing social situation, the more important personal issues become and the greater the risk of "going native." Even when researchers acknowledge their role, "increased contact brings sympathy, and sympathy in its turn dulls the edge of criticism" (Fenno, 1978:277). Fenno minimized this problem by returning frequently to the university and by avoiding involvement in the personal lives of the congressional representatives he was studying. To study the social life of "corner boys," however, Whyte could not stay so disengaged. He moved into an apartment with a Cornerville family and lived for about four years in the community he was investigating:

> The researcher, like his informants, is a social animal. He has a role to play, and he has his own personality needs that must be met in some degree if he is to function successfully. Where the researcher operates out of a university, just going into the field for a few hours at a time, he can keep his personal social life separate from field activity. His problem of role is not quite so complicated. If, on the other hand, the researcher is living for an extended period in the community he is studying, his personal life is inextricably mixed with his research. (Whyte, 1955:279)

The correspondence between researchers' social attributes—age, sex, race, and so on—and those of their subjects also shapes personal relationships, as Diamond noted:

> The staff were mostly people of color, residents mostly white. . . . Never before, or since, have I been so acutely aware of being a white American man. At first the people who lived in the homes stared at me, then some approached to get a closer look, saying that I reminded them of a nephew, a son, a grandson, a brother, a doctor. This behavior made more sense as time went on: except for the few male residents and occasional visitors, I was the only white man many would see from one end of the month to the next. (Diamond, 1992:39)

Thorne wondered whether "my moments of remembering, the times when I felt like a ten-year-old girl, [were] a source of distortion or insight?" She concluded they were both: "Memory, like observing, is a way of knowing and can be a rich resource." But "When my own responses, . . . were driven by emotions like envy or aversion, they clearly obscured my ability to grasp the full social situation" (Thorne, 1993:26).

There is no formula for successfully managing the personal dimension of field research. It is much more art than science and flows more from the researcher's own personality and natural approach to other people than from formal training. But novice field researchers often neglect to consider how they will manage personal relationships when they plan and carry out their projects. Then suddenly they find themselves doing something they don't believe they should, just to stay in the good graces of research subjects, or juggling the emotions resulting from conflict within the group. As Whyte noted:

> The field worker cannot afford to think only of learning to live with others in the field. He has to continue living with himself. If the participant observer finds himself engaging in behavior that he has learned to think of as immoral, then he is likely to begin to wonder what sort of a person he is after all. Unless the field worker can carry with him a reasonably consistent picture of himself, he is likely to run into difficulties. (Whyte, 1955:317)

If you plan a field research project, follow these guidelines (Whyte, 1955:300–317):

- Take the time to consider how you want to relate to your potential subjects as people.
- Speculate about what personal problems might arise and how you will respond to them.

- Keep in touch with other researchers and personal friends outside the research setting.

- Maintain standards of conduct that make you comfortable as a person and that respect the integrity of your subjects.

When you evaluate participant observers' reports, pay attention to how they defined their role in the setting and dealt with personal problems. Don't place too much confidence in such research unless the report provides this information.

■ ■ ■ ■ Intensive Interviewing

Asking questions is part of almost all participant observation (Wolcott, 1995:102–105). However, many qualitative researchers employ intensive interviewing exclusively, without systematic observation of respondents in their natural setting.

Unlike the more structured interviewing that may be used in survey research (discussed in Chapter 7), **intensive interviewing** relies on open-ended questions. Qualitative researchers do not presume to know the range of answers that respondents might give and seek to hear these answers in the respondents' own words. Rather than asking standard questions in a fixed order, intensive interviewers allow the specific content and order of questions to vary from one interviewee to another.

What distinguishes intensive interviewing from less structured forms of questioning is consistency and thoroughness. The goal is to develop a comprehensive picture of the interviewee's background, attitudes, and actions, in his or her own terms; to "listen to people as they describe how they understand the worlds in which they live and work" (Rubin & Rubin, 1995:3). For example, Sharon Kaufman (1986:6) sought through intensive interviewing to learn how old people cope with change. She wanted to hear the words of the elderly themselves, for "the voices of individual old people can tell us much about the experience of being old."

Intensive interview studies do not reveal as directly as does participant observation the social context in which action is taken and opinions are formed. But like participant observation studies, intensive interviewing engages researchers more actively with subjects than does standard survey research. The researchers must listen to lengthy explanations, ask follow-up questions tailored to the preceding answers, seek to learn about interrelated belief systems or personal approaches to things—rather than measure a limited set of variables. As a result, intensive interviews are often much longer than standardized interviews, sometimes as long as 15 hours, conducted in several different sessions (Kaufman, 1986:22).

The intensive interview becomes more like a conversation between partners than between a researcher and a subject.

> I tried to place my informants in the role of teacher. I think I was most often put in the role of empathetic acquaintance. For a number of people, I was a confidant. From my viewpoint, and I think from that of my informants as well, our conversations were undertaken in a spirit of friendliness, honesty, and enjoyment. Data that I obtained in this manner were spontaneous, thoughtful, and usually self-reflective. Anyone overhearing one of my "interviews" (except another anthropologist) probably would have thought that we were friends carrying on a conversation, or that we were acquaintances, and that I was simply trying to get to know the other person better. This is the context in which I acquired information about [older persons'] identity. (Kaufman, 1986:23)

Intensive interviewers actively try to probe understandings and engage interviewees in a dialogue about what they mean by their comments. Robert Bellah, Richard Madsen, William Sullivan, Ann Swidler, and Steven Tipton (1985) elaborate on this aspect of intensive interviewing in a methodological appendix to their national best-seller about American individualism, *Habits of the Heart*:

> We did not, as in some scientific version of "Candid Camera," seek to capture their beliefs and actions without our subjects being aware of us. Rather, we sought to bring our preconceptions and questions into the conversation and to understand the answers we were receiving not only in terms of the language but also, so far as we could discover, in the lives of those we were talking with. Though we did not seek to impose our ideas on those with whom we talked . . . , we did attempt to uncover assumptions, to make explicit what the person we were talking to might rather have left implicit. The interview as we employed it was active, Socratic. (Bellah et al., 1985:304)

The intensive interview follows a preplanned outline of topics, which often are asked in a reasonably consistent manner of selected group members or other participants. Some projects may use relatively structured interviews, particularly when the focus is on developing knowledge about prior events or some narrowly defined topic. But more exploratory projects, particularly those aiming to learn about interviewees' interpretations of the world, may let each interview flow in a unique direction in response to the interviewee's experiences and interests (Kvale, 1996:3–5; Rubin & Rubin, 1995:6; Wolcott, 1995:113–114). In either case, qualitative interviewers must adapt nimbly throughout the interview, paying attention to nonverbal cues, expressions with symbolic value, and the ebb and flow of the interviewee's

Exhibit 8.5   **The Saturation Point in Intensive Interviewing**

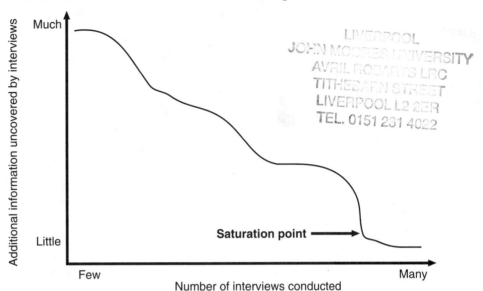

feelings and interests. "You have to be free to follow your data where they lead" (Rubin & Rubin, 1995:64).

Random selection is rarely used to select respondents for intensive interviews, but the selection method still must carefully be considered. If interviewees are selected in a haphazard manner, as by speaking just to those who happen to be available at the time that the researcher is on site, the interviews are likely to be of less value than when a more purposive selection strategy is used. Researchers should try to select interviewees who are knowledgeable about the subject of the interview, who are open to talking, and who represent the range of perspectives (Rubin & Rubin, 1995:65–92). Selection of new interviewees should continue, if possible, at least until the **saturation point** is reached, the point when new interviews seem to yield little additional information (see Exhibit 8.5). As new issues are uncovered, additional interviewees may be selected to represent different opinions about these issues.

Establishing and Maintaining a Partnership

Because intensive interviewing does not engage researchers as participants in subjects' daily affairs, the problems of entering the field are much reduced. However, the logistics of arranging long periods for personal interviews can still be pretty complicated. It also is important to establish rapport with subjects by considering in advance how they will react to the interview arrangements and by developing an approach that does not violate their standards for social behavior. Interviewees should be treated with respect, as knowledgeable partners whose time is valued (in other words, avoid coming late for appointments). A commitment to confidentiality should be stated and honored (Rubin & Rubin, 1995).

But the intensive interviewer's relationship with the interviewee is not an equal partnership, for the researcher seeks to gain certain types of information and strategizes throughout to maintain an appropriate relationship (Kvale, 1996:6). In the first few minutes of the interview, the goal is to show interest in the interviewee and to explain clearly what the purpose of the interview is (Kvale, 1996:128). During the interview, the interviewer should maintain an appropriate distance from the interviewee, one that doesn't violate cultural norms; the interviewer should maintain eye contact and not engage in distracting behavior. An appropriate pace is also important; pause to allow the interviewee to reflect, elaborate, and generally not feel rushed (Gordon, 1992). When an interview covers emotional or otherwise stressful topics, the interviewer should give the interviewee an opportunity to unwind at the interview's end (Rubin & Rubin, 1995:138).

Asking Questions and Recording Answers

Intensive interviewers must plan their main questions around an outline of the interview topic. The questions should generally be short and to the point. More details can then be elicited through nondirective probes (such as "Can you tell me more about that?") and follow-up questions tailored to answers to the main questions. Interviewers should strategize throughout an interview about how best to achieve their objectives while taking into account interviewees' answers.

Habits of the Heart again provides a useful illustration:

[Coinvestigator Steven] Tipton, in interviewing Margaret Oldham [a pseudonym], tried to discover at what point she would take responsibility for another human being:

Q: So what are you responsible for?
A: I'm responsible for my acts and for what I do.
Q: Does that mean you're responsible for others, too?
A: No.
Q: Are you your sister's keeper?
A: No.
Q: Your brother's keeper?
A: No.
Q: Are you responsible for your husband?
A: I'm not. He makes his own decisions. He is his own person. He acts his own acts. I can agree with them, or I can disagree with them. If I

ever find them nauseous enough, I have a responsibility to leave and not deal with it any more.

Q: What about children?

A: I . . . I would say I have a legal responsibility for them, but in a sense I think they in turn are responsible for their own acts. (Bellah et al., 1985:304)

Do you see how the interviewer actively encouraged the subject to explain what she meant by "responsibility"? This sort of active questioning undoubtedly did a better job of clarifying her concept of responsibility than a fixed set of questions would have.

Tape recorders commonly are used to record intensive and focus group interviews. Most researchers who have tape recorded interviews (including me) feel that that they do not inhibit most interviewees and, in fact, are routinely ignored. The occasional respondent is very concerned with his or her public image and may therefore speak "for the tape recorder," but such individuals are unlikely to speak frankly in any research interview. In any case, constant note-taking during an interview prevents adequate displays of interest and appreciation by the interviewer and hinders the degree of concentration that results in the best interviews.

Of course, there are exceptions to every rule. Fenno presents a compelling argument for avoiding the tape recorder when interviewing public figures who are concerned with their public image:

My belief is that the only chance to get a nonroutine, nonreflexive interview [from many of the members of Congress] is to converse casually, pursuing targets of opportunity without the presence of a recording instrument other than myself. If [worse] comes to worst, they can always deny what they have said in person; on tape they leave themselves no room for escape. I believe they are not unaware of the difference. (Fenno, 1978:280)

Combining Participant Observation and Intensive Interviewing

Eric Hirsch (1990) used a combination of methodologies—including participant observation, intensive interviewing, and a standardized survey—to study the 1985 student movement that attempted to make Columbia University divest its stock in companies dealing with South Africa. The study illustrates the value of combining methods.

One point Hirsch tried to establish in his study was the importance of "consciousness raising" for social movements. Participant observation revealed that

consciousness-raising was done in a variety of small group settings, including dormitory rap sessions, forums, and teach-ins. Coverage of [Coalition for a Free South Africa] activities in the Columbia student newspaper and television reports on the violent repression of the anti-apartheid movement in South Africa increased student consciousness of apartheid and encouraged many students to support divestment. (E. Hirsch, 1990:247)

Hirsch also found an association between student questionnaire responses indicating "raised consciousness" about apartheid in South Africa and those indicating support for the divestment campaign. Comments from intensive interviews then deepened Hirsch's understanding of how consciousness was raised and the role that it played. Here's one example of a subject's observations:

I remember in '83 when the [Columbia University Student] Senate voted to divest. I was convinced that students had voiced their opinion and had been able to convince the minority of administrators that what they wanted was a moral thing. It hadn't been a bunch of radical youths taking buildings and burning things down, to destroy. But rather, going through the system, and it seemed to me that for the first time in a really long time the system was going to work. And then I found out that it hadn't worked, and that just reaffirmed my feelings about how the system at Columbia really did work. (E. Hirsch, 1990:247)

Comments like these, combined with survey responses and Hirch's own observations, provided a comprehensive picture of students' motivations.

Focus Groups

Focus groups are groups of unrelated individuals that are formed by a researcher and then led in group discussion of a topic. The researcher asks specific questions and guides the discussion to ensure that group members address these questions, but the resulting information is qualitative and relatively unstructured. Unlike most other survey designs, focus groups do not involve representative samples; instead, a few individuals are recruited for the group who have the time to participate and who share key characteristics with the target population.

Focus groups have their roots in the interviewing techniques developed in the 1930s by sociologists and psychologists who were dissatisfied with traditional surveys. Traditionally, in a questionnaire survey, subjects are directed to consider certain issues and particular response options in a predetermined order. The spontaneous exchange and development of ideas that characterize social life outside the survey situation is lost—and with it, some social scientists feared, the prospects for validity.

Focus groups were used by the military in World War II to investigate morale and then were popularized by the great American sociologist Robert K. Merton and two collaborators, Marjorie Fiske and Patricia Kendall, in *The Focused Interview* (1956). But marketing researchers were the first to adopt focus groups as a widespread methodology. Marketing researchers use focus groups to investigate likely popular reactions to possible advertising themes and techniques. Their success has prompted other social scientists to use focus groups to evaluate social programs and to assess social needs (Krueger, 1988:18–22).

Most focus groups involve 7 to 10 people, a number that facilitates discussion by all in attendance. Although participants usually do not know one another, they are chosen so that they are relatively homogeneous, which tends to reduce their inhibitions in discussion. (Some researchers conduct discussions among groups of people who know one another, which may further reduce inhibitions.) Of course, the characteristics of individuals that determine their inclusion are based on the researcher's conception of the target population for the study. Focus group leaders must begin the discussion by creating the expectation that all will participate and that the researcher will not favor any particular perspective or participant.

Focus groups are used to collect qualitative data, using open-ended questions posed by the researcher (or group leader). Thus a focused discussion mimics the natural process of forming and expressing opinions—and may give some sense of validity. The researcher may also want to conduct a more traditional survey, asking a representative sample of the target population to answer closed-ended questions, to weigh the validity of data obtained from the focus group. No formal procedure exists for determining the generalizability of focus group answers, but the careful researcher should conduct at least several focus groups on the same topic and check for consistency in the findings as a partial test of generalizability.

Richard Krueger provides a good example of a situation in which focus groups were used effectively:

> [A] University recently launched a $100 million fund drive. The key aspect of the drive was a film depicting science and research efforts. The film was shown in over two dozen focus groups of alumni, with surprising results to University officials. Alumni simply did not like the film and instead were more attracted to supporting undergraduate humanistic education. (Krueger, 1988:33–37)

Focus groups are now used extensively in political campaigns, as a quick means of generating insight into voter preferences and reactions to possible candidate positions. For example, focus groups were used by Michigan Democratic legislators to determine why voters were turning away from them in 1985. Elizabeth Kolbert found that white, middle-class

Democrats were shifting to the Republican Party because of their feelings about race:

> These Democratic defectors saw affirmative action as a direct threat to their own livelihoods, and they saw the black-majority city of Detroit as a sinkhole into which their tax dollars were disappearing. . . . [T]he participants listen[ed] to a quotation from Robert Kennedy exhorting whites to honor their "special obligation" to blacks. Virtually every participant in the four groups—37 in all—reacted angrily. (Kolbert, 1992:21).

Focus group methods share with other field research techniques an emphasis on discovering unanticipated findings and exploring hidden meanings. Although they do not provide a means for developing reliable, generalizable results (the traditional strong suits of survey research), focus groups can be an indispensable aid for developing hypotheses and survey questions, for investigating the meaning of survey results, and for quickly assessing the range of opinion about an issue.

■ ■ ■ ■ **Analysis of Qualitative Data**

The data for a qualitative study most often are notes jotted down in the field or during an interview, from which the original comments are reconstructed, or text transcribed from an audiotape. Diamond's (1992:7) procedure is typical: "Off duty I assembled the notes and began to search for patterns in them. The basic data are these observations and conversations, the actual words of people reproduced to the best of my ability from the field notes."

Many are the projects that have slowed to a halt because a novice researcher becomes overwhelmed by the quantity of information that has been collected. A one hour interview can generate 20 to 25 pages of single-spaced text (Kvale, 1996:169). Analysis is less daunting, however, if the process is broken into smaller steps.

The Phases of Analysis

The analysis of qualitative research notes typically proceeds sequentially, with the researcher first identifying problems and concepts that appear likely to help in understanding the situation. This phase of the analysis should begin while the researcher is still engaged in the field or conducting interviews, so analytic insights can be tested against new observations—as in this study of medical students:

When we first heard medical students apply the term "crock" to patients, we made an effort to learn precisely what they meant by it. We found, through interviewing students about cases both they and the observer had seen, that the term referred in a derogatory way to patients with many subjective symptoms but no discernible physical pathology. Subsequent observations indicated that this usage was a regular feature of student behavior and thus that we should attempt to incorporate this fact into our model of student-patient behavior. The derogatory character of the term suggested in particular that we investigate the reasons students disliked these patients. We found that this dislike was related to what we discovered to be the students' perspective on medical school: the view that they were in school to get experience in recognizing and treating those common diseases most likely to be encountered in general practice. "Crocks," presumably having no disease, could furnish no such experience. We were thus led to specify connections between the student-patient relationship and the student's view of the purpose of his professional education. Questions concerning the genesis of this perspective led to discoveries about the organization of the student body and communication among students, phenomena which we had been assigning to another [segment of the larger theoretical model being developed]. Since "crocks" were also disliked because they gave the student no opportunity to assume medical responsibility, we were able to connect this aspect of the student-patient relationship with still another tentative model of the value system and hierarchical organization of the school, in which medical responsibility plays an important role. (H. S. Becker, 1958:658)

This excerpt shows how the researcher first was alerted to a concept by observations in the field, then refined his understanding of this concept by investigating its meaning. By observing the concept's frequency of use, he came to realize its importance. Then he incorporated the concept into an explanatory model of student-patient relationships.

Development of theory occurs continually in qualitative research and occurs explicitly in interaction with analysis of the data (Coffey & Atkinson, 1996:23). The goal of many qualitative researchers is to create **grounded theory**—that is, to build up inductively a systematic theory that is "grounded" in, or based on, the observations. The observations are summarized into conceptual categories, which are tested directly in the research setting with more observations. Over time, as the conceptual categories are refined and linked, a theory evolves (Glaser & Strauss, 1967; Huberman & Miles, 1994:436). Exhibit 8.6 diagrams this process. Notice that it corresponds to the inductive portion of the research circle, which was introduced in Chapter 2 (see Exhibit 2.4).

Exhibit 8.6   **The Development of Grounded Theory**

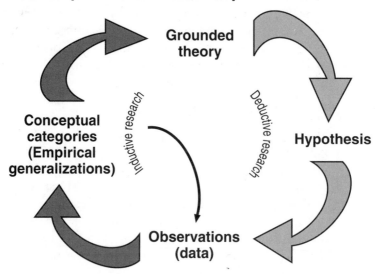

Simply reading the notes or transcripts is an important step in the analytic process. Researchers should make frequent notes in the margins to identify important statements and to propose ways of coding the data: "husband/wife conflict," perhaps, or "tension reduction strategy." An interim stage may consist of listing the concepts reflected in the notes and diagramming the relationships among concepts (Maxwell, 1996:78–81).

As observation, interviewing, and reflection continue, researchers refine their definitions of problems and concepts and select indicators. They can then check the frequency and distribution of phenomena. How many people made a particular type of comment? How often did social interaction lead to arguments? Social system models may be developed, which specify the relationships among different phenomena. These models are modified as researchers gain experience in the setting. For the final analysis, the researchers check their models carefully against their notes and make a concerted attempt to discover negative evidence that might suggest the model is incorrect.

Finally, the researchers should add a "natural history" of the development of the evidence so that others can evaluate their findings. Thorne provides a good example of this final element of the analysis:

> Many of my observations concern the workings of gender categories in social life. For example, I trace the evocation of gender in the organization of everyday interactions, and the shift from boys and girls as loose aggregations to "the boys" and "the girls" as self-aware, gender-based groups. In writing about these processes, I discovered that different angles of vision lurk within seemingly simple choices of language.

How, for example, should one describe a group of children? A phrase like "six girls and three boys were chasing by the tires" already assumes the relevance of gender. An alternative description of the same event—"nine fourth-graders were chasing by the tires"—emphasizes age and downplays gender. Although I found no tidy solutions, I have tried to be thoughtful about such choices. . . . After several months of observing at Oceanside, I realized that my fieldnotes were peppered with the words "child" and "children," but that the children themselves rarely used the term. "What do they call themselves?" I badgered in an entry in my fieldnotes. The answer it turned out, is that children use the same practices as adults. They refer to one another by using given names ("Sally," "Jack") or language specific to a given context ("that guy on first base"). They rarely have occasion to use age-generic terms. But when pressed to locate themselves in an age-based way, my informants used "kids" rather than "children." (Thorne, 1993:8–9)

Use of Computers

The analysis process can be enhanced in various ways by using a computer. Programs designed for qualitative data can speed up the analysis process, make it easier for researchers to experiment with different codes and test different hypotheses about relationships, and facilitate diagrams of emerging theories and preparation of research reports (Coffey & Atkinson, 1996:165–188; Richards & Richards, 1994). The steps involved in computer-based qualitative analysis parallel those used traditionally to analyze such text as notes, documents, or interview transcripts: preparation, coding, analysis, and reporting. I use two of the most popular programs, HyperRESEARCH™ and QSR NUD*IST™, to illustrate these steps.

Text preparation begins with typing or scanning text in a word processor. Both systems require that your text be saved as a text file ("as ASCII" in most word processors) before you transfer it into the analysis program. QSR NUD*IST also requires that you identify all the text units that you will use for coding, by inserting carriage returns after each one. The text units could be lines, sentences, or paragraphs. HyperRESEARCH expects your text data to be stored in separate files corresponding to each unique case, such as an interview with one subject. (See Appendix G to learn about some other capabilities in QSR NUD*IST.)

Coding the text involves categorizing particular text segments. This is the foundation for qualitative analysis. You assign codes with QSR NUD*IST to the predesignated text units (lines, sentences, or paragraphs), while HyperRESEARCH allows you to assign a code to any segment of text (you simply click on the first and last words of the selected text). You can both make up codes as you go through a document and assign codes that you have already developed to text segments. Exhibit 8.7 shows the screens

Exhibit 8.7a **HyperRESEARCH Coding Stage**

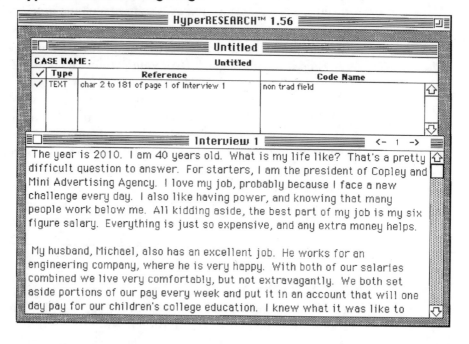

Exhibit 8.7b **QSR NUD*IST Coding Stage**

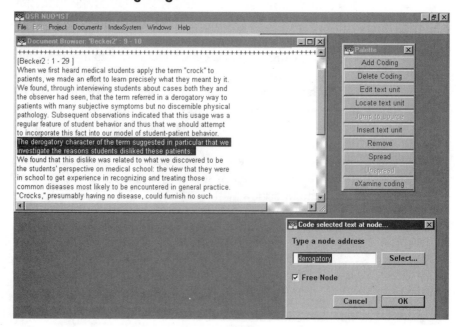

that appear in the two programs at the coding stage, when a particular text segment is being labeled. You can also have the programs "autocode" text if you can identify a word or phrase that should always receive the same code (of course, you should check carefully the results of autocoding). Both programs also let you examine the coded text "in context"—embedded in its place in the original document.

In qualitative data analysis, coding is not a one-time-only or one-code-only procedure. Both programs allow you to be inductive and holistic in your coding: you can revise codes as you go along, assign multiple codes to text segments, and link your own comments ("memos") to text segments.

Analysis focuses on reviewing cases or text segments with similar codes and examining relationships among different codes. You may decide to combine codes into larger concepts. You may specify additional codes to capture more fully the variation among cases. You can test hypotheses about relationships among codes. QSR NUD*IST encourages development of an indexing system that shows relationships among codes in a hierarchical "tree display" (Exhibit 8.8). This facilitates thinking about the relations among concepts and the overarching structure of these relations. In HyperRESEARCH, you can specify combinations of codes that identify

Exhibit 8.8 **QSR NUD*IST Indexing System**

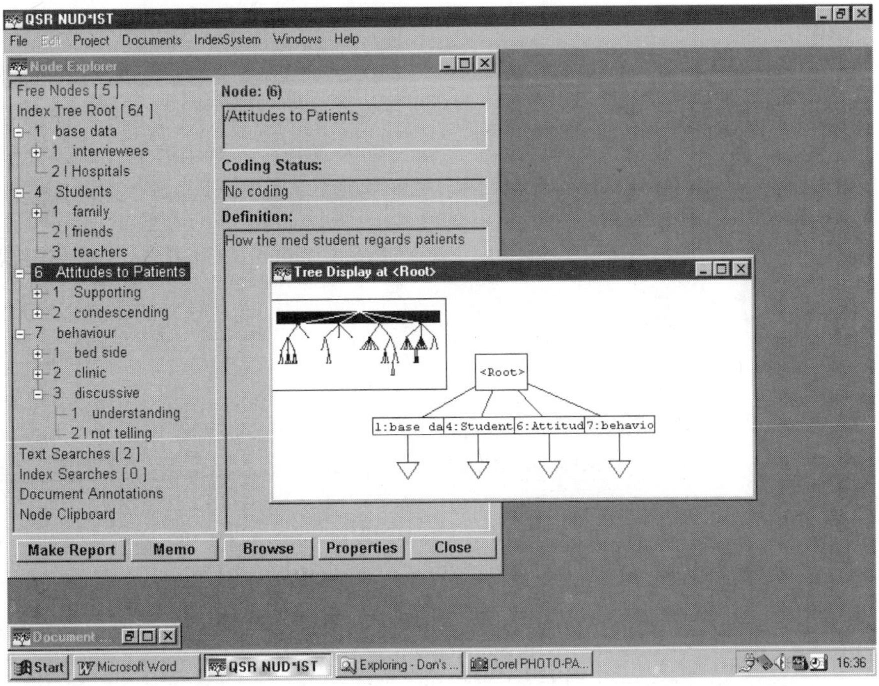

Exhibit 8.9   **Hypothesis Testing in HyperRESEARCH**

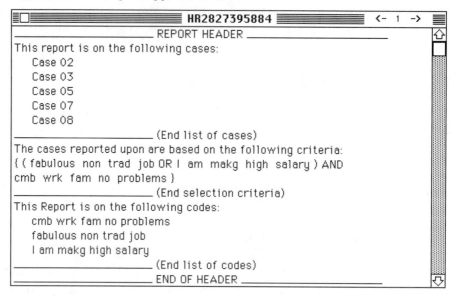

```
▤☐▤▤▤▤▤▤▤▤▤▤▤▤▤▤▤ HR2827395884 ▤▤▤▤▤▤▤▤  <- 1 -> ▤
_____ REPORT HEADER _____    ⇧
This report is on the following cases:                           ☐
    Case 02
    Case 03
    Case 05
    Case 07
    Case 08
_____ (End list of cases)
The cases reported upon are based on the following criteria:
{ ( fabulous  non  trad  job OR I  am  makg  high  salary ) AND
cmb  wrk  fam  no  problems }
_____ (End selection criteria)
This Report is on the following codes:
    cmb wrk fam no problems
    fabulous non trad job
    I am makg high salary
_____ (End list of codes)
_____ END OF HEADER _____    ⇩
```

cases that you wish to examine. For example, as indicated in Exhibit 8.9, you might want to see all cases in which respondents combine work and family with no problems and are also making a high salary or have a "fabulous" nontraditional job. You can count the frequency of different codes and of the combinations of codes you have identified.

Reports from both programs can include text that illustrates the cases, codes, and relationships that you specify. You can also generate counts of code frequencies and then import these counts into a statistical program for quantitative analysis. However, the many types of analyses and reports that can be developed with qualitative analysis software do not lessen the need for a careful evaluation of the quality of the data on which conclusions are based.

Evaluation of Conclusions

No set standards exist for evaluating the validity of conclusions in a qualitative study, but the need to consider carefully the evidence and methods on which conclusions are based is just as great as with other types of research. Individual items of information can be assessed in terms of at least three criteria (H. S. Becker, 1958):

■ *How credible was the informant?* Were statements made by someone with whom the researcher had a relationship of trust, or by someone the researcher had just met? Did the informant have reason to lie? If the statements do not seem to be trustworthy as indicators of actual events, can they at least be used to help understand the informant's perspective?

- *Were statements made in response to the researcher's questions, or were they spontaneous?* Spontaneous statements are more likely to indicate what would have been said had the researcher not been present.

- *How does the presence or absence of the researcher or the researcher's informant influence the actions and statements of other group members?* Reactivity to being observed can never be ruled out as a possible explanation for some directly observed social phenomenon. However, if the researcher carefully compares what the informant says goes on when the researcher is not present, what the researcher observes directly, and what other group members say about their normal practices, the extent of reactivity can be assessed to some extent.

A qualitative researcher's conclusions should also be assessed by their ability to provide a credible explanation for some aspect of social life. That explanation should capture group members' **tacit knowledge** of the social processes that were observed, not just their verbal statements about these processes. Tacit knowledge—"the largely unarticulated, contextual understanding that is often manifested in nods, silences, humor, and naughty nuances"—is reflected in participants' actions as well as their words and in what they fail to state but nonetheless feel deeply and even take for granted (Altheide & Johnson, 1994:492–493). These features are evident in Whyte's analysis of Cornerville social patterns:

> The corner-gang structure arises out of the habitual association of the members over a long period of time. The nuclei of most gangs can be traced back to early boyhood. . . . Home plays a very small role in the group activities of the corner boy. . . .
> . . . The life of the corner boy proceeds along regular and narrowly circumscribed channels. . . . Out of [social interaction within the group] arises a system of mutual obligations which is fundamental to group cohesion. . . . The code of the corner boy requires him to help his friends when he can and to refrain from doing anything to harm them. When life in the group runs smoothly, the obligations binding members to one another are not explicitly recognized. (Whyte, 1955:255–257)

In *Gender Play*, Thorne notes how the tacit knowledge of her young subjects contributed to her conclusions:

> I have argued that kids, as well as adults, take an active hand in constructing gender, and that collective practices—forming lines, choosing seats, teasing, gossiping, seeking access to or avoiding particular activities—animate the process. . . . Gender is not only a category of individual identity and the focus of symbolic constructions, but also a

> dimension of *social relations and social organization.* I have traced the
> weaving of gender in the creation of groups, and, at a more abstract
> level, institutions. The organization and meanings of gender vary from
> one social context to another, from families to neighborhoods to
> schools, and, within schools, from foursquare to scenes of chasing to
> classrooms and lunchrooms. . . . [A]t the level of social situations,
> gender has a fluid quality. (Thorne, 1993:157–158)

Her logic is compelling, although she offers no test of rival explanations for
what she observed. Subsequent research would be useful to evaluate these
propositions more systematically.

Confidence in the conclusions from a field research study is also
strengthened by an honest and informative account about how the researcher interacted with subjects in the field, what problems he or she encountered, and how these problems were or were not resolved. Such an account is important first and foremost because of the evolving and variable
nature of field research: To an important extent, the researcher "makes up"
the method in the context of a particular investigation rather than applying
standard procedures that are specified before the investigation begins.

In recent years qualitative researchers also have become increasingly
sensitive to the idea that a social situation or process is interpreted from a
particular background and values and not simply from the situation itself
(Altheide & Johnson, 1994). Researchers are only human, after all, and must
rely on their own senses and process all information through their own
minds. By reporting how and why they think they did what they did, they
can help others determine whether, or how, the researchers' perspectives influenced their conclusions. "There should be clear 'tracks' indicating the attempt [to show the hand of the ethnographer] has been made" (Altheide &
Johnson, 1994:493).

Can the participant observer truly gain access to the minds and behaviors of other people? Can participant observation really lead to insights into
the social world? Consider Thorne's (1993:12) reflection on her experiences
with children: "Like Westerners doing fieldwork in colonized Third World
cultures, or academics studying the urban poor, when adults research children, they 'study down,' seeking understanding across lines of difference
and inequality." Most field researchers now believe that no outsider can really see the world just as an insider does. We all filter our observations
through a subjective mental apparatus. But doesn't Thorne's qualitative approach seem to get us closer to the reality of ongoing social life than a survey or experiment would?

In general, the usual approach to the analysis of qualitative data contrasts markedly with the procedures used to analyze quantitative data collected in experimental and survey research. Qualitative researchers seek to

- *Confidentiality.* Field researchers normally use fictitious names for the characters in their reports, but doing so does not always guarantee confidentiality to their research subjects. Individuals in the setting studied may be able to identify those whose actions are described and may thus become privy to some knowledge about their colleagues or neighbors that had formerly been kept from them. Researchers should thus make every effort to expunge possible identifying material from published information and to alter unimportant aspects of a description when necessary to prevent identity disclosure. In any case, no field research project should begin if some participants clearly will suffer serious harm by being identified in project publications.

These ethical issues cannot be evaluated independently. The final decision to proceed must be made after weighing the relative benefits and risks to participants. Few qualitative research projects will be barred by consideration of these ethical issues, however, except for those involving covert participation. The more important concern for researchers is to identify the ethically troublesome aspects of their proposed research and resolve them before the project begins and to act on new ethical issues as they come up during the project. Combining methods is often the best strategy.

■ ■ ■ ■ Conclusion

Qualitative research allows the careful investigator to obtain a richer and more intimate view of the social world than with more structured methods. It is not hard to understand why so many qualitative studies have become classics in the sociological literature. And the emphases in qualitative research on inductive reasoning and incremental understanding help to stimulate and inform other research approaches. Exploratory research to chart the dimensions of previously unstudied social settings and intensive investigations of the subjective meanings that motivate individual action are particularly well served by the techniques of participant observation, intensive interviewing, and focus groups.

The very characteristics that make qualitative research techniques so appealing restrict their use to a limited set of research problems. It is not possible to draw representative samples for study using participant observation, and for this reason the generalizability of any particular field study's results cannot really be known. Only the cumulation of findings from numerous qualitative studies permits confident generalization, but here again the time and effort required to collect and analyze the data make it unlikely that many particular field research studies will be replicated.

Even if qualitative researchers made more of an effort to replicate key studies, their notion of developing and grounding explanations inductively in the observations made in a particular setting would hamper comparison of findings. Measurement reliability is thereby hindered, as are systematic tests for the validity of key indicators and formal tests for causal connections.

In the final analysis, qualitative research involves a mode of thinking and investigating different from that used in experimental and survey research. Qualitative research is inductive and idiographic; experiments and surveys tend to be conducted in a deductive, quantitative, and nomothetic framework. Both approaches can help social scientists learn about the social world; the proficient researcher must be ready to use either. Qualitative data are often supplemented with counts of characteristics or activities. And as you have already seen, quantitative data are often enriched with written comments and observations, and focus groups have become a common tool of survey researchers seeking to develop their questionnaires. Thus the distinction between qualitative and quantitative research techniques is not always clear-cut.

KEY TERMS

Complete observation
Complete participation
Covert participation
Experience sampling method (ESM)
Field notes
Field research
Focus group
Grounded theory

Intensive interviewing
Participant observation
Qualitative method
Reactive effects
Saturation point
Tacit knowledge
Theoretical sampling

HIGHLIGHTS

■ Qualitative methods are most useful in exploring new issues, investigating hard-to-study groups, and determining the meaning people give to their lives and actions. In addition, most social research projects can be improved in some respects by taking advantage of qualitative techniques.

■ Qualitative researchers tend to develop ideas inductively, try to understand the social context and sequential nature of attitudes and actions, and explore the subjective meanings that participants attach to events. They rely primarily on participant observation, intensive interviewing, and in recent years, focus groups.

■ Participant observers may adopt one of several roles for a particular research project. Each role represents a different balance between observing and participating, which may or may not include public acknowledgment of the researcher's real identity. Many field researchers prefer a moderate role, participating as well as observing in a group but acknowledging publicly the researcher role. Such a role avoids the ethical issues posed by covert participation while still allowing the customary insights into the social world derived from participating directly in it. The role that the participant observer chooses should be based on an evaluation of the problems likely to arise from reactive effects, the ethical dilemmas of covert observation, and the consequences of identity disclosure in the particular setting.

■ Field researchers must develop strategies for entering the field, developing and maintaining relations in the field, sampling, and recording and analyzing data. Sampling techniques commonly used in field research include theoretical sampling, purposive sampling, snowball sampling, quota sampling, and in special circumstances, random selection with the experience sampling method.

■ Recording and analyzing notes is a crucial step in field research. Detailed notes should be recorded and analyzed daily to refine methods and to develop concepts, indicators, and models of the social system observed.

■ Intensive interviews involve open-ended questions and follow-up probes, with specific question content and order varying from one interview to another. Intensive interviews can supplement participant observation data.

■ Focus groups combine elements of participant observation and intensive interviewing. They can increase the validity of attitude measurement by revealing what people say when presenting their opinions in a group context, instead of the artificial one-on-one interview setting.

■ The four main ethical issues in field research concern voluntary participation, subject well-being, identity disclosure, and confidentiality.

EXERCISES

1. The April 1992 issue of the *Journal of Contemporary Ethnography* is devoted to a series of essays reevaluating Whyte's classic field study, *Street Corner Society*. A social scientist interviewed some of the people described in Whyte's book and concluded that the researcher had made methodological and ethical errors. Whyte and others offer able rejoinders and further commentary. Reading the entire issue of this journal will improve your appreciation of the issues that field researchers confront.

2. Conduct a brief observational study in a public location on campus where students congregate. A cafeteria, a building lobby, or a lounge would be ideal. You can sit and observe, taking occasional notes unobtrusively, without violating any expectations of privacy. Observe for 30 minutes. Write up field notes, being

sure to include a description of the setting and a commentary on your own behavior and your reactions to what you observed.

3. Review the experiments and surveys described in previous chapters. Pick one,
and propose a field research design that would focus on the same research
question but with participant observation techniques in a local setting. Propose
the role that you would play in the setting, along the participant observation
continuum, and explain why you would favor this role. Describe the stages of
your field research study, including your plans for entering the field, developing and maintaining relationships, sampling, and recording and analyzing data.
Then discuss what you would expect your study to add to the findings resulting from the study described in the book.

4. Develop an interview guide that focuses on a research question addressed in
one of the studies in this book. Using this guide, conduct an intensive interview
with one person who is involved with the topic in some way. Take only brief
notes during the interview, and then write up as complete a record of the interview as you can immediately afterward. Turn in an evaluation of your performance as an interviewer and note-taker, together with your notes.

5. Read about focus groups in one of the references cited in this chapter. Then devise a plan for using a focus group to explore and explain student perspectives
on some current event. How would you recruit students for the group? What
type of students would you try to include? How would you introduce the topic
and the method to the group? What questions would you ask? What problems
would you anticipate, such as discord between focus group members or digres-
sions from the chosen topic? How would you respond to these problems?

6. Read and summarize one of the qualitative studies discussed in this chapter or
another classic study recommended by your instructor. Review and critique the
study using the article review questions presented in Appendix C. What questions are answered by the study? What questions are raised for furthur investigation?

7. Write a short critique of the ethics of Whyte's or Van Maanen's study or of some
field research that has been challenged as ethically questionable (Alfred, 1976,
and Humphreys, 1970, are good choices). Read their books ahead of time to
clarify the details, and then focus on each of the ethical guidelines presented in
this chapter: voluntary participation, subject well-being, identity disclosure,
and confidentiality. Conclude with a statement about the extent to which field
researchers should be required to disclose their identities and the circumstances
in which they should not be permitted to participate actively in the social life
they study.

WEB EXERCISES

1. Go to the *Annual Review of Sociology*'s Web site by following the publications
link at

   http://www.annurev.org/ari

   Search for articles that use field research as the primary method of gathering
   data on any one of the following subjects: child development/socialization;

gender/sex roles; aging/gerontology. Find at least five articles and report on the specific method of field research used in each.

2. Go to the Social Science Information Gateway (SOSIG) at

   http://sosig.esrc.bris.ac.uk/Welcome.html

   Choose "Search SOSIG."
   Enter "field research" as your search term.
   Out of the matches for the query "field research" that SOSIG provides, choose three or four sites that look interesting to find out more about field research. Explore the sites to find out what information they provide regarding field research, what kinds of projects are being done that involve field research, and the purposes that specific field research methods are being used for.

3. You have been asked to do field research on the World Wide Web's impact on the socialization of children in today's world. The first part of the project involves your writing a compare and contrast report on the differences between how you and your generation were socialized as children and the way children today are being socialized. Collect your data by surfing the Web "as if you were a kid." The Web is your "field" and you are the "field researcher."

   Using any of the major search engines, explore the Web within the "Kids" or "Children" subject heading, keeping "field notes" on what you observe.

   Write a brief report based on the data you have collected. How has the Web impacted child socialization in comparison to when you were a kid?

SPSS EXERCISES

The GSS96 includes some questions about care of the elderly and a number about gender roles. Focus on one of these two areas for these SPSS exercises.

1. Describe attitudes and behavior involving care of the elderly, or attitudes about gender roles, based on the frequencies for related variables in the GSS96.

   STATISTICS
   SUMMARIZE
   FREQUENCIES aidold,famgen,needyrel,spretire

   or

   fechld,fefam,fehelp,fepres,fepol,fework

2. What explanation can you develop (inductively) for these attitudes? Consider the differences as well as the similarities in the distributions of the set of variables.

3. Propose a participant observation study or an intensive interview study to explore these attitudes further. Identify the setting or sample for the study and describe how you would carry out your observations or interviews.

9 Historical and Comparative Methods

Overview of Historical and Comparative Methods

Historical Social Science Methods

Historical Events Research

A Quantitative Case Study: Citizenship and Public Schools
A Qualitative Case Study: Petitions in the English Revolution
Methodological Issues: Historical Events Research

Historical Process Research

A Quantitative Case Study: Explaining Variation in Race Riots
A Qualitative Case Study: Breakdown of Chilean Democracy
Methodological Issues: Historical Process Research

Comparative Social Science Methods

Cross-Sectional Comparative Research

A Quantitative Case Study: Voter Turnout
A Qualitative Case Study: Mass Conscription in Modern Democracies
Methodological Issues: Cross-Sectional Comparative Research

Comparative Historical Research

A Quantitative Case Study: Democratization and Modernization
Two Qualitative Case Studies: Democracy and Development
Methodological Issues: Comparative Historical Research

Data Sources

U.S. Bureau of the Census
Bureau of Labor Statistics (BLS)
Other U.S. Government Sources
International Data Sources
Survey Datasets
Methodological Issues: Secondary Data Sources

Special Techniques

Demographic Analysis

Although the United States and several European nations have maintained democratic systems of governance for over 100 years, democratic rule has more often been brief and unstable, when it has occurred at all. What explains the presence of democratic practices in one country, their absence in another? Are democratic politics a realistic option for every nation? What about Bosnia? Congo? Iraq? Are there some prerequisites in historical experience, cultural values, or economic resources? Historical and comparative methods seek to answer research questions like these about democratization, as well as questions about other aspects of political processes, about stratification systems and economic development, about religion, world trade, wars, and migration.

Historical and comparative methods can generate new insights into social processes by focusing attention on aspects of the social world beyond recent events in one country. They involve several different approaches, a diverse set of techniques, and they may have qualitative and/or quantitative components. They provide means for investigating topics that usually cannot be studied with experiments, participant observation, or surveys. However, because this broader focus involves collecting data from records on the past or from other nations, historical and comparative methods present unique challenges to social researchers.

I will review in this chapter the major approaches used by social scientists to understand historical processes and to compare different societies or regions. I will also introduce several methodological techniques that are particularly useful in these types of investigations: secondary data analysis, demographic methods, content analysis, and oral life history interviews. Throughout the chapter, I will draw examples from research on democracy and the process of democratization.

■ ■ ■ ■ Overview of Historical and Comparative Methods

The central insight behind historical and comparative methods is that we can improve our understanding of social processes when we make comparisons to other times and places. Max Weber's comparative study of world religions, Emile Durkheim's historical analysis of the division of labor, Karl Marx's investigation of political and economic change—each affirms the value of this insight. Beyond this similarity, however, historical and comparative methods are a diverse collection of approaches. Research may be historical, comparative, or both historical and comparative. Historical and comparative methods can be quantitative or qualitative, or a mixture of both. Both nomothetic and idiographic approaches to establishing causal effects can be used.

The boundaries around historical and comparative research are not defined rigidly. There are no hard-and-fast rules for determining how far in the past the focus of research must be in order to consider it historical, nor what type of comparisons are needed to warrant calling research comparative. In practice, research tends to be considered historical when it focuses on a period prior to the experience of most of those conducting research (Abbott, 1994:80). Research involving different nations is usually considered comparative, but so are studies of different regions within one nation if they emphasize interregional comparison. Thus, Mildred A. Schwartz's (1974) study of Canadian regions is comparative, as is Seymour Martin Lipset's (1990) comparison of popular attitudes in the United States and Canada. Research focusing on more than one smaller geographic or political unit, such as states or towns, can also be considered comparative.

Distinguishing research in terms of a historical and/or comparative focus results in four basic types: **historical events research, historical process research, cross-sectional comparative research,** and **comparative historical research** (see definition box). Research focusing on events in one short historical period is historical events research, while research that traces a sequence of events over a number of years is historical process research (cf. Skocpol, 1984:359). There are also two types of comparative research, the first involving cross-sectional comparisons and the second combining historical process data on multiple cases. The resulting four types of research are displayed in Exhibit 9.1.

Historical events research and historical process research often use qualitative methods and can be termed **case-oriented.** They focus attention on the nation or other unit as a whole. Much comparative research and some historical comparative research is quantitative and variable-oriented. **Variable-oriented studies** focus attention on variables representing particular aspects of the units studied and then examine the relations among these variables across sets of cases. However, any of the four research types can contain elements of both case-oriented and variable-oriented approaches.

Exhibit 9.1 **Types of Historical and Comparative Research**

	Cross-Sectional	**Historical**
Single Case	Historical Events Research	Historical Process Research
Multiple Cases	Cross-Sectional Comparative Research	Comparative/ Historical Research

Historical events research Research in which social events are studied at one past time period.

Historical process research Research in which historical processes are studied over a long period of time.

Cross-sectional comparative research Research comparing data from one time period between two or more nations.

Comparative historical research Research comparing data from more than one time period in more than one nation.

Case-oriented research Research that focuses attention on the nation or other unit as a whole.

Variable-oriented research Research that focuses attention on variables representing particular aspects of the units studied and then examines the relations among these variables across sets of cases.

Historical Social Science Methods

Both historical events research and historical process research investigate questions concerning past times. These methods are used increasingly by social scientists in sociology, anthropology, political science, and economics, as well as by many historians (Monkkonen, 1994). The late 20th century has seen so much change in so many countries that many scholars have felt a need to investigate the background of these changes and to refine their methods of investigation (Hallinan, 1997; Robertson, 1993). The accumulation of large bodies of data about the past has also stimulated more historically oriented research.

The methods of history in the social sciences differ from traditional historical research by seeking to develop general theoretical explanations of historical events and processes instead of just detailed, "fact centered," descriptions of them (Monkkonen, 1994:8). Social scientists do not ignore the details of historical events; rather, they "unravel" unique events in order to identify general patterns (Abrams, 1982:200). However, as in traditional history, the focus on the past presents special methodological challenges. Documents and other evidence may have been lost or damaged and what evidence there is may represent a sample biased toward those who were more newsworthy figures or who were more prone to writing. The feelings of individuals involved in past events may be hard, if not impossible, to reconstruct. Nonetheless, in many situations the historical record may support very systematic research on what occurred in the past. I will first discuss historical events research.

Historical Events Research

When research on past events does not follow processes for some long period of time, when it is basically cross-sectional, then it is historical events research rather than historical process research. Investigations of past events may be motivated by the belief that they had a critical impact on subsequent developments or because they provide opportunities for testing the implications of a general theory (Kohn, 1987).

A Quantitative Case Study: Citizenship and Public Schools

How do political rights affect access to public goods such as education? More specifically, how does the right to vote influence the distribution of educational opportunity? Pamela Walters, David James, and Holly McCammon (1997) saw an opportunity to answer this research question by examining the period of 1890 to 1910, when blacks were disfranchised in the South. Several measures indicate that educational opportunities for Southern blacks eroded during this period: for example, salaries for white teachers rose to much higher levels than salaries for black teachers and the rate of enrollment for black children declined relative to that for whites. However, prior research had not identified how this change occurred.

Walters, James, and McCammon obtained U.S. census data for the years 1890 and 1910 for counties in Alabama, Florida, Georgia, Louisiana, North Carolina, and South Carolina—the only southern states having census data on teacher availability and public school enrollments in both years. Then,

Exhibit 9.2 **Teacher Availability and Public School Enrollments: Hypothesized Relationships**

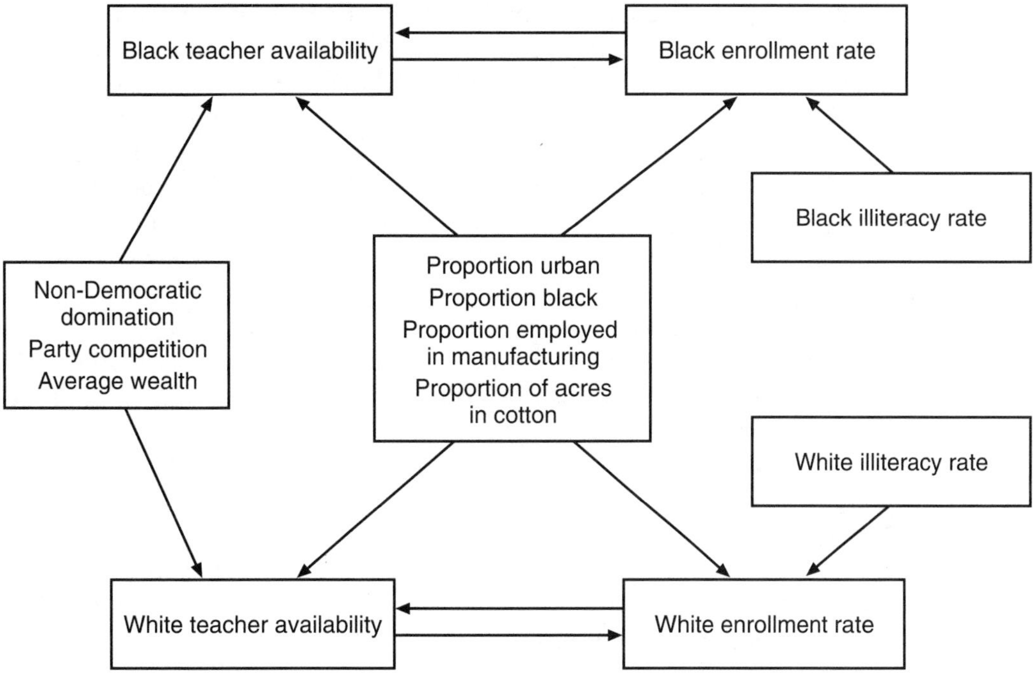

Source: Walters et al., 1997:40.

they tested a number of relationships in order to determine which county characteristics influenced teacher availability and enrollment rate for black and white schools (see Exhibit 9.2). Their statistical analysis indicated several ways in which disfranchisement led to fewer educational opportunities for black children. For example, higher rates of literacy and education in a county tended to be associated with getting more teachers, but the advantage that black counties received for higher rates of literacy and education declined sharply after blacks were disfranchised.

A Qualitative Case Study: Petitions in the English Revolution

The ability "to petition the government for a redress of grievances" is the first right protected by the United States' Bill of Rights. It is one of the key conditions for the open political debate and concern with public opinion that are hallmarks of democratic governance. However, scholars disagree about why public opinion became important in political affairs and what role petitions to the government played. Indiana University sociologist David Zaret (1996) investigated this question with historical research on early 17th-century England.

In England before 1640, signed petitions to Parliament or some other government body were often used to present grievances and requests for help, but they were not made public (Zaret, 1996). To understand how petitions became public documents after that, Zaret sampled 500 petitions in government archives that were published between 1640 and 1660. Zaret's basic method of investigation was reading the selected petitions and other relevant documents. He noted that sometimes petitions were deceptive, designed more as propaganda than as statements about public opinion. Sometimes petitions in the files were outright forgeries. So Zaret did not rely solely on the petitions themselves. He also read through collections of private letters, pamphlets, diaries, and newspapers that included debates about the appropriate role for petitions.

The content of the petitions and the debate over them indicated that the widespread use of printing played a critical role in turning petitions into public documents. By 1640, printing had become widely available in England, and Zaret found that after this point large numbers of petitions were circulated before they were submitted to the government. As opposing sides began to use petitions to publicize their views, the rights of people to exchange ideas openly and to sign petitions voluntarily were recognized. Public opinion became a political force to be reckoned with, and the stage was set for a robust democracy.

Methodological Issues: Historical Events Research

These examples of historical events research illustrate some of the important methodological issues to consider when conducting historical research:

- *The meaning of words and phrases can differ across historical periods* (Erikson, 1966:xi). The analyst must strive for the right balance between preserving the words of the original and conveying their meaning to a modern audience.

- *The accuracy of original source documents (as well as of secondary documents) cannot simply be assumed.* What remains in the historical archives may be an unrepresentative selection of materials that still remain from the past. "Original" documents may be transcriptions of spoken words or handwritten pages and could have been modified slightly in the process; they could also be outright distortions (Erikson, 1966:172, 209–210; Zaret, 1996). Developing a systematic plan for identifying relevant documents and evaluating them is very important.

- *Critical data are often unavailable* (Walters, James, & McCammon, 1997). Zaret (1996) had to supplement the record from petitions with other documents. The researcher must assess the problem honestly and openly.

- *The restriction of this type of research to one setting in the past limits possibilities for assessing validity.* Explanations applied to these events can seem arbitrary (Skocpol, 1984:365). The researcher can reduce the problem by making some comparisons to other events in the past or present.

Historical Process Research

Historical process research extends historical events research by focusing on a series of events that happened over some period of time. This longitudinal component allows for idiographic causal explanations and a much more complete understanding of historical developments than is the case with historical events research. It can enable us to identify "the long chain of causes and effects of which [the present] is the result" (Durkheim, 1906/1956:152–153, as quoted in Emirbayer, 1996:265).

Understanding time and its relation to events is the central challenge of historical process research. The simplest way to think about time is as an independent variable that may influence events. For example, you might test the hypothesis: Countries that industrialize early are more likely to develop democratic practices than countries that industrialize at a later time. However, the timing of an event may not be as important as some other time-related variable. At least five aspects of time may be important for understanding historical processes (Aminzade, 1992):

- The *duration* of an event—how long it takes—may shape the consequences of that event. A hotly contested election may shape national politics for years to come if it lasts for many months, but its impact may be minor if the contest is limited to a few weeks.

- The *pace* of change may be important: Industrialization may encourage democratic politics when its pace is gradual, but not when its pace is fast.

- Historical sociologists also may take into account the *trajectory*, or sequential order of events. The end of colonial rule may result in democratization only if it is part of a long-term trajectory of events that diminish the power of the socioeconomic elite.

- *Cyclical processes*, involving a series of events that recur, must be taken into account in explaining the consequences of particular events within a cycle. If we see grassroots activism as one stage of an ongoing cycle of protest, we will explain it differently than if we believe such activism is a unique historical event.

- *The subjective perception of time* may prove to be more important than objective time for understanding some historical processes. A process that takes the same time according to the calendar may have very different consequences in a society that "lives by the clock" than in a society that pays little attention to the passage of time.

A Quantitative Case Study: Explaining Variation in Race Riots

Even in democratic societies, conflict sometimes bursts outside the bounds of routine politics in demonstrations, riots, and other forms of civil disobedience. The political history of a nation is incomplete without an understanding of the historical processes associated with such events. It was these processes that Susan Olzak, Suzanne Shanahan, and Elizabeth McEneaney (1996) sought to understand in their examination of race riots in the United States from 1960 to 1993. Alternative theories pointed to high levels of deprivation, residential segregation and inter-ethnic competition, and experience with prior unrest, but prior research had not determined the relative importance of these variables as precursors to riots.

Olzak, Shanahan, and McEneaney (1996:600–601) coded information on 1,770 ethnic or racial events that were reported in *The New York Times* in 55 cities (Standard Metropolitan Statistical Areas) between 1960 and 1993. (These SMSAs were used because they had complete information available on key variables from 1960 to 1993.) Information on population size, segregation levels, and economic variables was also obtained from census and other sources. Time-related variables in their analysis included change in racial segregation, number of previous riots, and change in racial isolation. Their analysis focused on 154 riots driven by racial grievances in which blacks were the main instigators of the riot (Olzak, Shanahan, & McEneaney, 1996:599). Exhibit 9.3 shows that these events peaked in the late 1960s and then declined to no more than one or two per year.

Statistical analysis indicated that riots were more likely when racial segregation had been high but was declining in cities, and when cities had previously experienced race riots. Levels of poverty and unemployment in themselves were not related to the likelihood of rioting.

A Qualitative Case Study: Breakdown of Chilean Democracy

Qualitative historical research takes a very different, narrative approach to linking events and the passage of time. **Narrative explanations** rely on an idiographic concept of causation (see Chapter 5), in which historical events are treated as part of a developing "story" (Abbott, 1994:102). Events such as wars, revolutions, and elections are understood only in relation to other events and by taking into account their position in time and in a unique historical context (Griffin, 1992). A narrative explanation for a military coup, for example, might take into account the sequence of events that led up to the coup, examine the actions of individuals and of political groups, and review the national culture and the positions of different economic classes.

A narrative explanation is case-based, meaning that it seeks historically specific explanations for a particular case. The goal is a story involving specific actors and other events occurring at the same time, rather than a general

Exhibit 9.3   **Black Riots Reported in *The New York Times*, 1960–1993, in 55 SMSAs**

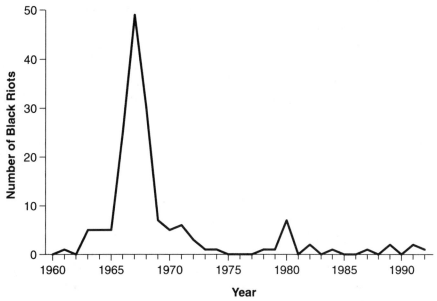

Source: Olzak, Shanahan, & McEneaney, 1996:602.

explanation involving relations among variables (Abbott, 1994:102). This type of explanation has three key features (Abbott, 1994; Griffin, 1992). It is

■ **Temporal,** taking into account a related series of events that unfold over time

■ **Holistic,** looking at "how different conditions or parts fit together" (Ragin, 1987:25–26)

■ **Conjunctural,** because "no cause ever acts except in complex conjunctions with others" (Abbot, 1994:101)

Each of these features is apparent in Arturo Valenzuela's (1990) analysis of the history of democracy in Chile.

Chilean Army Commander-in-Chief General Pinochet and other military commanders seized power from a democratically elected government on September 11, 1973. From a distance, it might have seemed to be just one more military coup in a country without established democratic traditions. Valenzuela's (1990) historical process research shows just how wrong such an explanation would be. In fact, Chile had maintained democratic practices since 1830. With only brief exceptions, the Chilean people were used to "an open and participatory political system," which was completely foreign to the ensuing dictatorship (Valenzuela, 1990:67–68).

"How could this transformation have taken place?" (Valenzuela, 1990: 68). Valenzuela's (1990) historical process research focuses on the events in Chilean history that allow comparisons between competing theoretical predictions about the course of democracy: the colonial-continuity thesis, the political culture thesis, the economic development thesis, and the political-determinants thesis.

Does the continuance of traditions developed under colonial rule explain the breakdown of democracy in Chile? Valenzuela finds that Chile broke decisively with the colonial period of monarchical rule. Did Chilean democracy reflect a liberal political culture, distinct from other Latin American countries? Apparently not. Chile's stratification system "was one of the most rigid and traditional on the continent" (Valenzuela, 1990:55). Another explanation for the development of democracy focuses on economic development, but this explanation also seems to fail in the case of Chile, which throughout the nineteenth century "was a rural, pre-industrial society with very low levels of personal wealth and literacy" (Valenzuela, 1990:57).

Valenzuela argues that the historical evidence fits with the predictions of the political-determinants thesis. He concludes that elite groups in Chile helped to develop a national identity, government structures that were not subordinate to the military or to a particular elite group, and rules allowing widespread political participation. Democratic practices served the interests of particular elite groups at particular times, resulting in acceptance by all of compromises and of democratic "rules of the [political] game" (Valenzuela, 1990:62). Democratic rule failed in Chile when these rules were changed, a new (centrist) party proved unwilling to compromise, and a leftist president (Allende), elected with just 36.2 percent of the vote, tried rapidly to change established political and economic practices (Valenzuela, 1990:62–66).

Can you see the three key features of narrative explanation in Valenzuela's research? It is temporal, telling a story that develops over time. It is holistic, tying together economic, political, military, and cultural factors. Valenzuela's explanation is also conjunctural since it shows that the occurrence of several events together resulted in the demise of democratic politics. Although it might be tempting to say that "a military coup" caused the end of democratic politics, Valenzuela's research reveals the coup as only one element, albeit a critical one.

Methodological Issues: Historical Process Research

The strength of historical process research is its ability to trace idiographic causal connections between events and to consider alternative explanations for these historical processes. Nonetheless, the method has several limitations:

■ *The focus on a single case can lead to explaining historical events in terms of political actors' decisions* (like Valenzuela's political-determinants explanation), *rather than in terms of social structures* like the level of social inequality, which don't vary much between nations (Rueschemeyer, Stephens, & Stephens, 1992:31–36). Comparisons across nations may reveal that differences in social structures are much more important than voluntary decisions by individual political actors. It is only when structural factors change over time within one nation that the impact of these factors can empirically be evaluated (Rueschemeyer, Stephens, & Stephens, 1992:29).

■ *Historical process research can also be criticized for selecting cases (nations) for study on arbitrary grounds,* such as the researcher's familiarity with the case or the availability of data. The appropriateness of cases for testing a particular theoretical explanation may be neglected.

■ *Operational definitions of variables and geographic units may change over time, resulting in a need for various types of adjustments.* For example, Walters, James, and McCammon (1997) found that the boundaries of many southern counties changed between 1890 and 1910. Olzak, Shanahan, and McEneaney (1996:597) had to overcome problems due to changes in SMSA boundaries during the period they studied.

■ *Long-term records often have gaps or must be compiled from multiple sources.* Olzak, Shanahan, and McEneaney (1996:598) concluded that *The New York Times* was a reliable source about race riots after carefully comparing reports of riots in the *Times* with reports in local newspapers about the same events (1996:594). Nonetheless, they were only able to include 55 out of a total of 212 SMSAs in their analysis because some data were missing for the others.

■ *Narrative explanations can seem like purely inductive efforts to account for the historical record, tailored to fit the particulars of that record and unlikely to be confirmed by other cases* (Rueschemeyer, Stephens, & Stephens, 1992:30).

In spite of these limitations, analyses like Valenzuela's and Olzak, Shanahan, and McEneaney's can generate great insights into historical process. By comparing carefully the historical process in one country to the predictions of a theoretical framework that incorporates findings from research on many countries, they inject a valuable comparative element that allows stronger causal inferences (Rueschemeyer, Stephens, & Stephens, 1992:38).

Counterfactual thought experiments are a more systematic method for adding a comparative element to studies of single historical cases. Such an "experiment" involves asking a "what if" question. One possibility might be to ask "What if President Kennedy had decided to invade Cuba during the

Cuban missile crisis?" The analysis then focuses on determining which of the series of events that occurred when Kennedy decided NOT to invade Cuba would have been altered if he had decided to invade Cuba. Of course, it is easy to imagine silly "what if" questions and very unrealistic arguments about what might have changed. Such a counterfactual analysis becomes more plausible when the focus is on differences in potential causes that have been clearly identified, on effects that are logically connected with the potential cause and with each other, and on sequences of events that are consistent with established historical facts and theory (Tetlock & Belkin, 1996).

■ ■ ■ ■ Comparative Social Science Methods

The limitations of single-case historical research have encouraged many social scientists to turn to comparisons between nations. In fact, Valenzuela's case study of Chile using historical process methods was published in a book with 10 case studies of different developing countries. Larry Diamond, Juan Linz, and Seymour Martin Lipset (1990:1–37), the book's editors, then compared the findings from these 10 studies in order to gain richer insights into the process of democratization. Other social scientists have developed comparative studies to broaden the scope of cross-sectional research. These studies allow for a broader vision about social relations than is possible with cross-sectional research limited to one country.

From 1985 to 1990, more than 80 research articles in top sociology journals and 200 nonedited books were published in which the primary purpose was the comparison of two or more nations (Bollen, Entwisle, & Alderson, 1993). Most of the authors (88%) used their research to draw general rather than historically specific conclusions—they were writing social science, not history. About half of this research used cross-sectional data rather than longitudinal data collected over a period of time.

Cross-Sectional Comparative Research

Comparisons between countries during one time period can help social scientists to identify the limitations of explanations based on single-nation research. The focus of these comparative studies may be on a period either in the past or the present.

A Quantitative Case Study: Voter Turnout

Research on voter turnout illustrates the value of cross-sectional comparative research. This research focuses on a critical issue in political science: Although free and competitive elections are a defining feature of democratic politics, elections themselves cannot orient governments to popular sentiment if citizens do not vote (LeDuc, Niemi, & Norris, 1996). As a result, the

Exhibit 9.4　**Percent of Voters Who Participate in Elections, 1960–1995**

Australia	95	Norway	81
Malta	94	Bulgaria	80
Austria	92	Israel	80
Belgium	91	Portugal	79
Italy	90	Finland	78
Luxembourg	90	Canada	76
Iceland	89	France	76
New Zealand	88	United Kingdom	75
Denmark	87	Ireland	74
Venezuela	85	Spain	73
Germany	86	Japan	71
Greece	86	Estonia	69
Latvia	86	Hungary	66
Lithuania	86	Russia	61
Sweden	86	India	58
Czech Republic	85	Switzerland	54
Brazil	83	United States	54
Netherlands	83	Poland	51
Costa Rica	81		

Source: Franklin, 1996:218.

low levels of voter participation in U.S. elections have long been a source of practical concern and research interest.

International data give our first clue for explaining voter turnout: the rate of voter participation in the United States (54%, on average) is much lower than it is in many other countries that have free, competitive elections; in Australia, for example, 95% of voters usually turn out to vote (Exhibit 9.4).

Is this variation due to differences among voters in knowledge and wealth? Do media and political party get-out-the-vote efforts matter? Mark Franklin's (1996:219–222) analysis of these international data indicates that neither explanation accounts for much of the international variation in voter turnout. Instead, it is the structure of competition and the importance of issues that are important. Voter turnout is maximized where structural features maximize competition: compulsory voting, mail and Sunday voting, and multiday voting. Voter turnout also tends to be higher where the issues being voted on are important and where results are decided by proportional representation rather than on a winner-take-all basis—so individual votes are more important.

Franklin concludes that it is these characteristics that explain the low level of voter turnout in the United States, not the characteristics of individual voters. The United States lacks the structural features that make voting easier, the proportional representation that increases the impact of individuals' votes, and, often, the sharp differences between candidates that are found in countries with higher turnout. Since these structural factors generally do not vary within nations, we would never realize their importance if our analysis was limited to data from individuals in one nation.

A Qualitative Case Study: Mass Conscription in Modern Democracies

Cross-sectional comparative research may focus on a past period and involve qualitative methods. Both of these two features are illustrated in Margaret Levi's (1996) study of the institution of mass conscription in five Western democracies.

Levi sought to understand influences on government conscription policy in a democratic nation. For this purpose, she compared Great Britain, the United States, Canada, New Zealand, and Australia during the period during World War I when each attempted to institute a compulsory draft. Some of these countries were successful in instituting conscription, while some failed. Levi's analysis sought to identify the reasons for these differences, drawing on the history of events documented in previously published histories.

Levi's comparison points out similarities and differences among the five countries in terms of the success of voluntary military recruiting, the strength of opposition groups, manpower shortages, and popular trust in the government. This comparison led to the elimination of several possible explanations: geographic distance to the military conflict; cultural differences; the strength of ideological opponents to the draft. These explanations "simply do not fit the evidence" (Levi, 1996:154). Instead, conscription was accepted in countries where the working class and ethnic groups had less political clout, where groups tended to trust the central government, and where the government was able to deliver on its promises. In Australia, for example, where a draft was not instituted, "the most vociferous opponents of conscription, the working class and the Irish organizations . . . were sufficiently numerous and dispersed throughout the country that they could use existing institutional arrangements effectively" and "the Australian Labor party provided the Australian opposition with a means to veto policies they strongly disliked" (Levi, 1996:138).

Methodological Issues: Cross-Sectional Comparative Research

In spite of its evident value for broadening our vision and enriching our explanations, the ability of cross-sectional comparative research to evaluate causal explanations is limited.

■ *One problem is simply the lack of longitudinal data* (Rueschemeyer, Stephens, & Stephens, 1992:4). Levi concludes that the strength of opposition groups led, in part, to failure of national conscription efforts. But perhaps, instead, earlier failures to impose military conscription resulted in variation in the strength of opposition groups.

■ *Another common problem in comparative investigations is the lack of adequate measures.* Data for many measures are often missing; there is often no way to use multiple measures of the same concept; and there may be few opportunities to test measurement reliability and validity. Although these problems are often not acknowledged, they weaken the confidence that can be placed in the conclusions of most comparative research (Bollen, Entwisle, & Alderson, 1993).

■ *Even when measures of key variables are available, they may be operationalized in quite different ways in different nations.* Rates of physical disability cannot be compared among nations due to a lack of standard definitions (Martin & Kinsella, 1995:364–365). Individuals in different cultures may respond differently to the same questions (Martin & Kinsella, 1995:385).

In spite of these limitations, data of increasingly good quality are available on a rapidly expanding number of nations, creating many opportunities for comparative research.

Comparative Historical Research

Comparative historical research combines the advantages of both historical process research and cross-sectional comparative research. Historical social scientists may use comparisons between cases "to highlight the particular features of each case" (Skocpol, 1984:370). Comparative historical research can help to identify the causal processes at work within the nations compared (Lipset, 1968:34; Skocpol, 1984:374–386). This type of research can also identify general historical patterns across nations.

The comparative historical approach focuses on sequences of events, rather than on some single past (or current) occurrence that might have influenced an outcome in the present. Comparisons of these sequences may be either quantitative or qualitative. Some studies collect quantitative longitudinal data about a number of nations and then use these data to test hypotheses about influences on national characteristics (Theda Skocpol [1984:375] terms this "analytic historical sociology"). Others compare the histories or particular historical experiences of nations in a narrative form, noting similarities and differences and inferring explanations for key national events ("interpretive historical sociology" in Skocpol's terminology [1984:368]).

A Quantitative Case Study: Democratization and Modernization

Which prior historical processes increase the chances of democratization in nations? Edward Crenshaw (1995) sought to answer this question with a quantitative study of the relation between the level of political democracy in 83 countries and their social and economic characteristics. Drawing from a variety of sources, he was able to measure the level of political democracy in 1965 and 1980, as well as such features of nations as GDP per capita, secondary school enrollment, armed forces per 1,000 population, agricultural density, and income inequality.

A shift toward more democratic practices between 1965 and 1980 was due in large part to the level of societal complexity. This meant that societies that were larger and more densely settled, had a complex division of labor, and used elaborate, decentralized political structures were more likely to develop in a democratic direction, whether their economies were primarily agrarian or industrial. These results support political modernization theory, and call into question other theories that focus on the impact of class conflict or on industrial countries' exploitation of less developed countries.

This research approach extends cross-sectional comparative research with longitudinal data. Like other types of historical and comparative research, it requires adequate measures of theoretically relevant variables. Missing information on some indicators reduced the number of nations in some of Crenshaw's analyses from 83 to 56; similar data problems are common in historical comparative research.

Two Qualitative Case Studies: Democracy and Development

Charles Ragin (1987:44–52) proposed several stages for a systematic qualitative comparative historical study:

- Specify a theoretical framework and identify key concepts or events that should be examined to explain a phenomenon.

- Select cases (such as nations) that vary in terms of the key concepts or events.

- Identify similarities and differences between the cases in terms of these key concepts or events and the outcome to be explained.

- Propose a causal explanation for the historical outcome and check it against the features of each case. The criterion of success in this method is to explain the outcome for each case, without allowing deviations from the proposed causal pattern (Rueschemeyer, Stephens, & Stephens, 1992:36–39).

The core of this approach is the comparison of nations ("cases") in terms of similarities and differences on potential causal variables and the phenomenon to be explained. For example, suppose three nations that have all developed democratic political systems are compared in terms of four socioeconomic variables hypothesized by different theories to influence democratization. If the nations differ in terms of three of the variables but are similar in terms of the fourth, this is evidence that the fourth variable influences democratization. This is what John Stuart Mill (1872), the English philosopher, called the **"method of agreement"** (Exhibit 9.5).

The comparison can instead focus on differences—Mill's **"method of difference."** If two cases differ in terms of an outcome, such as development of democratic practices, then any variable that causes this difference must itself differ between the cases (Exhibit 9.5). Presumably, variables having the same value in the different nations cannot be the cause of the difference in democratization between them. Ragin (1987) has developed a systematic procedure for these qualitative comparisons.

Rueschemeyer, Stephens, and Stephens (1992) used a method like this to explain why some nations in Latin America developed democratic politics, while others became authoritarian states. First, Rueschemeyer, Stephens, and Stephens developed a theoretical framework that gave key attention to the power of social classes, state (government) power, and the interaction between social classes and the government. They then classified the political regimes in each nation over time (Exhibit 9.6). Next, they noted how

Exhibit 9.5 **John Stuart Mill's Methods of Agreement and Difference**

The Method of Agreement*

Variable	Case 1	Case 2	Case 3
A	Different	Different	Different
B	Different	Same	Same
C	Different	Different	Different
D	Same	Same	Same
Outcome	Same	Same	Same

*D is considered the cause of the outcome.

The Method of Difference**

Variable	Case 1	Case 2	Case 3
A	Same	Same	Same
B	Different	Different	Different
C	Different	Same	Same
D	Same	Different	Same
Outcome	Different	Different	Different

**B is considered the cause of the outcome.

Source: Adapted from Skocpol, 1984:379.

Exhibit 9.6 **Classification of Regimes Over Time**

	Constitutional Oligarchic	Authoritarian; Traditional, Populist, Military, or Corporatist	Restricted Democratic	Fully Democratic	Bureaucratic Authoritarian
Argentina	Before 1912	1930–46 1951–55 1955–58 1962–63	1958–62 1963–66	1912–30 1946–51 1973–76 1983–90	1966–73 1976–83
Brazil	Before 1930	1930–45	1945–64 1985–90		1964–85
Bolivia	Before 1930	1930–52 1964–82	1982–90	1952–64	
Chile	Before 1920	1924–32	1920–24 1932–70 1990	1970–73	1973–89
Colombia	Before 1936	1949–58	1936–49 1958–90		
Ecuador	1916–25	Before 1916 1925–48 1961–78	1948–61 1978–90		
Mexico		Up to 1990			
Paraguay		Up to 1990			
Peru		Before 1930 1930–39 1948–56 1962–63 1968–80	1939–48 1956–62 1963–68	1980–90	
Uruguay		Before 1903 1933–42	1903–19	1919–33 1942–73 1984–90	1973–84
Venezuela		Before 1935 1935–45	1958–68	1945–48 1968–90	

Source: Rueschemeyer, Stephens, & Stephens, 1992.

each nation varied over time in terms of the variables they had identified as potentially important for successful democratization.

Their analysis identified several conditions for initial democratization: consolidation of state power (ending overt challenges to state authority); expansion of the export economy (reducing conflicts over resources); industrialization (increasing the size and interaction of middle and working

Exhibit 9.7   **Achievement of Objectives in Three Free Economic Zones**

Objective	Kaohsiung (Taiwan)	Masan (South Korea)	Shenzhen (China)
Foreign investment attraction	Strong early, weak later	Strong early, weak later	Strong early, weak later
Employment generation	Strong early, weak later	Strong early, weak later	Weak early, strong later
Export promotion	Strong early, weak later	Strong early, weak later	Weak early, strong later
Technology transfer	Weak early, strong later	Weak early, strong later	Weak
Domestic integration	Weak early, strong later	Weak early, strong later	Strong
Regional development	Weak early, strong later	Weak early, strong later	Weak early, strong later

Source: Chen, 1994:19.

classes); and some agent of political articulation of the subordinate classes (which could be the state, political parties, or mass movements). Historical variation in these conditions was then examined in detail.

Xiangming Chen's (1994) study of the role of free economic zones in East Asian countries used quantitative data to develop a historical comparative analysis of three nations: Taiwan, South Korea, and China. His analysis represents several elements of Ragin's approach. Chen described key characteristics of these zones and presented selected economic indicators. After comparing the course of development of the free economic zones, he classified each in terms of its success in achieving six development objectives (Exhibit 9.7). The last stage in the analysis compared the types of patterns found with the predictions of alternative development theories. He concludes that free economic zones are capable of stimulating surrounding areas, as predicted by neoclassical economics, but state planning and regulation also can have an important impact.

Methodological Issues: Comparative Historical Research

Comparative historical analyses can yield rich insights into the combination of factors that explain historical processes, such as how nations have developed. Use of both historical and comparative perspectives allows for much more attention to the actual unfolding of events than is possible with cross-sectional or single-case studies. By blending variable-oriented and case-oriented approaches (see Chapter 5), comparative historical methods can involve systematic tests of causal explanations as well as intensive examinations of the historical record (Rueschemeyer, Stephens, & Stephens, 1992:225). However, when we use or review these methods, we must be sensitive to several problems:

■ *Historical research requires detailed knowledge of the nation investigated* (Kohn, 1987). This is as it should be, but it also serves as a barrier to in-depth historical research comparing many nations.

■ *The selection of cases for comparison has a critical impact on the conclusions reached.* If the goal of the analysis is to isolate the influence of certain key factors on the outcome of interest, cases should be chosen for their difference on these factors and their similarity on other, possibly confounding, factors (Skocpol, 1984:383). It is easy to select cases for comparison in a way that undermines causal analysis. For example, in order to understand how industrialization influences democracy, you might be tempted to compare an industrial nation that is democratic to a nonindustrial nation that is authoritarian. This selection of cases would make it impossible to determine whether industrialization influences democratization. You would need to select cases for comparison that differ in industrialization, so that you could then see if they differ in democratization (King, Keohane, & Verba, 1994:148–152).

■ *The goal of the type of historical comparative analysis recommended by Ragin* (1987:44–52) *is to explain completely the outcome of interest in each nation in terms of the factors examined.* This **deterministic causal approach** requires that there be no deviations from the combination of factors that are identified as determining the outcome for each nation. Yet there are likely to be exceptions to any explanatory rule that we establish (Lieberson, 1991). A careful analyst will evaluate the extent to which exceptions should be allowed in particular analyses.

■ *When a nation is coded as "democratic" or "authoritarian," the values of the underlying continuous variables are being dichotomized.* This introduces an imprecise and arbitrary element into the analysis (Lieberson, 1991). On the other hand, for some comparisons, qualitative distinctions, such as "simple majority rule" or "unanimity required," may capture the important differences between cases better than quantitative distinctions. It is essential to inspect carefully the categorization rules for any such analysis and to consider what form of measurement is both feasible and appropriate for the research question being investigated (King, Keohane, & Verba, 1994:158–163).

■ *Although comparative historical methods encourage examination of complex multidimensional processes, it often is difficult to conclude that one particular set of factors is critical for a given outcome.* There are just too many possible combinations. Alternative explanations for the evidence examined should be carefully weighed.

■ *The comparative strategy assumes that the nations examined are independent of each other in terms of the variables examined.* Yet in a very interdependent world, this assumption may be misplaced—nations may develop as they do because of how other nations are developing. As a result, comparing the particular histories of different nations may overlook the influence of global culture, international organizations, or economic dependency (Skocpol, 1984:384; cf. Chase-Dunn & Hall, 1993). The possibility of such complex interrelations should always be considered when evaluating the plausibility of a causal argument based on a comparison between two apparently independent cases (Jervis, 1996).

With these cautions in mind, the combination of historical and comparative methods allows for rich descriptions of social and political processes in different nations or regions as well as for causal inferences that reflect a systematic, defensible weighing of the evidence. We cannot expect one study comparing the histories of a few nations to control adequately for every plausible alternative causal influence, but repeated investigations can increasingly refine our understanding and lead to increasingly accurate causal conclusions (King, Keohane, & Verba, 1994:33).

Data Sources

After choosing one of the four research designs and deciding to use a quantitative or qualitative approach, a historical and comparative researcher must also select a data collection technique. Quantitative studies like Walters, James, and McCammon's (1997) often use data available from the U.S. Bureau of the Census or other government agencies. Similar data are also available from many other countries as well as from world bodies like the World Bank, as reflected in Franklin's (1996) study of international voting patterns, Crenshaw's (1995) comparative study of democracy, and Chen's (1994) study of free economic zones in East Asia. Historical and comparative research may also rely on previously collected survey data.

Qualitative research often relies on information in published histories, as did Levi's (1996) conscription study, or other secondary sources, such as the documents Zaret (1996) found in archival collections. Rueschemeyer, Stephens, and Stephens (1992) used a variety of sources to code key events in the histories of the nations they studied.

U.S. Bureau of the Census

The U.S. government has conducted a census of the population every 10 years since 1790; since 1940, this census also has included a census of housing (see also Chapter 4). This decennial Census of Population and Housing is a rich source of social science data (Lavin, 1994). The Census Bureau's monthly *Current Population Survey* (CPS) provides basic data on labor force activity that is then used in Bureau of Labor Statistics reports (see U.S. Bureau of Labor Statistics). The Census Bureau also collects data on agriculture, manufacturers, construction and other business, foreign countries, and foreign trade.

The U.S. Census of Population and Housing aims to survey an adult in every household in the United States. The basic "complete-count" census contains questions about household composition as well as ethnicity and income. More questions are asked in a longer form of the census that is administered to a sample of the households. A separate census of housing characteristics is conducted at the same time (Rives & Serow, 1988:15). Participation in the census is required by law, and confidentiality of the information obtained is mandated by law for 72 years after collection. Census data are reported for geographic units, including states, metropolitan areas, counties, and, in metropolitan areas, census tracts (small, relatively permanent areas with counties) and even blocks (see Exhibit 9.8). These different units allow units of analysis to be tailored to research questions.

Census data are used to apportion seats in the U.S. House of Representatives and to determine federal and state legislative district boundaries, as well as to inform other decisions by government agencies. Thousands of printed reports make census results available to the public in a variety of formats, including statistics for specific states and regions (Rives & Serow, 1988:24–32; U.S. Bureau of the Census, 1996). The U.S. Census Web site (*http:*

Exhibit 9.8 **Census Small-Area Geography**

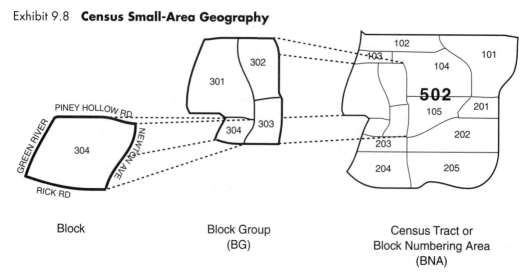

Block   Block Group (BG)   Census Tract or Block Numbering Area (BNA)

Source: U.S. Bureau of the Census, 1994:8.

//www.census.gov) provides direct access to many of these statistics (as do Internet service providers like Compuserve) and the catalog of the Inter-University Consortium for Political and Social Research (*http://www.icpsr. umich.edu*) lists the available reports. Some detailed information is only available with a subscription fee of $40 per quarter for individuals (as of 1997). Summary tapes and CD-ROM disks also can be purchased with census data in various geographic levels, including cities, census tracts, and even blocks (see Exhibit 9.9).

States also maintain census bureaus and may have additional resources. Some contain the original census data collected in the state 100 or more years ago. The ambitious historical researcher can use these returns to conduct detailed comparative studies at the county or state level (Lathrop, 1968:79).

Bureau of Labor Statistics (BLS)

Another good source of data is the Bureau of Labor Statistics of the U.S. Department of Labor, which collects and analyzes data on employment, earnings, prices and living conditions, industrial relations, productivity and technology, and occupational safety and health (U.S. Bureau of Labor Statistics, 1997b; U.S. BLS, 1991). Some of these data are collected by the Bureau of the Census in the monthly *Current Population Survey*, while other data are collected through surveys of establishments (U.S. Bureau of Labor Statistics, 1997a).

The *Current Population Survey* provides a monthly record for the United States of employment and unemployment, classified by age, sex, race, and other characteristics. The CPS uses a stratified random sample of about 60,000 households (with separate forms for about 120,000 individuals). Detailed questions are included to determine the precise labor force status of each household member over the age of 16, whether they are currently working or not. Statistical reports are published each month in the BLS's *Monthly Labor Review* and can also be inspected at their Web site (*http:// stats.bls.gov*). Datasets are available on computer tapes and disks from the BLS and services like the ICPSR.

Other U.S. Government Sources

Many more datasets useful for historical and comparative research have been collected by federal agencies and other organizations. The National Technical Information Service (NTIS) of the U.S. Department of Commerce maintains a Federal Computer Products Center that collects and catalogs many of these datasets and related software.

By 1993, more than 1,850 datasets from 50 agencies were described in the NTIS *Directory*. The *Directory* is the essential source of information about

Exhibit 9.9 **U.S. Census County Profile**

USA Counties 1996

GENERAL PROFILE

Cecil County, Maryland

From the *USA Counties 1996 CD-ROM*

Note: The actual application allows customers to compare an item for this county to other counties in the same state. See the test drive of *USA Counties 1996, Resident Population Table* for a sample of this feature.

POPULATION AND HOUSING (Bureau of the Census)	
Total Resident Population, 1995...................	78,174
Percent Of Population 65 Years And Over, 1995.....	10.4
Total Resident Population, 1990...................	71,347
Total Resident Population, 1980...................	60,430
Occupied Housing Units, 1990.....................	24,725
Percent Of Housing Units Owner Occupied, 1990.....	75.0
BIRTHS AND DEATHS (National	
Center for Health Statistics)	
Births, 1993......................................	1,113
Births Per 1,000 Resident Population, 1993........	14.7
Percent To Mothers Under 20 Years Of Age, 1993....	11.3
Deaths, 1993......................................	604
Per 1,000 Resident Population, 1993...............	8.0
Infant Deaths Per 1,000 Live Births, 1993.........	7.2
EDUCATION (Bureau of the Census)	
Persons 25 Years And Over, 1990...................	44,944
Percent Of Persons 25 And Over	
And High School Graduates, 1990.................	72.2

Source: http://www.census.gov/apsd/www/TestDrive/usaprof.htm

the datasets and can be purchased from the U.S. Department of Commerce (National Technical Information Service, 1993). Dataset summaries can be searched in the *Directory* by either subject or agency. Government research reports catalogued by NTIS can be searched on-line at the NTIS Web site (*http://www.fedworld.gov*), through services such as Compuserve, and in a CD-ROM catalog available in some libraries.

International Data Sources

Comparative researchers can find datasets on population characteristics, economic and political features, and political events in many nations. Some of these are available from U.S. government agencies. For example, the Social Security Administration reports on the characteristics of social security throughout the world (Wheeler, 1995). This comprehensive report classifies nations in terms of their type of social security program and provides detailed summaries of the characteristics of each nation's programs. It is available on the Internet at *http://www.ssa.gov/statistics/ssptw97.html*.

Many other sources of historical and comparative data are archived at the University of Michigan's Inter-University Consortium for Political and Social Research. A dataset collected in the "National Capability" study by Charles Taylor and Joachim Amm describes features of 155 nations between 1950 and 1988. Indicators include size of armed forces, military expenditures, economic productivity, and population characteristics. A broader range of data are available in the *World Handbook of Political and Social Indicators*, with political events coded from 1978 to 1982 and political, economic, and social data from 1950 to 1975 (*http://www.icpsr.umich.edu/cgi/ab.prl?file=7761*).

The history of military interventions in nations around the world between 1946 and 1988 is coded in a dataset developed by Frederic Pearson and Robert Baumann. The dataset identifies the intervener and target countries, the starting and ending dates of military intervention, and a range of potential motives (such as foreign policies, related domestic disputes, and pursuit of rebels across borders). Do you have an interest in international events, that is, in "words and deeds communicated between nations, such as threats of military force between nations"? A dataset collected by Charles McClelland includes characteristics of 91,240 such events (*http://www.icpsr.umich.edu/cgi/ab.prl?file=5211*).

Census data from other nations is also available through the ICPSR, as well as directly through the Internet. You can find in the ICPSR archives a dataset from the Statistical Office of the United Nations on the 1966–1974 population of 220 nations throughout the world (*http://www.icpsr.umich.*

edu/cgi/ab.prl?file=7623). More current international population data are provided by the Center for International Research and the U.S. Census Bureau (*http://www.icpsr.umich.edu/cgi/ab.prl?file=8490*).

Survey Datasets

Many survey datasets are also available on the Internet. These can be used by historical and comparative researchers to compare national attitudes and to examine trends over time. The Inter-University Consortium for Political and Social Research (1996) provides access to such surveys to researchers (including students) at many universities (*http://www.icpsr.umich.edu*). ICPSR was founded in 1962 by 21 universities collaborating with the University of Michigan's Survey Research Center. More than 370 colleges and universities around the world had joined by 1994, and the ICPSR archives include data from over 9,000 studies in more than 130 countries.

Survey datasets obtained in the United States and in many other countries that are stored at the ICPSR provide data on topics ranging from elite attitudes to consumer expectations. For example, data collected in the British Social Attitudes Survey in 1986, designed by the University of Chicago's National Opinion Research Center, are available through the ICPSR (*http://www.icpsr.umich.edu/cgi/ab.prl?file=8910*).

Data collected in a monthly survey of Spaniards' attitudes, by the Center for Research on Social Reality [Spain] Survey, are also available (*http://www.icpsr.umich.edu/cgi/ab.prl?file=6267*). Survey data from Russia, Germany, and other countries can also be found in the ICPSR collection.

The ICPSR archives also include data from the U.S. census, election results, 19th-century French census materials, popular organizations, international events, and roll call votes in the U.S. House and Senate since 1790. More than 6 million variables are represented in the collection.

Methodological Issues: Secondary Data Sources

No matter what the source of data, a researcher who relies on **secondary data**—data that he or she has not collected to answer the research question of interest—must have a good understanding of that source. The researcher should be able to answer the following questions (Stewart, 1984:23–30):

1. What was the study's purpose?
2. Who was responsible for data collection and what were their qualifications?
3. What data were collected and what was it intended to measure?
4. When was the information collected?

5. What methods were used for data collection?

6. How consistent are the data with data available from other sources?

Answering these questions helps to ensure that the researcher is familiar with the data he or she will analyze and can help to identify any problems with it.

Data quality is always a concern with secondary data, even when the data are collected by an official government agency. Census counts can be distorted by incorrect answers to census questions as well as by inadequate coverage of the entire population (see Chapter 4; Rives & Serow, 1988:32–35). Both historical and comparative analyses can be affected. For example, the percentage of the U.S. population not counted in the U.S. Census appears to have declined since 1880 from about 7% to 1%, but undercounting continues to be more common among poorer urban dwellers and recent immigrants (King & Magnuson, 1995; and see Chapter 4).

Data sources that we take for granted today are often unavailable for early years or other nations. For example, the widely used U.S. Uniform Crime Reporting System did not begin until 1930 (Rosen, 1995). It is easy to overlook problems of data quality when relying on previous publications that report relevant data, but this simply makes it all the more important to evaluate the primary sources themselves.

Special Techniques

Quantitative analysis of historical and comparative data can involve special techniques, such as demographic statistics for the analysis of census data and content analysis for studies that rely on news stories or other documents. Historical quantitative research like Olzak, Shanahan, and McEneaney's (1996) study of race riots may also use content analysis techniques to document the occurrence of events. Oral history interviews may be useful in studies of the recent past.

Demographic Analysis

The social processes that are the focus of historical and comparative research are often reflected in and influenced by changes in the makeup of the population being studied. **Demography** is the field that studies these dynamics. *Demography is the statistical and mathematical study of the size, composition, and spatial distribution of human populations and how these features change over time.* Demographers explain population change in terms of five processes: fertility, mortality, marriage, migration, and social mobility (Bogue, 1969:1).

Demographers obtain data from a census of the population (see Chapter 4) and from registries—records of events like births, deaths, migrations, marriages, divorces, diseases, and employment (Anderton, Barrett, & Bogue, 1997:54–79; Baum, 1993). They compute various statistics from these data to facilitate description and analysis (Wunsch & Termote, 1978). In order to use these data you need to have an understanding of how they are calculated and the questions they are used to answer. Four concepts are key to understanding and using demographic methods: population change, standardization of population numbers, the demographic bookkeeping equation, and population composition.

- *Population change* is a central concept in demography. The absolute population change is calculated simply as the difference between the population size in one census minus the population size in an earlier census. This measure of absolute change is of little value, however, because it does not take into account the total size of the population that was changing (Bogue, 1969:32–43). This is accomplished with the "intercensal percent change," which is the absolute change in population between two censuses divided by the population size in the earlier census (and multiplied by 100 to obtain a percent). With the percent change statistic, we can meaningfully compare the growth in two or more nations that differ markedly in size (as long as the intercensal interval does not vary between the nations) (White, 1993:1–2).

- *Standardization* of population numbers, as with the calculation of intercensal percent change, is a key concern of demographic methods (Gill, Glazer, & Thernstrom, 1992:478–482; Rele, 1993). In order to make meaningful comparisons between nations and over time, numbers that describe most demographic events must be adjusted for the size of the population at risk for the event. The fertility rate is calculated as the ratio of the number of births to women of childbearing age to the total number of women in this age range (multiplied by 1,000). Unless we make such adjustments, we will not know if a nation with a much higher number of births or deaths in relation to its total population size simply has more women in the appropriate age range or has more births per "eligible" woman.

- The *demographic bookkeeping (or balancing) equation* is used to identify the four components of population growth during a time interval ($P_2 - P_1$): births (B), deaths (D), and in- (M_i) and out-migration (M_o). The equation is written as follows: $P_2 = P_1 + (B - D) + (M_i - M_o)$. That is, population at a given point in time is equal to the population at an earlier time plus the excess of births over deaths during the interval and the excess of in-migration over out-migration (White, 1993:1–4). Whenever you see population size or change statistics used in a comparative analysis, you will want to ask yourself whether it is also important to know which component in the equation was responsible for the change over time or for the difference between countries (White, 1993:1–4).

■ *Population composition* refers to a description of a population in terms of such basic characteristics as age, race, sex, or marital status (White, 1993:1-7). Descriptions of population composition at different times or in different nations can be essential for understanding social dynamics identified in historical and comparative research. For example, Exhibit 9.10 compares the composition of the population in more and less developed regions of the world by age and sex in 1995, using United Nations data. By comparing these "population pyramids," we see the much greater proportion that children comprise of the population in less developed regions. The more developed regions' population pyramid also shows the greater proportion of women at older ages and the post–World War II "baby boom" bulge in the population.

Demographic analysis can be an important component of historical research (Bean, Mineau, & Anderton, 1990), but problems of data quality must be carefully evaluated (Vaessen, 1993). The hard work that can be required to develop demographic data from evidence that is hundreds of years old does not always result in worthwhile information. The numbers

Exhibit 9.10 **Population Pyramids for More Developed and Developing Regions of the World: 1995**

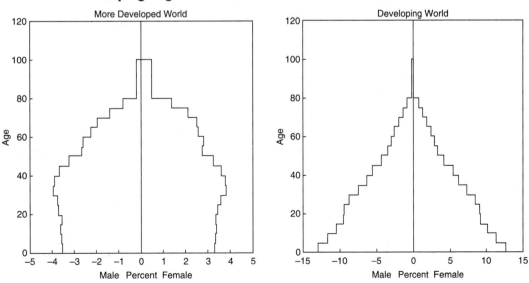

Source: Bogue, Arriega, & Anderton, 1993:1–19.

of people for which data are available in particular areas may be too small for statistical analysis; data that are easily available (such as a list of villages in an area) may not provide the information that is important (such as population size); lack of information on the original data collection procedures may prevent assessment of data quality (Hollingsworth, 1972:77).

Content Analysis

Content analysis is a research method for systematically analyzing and making inferences from text (cf., Weber, 1985:9). You can think of a content analysis as a "survey" of some documents or other records of prior communication. This method was first applied to the study of newspaper content and then to the analysis of Nazi propaganda broadcasts in World War II, but it can also be used to study historical documents, records of speeches, and other "voices from the past."

The units that are "surveyed," or coded in a content analysis can range from newspapers, books, or TV shows to persons referred to in other communications, themes expressed in documents or propositions made in different statements. Whatever the particular units surveyed, content analysis proceeds through several stages (Weber, 1985):

- *Identify a population of documents or other textual sources for study.* This population should be selected so that it is appropriate to the research question of interest. Perhaps the population will be all newspapers published in the United States, college student newspapers, nomination speeches at political party conventions, or "state of the nation" speeches by national leaders.

- *Determine the units of analysis,* such as newspaper articles, whole newspapers, speeches, or political conventions.

- *Select a sample of units from the population.* The simplest strategy might be simple random sample of documents. However, a stratified sample might be needed to ensure adequate representation of large and small cities, or of weekday and Sunday papers, or of political speeches during election years and in off-years (see Chapter 4).

- *Design coding procedures for the variables to be measured.* This requires deciding what unit of text to code, such as words, sentences, themes, or paragraphs. Then the categories into which the text units are to be coded must be defined. These categories may be broad, such as "supports democracy," or narrow, such as "supports universal suffrage."

- *Test and refine the coding procedures.* Clear instructions and careful training of coders are essential.

- *Base statistical analyses on counting occurrences of particular words, themes, or phrases, and test relations between different variables.*

Developing reliable and valid coding procedures is not an easy task. The meaning of words and phrases is often ambiguous. Homographs create special problems (words such as *mine* that have different meanings in different contexts), as do many phrases that have special meanings (such as "point of no return") (Weber, 1984:30). As a result, coding procedures cannot simply categorize and count words. Text segments in which the words are embedded must also be inspected before codes are finalized. Since different coders may perceive different meanings in the same text segments, explicit coding rules are required to ensure coding consistency. Special dictionaries can be developed to keep track of how the categories of interest are defined in the study (Weber, 1984:24–34).

Once coding procedures are developed, their reliability can be assessed by comparing coding done by different coders. Computer programs for content analysis can be used to enhance reliability (Weber, 1984). Whatever the rules that the computer is programmed to use to code text, these rules will be applied consistently. Validity can be assessed with a construct validation approach by determining the extent to which theoretically predicted relationships occur (see Chapter 3).

Exhibit 9.11 is a segment of the coding form I developed for a content analysis of union literature that I collected during a study of union political processes (Schutt, 1986). My sample was of 362 documents: all union newspapers and a stratified sample of union leaflets to members during the years of my investigation. My coding scheme included measures of the source and target for the communication, as well as of concepts that my theoretical framework indicated were important in organizational development: type of goals; tactics for achieving goals; organizational structure; forms of participation. The analysis documented a decline in concern with client issues and an increase in focus on organizational structure, which were both trends that also emerged in interviews with union members.

Oral History

History that is not written down is mostly lost to posterity (and social researchers). However, when a research question focuses on a time period within the lifetimes of living individuals, interviews—**"oral histories"**—can be useful. Thanks to a Depression-era writers project, Deanna Pagnini and S. Philip Morgan (1996) found that they could use oral histories to study attitudes toward births out of wedlock among African-American and white women in the South during the 1930s.

Almost 70% of African-American babies are born to unmarried mothers, compared to 22% of white babies (Pagnini & Morgan, 1996:1696). This difference often is attributed to contemporary welfare policies or problems in the inner city, but Pagnini and Morgan thought it might be due to more

Exhibit 9.11 **Union Literature Coding Form***

I. *Preliminary Codes*

  1. Document # _____

  2. Date _____
         mo   yr

  3. Length of text _____ pp. (round up to next 1/4 page;
     count legal size as 1.25)

  4. Literature Type

     1. General leaflet for members/employees

     2. Newspaper/Newsletter article

     3. Rep Council motions

     4. Other material for Reps, Stewards, Delegates (e.g., budget, agenda)

     5. Activity reports of officers, President's Report

     6. Technical information-filing grievances, processing forms

     7. Buying plans/Travel packages

     8. Survey Forms, Limited Circulation material (correspondence)

     9. Non-union

    10. Other _____ (specify)

4A. If newspaper article
    Position

     1. Headline story

     2. Other front page

     3. Editorial

     4. Other

4B. If Rep Council motion
    Sponsor

     1. Union leadership

     2. Office

     3. Leadership faction

     4. Opposition faction

     5. Other

  5. Literature content—Special issues

     1. First strike (1966)

     2. Second strike (1967)

     3. Collective bargaining (1977)

     4. Collective bargaining (1979)

     5. Election/campaign literature

     6. Affiliation with AFSCME/SEIU/other national union

     7. Other

II. *Source and Target*

  6. Primary source (code in terms of those who prepared this literature for distribution).

     1. Union—newspaper (Common Sense; IUPAE News)

     2. Union—newsletter (Info and IUPAE Bulletin)

     3. Union—unsigned

     4. Union officers

     5. Union committee

     6. Union faction (the Caucus; Rank-and-Filers; Contract Action, other election slate; PLP News; Black Facts)

     7. Union members in a specific work location/office

     8. Union members—other

*Coding instructions available from the author.

(continued on next page)

Exhibit 9.11 **Union Literature Coding Form** *(continued)*

      9. Dept. of Public Aid/Personnel

    10. DVR/DORS

    11. Credit Union

    12. Am. Buyers' Assoc.

    13. Other non-union

 7. Secondary source (use for lit. at least in part reprinted from another source, for distribution to members).

    1. Newspaper—general circulation

    2. Literature of other unions, organizations

    3. Correspondence of union leaders

    4. Correspondence from DPA/DVR—DORS/Personnel

    5. Correspondence from national union

    6. Press release

    7. Credit Union, Am. Buyers'

    8. Other _____ (specify)

    9. None

 8. Primary target (the audience for which the literature is distributed)

    1. Employees—general (if mass-produced and unless otherwise stated)

    2. Employees—DVR/DORS

    3. Union members (if refers *only* to members or if about union elections)

    4. Union stewards, reps, delegates committee

    5. Non-unionized employees (recruitment lit., etc.)

    6. Other _____ (specify)

    7. Unclear

III. *Issues*

  A. Goal

 9. Employee conditions/benefits (Circle up to 5)

    1. Criteria for hiring

    2. Promotion

    3. Work out of Classification, Upgrading

    4. Step increases

    5. Cost-of-living, pay raise, overtime pay, "money"

    6. Layoffs (non-disciplinary); position cuts

    7. Workloads, Redeterminations, "30 for 40", GA Review

    8. Office physical conditions, safety

    9. Performance evaluations

   10. Length of workday

   11. Sick Benefits/Leave—holidays, insurance, illness, vacation, voting time

   12. Educational leave

   13. Grievances—change in procedures

   14. Discrimination (race, sex, age, religion, national origin)

   15. Discipline—political (union-related)

   16. Discipline—performance, other

   17. Procedures with clients, at work

   18. Quality of work, "worthwhile jobs"—other than relations with clients

Source: Schutt, 1986:208–209.

enduring racial differences in marriage and childbearing. To investigate these historical differences, they read 1,170 life histories recorded by almost 200 writers who worked for a New Deal program during the Depression of the 1930s, the Federal Writers' Project Life History Program for the Southeast. The interviewers had used a topic outline that included family issues, education, income, occupation, religion, medical needs, and diet.

In 1936, the divergence in rates of nonmarital births was substantial in North Carolina: 2.6% of white births were to unmarried women, compared to 28.3% of nonwhite births. The oral histories gave some insight into community norms that were associated with these patterns. A white seamstress who became pregnant at age 16 recalled that "I'm afraid he didn't want much to marry me, but my mother's threats brought him around" (Pagnini & Morgan, 1996:1705) There were some reports of suicides by unwed young white women who were pregnant. In comparison, African-American women who became pregnant before they were married reported regrets, but rarely shame or disgrace. There were no instances of young black women committing suicide or getting abortions in these circumstances.

> We found that bearing a child outside a marital relationship was clearly not the stigmatizing event for African-Americans that it was for whites. . . . When we examine contemporary family patterns, it is important to remember that neither current marriage nor current childbearing patterns are "new" for either race. Our explanations for why African-Americans and whites organize their families in different manners must take into account past behaviors and values. (Pagnini & Morgan, 1996:1714–1715)

Whether oral histories are collected by the researcher or obtained from an earlier project, the stories they tell can be no more reliable than the memories that are recalled. Unfortunately, memories of past attitudes are "notoriously subject to modifications over time" (Banks, 1972:67), as are memories of past events, relationships, and actions. Use of corroborating data from documents or other sources should be used when possible to increase the credibility of descriptions based on oral histories.

■ ■ ■ ■ Conclusion

Historical and comparative social science investigations use a variety of techniques that range from narrative histories having much in common with qualitative methods to analyses of secondary data that are in many respects like traditional survey research. Each of these methods can help to gain new insights into processes like democratization. They encourage intimate familiarity with the course of development of the nations studied and thereby stimulate inductive reasoning about the interrelations among different historical events. Systematic historical and comparative techniques can be used to test deductive hypotheses concerning international differences as well as historical events.

Most historical and comparative methods encourage causal reasoning. They require the researcher to consider systematically the causal mechanism, or historical sequences of events, by which earlier events influence later outcomes. They also encourage attention to causal context, with a particular focus on the ways in which different cultures and social structures may result in different effects of other variables. There is much to be gained by continuing to use and develop these methods.

KEY TERMS

Case-oriented research
Comparative historical research
Conjunctural
Content analysis
Cross-sectional comparative research
Demography
Deterministic causal approach
Historical events research
Historical process research

Holistic
Method of agreement
Method of difference
Narrative explanation
Oral history
Secondary data
Temporal
Variable-oriented research

HIGHLIGHTS

- The central insight behind historical and comparative methods is that we can improve our understanding of social processes when we make comparisons to other times and places.

- There are four basic types of historical and comparative research methods: historical events research, historical process research, cross-sectional comparative research, and comparative historical research. Historical events and historical process research are likely to be qualitative, and comparative studies are often quantitative, although research of each type may be either quantitative or qualitative.

- Methodological challenges for historical research often include variation in the meaning of words and phrases across historical periods, bias or inaccuracy of historical documents, missing data, and the limitations of focusing on one case.

- Five important aspects of time for understanding historical processes are the duration of an event, the pace of change, the trajectory of events, cyclical processes, and the subjective perception of time.

- Qualitative historical process research uses a narrative approach to causal explanation, in which historical events are treated as part of a developing story. Narrative explanations are temporal, holistic, and conjunctural.

■ Methodological challenges for comparative and historical research include the need for detailed knowledge of the cases chosen, identification of changing definitions of variables and geographic units, selection of cases on the basis of the theoretical framework, sensitivity to the limitations of a deterministic causal approach and reliance on dichotomous categorizations of cases, and openness to alternative explanations.

■ Secondary data analysts should have a good understanding of the research methods used to collect the data they analyze. Data quality is always a concern, particularly with historical data.

■ Central concepts for demographic research are population change, standardization of population numbers, the demographic bookkeeping equation, and population composition.

■ Content analysis is a tool for systematic analysis of documents and other textual data. It requires careful testing and control of coding procedures to achieve reliable measures.

■ Oral history provides a means of reconstructing past events. Data from other sources should be used whenever possible to evaluate the accuracy of memories.

EXERCISES

1. Read the original article reporting one of the studies described in this chapter. Critique the article, using the article review questions presented in Appendix C as your guide. Focus particular attention on procedures for measurement, sampling, and establishing causal relations.

2. What historical events have had a major influence on social patterns in the nation? The possible answers are too numerous to list, ranging from any of the wars to major internal political conflicts, economic booms and busts, scientific discoveries, and legal changes. Pick one such event in your own nation for this exercise. Find one historical book on this event and list the sources of evidence used. What additional evidence would you suggest for a social science investigation of the event?

3. The journals *Journal of Social History* and *Social Science History* report many studies of historical processes. Select one article from a recent journal issue about a historical process used to explain some event or other outcome. Summarize the author's explanation. Identify any features of the explanation that are temporal, holistic, and conjunctural. Prepare a chronology of the important historical events in that process. Do you agree with the author's causal conclusions? What additional evidence would strengthen the author's argument?

4. The table on the facing page identifies voting procedures and the level of turnout in one election for 10 countries. Do voting procedures appear to influence turnout in these countries? In order to answer this question using Mill's

	Voting Age	Number of Days Polling Booth Open	Voting Day on Work Day or Rest Day	Postal Voting	Proxy Voting	Constituency Transfer	Advance Voting	Voter Turnout (in %)	Year (P=presidential, L=Legislative Election)
Switzerland	20	2	Rest day	Automatic for armed forces, otherwise by application 4 days before voting	Varies by canton	No	No	46	1991L
Taiwan	20	1	Rest day					72	1992L
Thailand	20	1	Rest day	No				62	1995L
Turkey	20	1	Rest day	No	No	Special polling stations at border posts for citizens residing abroad	No	80	1991L
Ukraine	18	1	Rest day					71.6	1994P
United Kingdom	18	1	Work day	On application	On application	No	No	77.8	1992L
United States	18	1	Work day	By application; rules vary across states	In some states for blind and disabled	No		51.5	1992P
Uruguay	18	1	Rest day	No	No	No	No	89.4	1994P
Venezuela	18	1	Rest day	No	"Assisted" voting for blind and disabled	No	No	60	1993P
Zambia		1	Work day		No			50	1991P

Source: LeDuc, Niemi, & Norris, 1996:19 [Figure 1.3].

methods, you will first have to decide how to dichotomize the values of variables that have more than two values (postal voting, proxy voting, and turnout). You must also decide what to do about missing values. Apply Mill's method of agreement to the pattern in the table. Do any variables emerge as likely causes? Now apply Mill's method of difference to the pattern in the table. Do any variables emerge as likely causes? What additional information would you like to have for your causal analysis?

5. Compare the historical process research by Valenzuela (1990) on the breakdown of democracy in Chile and the comparative historical research by Rueschemeyer, Stephens, and Stephens (1992) on democratic politics in Latin America. What does comparison among nations add to the researcher's ability to develop causal explanations? What comparisons would help to test the explanation that Valenzuela uses for the case of Chile?

6. Olzak, Shanahan, and McEneaney (1996) developed a nomothetic causal explanation of variation in racial rioting in the United States over time, while Valenzuela's explanation of the breakdown in democracy in Chile can be termed idiographic. Discuss the similarities and differences between these types of causal explanation. Use these two studies to illustrate the strengths and weaknesses of each.

7. Select one of the four types of historical and comparative methods for further study. Now search recent issues of journals like the *American Journal of Sociology*, the *American Sociological Review*, the *American Political Science Review*, the *Journal of Social History*, and *Social Science History* to find an article that uses this method. Read the abstracts of articles that appear to be historical and/or comparative. What difficulties do you have in classifying articles as historical or comparative? What rules would you suggest for making this classification? Now focus on the one article you have chosen. What strengths and limitations of the method you focused on does the article illustrate? (Refer to the "methodological issues" section in the text's discussion of this method.)

8. Using your library's government documents collection or the Census site on the Web, select one report by the Bureau of the Census about the population of the United States or some segment of it. Outline the report and list all of the tables included in it. Summarize the report in two paragraphs. Suggest a historical or comparative study for which this report would be useful.

9. Review the survey datasets available through the Inter-University Consortium for Political and Social Research (ICPSR) (1996), using either their published directory or their Internet site. Select two such datasets that might be used to study a research question in which you are interested. Use the information ICPSR reports about them to answer Questions 1–5 in the text section on methodological issues with secondary data sources. Is the information adequate to answer these questions? What are the advantages and disadvantages of using one of these datasets to answer your research question compared to designing a new study?

10. Find a magazine or newspaper report on a demographic issue, such as population change or migration. Explain how one of the key demographic concepts could be used or was used to improve understanding of this issue.

11. Select a current social or political topic that has been the focus of news articles. Propose a content analysis strategy for this topic, using newspapers or newspaper articles or editorials as your units of analysis. Your strategy should include a definition of the population, selection of the units of analysis, a sampling plan, and coding procedures for key variables. Now find an article on this topic and use it to develop your coding procedures. Test and refine your coding procedures with another article on the same topic.

WEB EXERCISES

1. You've been asked to be a research assistant for a professor in your sociology department who is doing a cross-sectional comparative study of social inequality. She has asked you to get information regarding birth rate, death rate, life expectancy, and literacy for five countries in various parts of the world. She also wants to supplement the information with some qualitative data about each country. Use the City.Net Web site at

   http://www.city.net

   Gather the requested information for five countries of your choosing from different regions of the earth.

2. Using the Web as your information source, find quantitative *and* qualitative data about a topic of your choice relating to social inequality. For example, if you choose "income inequality," you may find social science survey sites to gather information regarding statistics reporting income distribution in the United States as well as sites sponsored by social service organizations that give information regarding the disparity in quality of life between the "rich" and the "poor" in the United States. In writing up your results, list the Web sites you used as references and the types of data each gave you access to.

3. Go to the Pathfinder homepage at

   http://www.pathfinder.com

   Using the Pathfinder site as your data source, do a content analysis study of major stories in U.S. popular magazines, newspapers, and/or other on-line sources. Your content analysis strategy should involve choosing 10–12 different sources from the Pathfinder menus (magazines, newspapers, Web sites, etc.), looking at each source, and writing down the headlines and basic subject of the major story (or stories) they are reporting. Can you find any trends or patterns in what you see? Are there certain stories that all of the sources are reporting on? What themes do you see running through the different stories? Write up your results in a one-page report.

   On a second page, answer the following questions: How many sources are you relying on? What is the sample size (the number of sources you used)? Explain how you chose your sample. What type of sampling have you chosen (availability, cluster, snowball, random, etc.)? Is your sample a representative one? How generalizable are your results? Explain.

4. The U.S. Census Bureau's homepage can be found at

   http://ftp.census.gov/

This site contains extensive reporting of census data including population data, economic indicators, and other information acquired through the Census. This Web site allows you to collect information on numerous subjects and topics. This information can then be used to make comparisons between different states or cities. Choose a subject that you find interesting and use the U.S. Census Bureau's homepage as a resource to collect data about that subject for your state or your city. Next choose two other states or cities to compare yours with, and collect the appropriate data for each of them. Use the data you have collected to compare your state or city with other states or cities. Write a one-page report summarizing your findings. Make sure to include some of the data you collected from the Web.

SPSS EXERCISES

1. You can use the 1996 General Social Survey dataset for a cross-sectional comparative description of different regions in the United States: East, Midwest, South, and West. We will focus on social and political attitudes.
   a. First, examine the distributions of the following variables: attend, bible, chldben, family16, fefam, rifle, usworry, and jobsall. (I have recoded some of the variables so there are fewer categories in the tables.) Would you expect any of these attitudes to vary among the four U.S. regions? Write hypotheses to indicate your expectations.

   STATISTICS
     DESCRIPTIVE
       FREQUENCIES (attend,bible,chldben…)

   b. Now, request crosstabs by region4, with percentages based on regional totals.

   STATISTICS
     CROSSTABS
       DOWN [attend,bible,chldben,family16,fefam,
       rifle,usworry,jobsall]
       ACROSS [region4]
        STATISTICS [COLUMN %].

   c. Now read the tables by comparing the percentages in the regions, column by column.
   d. Describe the apparent differences among the regions in these attitudes and behaviors. Are your hypotheses supported?

2. How do the attitudes of immigrants to the United States compare to those of people born in the United States? Request the crosstabulations (in percentage form) of nafta1, nafta2, refugees, nataid, wrldgovt, and jobsall by born (with BORN as the column variable).

   Inspect the output. Describe the similarities and differences you have found.

3. Since the GSS file is cross-sectional, we cannot use it to conduct historical research. However, we can develop some interesting historical questions by examining differences in the attitudes of Americans in different cohorts.

a. Inspect the distributions of the following variables: attend, bible, chldben, family16, fefam, rifle, usworry, jobsall. Would you expect any of these attitudes and behaviors to have changed over the twentieth century? State your expectations in the form of hypotheses.

b. Request a crosstabulation of several attitudinal and behavioral variables by birth COHORT (choose your dependent variables from this list: ATTEND, BIBLE, CHLDBEN, FAMILY16, FEFAM, RIFLE, USWORRY, JOBSALL).

c. Read the crosstabulations by comparing the percentage distribution in each cohort, column by column, for each table. What appear to be the differences among the cohorts? Which differences do you think are due to historical change and which do you think are due to the aging process? Which attitudes and behaviors would you expect to still differentiate the baby-boom generation and the post-Vietnam generation in 20 years?

10 Multiple Methods in Context: Integration and Review

Conclusion

KEY TERMS
HIGHLIGHTS
EXERCISES
WEB EXERCISES
SPSS EXERCISES

■ ■ ■ ■ Designing research means deciding how to measure empirical phenomena, how to identify causal connections, and how to generalize findings—not as separate decisions, but in tandem, with each decision having implications for the others. A research design is an integrated whole involving both fruitful conjunctions and necessary compromises. The carefully controlled laboratory conditions that increased the causal validity of Bushman's (1995) experiments on TV violence decreased the generalizability of his conclusions (Chapter 6). The representative sampling plan that increased the generalizability of Ross's (1990) national health study limited her options for estimating causal effects (Chapter 7). The observations that underlay Diamond's (1992) descriptions of nursing home staff would not be feasible in a national sample of nursing homes (Chapter 8). Few measures are available for large representative samples of nations (Chapter 9).

The goals of this chapter are to deepen your understanding of research designs and their consequences for achieving valid results and to alert you to the value of using multiple methods within a single research project. First, I review the design of two studies of AIDS awareness, noting their relative merits and drawing from this comparison 10 lessons about research designs. Next, I discuss the value of using multiple methods and give examples of combined designs. We will also see how social science research designs can be extended to take account of context and to identify the influence of natural processes. The chapter concludes with a summary of different theoretical perspectives on combining research designs.

■ ■ ■ ■ Analysis of Research Designs

It is not enough to ask of a study you critique, or one that you plan, such questions as how valid the measures were and whether the causal conclusions were justified. In addition, you must consider how the measurement approach might have affected the causal validity of the researcher's conclusions and how the sampling strategy might have altered the quality of measures. In fact, you must be concerned with how each component of the research design influenced the others. My goal here is to illustrate the process of thinking about the relations among selected design elements.

This section guides you through a critique and comparison of two studies. The questions that will guide our critiques—the questions that you should ask when you critique any social research study—are listed in Appendix C. Throughout the critiques, bracketed numbers indicate which questions in Appendix C I am answering. Since I am most concerned with pointing out certain features of the studies, my critiques will not answer each of the questions, nor will they provide complete answers to those questions I do answer. You will find that several questions (17–20) are best answered after you have studied this chapter and Chapters 11 and 12. In any case, remember that your goal is to evaluate research projects as integrated wholes rather than as marriages of convenience among discrete techniques. To this end, I follow the separate critiques with some lessons that apply to the relations among design components.

Case Study: AIDS Education Among the Homeless

I served as a consultant for several years to a Massachusetts AIDS prevention program for homeless persons, which was funded by the U.S. Centers for Disease Control. My role was to evaluate the need for and effectiveness of particular prevention strategies. One of the studies I conducted involved interviewing homeless persons living in shelters in order to determine what they knew about HIV transmission and AIDS, whether they had been exposed to any prevention activities, and what effect the exposure might have had on their knowledge and on their risk-related behaviors (Schutt, Gunston, & O'Brien, 1992).[1,16] The study thus had both descriptive and evaluative purposes; in addition, I explored unanticipated patterns in the data.[2]

The Research Design

The survey measured knowledge about HIV/AIDS, fear of contracting AIDS, awareness of shelter-based efforts to increase AIDS awareness, and a host of other variables that I thought might influence how likely people were to understand and act on prevention information—age, gender, education, substance abuse, and mental and physical illness among them.[7,9] Using systematic random sampling procedures, respondents were selected from lists of those sleeping in three large shelters, with 80% of those selected agreeing to participate in the survey.[14,15] One of these three shelters had hosted an active AIDS prevention program; the other two had not.

The interview schedule about AIDS that I constructed with my project collaborators was based on similar instruments used in other studies.[4] It included questions about how HIV is transmitted, how the illness progresses, and what prospects for a cure exist. From these questions I constructed an index of knowledge about AIDS that was internally reliable. I measured awareness of shelter-based AIDS educational efforts and self-reported behavioral change with other questions. When I compared awareness of shelter-based AIDS educational efforts between the shelter that had an active AIDS educational program and other shelters, I found that awareness was much higher in the shelter with the active AIDS educational program, thus suggesting the validity of the questions measuring awareness of shelter-based AIDS educational efforts.[10]

Knowledge of basic AIDS transmission facts was quite high in all the shelters; 80 to 90% of those questioned knew that sexual contact and exchange of dirty drug needles are the primary means of transmission, although many mistakenly feared transmission through insect bites and being near people with AIDS. But a comparison of the average knowledge index score among the shelters did not detect a difference, nor was there a relation between the number of prevention activities respondents had been exposed to and their knowledge index score. It seemed that the prevention work had not had an impact on overall knowledge.

But there were some indications of program effects. Individuals in the prevention-oriented shelter—called the experimental shelter—were more likely to be aware of the value of the primary tools, other than abstinence, for avoiding transmission through sexual contact (use of condoms) and sharing drug needles (cleaning needles with bleach). It was this awareness that was the primary focus of the prevention campaign (see Exhibit 10.1). Also, individuals exposed to more prevention activities were more likely to report having changed their behavior to reduce their risk of contracting AIDS, irrespective of their other characteristics.[17]

Analysis of the Design

After looking at the data, I rejected our initial hypothesis that persons staying in the shelter with the active AIDS education program would have a higher level of knowledge about AIDS than persons staying in the other shelters, although tests of related, derivative hypotheses yielded some indications of program effects.[8]

Were the conclusions valid? The AIDS knowledge index questions seemed valid on their face as a test of relevant knowledge, although, as with any multiple choice test, the level of understanding of issues might vary significantly from what the index score suggested.[10] More important, the self-reports of behavioral change are suspect as valid indicators of actual behavioral change, as indicated in the following excerpt:

> We did not measure behavior change itself, and . . . the likelihood of
> reporting behavior change retrospectively undoubtedly increases more
> readily in response to prevention efforts than would actual behavior
> change assessed in a longitudinal study. Moreover, these results do not

Exhibit 10.1　**Agreement with AIDS Knowledge Questions***

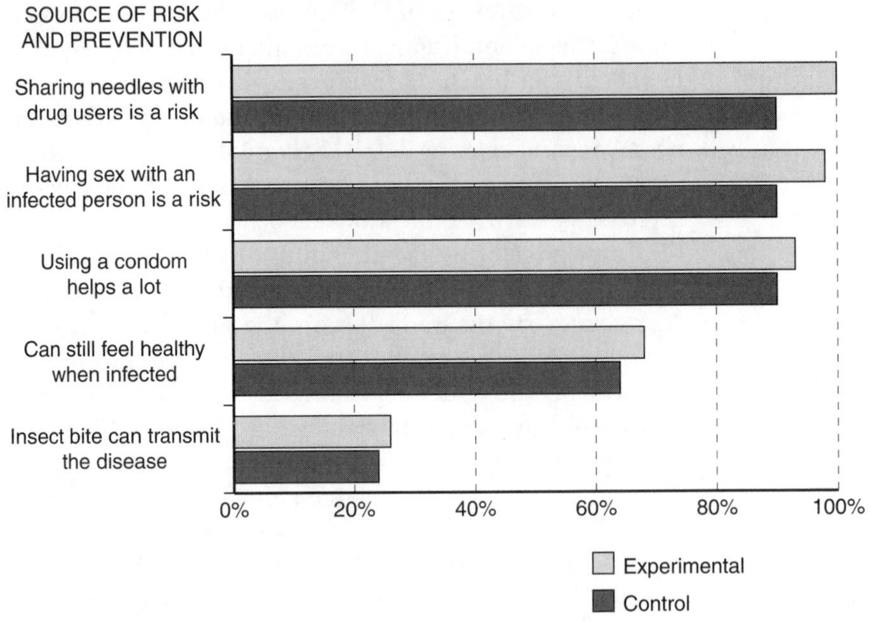

SOURCE OF RISK
AND PREVENTION

*Experimental data based on 58 to 60 cases, control data on 135 to 146 cases.

Source: Schutt, Gunston, & O'Brien, 1992.

specify which behaviors were thought to have been altered, or how consistent and how prolonged the alleged behavior change was. (Schutt et al., 1992:6)

Given the use of a random sampling technique and a relatively high rate of response, the results were probably generalizable to the shelter population surveyed, although the 20% who refused to participate could have been different from those who did respond. If those who refused were more likely to engage in risky behaviors (drug use, in particular) and to have less knowledge about AIDS, our causal conclusions would have been affected. In any case, there is no way of knowing with confidence that the results are generalizable to other groups of homeless persons.[14,15]

The causal conclusions, that prevention efforts did not affect overall AIDS knowledge but did influence knowledge about preventing high-risk activities, must remain suspect.[13] One possible source of invalidity in this case is that the shelter residents exposed to more prevention activity were more knowledgeable about some issues because they differed in some individual respects from those who had been exposed to less prevention activity. I tested for this possibility by statistically controlling for such individual characteristics as education and health status, and the findings did not change; so the relationship between exposure to prevention activities and knowledge about high-risk activities was not spurious due to these variables. But perhaps other variables should have been controlled. Perhaps drug users were more aware of the distribution of bleach for cleaning needles and also more likely to know that unclean needles can result in HIV infection. If this were true, being aware that bleach was being distributed might itself have had no educational benefit. The association between being aware of bleach distribution and knowing about the hazards of unclean needles would then have been spurious. Our confidence in the conclusion that there were some limited effects of exposure to AIDS-prevention activities also is lessened by the fact that these specific relationships were identified through an exploratory analysis planned after the data were collected and the initial hypothesis tested. Such an approach, as I noted in Chapter 2, gives us less confidence in the results than a test of a hypothesis stated in advance of data analysis.[18]

Another possible explanation for the lack of effect of prevention activities on overall knowledge of AIDS-transmission facts might have been discovered if we had investigated the way in which respondents actually made sense of these facts and then acted on them. Greater elaboration of the mechanism by which knowledge is translated into behavior is needed.[13]

Were there any ethical problems with this research?[6] All persons selected for the sample were read a statement describing the survey and making it clear that their participation was voluntary. Before an interview could begin, the respondents had to sign a statement indicating their consent to be interviewed. In addition, the interviews were anonymous. The consent forms were kept separately and could not be linked to the interview schedules on which answers were recorded; no identifying information was recorded on the interview schedules themselves.

I did not expect that the interview process itself would cause any harm to subjects. In fact, the interviewers reported that many respondents enjoyed the chance to talk with someone (a common reaction to in-person interviews), but interviewers also found that a few respondents became sad when asked questions about their social contacts. All respondents who expressed emotional or other needs during the interviews were invited to speak with trained shelter staff. Other sensitive personal information was requested in the interview about substance abuse, past arrests, and abuse history; but the anonymity of the interviews ensured that disclosing this information could not harm the subjects.

The only tangible benefits to the actual research subjects were the small rewards distributed (money, socks, or cigarettes) and the sociability provided by the interview process. However, the research had some potential general benefits to homeless persons as a result of the knowledge it developed about preventing AIDS. In fact, the director of the AIDS prevention project modified her approach based on the research findings so as to emphasize those prevention strategies that seemed most effective. Given the negligible risk to subjects posed by the interviews and the attention to ethical practice in carrying out the study, the study seems to conform to current ethical standards. I should note, however, that some people who work with or advocate for homeless persons object to any research with homeless persons, including interviewing, because they believe it exploits the vulnerable position of these persons. This issue is worth discussing. My own position, and that of most university and agency review boards, is that responsible interview studies are appropriate in these circumstances. In fact, well-designed research can result in more effective service programs.

Case Study: AIDS Education Among College Students

A study by Eleanor Maticka-Tyndale (1992) explored the mechanism by which formal knowledge about AIDS influences behavior.[1,2] Maticka-Tyndale surveyed 1,000 students in selected courses in Montreal colleges, 866 of whom completed her questionnaire about their knowledge of AIDS and their behaviors that might put them at risk of infection.[16]

Of these students, 200 returned forms indicating their consent to in-depth interviews, and Maticka-Tyndale then interviewed 25 of them. (Interviewees were chosen to represent the different characteristics that theory suggested might lead to different orientations to AIDS, such as gender, French or English cultural background, and sexual experience.)[14]

The Research Design

Responses to the fixed-choice questionnaire indicated a high level of knowledge about basic AIDS transmission and prevention facts, but high rates of risky behavior nonetheless. The in-depth interviews helped to explain this apparent disjuncture between knowledge and behavior. Through casual conversation with their peers, students transformed the way they understood the facts they had learned about AIDS into a commonsense approach that minimized their risk. Many came to see AIDS as just another risk in their lives, requiring no special action, or just requiring that they restrict intimate activities to those they could "trust."[13]

> But then, like you don't really believe it will ever happen. At least, not to you. . . . Anyway, there are a lot more common things women have to worry about. (Maticka-Tyndale, 1992: 243)

Analysis of the Design

Measurement in this study represented an improvement over my study in the homeless shelters because it included responses to in-depth interview questions, but it was possible to collect the in-depth information on AIDS knowledge only from a tiny sample of volunteers.[10] Although the sample selection is justified as being theoretically based, representing the different perspectives in the entire population studied, there really is no way to verify that this representation was achieved. More important, the rate of nonresponse became a very large concern with the in-depth interview sample. Since 86.6% of the original sample of 1,000 returned question-naires, and only 200 of these indicated their willingness to be interviewed, the interview sample represents at best a response rate of just 20%. There is no reason to believe that those who did not give their consent to be inter-viewed were like those who did. Generalization of the findings from even the larger sample of college students used in the questionnaire survey to the target population of college students in general is, of course, hazard-ous, because the sample was drawn just from certain types of classes and from schools in one city. And there is no way to know from the study itself whether the general process identified applies to homeless people or others.[14]

But the focus of the Maticka-Tyndale study on the mechanism of trans-mission of scientific facts into actual behavior, through the process of so-cially determining the meaning of those facts, sheds light on other studies of the impact of AIDS prevention efforts.[19] These findings suggest the im-portance of incorporating measures of a broader range of AIDS-related atti-tudes into larger surveys, and of designing education campaigns that target the misunderstandings supported by peer groups, as indicated in a con-cluding comment:[20]

> For the young adults in this study, commonsense knowledge coincided with the medical perspective of AIDS as fearsome and deadly. It diverged from the medical understanding of AIDS, however, in its personalization of risk and safety. . . . The first personalization was the faith that the scientific and medical communities will find a cure "in time" for these young adults, should they need one. The seriousness of AIDS is thus attenuated, since these young adults do not expect its deadliness to directly affect them. The second personalization is of the source of risk. AIDS is conceptualized as caused by *individuals* rather than by a virus. Individuals who engage in particular types of sexual encounters, unlike those engaged in by the study participants and their peers, are considered a threat. . . . [This personalization] made it difficult for these young adults to perceive of themselves as "at risk." (Maticka-Tyndale, 1992:248)

This study does not appear to raise problematic ethical concerns, although it did deal with sensitive personal issues.[6] Participation was completely voluntary, and the college students surveyed could not be considered a vulnerable population (and I presume that none were coerced into completing their questionnaires by their instructors). In a study like this, it would have been critical to maintain the confidentiality of all information disclosed in the questionnaires and interviews.

Evaluating Research Designs

These two examples show that the boundaries separating different methods of data collection are not sharp: Experiments may be conducted in the field; surveys may involve some intensive open-ended questioning; field research may utilize quantitative counts of phenomena or random samples of events. But the central features of experiments, surveys, and qualitative methods provide distinct perspectives even when used to study the same social processes. Comparing subjects randomly assigned to a treatment and a comparison group, asking standard questions of the members of a random sample, and observing while participating in a natural social setting involve markedly different decisions about measurement, causality, and generalizability. As you can see in Exhibit 10.2, not one of these methods can reasonably be graded as superior to the others in all respects, and each varies in its suitability to different research questions and goals.

Exhibit 10.2 **Comparison of Research Methods**

Design	Measurement Validity	Generalizability	Type of Causal Assertions	Causal Validity
Experiments	+	−	Nomothetic	+
Surveys	+	+	Nomothetic	−/+[a]
Participant observation	−/+[b]	−	Idiographic	−
Comparative[c]	−	−/+	Idiographic or nomothetic	−

[a]Surveys are a weaker design for identifying causal effects than true experiments, but use of statistical controls can strengthen causal arguments.
[b]Reliability is low compared to surveys, and systematic evaluation of measurement validity is often not possible. However, direct observations may lead to great confidence in the validity of measures.
[c]All conclusions about this type of design vary with the specific approach used. See Chapter 9.

Lessons About Research Designs

What general lessons can we learn from these examples about research designs and the difficulties and tradeoffs involved in attempting to maximize validity?

Some lessons have to do with the fundamentals of developing research problems and deciding on research purposes:

1. **The research problem guides all subsequent decision making.**

    Measures that might appear weak in one context may be quite appropriate given the research problem in another context. The evaluative focus of the AIDS prevention study made it important to select purposively as one site for study the shelter with the CDC-funded AIDS prevention program.

2. **Deductive research strategies should not preclude inductive efforts to elaborate on and explain unanticipated findings.**

    The studies just reviewed yielded their richest insights from some degree of inductive exploration, although the inductively derived conclusions must be confirmed in subsequent deductive research. For example, the study of AIDS prevention in homeless shelters found several relationships between knowledge of specific AIDS prevention activities and knowledge of certain risk factors, even though the hypothesized relationship between exposure and overall knowledge was not supported.

    Sampling decisions and decisions about units of analysis have multiple ramifications:

3. **The most readily available data, and the data that are most feasible to collect from a large sample, may not provide the best measures of some important concepts.**

    The small sample used for in-depth interviews about students' conceptions of vulnerability to AIDS allowed sensitive measures that were not possible with the larger sample of homeless persons using several Boston shelters. This problem also occurs when secondary data are used, even when they were collected in a well-designed survey, since we must rely on the measures devised by another researcher to answer a different research question than ours. When we rely on official records, the possibilities for inappropriate or insufficient data are multiplied. Whenever we obtain a secondary dataset, we must familiarize ourselves with the procedures used and the results obtained in sampling, survey design, and survey administration.

4. **Some research questions are most suited to group-level data.**

Social processes at different levels of reality (individuals, groups, political units, and so on) are interrelated, and we often can understand the social world better when we do not restrict our vision to just one level. It was because Sampson and Laub (1993) used counties as the units of analysis that their work contributed so much more to understanding the operation of the criminal justice system than would just one more study using individuals as the units of analysis. The lesson can be stated in a slightly different way: **microlevel research** on social processes (concerning individuals) should be complemented by **macrolevel research** (concerning societies or other aggregates).

Research designs that can effectively identify causal influences are hard to achieve. This is partly because it is often difficult to design research that can meet the criteria for establishing causal relationships, and also because causal relationships can be obscured of misidentified due to invalid measures or inappropriate samples:

5. **It is difficult to test hypotheses about the effects of historical events, even with longitudinal data, unless a comparison group that was not exposed to those events is available.**

When all individuals or groups in a study have been exposed to the same event, before/after comparisons are risky since other events may account for any changes in the individuals or events. Trying to identify the effects of AIDS prevention efforts funded by the CDC would have been pointless in a study of just the one shelter where these efforts occurred, because much attention to AIDS was being paid in the media and other sources during this period. Data from multiple time points can partly make up for the lack of a comparison group since longer time series make it possible to see whether there was any trend before and after the event hypothesized as causing a change.

6. **Causal conclusions often rest on questionable evidence of non-spuriousness.**

Many research questions cannot be studied directly with experimental designs. For example, the effectiveness of the AIDS prevention program could not have been studied after the fact with a design requiring random assignment of persons. It is easy to statistically control for a few variables when testing a causal hypothesis in a nonexperimental design, but it is important to realize that nonspuriousness cannot be ruled out until all the variables that might produce spurious effects have been controlled. Of course, it is impossible in nonexperimental research to rule out all *possible* sources of spuriousness; so the goal should be to identify, measure, and control for all *plausible* sources.

7. **Causal hypotheses cannot be tested with invalid measures.**

   If a variable is measured unreliably, its association with other variables will be lessened. So a researcher might find no association where one had been hypothesized and conclude mistakenly that no causal connection exists. Similarly, if the measure of an extraneous variable is invalid, a procedure that statistically controls for this variable will, in fact, not control for the intended source of spuriousness. For example, after additional research I now suspect the validity of the self-report measure of substance abuse that I used in the study of AIDS prevention. If this measure was invalid, it means that I actually did not control for substance abuse when I attempted to determine whether the relation between exposure to some AIDS prevention activities and indicators of AIDS knowledge was spurious. In the same way, causal influences can be obscured by the use of composite measures of dependent or independent variables, or both. The use of a composite measure of AIDS knowledge obscured the apparent effects of prevention efforts on the specific beliefs that had been targeted by the prevention campaign.

8. **Causal explanations are strengthened by identification of causal mechanisms.**

   Such identification can require more intensive styles of investigation that preclude large samples. The increased understanding of the effect (actually the noneffect) of traditional AIDS education was substantially clarified by the investigation of how students interpreted AIDS facts.

9. **Problems in sampling and nonresponse can prevent identification of causal relationships.**

   Perhaps those students who did not volunteer to participate in the AIDS awareness study were more likely to engage in risky behavior and to have less knowledge of AIDS than those who did volunteer. If these students had been included in the sample, the researcher might have found that less AIDS knowledge was associated with more risky behavior, rather than that there was no relationship between the two. In the study of AIDS knowledge among homeless persons in three shelters, I might also have sampled homeless persons staying in other shelters and on the streets, where there were no AIDS education efforts at all. If these persons had a measurably lower level of knowledge about AIDS, I might have found that for the sample overall there was an association between AIDS education efforts and overall AIDS knowledge. Drawing a very large and diverse sample, however, may preclude more intensive measures needed to test some hypotheses.

10. **Ethical considerations must often be weighed against the value of more powerful research designs.**

You recall how Sherman and Berk's (1984) experimental research design allowed a powerful test of the influence of arrest on those accused of domestic violence, because the possibility of spuriousness was lessened through random assignment to the arrest or warning conditions (see Chapter 2). But some would object to this manipulation of police practices, even though it produced a more sound basis for police decision making. Would you endorse such a manipulation in a study of police decisions with juveniles?

Comparing Research Designs

Experimental designs are strongest for testing nomothetic causal hypotheses and most appropriate for studies of treatment (see Chapter 5). Because random assignment reduces the possibility of preexisting differences between treatment and comparison groups to small, specifiable, chance levels, many of the variables that might create a spurious association are controlled. But in spite of this clear advantage, an experimental design requires a degree of control that cannot always be achieved outside of the laboratory (see Chapter 6). It can be difficult to ensure in real-world settings that a treatment was delivered as intended and that other influences did not intrude. As a result, what appears to be a treatment effect or noneffect may be something else altogether. Field experiments thus require careful monitoring of the treatment process.

Laboratory experiments permit much more control over conditions, but at the cost of less generalizable findings. People must volunteer for most laboratory experiments, and so there is a good possibility that experimental subjects differ from those who do not volunteer. The problem of generalizability in an experiment using volunteers lessens only when the object of investigation is an orientation, behavior, or social process that is relatively invariant among people. But it is difficult to know which orientations, behaviors, or processes are so invariant.

Both surveys and experiments typically use standardized, quantitative measures of attitudes, behaviors, or social processes. Closed-ended questions are most common and are well suited for the reliable measurement of variables that have been studied in the past and whose meaning is well understood (see Chapter 3). Of course, surveys often include measures of many more variables than are included in an experiment, but this quality is not inherent in either design. Phone surveys may be quite short, and some experiments can involve very lengthy sets of measures (see Chapter 7). The set of interview questions we used in the Boston housing study, for example, required more than 10 hours to complete.

Most social science surveys rely on random sampling for their selection of cases from some larger population, and it is this feature that makes them preferable for maximizing generalizability (see Chapter 4). When description of a particular large population is a key concern, survey research is likely to be the method of choice. But because many variables can be measured within a given survey, and repeated measurements are possible over time, surveys are also often used to investigate hypothesized causal relationships. If variables that might create spurious relations are included in the survey, they can be controlled statistically in the analysis, thus strengthening the evidence for or against a hypothesized causal relationship.

Qualitative methods presume an intensive measurement approach in which indicators of concepts are drawn from direct observation or in-depth commentary (see Chapter 8). This approach is most appropriate when it is not clear what meaning people attach to a concept or what sense they might make of particular questions about it. Qualitative methods are also admirably suited to the exploration of new or poorly understood social settings, when it is not even clear what concepts would help to understand the situation. For these reasons, qualitative methods tend to be preferred when exploratory research questions are posed. But, of course, intensive measurement necessarily makes the study of large numbers of cases or situations difficult, resulting in the limitation of many field research efforts to small numbers of people or unique social settings.

When qualitative methods can be used to study several individuals or settings that provide marked contrasts in terms of a presumed independent variable, it becomes possible to evaluate nomothetic causal hypotheses with these methods. However, the impossibility of taking into account many possible extraneous influences in such limited comparisons makes qualitative methods a weak approach to hypothesis testing. What qualitative methods are more suited to is the elucidation of causal mechanisms. In addition, qualitative methods can be used to identify the multiple successive events that might have led to some outcome, thus identifying idiographic causal processes.

Historical and comparative methods range from cross-national quantitative surveys to qualitative comparisons of social features and political events. Their suitability for description, explanation, and generalization varies accordingly, but in every case the inclusion of historical or international data, or both, can strengthen the potential validity of research findings. If the same methods are used in a study involving multiple eras or nations as are used in a study of the same research question at one time, within one nation, the result will be a major gain in the significance of the study's conclusions. If different methods must be used in order to gather historical or cross-national data, there may be a net loss in measurement or causal validity that will have to be weighed against gains in generalizability or, perhaps, depth of understanding.

■ ■ ■ ■ Triangulating Research Designs

In spite of their different advantages and disadvantages, none of these methods of data collection provides a foolproof means for achieving measurement validity, causal validity, or generalizability. Each will have some liabilities in a specific research application, and all can benefit from combination with one or more other methods (Sechrest & Sidani, 1995). The use of multiple methods to study one research question is termed **triangulation.** The term suggests that a researcher can get a clearer picture of the social reality being studied by viewing it from several different perspectives.

> *Triangulation* The use of multiple methods to study one research question.

I can provide a good example of triangulation's value from my work on the Goldfinger, Schutt, et al. (1997) housing study (Chapter 1). I had expected that we would surely be able to detect increasing feelings of self-confidence among the residents of our "evolving consumer households" with a well-known index of mastery based on closed-ended questions. Two years after we had added this measure to our proposal, however, I found that scores on this mastery index remained relatively stable throughout the 18-month follow-up period. This result would have led us to reject the hypothesis that our evolving consumer households would increase feelings of self-confidence were it not for the fact that anthropologists observing in the houses had recorded in their notes a great many indications of residents' development of self-confidence. Was our survey-based outcome measure flawed, or was our treatment truly ineffective? If we had not supplemented our survey with participant observation techniques, we might not have realized that this question still needed an answer.

Quantifying Observational Data

We already have studied some of the possibilities for enriching qualitative research with quantitative methods. The Experience Sampling Method added a survey sampling component to field research methods (Chapter 8); some quasi-experimental designs combined elements of survey research with experimental methods (Chapter 6); and comparative studies often used survey data collected from multiple nations (Chapter 9). In each case, quantitative data allowed more systematic comparisons and more confident generalizations.

Adding Qualitative Data

It makes sense to use official records to study the treatment of juveniles accused of illegal acts since these records document the critical decisions to arrest, to convict, or to release (Dannefer & Schutt, 1982). But research based on official records can be only as good as the records themselves. In contrast to the interview process in a research study, there is no guarantee that officials' acts and decisions were recorded in a careful and unbiased manner.

Case Study: Juvenile Court Records

Research on official records can be strengthened by interviewing officials who create the records or by observing them while they record information. A participant observation study of how probation officers screened cases in two New York juvenile court intake units shows how important such information can be (Needleman, 1981). As indicated in Exhibit 10.3, Needleman (1981) found that the concepts most researchers believe they are measuring with official records differ markedly from the meaning attached to these records by probation officers. Researchers assume that sending a juvenile case to court indicates a more severe disposition than retaining a case in the intake unit, but probation officers often diverted cases from court because they thought the court would be too lenient. Researchers assume that probation officers evaluate juveniles as individuals, but in these settings probation officers often based their decisions on juveniles' current social situation (whether they were living in a stable home, for example), without learning

Exhibit 10.3   **Researchers' and Juvenile Court Workers' Discrepant Assumptions**

Researchers' Assumptions	Intake Workers' Assumptions
■ Being sent to court is a harsher sanction than diversion from court	■ Being sent to court often results in more lenient and less effective treatment
■ Screening involves judgments about individual juveniles	■ Screening centers on the juvenile's social situation
■ Official records accurately capture case facts	■ Records are manipulated to achieve the desired outcome

Source: Needleman, 1981:248–256.

anything about the individual juvenile. Perhaps most troubling for research using case records, Needleman (1981) found that probation officers decided how to handle cases first and then created an official record that appeared to justify their decisions.

This one example certainly does not call into question all legal records or all other types of official records. But it does highlight the value of using multiple methods, particularly when the primary method of data collection is analysis of records generated by **street-level bureaucrats**—officials who serve clients and have a high degree of discretion (Lipsky, 1980). When officials both make decisions and record the bases for their decisions without much supervision, records may diverge considerably from the decisions they are supposed to reflect. More generally, Needleman's (1981) research indicates how important it is to learn how people make sense of the social world when we want to describe their circumstances and explain their behavior (see Chapter 8).

Case Study: Mental Health System Effectiveness

The same observation can be made about the value of supplementing fixed-choice survey questions with more probing, open-ended questions. For example, Renee Anspach (1991) wondered about the use of standard surveys to study the effectiveness of mental health systems. Instead of drawing a large sample and asking a set of closed-ended questions, Anspach used snowball sampling techniques to select some administrators, case managers, clients, and family members in four community mental health systems, and then asked these respondents a series of open-ended questions. When asked whether their programs were effective, the interviewees were likely to respond in the affirmative. Their comments in response to other questions, however, pointed to many program failings. Anspach concluded that the respondents simply wanted the interviewer (and others) to believe in the program's effectiveness, for several reasons: administrators wanted to maintain funding and employee morale; case managers wanted to ensure cooperation by talking up the program with clients and their families; and case managers also preferred to deflect blame for problems to clients, families, or system constraints.

Case Study: Obedience to Authority

Even the results of laboratory experiments can be enriched by incorporating some field research techniques. For example, you may recall from Chapter 6 Stanley Milgram's (1965) study of obedience to authority. Many subjects obeyed the authority in the study (the experimenter), even when their obedience involved administering potentially lethal shocks to another person. But did the experimental subjects actually believe that they were harming someone? Observational data suggest they did: "Persons were observed to sweat, tremble, stutter, bite their lips, and groan as they found themselves increasingly implicated in the experimental conflict" (Milgram, 1965:66). And verbatim transcripts of the sessions also clarified what participants were thinking as they disobeyed or complied with the experimenter's instructions:

> *150 volts delivered.* You want me to keep going?
>
> *165 volts delivered.* That guy is hollering in there. There's a lot of them here. He's liable to have a heart condition. You want me to go on?
>
> *180 volts delivered.* He can't stand it! I'm not going to kill that man in there! You hear him hollering? He's hollering. He can't stand it. . . . I mean who is going to take responsibility if anything happens to that gentleman?
>
> *[The experimenter accepts responsibility.]* All right.
>
> *195 volts delivered.* You see he's hollering. Hear that. Gee, I don't know. *[The experimenter says: "The experiment requires that you go on."]* I know it does, sir, but I mean—uhh—he don't know what he's in for. He's up to 195 volts. . . . (Milgram, 1966:67)

In each of these studies, qualitative data resulted in an understanding of social processes that was better than that based solely on quantitative data. In both Needleman's and Anspach's studies involving official records and the officials who record such records, qualitative methods called into question common assumptions about the validity of measures and causal conclusions. Milgram's use of qualitative data serves to increase confidence in his conclusions.

Conducting Factorial Surveys

Factorial surveys combine those features of true experiments that maximize causal validity with the features of surveys that maximize generalizability. In the simplest type of factorial survey, randomly selected subsets of survey respondents are asked different questions. These different questions represent, in effect, different experimental treatments; the goal is to determine the impact of these questions on answers to other questions. For example, Howard Schuman and Stanley Presser (1981) used factorial surveys to assess how different ways of wording survey questions influenced respondents' answers. In another type of factorial survey, respondents are asked for their likely responses to one or more vignettes about hypothetical situations. The content of these vignettes is varied randomly among survey respondents so as to create "treatment groups" that differ in terms of particular variables reflected in the vignettes.

Case Study: Wrongdoing in Japan and Detroit

V. Lee Hamilton and Joseph Sanders (1983) used a factorial survey to test the effect of people's deeds and social roles on judgments of wrongdoing in Japan and Detroit. For example, one set of vignettes involved friends who are in what is termed the *equal/status condition* (they are in equal positions of authority and have a status relation to each other rather than a contractual relation) and who get into a fight.

> In the *equal/status* story two twin brothers are playing baseball with a friend. Either Billy, the protagonist, or the friend . . . decides that it is Billy's turn to bat. Billy grabs the bat and the brothers begin fighting. The brother is then hit with the bat; the hit is described as accidental in the low mental state condition, and done out of anger in the high condition. Billy has either often or rarely gotten into fights before (past pattern). The consequence is a large bump on the head or a head injury requiring a hospital visit. (Hamilton & Sanders, 1983:201–202)

The variations of this vignette allowed Hamilton and Sanders to test a hypothesis about how aspects of the deed at the focus of the dispute influenced judgments of responsibility.

> We hypothesize that Japanese respondents, like their American counterparts, use information about an actor's mental state in determining responsibility for wrongdoing [whether the injury was accidental or not and whether the actor had a history of bad behavior] but make little, if any, use of information about consequence severity [whether the fight resulted in an injury requiring a hospital visit]. (Hamilton & Sanders, 1983:202)

This hypothesis was supported in both Japan and Detroit.

Another set of vignettes allowed a test of the same hypothesis for people in a social relationship termed *authority/contract.* This relationship involved a foreman and a worker, two individuals of unequal authority whose social roles are defined by contract.

> In the *authority/contract* story, Joe is a foreman on an assembly line. The company is trying to fill a large order and Joe either does not want to stop the line, or is told by his supervisor not to let the line stop. . . . Joe is described as always being careful about safety procedure in the past or sometimes being careless (past pattern) . . . a worker suffers a bruised hand or loses two fingers. (Hamilton & Sanders, 1983:202)

As in the baseball field fight, evaluations by respondents of who was responsible in this story provided support for the importance of the actor's (the foreman's) mental state but indicated that little importance was placed on the severity of the action's consequence. By comparing responses to these two sets of vignettes, Hamilton and Sanders were also able to test hypotheses about the importance of role variables:

Concerning hierarchy: Authorities are held more responsible than equals because authority positions carry with them greater social obligations. . . . Concerning solidarity: More responsibility is assigned to wrongdoing in contract relations than status relations. (Hamilton & Sanders, 1983:202)

The findings indicated that in both Japan and Detroit, as hypothesized, people in positions of authority were judged as more responsible than were equals, whereas actors tied by contract were seen as more responsible than actors related by status (friends or family). Since the research was based on random samples from cities in both countries, the findings are generalizable to those populations (except for the possibility of sampling error).

There is still an important limitation to the generalizability of factorial surveys: they only indicate what respondents *say* they would do in situations that have been described to them. If these individuals had to make decisions in comparable real-life situations, we cannot be sure that they would act in accord with their stated intentions. So factorial surveys do not completely resolve the problems caused by the difficulty of conducting true experiments with representative samples. Nonetheless, by combining some of the advantages of experimental and survey designs, factorial surveys can provide stronger tests of causal relations than surveys and more generalizable findings than experiments.

■ ■ ■ ■ **Extending Social Science Investigations**

Even when an individual study combines multiple methods, focusing on people and processes in one setting can obscure or distort important social processes. Concluding, on the basis of one study, that arrest deters spouse abuse is very different from concluding, after several studies, that arrest deters spouse abuse *only* if the abuser is employed. Taking social context into account will not only improve our understanding of important concepts and causal processes; it will also identify the limits to our generalizations. We also need to consider the possibility of influence from the natural world in which social life takes place. Are there biological processes or ecological relationships that influence particular social processes? New quantitative procedures give us techniques for analyzing the impact of context and other factors across many studies.

Taking Context into Account

We have seen the rich insights that can be gained with historical and comparative methods that focus attention on the impact of historical and national context (see Chapter 9). We can reap the same type of benefits from taking other types of social context into account. Do the processes in which we are interested vary across neighborhoods? Among organizations? Across regions? These are the types of questions we seek to answer by taking social context into account. When relationships among variables differ across geographic units like counties or across other contexts, researchers say there is a **contextual effect.**

Case Study: Juvenile Justice

Robert Sampson and John Laub (1993) drew a large sample of 538,000 juvenile justice cases from 322 counties across the United States. They then matched these case data from official records with census data on county social characteristics. They hypothesized that juvenile justice would be harsher in areas characterized by racial poverty and a large underclass (see Chapter 3). Statistical analysis of their data supported the hypothesis: in counties having a relatively large underclass and poverty concentrated among minorities, juvenile cases were more likely to be treated harshly. These relationships occurred for both African-American and white juveniles, but were particularly strong for African-Americans. Since counties' average income levels and criminal justice system resources were not related to juvenile justice case processing, it seems that racial polarization and underclass poverty, rather than the overall affluence of the county, were critical.

The results of this research suggest the importance of taking social context into account when examining criminal justice processes. Studies limited to one social context would not be generalizable to the entire country and would seriously misrepresent the role of race and other factors. Awareness of contextual differences helps to make sense of the discrepant findings from many purely local studies of juvenile justice case processing.

Recognizing Natural Processes

Although the social world is sufficiently complex to challenge the most able researcher, features of the natural world must also be taken into account in order to explain some social phenomena. The natural environment in which people live and the biology of the human body influence the social world in many ways.

Case Study: Adolescent Sexuality

J. Richard Udry's (1988) study of adolescent sexuality is a good example of the influence of natural processes. Udry studied 8th-, 9th-, and 10th-grade public school students in a southern U.S. city. After signing a consent form (their parents also had to sign a consent form), the students completed a questionnaire about their sexual behavior and attitudes and gave blood samples. Udry was then able to identify effects of both social environment and hormone levels in the blood on sexual behavior and attitudes. Such social variables as church attendance, best (same-sex) friend's attitude toward sexual permissiveness, and the permissiveness of the respondent's own sexual attitudes were related to sexual behavior, as were levels of testosterone and other hormones. There were major differences between boys and girls in the importance of these variables. For example, testosterone levels influenced boys' sexuality irrespective of other variables, but it influenced only the sexuality of girls who were not involved in sports—not the sexuality of girls who were involved in sports. Biological factors thus helped to explain sexual behavior and attitudes, and enriched our understanding of the role of social variables.

Tracing the relations between biological and social processes only begins to identify the many ways in which the natural world provides the context for social life. Microorganisms that spread disease, pollutants that stunt growth, and rivers that power electric generators all shape the context of social life in ways too numerous to list. Research in collaboration with scientists who study the natural world can often generate insights into these connections and is itself another form of triangulation (Janesick, 1994: 215).

Performing Meta-Analyses

We also can gain insights into the impact of social context and the consequences of particular methodologies with meta-analysis. A **meta-analysis** is a quantitative method for identifying patterns in findings across multiple studies of the same research question. Unlike a traditional literature review, which describes previous research studies verbally, meta-analyses treat previous studies as cases whose features are measured as variables and are then analyzed statistically. Whereas a macrolevel analysis like Sampson and Laub's (1993) shows how social processes vary across social contexts, meta-analysis shows how evidence about social processes varies across research studies. If the methods used in these studies varied, then meta-analysis can describe how this variation affected study findings. If social contexts varied across the studies, then meta-analysis will indicate how social context affected study findings.

Meta-analysis can be used when a number of studies have attempted to answer the same research question with some quantitative method, most often experiments. Once a research problem is formulated about the findings of such research, then the literature must be searched systematically to identify the entire population of relevant studies. Typically, multiple bibliographic databases are used; some researchers also search for relevant dissertations and conference papers. Once the studies are identified, their findings, methods, and other features are coded (for example, sample size, location of sample, strength of the association between the independent and dependent variables). Statistics are then calculated to identify the average effect of the independent variable on the dependent variable, as well as the effect of methodological and other features of the studies (Cooper & Hedges, 1994).

The meta-analytic approach to synthesizing research results can result in much more generalizable findings than those obtained with just one study. Methodological weaknesses in the studies included in the meta-analysis are still a problem, however; it is only when other studies without particular methodological weaknesses are included that we can estimate effects with some confidence. In addition, before we can place any confidence in the results of a meta-analysis, we must be confident that all (or almost all) relevant studies were included and that the information we need to analyze was included in all (or most) of the studies (Matt & Cook, 1994).

Case Study: Broken Homes and Delinquency

Many studies have tested the hypothesis that juveniles from broken homes have higher rates of delinquency than those from homes with intact families, but findings have been inconclusive. L. Edward Wells and Joseph Rankin (1991) were able to find 50 studies that tested this hypothesis, with estimates of the increase in delinquency among juveniles from broken homes ranging from 1% to 50%. In order to explain this variation, Wells and Rankin coded key characteristics of the research studies, such as the population sampled—the general population? a specific age range?—and the measures used: Did researchers take account of stepparents? Did they measure juveniles' relations with the absent parent? Was delinquency measured with official records or by self-report? What types of delinquency were measured?

The average effect of broken homes across the studies was to increase the likelihood of delinquency by about 10 to 15% (see Exhibit 10.4). Effects varied with the studies' substantive features and their methods, however. Juveniles from broken homes were more likely to be involved in status offenses (such as truancy and running away) and drug offenses but were no more likely to commit crimes involving theft or violence than were juveniles from intact homes. Juveniles' race, sex, and age and whether a stepparent was present did not have consistent effects. On the other hand, differences in methods accounted for much of the variation among the studies in the estimated effect of broken homes. The effect of broken homes on delinquency tended to be greater in studies using official records rather than surveys and in studies of smaller special populations rather than of the general population. In general, the differences in estimates of the association between broken homes and delinquency were due primarily to differences in study methods and only secondarily to differences in the social characteristics of the people studied.

Meta-analyses like the Wells and Rankin study make us aware how hazardous it is to base understanding of social processes on single studies that are limited in time, location, and measurement. Although one study may

Exhibit 10.4 **Delinquency by Broken Homes**

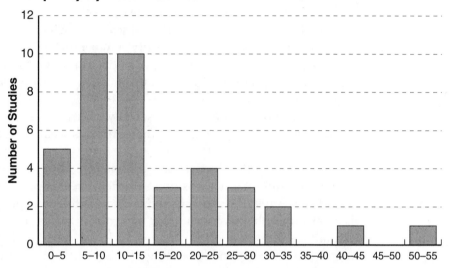

Percent Difference in Delinquency Between Intact and Broken Families

Source: Adapted from Wells & Rankin, 1991:80.

not support the hypothesis that we deduced from what seemed to be a compelling theory, this is not a sufficient basis for discarding the theory itself, nor even for assuming that the hypothesis is no longer worthy of consideration in future research. You can see that a meta-analysis combining the results of many studies may identify conditions when the hypothesis is supported and others when it is not.

■ ■ ■ ■ **Theoretical Perspectives on Research Designs**

A researcher's choice of a design, or decision to combine research designs, is not just a matter of matching appropriate techniques to a particular research problem. Methodological preferences also reflect theoretical perspectives on reality and the role of the researcher. Most social scientists accept a perspective that is similar to the approach of natural scientists, and this is the perspective I presented with the research circle in Chapter 2. Since the development of modern science in the 17th century, however, this perspective has not gone unchallenged (Tarnas, 1991).

Positivism

Most scientists define themselves as positivists. **Positivism** is the view that there is a reality that exists quite apart from our own perception of it. Valid ideas about the empirical world are those that reflect accurately the natural world and processes within it, without distortion by the observer. The goal of the scientist is to develop these ideas, continually testing them against empirical evidence: "The type of social science in which we are interested is an empirical science of concrete reality" (Weber, 1949:72).

Whether in physics or sociology, positivists believe "in the objective reality of the ingredients of our scientific theories . . . that the laws of physics have an existence of their own" (Davies, 1993:12). "We affirm that there are eternal, objective, extrahistorical, socially neutral, external and universal truths and that the assemblage of these truths is what we call physical science" (Glashow, 1989:E24).

The positivist perspective has been modified by some philosophers of science who adopt a postpositivist or critical realist perspective (Guba & Lincoln, 1994:109–111). **Postpositivism** accepts the basic premise that there is an external, objective reality, but recognizes that its complexity, and the limitations of human observers, preclude us from developing anything more than a partial understanding of this reality. In this perspective, the goal of science should be seen as seeking to achieve **intersubjective agreement** about the nature of reality, rather than certainty about what objective reality is:

> Whatever nature "really" is, we assume that it presents itself in precisely the same way to the same human observer standing at different points in time and space. . . . We assume that it also presents itself in precisely the same way across different human observers standing at the same point in time and space. (Wallace, 1983:461)

Social scientists are more likely to accept this postpositivist view than the simple positivist perspective because of the special challenges posed by the scientific study of people. First, human beings have the capacity to think and to reflect, to create mental interpretations of themselves and their world that have no concrete manifestation nor any necessary relation to subsequent action. Second, scientists are themselves human beings, and therefore when they study other people, they are studying others like themselves, onto whom they may project their own interpretations (D. L. Phillips, 1971:144–145). Max Weber (1949:81), the German sociologist who helped to establish the discipline about 100 years ago, put it this way: "All knowledge of cultural reality [the focus of sociology, according to Weber], as may be seen, is always knowledge from particular points of view."

In addition, the social sciences must cope with very diverse cases for which "universal" laws tend not to hold (Lieberson, 1992; Mayr, 1982:846). This perspective encourages triangulation of methods in order to achieve an ever better understanding of the complex, variable social world (Guba & Lincoln, 1994:110; Shadish, 1995).

Positivism The belief, shared by most scientists, that there is a reality that exists quite apart from our own perception of it, although our knowledge of this reality may never be complete.

Intersubjectivity Different observers agree on what is happening in the natural or social world.

Objective ideas Ideas that reflect properly the natural world and processes within it; ideas that are not distorted by the perspective of the scientist or other observer. Most scientists do not believe that we can ever be sure of the objectivity of an idea, and so instead seek to achieve intersubjectively shared ideas.

Constructivism

Constructivism is a theoretical perspective challenging the notion that there is a concrete, objective reality that scientific methods help us to understand (Lynch & Bogen, 1997). In the view of constructivists, scientists construct an image of reality that reflects their own preferences and prejudices and their interactions with others. From this standpoint, the goal of validity becomes meaningless: "truth is a matter of the best-informed and most sophisticated construction on which there is consensus at a given time" (Schwandt, 1994:128). "Does science reflect the real world? Does it tell one true story that is readymade and is out there for reflecting by our glassy mirror minds? . . . this peculiar notion of objectivity" (Harding, 1989:E24).

For constructivists, the goals of social research should be to discover what is meaningful to individuals and how and why they orient themselves to particular meaningful objects and values at particular times and places (Larson, 1993). These goals are seen by many qualitative researchers as appropriate to their method, with its emphasis on interpretations and the particulars of social situations (see Chapter 8).

> Searching for universally applicable social laws can distract from learning what people know and how they understand their lives. The interpretive social researcher examines meanings that have been socially constructed. . . . There is not one reality out there to be measured; objects and events are understood by different people differently, and those perceptions are the reality—or realities—that social science should focus on. (Rubin & Rubin, 1995:35)

Constructivist perspectives are sometimes called **interpretivist**, as in the preceding quote (Goldenberg, 1992). Some researchers who adopt this perspective feel that the primary task of researchers is to present the interpretations of the people that they study. The perspective known as **ethnomethodology** is also a type of constructivist perspective, but it views the primary task of researchers as developing an understanding of a social setting that may be quite different than that of the participants in that setting. Ethnomethodologists seek to understand how people create the reality that they experience in social interactions, with a focus on talk and the construction of shared meanings (Gubrium & Holstein, 1997:38–56).

If you are impressed by the contrast between the positivist and constructivist perspectives on research methods, then you probably have understood this section. There is quite a difference between believing that there is an empirical reality that scientists seek to understand and claiming that there are only subjective realities that all people, including scientists, create. You have to decide for yourself how useful these perspectives are, but I should point out that this entire book reflects the postpositivist perspective that I and most social scientists share—that the social world is one part of a reality that shapes and constrains our lives, but that this is a reality that we can only hope to partially understand.

There is great merit to investigating the meanings that social actors give to their lives and the world that they perceive, and the constructivist perspective can be a useful guide for these investigations. It is also a perspective that encourages us to consider honestly how much our own interpretations of the reality that others experience reflects our own subjective perspective more than it does the reality that research subjects feel they have experienced. However, ask yourself how the experiences of poor people differ from those of people who are wealthy; what distinguishes physical illness and health; how drinking impairs driving and when police practices can influence the crime rate. If you find yourself thinking that there is a physical and social reality that you need to understand better to answer these questions, you are indicating that you share a positivist or postpositivist perspective.

Paradigm Shifts

Scientific understandings of the world can change, sometimes dramatically. In his classic work, *The Structure of Scientific Revolutions*, Thomas S. Kuhn (1970) distinguished two types of scientific change. One involves gradual, incremental additions to the body of knowledge. Kuhn termed this "normal science," and it is what most research involves: the nuts and bolts of science. But some research also contributes to a major change in scientific understanding and has broad implications for many areas of research. Kuhn discussed this as the process of **scientific revolution,** when sudden, radical change overturns the prevailing wisdom in a scientific field, including its accepted theories, research findings, and presuppositions—in other words, an entire body of knowledge, a **scientific paradigm.** Scientific revolutions, or **paradigm shifts**, are often rejected by many scientists when they are first proposed; but they come to be seen as exceptional contributions as they are publicized and begin to inform new research.

Several popular social science paradigms have been overturned by subsequent research and theorizing. Most psychologists now reject the formerly dominant Freudian view of human intrapsychic development, although newer theories usually incorporate some of Freud's ideas. The Marxist paradigm for understanding societal development has been rejected by many students of social history since the late 19th century, and the ambitious structural-functional theory of Talcott Parsons, widely accepted in the 1950s and 1960s, has had an even shorter half-life among sociologists. Yet these paradigms continue to stimulate debate as well as new research and theorizing.

Scientific paradigm A set of beliefs that guide scientific work in an area, including unquestioned presuppositions, accepted theories, and exemplary research findings. *Examples:* Structural-functional theory; Marxism; Freudian theory.

Think of paradigm shifts when you find yourself feeling very confident about particular interpretations of the social world. Ask yourself whether there is perhaps some basis for changing a dominant interpretation, the current paradigm. Consider whether the accumulating body of research suggests a new direction is necessary. Would the same assumptions be likely to guide social scientists in other nations or cultures? Might your understanding be challenged or tested with greater rigor if you used multiple methods of investigation?

■ ■ ■ ■ **Conclusion**

Choice of a method of data collection should be guided in part by the aspect of validity that is of most concern, but each aspect of validity must be considered in attempting to answer every research question. Experiments may be the preferred method when causal validity is a paramount concern, and surveys the natural choice if generalizability is critical. But generalizability must still be a concern when assessing the results of an experiment, and causal validity is a key concern in most social science surveys. Field research has unique value for measuring social processes as they happen, but the causal validity and generalizability of field research results are often open to question. A researcher should always consider whether data of another type should be collected in what is basically a single-method study and whether additional research using different methods is needed before the research question can be answered with sufficient confidence.

The ability to apply diverse techniques to address different aspects of a complex research question is one mark of a sophisticated social researcher. Awareness that one study's findings must be understood in the context of a larger body of research is another. And the ability to speculate on how the use of different methods might have altered a study's findings is a prerequisite for informed criticism of social research. As social research methods and substantive findings continue to grow in number, these insights should stimulate more ambitious efforts to combine research methods and integrate many studies' findings.

But the potential for integrating methods and combining findings does not decrease the importance of single studies using just one method of data collection. The findings from well-designed studies in carefully researched settings are the necessary foundation for broader, more integrative methods. There is little point in combining methods that are poorly implemented or in merging studies that produced invalid results. Whatever the research question, consider the full range of methodological possibilities, make an informed and feasible choice, and then carefully carry out your strategy.

Finally, realistic assessment of the weaknesses as well as the strengths of each method of data collection should help you to remember that humility is a virtue in science. Advancement of knowledge and clear answers to specific research questions are attainable with the tools you now have in your methodological toolbox. Perfection, however, is not a realistic goal. No matter what research method we use, our mental concepts cannot reflect exactly what we measured, our notions of causation cannot reveal a tangible causal force, and our generalizations always extend beyond the cases that were actually studied. This is not cause for disillusionment, but it should keep us from being excessively confident in our own interpretations or unreasonably resistant to change. Final answers to every research question we pose cannot be achieved; what we seek are new, ever more sophisticated questions for research and additional propositions for social theory.

KEY TERMS

Constructivism

Contextual effect

Ethnomethodology

Factorial survey

Interpretivism

Intersubjective agreement

Macrolevel research

Meta-analysis

Microlevel research

Paradigm shift

Positivism   *Scientific revolution*
Postpositivism   *Street-level bureaucrat*
Scientific paradigm   *Triangulation*

HIGHLIGHTS

■ The three dimensions of validity (measurement, causality, and generalizability) must be considered as an integrated whole when evaluating and planning research projects. Decisions about each dimension have implications for the others.

■ Questions to guide evaluations of research reports and articles are listed in Appendix C. You should keep this list as a guide to use whenever you critique research articles.

■ Ten lessons about research designs appear in this chapter. You should consider them when you review or design research.

■ Factorial surveys combine features of experimental design with survey research methods. Variation of hypothetical vignettes or particular questions across randomly assigned survey subgroups can strengthen the validity of conclusions about causal processes if these processes can be modeled with vignettes or questions.

■ Researchers can test statistically for patterns across multiple studies with meta-analysis. This technique can be used only in areas of research in which there have been many prior studies using comparable methods.

■ Understanding of many social processes can be enriched by taking into account related biological and physical processes.

EXERCISES

1. A good place to start developing your critical skills would be with one of the two articles reviewed in this chapter. Try reading one, and fill in the answers to the article review questions that I did not cover (Appendix C). Do you agree with my answers to the other questions? Could you add some points to my critique, or to the lessons on research designs that I drew from these critiques?

2. Try your hand at critiquing an article on your own. In a professional journal, find a research article that uses a method of data collection like one in the studies we have reviewed in this or previous chapters. Review the article, using the questions in Appendix C as a guide. See whether you can add one or two lessons to my list in this chapter after you complete your critique.

3. Evaluate the ethics of one of the studies reviewed in which human subjects were used. Sherman and Berk's (1984) study of domestic violence raises some interesting ethical issues, but there are also points to consider in most of the other studies. Which ethical guidelines (see Chapter 2) seem most difficult to adhere to? Where do you think the line should be drawn between not taking

any risks at all with research participants and developing valid scientific knowledge? Be sure to consider various costs and benefits of the research.

4. You may now find it informative to read the articles by Udry (1988), Sampson and Laub (1993), Wells and Rankin (1991), and Needleman (1981) that were discussed in this chapter. What can you add to the description of these studies? Do they suggest other lessons about research designs to you? Use the article review questions (Appendix C) as your guide.

5. Try your hand at developing a meta-analysis of research testing one hypothesis. Review several journals in social psychology or evaluation research, and identify a hypothesis that has been tested in multiple studies of individuals. Develop a one-page form for recording the characteristics of each study's social setting, methods, and findings. Code about five studies on this form, and summarize their features and findings with statistics and graphs.

WEB EXERCISES

1. How do law enforcement agencies define gang activity? Go to:

   http://www.fbi.gov/kids/gang/gang.htm

   Read the FBI's descriptions of different types of gang activity. How could you study these with qualitative methods? What would this study add to the statistical information included in the report on the site? What indicators could you use to differentiate the different types? Do you think the distinction among the types is conceptually useful?

2. How adequate are juvenile court records? Go to the Bureau of Justice Statistics:

   http://www.ojp.usdoj.gov/pub/bjs/ascii/pjjr.txt

   Read the report and write a brief summary.

3. The Substance Abuse and Mental Health Services Administration site offers summaries of reports as well as statistical information on services research. Visit the site and check the list of publications, reports, and statistical information.

   http://www.samsha.gov

   What data sources are available on mental health services? Describe one and suggest a related multi-method research project. What research is SAMHSA supporting? Which use multiple methods?

SPSS EXERCISES

1. Have any particular groups in the United States benefited more than others in the economy of the late 1990s? You can explore this issue in the 1996 GSS by examining the associations between perceptions of change in finances and such social characteristics as race, sex, income, and education.
   a. What associations would you predict?
   b. Enter the following SPSS menu commands:
      STATISTICS
      TABLES

DOWN [FINALTER]
ACROSS [RACED,SEX,INCOM91Z,EDUCR3]
    STATISTICS [COLUMN %]
    TOTALS [OVER GROUPS]

    c. Describe the findings. What lessons should you consider as you think about how to interpret these associations? Unanticipated relationships (Lesson 2)? Evidence of nonspuriousness (Lesson 6)? Identification of causal mechanisms (Lesson 8)? What other associations would you like to examine to take these lessons into account?

2. How close do people feel to their neighborhoods, towns, state, and the nation? Would you predict any differences in these feelings between these different geographic units?

    a. Use SPSS to compare the distributions of the closeness variables:

        STATISTICS
            FREQUENCIES [CLSETOWN, CLSENEI, CLSESTAT, CLSEUSA, CLSENOAM]

    b. You can consider this as if it were a factorial experiment (although it isn't) and discuss the extent to which the different wordings of these statements made a difference in people's responses. What do you think explains the pattern you have identified?

11   Data Analysis

Introducing Statistics
Case Study: The Likelihood of Voting

Preparing Data for Analysis

Displaying Univariate Distributions
Graphs
Frequency Distributions
Ungrouped Data
Grouped Data

Summarizing Univariate Distributions
Measures of Central Tendency
Mode
Median
Mean
Median or Mean?
Measures of Variation
Range
Interquartile Range
Variance
Standard Deviation
Analyzing Data Ethically: How Not to Lie with Statistics

Crosstabulating Variables
Describing Association
Evaluating Association
Controlling for a Third Variable
Intervening Variables
Extraneous Variables
Specification
Analyzing Data Ethically: How Not to Lie About Relationships

Conclusion

KEY TERMS
HIGHLIGHTS
EXERCISES
WEB EXERCISES
SPSS EXERCISES

■ ■ ■ ■ *Social Science Exposed: How Warm People Are Turned into Cold Numbers.* I suppose a spoof on social science might have a title like that. Most social science research starts by collecting information from people and ends by expressing this information in the form of statistics. Cold or not, these numbers seem not half so interesting as the people or groups whose actions and orientations they represent. A book on the life and times of Jack Olson, whose story you read in Chapter 1, would outsell by far another statistical report on homelessness.

Of course, this critique of statistics is superficial, but only partially so. To use statistics is not to head off into some strange world of equations and numbers, but rather to investigate the social world with new tools for describing, explaining, and exploring. But it is true that the complexity of the social world and its participants can never be captured entirely with numbers; using statistics responsibly means considering carefully in each application how to strike the right balance between numerical summary and verbal discussion. And using statistics intelligently means continuing to focus on the role of theory, the goal of validity, and the particular research methods used to generate the numbers for data analysis.

This chapter will introduce several common statistics in social research and highlight the factors that must be considered in using and interpreting statistics. Think of it as a review of fundamental social statistics, if you have already studied them, or as an introductory overview, if you have not. Two preliminary sections lay the foundation for studying statistics. In the first I will discuss the role of statistics in the research process, returning to themes and techniques with which you are already familiar. In the second preliminary section, I will outline the process of acquiring data for statistical analysis. In the rest of the chapter, I will explain how to describe the distribution of single variables and the relationship between variables. Along the way, I will address ethical issues related to data analysis. This chapter will have been successful if it encourages you to use statistics responsibly, to evaluate statistics critically, and to seek opportunities for extending your statistical knowledge.

■ ■ ■ ■ **Introducing Statistics**

Statistics play a key role in achieving valid research results, in terms of measurement and causal validity and generalizability. Some statistics are useful primarily to describe the results of measuring single variables and to construct and evaluate multi-item scales. These statistics include frequency distributions, graphs, measures of central tendency and variation, and reliability tests. Other statistics are useful primarily in achieving causal validity, by helping us to describe the association among variables and to control for or otherwise take account of other variables. Crosstabulation is the technique for measuring association and controlling other variables that is introduced in this chapter. All of these statistics are termed **descriptive statistics** because they are used to describe the distribution of and relationship among variables.

You already learned in Chapter 4 that it is possible to estimate the degree of confidence that can be placed in generalizations from a sample to the population from which the sample was selected. The statistics used in making these estimates are termed **inferential statistics,** and they include confidence intervals, to which you were exposed in Chapter 4. In this chapter I will refer only briefly to inferential statistics, but I will emphasize later their importance for testing hypotheses involving sample data.

Social theory and the results of prior research should guide our statistical choices, as they guide the choice of other research methods. There are so many particular statistics and so many ways for them to be used in data analysis that even the best statistician can become lost in a sea of numbers if she does not use prior research and theorizing to develop a coherent analysis plan. It is also important to choose for an analysis statistics that are appropriate to the level of measurement of the variables to be analyzed. As you learned in Chapter 3, numbers used to represent the values of variables may not actually signify different quantities, meaning that many statistical techniques will be inapplicable.

Case Study: The Likelihood of Voting

In this chapter I will use for examples data from the General Social Survey on voting and the variables associated with it; and I will focus on a research question about political participation: What influences the likelihood of voting? Prior research on voting in both national and local settings provides a great deal of support for one hypothesis: the likelihood of voting increases with social status (Milbrath & Goel, 1977:92–95; Salisbury, 1975:326; Verba & Nie, 1972:8–92). Research suggests that social status influences likelihood of voting through the intervening variable of perceived political efficacy, or the feeling that one's vote matters (see Exhibit 11.1). But there have been some

Exhibit 11.1 **Voting and Social Status**

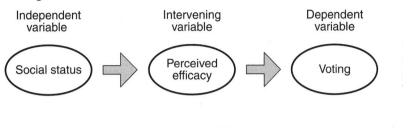

Independent variable → Social status ⇒ Intervening variable → Perceived efficacy ⇒ Dependent variable → Voting

research findings on political participation that are inconsistent with the social status–voting hypothesis. For example, African-Americans participate in politics at higher rates than do white Americans of similar social status (Verba & Nie, 1972; Verba, Nie, & Kim, 1978). This discrepant finding suggests that the impact of social status on voting and other forms of political participation varies with the social characteristics of potential participants.

If we are guided by prior research, a test of the hypothesis that likelihood of voting increases with social status should also take into account political efficacy and some social characteristics, such as race. We can find indicators for these variables in the 1996 General Social Survey (see Exhibit 11.2). I will use these variables to illustrate particular statistics throughout this chapter, drawing on complete 1996 GSS data. You can replicate my analysis with the subset of the 1996 GSS data that is included on your disk.

Preparing Data for Analysis

My analysis of voting in this chapter is an example of what is called **secondary data analysis.** It is secondary because I received the data secondhand; I did not design the data collection instrument. Using secondary data in this way has a major disadvantage: if you did not design the study yourself, it is unlikely that all the variables that you think should have been included actually were included *and* were measured in the way that you prefer. In addition, the sample may not represent just the population in which you are interested, and the study design may be only partially appropriate to your research question. For example, the 1991 GSS included only one question having to do with feelings of political efficacy, although the 1996 version included several. Because it is a survey of individuals, the 1996 GSS lacked measures of political context (such as the dominant party in an area). Because the survey sample is selected only from the United States and because the questions concern just one presidential election, we will not be able to address directly the larger issues of political context that are represented in cross-national and longitudinal research (Verba et al., 1978).

Exhibit 11.2 **List of GSS Variables for Analysis of Voting**

Variable	SPSS Variable Name	Description
Social Status		
Family income	INCOME91	Family income in 1996 (categories)
Education	EDUC	Years of education completed
Age	AGE	Years old
Gender	SEX	Sex
Marital status	MARITAL	Married, never married, widowed, divorced,
Race	RACE	White, black, other
Politics		
Voting	VOTE92	Voted in 1992 presidential election
Political views	POLVIEWS	Liberal to conservative rating
Political efficacy	POLEFF11	Believe people like me don't have any say in what the government does

It is the availability of secondary data that makes their use preferable for many purposes. A great many high-quality datasets are available for re-analysis from the Inter-University Consortium for Political and Social Research at the University of Michigan, and many others can be obtained from the government, individual researchers, and other research organizations. Most of these datasets are stored on computer tapes, disks, or CD-ROM, ready for use without any further effort. For a great many research problems, therefore, a researcher should first check what datasets on the question already are available. An enormous savings in time and resources may be the result.

If you have conducted your own survey or experiment, your quantitative data must be prepared in a format suitable for computer entry. You learned in Chapter 7 that questionnaires and interview schedules can be precoded in order to facilitate data entry by representing each response with a unique number (see Exhibit 11.3). This method allows direct entry of

Exhibit 11.3 **1996 GSS Survey Questions: Voting in 1992 Presidential Election**

86.   In 1992, you remember that Clinton ran for President on the Democratic ticket against George Bush for the Republicans and Perot as an Independent. Do you remember for sure whether or not you voted in that election?

Voted	(ASK A)	1
Did not vote	(ASK B)	2
Ineligible	(ASK B)	3
REFUSED TO ANSWER	(GO TO Q.87)	4
DON'T KNOW, CAN'T REMEMBER	(GO TO Q.87)	8

IF VOTED:

A.   Did you vote for Clinton, Bush, or Perot?

Clinton	(GO TO Q.87)	1
Bush	(GO TO Q.87)	2
Perot	(GO TO Q.87)	3
Other candidate (SPECIFY)_____	(GO TO Q.87)	4
DIDN'T VOTE FOR PRESIDENT	(ASK B)	6
DON'T KNOW, CAN'T REMEMBER	(GO TO Q.87)	8

IF DID NOT VOTE OR INELIGIBLE:

Who would you have voted for, for President, if you had voted?

Clinton	1
Bush	2
Perot	3
Other	4
DON'T KNOW, CAN'T REMEMBER	8

the precoded responses into a computer file, after responses are checked to ensure that only one valid answer code has been circled (extra written answers can be assigned their own numerical codes). Most survey research organizations now use a database management program to control data entry. The program prompts the data entry clerk for each response, checks the response to ensure that it is a valid response for that variable, and then saves the response in the data file. Exhibit 11.4 is an example of a computer data entry screen.

Of course, numbers stored in a computer file are not yet numbers that can be analyzed with statistics. After the data are entered, they must be checked carefully for errors—a process called **data cleaning.** If a data entry

Exhibit 11.4 **Example of a Data Entry Screen from SPSS**

program has been used and programmed to flag invalid values, the cleaning process is much easier. If data are read in from a text file, a computer program must be written that defines which variables are coded in which columns, that attaches meaningful labels to the codes, and that distinguishes values representing missing data (such as 8 in the preceding example). The procedures for doing so vary with the specific statistical package used. I used the Statistical Package for the Social Sciences (SPSS) for the analysis in this chapter; you will find examples of SPSS commands required to define and analyze data in Appendix E. More detailed information on using SPSS is contained in SPSS manuals and in the Pine Forge Press volume, *Adventures in Social Research: Data Analysis Using SPSS for Windows* by Earl Babbie and Fred Halley (1995).

Displaying Univariate Distributions

The first step in data analysis is usually to display the variation in each variable of interest—univariate distributions. For many descriptive purposes, the analysis may go no further. Graphs and frequency distributions are the two most popular approaches; both allow the analyst to display the distribution of cases across the categories of a variable. Graphs have the advantage of providing a picture that is easier to comprehend, although frequency distributions are preferable when exact numbers of cases having particular values must be reported and when many distributions must be displayed in a compact form.

Whichever type of display is used, the primary concern of the data analyst is to display accurately the distribution's shape—that is, to show how cases are distributed across the values of the variable. Three features of shape are important: **central tendency**, **variability**, and **skewness** (lack of symmetry). All three features can be represented in a graph or in a frequency distribution.

> *Central tendency* The most common value (for variables measured at the nominal level) or the value around which cases tend to center (for a quantitative variable).
>
> *Variability* The extent to which cases are spread out through the distribution or clustered in just one location.
>
> *Skewness* The extent to which cases are clustered more at one or the other end of the distribution of a quantitative variable, rather than in a symmetric pattern around its center. Skew can be positive (a "right skew"), with the number of cases tapering off in the positive direction, or negative (a "left skew"), with the number of cases tapering off in the negative direction.

These features of a distribution's shape can be interpreted in several different ways, and they are not all appropriate for describing every variable. In fact, all three features of a distribution can be distorted if graphs, frequency distributions, or summary statistics are used inappropriately.

A variable's level of measurement is the most important determinant of the appropriateness of particular statistics. For example, we cannot talk about the skewness (lack of symmetry) of a qualitative variable (those measured at the nominal level). If the values of a variable cannot be ordered from lowest to highest—if the ordering of the values is arbitrary—we cannot say that the distribution is not symmetric because we could just reorder the values to make the distribution more (or less) symmetric. Some measures of central tendency and variability are also inappropriate for qualitative variables.

The distinction between variables measured at the ordinal level and those measured at the interval or ratio level should also be considered when selecting statistics to use, but social researchers differ in just how much importance they attach to this distinction. Many social researchers think of ordinal variables as imperfectly measured interval level variables and believe that in most circumstances statistics developed for interval level variables also provide useful summaries for ordinal variables. Other social researchers believe that variation in ordinal variables will often be distorted by statistics that assume an interval level of measurement. We will touch on some of the details in the following sections on particular statistical techniques.

We will now examine graphs and frequency distributions that illustrate these three features of shape. Summary statistics used to measure specific aspects of central tendency and variability will be presented in a separate section. There is a summary statistic for the measurement of skewness, but it is used only rarely in published research reports and will not be presented here.

Graphs

A picture often is worth some unmeasurable quantity of words. Even for the uninitiated, graphs can be easy to read, and they highlight a distribution's shape. They are useful particularly for exploring data since they show the full range of variation and identify data anomalies that might be in need of further study. And good, professional-looking graphs can now be produced relatively easily with software available for personal computers. There are many types of graphs, but the most common and most useful are bar charts, histograms, and frequency polygons. Each has two axes, the vertical axis (the y-axis) and the horizontal axis (the x-axis), and labels to identify the variables and the values—with tick marks showing where each indicated value falls along the axis.

A **bar chart** contains solid bars separated by spaces. It is a good tool for displaying the distribution of variables measured at the nominal level and other discrete categorical variables since there is, in effect, a gap between each of the categories. The bar chart of marital status in Exhibit 11.5 indicates that almost half of adult Americans were married and about one in five was single at the time of the survey. Smaller percentages were divorced, separated, or widowed. The most common value in the distribution is married, so this would be the distribution's central tendency. There is a moderate amount of variability in the distribution, as the half who are not married are spread across the categories of widowed, divorced, separated, and never married. Because marital status is not a quantitative variable, the order in which the categories are presented is arbitrary, and skewness is not defined.

Histograms, in which the bars are adjacent, are used to display the distribution of quantitative variables that vary along a continuum that has no necessary gaps. Exhibit 11.6 shows a histogram of years of education from the 1996 GSS data. The distribution has a clump of cases represented

Exhibit 11.5   **Bar Chart of Marital Status**

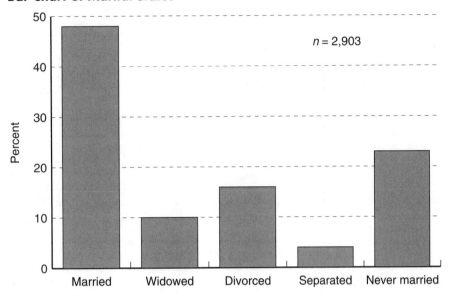

Source: General Social Survey, 1996.

Exhibit 11.6   **Histogram of Years of Education**

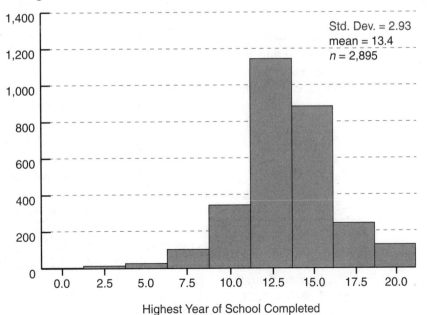

Source: General Social Survey, 1996.

Exhibit 11.7   **Frequency Polygon of Years of Education**

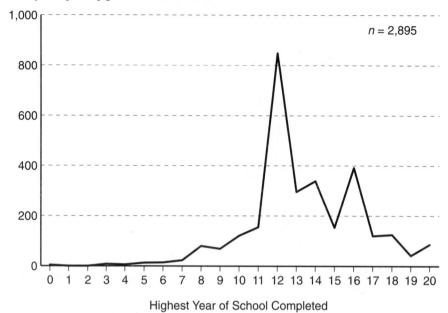

Highest Year of School Completed

Source: General Social Survey, 1996.

between about 12 and 15 years, with a modal value of 12. The distribution is not symmetric, since there are more cases just above the central point than below it.

In a **frequency polygon,** a continuous line connects the points representing the number or percentage of cases with each value. The frequency polygon is an alternative to the histogram when the distribution of a quantitative, continuous variable must be displayed; this alternative is particularly useful when the variable has a wide range of values. It is easy to see in the frequency polygon of years of education in Exhibit 11.7 that the most common value is 12 years, high school completion, and that this value also seems to be the center of the distribution. There is moderate variability in the distribution, with many cases having more than 12 years of education and about one-quarter having completed at least 4 years of college (16 years). The distribution is highly skewed in the negative direction, with few respondents reporting less than 10 years of education. This same type of graph can use percentages rather than frequencies.

If graphs are misused, they can distort, rather than display, the shape of a distribution. Compare, for example, the two graphs in Exhibit 11.8. The first graph shows that high school seniors reported relatively stable rates of lifetime use of cocaine between 1980 and 1985. The second graph, using exactly the same numbers, appeared in a 1986 *Newsweek* article on the coke plague

Exhibit 11.8 **Two Graphs of Cocaine Usage**

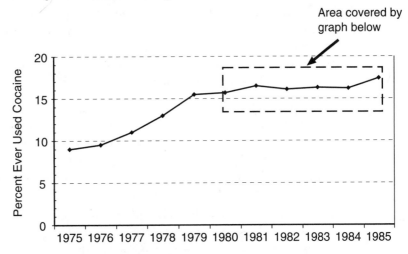

A. University of Michigan Institute for Social Research,
Time Series for Lifetime Prevalence of Cocaine Use

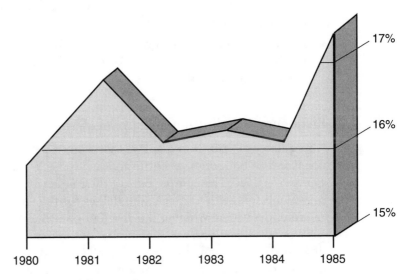

B. Final Stages of Construction

Source: Orcutt & Turner, 1993:196, 197.

(Orcutt & Turner, 1993). To look at this graph, you would think that the rate of cocaine usage among high school seniors increased dramatically during this period. But, in fact, the difference between the two graphs is due simply to changes in how the graphs are drawn. In the plague graph, the percentage scale on the vertical axis begins at 15 rather than at 0, making what was about a 1 percentage point increase look very big indeed. In addition, omission from the plague graph of the more rapid increase in reported usage between 1975 and 1980 makes it look as if the tiny increase in 1985 were a new, and thus more newsworthy, crisis.

Adherence to several guidelines (Tufte, 1983) will help you to spot these problems and to avoid them in your own work:

- The difference between bars can be exaggerated by cutting off the bottom of the vertical axis and displaying less than the full height of the bars. Instead, begin the graph of a quantitative variable at 0 on both axes. It may at times be reasonable to violate this guideline, as when an age distribution is presented for a sample of adults, but in this case be sure to mark the break clearly on the axis.

- Bars of unequal width, including pictures instead of bars, can make particular values look as if they carry more weight than their frequency warrants. Always use bars of equal width.

- Either shortening or lengthening the vertical axis will obscure or accentuate the differences in the number of cases between values. The two axes usually should be of approximately equal length.

- Avoid chart junk that can confuse the reader and obscure the distribution's shape (a lot of verbiage or umpteen marks, lines, lots of crosshatching, and the like).

Frequency Distributions

A **frequency distribution** displays the number, percentage (the relative frequencies), or both of cases corresponding to each of a variable's values or group of values. The components of the frequency distribution should be clearly labeled, with a title, a stub (labels for the values of the variable), a caption (identifying whether the distribution includes frequencies, percentages, or both), and perhaps the number of missing cases. If percentages are presented rather than frequencies (sometimes both are included), the total number of cases in the distribution (the **base N**) should be indicated (see Exhibit 11.9).

Ungrouped Data

Constructing and reading frequency distributions for variables with few values is not difficult. The frequency distribution of voting in Exhibit 11.9, for example, shows that 65.7% of the respondents eligible to vote said they voted and that 26.2% reported they did not vote. The total number of respondents to this question was 2,671, although 2,904 actually were interviewed. The rest were ineligible to vote, just refused to answer the question, said they did not know whether they had voted or not, or gave no answer.

Exhibit 11.9 **Frequency Distribution of Voting in 1992 Presidential Election**

Value	Frequency	Valid Percent
Voted	1,909	71.5%
Did not vote	762	28.5
Not eligible	183	—
Refused	10	—
Don't know	38	—
No answer	2	—
Total	2,904	100.0%

Source: General Social Survey, 1996.

Political ideology was measured with a question having seven response choices, resulting in a longer but still relatively simple frequency distribution (see Exhibit 11.10). The most common response was moderate, with 38% of the sample choosing this label to represent their political ideology. The distribution has a symmetric shape, with about equal percentages of respondents identifying themselves as liberal and conservative. About 3% of the respondents identified themselves as extremely conservative and about 2% as extremely liberal.

If you compare Exhibits 11.10 and 11.6, you can see that a frequency distribution (Exhibit 11.10) can provide more precise information than a graph about the number and percentage of cases in a variable's categories. Often, however, it is easier to see the shape of a distribution when it is graphed.

Exhibit 11.10 **Frequency Distribution of Political Views**

Value	Frequency	Percent
Extremely liberal	59	2.2%
Liberal	303	11.0
Slightly liberal	338	12.3
Moderate	1,043	38.0
Slightly conservative	450	16.4
Conservative	457	16.7
Extremely conservative	93	3.4
Total	2,743	100.0%

Source: General Social Survey, 1996.

When the goal of a presentation is to convey a general sense of a variable's distribution, particularly when the presentation is to an audience that is not trained in statistics, the advantages of a graph outweigh those of a frequency distribution.

Grouped Data

Many frequency distributions (and graphs) require grouping of some values after the data are collected. There are two reasons for grouping:

- There are more than 15–20 values to begin with, a number too large to be displayed in an easily readable table.
- The distribution of the variable will be clearer or more meaningful if some of the values are combined.

Inspection of Exhibit 11.11 should clarify these reasons. In the first distribution, which is only a portion of the entire ungrouped GSS age distribution, it is very difficult to discern any shape, much less the central tendency. In the second distribution, age is grouped in the familiar 10-year intervals (except for the first, abbreviated category), and the distribution's shape is immediately clear.

Once we decide to group values, or categories, we have to be sure that in doing so we do not distort the distribution. Adhering to the following guidelines for combining values in a frequency distribution will prevent many problems.

- Categories should be logically defensible and preserve the distribution's shape.
- Categories should be mutually exclusive and exhaustive, so that every case should be classifiable in one and only one category.

Violating these two guidelines is easier than you might think. If you were to group all the ages above 59 together, as 60 or higher, it would create the appearance of a bulge at the high end of the age distribution, with 25% of the cases. The same type of misleading impression could be created by combining other categories so that they include a wide range of values. In some cases, however, the most logically defensible categories will vary in size. A good example would be grouping years of education as less than 8 (did not finish grade school), 8–11 (finished grade school), 12 (graduated high school), 13–15 (some college), 16 (graduated college), and 17 or more (some postgraduate education). Such a grouping captures the most meaningful distinctions in the educational distribution and preserves the information that would be important for many analyses (see Exhibit 11.12).

It is also easy to imagine how the requirement that categories be mutually exclusive can be violated. You sometimes see frequency distributions or

Exhibit 11.11 **Ungrouped and Grouped Age Distributions**

Ungrouped		Grouped	
Age	**Percent**	**Age**	**Percent**
18	0.2%	18–19	1.4%
19	1.2	20–29	19.0
20	1.4	30–39	24.0
21	1.3	40–49	21.5
22	1.6	50–59	13.6
23	2.0	60–67	9.6
24	2.3	70–79	7.3
25	2.3	80–89	3.6
26	2.0		100.0%
27	1.8		(2,898)
28	2.3		
29	2.0		
30	2.5		
31	2.1		
32	2.6		
33	2.6		
34	2.2		
35	2.1		
36	2.1		
37	3.1		
38	2.8		
39	2.0		
40	2.3		
41	2.0		
42	2.3		
43	2.6		
44	1.8		
45	1.9		
46	1.8		
. . .	. . .		

Source: General Social Survey, 1996.

categories in questionnaires that use such overlapping age categories as 20–30, 30–40, and so on, instead of mutually exclusive categories like those in Exhibit 11.11. The problem is that we then can't tell which category to place someone in who is age 30, age 40, and so on.

Exhibit 11.12 **Years of Education Completed**

Years of Education	Percent
Less than 8	2.3%
8–11	14.7
12	29.3
13–15	27.2
16	13.5
17 or more	12.9
	100.0%
	(2,895)

Source: General Social Survey, 1996.

Summarizing Univariate Distributions

Summary statistics focus attention on particular aspects of a distribution and facilitate comparison among distributions. For example, if your purpose is to report variation in income by state in a form that is easy for most audiences to understand, you would usually be better off presenting average incomes; many people would find it difficult to make sense of a display containing 50 frequency distributions, although they could readily comprehend a long list of average incomes. A display of average incomes would also be preferable to multiple frequency distributions if your only purpose was to provide a general idea of income differences among states.

Of course, representing a distribution in one number loses information about other aspects of the distribution's shape, and so creates the possibility of obscuring important information. If you need to inform a discussion about differences in income inequality among states, for example, measures of central tendency and variability would miss the point entirely. You would either have to present the 50 frequency distributions or use some special statistics that represent the unevenness of a distribution. For this reason, analysts who report summary measures of central tendency usually also report a summary measure of variability, and sometimes several measures of central tendency, variability, or both.

Measures of Central Tendency

Central tendency is usually summarized with one of three statistics: the mode, the median, or the mean. For any particular application, one of these statistics may be preferable, but each has a role to play in data analysis. In order to choose an appropriate measure of central tendency, the analyst must consider a variable's level of measurement, the skewness of a quantitative variable's distribution, and the purpose for which the statistic is used. In addition, the analyst's personal experiences and preferences inevitably will play a role.

Mode

The **mode** is the most frequent value in a distribution. It is also termed the **probability average** because, being the most frequent value, it is the most probable. For example, if you were to pick a case at random from the distribution of political views (refer back to Exhibit 11.10), the probability of the case being a moderate would be .38 out of 1, or 38%—the most probable value in the distribution.

The mode is used much less often than the other two measures of central tendency because it can so easily give a misleading impression of a distribution's central tendency. One problem with the mode occurs when a distribution is bimodal, in contrast to being **unimodal.** A **bimodal** (or trimodal, and so on) distribution has two or more categories with an equal number of cases and with more cases than any of the other categories. There is no single mode. Imagine that a particular distribution has two categories each having just about the same number of cases (and these are the two most frequent categories). Strictly speaking, the mode would be the one with more cases, even though the other frequent category had only slightly fewer cases. Another potential problem with the mode is that it might happen to fall far from the main clustering of cases in a distribution. It would be misleading in most circumstances to say simply that the variable's central tendency was whatever the modal value was.

Nevertheless, there are occasions when the mode is very appropriate. Most important, the mode is the only measure of central tendency that can be used to characterize the central tendency of variables measured at the nominal level. We can't say much more about the central tendency of the distribution of marital status in Exhibit 11.5 than that the most common value is married. The mode also is often referred to in descriptions of the shape of a distribution. The terms *unimodal* and *bimodal* appear frequently, as do descriptive statements like "The typical [most probable] respondent was in her 30s." Of course, when the issue is what is the most probable value, the mode is the appropriate statistic. Which ethnic group is most common in a given school? The mode provides the answer.

Median

The **median** is the position average, or the point that divides the distribution in half (the 50th percentile). The median is inappropriate for variables measured at the nominal level because their values cannot be put in order and so there is no meaningful middle position. In order to determine the median, we simply array a distribution's values in numerical order and find the value of the case that has an equal number of cases above and below it. If the median point falls between two cases (which happens if the distribution has an even number of cases), the median is defined as the average of the two middle values and is computed by adding the values of the two middle cases and dividing by 2.

The median in a frequency distribution is determined by identifying the value corresponding to a cumulative percentage of 50. Starting at the top of the years of education distribution in Exhibit 11.12, for example, and adding up the percentages, we find that we have reached 46.3% in the 12 years category and then 73.5 in the 13–15 years category. The median is therefore 13–15.

With most variables, it is preferable to compute the median from ungrouped data since that method results in an exact value for the median, rather than an interval. In the grouped age distribution in Exhibit 11.11, for example, the median is in the 40s interval. But if we determine the median from the ungrouped data, we can state the exact value of the median as 41.

Mean

The **mean,** or arithmetic average, takes into account the values of each case in a distribution—it is a weighted average. The mean is computed by adding up the value of all the cases and dividing by the total number of cases, thereby taking into account the value of each case in the distribution:

Mean = Sum of value of cases/Number of cases

In algebraic notation, the equation is: $\overline{Y} = \Sigma Y_i / N$. For example,

$(28 + 117 + 42 + 10 + 77 + 51 + 64 + 55) /8 = 444/8 = 55.5$

Since computing the mean requires adding up the values of the cases, it makes sense to compute a mean only if the values of the cases can be treated as actual quantities—that is, if they reflect an interval or ratio level of measurement, or if they are ordinal and we assume that ordinal measures can be treated as interval (see page 408). It would make no sense to calculate the mean religion, for example. Imagine a group of four people in which there were two Protestants, one Catholic, and one Jew. To calculate the mean you would need to solve the equation (Protestant + Protestant + Catholic + Jew)/4 = ?????. Even if you decide that Protestant = 1, Catholic = 2, and Jewish = 3 for data entry purposes, it still doesn't make sense to add these numbers because they don't represent quantities.

Median or Mean?

Both the median and the mean are used to summarize the central tendency of quantitative variables, but their suitability for a particular application must be carefully assessed. The key issues to be considered in this assessment are the variable's level of measurement, the shape of its distribution, and the purpose of the statistical summary. Consideration of these issues will sometimes result in a decision to use both the median and the mean, and will sometimes result in neither measure being seen as preferable. But in many other situations, the choice between the mean and median will be clear-cut as soon as the researcher takes the time to consider these three issues.

Level of measurement is a key concern because to calculate the mean, we must add up the values of all the cases—a procedure that assumes the variable is measured at the interval or ratio level. So even though we know that coding Agree as 2 and Disagree as 3 does not really mean that Disagree is 1 unit more of disagreement than Agree, the mean assumes this evaluation to be true. Since calculation of the median requires only that we order the values of cases, we do not have to make this assumption. Technically speaking, then, the mean is simply an inappropriate statistic for variables measured at the ordinal level (and you already know that it is completely meaningless for qualitative variables). In practice, however, many social researchers use the mean to describe the central tendency of variables measured at the ordinal level, for the reasons outlined earlier (see page 408).

The shape of a variable's distribution should also be taken into account when deciding whether to use the median or mean. When a distribution is perfectly symmetric, so that the distribution of values below the median is a mirror image of the distribution of values above the median, the mean and median will be the same. But the values of the mean and median are affected differently by skewness, or the presence of cases with extreme values on one side of the distribution but not the other side. Because the median takes into account only the number of cases above and below the median point, not the value of these cases, it is not affected in any way by extreme values. Because the mean is based on adding the value of all the cases, it will be pulled in the direction of exceptionally high (or low) values. When the value of the mean is larger than the median, we know that the distribution is skewed in a positive direction, with proportionately more cases with higher than lower values. When the mean is smaller than the median, the distribution is skewed in a negative direction.

This differential impact of skewness on the median and mean is illustrated in Exhibit 11.13. On the first balance beam, the cases (bags) are spread out equally, and the median and mean are in the same location. On the second and third balance beams, the median corresponds to the value of the middle case, but the mean is pulled toward the value of the one case with an extremely low value. For this reason, the mean age (44.78) for the 2,898 cases represented partially in the detailed age distribution in Exhibit 11.11 is higher than the median age (42). Although in this instance the difference is small, in some distributions the two measures will have markedly different values, and in such instances the median may be preferred.

Exhibit 11.13   **The Mean as a Balance Point**

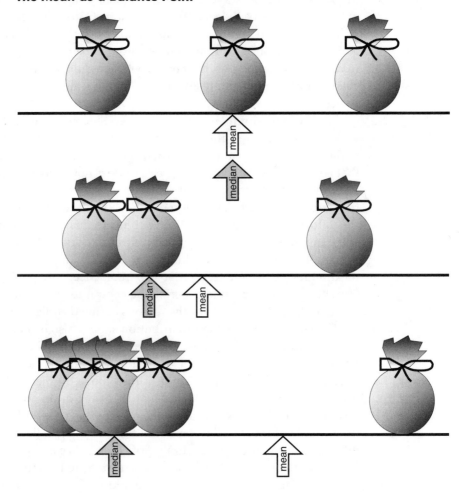

The single most important influence on the choice of the median or the mean should be the purpose of the statistical summary. If the purpose is to report the middle position in one or more distributions, then the median is the appropriate statistic, whether or not the distribution is skewed. For example, with respect to the age distribution from the GSS, you could report that half the American population is younger than 41 years old and half the population is older than that. But if the purpose is to show how likely different groups are to have age-related health problems, the measure of central tendency for these groups should take into account people's ages, not just the number who are older and younger than a particular age. For this purpose, the median would be inappropriate because it would not distinguish the two distributions like those represented in Exhibit 11.14. In the top distribution, everyone is between the ages of 35 and 45, with a median

Exhibit 11.14   **Insensitivity of Median to Variation at End of Distribution**

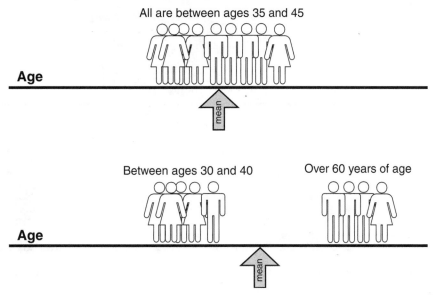

of 41. In the bottom distribution, the median is still 41 but half of the cases have ages above 60. The higher mean in the second distribution reflects the fact that it has more older people.

In general, the mean is the most commonly used measure of central tendency for quantitative variables, both because it takes into account the value of all cases in the distribution and because it is the foundation for many other more advanced statistics. However, the mean's very popularity results in its use in situations for which it is inappropriate. Keep an eye out for this problem.

Measures of Variation

You already have learned that central tendency is only one aspect of the shape of a distribution—the most important aspect for many purposes, but still just a piece of the total picture. A summary of distributions based only on their central tendency can be very incomplete, even misleading. For example, three towns might have the same mean and median income but still be very different in their social character due to the shape of their income distributions. As illustrated in Exhibit 11.15, town A is a homogeneous middle-class community; town B is very heterogeneous; and town C has a polarized, bimodal income distribution, with mostly very poor and very rich people and few in between.

The way to capture these differences is with statistical measures of variation. Four popular measures of variation are the range, the interquartile

Exhibit 11.15   **Distributions Differing in Variability by Not Central Tendency**

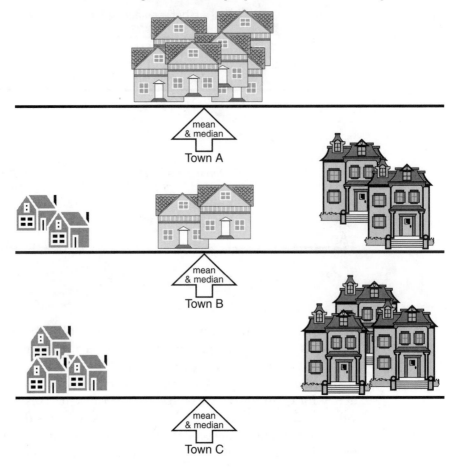

range, the variance, and the standard deviation (which is the most popular measure of variability). In order to calculate each of these measures, the variable must be at the interval or ratio level. Statistical measures of variation are used infrequently with qualitative variables, so these measures will not be presented here.

Range

The **range** is a simple measure of variation, calculated as the highest value in a distribution minus the lowest value, plus 1):

    Range = Highest value – Lowest value + 1

It often is important to report the range of a distribution, to identify the whole range of possible values that might be encountered. However, since the range can be drastically altered by just one exceptionally high or low value (termed an **outlier**), it does not do an adequate job of summarizing the extent of variability in a distribution.

Interquartile Range

A version of the range statistic, the **interquartile range,** avoids the problem created by outliers. **Quartiles** are the points in a distribution corresponding to the first 25% of the cases, the first 50% of the cases, and the first 75% of the cases. You already know how to determine the second quartile, corresponding to the point in the distribution covering half of the cases—it is another name for the median. The first and third quartiles are determined in the same way, but by finding the points corresponding to 25% and 75% of the cases, respectively. The interquartile range is the difference between the first quartile and the third quartile (plus 1).

Variance

The **variance** is the average squared deviation of each case from the mean, so it takes into account the amount by which each case differs from the mean. An example of how to calculate the variance, using the following formula, appears in Exhibit 11.16.

$$\sigma^2 = \frac{\Sigma(Y_i - \overline{Y})^2}{N}$$

Symbol key: $\overline{Y}$ = mean; N = number of cases; Σ = sum over all cases; — = division; Y_i = value of case i on variable Y.

Exhibit 11.16 **Calculation of the Variance**

Case #	Score (Y_i)	$Y_i - \overline{Y}$	$(Y_i - \overline{Y})^2$
1	21	−3.27	10.69
2	30	5.73	32.83
3	15	−9.27	85.93
4	18	−6.27	39.31
5	25	0.73	0.53
6	32	7.73	59.75
7	19	−5.27	27.77
8	21	−3.27	10.69
9	23	−1.27	1.61
10	37	12.73	162.05
11	26	1.73	2.99
	267		434.15

Mean: $\overline{Y}$ = 267/11 = 24.27
Sum of squared deviations = 434.15
Variance: σ^2_Y = 434.15/11 = 39.47

The variance is used in many other statistics, although it is more conventional to measure variability with the closely related standard deviation than with the variance.

Standard Deviation

The **standard deviation** is simply the square root of the variance. It is the square root of the average squared deviation of each case from the mean:

$$\sigma = \sqrt{\frac{\Sigma(Y_i - \overline{Y})^2}{N}}$$

Symbol key: $\overline{Y}$ = mean; N = number of cases; Σ = sum over all cases; — = division; Y_i = value of case i on variable Y; $\sqrt{}$ = square root.

When the standard deviation is calculated from sample data, the denominator is supposed to be $N - 1$, rather than N, an adjustment that has no discernible effect when the number of cases is reasonably large. You also should note that the use of *squared* deviations in the formula accentuates the impact of relatively large deviations, since squaring a large number makes that number count much more.

The standard deviation has mathematical properties that make it the preferred measure of variability in many cases. In particular, the calculation of confidence intervals around sample statistics, which you learned about in Chapter 4, relies on an interesting property of normal curves (see pages 136–137): areas under the normal curve correspond to particular distances from the mean, expressed in standard deviation units. If a variable is normally distributed, 68% of the cases will lie between plus and minus 1 standard deviation from the distribution's mean, and 95% of the cases will lie between 1.96 standard deviations above and below the mean. Because of this property, the standard deviation tells us quite a bit about a distribution, if the distribution is normal. And this same property of the standard deviation enables us to infer how confident we can be that the mean (or some other statistic) of a population sampled randomly is within a certain range of the sample mean (see Chapter 4).

Analyzing Data Ethically: How Not to Lie with Statistics

Using statistics ethically means first and foremost being honest and open. Findings should be reported honestly, and the researcher should be open about the thinking that guided her decision to use particular statistics. Although this section has a humorous title (after Darrell Huff's [1954] little classic, *How to Lie with Statistics*), make no mistake about the intent. It is possible to distort social reality with statistics, and it is unethical to do so knowingly, even when the error is due more to carelessness than deceptive intent.

Summary statistics can easily be used unethically, knowingly or not. When we summarize a distribution in a single number, even in two numbers, we are losing much information. Neither central tendency nor variation describe a distribution's overall shape. And taken separately, neither measure tells us about the other characteristic of the distribution (central tendency or variation). So reports using measures of central tendency should normally also include measures of variation. And we also should inspect the shape of any distribution for which we report summary statistics in order to ensure that the summary statistic does not mislead us (or anyone else) because of an unusual degree of skewness.

It is possible to mislead those who read statistical reports by choosing summary statistics that accentuate a particular feature of a distribution. For example, imagine an unscrupulous realtor trying to convince a prospective home buyer in community B that it is a community with very high property values, when it actually has a positively skewed distribution of property values (see Exhibit 11.17). The realtor compares the mean price of homes in

Exhibit 11.17   **Using the Mean to Create a More Favorable Impression**

Town A
4 houses @ $150,000 each

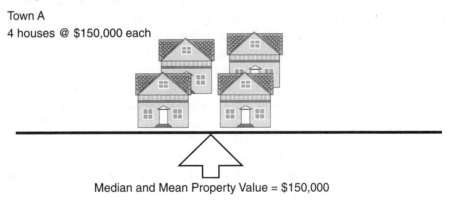

Median and Mean Property Value = $150,000

Town B
7 houses @ $30,000–$60,000 each
1 house @ $1,100,000

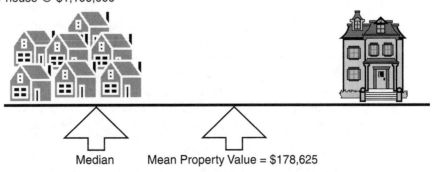

Median   Mean Property Value = $178,625

"Yes, our lovely town B has a higher average property value than town A."

community B to that for community A (one with a homogeneous mid-priced set of homes) and therefore makes community B look much better. In truth, the higher mean in community B reflects a very skewed, lopsided distribution of property values; most residents own small, cheap homes. A median would provide a better basis for comparison.

You have already seen that it is possible to distort the shape of a distribution by ignoring some of the guidelines for constructing graphs and frequency distributions. Whenever you need to group data in a frequency distribution or graph, you can reduce the potential for problems by inspecting the ungrouped distributions and then using a grouping procedure that does not distort the distribution's basic shape. When you create graphs, be sure to consider how the axes you choose may change the distribution's apparent shape.

■ ■ ■ ■ **Crosstabulating Variables**

Most data analyses focus on relationships among variables in order to test hypotheses or just to describe or explore relationships. For each of these purposes, we must examine the association among two or more variables. **Crosstabulation (crosstab)** is one of the simplest methods for doing so. A crosstabulation displays the distribution of one variable for each category of another variable; it can also be termed a *bivariate distribution*. Crosstabs also provide a simple tool for statistically controlling one or more variables while examining the associations among others. In the next section you will learn how crosstabs used in this way can help to test for spurious relationships and to evaluate causal models.

Exhibit 11.18 displays the crosstabulation of voting by income, so that we can test the hypothesis that likelihood of voting increases with this one social status indicator (see page 402). The table is presented first with frequencies, and then again with percentages. In both tables, the *body* of the table is the part between the row and column labels and the row and column totals. The *cells* of the table are defined by combinations of row and column values. Each cell represents cases with a unique combination of values of the two variables, corresponding to that particular row and column. The **marginal distributions** of the table are on the right (the *row marginals*) and underneath (the *column marginals*). These are just the frequency distributions for the two variables (in number of cases, percentages, or both), considered separately (the column marginals in Exhibit 11.18 are for family income; the row marginals are for the distribution of voting). The independent variable is usually the column variable; the dependent variable then is the row variable.

The first table in Exhibit 11.18 shows the number of cases with each combination of values of voting and family income. It is hard to look at the

Exhibit 11.18 **Crosstabulation of Voting in 1992 by Family Income**

		FAMILY INCOME			
VOTING	<$17,500	$17,500–$34,999	$35,000–$59,999	$60,000+	Total
Voted	342	482	461	409	1,694
Did not vote	242	184	165	83	674
Total (*n*)	(584)	(666)	(626)	(492)	(2,368)

Source: General Social Survey, 1996.

		FAMILY INCOME			
VOTING	<$17,500	$17,500–$34,999	$35,000–$59,999	$60,000+	Total
Voted	59%	72%	74%	83%	71%
Did not vote	41%	28%	26%	17%	29%
Total (*n*)	100%	100%	100%	100%	100%

Source: General Social Survey, 1996.

table in this form and determine whether there is a relationship between the two variables. We need to convert the cell frequencies into percentages, as in the second table in Exhibit 11.18. This table presents the data as **percentages** within the categories of the independent variable (the column variable, in this case). In other words, the cell frequencies have been converted into percentages of the column totals (the *n* in each column). For example, in Exhibit 11.18, the number of people earning less than $17,500 who voted is 342 out of 584, or 58.6%. Because the cell frequencies have been converted to percentages of the column totals, the numbers add up to 100 in each column but not across the rows.

To read the percentage table, compare the percentage distribution of voting across the columns, starting with the lowest income category (in the left column). There is a strong association. As income increases, the percentage who voted also rises, from about 59% of those with annual incomes under $17,500 (in the first cell in the first column) up to 83% of those with incomes of $60,000 or more (the last cell in the body of the table in the first row). This result is consistent with the hypothesis.

When a table is percentaged, usually just the percentages in each cell should be presented, not the number of cases in each cell. Include 100% at the bottom of each column (if the independent variable is the column variable) to indicate that the percentages add up to 100, as well as the base number (*n*) for each column (in parentheses). If the percentages add up to 99 or 101 due to rounding error, just indicate so in a footnote.

Exhibit 11.19 **Crosstabulation of Voting in 1992 by Age (with row percents)**

	VOTING		
AGE	**Voted**	**Did Not Vote**	**Total (n)**
20–29	54%	46%	100% (445)
30–39	66%	34%	100% (663)
40–49	76%	24%	100% (599)
50–59	79%	21%	100% (381)
60–69	81%	19%	100% (270)
70–79	84%	16%	100% (207)
80–89	79%	21%	100% (100)

Source: General Social Survey, 1996.

There is no requirement that the independent variable always be the column variable, although consistency within a report or paper is a must. If the independent variable is the row variable, we percentage the table on the row totals (the *n* in each row), and so the percentages add up to 100 across the rows (see Exhibit 11.19). When you read the table in Exhibit 11.19, you find that 54% of those under 30 voted, compared to 66% of those in their 30s, 76% of those in their 40s, and about 80% for those between 50 and 80 (the cell frequencies were omitted from this table).

Describing Association

A crosstabulation table reveals four aspects of the association between two variables:

■ *Existence.* Do the percentage distributions vary at all between categories of the independent variable?

■ *Strength.* How much do the percentage distributions vary between categories of the independent variable?

■ *Direction.* For quantitative variables, do values on the dependent variable tend to increase or decrease with an increase in value on the independent variable?

■ *Pattern.* For quantitative variables, are changes in the percentage distribution of the dependent variable fairly regular (simply increasing or decreasing), or do they vary (perhaps increasing, then decreasing, or perhaps gradually increasing, then rapidly increasing)?

In Exhibit 11.18, an association exists; it is moderately strong (the difference in percentages between the first and last column is about 25 per-

Exhibit 11.20 **Voting in 1992 by Perceived Political Efficacy**

	"People like me don't have any say about what the government does."	
VOTING	**Agree**	**Disagree**
Voted	65%	77%
Did not vote	35%	23%
Total	100%	100%
(n)	(556)	(637)

Source: General Social Survey, 1996.

centage points); and the direction of association between likelihood of voting and family income is positive. The pattern in this table is close to what is termed monotonic. In a **monotonic** relationship, the value of cases consistently increases (or decreases) on one variable as the value of cases increases on the other variable. Monotonic is often defined a bit less strictly, with the idea being that as the value of cases on one variable increases (or decreases), the value of cases on the other variable tends to increase (or decrease), and at least does not change direction. This describes the relationship between voting and income: the likelihood of voting increases as family income increases, although the increase levels off in the middle two categories, with the result that the association is not strictly monotonic. There is also a moderate positive association between age and voting in Exhibit 11.19, with likelihood of voting rising more than 20 percentage points. However, the pattern of this relationship is **curvilinear** rather than monotonic: the increase in voting with age occurs largely between the ages of 20 and 40, before leveling off and then declining in the oldest age category.

The relationship between our measure of perceived efficacy and voting (pages 402–403) appears in Exhibit 11.20. There is an association, and in the direction I hypothesized: 65% of those who agreed that they have no say about government decisions voted, compared to 77% of those who disagreed. Since both variables are dichotomies, there can be no pattern to the association beyond the difference between the two percentages. (Comparing the column percentages in either the first or the second row gives the same picture.)

Exhibit 11.21, by contrast, gives no evidence of an association between gender and voting. There is little difference between the percentage of men and women who voted. So that's all there is to say about the relationship.

Exhibit 11.21   **Voting in 1992 by Gender**

	GENDER	
VOTING	**Male**	**Female**
Voted	70%	72%
Did not vote	30%	28%
Total	100%	100%
(n)	(1,173)	(1,498)

Source: General Social Survey, 1996.

Evaluating Association

You will find when you read research reports and journal articles that social scientists usually make decisions about the existence and strength of association on the basis of more statistics than just a crosstabulation table.

A **measure of association** is a type of descriptive statistic used to summarize the strength of an association. There are many measures of association, some of which are appropriate for variables measured at particular levels. One popular measure of association in crosstabular analyses with variables measured at the ordinal level is **gamma.** As with many measures of association, the possible values of gamma vary from –1, meaning the variables are perfectly associated in an inverse direction; to 0, meaning there is no association of the type that gamma measures; to +1, meaning there is a perfect positive association of the type that gamma measures.

Inferential statistics are used in deciding whether it is likely that an association exists in the larger population from which the sample was drawn. Even when the association between two variables is consistent with the researcher's hypothesis, it is possible that the association was just due to chance—the vagaries of sampling on a random basis (of course, the problem is even worse if the sample is not random). It is conventional in statistics to avoid concluding that an association exists in the population from which the sample was drawn unless the probability that the association was due to chance is less than 5%. In other words, a statistician normally will not conclude that an association exists between two variables unless he or she can be at least 95% confident that the association was not due to chance. This is the same type of logic that you learned about in Chapter 4, which introduced the concept of 95% confidence limits for the mean. Estimation of the probability that an association is not due to chance will be based on one of several inferential statistics, **chi-square** being the one used in most crosstabular analyses. The probability is customarily reported in a summary form such as "$p < .05$," which can be translated as: "The probability that the association was due to chance is less than 5 out of 100 [5%]."

When an association passes muster in this way—when the analyst feels reasonably confident (at least 95% confident) that it was not due to chance—it is said that the association is statistically significant. **Statistical significance** means that an association is not likely to be due to chance, according to some criterion set by the analyst. Convention (and the desire to avoid concluding that an association exists in the population when it doesn't) dictates that the criterion be a probability less than 5%.

But statistical significance is not everything. You may remember from Chapter 4 that sampling error decreases as sample size increases. For this same reason, an association is less likely to appear on the basis of chance in a larger sample than in a smaller sample. In a table with more than 1,000 cases, such as those involving the full 1996 GSS sample, the odds of a chance association are often very low indeed. For example, with our table based on 2,368 cases, the probability that the association between income and voting (Exhibit 11.18) was due to chance was less than 1 in 1,000 ($p < .001$)! The association in that table was only moderate, as indicated by a gamma of .29. Even weak associations can be statistically significant with such a large random sample, which means that the analyst must be careful not to assume that just because a statistically significant association exists, it is therefore important. In a large sample, an association may be statistically significant but still be too weak to be substantively significant. All this boils down to another reason for evaluating carefully *both* the existence and the strength of an association.

Controlling for a Third Variable

Crosstabulation can also be used to study the relationship between two variables while controlling for other variables. We will focus our attention on controlling for a third variable in this section, but I will say a bit about controlling for more variables at the section's end. We will examine three different uses for three-variable crosstabulation: identifying an intervening variable, testing a relationship for spuriousness, and specifying the conditions for a relationship. Each of these uses for three-variable crosstabs helps to determine the validity of our findings, either by evaluating criteria for causality (nonspuriousness and identification of a causal mechanism) or by increasing our understanding of the conditions required for a relationship to hold—an indication of the cross-population generalizability of the findings. All three uses are aspects of **elaboration analysis**: the process of introducing control variables into a bivariate relationship in order to better understand—to elaborate—the relationship (Rosenberg, 1968). We will examine the gamma and chi-square statistics for each table in this analysis.

Exhibit 11.22 **Crosstabulation of Political Efficacy by Family Income**

"No say about government"	FAMILY INCOME			
	<$17,500	$17,500–$34,999	$35,000–$59,999	$60,000+
Agree	57%	49%	42%	39%
Disagree	43%	51%	58%	61%
Total	100%	100%	100%	100%
(n)	(278)	(316)	(317)	(235)

Source: General Social Survey, 1996.

Intervening Variables

We will first complete our test of one of the implications of the causal model of voting in Exhibit 11.1 (page 403): that perceived efficacy intervenes in the relationship between social status and voting. You already have seen that both income (one of our social status indicators) and the belief that people like the respondent can influence government decisions (our indicator of perceived efficacy) are associated with likelihood of voting. Both relationships are predicted by the model: so far, so good. You can also see in Exhibit 11.22 that perceived efficacy is related, though weakly, to income: higher income is associated with the belief that ordinary people can influence government decisions (gamma = .2; $p < .001$). Another prediction of the model is confirmed. But in order to determine whether the perceived interest variable *intervenes* in the relationship between income and voting—whether it explains this relationship—we must examine the relationship between income and voting while controlling for the respondent's belief that ordinary people can or cannot influence government decisions.

If belief in ordinary people's ability to influence government intervened in the income-voting relationship, the effect of controlling for this third variable would be to eliminate, or at least substantially reduce, this relationship. According to the causal model, income (social status) influences voting (political participation) by influencing perceived ability to influence the government (perceived efficacy), which in turn influences voting. We can evaluate this possibility by reading the two subtables in Exhibit 11.23. **Subtables** like those in Exhibit 11.23 describe the relationship between two variables within the discrete categories of one or more other control variables. The control variable in Exhibit 11.23 is belief in the ability to influence government decisions, and the first subtable is the income-voting crosstab for only those respondents who agreed that ordinary people *can't* influence government decisions. The second subtable is for those respondents who

Exhibit 11.23 **Voting in 1992 by Family Income by Perceived Political Efficacy**

"People like me don't have a say in what the government does"

		FAMILY INCOME		
VOTING	<$17,500	$17,500–$34,999	$35,000–$59,999	$60,000+
Voted	56%	65%	68%	80%
Did not vote	44%	35%	32%	20%
Total	100%	100%	100%	100%
(n)	(142)	(144)	(125)	(137)

"People like me do have a say in what the government does"

		FAMILY INCOME		
VOTING	<$17,500	$17,500–$34,999	$35,000–$59,999	$60,000+
Voted	56%	84%	78%	86%
Did not vote	44%	16%	22%	14%
Total	100%	100%	100%	100%
(n)	(111)	(155)	(170)	(137)

Source: General Social Survey, 1996.

agreed that they *can* influence government decisions. They are called sub-tables because together they make up the table in Exhibit 11.18.

A quick inspection of the subtables reveals only a modest difference in the strength of the income-voting association in the subtables (gamma is .25 in the first subtable and .33 in the second). Perceived ability to influence government decisions does not intervene in the relationship between income and voting. Of course, this finding does not necessarily mean that the causal model was wrong. This one measure seems on its face to be a weak measure of perceived political efficacy; a better measure, from a different survey, might function as an intervening variable. But for now we should be less confident in the model.

Extraneous Variables

Another reason for introducing a third variable into a bivariate relationship is to see whether that relationship is spurious due to the influence of an **extraneous variable**—a variable that influences both the independent and dependent variables, creating an association between them that disappears when the extraneous variable is controlled. Ruling out possible extraneous

Exhibit 11.24 **A Causal Model of a Spurious Effect**

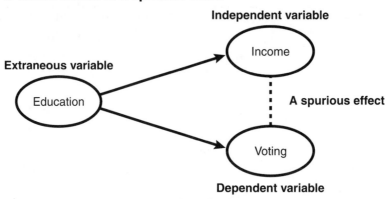

variables will help to strengthen considerably the conclusion that the relationship between the independent and dependent variables is causal, particularly if all the variables that seem to have the potential for creating a spurious relationship can be controlled.

One variable that might create a spurious relationship between income and voting is education. You have already seen that the likelihood of voting increases with income. Is it not possible, though, that this association is spurious due to the effect of education? Education, after all, is associated with both income and voting, and we might surmise that it is what students learn in school about civic responsibility that increases voting, not income itself. Exhibit 11.24 diagrams this possibility, and Exhibit 11.25 shows the bivariate associations among education, income, and voting as predicted by the model. If this model is correct, there should be no association between income and voting after controlling for education. Since we are using crosstabs, this means there should be no association in any of the income-voting subtables for any value of education.

The trivariate crosstabulation in Exhibit 11.26 (page 436) shows that the relationship between voting and income may be spurious due to the effect of education—as perhaps you can see more readily in the graph in Exhibit 11.27 (page 437). The association between voting and income is particularly weak in the first subtable, and the strength of that association is weaker in each subtable than it was in the original bivariate table (Exhibit 11.18). Gamma ranges from .004 for the first subtable to .15 and .27 in the second and third subtables. So our hypothesis, that income as a social status indicator has a causal effect on voting, is weakened. However, we must note that there still is a moderate relationship between income and voting at the level

Exhibit 11.25 **Voting in 1992 by Education, Income by Education**

VOTING BY EDUCATION

		EDUCATION	
VOTING	**Grade School**	**High School**	**Some College**
Voted	52%	66%	80%
Did not vote	48%	34%	20%
Total	100%	100%	100%
(n)	(431)	(773)	(1,461)

INCOME BY EDUCATION

		EDUCATION	
INCOME	**Grade School**	**High School**	**Some College**
<$17,500	52%	27%	17%
$17,500– $34,999	28%	33%	25%
$35,000– $59,999	15%	26%	30%
$60,000+	6%	14%	28%
Total	101%*	100%	100%
(n)	(410)	(736)	(1,407)

*Percents do not add to 100 due to rounding error.
Source: General Social Survey, 1996.

of some college. The association between income and voting may be due to the influence of education on both of these variables, but the more complex pattern we have identified suggests that education does not entirely account for the relationship between voting and income at higher income levels. The next section elaborates on this possibility.

Specification

By adding a third variable to an evaluation of a bivariate relationship, the data analyst can also specify the conditions under which the bivariate relationship occurs. A **specification** occurs when the association between the independent and dependent variables varies across the categories of one or more other control variables.

Exhibit 11.26   **Voting in 1992 by Income by Education**

EDUCATION = GRADE SCHOOL

		FAMILY INCOME		
VOTING	**<$17,500**	**$17,500–$34,999**	**$35,000–$59,999**	**$60,000+**
Voted	50%	54%	43%	60%
Did not vote	50%	46%	57%	40%
Total	100%	100%	100%	100%
(n)	(213)	(339)	(396)	(20)

EDUCATION = HIGH SCHOOL

		FAMILY INCOME		
VOTING	**<$17,500**	**$17,500–$34,999**	**$35,000–$59,999**	**$60,000+**
Voted	58%	68%	71%	68%
Did not vote	42%	32%	29%	32%
Total	100%	100%	100%	100%
(n)	(184)	(225)	(173)	(88)

EDUCATION = SOME COLLEGE

		FAMILY INCOME		
VOTING	**<$17,500**	**$17,500–$34,999**	**$35,000–$59,999**	**$60,000+**
Voted	67%	81%	79%	88%
Did not vote	33%	19%	21%	12%
Total	100%	100%	100%	100%
(n)	(213)	(339)	(396)	(384)

Source: General Social Survey, 1996.

The subtables in Exhibit 11.28 (page 438) allow an evaluation of whether race specifies the effect of income on voting, as found in some previous research (see page 403). The percentages who voted in each of the income categories vary in just about the same pattern for minorities (gamma = .30) as for whites (gamma = .20). Race therefore does not appear to specify the association between income and voting, although the finding of a small dif-

DATA ANALYSIS ■ 437

Exhibit 11.27 **Bar Chart of Voting in 1992 by Income by Education**

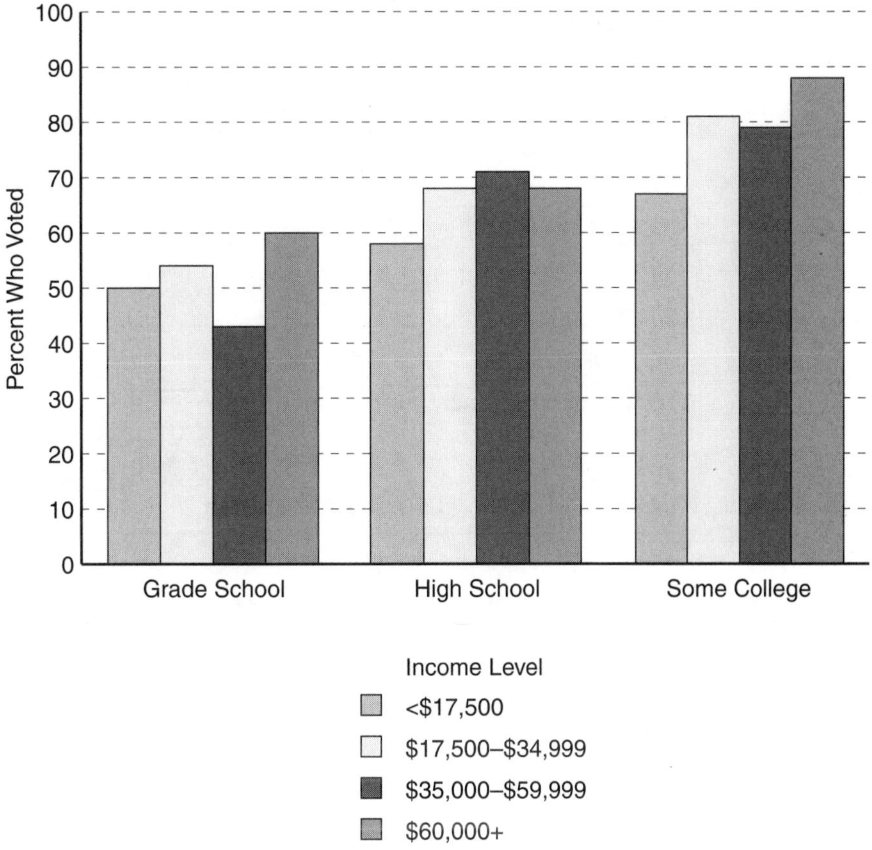

Source: General Social Survey, 1996.

ference in the strength of the association might encourage us to reexamine this possibility in another sample.

I should add one important caution about constructing tables involving three or more variables. Because the total number of cells in the subtables becomes large as the number of categories of the control (third) variable increases, the number of cases that each cell percentage is based on will become correspondingly small. This effect has two important consequences. First, the number of comparisons that must be made in order to identify the patterns in the table as a whole becomes very substantial—and the patterns may become too complex to make much sense of. Second, as the number of cases per category decreases, the odds that the distributions within these categories could be due to chance becomes greater. This problem of having too many cells and too few cases can be lessened by making sure that the control variable has only a few categories, and by drawing a large sample,

Exhibit 11.28 **Voting in 1992 by Income by Race**

RACE = WHITE

VOTING	FAMILY INCOME			
	<$17,500	$17,500–$34,999	$35,000–$59,999	$60,000+
Voted	60%	73%	75%	84%
Did not vote	40%	27%	25%	16%
Total	100%	100%	100%	100%
(n)	(424)	(550)	(541)	(433)

RACE = AFRICAN-AMERICAN AND OTHER MINORITY

VOTING	FAMILY INCOME			
	<$17,500	$17,500–$34,999	$35,000–$59,999	$60,000+
Voted	55%	69%	62%	75%
Did not vote	45%	31%	38%	25%
Total	100%	100%	100%	100%
(n)	(160)	(116)	(85)	(59)

Source: General Social Survey, 1996.

but often neither of these steps will be sufficient to resolve the problem completely.

My goal in introducing you to crosstabulation has been to help you think about the association among variables and to give you a relatively easy tool for describing association. In order to read most statistical reports and to conduct more sophisticated analyses of social data, you will have to extend your statistical knowledge. In addition to the statistical techniques we have considered here and the inferential statistics I discussed previously, you should learn about the summary descriptive statistics used to indicate the strength and direction of association. Until you do so, you will find it difficult to state with precision just how strong an association is. You also should learn about a different statistical approach to characterizing the association between two quantitative variables, called *regression* or *correlation analysis*. Statistics based on regression and correlation are used very often in social science and have many advantages over crosstabulation—as well as some disadvantages. You will need to take a course in social statistics in order to become proficient in the use of statistics based on regression and correlation.

Analyzing Data Ethically: How Not to Lie About Relationships

When the data analyst begins to examine relationships among variables in some real data, social science research becomes most exciting. The moment of truth, it would seem, has arrived. Either the hypotheses are supported or not. But, in fact, this is also a time to proceed with caution, and to evaluate the analyses of others with even more caution. Once large datasets are entered into a computer, it becomes very easy to check out a great many relationships; when relationships are examined among three or more variables at a time, the possibilities become almost endless.

This range of possibilities presents a great hazard for data analysis. It becomes very tempting to search around in the data until something interesting emerges. Rejected hypotheses are forgotten in favor of highlighting what's going on in the data. It's not wrong to examine data for unanticipated relationships; the problem is that inevitably some relationships between variables will appear just on the basis of chance association alone. If you search hard and long enough, it will be possible to come up with something that really means nothing.

A reasonable balance must be struck between deductive data analysis to test hypotheses and inductive analysis to explore patterns in a dataset. Hypotheses formulated in advance of data collection must be tested as they were originally stated; any further analyses of these hypotheses that involve a more exploratory strategy must be labeled in research reports as such. Serendipitous findings do not need to be ignored, but they must be reported as such. Subsequent researchers can try to test deductively the ideas generated by our explorations.

We also have to be honest about the limitations of using survey data to test causal hypotheses. The usual practice for those who seek to test a causal hypothesis with nonexperimental survey data is to test for the relationship between the independent and dependent variables, controlling for other variables that might possibly create a spurious relationship. This is what we did by examining the relationship between income and voting while controlling for education (Exhibit 11.26). But finding that a hypothesized relationship is not altered by controlling for just one variable does not establish that the relationship is causal. Nor does controlling for two, three, or many more variables. There always is a possibility that some other variable that we did not think to control, or that was not even measured in the survey, has produced a spurious relationship between the independent and dependent variables in our hypothesis (Lieberson, 1985). We have to think about the possibilities and be cautious in our causal conclusions.

■ ■ ■ ■ ■ **Conclusion**

This chapter has demonstrated how a researcher can describe social phenomena, identify relationships among them, explore the reasons for these relationships, and test hypotheses about them. Statistics provide a remarkably useful tool for developing our understanding of the social world, a tool that we can use both to test our ideas and to generate new ones.

Unfortunately, to the uninitiated, the use of statistics can seem to end debate right there—you can't argue with the numbers. But you now know better than that. The numbers will be worthless if the methods used to generate the data are not valid; and the numbers will be misleading if they are not used appropriately, taking into account the type of data to which they are applied. And even assuming valid methods and proper use of statistics, there's one more critical step, for the numbers do not speak for themselves. Ultimately, it is how we interpret and report the numbers that determines their usefulness. It is to this topic that we now turn.

KEY TERMS

Bar chart	Measure of association
Base N	Median
Bimodal	Mode
Central tendency	Monotonic
Chi-square	Outlier
Crosstabulation (crosstab)	Percentage
Curvilinear	Probability average
Data cleaning	Quartile
Descriptive statistics	Range
Elaboration analysis	Secondary data analysis
Extraneous variable	Skewness
Frequency distribution	Specification
Frequency polygon	Standard deviation
Gamma	Statistical significance
Histogram	Subtables
Inferential statistics	Unimodal
Interquartile range	Variability
Marginal distribution	Variance
Mean	

HIGHLIGHTS

- Data collection instruments should be precoded for direct entry, after verification, into a computer. Use of secondary data can save considerable time and resources, but may limit data analysis possibilities.

- Bar charts, histograms, and frequency polygons are useful for describing the shape of distributions. Care must be taken with graphic displays to avoid distorting a distribution's apparent shape.

- Frequency distributions display variation in a form that can be easily inspected and described. Values should be grouped in frequency distributions in a way that does not alter the shape of the distribution. Following several guidelines can reduce the risk of problems.

- Summary statistics are often used to describe the central tendency and variability of distributions. The appropriateness of the mode, mean, and median vary with a variable's level of measurement, the distribution's shape, and the purpose of the summary.

- The variance and standard deviation summarize variability around the mean. The interquartile range is usually preferable to the range to indicate the interval spanned by cases, due to the effect of outliers on the range. The degree of skewness of a distribution is usually described in words rather than with a summary statistic.

- Honesty and openness are the key ethical principles that should guide data summaries.

- Crosstabulations should normally be percentaged within the categories of the independent variable. A crosstabulation can be used to determine the existence, strength, direction, and pattern of an association.

- Elaboration analysis can be used in crosstabular analysis to test for spurious and mediating relationships and to identify the conditions under which relationships occur.

- Inferential statistics are used with sample-based data to estimate the confidence that can be placed in a statistical estimate of a population parameter. Estimates of the probability that an association between variables may have occurred on the basis of chance are also based on inferential statistics.

EXERCISES

1. Create frequency distributions from lists in U.S. Bureau of the Census reports on the characteristics of cities or counties, or any similar listing of data for at least 100 cases. You will have to decide on a grouping scheme for the distribution of variables like average age and population size, how to deal with outliers in the frequency distribution, and how to categorize qualitative variables like the predominant occupation. Decide what summary statistics to use for each

variable. How well were the features of each distribution represented by the summary statistics? Describe the shape of each distribution. Propose a hypothesis involving two of these variables and develop a crosstab to evaluate the support for this hypothesis. Describe each relationship in terms of the four aspects of an association, after percentaging each table within the categories of the independent variable. Which hypotheses appear to have been supported?

2. Become a media critic. For the next week, scan a newspaper or some magazines for statistics. How many can you find using frequency distributions, graphs, and the summary statistics introduced in this chapter? Are these statistics used appropriately and interpreted correctly? Would any other statistics have been preferable, or useful in addition to those presented?

3. Exhibit 11.29 shows a frequency distribution as produced by the Statistical Package for the Social Sciences (SPSS). As you can see, the table includes a shorthand name (POLEF11D) that SPSS uses to identify variables. The table also includes the numerical values assigned to the values, the raw frequencies, and three percentage columns. The first percentage column shows the percentage responding in each category; the next percentage is based on the total number of respondents who gave valid answers (1,285 in this instance). The last percentage column is cumulative, adding up the valid percents from top to bottom. Since there were only two legitimate values for this variable, no additional information is contained in this column.

Redo the table for presentation, using the format of the frequency distributions presented in the text.

Exhibit 11.29 **Frequency Distribution in SPSS**

Frequencies

Statistics

	N	
	Valid	Missing
POLEF11D No Say About Govt	1285	1619

POLEF11D No Say About Govt

		Frequency	Percent	Valid Percent	Cumulative Percent
Valid	1.00 Agree	610	21.0	47.5	47.5
	2.00 Disagree	675	23.2	52.5	100.0
	Total	1285	44.2	100.0	
Missing	9.00	1619	55.8		
	Total	1619	55.8		
Total		2904	100.0		

4. Try your hand at recoding. Start with the distribution of the political ideology variable from Exhibit 11.10. It is named POLVIEWS in the GSS. Recode it to just three categories. What decision did you make about grouping? What was the consequence of this decision for the shape of the distribution? For the size of the middle category?

5. Exhibit 11.30 contains a crosstabulation of voting by education (recoded) directly as output by SPSS from the 1996 GSS dataset. Describe the row and column marginal distributions. Try to calculate one of the cell percentages using the frequency in that cell and the appropriate base number of cases.

6. Crosstabulations produced by most statistical packages are not in the proper format for inclusion in a report, and so they have to be reformatted. Referring again to Exhibit 11.30, state a hypothesis that the table might have been produced to test. Then pick the appropriate percentages to use given the variable you treated as independent in the hypothesis. Next rewrite the table in presentational format, using one of the other tables as your guide. Describe the association in the table in terms of each of the four aspects of association. A

Exhibit 11.30 Crosstabulation of Voting by Education (Recoded) as Output by SPSS

VOTE92D Vote in 1992 Election, Dichotomy * EDUCR3 Education Trichotomized
Crosstabulation

			EDUCR3 Education Trichotomized			
			1.00 Grade School	2.00 High School	3.00 Some College	Total
VOTE92D Vote in 1992 Election, Dichotomy	1.00 Voted	Count	223	508	1175	1906
		Row %s — % within VOTE92D Vote in 1992 Election, Dichotomy	11.7%	26.7%	61.6%	100.0%
		Column %s — % within EDUCR3 Education Trichotomized	51.7%	65.7%	80.4%	71.5%
	2.00 Did Not Vote	Count	208	265	286	759
		% within VOTE92D Vote in 1992 Election, Dichotomy	27.4%	34.9%	37.7%	100.0%
		% within EDUCR3 Education Trichotomized	48.3%	34.3%	19.6%	28.5%
Total		Count	431	773	1461	2665
		% within VOTE92D Vote in 1992 Election, Dichotomy	16.2%	29.0%	54.8%	100.0%
		% within EDUCR3 Education Trichotomized	100.0%	100.0%	100.0%	100.0%

chi-square test of statistical significance resulted in a p value of .000, meaning that the actual value was less than .001. State the level of confidence that you can have that the association in the table is not due to chance.

7. What if you had to answer this question: What was the income distribution of voters in the 1992 presidential election, and how did it compare to the income distribution for those who didn't vote? Can you answer this question exactly with Exhibit 11.18? If not, change the column percentages in the table to row percentages. In order to do this, you will first have to convert the column percentages back to cell frequencies (although the frequencies are included in the table, so you can check your work). You can do this by multiplying the column percentage by the number of cases in the column, and then dividing by 100 (you will probably have fractional values because of rounding error). Then compute the row percentages from these frequencies and the row totals.

WEB EXERCISES

1. Search the Web for a social science example of statistics. Using the key terms from this chapter, describe the set of statistics you have identified. What social phenomena does this set of statistics describe? What relationships, if any, do the statistics identify?

2. Go to the Roper Center for Public Opinion Research Web site at

   http://www.ropercenter.uconn.edu/

   Choose any two U.S. presidents from F. D. Roosevelt to the present. By using the Web site links, locate the presidential job performance poll data for the two presidents you have chosen. Based on poll data on presidential job performance, create a brief report that includes the following for each president you chose: the presidents you chose and their years in office; the questions asked in the polls; bar charts showing years when polls were taken, average of total percentage approving of job performance, average of total percentage disapproving of job performance, average of total percentage with no opinion on job performance. Write a brief summary comparing and contrasting your two bar charts.

3. Do a Web search for information on a social science subject you are interested in. How much of the information you find relies on statistics as a tool for understanding the subject? How do statistics allow researchers to test their ideas about the subject and generate new ideas? Write your findings in a brief report, referring to the Web sites that you relied on.

SPSS EXERCISES

1. Develop a description of the basic social and demographic characteristics of the U.S. population in 1996. Examine each characteristic with three statistical techniques: a graph, a frequency distribution, and a measure of central tendency (and a measure of variation, if appropriate).

   a. Select the following SPSS commands:

GRAPHS
    BAR
        SIMPLE [MARITAL]
            %
        HISTOGRAM [EDUC,EARNRS,TVHOURS,ATTEND]

b. Describe the distribution of each variable.

c. Generate frequency distributions and descriptive statistics for these variables.

STATISTICS
    SUMMARIZE
        FREQUENCIES[MARITAL,EDUC,EARNRS,TVHOURS,ATTEND]
        Statistics[mean, median,range, std deviation]

d. Collapse the categories for each distribution. Be sure to adhere to the guidelines on page 414. Does the general shape of any of the distributions change as a result of changing the categories?

e. Which statistics are appropriate to summarize the central tendency and variation of each variable? Do the values of any of these statistics surprise you?

2. Do other forms of civic involvement have the same predictors as voting? You can check this with the GSS96 data using a variable I created. This variable, VOL2, indicates whether the respondent volunteered in any of 13 civic activities within the preceding year. Try to reproduce the crosstabulations in this chapter using VOL2 rather than VOTE92D.

STATISTICS
    SUMMARIZE
        CROSSTABS
        ROWS [VOL2]
        COLUMNS [INCOM91Z,AGER,POLEF11D,SEX]
            CELLS [Percentages Column]

3. If you have the disk that came with this book, with a copy of a subset of the 1996 General Social Survey, it will be easy for you to replicate the tables in this chapter. It would be a good exercise for you to do so, but remember that your tables will contain only a sample of cases from the complete GSS96 file that I used. The computer output you get will probably not look like the tables shown here, since I reformatted the tables for presentation, as you should do before preparing a final report. At this point, I'll let you figure out the menu commands required to generate these graphs, frequency distributions, and cross–tabulations.

4. Propose a variable that might have created a spurious relationship between income and voting. Explain your thinking. Propose a variable that might result in a conditional effect of income on voting, so that the relationship between income and voting would vary across the categories of the other variable. Test these propositions with three-variable crosstabulations. Were any supported? How would you explain your findings?

12   Reporting Research Results

The Research Proposal
Case Study: Treating Substance Abuse
A Methodologist's Toolchest

Research Report Goals
Advance Scientific Knowledge
Shape Social Policy
Organize Social Action
Dialogue with Research Subjects

Research Report Types
Student Papers and Theses
  Group Projects
  The Thesis Committee
Applied Reports
  Case Study: The Diaper Debate
  An Advisory Committee
Journal Articles
  Case Study: Distress and Social Support

Writing and Organization

Data Displays

Ethics and Reporting

Conclusion

KEY TERMS
HIGHLIGHTS
EXERCISES
WEB EXERCISES
SPSS EXERCISES

The goal of research is not just to discover something, but to communicate that discovery to a larger audience: other social scientists, government officials, your teachers, the general public; perhaps several of these audiences. Whatever the study's particular outcome, if the research report enables the intended audience to comprehend the results and learn from them, the research can be judged a success. If the intended audience is not able to learn about the study's results, the research should be judged a failure—no matter how expensive the research, how sophisticated its design, or how much of yourself you invested in it.

This conclusion may seem obvious, and perhaps a bit unnecessary. After all, you may think, of course researchers write up their results for other people to read. But the fact is that many research projects fail to produce a research report and thus can be judged complete failures. Sometimes the problem is that the research was poorly designed to begin with and couldn't be carried out in a satisfactory manner; sometimes unanticipated difficulties derail a viable project. But too often the researcher just never gets around to writing a report. And then there are many research reports that are very incomplete or poorly written, or that speak to only one of several interested audiences. The failure may not be complete, but the project's full potential is not achieved.

Remember that the time for congratulations is when credible results are released and they serve some useful function—not when the research project is first approved. Give careful attention to the research report, whatever type it is, before breaking out the bottle of champagne. And if you've conducted a worthwhile research project, consider whether some of the results might be appropriate for more than one report—to different audiences.

The primary goals of this chapter are to help you develop worthwhile reports for any research you conduct and to guide you in evaluating reports produced by others. We begin by learning how to write research proposals, since a formal proposal lays the groundwork for a final research report. We then consider some of the different options that have been proposed for involving research subjects in designing the research project and the final report. The next section highlights problems that are unique to the main types of reports: journal articles, unpublished reports for specific clients, and student papers and theses. The chapter's final sections present suggestions for writing and organizing reports, techniques for displaying statistical results, and ethical issues to be considered.

The Research Proposal

Be grateful for those who require you to write a formal research proposal—and even more for those who give you constructive feedback. Whether your proposal is written for a professor, a thesis committee, an organization seeking practical advice, or a government agency that funds basic research, the proposal will force you to set out a problem statement and a research plan. Too many research projects begin without a clear problem statement or with only the barest of notions about which variables must be measured or what the analysis should look like. Such projects often wander along, lurching from side to side, then collapse entirely or just peter out with a report that is ignored—and should be. So even in circumstances when a proposal is not required, you should prepare one and present it to others for feedback. Just writing your ideas down will help you to see how they can be improved, and feedback in almost any form will help you to refine your plans.

A well-designed proposal can go a long way toward shaping the final research report and will make it easier to progress at later research stages. Every research proposal should have at least five sections:

- *An introductory statement of the research problem*, in which you clarify what it is that you are interested in studying.

- *A literature review*, in which you explain how your problem and plans build on what has already been reported in the literature on this topic.

- *A methodological plan*, detailing just how you will respond to the particular mix of opportunities and constraints you face.

- *A budget*, presenting a careful listing of the anticipated costs.

- *An ethics statement*, identifying human subjects issues in the research and how you will respond to them in an ethical fashion.

If your research proposal will be reviewed competitively, it must present a compelling rationale for funding. It is not possible to overstate the importance of the research problem that you propose to study (see Chapter 2). If you propose to test a hypothesis, be sure that it is one for which there are plausible alternatives: "a boring hypothesis is one which, although likely to be correct, has no credible alternatives" (Dawes, 1995:93).

Case Study: Treating Substance Abuse

Particular academic departments, grant committees, and funding agencies will have more specific proposal requirements. As an example, Exhibit 12.1 lists the primary required sections of the "Research Plan" for proposals to the National Institutes of Health (NIH), together with excerpts from a proposal I submitted in this format to the National Institute of Mental Health (NIMH) with colleagues from the University of Massachusetts Medical School. The Research Plan is limited by NIH guidelines to 25 pages. It must be preceded by an abstract (which I have excerpted), a proposed budget, biographical sketches of project personnel, and a discussion of the available resources for the project. Appendixes may include research instruments, prior publications by the authors, and findings from related work.

Exhibit 12.1   **A Grant Proposal to the National Institute of Mental Health**

Relapse Prevention for Homeless Dually Diagnosed

Abstract

This project will test the efficacy of shelter-based treatment that integrates Psychosocial Rehabilitation with Relapse Prevention techniques adapted for homeless mentally ill persons who abuse substances. Two hundred and fifty homeless persons, meeting . . . criteria for substance abuse and severe and persistent mental disorder, will be recruited from two shelters and then randomly assigned to either an experimental treatment condition . . . or to a control condition.

For one year, at the rate of three two-hour sessions per week, the treatment group ($n = 125$) will participate for the first six months in "enhanced" Psychosocial Rehabilitation . . . , followed by six months of Relapse Prevention training. . . . The control group will participate in a Standard Treatment condition (currently comprised of a twelve-step peer-help program along with counseling offered at all shelters). . . .

Outcome measures include substance abuse, housing placement and residential stability, social support, service utilization, level of distress. . . . The integrity of the experimental design will be monitored through a process analysis. Tests for the hypothesized treatment effects . . . will be supplemented with analyses to evaluate the direct and indirect effects of subject characteristics and to identify interactions between subject characteristics and treatment condition. . . .

Research Plan
1. Specific Aims

The research demonstration project will determine whether an integrated clinical shelter-based treatment intervention can improve health and well-being among homeless persons who abuse both alcohol and/or drugs and who are seriously and persistently ill—the so-called "dually diagnosed." . . . We aim to identify the specific attitudes and behaviors that are most affected by the integrated psychosocial rehabilitation/relapse prevention treatment, and thus to help guide future service interventions.

2. Background and Significance

Relapse is the most common outcome in treating the chronically mentally ill, including the homeless. . . . Reviews of the clinical and empirical literature published to date indicate that treatment interventions based on social learning experiences are associated with more favorable outcomes than treatment interventions based on more traditional forms of psychotherapy and/or chemotherapy. . . . However, few tests of the efficacy of such interventions have been reported for homeless samples.

3. Progress Report/Preliminary Studies

Four areas of Dr. Schutt's research help to lay the foundation for the research demonstration project here proposed. . . . The 1990 survey in Boston shelters measured substance abuse with selected ASI [Addiction Severity Index] questions. . . . About half of the respondents evidenced a substance abuse problem.

(continued on next page)

Exhibit 12.1 **A Grant Proposal to the NIMH** *(continued)*

Just over one-quarter of respondents had ever been treated for a mental health problem. . . . At least three-quarters were interested in help with each of the problems mentioned other than substance abuse. Since help with benefits, housing, and AIDS prevention will each be provided to all study participants in the proposed research demonstration project, we project that this should increase the rate of participation and retention in the study. . . . Results [from co-investigator Dr. Walter Penk's research] . . . indicate that trainers were more successful in engaging the dually diagnosed in Relapse Prevention techniques. . . .

4. Research Design and Methods

Study Sample.
Recruitment. The study will recruit 350 clients beginning in month 4 of the study and running through month 28 for study entry. The span of treatment is 12 months and is followed by 12 months of follow-up. . . .

Study Criteria.
Those volunteering to participate will be screened and declared eligible for the study based upon the following characteristics:

1. Determination that subject is homeless using criteria operationally defined by one of the accepted definitions summarized by . . .

Attrition.
Subject enrollment, treatment engagement, and subject retention each represent potentially significant challenges to study integrity and have been given special attention in all phases of the project. Techniques have been developed to address engagement and retention and are described in detail below. . . .

Research Procedures.
All clients referred to the participating shelters will be screened for basic study criteria. . . . Once assessment is completed, subjects who volunteer are then randomly assigned to one of two treatment conditions—RPST or Standard Treatment. . . .

Research Variables and Measures.
Measures for this study . . . are of three kinds: subject selection measures, process measures, and outcome measures. . . .

5. Human Subjects

Potential risks to subjects are minor . . . acute problems identified . . . can be quickly referred to appropriate interventions. Participation in the Project is voluntary, and all subjects retain the option to withdraw . . . at any time, without any impact on their access to shelter care or services regularly offered by the shelters. Confidentiality of subjects is guaranteed. . . . [They have] . . . an opportunity to learn new ways of dealing with symptoms of substance abuse and mental illness.

As you can see from the excerpts, our proposal was to study the efficacy of a particular treatment approach for homeless mentally ill persons who abuse substances. The proposal included a procedure for recruiting subjects in two cities, randomly assigning half of the subjects to a recently developed treatment program, and measuring a range of outcomes. The NIMH review committee (composed of social scientists expert in these issues) approved the project for funding but did not rate it highly enough so that it actually was awarded funds (it often takes several resubmissions before even a worthwhile proposal is funded). The committee members recognized the proposal's strengths, but also identified several problems that they believed had to be overcome before the proposal could be funded. The problems were primarily methodological, stemming from the difficulties associated with providing services to, and conducting research on, this particular segment of the homeless population.

> The proposal has many strengths, including the specially tailored intervention derived from psychiatric rehabilitation technology developed by Liberman and his associates and relapse prevention methods adapted from Marlatt. [T]his fully documented treatment . . . greatly facilitates the generalizability and transportability of study findings. . . . The investigative team is excellent . . . also attuned to the difficulties entailed in studying this target group. . . . While these strengths recommend the proposal . . . eligibility criteria for inclusion of subjects in the study are somewhat ambiguous. . . . This volunteer procedure could substantially underrepresent important components of the shelter population. . . . The projected time frame for recruiting subjects . . . also seems unrealistic for a three-year effort. . . . Several factors in the research design seem to mitigate against maximum participation and retention. . . .

If you get the impression that researchers cannot afford to leave any stone unturned in working through procedures in an NIMH proposal, you are right. It is very difficult to convince a government agency that a research project is worth spending a lot of money on (we requested about $2 million). And that is as it should be: your tax dollars should be used only for research that has a high likelihood of yielding findings that are valid and useful. But even when you are proposing a smaller project to a more generous funding source—or even presenting a proposal to your professor—you should scrutinize the proposal carefully before submission and ask others to comment on it. Other people will often think of issues you neglected to consider, and you should allow yourself time to think about these issues and to reread and redraft the proposal. Besides, you will get no credit for having thrown together a proposal as best you could in the face of an impossible submission deadline.

When you develop a research proposal, it will help to ask yourself a series of questions like those in Exhibit 12.2 (also see Herek, 1995). It is too easy to omit important details and to avoid being self-critical while rushing to put a proposal together. And it is too painful to have a proposal rejected (or to receive a low grade). Better to make sure the proposal covers what it should and confronts the tough issues that reviewers (or your professor) will be sure to spot.

The series of questions in Exhibit 12.2 can serve as a map to preceding chapters in this book as well as a checklist of decisions that must be made throughout any research project. The questions are organized in five sections, each concluding with a *checkpoint* at which you should consider whether to proceed with the research as planned, modify the plans, or stop the project altogether. The sequential ordering of these questions obscures a bit the way in which they should be answered: not as single questions, one at a time, but as a unit—first as five separate stages, and then as a whole. Feel free to change your answers to earlier questions on the basis of your answers to later questions.

A brief review of how the questions in Exhibit 12.2 might be answered with respect to my NIMH relapse prevention proposal should help you to review your own work. Our research problem on treating substance abuse certainly was suitable for social research, and it was one that could have been handled for the money we requested [Question 1]. Prior research demonstrated clearly that our proposed treatment had potential and also that it had not previously been tried with homeless persons [2]. The treatment approach was connected to psychosocial rehabilitation theory [3] and, given prior work in this area, a deductive, hypothesis-testing stance was called for [4]. So it seemed reasonable to continue to develop the proposal (Checkpoint I). The problem was best addressed with longitudinal data [5], involved individuals [6], and was well suited to a randomized, experimental design [9]. Measures were to include direct questions, observations by field researchers, and laboratory tests (of substance abuse) [7].

The proposal's primary weakness was in the area of generalizability [8]. We proposed to sample persons in only two homeless shelters, in two cities, and we could offer only weak incentives to encourage potential participants to start and stay in the study. The review committee believed that these procedures might result in an unrepresentative group of initial volunteers beginning the treatment and perhaps an even less representative group continuing through the entire program. Clearly we should have modified the proposal with some additional recruitment and retention strategies—although it may be that the research could not actually be carried out without some major modification of the research question (Checkpoint II).

An experimental design was preferable because this was to be a treatment-outcome study, but we did include a field research component so that we could evaluate treatment implementation [10]. Since the effectiveness of

Exhibit 12.2 **Decisions in Research**

PROBLEM FORMULATION (Chapters 1–2)
1. Assessing researchability of the problem
2. Consulting prior research
3. Relating to social theory
4. Choosing an approach:
   Deductive? Inductive? Descriptive?

> Checkpoint I
>
> Alternatives: • Continue as planned;
> • Modify the plan;
> • STOP. Abandon the plan.

RESEARCH VALIDITY (Chapters 3–5)
5. Data required: longitudinal or cross-sectional?
6. Units of analysis: individuals or groups?
7. Strategy for measuring variables:
   Records, direct questions, observations, unobtrusive measures?
8. Establishing generalizability:
   Was a representative sample used?
   Are the findings applicable to particular subgroups?
   Does the population sampled correspond to the population of interest?
9. Establishing causality:
   Possibility of experimental or statistical controls?
   How to assess the causal mechanism?
   Consider the causal context.

> Checkpoint II
>
> Alternatives: • Continue as planned;
> • Modify the plan;
> • STOP. Abandon the plan.

RESEARCH DESIGN (Chapters 6–10)
10. Choosing a research design:
    Experimental? Survey? Participant observation?
    Historical, comparative? Multiple methods?
11. Secondary analysis? Availability of suitable datasets?
12. Assessing ethical concerns

> Checkpoint III
>
> Alternatives: • Continue as planned;
> • Modify the plan;
> • STOP. Abandon the plan.

(continued on next page)

Exhibit 12.2   **Decisions in Research *(continued)***

DATA ANALYSIS (Chapter 11)
13. Choosing a statistical approach
        Statistics and graphs for describing data
        Deciding about statistical controls
        Testing for interaction effects
        Evaluating inferences from sample data to the population

Checkpoint IV

Alternatives: • Continue as planned;
                • Modify the plan;
                • STOP. Abandon the plan.

REPORTING RESEARCH FINDINGS (Chapter 12)
14. Identifying the intended audience: Multiple reports for different audiences?
15. Distribution of the report: What restrictions?
16. Report deadline: Is it feasible?

Checkpoint V

Alternatives: • Continue as planned;
                • Modify the plan;
                • STOP. Abandon the plan.

our proposed treatment strategy had not been studied before among homeless persons, we could not propose doing a secondary data analysis or meta-analysis [11]. Because participation in the study was to be voluntary and everyone received *something* for participation, the research design seemed ethical (and it was approved by the University of Massachusetts Medical School's Institutional Review Board and by the state mental health agency's human subjects committee) [12]. We planned several statistical tests, but here the review committee remarked that we should have been more specific [13]. Our goal was to use our research as the basis for several academic articles, and we expected that the funding agency would also require us to prepare a report for general distribution. As is typical in most research proposals, we did not develop our research reporting plans any further [14].

A Methodologist's Toolchest

You may also find it useful when preparing a research proposal to have a computer program identify and review key decisions that you have to make. The *Methodologist's Toolchest*™ (Brent & Thompson, 1996) is an expert decision support system containing detailed information on the major components of research proposals. You can review the issues that should be considered for such critical stages as designing a sample, developing measures, and choosing statistics. The software shows you what the alternatives are and asks you which one you prefer. It then can give you feedback to indicate possible consequences of your decision.

This process is represented in Exhibit 12.3. First you see the *Toolchest* outline of major proposal sections. Then you see the different types of threats to validity that you can review, if these are what you are interested in. Next you see some background information to help you choose a research design, and then feedback indicating the consequences of your design choice for the validity threat on which you focused (history, in the example). The last screens provide suggestions for reducing the threat and a quantitative rating of the extent to which your design has addressed the validity threat. Of course, this information and feedback is useful only if you treat it as an additional source of suggestions, not as the ultimate authority. You may sometimes receive inappropriate advice from a system like the *Toolchest* because it doesn't understand all the aspects of the research problem. You still must be in charge. Nonetheless, a structured procedure for reviewing decisions and thinking about alternatives can only help to improve your proposals.

Exhibit 12.3   **Methodologist's Toolchest™**

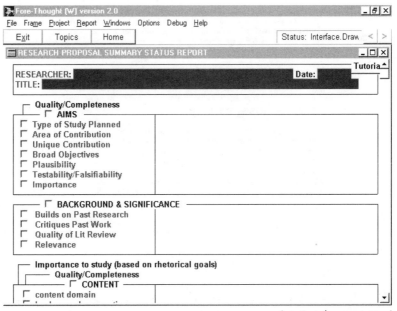

(continued on next page)

Exhibit 12.3   **Methodologist's Toolchest™ *(continued)***

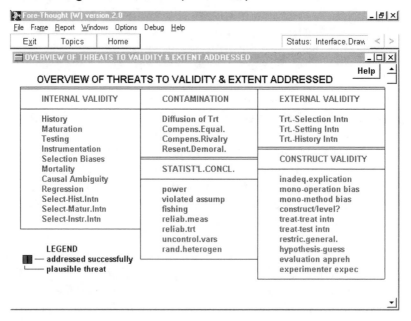

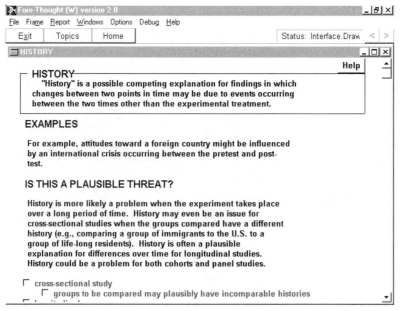

(continued on next page)

Exhibit 12.3   **Methodologist's Toolchest™ (continued)**

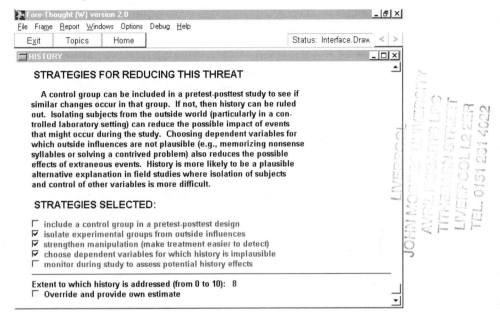

STRATEGIES FOR REDUCING THIS THREAT

A control group can be included in a pretest-posttest study to see if similar changes occur in that group. If not, then history can be ruled out. Isolating subjects from the outside world (particularly in a controlled laboratory setting) can reduce the possible impact of events that might occur during the study. Choosing dependent variables for which outside influences are not plausible (e.g., memorizing nonsense syllables or solving a contrived problem) also reduces the possible effects of extraneous events. History is more likely to be a plausible alternative explanation in field studies where isolation of subjects and control of other variables is more difficult.

STRATEGIES SELECTED:

☐ include a control group in a pretest-posttest design
☑ isolate experimental groups from outside influences
☑ strengthen manipulation (make treatment easier to detect)
☑ choose dependent variables for which history is implausible
☐ monitor during study to assess potential history effects

Extent to which history is addressed (from 0 to 10): 8
☐ Override and provide own estimate

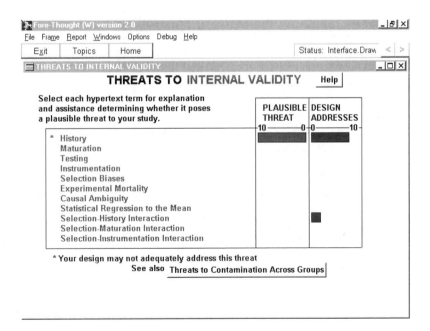

THREATS TO INTERNAL VALIDITY   Help

Select each hypertext term for explanation and assistance determining whether it poses a plausible threat to your study.

	PLAUSIBLE THREAT	DESIGN ADDRESSES
* History		
Maturation		
Testing		
Instrumentation		
Selection Biases		
Experimental Mortality		
Causal Ambiguity		
Statistical Regression to the Mean		
Selection-History Interaction		
Selection-Maturation Interaction		
Selection-Instrumentation Interaction		

* Your design may not adequately address this threat
See also Threats to Contamination Across Groups

Source: Brent & Thompson, 1996: 3-8, 6-9, 6-10, 6-12, 6-14.

■ ■ ■ ■ **Research Report Goals**

The research report will present research findings and interpretations in a way that reflects some combination of the researcher's goals, the research sponsor's goals, the concerns of the research subjects, and—perhaps—those of a wider anticipated readership. Understanding the goals of these different groups will help the researcher begin to shape the final report even at the start of the research. In designing a proposal and in negotiating access to a setting for the research, commitments often must be made to produce a particular type of report, or at least to cover certain issues in the final report. As the research progresses, feedback about the research from its subjects, from sponsoring agencies, and from collaborators or other interested parties may suggest the importance of focusing on particular issues in the final report. Social researchers traditionally have tried to distance themselves from the concerns of such groups, paying attention only to what is needed to advance scientific knowledge, but in recent years some social scientists have recommended bringing these interested parties into the research and reporting process itself.

Advance Scientific Knowledge

Since most social science research reports are directed to other social scientists working in the area of study, they reflect orientations and concerns that are shared within this community of interest. The traditional scientific approach encourages a research goal of advancing scientific knowledge with reports to other scientists. This approach also treats value considerations as beyond the scope of science:

> An empirical science cannot tell anyone what he should do—but rather what he can do—and under certain circumstances—what he wishes to do. (Weber, 1949:54)

The idea is that developing valid knowledge about how society *is* organized, or how we live our lives, does not tell us how society *should* be organized or how we *should* live our lives. There should, as a result, be a strict separation between the determination of empirical facts and the evaluation of these facts as satisfactory or unsatisfactory (Weber, 1949:11). The idea is not that social scientists must ignore value considerations. Value-based considerations are viewed as a legitimate basis for selecting a research problem to study. After the research is over and a report has been written, many scientists also consider it acceptable to encourage government officials or private organizations to implement the findings. During a research project, however, value considerations are to be held in abeyance.

Shape Social Policy

Many social scientists seek through their writing to influence social policy. You have been exposed to several examples in this text, including Rossi's (1989) study of homelessness (Chapter 1), Sherman and Berk's (1984) study of arrest and domestic violence (Chapter 2), and Drake et al.'s (1996) study of employment services (Chapter 6). These particular studies, like much policy-oriented social science research, are similar to those that aim strictly to increase knowledge. In fact, these studies might even be considered contributions to knowledge first, and to social policy debate second. What distinguishes the reports of these studies from strictly academic reports is their attention to policy implications. Most of Jencks's book *The Homeless* (1994), for example, reviews current research and presents some new analyses of data pertaining to homelessness, but the book concludes with a section entitled "Reversing the Trend" and a chapter entitled "Some Partial Solutions."

Other social scientists who seek to influence social policy explicitly reject the traditional scientific, rigid distinction between facts and values (Sjoberg & Nett, 1968). Bellah and colleagues (1985) have instead proposed a model of "social science as public philosophy," in which social scientists focus explicit attention on achieving a more just society:

> Social science makes assumptions about the nature of persons, the nature of society, and the relation between persons and society. It also, whether it admits it or not, makes assumptions about good persons and a good society and considers how far these conceptions are embodied in our actual society.
>
> Social science as public philosophy, by breaking through the iron curtain between the social sciences and the humanities, becomes a form of social self-understanding or self-interpretation. . . . By probing the past as well as the present, by looking at "values" as much as at "facts," such a social science is able to make connections that are not obvious and to ask difficult questions. (p. 301)

This perspective suggests more explicit concern with public policy implications when reporting research results. But it is important to remember that we all are capable of distorting our research and our interpretations of research results so that they correspond to our own value preferences. The temptation to see what we want to see is enormous, and research reports cannot be deemed acceptable unless they avoid this temptation.

Organize Social Action

For the same reasons that value questions are traditionally set apart from the research process, many social scientists consider the application of research to be a nonscientific concern. William Foote Whyte (1991), whose *Street Corner Society* (1955) study you encountered in Chapter 8, has criticized this belief and proposed an alternative research and reporting strategy, **participatory action research.** Whyte (1991:285) argues that social scientists must get "out of the academic rut" and engage in applied research in order to develop better understanding of social phenomena.

In participatory action research, the researcher involves some organizational members as active participants. Both the organizational members and the researcher are assumed to want to develop valid conclusions, to bring unique insights, and to desire change. For example, many academic studies of employee participation have found that it is associated with job satisfaction, but not with employee productivity. After some discussions about this finding with employees and managers, Whyte (1991:278–279) realized that researchers had been using a general concept of employee participation that did not distinguish those aspects of participation that were most likely to influence productivity. For example, occasional employee participation in company meetings had not been distinguished from ongoing employee participation in and control of production decisions. When these and other concepts were defined more precisely, it became clear that certain forms of employee participation had substantially increased overall productivity. This discovery would not have occurred without the active involvement of company employees in planning the research.

Dialogue with Research Subjects

Egon Guba and Yvonna Lincoln (1989:44–45) have carried the notion of involving research subjects and others in the design and reporting of research one step further. What they call the **constructivist paradigm** is a methodology that emphasizes the importance of exploring how different stakeholders in a social setting construct their beliefs. This approach rejects the assumption that there is a reality around us to be studied and reported on. Instead, social scientists operating in the constructivist paradigm try to develop a consensus among participants in some social process about how to understand the focus of inquiry, often a program that is being evaluated. A research report will then highlight different views of the social program and explain how a consensus can be reached among them.

Constructivist inquiry uses an interactive research process, in which a researcher begins an evaluation in some social setting by identifying the different interest groups in that setting—the stakeholder groups. The researcher goes on to learn what each group thinks, and then gradually tries to develop a shared perspective on the problem being evaluated (Guba & Lincoln, 1989:42). This process involves four steps that can each be repeated many times in a given study:

1. Identify stakeholders and solicit their "claims, concerns, and issues."

2. Introduce the claims, concerns, and issues of each stakeholder group to the other stakeholder groups and ask for their reactions.

3. Focus further information collection on claims, concerns, and issues about which there is disagreement among stakeholder groups.

4. Negotiate with stakeholder groups about the information collected and attempt to reach consensus on the issues about which there is disagreement.

These steps are diagrammed as a circular process in Exhibit 12.4. In this process,

> the constructions of a variety of individuals—deliberately chosen so as to uncover widely variable viewpoints—are elicited, challenged, and exposed to new information and new, more sophisticated ways of interpretation, until some level of consensus is reached (although there may be more than one focus for consensus). (Guba & Lincoln, 1989:181)

The researcher conducts an open-ended interview with the first respondent (R_1) to learn about her thoughts and feelings on the subject of inquiry—her

Exhibit 12.4   **Popular Beliefs About Why People Become Homeless**

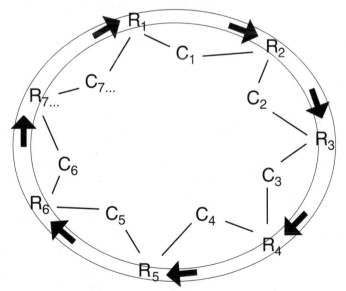

KEY: R = Respondent
C = Construction

Source: Adapted from Guba & Lincoln, 1989:152.

"construction" (C_1). The researcher then asks this respondent to nominate a second respondent (R_2), who feels very differently. The second respondent is then interviewed in the same way, but also is asked to comment on the themes raised by the previous respondent. The process continues until all major perspectives are represented, and then may be repeated again with the same set of respondents.

The final product is a "case report."

> A case report is very unlike the technical reports we are accustomed to seeing in positivist inquiries. It is not a depiction of a "true" or "real" state of affairs. . . . it does not culminate in judgments, conclusions, or recommendations except insofar as these are concurred on by relevant respondents.
>
> The case report helps the reader come to a realization (in the sense of making real) not only of the states of affairs that are believed by constructors [research respondents] to exist but also of the underlying motives, feelings, and rationales leading to those beliefs. The case report is characterized by a thick description that not only clarifies the all-important context, but that makes it possible for the reader vicariously to experience it. (Guba & Lincoln, 1989:180–181)

Although it is off the beaten social scientific track, the constructivist approach provides a useful way of thinking about how best to make sense of the complexity and subjectivity of the social world. Other researchers who write reports intended to influence public policy often find that their findings are ignored. Such neglect would be less common if social researchers gave more attention to the different meanings attached by participants to the same events, in the spirit of constructivist case reports.

■ ■ ■ ■ ■ **Research Report Types**

Research projects designed to produce student papers and theses, applied research reports, and academic articles all have unique features that will influence the final research report. For example, student papers are written for a particular professor or for a thesis committee and often are undertaken with almost no financial resources and in the face of severe time constraints. Applied research reports are written for an organization or agency that usually also has funded the research and that has expectations for a particular type of report. Journal articles are written for the larger academic community and will not be published until they are judged acceptable by some representatives of that community.

These unique features do not really match up so neatly with the specific types of research product: the issue is more one of degree. For example, a student paper that is based on a research project conducted in collaboration with a work organization may face some of the constraints of a project designed to produce an applied research report. An academic article may stem from an applied research project conducted for a government agency. An applied research report often can be followed by an academic article on the same topic. In fact, one research study may lead to all three types of research report, as students write course papers or theses for a professor who writes both academic articles and applied research reports.

Student Papers and Theses

What is most distinctive about a student research paper or thesis is the audience for the final product: a professor or, for a thesis, a committee of professors. In light of this, it is important for you to seek feedback early and often about the progress of your research and about your professor's expectations for the final paper. Securing approval of a research proposal is usually the first step, but it should not be the last occasion for seeking advice prior to writing the final paper. Don't become too anxious for guidance, however. Professors require research projects in part so that their students can work through the many issues they confront at least somewhat independently. A great deal of insight into the research process can be gained in this way. So balance your requests for advice with some independent decision making.

Most student research projects can draw on few resources beyond the student's own time and effort, so it is important that the research plan not be overly ambitious. Keep the paper deadline in mind when planning the project, and remember that almost every researcher tends to underestimate the time required to carry out a project.

Group Projects

Pooling your resources with those of several students in a group project can make it possible to collect much more data, but these projects can lead to other problems. Each student's role should be clarified at the outset and written into the research proposal as a formal commitment. Group members should try to help each other out, rather than competing to do the least work possible or to receive the most recognition. Complaints about other group members should be made to the professor when things just can't be worked out among group members. Each group member should have a clear area of responsibility in the final report, and one may want to serve as the final editor.

The Thesis Committee

Students who are preparing a paper for a committee, usually at the M.A. or Ph.D. level, must be prepared to integrate the multiple perspectives and comments of committee members into a plan for a coherent final report.

(The thesis committee chair should be the primary guide in this process; careful selection of faculty to serve on the committee is also important.) As much as possible, committee members should have complementary areas of expertise that are each important for the research project: perhaps one methodologist, one specialist in the primary substantive area of the thesis, and one specialist in a secondary area. Theses using data collected by service agencies or other organizations often benefit from inclusion of an organizational representative on the committee.

I directed for six years the University of Massachusetts at Boston's Graduate Program in Applied Sociology. In that capacity I conducted a survey about students' M.A. thesis projects. The following are contrasting student comments about their thesis committees:

> The research plan came about after much reading and talk among my advisors. My advisors were excellent in narrowing my focus. My biggest problem was making my research design manageable. What helped were:
>
>> Availability of my committee members.
>>
>> Their willingness to help.
>>
>> Their support and help outside the thesis.
>>
>> Their guidelines and simplicity.
>>
>> In general, they were there.
>
> One of the main problems was not due to the topic or the setting but the process of trying to satisfy three people, all of whom have their own concerns or interests in the area.

Applied Reports

The most important problem that applied researchers confront is the need to produce a final report that meets the funding organization's expectations. This is called the hired gun problem. Of course, the extent to which being a hired gun is a problem varies greatly with the research orientation of the funding organization and with the nature of the research problem posed. The ideal situation is to have few constraints on the nature of the final report, but sometimes research reports are suppressed or distorted because the researcher comes to conclusions that the funding organization does not like.

Case Study: The Diaper Debate

The problems of hired gun research have become most apparent in the reports of dueling researchers defending, and challenging, the claims of companies seeking to market their products. Such research has been called **tac-**

tical research and was the subject of a book review in *The Wall Street Journal* (Crossen, 1994):

> The diaper debate of the late 1980s was emblematic of the corporate-sponsored, research-driven policy duel. It was actually fought with four studies, . . .
>
> ■ A 1988 study, sponsored by the cloth diaper industry, appraising disposable diapers as garbage. . . .
>
> ■ A 1990 study, sponsored by the diaper arm of the American Paper Institute . . . , which showed that disposables and reusables were, environmentally speaking, equivalent.
>
> ■ A 1991 study, sponsored by the cloth diaper industry . . . found cloth diapers environmentally superior.
>
> ■ A study by Arthur D. Little, Inc., showed that disposable diapers were actually no worse for the environment than the reusable cloth kind. The study all but ended the highly visible campaign against disposable diapers. . . .

Applied reports that are written in a less highly charged environment can face another problem, even when they are favorably received by the funding organization: their conclusions are often ignored. This problem can be more a matter of the organizations not really knowing *how* to use research findings than not *wanting* to use them. And this is not just a problem of the funding organization; many researchers are prepared only to present their findings, without giving any thought to how research findings can be translated into organizational policies or programs.

An Advisory Committee

An advisory committee can help the applied researcher avoid the problems of incompatible expectations for the final report and insufficient understanding of how to use the research results, without adopting the more engaged strategy of Whyte's participatory action research or Guba and Lincoln's constructivist inquiry. An advisory committee should be formed before the project begins and should represent the various organizational segments. The researcher can use the committee as a source of intelligence about how particular findings may be received and as a sounding board for ideas about how the organization can use research findings. Perhaps most important, an advisory committee can help the researcher work out many problems in research design and implementation. I have worked with advisory committees in many applied research projects, and in every case the committee has provided invaluable assistance. Conflicts do at times arise, but they almost invariably can be used to learn more about the sponsoring organization and to strategize more effectively about the research design and the final product.

In one instance, a local church approved my proposal for a systematic survey of church members to identify their orientations toward and needs from the church. Funds were allocated for general survey expenses, and a research committee was formed. One committee member was a professional editor who prepared the survey and final report with a good word processor, much improving their appearance. Another member was a church leader, who was initially opposed to the survey project but soon became one of the project's strongest supporters. Results were presented in a detailed research report and in a special service designed by the entire research committee.

Another research effort that I was invited to participate in ended shortly after what was intended to be a first research committee meeting. Some local officials wanted to develop a combined database on homeless persons, using all shelters in the city. The research committee was charged with designing a data collection approach that would be suitable for each shelter. The problem was that at the time some participants objected to the collection of any survey data whatsoever on the persons using shelters, and some shelters were not interested in modifying their current operating procedures. Interests were too divergent to support a standardized cross-shelter survey effort and there was no authority with sufficient influence to require that one be administered.

A member of the research committee for another organizational survey disagreed with others about one important decision. After extended discussion during a very long evening meeting, the dissident member accepted the majority's decision. As the meeting progressed, a slight in-group spirit among the majority was expressed in some "good-natured" kidding of the dissident. Suspecting that working relations in the committee had been harmed, I later phoned the dissident member. Our discussion proved to be essential to restoring the member's confidence in the committee and his ability to continue to work with it. Although this discussion was not a part of the research itself, it was a crucial element in making the results useful.

Journal Articles

It is the **peer review** process that makes preparation of an academic journal article most unique. The journal's editor sends submitted articles to two or three experts—peers—who are asked whether the paper should be accepted more or less as is, revised and then resubmitted, or rejected. Reviewers also provide comments, sometimes quite lengthy, to explain their decision and to guide any required revisions. The process is an anonymous one at most journals: reviewers are not told the author's name, and the author is not told the reviewers' names. Although the journal editor has the final say, editors' decisions are normally based on the reviewers' comments.

This peer review process must be anticipated in designing the final report. Peer reviewers are not pulled out of a hat. They are experts in the field or fields represented in the paper and usually have published articles themselves in that field. It is critical that the author be familiar with the research literature and be able to present the research findings as a unique contribution to that literature. In most cases, this hurdle is much harder to jump with journal articles than with student papers or applied research reports. Of course, there is also a certain luck of the draw in peer review. One set of two or three reviewers may be inclined to reject an article that another set of reviewers would accept. But in general, the anonymous peer review process results in higher quality research reports because articles are revised prior to publication in response to suggestions and criticisms of other experts.

Case Study: Distress and Social Support

I have reprinted below the comments of three anonymous reviewers on a paper (Schutt, Meschede, & Rierdan, 1994) that I submitted to the *Journal of Health and Social Behavior,* the American Sociological Association's journal for medical sociology:

> In your call for future research, I wonder if you might not speculate briefly on the sort of sample that might be useful in studies of the homeless. By that I mean, should we use shelters, seek them out on the street, disregard families (like you have), or what?

> Give examples of the items in the Interpersonal Support Evaluation List, for the benefit of readers who do not have Cohen and Symes immediately at hand.
> Your discussion of "buffering" and "mediating" should refer to Wheaton's 1985 JHSB paper on "Models for the Stress-Buffering Functions of Coping Resources." Your social support results seem consistent with his model of independent stress deterrence.
> I appreciate your desire to try the Mirowsky and Ross model [of age effects] in a different sample. However, age is mostly just a control variable in your analysis, and not the central focus. It might be better to use a model that is similar to the Mirowsky and Ross one in form but that is both more common and easier to interpret. . . .

> The current paper finds a substantial direct benefit of social support in mediating distress, as well as buffering effects. . . . The disparity between findings here and those reported elsewhere is explained as the consequence of "more refined measures of social support." It is quite possible, though, that the social support measures used here are less refined and exhaustive. . . . They [the authors] should simply acknowledge differences in measurements, and explain how they lead to discrepancies between their findings and those of other studies.

You can see why I think that these comments helped my coauthors and me to improve the final version that the journal published. For example, the reviewer's suggestion that we "speculate briefly on the sort of sample that might be useful" led to the following discussion in our concluding section:

> The difficulty of sampling homeless persons makes it unlikely that any single study will yield broadly generalizable results about the questions on which we have focused. Generalizability will instead be increased through the cumulation of findings from limited samples. It is particularly important to sample homeless persons who do not use shelters and thus are exposed to circumstances most likely to elicit high levels of distress and suicidal thinking. Homeless mothers and their children are a distinct population in which the factors increasing psychological distress and suicidality may differ. But the comparability of our results with those obtained in general population studies leads us to suspect that the origins of distress are similar across a wide range of populations. (Schutt et al., 1994:141)

■ ■ ■ ■ Writing and Organization

You began writing your research report when you worked on the research proposal; and you will find that the final report is much easier to write, and more adequate, if you write more material for it as you work out issues during the project. It is very disappointing to discover that something important was left out when it is too late to do anything about it. And I don't need to point out that students (and professional researchers) often leave final papers (and reports) until the last possible minute (often for understandable reasons, including other coursework and job or family responsibilities). But be forewarned: *the last-minute approach does not work for research reports.*

A successful report must be well organized and clearly written. Getting to such a product is a difficult but not impossible goal. Consider the following principles formulated by experienced writers (Booth, Colomb, & Williams, 1995:150–151):

- Respect the complexity of the task and dont expect to write a polished draft in a linear fashion. Your thinking will develop as you write, causing you to reorganize and rewrite.

- Leave enough time for dead ends, restarts, revisions, and so on and accept the fact that you will discard much of what you write.

- Write as fast as you comfortably can. Don't worry about spelling, grammar and so on until you are polishing things up.

- Ask anyone whom you trust for their reactions to what you have written.
- Write as you go along, so you have notes and report segments drafted even before you focus on writing the report.

This is not the place for a detailed review of writing techniques—see Becker (1986), Booth et al. (1995), Mullins (1977), Strunk and White (1979), and Turabian (1967) for tips—but I will discuss how to organize a research report.

Any research report should include an introductory statement of the research problem, a literature review, and a methodology section. These are the same three sections that should begin a research proposal. In addition, a research report must include a findings section with pertinent data displays. A conclusions section should summarize evidence pertaining to the study's hypotheses and research questions and then draw implications for the theoretical framework used. Any weaknesses in the research design and ways to improve future research should also be identified in the conclusions section. Journal articles often also include a discussion section prior to the conclusions. The discussion section may include more of the review of hypotheses and perhaps a discussion of the primary weaknesses of the research, leaving the theoretical implications and suggestions for future research to the conclusions section.

Exhibit 12.5 presents an outline of the sections in an academic journal article, with some illustrative quotes. The article's introduction highlights the importance of the problem selected—the relation between marital disruption (divorce) and depression. The introduction also states clearly the gap in the research literature that the article is meant to fill—the untested possibility that depression might cause marital disruption, rather than, or in addition to, marital disruption causing depression. The findings section (labeled Results) begins by presenting the basic association between marital disruption and depression. Then it elaborates on this association by examining sex differences, the impact of prior marital quality, and various mediating and modifying effects. As indicated in the combined discussion and conclusions section, the analysis shows that marital disruption does indeed increase depression and specifies the time frame (three years) during which this effect occurs.

These basic report sections present research results well, but many research reports include subsections tailored to the issues and stages in the specific study being reported. Lengthy applied reports on elaborate research projects may, in fact, be organized somewhat differently, around the research project's different stages or foci.

What can be termed the *front matter* and the *back matter* of an applied report also are important. Most journals require a short abstract at the beginning that summarizes the research question and findings. Applied

Exhibit 12.5 **Sections in a Journal Article**

Aseltine, Robert H., Jr. and Ronald C. Kessler. 1993. "Marital Disruption and Depression in a Community Sample." Journal of Health and Social Behavior, *34 (September): 237–251.*

INTRODUCTION
Despite 20 years of empirical research, the extent to which marital disruption causes poor mental health remains uncertain. The reason for this uncertainty is that previous research has consistently overlooked the potentially important problems of selection into and out of marriage on the basis of prior mental health. (p. 237)

SAMPLE AND MEASURES
Sample
Measures

RESULTS
The Basic Association Between Marital Disruption and Depression
Sex Differences
The Impact of Prior Marital Quality
The Mediating Effects of Secondary Changes
The Modifying Effects of Transitions to Secondary Roles
DISCUSSION [includes conclusions]

. . . According to the results, marital disruption does in fact cause a significant increase in depression compared to pre-divorce levels within a period of three years after the divorce. (p. 245)

---

reports usually begin with an executive summary: a summary list of the study's main findings, often in bullet fashion. Appendixes, the *back matter*, may present tables containing supporting data that were not discussed in the body of the report. Applied research reports also often append a copy of the research instrument(s).

Exhibit 12.6 outlines the sections in an applied research report. This particular report was mandated by the California State Legislature in order to review a state-funded program for the homeless mentally disabled. The goals of the report are described as both description and evaluation. The body of the report presents findings on the number and characteristics of homeless persons and on the operations of the state-funded program in each of 17 counties. The discussion section highlights service needs that are not being met. Nine appendixes then provide details on the study methodology and the counties studied.

Exhibit 12.6 **Sections in an Applied Report**

Vernez, Georges, M. Audrey Burnam, Elizabeth A. McGlynn, Sally Trude, and Brian S. Mittman. 1988. Review of California's Program for the Homeless Mentally Disabled. *Santa Monica, CA: The RAND Corporation.*

SUMMARY

In 1986, the California State Legislature mandated an independent review of the HMD programs that the counties had established with the state funds. The review was to determine the accountability of funds; describe the demographic and mental disorder characteristics of persons served; and assess the effectiveness of the program. This report describes the results of that review. (p. v)

INTRODUCTION

Background

California's Mental Health Services Act of 1985 . . . allocated $20 million annually to the state's 58 counties to support a wide range of services, from basic needs to rehabilitation. (pp. 1–2)

Study Objectives

Organization of the Report

HMD PROGRAM DESCRIPTION AND STUDY METHODOLOGY

The HMD Program

Study Design and Methods

Study Limitations

COUNTING AND CHARACTERIZING THE HOMELESS

Estimating the Number of Homeless People

Characteristics of the Homeless Population

THE HMD PROGRAM IN 17 COUNTIES

Service Priorities

Delivery of Services

Implementation Progress

Selected Outcomes

Effects on the Community and on County Service Agencies

Service Gaps

DISCUSSION

Underserved Groups of HMD

Gaps in Continuity of Care

A particularly large gap in the continuum of care is the lack of specialized housing alternatives for the mentally disabled. The nature of chronic mental illness limits the ability of these individuals to live completely independently. But their housing needs may change, and board-and-care facilities that are acceptable during some periods of their lives may become unacceptable at other times. (p. 57)

(continued on next page)

Exhibit 12.6   **Sections in an Applied Report** *(continued)*

Improved Service Delivery
Issues for Further Research

Appendix
A. SELECTION OF 17 SAMPLED COUNTIES
B. QUESTIONNAIRE FOR SURVEY OF THE HOMELESS
C. GUIDELINES FOR CASE STUDIES
D. INTERVIEW INSTRUMENTS FOR TELEPHONE SURVEY
E. HOMELESS STUDY SAMPLING DESIGN, ENUMERATION, AND SURVEY WEIGHTS
F. HOMELESS SURVEY FIELD PROCEDURES
G. SHORT SCREENER FOR MENTAL AND SUBSTANCE USE DISORDERS
H. CHARACTERISTICS OF THE COUNTIES AND THEIR HMD-FUNDED PROGRAMS
I. CASE STUDIES FOR FOUR COUNTIES' HMD PROGRAMS

It is important to outline a report before writing it, but neither the report's organization nor the first written draft should be considered fixed. As you write, you will get new ideas about how to organize the report. Try them out. As you review the first draft, you will see many ways to improve your writing. Focus particularly on how to shorten and clarify your statements. Make sure each paragraph concerns only one topic. Remember the golden rule of good writing: writing is revising!

You can ease the burden of report writing in several ways:

■ Draw on the research proposal and on project notes.

■ Use a word processing program on a computer to facilitate reorganizing and editing.

■ Seek criticism from friends, teachers, and other research consumers before turning in the final product.

I often find it helpful to use what I call *reverse outlining:* After you have written a first complete draft, outline it on a paragraph-by-paragraph basis, ignoring the actual section headings you used. See if the paper you wrote actually fits the outline you planned. How could the organization be improved?

Most important, leave yourself enough time so that you *can* revise, several times if possible, before turning in the final draft. Here are one student's reflections on writing and revising:

I found the process of writing and revising my paper longer than I expected. I think it was something I was doing for the first time—

working within a committee—that made the process not easy. The overall experience was very good, since I found that I have learned so much. My personal computer also did help greatly.

Revision is essential until complete clarity is achieved. This took most of my time. Because I was so close to the subject matter, it became essential for me to ask for assistance in achieving clarity. My committee members, English editor, and fellow students were extremely helpful. Putting it on disk was also, without question, a timesaver. Time was the major problem.

The process was long, hard and time-consuming, but it was a great learning experience. I work full time so I learned how to budget my time. I still use my time productively and am very careful of not wasting it.

A well-written research report requires (to be just a bit melodramatic) blood, sweat, and tears—and more time than you will at first anticipate. But the process of writing one will help you to write the next. And the issues you consider, if you approach your writing critically, will be sure to improve your subsequent research projects and sharpen your evaluations of others.

■ ■ ■ ■ ■   **Data Displays**

You learned in Chapter 11 about some of the statistics that are useful in analyzing and reporting data, but there are some additional methods of presenting statistical results that can improve research reports. Combined and compressed displays are used most often in applied research reports, but they can also help to communicate findings more effectively in student papers and journal articles.

In a **combined frequency display,** the distributions for a set of conceptually similar variables having the same response categories are presented together, with common headings for the responses. For example, you could identify the variables in the leftmost column and the value labels along the top. Exhibit 12.7 is a combined display reporting the frequency distributions in percentage form for five variables that indicate shelter staff orientations to several AIDS prevention issues. By looking at the table, you can see quickly that almost all staff agree that people with AIDS should be more welcome in the shelter, while somewhat smaller percentages favor more AIDS prevention education. There is little support for avoiding contact with HIV-infected shelter users or making AIDS blood tests mandatory. Note the important information in the table's footnote.

Compressed displays can also be used to present crosstabular data and summary statistics more efficiently, by eliminating unnecessary percentages

Exhibit 12.7 **Combined Frequency Distribution Display:
Shelter Staff Preferences for Shelter AIDS Policy**

Options for Shelter AIDS Policy	STRENGTH OF AGREEMENT					
	Strongly Agree	Agree	Undecided	Disagree	Strongly Disagree	Total
People with AIDS should be more welcome	79%	14%	3%	3%	0%	99%
Do more to educate guests	45%	31%	10%	10%	3%	99%
Do more to inform staff	31%	41%	17%	7%	3%	99%
Staff should avoid contact with infected guests	10%	3%	3%	28%	55%	99%
Require AIDS testing of shelter guests	3%	3%	14%	31%	48%	99%

n = 29. Percents do not add to 100 due to rounding error.
Source: Schutt et al., 1991.

(such as those corresponding to the second value of a dichotomous variable) and by reducing the need for repetitive labels. Exhibit 12.8 presents a compressed display used in a report by Wornie L. Reed and his colleagues (1997) at Cleveland State University's Urban Child Research Center. The table shows that childhood immunization coverage varied among Ohio cities and among types of immunization. One city had achieved the state's 1996 goal for coverage of DTP3 (Cincinnati), while one large city (Cleveland) was lagging far behind. Note that this display omits the number of cases on which the percentages are based, thus violating a data-reporting convention.

Exhibit 12.9, another table in the Reed et al. (1997) report combines features of both combined and compressed data displays. The table shows the percentage of households that have three key characteristics in eight Ohio cities. We can see that Cleveland, which had a lower childhood immunization rate, has a relatively high percentage of households reporting no regular place for medical care and less than a high school education, but also few households reporting difficulty getting childhood immunization shots.

Combined and compressed statistical displays facilitate the presentation of a large amount of data in a relatively small space. To the experienced reader of statistical reports, such displays can convey much important information. They should be used with caution, however, since people who are not used to them may be baffled by the rows of numbers.

Graphs can also provide an efficient tool for summarizing relationships among variables. Exhibit 12.10 is from a Social Security Administration re-

Exhibit 12.8 **Percent Coverage for Children by City, Compared to Immunization Goals and Nation Coverage Rates**

Vaccination	Childhood Immunization Initiative 1996 Goal	2000 Goal	National Coverage Rates Fall 1995	Total 8 cities	Akron	Canton	Cincinnati	Cleveland	Columbus	Dayton	Toledo	Youngstown
4:3:1	—	90	78	53	44	51	68	41	63	56	48	48
4:3:1:3	—	90	76	50	43	48	66	39	62	53	43	39
3:3:1	—	—	—	65	65	64	76	52	68	66	59	65
DTP3	90	90	95	81	80	80	91	71	86	82	79	80
DTP4	—	—	80	58	49	56	73	47	69	62	54	48
OPV3	90	90	90	74	73	75	82	59	81	74	72	72
MMR1	90	90	92	75	75	76	82	64	80	76	70	74
Hib3	90	90	91	75	75	77	86	67	84	76	67	63
HepB3	70	90	78	68	68	71	81	67	65	70	55	68

Source: Reed et al., 1997:11.

Exhibit 12.9 **Medical Care Indicators and Education**

	PERCENT OF HOUSEHOLDS WITH		
City	**No Regular Medical Place**	**Difficulty Getting Shots**	**Less than High School Education**
Toledo	21.1	8.5	38.6
Youngstown	17.4	15.8	33.7
Cleveland	17.0	6.2	45.4
Akron	9.2	16.7	27.9
Dayton	8.1	8.1	39.5
Canton	8.0	22.2	33.5
Columbus	5.3	6.9	35.9
Cincinnati	3.4	12.7	48.3

Source: Reed et al., 1997:19.

port on income among the aged (Wheeler, 1996:14). It represents the relationship between race and source of income, showing that white aged persons are much more likely to have asset income and pension income than African-Americans and Hispanics, whereas African-Americans and Hispanics are much more likely to receive SSI (Social Security Income) funds.

Exhibit 12.10 **Receipt of Income from Major Sources Varies by Race and Hispanic Origin**

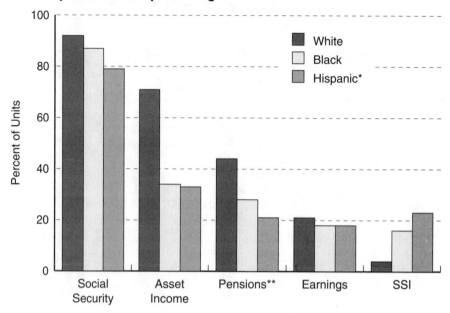

*Persons of Hispanic origin may be of any race.
**Includes private pensions or annuities, government employee pensions, Railroad Retirement, and IRA, Keogh, and 401(k) payments.

Source: Wheeler, 1996:14.

Another good example of the use of graphs to show relationships is provided by a Bureau of Justice Statistics report on criminal victimization (Rand, Lynch, & Cantor, 1997:1). Exhibit 12.11, taken from that report, shows how the rates of different violent crimes have varied over time, with most rates falling in the late 1980s, rising in the early 1990s, and then falling again by 1995.

■ ■ ■ ■ **Ethics and Reporting**

It is at the time of reporting research results that the researcher's ethical duty to be honest becomes paramount. Here are some guidelines:

■ *Provide an honest accounting of how the research was carried out and where the initial research design had to be changed.* Readers do not have to know about every change you made in your plans and each new idea you had,

Exhibit 12.11 **Violent Crime Rates, 1973–95***

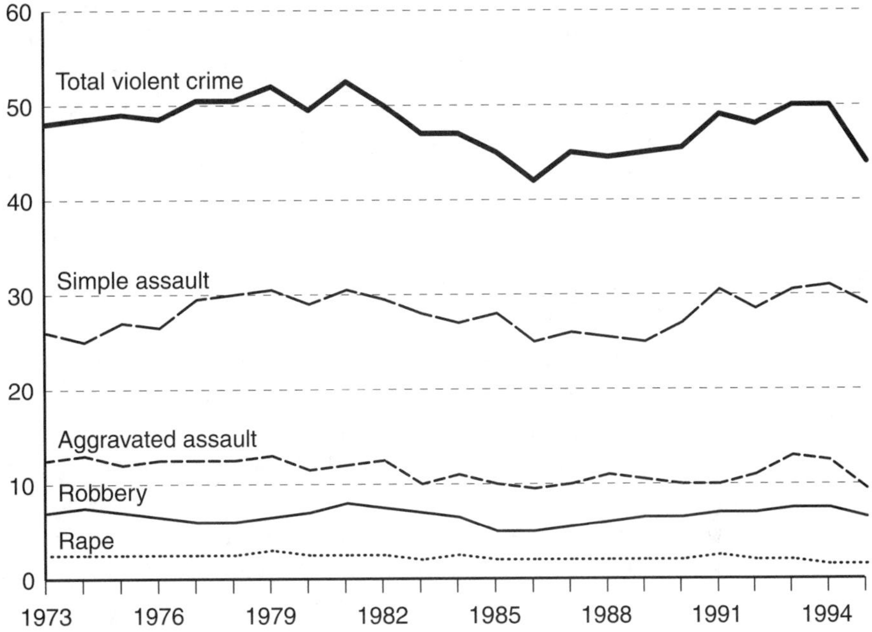

*Victimization rate per 1,000 persons age 12 or older.

Source: Rand, Lynch, & Cantor, 1997:1.

but they should be informed about major changes in hypotheses or research design.

■ *Maintain a full record of the research project so that questions can be answered if they arise.* Many details will have to be omitted from all but the most comprehensive reports, but these omissions should not make it impossible to track down answers to specific questions about research procedures that may arise in the course of data analysis or presentation.

■ *Avoid "lying with statistics" or using graphs to mislead* (see Chapter 11).

■ *Acknowledge the sponsors of the research*—in part so that others can consider whether this sponsorship may have tempted you to bias your results in some way—*and thank staff who made major contributions.*

■ *Be sure that the order of authorship for coauthored reports is discussed in advance and reflects agreed-upon principles.* Be sensitive to coauthors' needs and concerns.

Ethical research reporting should not mean ineffective reporting. You need to tell a coherent story in the report and to avoid losing track of the story in a thicket of minuscule details. You do not need to report every twist and turn in the conceptualization of the research problem or the conduct of the research. But be suspicious of reports that don't seem to admit to the possibility of any room for improvement. Social science is an ongoing enterprise in which one research report makes its most valuable contribution by laying the groundwork for another, more sophisticated research project. Highlight important findings in the research report, but use the research report also to point out what are likely to be the most productive directions for future researchers.

■ ■ ■ ■ ■ **Conclusion**

Good critical skills are essential when evaluating research reports, whether your own or those produced by others. There are *always* weak points in any research, even published research. It is an indication of strength, not weakness, to recognize areas where one's own research needs to be, or could have been, improved. And it is really not just a question of sharpening our knives and going for the jugular. You need to be able to weigh the strengths and weaknesses of particular research results, and to evaluate a study in terms of its contribution to understanding the social world—not in terms of whether it gives a definitive answer for all time.

But this is not to say that anything goes. Much research lacks one or more of the three legs of validity—measurement validity, causal validity, or generalizability—and contributes more confusion than understanding about the social world. Top journals generally maintain very high standards, partly because they have good critics in the review process and distinguished editors who make the final acceptance decisions. But some daily newspapers do a poor job of screening; and research reporting standards in many popular magazines, TV shows, and books are often abysmally poor. Keep your standards high and your view critical when reading research reports, but not so high or so critical that you turn away from studies that make tangible contributions to understanding the social world—even if they don't provide definitive answers. And don't be so intimidated by the need to maintain high standards that you shrink from taking advantage of opportunities to conduct research yourself.

The growth of social science methods from its infancy to adolescence, perhaps to young adulthood, ranks as a key intellectual accomplishment of the 20th century. Opinions about the causes and consequences of homelessness no longer need depend on the scattered impressions of individuals; criminal justice policies can be shaped by systematic evidence of their effectiveness; and changes in the distribution of poverty and wealth in populations can be identified and charted. Employee productivity, neighborhood cohesion, and societal conflict may each be linked to individual psychological processes and to international economic strains.

Of course, social research methods are no more useful than the commitment of researchers to their proper application. Research methods, like all knowledge, can be used poorly or well, for good purposes or bad, when appropriate or not. A claim that a belief is based on social science research in itself provides no extra credibility. As you have learned throughout this book, we must first learn which methods were used, how they were applied, and whether interpretations square with the evidence. To investigate the social world, we must keep in mind the lessons of research methods.

KEY TERMS

Combined frequency display
Compressed display
Constructivist paradigm

Participatory action research
Peer review
Tactical research

HIGHLIGHTS

- Proposal writing should be a time for clarifying the research problem, reviewing the literature, and thinking ahead about the report that will be required.

- Relations with research subjects and consumers should be developed in a manner that facilitates achievement of key research goals and preparation of an effective research report. The traditional scientific approach of minimizing the involvement of research subjects and consumers in research decisions has been challenged by proponents of participatory action research and adherents of the constructivist paradigm.

- Different types of reports typically pose different problems. Authors of student papers must be guided in part by the expectations of their professor. Thesis writers have to meet the requirements of different committee members, but can benefit greatly from the areas of expertise represented on a typical thesis committee. Applied researchers are constrained by the expectations of the research sponsor; an advisory committee from the applied setting can help to avoid problems. Journal articles must pass a peer review by other social scientists and often are much improved in the process.

- Research reports should include an introductory statement of the research problem, a literature review, a methodology section, a findings section with pertinent data displays, and a conclusions section that identifies any weaknesses in the research design and points out implications for future research and theorizing. This basic report format should be modified according to the needs of a particular audience.

- All reports should be revised several times and critiqued by others before being presented in final form.

- Some of the data in many reports can be displayed more efficiently by using combined and compressed statistical displays.

- The central ethical concern in research reporting is to be honest. This honesty should include providing a truthful accounting of how the research was carried out, maintaining a full record about the project, using appropriate statistics and graphs, acknowledging the research sponsors, and being sensitive to the perspectives of coauthors.

EXERCISES

1. Read the journal article "Marital Disruption and Depression in a Community Sample," by Aseltine and Kessler, in the September 1993 issue of *Journal of Health and Social Behavior.* How effective is the article in conveying the design and findings of the research? Could the article's organization be improved at all? Are there bases for disagreement about the interpretation of the findings?

2. Formulate a research problem, review the decision checklist (Exhibit 12.2), and *write a research proposal.* You will find that this is a major project, so you should attempt it only if you will have a month or more to work on it. Alternatively, just answer selected questions from the decision checklist about a research question you would like to pursue.

3. Convert frequency distributions and crosstabs you worked with in Chapter 11 into combined and compressed displays. Alternatively, do so with data presented in journal articles. Write a brief description of what your display shows.

4. Call a local social or health service administrator or a criminal justice official and arrange for an interview. Ask the official about his experience with applied research reports and his conclusions about the value of social research and the best techniques for reporting to practitioners.

5. Interview a student who has written an independent paper or thesis based on collecting original data. Ask her to describe her experiences while writing the thesis. Review the decisions she made in designing her research, and ask about the stages of research design, data collection and analysis, and report writing that proved to be difficult.

6. Rate four journal articles for overall quality of the research and for effectiveness of the writing and data displays. Discuss how each could have been improved.

7. How firm a foundation do social research methods provide for understanding the social world? Stage an in-class debate, with the pro and con arguments focusing on the variability of social research findings across different social contexts and the difficulty of understanding human subjectivity.

WEB EXERCISES

1. Go to the National Science Foundation's Sociology Program Web site at
   http://www.nsf.gov/sbe/sber/sociol/start.htm
   What are the components that the National Science Foundation's Sociology Pro-

gram looks for in a proposed piece of research? Write a detailed outline for a research proposal to study a subject of your choice to be submitted to the National Science Foundation for funding.

2. Go to the Ethics Site at

   http://www.uark.edu/depts/plscinfo/pub/ethics/ethics.html

   Choose "Cases."
   Choose "A Technical Adjustment."
   Read the case "A Technical Adjustment and a Matter of Conscience."
   Briefly describe the issues surrounding social science research, methods, reporting research results, and ethics in this case. Now click "back" twice to go to the original site listed above. Choose "Questions" and answer the "Questions for Consideration" in terms of the case "A Technical Adjustment and a Matter of Conscience."

3. Using the Web, find five different examples of social science research projects that have been completed. Briefly describe each. How does each differ in its approach to reporting the research results? Who do you think the author(s) of each is "reporting" to (i.e., who is the "audience")? How do you think the predicted audience has helped to shape the author's approach to reporting the results? Be sure to note the Web sites at which you located each of your five examples.

SPSS EXERCISES

1. How much do Americans support government assistance of various types? A combined frequency display of the distributions of a series of GSS96 variables will help you to answer this question.
   a. Inspect the labels for the variables AIDCOL to AIDUNEMP. Which forms of government assistance do you think would elicit the most support?
   b. Generate the appropriate frequency distributions. (If you have the TABLES option installed in SPSS, you can use the Table of Frequencies option instead.)

      STATISTICS
      FREQUENCIES [AIDCOL TO AIDUNEMP]
   c. Use the percentages in these distributions to prepare a combined frequency display.
   d. Discuss what you have learned about the distribution of support for government assistance.

2. How is social position and background related to feelings about abortion? A compressed tabular display using GSS96 variables can help you to answer this question.
   a. Pose hypotheses involving the relation between the following variables and attitude toward abortion: sex, education, and identification as a religious fundamentalist.
   b. Generate crosstabulations between SEX, EDUCR3, and FUND (the independent variables) and the following indicators of attitude toward abortion: ABANY TO ABSINGLE.

STATISTICS
  SUMMARIZE
    CROSSTABS
    ROWS [sex, educr3, fund]
    COLUMNS [abany to absingle]
      CELLS [Percentages Column]

c. Present three compressed crosstabulations to show the association between each of the independent variables and the abortion attitudes (displaying just the YES percentage for each).

d. Describe what you have learned about influences on attitudes toward abortion. Develop a tentative explanation for any of your hypotheses that were not supported.

3. Write a short proposal for a question module to be added in the General Social Survey in the year 2000. Your proposed questions should focus on some attitude or behavior that might be explained by other variables already measured in the GSS96. Present frequencies for these GSS96 variables as part of the proposal and include one crosstabulation that might be considered to be a preliminary or related study of the issue you are concerned with.

Appendix A
Summaries of Frequently Cited Research Articles

Actual research studies are used throughout the text to illustrate particular research approaches and issues. You can use the following summaries at any point to review the design of each study. The chapter number in brackets indicates the text chapter in which the study is introduced.

Bailey William C. 1990. "Murder, Capital Punishment, and Television: Execution Publicity and Homicide Rates." *American Sociological Review*, 55: 628–633. [Chapter 5]

Bailey (1990) used a nonexperimental approach to investigate the association between the monthly homicide rate in the United States from 1976 to 1987 (the dependent variable) and the amount of TV publicity given to public executions of murderers during this period (the independent variable). Since the homicide rate did not vary in relation to publicity, Bailey concluded that publicity about capital punishment does not cause variation in the homicide rate.

Bandura, Albert, Dorothea Ross, and Sheila A. Ross. 1963. "Imitation of Film-Mediated Aggressive Models." *Journal of Abnormal and Social Psychology*, 66:3–11. [Chapter 5]

A classic experimental study of children's aggressive behavior in response to media violence. The researchers found that effects of exposure to violence varied with the children's gender and with the gender of the opponent toward whom they acted aggressively but not with whether they saw a real (acted) or filmed violent incident.

Bushman, Brad J. 1995. "Moderating Role of Trait Aggressiveness in the Effects of Violent Media on Aggression." *Journal of Personality and Social Psychology*, 69:950–960. [Chapter 5]

Three laboratory experiments to test the hypothesis that high trait aggressive individuals are more affected by violent media than are low trait aggressive individuals. In the experiment cited in the text, participants (college students) viewed either a violent or a nonviolent videotape and then competed with an "opponent" on a reaction time task. The "loser" received a blast of unpleasant noise. High trait aggressive students displayed more aggression after watching the violent videotape than after watching the nonviolent videotape. Watching the violent videotape did not increase aggression among the low trait aggressive students.

Chen, Xiangming. 1994. "The Changing Roles of Free Economic Zones in Development: A Comparative Analysis of Capitalist and Socialist Cases in East Asia." *Studies in Comparative International Development*, 29:3–25. [Chapter 9]

A historical comparative analysis of free economic zones in three East Asian nations: Taiwan, South Korea, and China. Chen described key characteristics of these zones and presented selected economic indicators. After comparing the course of development of the free economic zones, he classified each in terms of its success in achieving six development objectives. The last stage in the analysis compared the types of patterns found with the predictions of alternative development theories. He concluded that free economic zones are capable of stimulating surrounding areas, as predicted by neoclassical economics, but that state planning and regulation also can have an important impact.

Cohen, Susan G. and Gerald E. Ledford, Jr. 1994. "The Effectiveness of Self-Managing Teams: A Quasi-Experiment." *Human Relations*, 47:13–43. [Chapter 6]

A study of the effectiveness of self-managing teams using an ex post facto design. Work teams were studied in a telecommunications company in which some work teams were self-managing and some were traditionally managed by a supervisor. Each work group identified as self-managing was matched with a traditionally managed work group that produced the same product or service. Self-reported quality of work life was higher in the self-managing groups than in the traditionally managed groups. Job performance also seemed higher in the self-managing groups in clerical and craft functions but not in small business offices. A special review of operations in the small business offices revealed that their work did not lend itself to a team approach. This finding helped to specify the context in which the hypothesized cause would have its effect.

Crenshaw, Edward M. 1995. "Democracy and Demographic Inheritance: The Influence of Modernity and Proto-Modernity on Political and Civil Rights, 1965 to 1980." *American Sociological Review*, 60:702–718. [Chapter 9]

A quantitative study of the relationship between the level of political democracy in 83 countries and the social and economic characteristics of these countries. The author drew on a variety of sources to measure the level of political democracy in 1965 and 1980, as well as such national features as GDP per capita, secondary school enrollment, armed forces per 1,000 population, agricultural density, and income inequality. The analysis indicated that a shift toward more democratic practices between 1965 and 1980 was due in large part to the level of societal complexity, as predicted by political modernization theory. This meant that societies that were larger and more densely settled, had a complex division of labor, and used elaborate, decentralized political structures were more likely to develop in a democratic direction, whether their economies were primarily agrarian or industrial.

Diamond, Timothy. 1992. *Making Gray Gold: Narratives of Nursing Home Care.* Chicago: University of Chicago Press. [Chapter 8]

A participant observation study of the inside of three Chicago nursing homes and the attitudes and actions of their staffs. The central research questions were, in Diamond's words, "What was life like inside, day in and day out? Who lived in nursing homes, and what did they do there?" He began the study by going to school for six months to obtain a required state certificate for nursing home employees; he then worked for several months at each of the three nursing homes. The nursing homes were selected to differ in location and in the proportion of their residents on Medicaid. Diamond's in-depth descriptions and idiographic connections of sequences of events enabled him to explore human experiences in depth and to carefully analyze the social contexts in which these experiences occurred.

Drake, Robert E., Gregory J. McHugo, Deborah R. Becker, William A. Anthony, and Robin E. Clark. 1996. "The New Hampshire Study of Supported Employment for People with Severe Mental Illness." *Journal of Consulting and Clinical Psychology*, 64:391–399. [Chapter 6]

A test of the value of two different approaches to providing employment services for people diagnosed with severe mental disorders that used a variant of the classic randomized comparative change design. One approach, Group Skills Training (GST), emphasized preemployment skills training and used separate agencies to provide vocational and mental health services. The other approach, Individual Placement and Support (IPS), provided vocational and mental health services in a single program and placed people directly into jobs without preemployment skills training. Both groups received posttests, at 6, 12, and 18 months. The researchers hypothesized that GST participants would be more likely to obtain jobs than would IPS participants, but the IPS participants proved to be twice as likely to obtain a competitive job as the GST participants.

Earley, P. Christopher. 1994. "Self or Group: Cultural Effects of Training on Self-Efficacy and Performance." *Administrative Science Quarterly*, 39:89–117. [Chapter 6]

A study of the effect of individual and group training on workers from different cultures. In one component of the investigation, managers from Hong Kong, the People's Republic of China, and the United States were recruited from training seminars for a laboratory study of the value of group training. Participants were assigned randomly to either individual or group training. The researchers expected that the group training would be more effective in the countries with a more collectivistic culture (Hong Kong and China) and the individual training would be more effective in the United States. This hypothesis was supported.

486 ■ APPENDIX A

Fenno, Richard F., Jr. 1978. *Home Style: House Members in Their Districts.* Boston: Little, Brown. [Chapter 8]

A field study of relations between members of the U.S. House of Representatives and their constituents. Fenno traveled with representatives when they visited their districts and conducted unstructured interviews. Representatives were selected with a theoretical sampling strategy in an attempt to ensure that commonly recognized types of representatives and districts were included.

Franklin, Mark N. 1996. "Electoral Participation." Pp. 216–235 in *Comparing Democracies: Elections and Voting in Global Perspective*, edited by Lawrence LeDuc, Richard G. Niemi, and Pippa Norris. Thousand Oaks, CA: Sage. [Chapter 9]

An analysis of international data to explain variation in voter turnout. Voter turnout is maximized where such structural features as compulsory voting and mail and Sunday voting maximize competition. Voter turnout also tends to be higher where the issues being voted on are important and where results are decided by proportional representation rather than on a winner-take-all basis—so individual votes are more important. Franklin concluded that it is the lack of these characteristics that explains the low level of voter turnout in the United States, not the characteristics of individual voters.

Goldfinger, Stephen M., Russell K. Schutt, Larry J. Seidman, Winston M. Turner, Walter E. Penk, and George S. Tolomiczenko. 1996. "Self-Report and Observer Measures of Substance Abuse Among Homeless Mentally Ill Persons in the Cross-Section and Over Time." *The Journal of Nervous and Mental Disease*, 184(11):667–672. [Chapter 3]

In our study of housing for homeless mentally ill persons, we assessed substance abuse with several different sets of direct questions as well as with reports from subjects' case managers and others. We found that the observational reports were often inconsistent with self-reports and that different self-report measures were not always in agreement—hence unreliable. A more reliable measure was initial reports of lifetime substance abuse problems, which identified all those who subsequently abused substances during the project. We concluded that the lifetime measure was a valid way to identify persons at risk for substance abuse problems. No single measure was adequate to identify substance abusers at a particular point in time during the project. Instead, we constructed a composite of observer and self-report measures that seemed to be a valid indicator of substance abuse over six-month periods.

Goldfinger, Stephen M., Russell K. Schutt, George S. Tolomicenko, Winston M. Turner, Norma Ware, Walter E. Penk, et al. 1997. "Housing Persons Who Are Homeless and Mentally Ill: Independent Living or Evolving Consumer Households?" Pp. 29–49 in *Mentally Ill and Homeless: Special Programs for Special Needs*, edited by William R. Breakey and James W. Thompson. Amsterdam, The Netherlands: Harwood Academic Publishers. [Chapter 1]

Field experiment to evaluate the impact of two types of housing on residential stability, health, and other outcomes for formerly homeless mentally ill persons.

Individuals living in shelters were assigned randomly to permanent housing in either an "Independent Living" site (an efficiency apartment) or in an "Evolving Consumer Household" site (a group home from which support staff were withdrawn as residents took over management responsibilities). Participants were evaluated with lengthy interview instruments, neuropsychological tests, and personality inventories for an 18-month period after housing placement. Anthropologists observed interaction in the group homes, and case managers reported on the services delivered to subjects. We found that residents assigned to group homes had a higher rate of housing retention than those assigned to independent apartments; that housing loss was higher among substance abusers and those whom clinicians recommended for group homes; and that individuals assigned to independent apartments were more satisfied with their residences. However, the type of housing did not affect residents' symptoms of mental illness or their feelings about the quality of their lives.

Griffin, Larry J. 1993. "Narrative, Event-Structure Analysis, and Causal Interpretation in Historical Sociology." *American Journal of Sociology*, 98: 1094–1133. [Chapter 5]

Analysis of the events leading up to a lynching in Mississippi in the 1930s. Event-structure analysis is used to develop an idiographic explanation that highlights the structure of action underlying the series of events.

Hamilton, V. Lee and Joseph Sanders. 1983. "Universals in Judging Wrongdoing: Japanese and Americans Compared." *American Sociological Review*, 48: 199–211. [Chapter 10]

A factorial survey to test the effect of people's deeds and social roles on judgments of wrongdoing using random samples of people in Japan and Detroit. Survey respondents read different vignettes describing hypothetical accidents and conflicts between people and then indicated who they thought was responsible in the situation. The responses indicated that Japanese respondents, like their American counterparts, use information about an actor's mental state to determine responsibility for wrongdoing but make little, if any, use of information about the severity of the consequences of the wrongdoing.

Horney, Julie, D. Wayne Osgood, and Ineke Haen Marshall. 1995. "Criminal Careers in the Short-Term: Intra-Individual Variability in Crime and Its Relation to Local Life Circumstances." *American Sociological Review*, 60:655–673. [Chapter 5]

An example of the use of retrospective data. The researchers interviewed 658 newly convicted male offenders sentenced to a Nebraska state prison. In a 45- to 90-minute interview, they recorded each inmate's report of his life circumstances and of his criminal activities for the previous two to three years. They then found that criminal involvement was related strongly to adverse changes in life circumstances, such as marital separation or drug use.

Lee, Barrett A., Sue Hinze Jones, and David W. Lewis. 1990. "Public Beliefs About the Causes of Homelessness." *Social Forces*, 69:253–265. [Chapter 1]

A representative sample of 293 Nashville residents was interviewed by phone about attitudes toward homelessness and experiences with homeless persons. Survey respondents emphasized structural forces and bad luck over individualistic factors as causes of homelessness. The survey results also give some idea of the basis for people's opinions about homelessness: Individuals who had less education and more conservative political beliefs were more likely than others to think that homelessness was a matter of personal choice. Personal contact also made a difference: People who had been panhandled by a homeless person were more likely to think that homelessness was a matter of personal choice, whereas those who had had an informal conversation with a homeless person about something other than money were less likely to believe that homelessness was a matter of personal choice.

Levi, Margaret. 1996. "The Institution of Conscription." *Social Science History*, 20:133–167. [Chapter 9]

Levi sought to understand influences on government conscription policy in democratic nations. She compared Great Britain, the United States, Canada, New Zealand, and Australia during the period in World War I when each attempted to institute a compulsory draft. Levi's analysis identified reasons for the success or failure of these attempts, drawing on the history of events documented in previously published accounts. She found that conscription was accepted in countries where the working class and ethnic groups had less political clout, where groups tended to trust the central government, and where the government was able to deliver on its promises.

Liang, Diane Wei, Richard Moreland, and Linda Argote. 1995. "Group versus Individual Training and Group Performance: The Mediating Role of Transactive Memory." *Personality and Social Psychology Bulletin*, 21:384–393. [Chapter 6]

An experimental study with undergraduate business students at Carnegie-Mellon University. Research goals were to determine whether groups whose members are trained together rather than alone would recall more about how to perform a task and whether a transactive memory system in a work group leads to this superior recall. In a laboratory, participants were asked to assemble the AM portion of an AM/FM radio. Half the students were randomly assigned to group training and half to individual training for about an hour. One week later, the students were placed in small groups to assemble the radios and told that those in the best work group would receive a $20 bonus. Students who had been trained in a group worked with that group to assemble the radios. As hypothesized, groups whose members were trained together remembered more about how to assemble the radio than groups whose members were trained alone. Videotapes of all work groups identified transactive memory as the causal mechanism behind the superior performance of the work groups.

Link, Bruce G., Jo C. Phelan, Ann Stueve, Robert E. Moore, Michaeline Brenahan, and Elmer L. Struening. 1996. "Public Attitudes and Beliefs About Homeless People." Pp. 143–148 in *Homelessness in America*, edited by Jim Baumohl. Phoenix: Oryx Press. [Chapter 4]

Link and his associates used random digit dialing to contact adult household members in the continental United States for an investigation of public attitudes and beliefs about homeless people. Sixty-three percent of the potential interviewees responded, and the sample actually obtained was not exactly comparable to the population sampled: Compared to U.S. Census figures, the sample overrepresented women, people ages 25 to 54, married people, and those with more than a high school education; it underrepresented Latinos. Over half of the respondents linked homelessness to a deviant status such as substance abuse, criminal background, or mental illness. Most Americans were optimistic about the impact of policies to reduce homelessness.

Lipset, Seymour Martin, Martin Trow, and James Coleman. 1956. *Union Democracy*. New York: Free Press. [Chapter 5]

Combined nomothetic and idiographic approaches to explain the preservation of a democratic form of government by the International Typographical Union (ITU). The researchers traced the history of the ITU over a century and also surveyed union members at one point in time. The historical and descriptive analyses complement each other and thus increase our confidence in the causal explanation the researchers developed. The preservation of democracy was in part due to a tradition of two-party conflict, the middle-class status of the printers, the lack of sharp differences in self-interest among the printers, and features of printers' workplaces. Specific historical events reinforced ideological cleavages between the two parties, thus helping to maintain electoral competition.

Maticka-Tyndale, Eleanor. 1992. "Social Construction of HIV Transmission and Prevention Among Heterosexual Young Adults." *Social Problems*, 39: 238–252. [Chapter 10]

Intensive interview study of how much Montreal students know about AIDS and HIV transmission and what impact this knowledge has on their attitudes and actions. A high level of knowledge was found, but students interpreted this knowledge in a way that made them feel they did not have to modify their own risky behavior.

Milgram, Stanley. 1965. "Some Conditions of Obedience and Disobedience to Authority." *Human Relations*, 18: 57–75. [Chapter 6]

Attempt to identify through laboratory experiments the conditions under which ordinary citizens would resist instructions from authority figures to inflict pain on others. Men were recruited through local newspaper ads. Each participant was told he was to participate in a study of the learning process. The recruit was then designated to play the role of the teacher while another "volunteer" (actually the researcher's confederate) went into another room for the rest of the experiment (in most versions of the experiment). The experimenter then instructed the teacher-subject to help the "student" memorize words by administering an electric shock (with a phony machine) every time the student failed to remember the correct word, increasing the voltage level for each successive shock. The researcher patiently encouraged the subject to continue administering the shocks even when the dial on the machine moved to "Extreme Intensity Shock" and "Danger: Severe Shock." Many subjects continued to administer shocks beyond the level they believed would hurt or even kill the subject.

Needleman, Carolyn. 1981. "Discrepant Assumptions in Empirical Research: The Case of Juvenile Court Screening." *Social Problems,* 28: 247–262. [Chapter 10]

Participant observation study of how probation officers screened cases in two New York juvenile court intake units. Revealed that the concepts most researchers believe they are measuring with official records differ markedly from the meaning attached to these records by probation officers. Probation officers often decided how to handle cases first and then created an official record that appeared to justify their decisions.

Olzak, Susan, Suzanne Shanahan, and Elizabeth H. McEneaney. 1996. "Poverty, Segregation, and Race Riots: 1960 to 1993." *American Sociological Review*, 61:590–613. [Chapter 9]

An examination of race riots in the United States from 1960 to 1993. Information on 1,770 ethnic or racial events in 55 cities was coded from reports in *The New York Times* between 1960 and 1993; information on population size, segregation levels, and economic variables was obtained from census and other sources. Statistical analysis indicated that riots were more likely when racial segregation had been high but was declining in cities, and when cities had previously experienced race riots. Levels of poverty and unemployment were not themselves related to the likelihood of rioting.

Pagnini, Deanna L. and S. Philip Morgan. 1996. "Racial Differences in Marriage and Childbearing: Oral History Evidence from the South in the Early Twentieth Century." *American Journal of Sociology*, 101:1694–1715. [Chapter 9]

Oral histories were studied to reveal attitudes toward births out of wedlock among African-American and white women in the South during the 1930s. Pagnini and Morgan read 1,170 life histories recorded by almost 200 writers who worked for a New Deal program during the Depression of the 1930s. The interviewers had used a topic outline that included family issues, education, income, occupation, religion, medical needs, and diet. The analysis gave some insight into community norms that were associated with higher rates of unwed births among African-American women. Bearing a child outside a marital relationship did not seem to be the stigmatizing event for African-Americans that it was for whites.

Paternoster, Raymond, Robert Brame, Ronet Bachman, and Lawrence W. Sherman. 1997. "Do Fair Procedures Matter? The Effect of Procedural Justice on Spouse Assault." *Law & Society Review*, 31(1):163–204. [Chapter 2]

A secondary analysis of data collected in the Milwaukee Domestic Violence Experiment, one of the replications of Sherman and Berk's study of the police response to domestic violence. Paternoster and his colleagues tested a prediction of procedural justice theory that people will comply with the law out of a sense of duty and obligation if they are treated fairly by legal authorities. The procedural justice hypothesis was supported: Persons who were arrested in the Milwaukee experiment became more likely to reoffend only if they had been treated unfairly by the police. Otherwise, their rate of rearrest was similar to that for the persons who were not arrested.

Phillips, David P. 1982. "The Impact of Fictional Television Stories on U.S. Adult Fatalities: New Evidence on the Effect of the Mass Media on Violence." *American Journal of Sociology*, 87: 1340–1359. [Chapter 6]

Quasi-experimental study of the effect of TV soap opera suicides on the number of actual suicides in the U.S., using a multiple group before-after design. Soap opera suicides in 1977 were identified and then the suicide rates in the week prior to and during the week of each suicide story were compared. Deaths due to suicide increased from the control period to the experimental period in 12 of the 13 comparisons.

Presley, Cheryl A., Philip W. Meilman, and Rob Lyerla. 1994. "Development of the Core Alcohol and Drug Survey: Initial Findings and Future Directions." *Journal of American College Health*, 42:248–255. [Chapter 3]

The Core Alcohol and Drug Survey was developed by a committee of grantees of the U.S. Department of Education's Fund for the Improvement of Postsecondary Education (FIPSE) to assist universities in obtaining reliable information about the effectiveness of their efforts to prevent substance abuse. The instrument measures the nature, scope, and consequences of the use of alcohol and other drugs among college students. It is administered annually on 800 campuses and has resulted in a database with over half a million respondents. Almost half of students report binge drinking within the preceding two weeks, and the average number of drinks declines with GPA. However, 87% of students report that they do not prefer to have drugs around, and 33% prefer not to have alcohol present on campus.

Price, Richard H., Michelle Van Ryn, and Amiram D. Vinokur. 1992. "Impact of a Preventive Job Search Intervention on the Likelihood of Depression Among the Unemployed." *Journal of Health and Social Behavior*, 33: 158–167. [Chapter 6]

Field experiment to test the hypothesis that a job search program to help newly unemployed persons could also reduce their risk of depression. Unemployed persons who volunteered for job search help at Michigan Employment Security Commission offices were randomly assigned either to participate in eight three-hour group training seminars over a two-week period (the treatment) or to receive self-help information on job search in the mail (the comparison condition). The authors found fewer depressive symptoms among the subjects who had participated in the group training seminars.

Reed, Wornie L., Jodi Nudelman, Robert W. Adams, Jane Dockery, Nicol Nealeigh, and Rodney W. Thomas. 1997. *Infant Immunization Coverage Cluster*

Survey. Cleveland: Urban Child Research Center, Cleveland State University. [Chapter 12]

A study of childhood immunization coverage in Ohio cities. Reed and his colleagues found that childhood immunization coverage varied among Ohio cities and among types of immunization. One city had achieved the state's 1996 goal for coverage of DTP3, while one large city lagged far behind.

Rosenthal, Rob. 1994. *Homeless in Paradise: A Map of the Terrain*. Philadelphia: Temple University Press. [Chapter 4]

A qualitative study of homeless persons living in Santa Barbara, California, which used snowball sampling. The researcher began by attending a meeting of homeless people he had heard about through housing advocate contacts. He then was invited by one homeless woman to meet another group. The process of snowballing continued as Rosenthal gained entree to new circles.

Ross, Catherine E. and Chia-ling Wu. 1995. "The Links Between Education and Health." *American Sociological Review*, 60:719–745. [Chapter 7]

1990 telephone survey of a random sample of 2,031 adult Americans to identify the psychological effects of changes in household structure. Ross proposed a theory to link women's and men's objective positions at home and in the labor force to their subjective sense of control over life, and in turn to emotional and physical well-being. The questionnaire measured conditions of work and home; sociodemographic characteristics such as employment and marital status, socioeconomic status, and age; the sense of control; and depression, anxiety, anger, and other psychological outcomes. She and her collaborators found that high educational attainment improves health directly, and it improves health indirectly through work and economic conditions, social-psychological resources, and health lifestyle.

Rossi, Peter H. 1989. *Down and Out in America: The Origins of Homelessness*. Chicago: University of Chicago Press. [Chapter 1]

Survey of homeless and other extremely poor persons in Chicago to determine, in part, why people become homeless. A random sample of shelter users was supplemented with a sample of all homeless persons found late at night on blocks selected for the likelihood that they would have homeless persons. Homeless persons were extremely poor but had more health problems, particularly substance abuse and mental illness, than extremely poor persons who were housed.

Roth, Dee. 1989. "Homelessness in Ohio: A Statewide Epidemiological Study." Pp. 145–163 in *Homelessness in the United States, Volume I: State Surveys*, edited by Jamshid A. Momeni. New York: Greenwood Press. [Chapter 1]

Multistage survey of homeless persons and service providers in Ohio. The "key informant" survey found wide variation among staff in shelters and mental health agencies about the number and characteristics of homeless persons. The survey of over 900 homeless persons selected in rural, urban, and mixed counties found a diverse population with many health problems.

Rueschemeyer, Dietrich, Evelyne Huber Stephens, and John D. Stephens. 1992. *Capitalist Development and Democracy*. Chicago: University of Chicago Press. [Chapter 9]

A comparative historical analysis to explain why some nations in Latin America developed democratic politics while others became authoritarian states. The researchers developed a theoretical framework that gave key attention to the power of social classes, state (government) power, and the interaction between social classes and the government. They then classified the political regimes in each nation over time, noting how each nation varied in terms of the variables they had identified as potentially important for successful democratization. Their analysis identified several conditions for initial democratization: consolidation of state power, expansion of the export economy, industrialization, and some agent of political articulation of the subordinate classes.

Sampson, Robert J. 1987. "Urban Black Violence: The Effect of Male Joblessness and Family Disruption." *American Journal of Sociology,* 93: 348–382. [Chapter 5]

Study of the causes of urban violence (rates of homicide and robbery) using city-level data from the 1980 U.S. Census. The specific hypothesis that higher rates of black family disruption (the percentage of black households with children headed by females) result in more violence was supported.

Sampson, Robert J. and John H. Laub. 1990. "Crime and Deviance over the Life Course: The Salience of Adult Social Bonds." *American Sociological Review,* 55: 609–627. [Chapter 5]

Longitudinal study of the effect of childhood deviance on adult crime. A sample of white males in Boston was first studied when they were between 10 and 17 years old and then again in their adult years. Data were collected from multiple sources, including interviews with the subjects themselves and criminal justice records. Children who had been committed to a correctional school for persistent delinquency were much more likely to have committed crimes as adults.

Sampson, Robert J. and John H. Laub. 1993. "Structural Variations in Juvenile Court Processing: Inequality, the Underclass, and Social Control." *Law and Society Review,* 27 (2): 285–311. [Chapter 10]

Analysis of official records to test the hypothesis that juvenile justice is harsher in areas characterized by racial poverty and a large underclass. A random sample of 538,000 cases from 322 counties was drawn and combined with census data on county social characteristics. In counties having a relatively large underclass and poverty concentrated among minorities, juvenile cases were more likely to be treated harshly. These relationships occurred for both black and white juveniles, but were particularly strong for blacks, and they were not related to counties' average income levels or to criminal justice system resources.

Sampson, Robert J., Stephen W. Raudenbush, and Felton Earls. 1997. "Neighborhoods and Violent Crime: A Multilevel Study of Collective Efficacy." *Science,* 277:918–924. [Chapter 5]

A survey-based study of influences on violent crime in Chicago neighborhoods. Collective efficacy was one variable hypothesized to influence the neighborhood crime rate. The variable is a characteristic of the neighborhood, but was measured with responses of individual residents to questions about their neighbors' helpfulness and trustworthiness. Neighborhood variation in collective efficacy explained variation in the rate of violent crime between neighborhoods.

Schutt, Russell K. 1986. *Organization in a Changing Environment: Unionization of Welfare Employees*. Albany: State University of New York Press. [Chapter 5]

My study of the development of a public employee union and how it changed over time from a participatory democratic structure to a more bureaucratic form of organization. I surveyed union members and other welfare employees with two mailed questionnaires, observed the delegate meetings of a public-employee union for about four years, and content-analyzed union literature. My explanation of union development combined a historical account of the union's development (an idiographic explanation) with survey findings that union members in expanding occupations were less likely than union members in stagnant or shrinking occupations to support a participatory democratic structure (a nomothetic explanation).

Schutt, Russell K., Suzanne Gunston, and John O'Brien. 1992. "The Impact of AIDS Prevention Efforts on AIDS Knowledge and Behavior Among Sheltered Homeless Adults." *Sociological Practice Review*, 3(1): 1–7. [Chapter 10]

Interview survey of homeless persons living in shelters to determine what they knew about HIV transmission and AIDS, whether they had been exposed to any prevention activities, and what effect the exposure might have had on their knowledge and on their risk-related behaviors. Respondents were selected from three large shelters using systematic random sampling procedures; one of these shelters had hosted an active AIDS prevention program. There was no association between the average AIDS knowledge score and exposure to prevention activities. However, exposure to specific prevention activities was associated with more knowledge about the specific risks the activities were designed to reduce.

Sherman, Lawrence W. and Richard A. Berk. 1984. "The Specific Deterrent Effects of Arrest for Domestic Assault." *American Sociological Review*, 49: 261–272. [Chapter 2]

A field experiment to determine whether arresting accused abusers on the spot would deter repeat incidents, as predicted by deterrence theory. Police in Minneapolis were randomly assigned domestic assault cases to either result in an arrest, in an order that the offending spouse leave the house for eight hours, or in some type of verbal advice by the police officers. Accused batterers who were arrested had lower recidivism rates than those who were ordered to leave the house or were just warned. Several replications of this experiment produced different results.

Snow, David A. and Leon Anderson. 1987. "Identity Work Among the Homeless: The Verbal Construction and Avowal of Personal Identities." *American Journal of Sociology*, 92: 1336–1371. [Chapter 1]

Field study of homeless persons in Austin, Texas, using participant observation method. Homeless persons were followed through their daily routines and asked about their lives over a period of one year. Six homeless persons were studied more intensively with taped, in-depth life-history interviews. The verbal forms used by homeless individuals to adjust to their homelessness included distancing, embracement, and fictive storytelling.

Sosin, Michael R., Paul Colson, and Susan Grossman. 1988. *Homelessness in Chicago: Poverty and Pathology, Social Institutions and Social Change.* Chicago: Chicago Community Trust. [Chapter 4]

A two-part study of homeless persons in Chicago. One part was a survey of 535 individuals randomly sampled from soup kitchens, shelters, and residential treatment programs for the indigent. The second part of the study examined social institutions in Chicago that focus on homelessness and poverty. The researchers found that social background characteristics of persons who were homeless and those who were housed but very poor were similar. Compared to very poor persons who were housed, homeless persons were more likely to have been in a mental hospital and to display symptoms of mental illness and substance abuse. However, these differences were small. More important were differences in current living arrangements: Persons who had experienced homelessness were less likely to have had another adult to live with and share expenses with and had been paying higher rents.

Thorne, Barrie. 1993. *Gender Play: Girls and Boys in School.* New Brunswick, NJ: Rutgers University Press. [Chapter 8]

A participant observation study of children's social interaction at two similar public elementary schools in California and Michigan. Thorne took the role of complete observer, after receiving permission from school authorities to observe in classrooms and on playgrounds. The research focused on children's social relations, how they organized and gave meaning to social situations, and how children and adults create and recreate gender in their daily interactions.

Valenzuela, Arturo. 1990. "Chile: Origins, Consolidation, and Breakdown of a Democratic Regime." Pp. 38–86 in *Politics in Developing Countries: Comparing Experiences with Democracy,* edited by Larry Diamond, Juan J. Linz, and Seymour Martin Lipset. Boulder, CO: Lynne Rienner Publishers. [Chapter 9]

Historical process research that traced the history of Chilean politics in order to explain variation in democratic practices. Valenzuela structured the research to allow a test of four competing theoretical predictions about the course of democracy: the colonial-continuity thesis, the political culture thesis, the economic development thesis, and the political-determinants thesis. His analysis indicated that democratic practices served the interests of particular elite groups at particular times, resulting in acceptance by all of compromises and of democratic "rules of the [political] game." Democratic rule failed in Chile when these rules were changed, a new (centrist) party proved unwilling to compromise, and a leftist president was elected with a minority of the popular vote and then tried rapidly to change established political and economic practices.

Valenzuela argued that this historical evidence fit with the predictions of the political-determinants thesis.

Walters, Pamela Barnhouse, David R. James, and Holly J. McCammon. 1997. "Citizenship and Public Schools: Accounting for Racial Inequality in Education for the Pre- and Post-Disfranchisement South." *American Sociological Review*, 62:34–52. [Chapter 9]

Quantitative historical events research to understand how the right to vote influences the distribution of educational opportunity. The researchers examined the period of 1890 to 1910, when blacks were disfranchised in the South. They obtained U.S. Census data for the years 1890 and 1910 for counties in Alabama, Florida, Georgia, Louisiana, North Carolina, and South Carolina—the only southern states having census data on teacher availability and public school enrollments in both years. They tested a number of relationships in order to determine which county characteristics influenced teacher availability and enrollment rate for black and white schools. Their statistical analysis indicated several ways in which disfranchisement led to fewer educational opportunities for black children.

Wechsler, Henry, Andrea Davenport, George Dowdall, Barbara Moeykens, and Sonia Castillo. 1994. "Health and Behavioral Consequences of Binge Drinking in College: A National Survey of Students at 140 Campuses." *The Journal of the American Medical Association*, 272(21):1672–1677. [Chapter 3]

A survey of 17,096 students attending 140 colleges about students' drinking behavior and its consequences. Binge drinking was operationalized in terms of both the quantity of alcohol consumed in one episode and the recency of that episode, with different quantities of alcohol specified for rating men and women as binge drinkers. Of the students, 16% did not drink, 41% drank but did not binge, and 44% were binge drinkers. The rates of binge drinking varied significantly by college. Binge drinkers reported significantly more alcohol-related problems than other students. Students at schools with moderate or high levels of binging were more likely than students at schools with low levels of binging to experience problems that result from the drinking behavior of other students.

Wells, L. Edward and Joseph H. Rankin. 1991. "Families and Delinquency: A Meta-Analysis of the Impact of Broken Homes." *Social Problems*, 38: 71–93. [Chapter 10]

Meta-analysis to test the hypothesis that juveniles from broken homes have higher rates of delinquency than those from homes with intact families. Features and findings of 50 previous studies of this hypothesis were coded. The average effect of broken homes was to increase the likelihood of delinquency by about 10 to 15%, but effects varied with the studies' features—primarily with their methods and secondarily with the social characteristics of the people studied.

Whyte, William Foote. 1955. *Street Corner Society*. Chicago: University of Chicago Press. [Chapter 8]

Classic exploratory field research study using participant observation of individuals in a poor Boston community. Whyte lived and socialized in the community, talking with many individuals and participating in a range of activities. He found a corner-gang structure that was relatively independent of the influence of older adults in the community and was based on long-term interaction and a system of mutual obligations.

Wickham-Crowley, Timothy P. 1992. *Guerrillas and Revolution in Latin America: A Comparative Study of Insurgents and Regimes Since 1956*. Princeton, NJ: Princeton University Press. [Chapter 5]

A study of Latin American guerrilla movements that combined elements of nomothetic and idiographic causal explanations. Wickham-Crowley hypothesized that revolutions succeed in Latin America when three conditions are met: peasant support, adequate military power by the guerrilla movement, and a weak political regime that tends to push diverse opposition elements into alliance with one another. He used idiographic analysis to review the history of the guerrilla movements in Latin America, comparing the situation in each country in terms of the three hypothesized causes. He used nomothetic methods to analyze changes over time in both the causal factors and in the strength of the guerrilla movements

Wright, James D. and Eleanor Weber. 1987. *Homelessness and Health*. New York: McGraw-Hill. [Chapter 4]

A massive study of homeless persons as part of the national Health Care for the Homeless program (HCH). Teams including doctors, nurses, and social workers filled out a contact form each time they delivered services to homeless persons in a variety of sites in 19 cities. After about a year, the resulting HCH database included information about 34,035 clients obtained on 90,961 contact forms. This database is a complete census of persons receiving care from HCH clinics, although these persons appeared to include only between one-quarter and one-third of the total homeless population in these cities.

Zaret, David. 1996. "Petitions and the 'Invention' of Public Opinion in the English Revolution." *American Journal of Sociology*, 101:1497–1555. [Chapter 9]

Qualitative historical events research to understand how petitions became public documents in England after 1640. Zaret sampled from 500 petitions in government archives that were published between 1640 and 1660. He read the selected petitions and other relevant documents. The content of the petitions and the debate over them indicated that the widespread use of printing played a critical role in turning petitions into public documents. By 1640, printing had become widely available in England, and Zaret found that after this point large numbers of petitions were circulated before they were submitted to the government. As opposing sides began to use petitions to publicize their views, the rights of people to exchange ideas openly and to sign petitions voluntarily were recognized.

Appendix B
Finding Information

All research is conducted in order to "find information" in some sense, but the focus of this section is more specific, on finding information to inform a central research project. This has often been termed "searching the literature," but the popularity of the World Wide Web for finding information sources requires that we broaden our focus beyond the traditional search of the published literature. It may sound trite, but we do indeed live in an "information age, " with an unprecedented amount of information of many types available to us with relatively little effort. Learning how to locate and use that information efficiently has become a prerequisite for social science.

Searching the Literature

It is most important to search the literature before we begin a research study. A good literature review may reveal that the research problem already has been adequately investigated, it may highlight particular aspects of the research problem most in need of further investigation, or it may suggest that the planned research design is not appropriate for the problem chosen. When we review previous research about our research question, we may learn about weaknesses in our measures, complexities in our research problem, and possible difficulties in data collection. The more of these problems that can be taken into account before, rather than after, data are collected, the better the final research product will be. Even when the rush to "find out" what people think or are doing creates pressure to just go out and ask or observe, it is important to take the time to search the literature and try to reap the benefit of prior investigations.

But the social science literature is not just a source for guidance at the start of an investigation. During a study, questions will arise that can be answered by careful reading of earlier research. After data collection has ceased, reviewing the literature can help to develop new insights into patterns in the data. Research articles published since a project began may suggest new hypotheses or questions to explore.

The best way of searching the literature will be determined in part by what library and bibliographic resources are available to you, but a brief review of some basic procedures and alternative strategies will help you get started on a productive search.

Preparing the Search

You should formulate a research question before you begin the search, although the question may change after you begin. Identify the question's parts and subparts and any related issues that you think might play an important role in the research. List the authors of relevant studies you are aware of, possible keywords that might specify the subject for your search, and perhaps the most important journals that you are concerned with checking. For example, if your research question is, "What is the effect of arrest on the likelihood of repeated domestic assault?" you might first consider searching the literature electronically for studies that mentioned domestic assault or violence and arrest. You might include in your initial list the names of Lawrence Sherman and Richard Berk. You could then plan to search for studies with these as keywords or as words used in their titles or abstracts or (for Sherman and Berk) as authors. If you are concerned with some particular aspects of this question, you should also include the relevant words in your list, such as *gender differences* or *police practices*.

Conducting the Search

Now you are ready to begin searching the literature. Of course, you should check for relevant books in your library and perhaps in the other college libraries in your area. This usually means conducting a search of an on-line catalog using a list of subject terms. But most scientific research is published in journal articles so that research results can quickly be disseminated to other scientists. The primary focus of your search must therefore be the journal literature.

The journal literature can be searched through paper indexes of research articles that include their abstracts (summaries), such as *Sociological Abstracts* and *Psychological Abstracts*, or with the *Social Science Citation Index*, in which you can find the articles that have cited a particular journal article or book. Articles can be searched in these compilations by subject and by standard indexing keywords, as well as by author, title, journal, and year. Exhibit B.1 shows a section of two pages from *Sociological Abstracts*.

Searching a computerized bibliographic database is by far the most efficient search strategy. The specifics of a database search will vary among libraries and according to your own computer resources (check with your librarian for help). Many libraries provide computerized versions of volumes such as *Sociological Abstracts* on CD-ROM. Others provide access to these or other volumes through dial-in services; all you need are your own computer, a modem, and appropriate communications software.

Once you have accessed the chosen index, either through a computer or in its paper version, you can locate the published articles pertaining to topics identified by your subject terms. When searching via a computer, you should choose your subject terms very carefully. A good rule is to cast a net wide enough to catch most of the relevant articles with your key terms but not so wide that it identifies many useless citations (see Exhibit B.2). You should give most attention to articles published in the leading journals in the field. Your professor can help you identify them. In any case, if you are searching a popular topic, you will need to spend a fair amount of time whittling down the list of citations.

Exhibit B.1 **A Page from *Sociological Abstracts***

Subject Index STUDIES IN VIOLENCE Sociological Abstracts

political/structural change, Venezuela,1992; 9302423

settlement patterns, Barí Indians, Venezuela; 16th-/17th-century documentary/20th-century fieldwork data; 9302713

sex ratios at birth/ages 1–5, Barí Indians, Venezuela/Colombia; 1988/89 interviews; 9302728

territorial exogamy, Venezuelan Barí Indians; 1982 census; 9302712

Verbal Accounts

accounts/excuses, organizational functions, blame remediation/impression management; questionnaires, task evaluations; financial institution employees, business students; 9302853

acquired immune deficiency syndrome, competing biomedical accounts' vocabulary/social construction, sociology of knowledge perspective; 9304247

emotion expression, cultural concepts relationship, "natural semantic language" approach; 9303517

French revolution, Robespierre's historical sequence reconstruction; 9303261

unidentified flying object accounts; Thomas E. Bullard's 1989 article summarized; 9302660

Verbal Communication

behavior disordered labeling, African-American adolescents, Theater Rehearsal Technique conduct management approach; 9303550

cognitive environments, audience relevance focus; 9303105

elaborated argumentative discourse production, cooperativeness role; debate experiment; children ages 10–17, France; 9302538

Subject searched

Violence

American Indian suicide/homicide/family violence; 8 chapter causal analysis; 9301760

attachment patterns, battering men, etiological implications; empirical data; 9304641

criminal victimization risk; lifestyle/neighborhood characteristics; survey data; residents, Seattle, Washington; 9304466

dating relationships violence, prevalence/correlates; scale/other data; undergraduates, Ontario; 9304651

homicide rates; divorce; 1983-1986 statistical data; North Dakota; 9304029

sexual horror films, adolescents' attitudes/acceptance; questionnaire data; 9303141

social inequality–violence relationship, deprivation vs rational choice theory; 1973–1977 cross-country data; 9302365

street violence, adolescent gang members, analytical methodology; interview/field data; western Canada; 9304644

violence, Republic South Africa, Sharpeville (1960–1963)/Soweto (1976/77)/current wave compared; published data; 9304642

violence/crime prevention efforts, at-risk youth; illustrative example; African-American youth, Dayton, Ohio; 9304643

violent crime against women, 1973-1989 trends, US National Crime Surveys; 9304655

violent crime rates; poverty/race/population interactive associations; 1988 county/city data; 9304650

Choose these to see more information

Exhibit B.1 **A Page from *Sociological Abstracts* (continued)**

930469   *STUDIES IN VIOLENCE*   *Sociological Abstracts*

tencing based on extensions beyond instant offense; & (4) targeting of certain offenses. Without adequate guidelines, the bifurcation policy simply leads to harsher criminal sentencing. 23 References. D. Generoli (Copyright 1993, Sociological Abstracts, Inc., all rights reserved.)

9304650

Neapolitan, Jerry (Tennessee Technological U, Cookeville 38505), **Poverty, Race, and Population Concentrations: Interactive Associations to Violent Crime, UM** *American Journal of Criminal Justice,* 1992, 16, 2, 143–153.

¶ The argument that nonlinear & interactive associations demonstrate the underlying theoretical links between various factors & violent crime better than single-factor links is examined, using the 1988 County & City Data File for 957 cities with populations of 25,000+. Results support the basic proposition that violent crime rates in cities are very high only when both % black & % in poverty are high in areas of concentrated populations. It is suggested that only under such conditions are both sub-cultural values conducive to violence & motivations toward violence likely to occur. 2 Tables, 33 References. Adapted from the source document. (Copyright 1993, Sociological Abstracts, Inc., all rights reserved.)

9304651

Pedersen, Patricia & Thomas, Cheryl D. (Dept Psychology U Saskatchewan, Saskatoon S7N 0W0), **Prevalence and Correlates of Dating Violence in a Canadian University Sample, UM** *Canadian Journal of Behavioral Science/Revue canadian des sciences du comportement,* 1992, 24, 4, Oct, 490-501 .

¶ Physical violence in their most recent dating relationship was examined

9304054

Schneider, Hans Joachim (Dept Criminology U Westfalia, D-4400 Muenster Federal Republic Germany), **Criminology of Riots, UM** *International Journal of Offender Therapy and Comparative Criminology,* 1992, 36, 3, fall, 173-186.

¶ An overview of the history of international riot research, highlighting psychological & sociological patterns underlying riots, the presentation of riots in the mass media, & various research problems. Recent causation theories are also reviewed, & suggestions offered for controlling riots. 31 References. Adapted from the source document. (Copyright 1993, Sociological Abstracts, Inc., all rights reserved.)

9304655

Smith, M. Dwayne & Kuchta, Ellen S. (Dept Sociology Tulane U, New Orleans LA70118-5698), **Trends in Violent Crime against Women, 1973-89, UM** *Social Science Quarterly,* 1993, 74, 1, Mar, 28-45.

¶ Data from the 1973-1989 National Crime Surveys (N = approximately 98,000 households annually) & criminal justice & vital statistics are used to document trends in violent crime against females (Fs) over the past two decades. Despite recent claims of increasing crime against Fs, generally downward trends in rates of victimization are found. However, a trend toward the greater representation of Fs in the victimized population is discovered, primarily because of more pronounced decreases in men's victimization rates; this finding holds across age categories, with younger Fs showing no trend toward higher victimization rates than previous cohorts. Implications for theory & future research are discussed. Adapted from the source document. (Copyright 1993, Sociological Abstracts, Inc., all rights reserved.)

Exhibit B.2 **Searching *Sociological Abstracts* On-Line: An Example**

Search: scid and (english in la)

| Previous 10 | Next 10 | Show Marked | Print... | Save... | E-mail... | Change Display |

Copyright Information

⬜ **Record 1 of 3 in sociofile 1/74-6/97**

TITLE (ENGLISH AND NON-ENGLISH) (TI)
  Validity of the **SCID** in Substance Abuse Patients
AUTHOR(S) (AU)
  Kranzler,-Henry-R.; Kadden,-Ronald-M.; Babor,-Thomas-F.; Tennen,-Howard;
  Rounsaville,-Burce-J.
INSTITUTIONAL AFFILIATION OF FIRST AUTHOR (IN)
  Dept Psychiatry U Connecticut Health Center, Farmington 06030-2103 [Tel: 860-679-4151]
JOURNAL NAME (JN)
  Addiction;1996, 91, 6, June, 859-868.;
DOCUMENT TYPE (DT)
  aja Abstract-of-Journal-Article
ABSTRACT (AB)
  Structured or semistructured interviews, including the Structured Clinical Interview (**SCID**) for
  DSM-III-R ([Diagnostic & Statistical Manual], third edition, revised), are used widely to maximize
  the reliability & validity of psychiatric diagnoses. Although the reliability of such interviews appears
  adequate, there has been little effort to evaluate their validity. Here, the concurrent, discriminant, &
  predictive validity of **SCID** substance use diagnoses are evaluated in a sample of 100 patients in
  Farmington, CT, as well as co-morbid disorders that occur commonly among these patients. The
  validity of current & life-time substance use diagnoses obtained by a research technician using the
  SCID was good; it was moderate for antisocial personality disorder & major depression, & poor
  for anxiety disorders. Although accurate diagnosis of substance use disorders can be accomplished
  by a research technician, the diagnosis of co-morbid psychiatric disorders requires either additional
  expertise or the use of a diagnostic instrument specially designed for that purpose. 3 Tables, 36
  References. Adapted from the source document. (Copyright 1997, Sociological Abstracts, Inc., all
  rights reserved.)
ACCESSION NUMBER (AN)
  9700058 .

Exhibits B.3 and B.4 show the results of a search for articles on domestic violence and arrest in two on-line bibliographies. The first database I used was UnCover. As you can see, its holdings are substantial, but the introductory description confronts us with the first limitation of many on-line sources: most include only relatively recently published sources. Social science research did not begin in 1988 (even Sherman and Berk's first articles on their domestic violence research were published before then), so we may have to search for relevant sources in paper volumes or in other computerized sources (some libraries offer the complete *Sociological Abstracts* through a dial-in service).

A second problem with computerized searching can be the sheer size of the resulting bibliography. Depending on the database you are working with and the purposes of your search, you may want to limit your search to English language publications, to journal articles rather than conference papers or dissertations (both of which are more difficult to acquire), and to materials published in recent years. Often you should use a more complex strategy that limits your subject search to articles containing certain combinations of words or phrases.

UnCover identified 786 articles on domestic violence since 1988. However, by including the requirement in our search that the article also deal with "arrest," the number of articles diminished to just 19. The first citation is printed in Exhibit B.3 as an example.

UnCover, like most computerized services, is very flexible, although the specific options you find will be determined by your local library. You can search on subject terms, journal names, or authors, or by reading tables of contents from journal issues. You can have an article you identify faxed to you or transmitted to your library's interlibrary loan desk. You also can register for a service (REVEAL Alert) that sends you new citations to the topic(s) of your choice on a weekly basis.

Exhibit B.3   **Results of a Search Using UnCover**

```
Welcome to UnCover at Healey Library

UnCover indexes over 17,000 serials from 1988 to the present.
Journal tables-of-contents are indexed for current-awareness
searches.

        .
        .
        .

>>domestic violence
DOMESTIC 6840 ITEMS UnCover at Healey Libr
DOMESTIC + VIOLENCE 786 ITEMS

DOMESTIC + VIOLENCE 786 ITEMS UnCover at Healey Libr

Result sets larger than 300 will not be sorted.

You may make your search more specific (and reduce the size of
the list) by adding another word to your search. The result will
be items in your current list that also contain the new word.

 to ADD a new word, enter it,

 <D>ISPLAY to see the current list, or

 <Q>UIT for a new search:
```

(continued on next page)

Exhibit B.3   **Results of a Search Using UnCover** *(continued)*

```
NEW WORD(S): arrest
DOMESTIC + VIOLENCE + ARREST 19 ITEMS

You now have: DOMESTIC + VIOLENCE + ARREST 19 ITEMS

 <D>ISPLAY to see the current list, or

NEW WORD(S): d

1  Wanless, Marion   (University of illinois law review. 1996 )
     Mandatory Arrest: A Step Toward Eradicating Domestic...

2  Zorza, Joan    (Criminal justice Fall 95 )
     Mandatory Arrest For Domestic Violence.

3  Wattendorf, George    (The police chief. 11/01/95)
     Chief's Counsel: Pro-Arrest Policy for Domestic Viol...

4  Tolman, Richard M.    (Crime & delinquency. ... 10/01/95)
     Coordinated Community Intervention for Domestic Viol...
     **FAX 1HR*

5  Saunders, Daniel G.    (Journal of interpersonal violence...
     06/01/95)
     The Tendency to Arrest Victims of Domestic Violence:...
     **FAX 1HR*

6  Smith, Dale T. (Journal of dispute resolution. 1995 )
     We Can Settle This Here or Downtown: Mediation of Ar...

7  Martin, Margaret E. (Criminal justice review. ... Fall 94 )
     Mandatory Arrest for Domestic Violence: The Courts' **FAX 1HR*

<RETURN> =CONTINUE LINE # =FULL<P>REVIOUS<Q>UIT//EXPRESS
Number + M to MARK for Order (ex: 4M)Number + F to FLAG for
Email (ex: 4F)
<G>GENERATE Email citations>> 4

AUTHOR(s):  Tolman, Richard M.
            Weisz, Arlene
TITLE(s):   Coordinated Community Intervention for Domestic
            Violence: The Effects of Arrest and Prosecution on
            Recidivism of Woman Abuse Perpetrators.
Summary:

 In: Crime & delinquency.
 OCT 01 1995 v 41 n 4
 Page: 481
 SICI Code: 0011-1287(19951001)41:4L.481:CCID;1-
```

(continued on next page)

Exhibit B.3   **Results of a Search Using UnCover** *(continued)*

```
CALL #: HV6001 .N2
LOCATION: Periodicals
NOTES: 6N3-15 (1960-1969) 17-18 (11971-1972) 20-28 (197
1982) 31-34 (1985-1988) 37 (1991) 38 (1992)-

ISSUE STATUS: Published

This article may be available in your library, at no cost to you.
To have it faxed from UnCover, the following charges apply:

Service Charge:  $  6.50     * 1 Hour Fax *
Fax Surcharge:   $   .00     15 pages
Copyright Fee:   $  6.00
_____

Total Delivery Cost:12.50
```

The second search example uses Medline, a database with information from medical journals. It also provides the abstract for articles.

Many other bibliographic databases are available. Check with your library, concentrate on the one database that your instructor recommends as most appropriate for your discipline, and try not to get swamped!

Exhibit B.4   **Results of a Search Using Medline**

```
MEDLINE is a registered trademark of the U.S. National Library of
Medicine.

COVERAGE: More than 3,500 journals published internationally,
covering all areas of medicine. 1985 to the present. Updated
monthly.

Some NLM produced data is from copyrighted publications of the
respective copyright claimants. Users of the NLM databases are
solely responsible for compliance with any copyright restrictions
and are referred to the publication data appearing in the
bibliographic citations, as well as to the copyright notices
appearing in the original publications, all of which are hereby
incorporated by reference.

NLM users are required to read additional terms contained under the
Help menu.

DATABASE: MEDLINE                          LIMITED TO:
SEARCH: su:domestic violence and arrest    FOUND 12 Records
```

(continued on next page)

Exhibit B.4   **Results of a Search Using Medline *(continued)***

```
* * * * * * * * * * * * Full Record Display * * * * * * * * * * *
DATABASE: MEDLINE                          LIMITED TO:
SEARCH: su:domestic violence and arrest

Record 1 of 12__YOUR LIBRARY (BMU) MAY OWN THIS ITEM___(Page 1 of 5)
|
| RECORD NO.: 97280615
|   AUTHOR: Brookoff D; O'Brien KK; Cook CS; Thompson TD; Williams C
|   ADDRESS: Department of Medical Education, Methodist Hospital,
|        Memphis, TN 38104, USA. brookofd@mhsgate.meth-mem.org
|   TITLE: Characteristics of participants in domestic violence.
|        Assessment at the scene of domestic assault [see comments]
|   SOURCE: JAMA (KFR), 1997 May 7; 277 (17): 1369-73
|   LANGUAGE: English
|   COUNTRY PUB.: UNITED STATES
|   ANNOUNCEMENT: 9707
|   PUB. TYPE: JOURNAL ARTICLE
| ABSTRACT: OBJECTIVE: To evaluate the characteristics of victims
| and perpetrators of domestic assault. DESIGN AND SETTING:
| Consecutive-sample survey study conducted at the scenes of
| police calls for domestic assault in Memphis, Tenn, in 1995.
| PARTICIPANTS: A total of 136 participants (72 victims and 64
| assailants) involved in 62 incidents of domestic violence
| and 75 adult family members at the scene. MAIN OUTCOME
| MEASURES: Participants' responses to a confidential survey
| and review of police records. RESULTS: Of 62 episodes of
| domestic assault, 42 (68%) involved weapons and 11 (15%)
| resulted in serious injury. Fifty-five (89%) of 62 assault
| victims reported previous assaults by their current
| assailants, 19 (35%) of them on a daily basis. Although
| nearly all assault victims had called the police for help on
| previous occasions, only 12 (22%) reported having ever
| sought medical care, counseling, or shelter because of
| domestic assault. Sixty (92%) of the 64 assailants
| reportedly used alcohol or other drugs on the day of the
| assault. Of the assailants, 28 (44%) had a history of arrest
| for charges related to violence, and 46 (72%) had an arrest
| for substance abuse. Eleven (15%) of the victims were
| children. Children directly witnessed 53 (85%) of the
| assaults. CONCLUSIONS: Most victims of domestic violence who
| had called the police rarely used medical or mental health
| facilities for problems related to family violence despite
| frequent assaults. Victims and assailants were willing to
| discuss their histories of family violence and undergo
| assessments at the scenes of police calls.
| NOTES: Comment in: JAMA , 1997 May 7;277(17 ):1400-1
| MESH HEADINGS: Domestic Violence—statistics & numerical data
| (*SN); Adolescence; Adult; Child; Child, Preschool; Crime; Middle
| Age; Police; Sampling Studies; Substance Abuse; Wounds and
| Injuries; Female; Human; Male; Support, Non-U.S. Gov't
| STANDARD NO.: 0098-7484
| DATES: Entered 970513
```

Checking the Results

Now it is time to find the actual articles—and find them you must. You may be tempted to write up a "review" of the literature just based on reading the abstracts, but you will be selling yourself short. Many crucial details about methods, findings, and theoretical implications will be found only in the body of the article. Remember that the authors themselves write the abstracts for their articles, so they may present a sanitized, as well as a very partial, summary of the research in the abstract. To understand, critique, and really benefit from previous research studies, you must read the articles. Don't stop with the articles you identified in your initial search of the *Abstracts* or other index. Always check the bibliographies of the articles that you read for additional relevant sources, and then expand your literature search by reading those articles and books. Continue this process as long as it identifies new and useful sources. You will be surprised (I always am) at how many important articles your initial search missed.

If you have done your job well, you will have more than enough literature as background for your own research, unless it is on a very obscure topic. (Of course, your search will also be limited by library holdings you have access to and perhaps by the time required to order copies of conference papers and dissertations you find in your search.) At this point, your main concern is to construct a coherent framework in which to develop your research problem, drawing as many lessons as you can from previous research. You may use the literature to identify a useful theory and hypotheses to be reexamined, to find inadequately studied specific research questions, to explicate the disputes about your research question, or to summarize the major findings of prior research. Be sure to take notes on each article you read, organizing your notes into the standard sections: theory, methods, findings, conclusions. In any case, write the literature review so that it contributes to your study in some concrete way, and try to avoid a common problem of beginning researchers: Don't feel that you have to discuss an article in your review just because you have read it. Be judicious. You are conducting only one study of one issue, and it will only obscure the value of that study if you try to relate it to everything that's been studied about related topics. Don't be diverted from your central concerns by tangential points in other studies.

In this "information age," you should not think of searching the literature as a one-time-only venture—something that you leave behind as you move on to your *real* research. You may encounter new questions or unanticipated problems as you conduct your research or as you burrow deeper into the research of others. Searching the literature to find out what others have found in response to these questions or what steps they have taken to resolve these problems can yield substantial improvements in your own research. There is so much literature on so many topics that it often is not possible to figure out in advance every subject you should search the literature for or what type of search will be most beneficial.

Another reason to make searching the literature an ongoing project is that the literature is always growing. During the course of one research study, whether it takes only one semester or several years, new findings will be published and relevant questions will be debated. Staying attuned to the literature and checking it at least when you are writing up your findings may save your study from being outdated. Of course, this does not make life any easier for researchers. For example, I am registered with a service that every week sends to my electronic mailbox citations of new journal articles on homelessness. Most are not very important, but even looking over the abstracts for between 5 and 15 new articles each week is quite a chore. Part of the price we pay for living in the information age!

■ ■ ■ ■ Searching the Web

The World Wide Web and other services available through the Internet provide tools for acquiring vast amounts of information of many different sorts. With the World Wide Web you can search the holdings of libraries around the country as well as the types of bibliographic databases that I have just described. You can also access the complete text of government reports and some conference papers, the text of articles from many newspapers, statements of local government policies, postings of advocacy groups and individuals on topics of interest, and advertisements for products related to many different interests.

In order to connect to the Web you first need computer hardware: a personal computer (check with a local store for technical requirements), a modem for communicating over the phone lines (or a card that allows you to connect directly to a communications cable on campus), and a printer. You also need the right software. If you must dial in through a modem, you need communications software to control the communications. You will then need to register with a company such as Compuserve, America Online, or Microsoft that provides access to the Web (unless your school provides access for free). To obtain information through the Web, you will also need a Web browser program such as Microsoft Internet Explorer or Netscape Navigator.

There are three basic strategies for finding information through the Web: direct addressing, indirect addressing, and searching. For some purposes, you will need to use only one strategy. For other purposes, you will want to use all three.

Direct addressing. Every Web information source is identified by an address (a "uniform resource locator," or URL). If you know the URL (address) of the information source(s) you want to use, you can instruct your browser to go directly to that source. This is by far the most efficient strategy for acquiring information on the Web, but it requires that you know in advance just what you are looking for. Appendix H and the student study guide for this text list many URLs relevant to social science research.

Sites you may be interested in include those of professional organizations, government publications, and on-line journals. For example,

http://www.asanet.org

is the American Sociological Association's Web site; it lists publications and includes links to sources of social science data. The URL

http://www.annurev.org/ari

will help you find abstracts from all volumes of the *Annual Review of Sociology*. This site allows you to download the full text of articles.

Indirect addressing. Many Web sites maintain lists of URLs that pertain to their site. When you visit one of these sites, you can browse their list of related URLs and then go directly to one of these other sites. If you share the interests of the person or organization that maintains such a list, and if they keep their URL list up-to-date, these sites can make Web searches much more efficient. Many government agencies and professional organizations and some universities and academic departments now maintain URL lists as part of their own Web sites. For example,

http://www.princeton.edu/~sociolog/links.html

provides search aids, lists of professional associations, URLs for sociology departments, university catalogs, and data archives.

Searching. Every Web browser gives you access to one or more "search engines." These are programs (and people who maintain them) that explore the Web, catalog its resources (URLs), and then let you search their catalog for resources on topics of interest. Popular search engines include Alta Vista, Infoseek, and Yahoo. Each search engine uses its own procedure for identifying and cataloging Web resources. You can ask your instructor for recent information about their advantages and disadvantages.

Exhibit B.5 shows some results from a search I conducted for Web resources on domestic violence. Netscape Navigator was my Web browser; Infoseek was my search engine; Windows 95 was my operating environment. You can see in Exhibit B.5 the framework provided by a Web browser: a box in which you can type a URL for direct or indirect addressing, arrows to click to go back or forward between screens, menu items that allow you to edit or download a file, an icon to click for starting a search, bookmarks that you can use to store frequently accessed URLs, and an icon to click when you want to start a search.

Within the Netscape Navigator window we find the first information provided by Infoseek: a count of the number of sites found, an annotated list of all the sites, and marginal links to related (or unrelated) sources or advertisements. I searched with Infoseek for resources containing the words *domestic, violence,* or *arrest*. Like most search engines, Infoseek then presented me with a list of resources that was ordered by the relevance of the resource to my request. Resources containing all three words are listed before those containing only two of the words, and so on.

This screen illustrates the first problem that you may encounter when searching the Web: the sheer quantity of resources that are available. Infoseek listed 288,616 sites that pertained in some way to my request. Ready to begin? If you wanted to inspect all these sites before you graduate, you would have to

Exhibit B.5   **Results of a Search Using Infoseek**

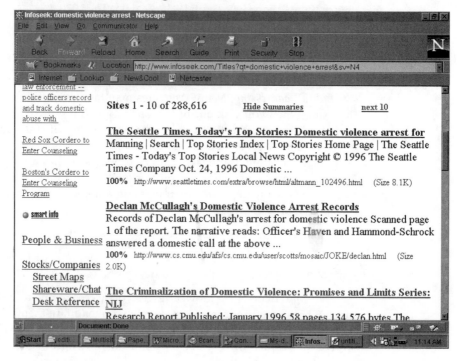

check two of these sites every minute—and that's only if you work on it 40 hours per week for 52 weeks for each of 4 years! Fortunately, most search engines now provide you with "intelligent search" features that help you limit your search to the types of sources in which you are really interested. Clearly that's the approach you would have to take here. Or you may decide that your information needs can be satisfied by the sources for which you already have URLs, entirely avoiding the need for unstructured searching.

A more complete listing of the first few sites found in my Infoseek search appears in Exhibit B.6. Five different types of information sources are identified:

1. *Newspaper articles.* For example, several are from a *Standard-Times* newspaper series on domestic volence. Articles within this series reported on police programs to reduce domestic violence in San Diego, Seattle, and other cities. There is a link to a news story about a baseball player (Cordero) accused in a domestic violence case.

2. *Government policies.* We can read the complete policy and procedure statement on domestic violence adopted by the Nashville, Tennessee, Metropolitan Police Department.

3. *Presented papers.* The complete text of a 58-page paper, "The Criminalization of Domestic Violence: Promises and Limits," presented by Dr. Jeffrey Fagan to a 1995 National Institute of Justice conference.

Exhibit B.6   **First Few Sites Found in the Infoseek Search**

```
[Infoseek] You searched for domestic violence arrest

[news center] Related Topics
            Support groups for survivors of abuse     Crime
The Aarell Co. to Domestic violence              Child abuse
help law
enforcement-- Sites 1-10 of 288,621    Hide Summaries     next 10
police officers
record and track  The Seattle Times, Today's Top Stories: Domestic
violence arrest for domestic abuse    Manning
| Search | Top Stories Index | Top Stories Home Page | The
with    Seattle Times - Today's Top Stories Local News Copyright ©
        1996 The Seattle Times Company Oct. 24, 1996 Domestic ...
Red Sox Cordero to100% http://www.seattletimes.com/extra/browse/
html/altmann_102496.html
Enter Counseling (Size 8.1K)

People & Business
      The Criminalization of Domestic Violence: Promises and Limits
      Series:
 Stocks/Companies NIJ
    Street Maps Research Report Published: January 1996 58 pages
    134,576 bytes The Shareware/ChatCriminalization of Domestic
    Violence: Promises and Limits by Jeffrey
    Desk Reference Fagan Presentation at the 1995 conference on ...
    100% http://aspensys3.aspensys.com:209/0/ncjrs/data/crimdom.txt
 Infoseek Investor (Size 15.8K)

    Domestic Violence
    menu San Diego program has reduced domestic slayings by half.
          By Maureen Boyle Standard-Times staff writer When San
          Diego Police Sgt. Anne O'Dell took the helm of the...
    100% http://www.s-t.com/projects/DomVio/sandiegoprogram.HTML
    (Size 9.6K)

    Metro Nashville Domestic Violence Policy
    >METROPOLITAN POLICE DEPARTMENT NASHVILLE, TENNESSEE General
    Order. No. 95-15 M.P.D FORM 101 SUBJECT:. DOMESTIC VIOLENCE
    RESCINDS:. G. O. 90-1, Memo 06-30-95 REFERENCE
       100% http://www.nashville.net/~police/citizen/policy.html
    (Size 37.2K)

National Domestic Violence Hotline
    Last Updated 22 July 1996 National Domestic Violence Hotline:
    1-800-799-SAFE TDD for the Hearing Impaired: 1-800-787-3224
    National Domestic Violence Hotline. Questions and ...
    100% http://www.usdoj.gov/vawo/hotlfs.htm (Size 10.1K)

[RocketMail. Free E-Mail for the Planet. Click here]
                    Click here
------------------------------------------------------------------
 Copyright © 1995-97 Infoseek Corporation. All rights reserved.
 Infoseek incorporates LinguistX technology from InXight.
 Disclaimer
```

4. *Sources of assistance.* There is a link to a hotline for domestic violence victims.

5. *Commercial advertisements.* Off to the side is an advertisement by the Aarell Co. for computer equipment designed to help police officers report domestic violence incidents efficiently, along with ads for unrelated products. The boundary between public and commercial information sources has become porous.

If you conduct unstructured Web searches like this, heed the following warnings:

■ *Clarify your goals.* Before you begin the search, jot down the terms that you think you need to search for and a statement of what you want to accomplish with your search. Then you will have a sense of what to look for and what to ignore.

■ *Use the best technology.* Take advantage of the more sophisticated search options available to refine your search so that it focuses on what you are really looking for.

■ *Quality is not guaranteed.* Anyone can post almost anything, so the accuracy and adequacy of the information you find are always suspect. There's no journal editor to monitor quality nor a librarian to estimate relevance.

■ *Anticipate change.* Web sites that are not maintained by stable organizations can come and go very quickly. Any search will result in attempts to link to some URLs that have gone out of business.

■ *One size does not fit all.* Different search engines use different procedures for identifying and cataloging Web sites. Some attempt to catalog every site, while others try to ignore sites that are likely to be of only marginal utility. As a result, you can get different results from different search engines even though you are searching for exactly the same terms. Try to read recent reviews of available search engines and learn how they work before deciding which one to use.

■ *Be concerned about generalizability.* You might be tempted to characterize police department policies by quoting from or summarizing the articles or documents you find. But how many police departments are there? How many have posted their policies on the Web? Are these policies representative of all police departments? How many policy statements can you locate and read among the 288,621 sites? In order to answer all these questions you would have to conduct a research project just on the Web sites themselves.

■ *Avoid Web addiction.* Another danger of the extraordinary quantity of information available on the Web is that one search will lead to another and to another and. . . . There are always more possibilities to explore and one more interesting source to check. Establish boundaries of time and effort to avoid the risk of losing all sense of proportion.

■ *Cite your sources.* Using text or images from Web sources without attribution is just as much plagiarism as copying someone else's work from a book or article and pretending that it is your own. Record the Web address (URL), the name of the information provider, and the date for any site from which you obtain material. Include this information in a footnote to the material that you use in a paper.

Appendix C
Questions to Ask About
a Research Article

1. What is the basic research question, or problem? Try to state it in just one sentence. (Chapter 2)

2. Is the purpose of the study explanatory, evaluative, exploratory, or descriptive? Did the study have more than one purpose? (Chapter 1)

3. Was a theoretical framework presented? What was it? Did it seem appropriate for the research question addressed? Can you think of a different theoretical perspective that might have been used? (Chapter 1)

4. What prior literature was reviewed? Was it relevant to the research problem? To the theoretical framework? Does the literature review appear to be adequate? Are you aware of (or can you locate) any important omitted studies? (Chapter 2)

5. How well did the study live up to the guidelines for science? Do you need additional information in any areas to evaluate the study? To replicate it? (Chapter 2)

6. Did the study seem consistent with current ethical standards? Were any tradeoffs made between different ethical guidelines? Was an appropriate balance struck between adherence to ethical standards and use of the most rigorous scientific practices? (Chapter 2)

7. What were the major concepts in the research? How, and how clearly, were they defined? Were some concepts treated as unidimensional that you think might best be thought of as multidimensional? (Chapter 3)

8. Were any hypotheses stated? Were these hypotheses justified adequately in terms of the theoretical framework? In terms of prior research? (Chapter 2)

9. What were the independent and dependent variables in the hypothesis or hypotheses? Did these variables reflect the theoretical concepts as intended? What direction of association was hypothesized? Were any other variables identified as potentially important? (Chapter 2)

10. Did the instruments used, the measures of the variables, seem valid and reliable? How did the authors attempt to establish this? Could any more have been done in the study to establish measurement validity? (Chapter 3)

11. What were the units of analysis? Were they appropriate for the research question? If some groups were the units of analysis, were any statements made at any point that are open to the ecological fallacy? If individuals were the units of analysis, were any statements made at any point that suggest reductionist reasoning? (Chapter 5)

12. Was the study design cross-sectional or longitudinal, or did it use both types of data? If the design was longitudinal, what type of longitudinal design was it? Could the longitudinal design have been improved in any way, as by collecting panel data rather than trend data, or by decreasing the dropout rate in a panel design? If cross-sectional data were used, could the research question have been addressed more effectively with longitudinal data? (Chapter 5)

13. Were any causal assertions made or implied in the hypotheses or in subsequent discussion? What approach was used to demonstrate the existence of causal effects? Were all four criteria for establishing causal relationships addressed? What, if any, variables were controlled in the analysis to reduce the risk of spurious relationships? Should any other variables have been measured and controlled? How satisfied are you with the internal validity of the conclusions? (Chapter 5)

14. Was a sample or the entire population of elements used in the study? What type of sample was selected? Was a probability sampling method used? Did the authors think the sample was generally representative of the population from which it was drawn? Do you? How would you evaluate the likely generalizability of the findings to other populations? (Chapter 4)

15. Was the response rate or participation rate reported? Does it appear likely that those who did not respond or participate were markedly different from those who did participate? Why or why not? Did the author(s) adequately discuss this issue? (Chapters 4, 7)

16. Was an experimental, survey, participant observation, or some other research design used? How well was this design suited to the research question posed and the specific hypotheses tested, if any? Why do you suppose the author(s) chose this particular design? How was the design modified in response to research constraints? How was it modified in order to take advantage of research opportunities? (Chapters 6–8)

17. Was a historical comparative design used? Which type was it? Were problems due to using historical and/or cross-national data addressed? (Chapter 9)

18. Were multiple methods used? Were findings obtained with different methods complementary? (Chapter 10)

19. Was any attention given to social context? To biological processes? If so, what did this add? If not, would it have improved the study? Explain. (Chapter 10)

20. Summarize the findings. How clearly were statistical and/or qualitative data presented and discussed? Were the results substantively important? (Chapters 11, 12)

21. Did the author(s) adequately represent the findings in the discussion and/or conclusions sections? Were conclusions well grounded in the findings? Are any other interpretations possible? (Chapter 12)

22. Compare the study to others addressing the same research question. Did the study yield additional insights? In what ways was the study design more or less adequate than the design of previous research? (Chapter 10)

23. What additional research questions and hypotheses are suggested by the study's results? What light did the study shed on the theoretical framework used? On social policy questions? (Chapters 10–12)

Appendix D
How to Read a Research Article

The discussions of research articles throughout the text may provide all the guidance you need to read and critique research on your own. But reading about an article in bits and pieces in order to learn about particular methodologies is not quite the same as reading an article in its entirety in order to learn what the researcher found out. The goal of this appendix is to walk you through an entire research article, answering the review questions introduced in Appendix C. Of course, this is only one article and our "walk" will take different turns than would a review of other articles, but after this review you should feel more confident when reading other research articles on your own.

We will use for this example an article by South and Spitze (1994) on housework in marital and nonmarital households. It focuses on a topic related to everyone's life experiences as well as to important questions in social theory And it is, moreover, a solid piece of research published in a top journal, the American Sociological Association's *American Sociological Review.*

I have reproduced below each of the article review questions from Appendix C, followed by my answers to them. After each question, I indicate the chapter where the question was discussed and after each answer I cite the article page or pages that I am referring to. You can also follow my review by reading through the article itself and noting my comments.

1. What is the basic research question, or problem? Try to state it in just one sentence. (Chapter 2)

The clearest statement of the research question—actually three questions—is that "we seek to determine how men and women in these [six] different situations [defined by marital status and living arrangement] compare in the amounts of time they spend doing housework, whether these differences can be attributed to differences in other social and economic characteristics, and which household tasks account for these differences" (p. 328). Prior to this point, the authors focus in on this research question, distinguishing it from the more general issue of how housework is distributed within marriages and explaining why it is an important research question.

2. Is the purpose of the study explanatory, evaluative, exploratory, or descriptive? Did the study have more than one purpose? (Chapter 1)

The problem statement indicates that the study will have both descriptive and explanatory purposes: it will "determine how men and women . . . compare" and then try to explain the differences in housework between them. The literature review that begins on p. 328 also makes it clear that the primary purpose of the research was explanatory since the authors review previous explanations for gender differences in housework and propose a new perspective (pp. 328–333).

3. Was a theoretical framework presented? What was it? Did it seem appropriate for the research question addressed? Can you think of a different theoretical perspective that might have been used? (Chapter 1)

The "gender perspective" is used as a framework for the research (p. 329). This perspective seems very appropriate to the research question addressed because it highlights the importance of examining differences between married and other households. The authors themselves discuss three other theoretical perspectives on the division of household labor that might have been used as a theoretical framework, but identify weaknesses in each of them (pp. 328–329).

4. What prior literature was reviewed? Was it relevant to the research problem? To the theoretical framework? Does the literature review appear to be adequate? Are you aware of (or can you locate) any important studies that have been omitted? (Chapter 2)

Literature is reviewed from the article's first page until the "data and methods" section (pp. 327–333). It all seems relevant to the particular problem as well as to the general theoretical framework. In the first few paragraphs, several general studies are mentioned to help clarify the importance of the research problem (pp. 327–328). In the "models of household labor" section, alternative theoretical perspectives used in other studies are reviewed and the strength of the support for them is noted (pp. 328–330). After identifying the theoretical perspective they will use, the authors then introduce findings from particular studies that are most relevant to their focus on how housework varies with marital status (pp. 330–333). I leave it to you to find out whether any important studies were omitted.

5. How well did the study live up to the guidelines for science? Do you need additional information in any areas to evaluate the study? To replicate it? (Chapter 2)

It would be best to return to this question after reading the whole article. The study clearly involves a test of ideas against empirical reality as much as that reality could be measured; it was carried out systematically and disclosed, as far as we can tell, fully. Since the authors used an available dataset, others can easily obtain the complete documentation for the study and try to replicate the authors' findings. The authors explicitly note and challenge assumptions made in other theories of the division of housework (p. 329), although they do not clarify their own assumptions as such. Two of their assumptions are that the appropriation of another's work is likely to occur "perhaps only" in hetero-sexual couple households (p. 329) and that "a woman cannot display love for or subordination to a man through housework when no man is present" (p. 330). The authors also assume that respondents' reports of the hours they have spent on various tasks are reasonably valid (p. 334). These seem to me to be reason-able assumptions, but a moment's reflection should convince you that they are, after all, unproved assumptions that could be challenged. This is not in itself a criticism of the research, since some assumptions must be made in any study The authors specified the meaning of key terms, as required in scientific re-search. They also searched for regularities in their data, thus living up to an-other guideline. A skeptical stance toward current knowledge is apparent in the literature review and in the authors' claim that they have found only "sugges-tive evidence" for their theoretical perspective (p. 344). They aim clearly to build social theory and encourage others to build on their findings, "to further specify the conditions" (p. 344). The study thus seems to exemplify adherence to basic scientific guidelines and to be very replicable.

6. Did the study seem consistent with current ethical standards? Were any tradeoffs made between different ethical guidelines? Was an appropriate balance struck between adherence to ethical standards and use of the most rigorous scientific practices? (Chapter 2)

The authors use survey data collected by others and so encounter no ethical problems in their treatment of human subjects. The reporting seems honest and open. Although the research should help inform social policy the authors' ex-plicit focus is on how their research can inform social theory. This is quite ap-propriate for research reported in a scientific journal, so there are no particular ethical problems raised about the uses to which the research is put. The original survey used by the authors does not appear at all likely to have violated any ethical guidelines concerning the treatment of human subjects, although it would be necessary to inspect the original research report to evaluate this.

7. What were the major concepts in the research? How, and how clearly, were they de-fined? Were some concepts treated as unidimensional that you think might best be thought of as multidimensional? (Chapter 3)

The key concept in the research is that of "doing gender"; it is discussed at length and defined in a way that becomes reasonably clear when it is said that "housework 'produces' gender through the everyday enactment of dominance, submission, and other behaviors symbolically linked to gender" (p. 329). The central concept of housework is introduced explicitly as "a major component of most people's lives" (p. 330), but it is not defined conceptually—presumably because it refers to a widely understood phenomenon. A conceptual definition would have helped to justify the particular operationalization used, and the decision to exclude child care from what is termed housework (p. 334). (A good practical reason for this exclusion is given in footnote 2.) The concept of housework is treated as multidimensional by distinguishing what are termed "male-typed" "female-typed," and "gender-neutral" tasks (p. 342). Another key concept is that of marital status, which the authors define primarily by identifying its different categories (pp. 330–333).

8. Were any hypotheses stated? Were these hypotheses justified adequately in terms of the theoretical framework? In terms of prior research? (Chapter 2)

Five primary hypotheses are stated, although they are labeled as "several important contrasts" that are suggested by the "doing gender" approach, rather than as hypotheses. For example, the first hypothesis is that "women in married-couple households [are expected] to spend more time doing housework than women in any other living situation" (p. 330). A more general point is made about variation in housework across household types before these specific hypotheses are introduced. Several more specific hypotheses are then introduced about variations among specific types of households (pp. 330–331). Some questions about patterns of housework in households that have not previously been studied are presented more as speculations than as definite hypotheses (pp. 332–333). Three additional hypotheses are presented concerning the expected effects of the control variables (p. 333).

9. What were the independent and dependent variables in the hypothesis(es)? Did these variables reflect the theoretical concepts as intended? What direction of association was hypothesized? Were any other variables identified as potentially important? (Chapter 2)

The independent variable in the first hypothesis is marital status (married versus other); the dependent variable is time spent doing housework. The hypothesis states that more time will be spent by married women than by other women, and it is stated that this expectation is "net of other differences among the household types" (p. 330). Can you identify the variables in the other hypotheses [the second and fourth hypotheses about men just restate the preceding hypotheses for women]? Another variable, gender differences in time spent on housework, is discussed throughout the article, but it is not in itself measured; rather, it is estimated by comparing the aggregate distribution of hours for men and women.

10. Did the instruments used, the measures of the variables, seem valid and reliable? How did the authors attempt to establish this? Could any more have been done in the study to establish measurement validity? (Chapter 3)

The measurement of the dependent variable was straightforward, but required respondents to estimate the number of hours per week they spent on various tasks. The authors report that some other researchers have used a presumably more accurate method—time diaries—to estimate time spent on household tasks, and that the results they obtain are very similar to those of the recall method used in their study This increases confidence in the measurement approach used, although it does not in itself establish the validity or reliability of the self-report data. Measures of marital status and other variables involved relatively straightforward questions and do not raise particular concerns about validity The researchers carefully explain in footnotes how they handled missing data.

11. What were the units of analysis? Were they appropriate for the research question? If some groups were the units of analysis, were any statements made at any point that are open to the ecological fallacy? If individuals were the units of analysis, were any statements made at any point that suggest reductionist reasoning? (Chapter 5)

The survey sampled adults, although it was termed a survey of families and households; and it is data on individuals (and the households in which they live) that are analyzed. You can imagine this same study being conducted with households forming the units of analysis, and the dependent variable being the percentage of total time in the family spent on housework, rather than the hours spent by individuals on housework. The conclusions generally are appropriate to the use of individuals as the units of analysis, but there is some danger in reductionist misinterpretation of some of the interpretations, such as that "men and women must be 'doing gender' when they live together" (p. 344). Conclusions like this would be on firmer ground if they were based on household-level data that revealed whether one person's approach to housework did, in fact, vary in relation to that of his or her partner's.

12. Was the study design cross-sectional or longitudinal, or did it use both types of data? If the design was longitudinal, what type of longitudinal design was it? Could the longitudinal design have been improved in any way, as by collecting panel data rather than trend data, or by decreasing the dropout rate in a panel design? If cross-sectional data were used, could the research question have been addressed more effectively with longitudinal data? (Chapter 5)

The survey was cross-sectional. The research question certainly could have been addressed more effectively with longitudinal data that followed people over their adult lives, since many of the authors' interpretations reflect their interest in how individuals' past experiences with housework shape their approach when they enter a new marital status (pp. 344–345).

13. Were any causal assertions made or implied in the hypotheses or in subsequent discussion? What approach was used to demonstrate the existence of causal effects? Were all four criteria for establishing causal relationships addressed? What, if any, variables were controlled in the analysis to reduce the risk of spurious relationships? Should any other variables have been measured and controlled? How satisfied are you with the internal validity of the conclusions? (Chapter 5)

The explanatory hypotheses indicate that the authors were concerned with causality. Mention is made of a possible causal mechanism when it is pointed out that "doing gender"—the presumed causal influence—may operate at both unconscious and conscious levels (p. 329). In order to reduce the risk of spuriousness in the presumed causal relationship (between marital status and housework time), variables such as age, education, earnings, and the presence of children are controlled (p. 335). There are, of course, other variables that might have created a spurious relationship, but at least several of the most likely contenders have been controlled. For example, the use of cross-sectional data leaves us wondering whether some of the differences attributed to marital status might really be due to generational differences—the never-married group is likely to be younger and the widowed group older; controlling for age gives us more confidence that this is not the case. On the other hand, the lack of longitudinal data means that we do not know whether the differences in housework might have preceded marital status: perhaps women who got married also did more housework even before they were married than women who remained single.

14. Was a sample or the entire population of elements used in the study? What type of sample was selected? Was a probability sampling method used? Did the authors think the sample was generally representative of the population from which it was drawn? Do you? How would you evaluate the likely generalizability of the findings to other populations? (Chapter 4)

The sample was a random (probability) sample of families and households. A disproportionate stratified sampling technique was used to ensure the representation of adequate numbers of single-parent families, cohabitors, and other smaller groups that are of theoretical interest (pp. 333–334). The sample is weighted in the analysis to compensate for the disproportionate sampling method and is said to be representative of the U.S. population. The large size of the sample (N = 11,016 after cases with missing values were excluded) indicates that the confidence limits around sample statistics will be very small. Do you think the findings could be generalized to other countries with different cultural values about gender roles and housework?

15. Was the response rate or participation rate reported? Does it appear likely that those who did not respond or participate were markedly different from those who did participate? Why or why not? Did the author(s) adequately discuss this issue? (Chapters 4, 7)

The response rate was not mentioned—a major omission, although it could be found in the original research report. The authors omitted 2,001 respondents from the obtained sample due to missing data and adjusted values of variables having missing data for some other cases. In order to check the consequences of these adjustments, the authors conducted detailed analyses of the consequences of various adjustment procedures. They report that the procedures they used did not affect their conclusions (pp. 333–334). This seems reasonable.

16. Was an experimental, survey, participant observation, or some other research design used? How well was this design suited to the research question posed and the specific hypotheses tested, if any? Why do you suppose the author(s) chose this particular design? How was the design modified in response to research constraints? How was it modified in order to take advantage of research opportunities? (Chapters 6–8)

Survey research was the method of choice, and probably was used for this article because the dataset was already available for analysis. Survey research seems appropriate for the research questions posed, but the limitation of the survey to one point in time was a major constraint (p. 333).

17. Was a historical comparative design used? Which type was it? Were problems due to using historical and/or cross-national data addressed? (Chapter 9)

This study did not use any type of historical or comparative design. It is interesting to consider how the findings might have differed if comparisons to other cultures or to earlier times had been made.

18. Were multiple methods used? Were findings obtained with different methods complementary? (Chapter 10)

This study used only survey methods.

19. Was any attention given to social context? To biological processes? If so, what did this add? If not, would it have improved the study? Explain. (Chapter 10)

In a sense, the independent variable in this study *is* social context: the combinations of marital status and living arrangements distinguish different social contexts in which gender roles are defined. However, no attention is given to the potential importance of larger social contexts, such as neighborhood, region, or nation. It is also possible to imagine future research that tests the influence of biological factors on the household division of labor, as in Udry's (1988) study of adolescents.

20. Summarize the findings. How clearly were statistical and/or qualitative data presented and discussed? Were the results substantively important? (Chapters 11,12)

Statistical data are presented clearly using descriptive statistics (multiple regression analysis (a multivariate statistical technique), and graphs that highlight the most central findings. In fact, the data displays are exemplary because they effectively convey findings to a wide audience and also subject the hypotheses to rigorous statistical tests. No qualitative data are presented. The findings seem substantively important, since they identify large differences in the household roles of men and women and in how these roles vary in different types of household (pp. 336–343).

21. Did the author(s) adequately represent the findings in the discussion and/or conclusions sections? Were conclusions well grounded in the findings? Are any other interpretations possible? (Chapter 12)

The findings are well represented in the discussion and conclusions section (pp. 343–345). The authors point out in their literature review that a constant pattern of gender differences in housework across household types would "cast doubt on the validity of the gender perspective" (p. 330), and the findings clearly rule this out. However, the conclusions give little consideration to the ways in which the specific findings might be interpreted as consistent or inconsistent with reasonable predictions from each of the three other theoretical perspectives reviewed. You might want to consider yourself what other interpretations of the findings might be possible. Remember that other interpretations always are possible for particular findings—it is a question of the weight of the evidence, the persuasiveness of the theory used, and the consistency of the findings with other research.

22. Compare the study to others addressing the same research question. Did the study yield additional insights? In what ways was the study design more or less adequate than the design of previous research? (Chapter 10)

The study investigated an aspect of the question of gender differences in housework that had not previously received much attention (variation in gender differences across different types of household). This helped the authors to gain additional insights into gender and housework, although the use of cross-sectional data and a retrospective self-report measure of housework made their research in some ways less adequate than others.

23. What additional research questions and hypotheses are suggested by the study's results? What light did the study shed on the theoretical framework used? On social policy questions? (Chapters 10–12)

The article suggests additional questions for study about "the conditions under which [the dynamics of doing gender] operate" and how equity theory might be used to explain the division of labor in households (p. 344). The authors make a reasonable case for the value of their "gender perspective." Social policy questions are not addressed directly, but the article would be of great value to others concerned with social policy.

HOUSEWORK IN MARITAL AND NONMARITAL HOUSEHOLDS*

Scott J. South
State University of New York at Albany

Glenna Spitze
State University of New York at Albany

Although much recent research has explored the division of household labor between husbands and wives, few studies have examined housework patterns across marital statuses. This paper uses data from the National Survey of Families and Households to analyze differences in time spent on housework by men and women in six different living situations: never married and living with parents, never married and living independently, cohabiting, married, divorced, and widowed. In all situations, women spend more time than men doing housework, but the gender gap is widest among married persons. The time women spend doing housework is higher among cohabitants than among the never-married, is highest in marriage, and is lower among divorcees and widows. Men's housework time is very similar across both never-married living situations, in cohabitation, and in marriage. However, divorced and widowed men do substantially more housework than does any other group of men, and they are especially more likely than their married counterparts to spend more time cooking and cleaning. In addition to gender and marital status, housework time is affected significantly by several indicators of workload (e.g., number of children, home ownership) and time devoted to nonhousehold activities (e.g., paid employment, school enrollment)—most of these variables have greater effects on women's housework time than on men's. An adult son living at home increases women's housework, whereas an adult daughter at home reduces housework for women and men. These housework patterns are generally consistent with an emerging perspective that view's housework as a symbolic enactment of gender relations. We discuss the implications of these findings for perceptions of marital equity.

Until 20 years ago, social science research on housework was largely nonexistent (Glazer-Malbin 1976; Huber and Spitze 1983), but since then, research on the topic has exploded. Patterns of housework and how housework is experienced by participants have been documented in both qualitative (e.g., Hochschild with Machung 1989; Oakley 1974) and quantitative studies (e.g., Berk 1985; Blair and Lichter 1991; Coverman and Sheley 1986; Goldscheider and Waite 1991; Rexroat and Shehan 1987; Ross 1987; Shelton 1990; Spitze 1986; Walker and Woods 1976). The vast majority of these studies have focused on married couples, but a few have examined cohabiting couples as well (e.g., Blumstein and Schwartz 1983; Shelton and John 1993; Stafford, Backman, and Dibona 1977). The rationale for fo-

cusing on couples is typically a research interest in equity (Benin and Agostinelli 1988; Blair and Johnson 1992; Ferree 1990; Peterson and Maynard 1981; Thompson 1991) and in how changes in women's employment and gender roles have changed, or failed to change, household production functions.

Very few studies have examined housework as performed in noncouple households composed of never-married, separated or divorced, or widowed persons (e.g., Grief 1985; Sanik and Mauldin 1986). Such studies are important for two reasons. First, people are spending increasing amounts of time in such households at various points in their lives due to postponed marriages, higher divorce rates, and a preference among adults in all age categories (including the later years) for independent living. For example, the proportion of households that includes married couples decreased from 76.3 percent to 60.9 percent between 1940 and 1980 (Sweet and Bumpass 1987), and the number of years adult women spend married has decreased by about seven years during the past several decades (Watkins, Menken, and Bon-

*Direct all correspondence to Scott J. South or Glenna Spitze, Department of Sociology, State University of New York at Albany, Albany, NY 12222. The authors contributed equally to this research and are listed alphabetically. We acknowledge with gratitude the helpful comments of several anonymous *ASR* reviewers.

gaarts 1987). It is important to learn how housework is experienced by this substantial segment of the population to understand the household production function in general and because performance of housework is related to decisions about paid work and leisure time for people in these categories.

Second, the housework experiences of single, divorced, and widowed persons go with them if they move into marriage or cohabitation— these experiences are part of the context in which they negotiate how to accomplish tasks jointly with a partner. People may use those prior experiences or assumptions about what they *would* do if the marriage or cohabiting relationship dissolved to set an alternative standard when assessing an equitable division of household labor, rather than simply comparing their own investment in housework to their partner's. Thus, by understanding factors affecting housework contributions by men and women not living in couple relationships, we can better understand what happens when they do form those relationships.

Our broadest objective in this paper is to analyze how time spent doing housework by men and women varies by marital status and to interpret this analysis in relation to the "gender perspective" on household labor. Focusing on six situations defined by marital status and living arrangement, we seek to determine how men and women in these different situations compare in the amounts of time they spend doing housework, whether these differences can be attributed to differences in other social and economic characteristics, and which household tasks account for these differences. We are particularly interested in those persons who are living independently and who are not married or cohabiting, since previous research has focused heavily on married persons and, to a lesser extent, on cohabiting couples (Shelton and John 1993; Stafford et al. 1977) and children still living at home (Benin and Edwards 1990; Berk 1985; Blair 1991; Goldscheider and Waite 1991; Hilton and Haldeman 1991).

MODELS OF HOUSEHOLD LABOR

Beginning with Blood and Wolfe's (1960) classic study, sociologists have attempted to explain the division of household labor between husbands and wives and to determine whether the division is changing over time. The *re-source-power perspective* originating in that work focuses on the economic and social contexts in which husbands and wives bring their individual resources (such as unequal earnings) to bear in bargaining over who will do which household chores. This resource-power theory has since been modified and elaborated upon in several ways, focusing on determining which resources are important and the conditions under which they are useful for bargaining. Rodman's (1967) theory of resources in cultural context and Blumberg and Coleman's (1989) theory of gender stratification (as applied to housework) suggest that there are limits on how effectively resources can be used, especially by women. Several observers suggest that wives' resources may be "discounted" by male dominance at the societal level (Aytac and Teachman 1992; Blumberg and Coleman 1989; Ferree 1991b; Gillespie 1971).

Two other perspectives are used frequently in the study of household labor. One focuses on *socialization and gender role attitudes*, suggesting that husbands and wives perform household labor in differing amounts depending upon what they have learned and have come to believe about appropriate behavior for men and women (see Goldscheider and Waite 1991). An alternative perspective, the *time availability hypothesis*, suggests that husbands and wives perform housework in amounts relative to the time left over after paid work time is subtracted. A variation on this, the demand response capability hypothesis (Coverman 1985), is somewhat broader and includes factors that increase the total amount of work to be done and spouses' availability to do it. The focus on time allocation as a rational process is akin to the economic perspective, most closely associated with Becker (1981; see also critique in Berk 1985). However, sociologists and economists differ in their views on this perspective: Economists assume that time allocation to housework and paid work is jointly determined and based on the relative efficiency of husbands and wives in both arenas; sociologists assume that decisions about paid work are causally prior (Godwin 1991; Spitze 1986).

The above three perspectives (power-resources, socialization-gender roles, and time availability) have guided much of the sociological research on household labor over the past 20 years (see reviews of these theories and their variations in Ferree 1991a; Godwin 1991; Shelton 1992; Spitze 1988). However, they have produced mixed results, and, as several reviewers have pointed out, much more variance is explained by gender per se than by any of the other factors in these models (Ferree 1991a; Thompson and Walker 1991). Moreover, studies show that women who earn more than their husbands often do a disproportionate share of the housework, perhaps in an attempt to prevent those earnings from threatening the husband's self-esteem (Thompson and Walker 1991). While both husbands' and wives' time in paid employment does affect the time they spend doing housework (Goldscheider and Waite 1991), it is argued that the basic distribution of household labor calls for an explanation of its gendered, asymmetrical nature (Thompson and Walker 1991).

A new direction in the explanation of household labor originates in West and Zimmerman's (1987) concept of "doing gender." They argue that gender can be understood as "a routine accomplishment embedded in everyday interaction" (1987:125). Berk (1985) applied their perspective to the division of household labor, observing that the current situation among husbands and wives is neither inherently rational (as the New Home Economics had argued; see Becker 1981) nor fair. Thus, Berk concludes that more than goods and services are "produced" through household labor. She describes the marital household as a "gender factory" where, in addition to accomplishing tasks, housework "produces" gender through the everyday enactment of dominance, submission, and other behaviors symbolically linked to gender (Berk 1985; see also Hartmann 1981; Shelton and John 1993).

Ferree (1991a) elaborates on the "gender perspective" and its application to household labor and argues that it challenges three assumptions of resource theory. First, as Berk pointed out in her critique of economic analyses of housework, housework is not allocated in the most efficient manner. Second, gender is more influential than individual resources in determining the division of household labor. And third, housework is not necessarily defined as "bad" and to be avoided. On the contrary, in addition to expressing subordination, housework can also express love and care, particularly for women (Ferree 1991a). Relatedly, DeVault (1989) describes in detail how the activities surrounding the planning and prepara-

tion of meals are viewed not only as labor but also as an expression of love. In support of the general argument that housework has important symbolic meanings, Ferree (1991a) points out that "housework-like chores are imposed in other institutions to instill discipline" (p. 113), such as KP in the army.

The process of "doing gender" is not assumed to operate at a conscious level; on the contrary, Berk (1985) points out that it goes on "without much notice being taken" (p. 207). Ferree (1991a) finds it "striking how little explicit conflict there is over housework in many families" (p. 113). Hochschild's (with Machung 1989) pathbreaking study shows how gender ideologies are enacted through the performance of housework and may operate in a contradictory manner at conscious and unconscious levels. She discovers through in-depth case studies that people's ideas about gender are often "fractured and incoherent" (p. 190) and that contradictions abound between what people say they believe, what they seem to feel, and how these beliefs and feelings are reflected in their household behavior.

This developing "doing gender" approach suggests several important contrasts between couple households (especially those of married couples) and other household types. Indeed, one could argue that *only* by examining a range of household types, including those *not* formed by couples, can one determine the usefulness of this explanation for the behavior of married or cohabiting persons. If gender is being "produced," one would expect this process to be more important in heterosexual couple households than in other household types—there would be less need or opportunity for either men or women to display dominance and subordination or other gender-linked behaviors when they are not involved in conjugal relations. Berk (1985) argues that "in households where the appropriation of *another's* work is possible, in practice the expression of work and the expression of gender become inseparable" (p. 204). Of course, we recognize that gender role socialization is likely to produce gender differentials, even among unmarried persons. However, this *appropriation* seems likely to occur mainly, or perhaps only, in heterosexual couple households, particularly when the couples are married. Berk observes a sharp contrast in the housework patterns of married couples versus same-sex roommate arrangements, the latter seeming "so uncomplicated" to respondents (1985:204).

If heterosexual couples indeed produce gender through performing housework, we would expect women in married-couple households to spend more time doing housework than women in any other living situation; we would expect men's time spent doing housework to be lower in married-couple households than in other household types. These expectations are net of other differences between the household types, such as the presence of children, that affect housework. We would expect women to display submission to and/or love for their husbands or male partners by performing a disproportionate share of the housework, whereas men would display their gender/dominance by avoiding housework that they might perform in other household settings—in particular female-typed housework that constitutes the vast majority of weekly housework time in households. Because a woman cannot display love for or subordination to a man through housework when no man is present, this avenue for displaying gender does not exist in one-adult households. Thus, we would predict smaller gender differences in noncouple than couple household settings once other relevant factors are controlled.

An alternative empirical outcome—one that would cast doubt on the validity of the gender perspective—would be a pattern across household type involving a more or less constant gender difference. We know that there is a gender gap in time spent doing housework between married men and women and between teenage boys and girls. We do not know, however, whether that gap is constant across other situations. If, for example, gender differences in childhood training produce standards or skill levels that vary with gender, one might argue that men and women would carry these attitudes or behaviors with them as they move among different household situations.

HOUSEWORK AND MARITAL STATUS

Housework is a major component of most people's lives, just as is paid work. It is first experienced in childhood as "chores" and continues into retirement. Yet, while housework is performed prior to marriage and after its dissolution, most studies of household labor focus exclusively on husbands and wives. This tends

to create the false impression that housework occurs only within marital households.

Our analysis of housework is based on a categorization by marital status. We focus on men and women who have *never married*, or are currently *married, divorced*, or *widowed*. However, because a key aspect of our theoretical argument focuses on gender relations in heterosexual households, we add a "cohabiting" category, which includes persons who are currently cohabiting whether or not they have ever been married, divorced, or widowed. Further, the situation of never-married persons (who are not cohabiting) varies greatly depending upon whether they are *living independently* or *living in a parental household*; thus we divide never-married persons into two groups based on living situation. In the sections below, we review studies of housework performed by persons in each of these six categories.

Never-Married Persons Living in Their Parents' Homes

The performance of household chores is one of many gender-differentiated socialization experiences gained in families of origin. A number of studies have examined housework performed by boys and girls up to the age of 18 who are living with their parents. These studies have focused on three kinds of questions: how parents define the meaning of housework (White and Brinkerhoff 1981a), how children's contributions relate to or substitute for mothers' or fathers' work (Berk 1985; Goldscheider and Waite 1991), and how housework varies by the gender of the child, mother's employment, and number of parents in the household (e.g., Benin and Edwards 1990; Blair 1991; Hilton and Haldeman 1991).

Housework done by boys and by girls mirrors that of adults, with girls doing stereotypical "female" chores and spending more time doing housework than boys (Benin and Edwards 1990; Berk 1985; Blair 1991; Goldscheider and Waite 1991; Hilton and Haldeman 1991; Timmer, Eccles, and O'Brien 1985; White and Brinkerhoff 1981b). Patterns by gender and age suggest that, under certain conditions, children (particularly older girls) actually assist their parents. Gender differences increase with age, so that in the teenage years girls are spending about twice as much time per week as boys doing housework (Timmer et al.

1985), and the gender-stereotyping of tasks is at a peak. This pattern holds even in single-father families, where one might expect less traditional gender-typed behavior (Grief 1985). Adolescent girls' housework time has been shown to substitute for that of their mothers, while boys' housework time does not (Bergen 1991; Goldscheider and Waite 1991). Differences between single-parent and two-parent families also suggest more actual reliance on girls' work: Boys in single-parent households do less housework than do boys in two-parent households, while girls in single-parent households do more (Hilton and Haldeman 1991). Similar differences have been found between single- and dual-earner two-parent families. Again, girls do more when parents' time is constrained (dual earners) while boys do less, suggesting that parents actually rely on girls to substitute for their mothers' time doing housework (Benin and Edwards 1990).

One would expect parallel differences in the behavior of young adult men and women who still live with their parents. To our knowledge, only three studies have examined housework performed by adult children living in parental households. Ward, Logan, and Spitze (1992) find that adult children living with parents perform only a small proportion of total household tasks when compared to their parents, and parents whose adult children do not live at home actually perform fewer household tasks per month than do parents whose adult children live with them. There are also major differences between adult sons and adult daughters in the amount of housework they do, with daughters performing more tasks than sons when they live in a parent's home. This holds for all parent age groups, particularly those under 65. These gender differences are consistent with results on adult children's share of household tasks reported by Goldscheider and Waite (1991). Hartung and Moore (1992) report qualitative findings that are consistent with the conclusion that adult children, especially sons, contribute little to household chores and typically add to their mothers' burdens.

Never-Married Persons Living Independently

We know of no empirical research that focuses specifically on never-married persons living independently, so we will speculate briefly about

factors affecting them. One likely consequence of experiences with housework in the parental home is that girls acquire the skills required for independent living, including shopping, cooking, cleaning, and laundry. To the extent that they have already been doing significant amounts of housework at home, girls' transitions to independent living may not create a major change in the amount or types of housework they perform. The skills boys are more likely to learn in the parental home (e.g., yard work) may be less useful, particularly if their first independent living experience is in an apartment. They may reach adulthood enjoying housework less than women, feeling less competent at household tasks, holding lower standards of performance, embracing gender-stereotyped attitudes about appropriateness of tasks, and preferring to pay for substitutes (e.g., laundry, meals eaten out). On the other hand, single men living independently (and not cohabiting) are forced, to a certain extent, to do their own housework (Goldscheider and Waite 1991), because their living situations are unlikely to provide household services. Thus, the time spent by single men doing housework should increase when they move out of parental households.

Cohabiters

Cohabiting couples share some characteristics of both married and single persons (Shelton and John 1993; Stafford et al. 1977). As Rindfuss and VandenHeuvel (1992) point out, most discussions have used married persons as the comparison group, viewing cohabitation as an alternative kind of marriage or engagement. The division of household labor between cohabiters may be closer to that of married persons, but in other areas such as fertility plans, employment, school enrollment, and home ownership, cohabiters more closely resemble single persons (Rindfuss and VandenHeuvel 1992). Thus, we would expect cohabiters to fall at an intermediate position, between never-married living independently and married persons, in the allocation of time to housework.

A few empirical studies have examined housework by heterosexual cohabiting couples. One early study (Stafford et al. 1977) uses a relative contribution measure of housework and finds cohabiting couples to be fairly "traditional" in their division of household labor. A more recent study using an absolute measure of time expenditure in housework (Shelton and John 1993) sheds more light on the comparison between cohabiting and married couples. Adjusted means of time spent doing housework for cohabiting men are not significantly different from those for married men, but cohabiting women do less housework than do married women. These results are consistent with Blumstein and Schwartz's (1983) comparisons of married and cohabiting men and women. Blair and Lichter (1991) find no significant differences between married and cohabiting men's housework time, but find less task segregation by gender among cohabitants. As is true of comparisons on other dimensions (Rindfuss and VandenHeuvel 1992), studies of housework among cohabiting couples have used married persons as the comparison group, and there have been few comparisons of housework patterns in cohabiting relationships to patterns in other marital statuses.

Married Persons

Marriage often entails a number of changes that increase housework, including parenthood and home ownership, but it also might increase housework for less tangible reasons. Marriage and parenthood entail responsibility for the well-being of others, which is likely to be reflected in higher standards of cleanliness and nutrition, and thus require that more time be devoted to housework. However, the net result of this increase in total work is different for men and for women, and this gender division of household labor has been the subject of much research and theorizing in recent years. Averages tend to range widely depending on the definitions of housework used, but women generally report performing over 70 percent of total housework, even if they are employed (Bergen 1991; Ferree 1991a). One recent study reported married women (including nonemployed) doing 40 hours of housework per week and men 19 hours (Shelton and John 1993), and countless studies have documented that wives' employment has little effect on married men's housework load (see reviews in Spitze 1988; Thompson and Walker 1991). Clearly, wives are responsible for the vast bulk of household chores and for maintaining standards of cleanliness and health in the family. Married men have been described as doing less

housework than they create (Hartmann 1981). Further, when they do contribute to household chores, men are more likely to take on those jobs which are more pleasant, leaving women with those than can be described as "unrelenting, repetitive, and routine" (Thompson and Walker 1991:86). Thus, past empirical results for married persons are consistent with the gender perspective, but comparative analyses that include persons in other marital statuses are needed.

Divorced Persons

To our knowledge there have been no studies of the time divorced persons spend doing housework except those studies focusing on children's housework. Divorced persons (who are not cohabiting) have had the prior experience of living with a heterosexual partner. Women may experience a decrease in housework hours if in fact their partner was creating more housework than he was doing. Men's experience, on the other hand, may be similar to that of moving out of the parental household, that is, of having to do some household tasks for themselves that were previously performed by others. Those who never lived independently before may have to do some of these chores for the first time. Gove and Shin (1989) point out that both divorced and widowed men have more difficulty carrying out their daily household routines than do their female counterparts, who are more likely to experience economic strains.

Widowed Persons

In empirical studies, housework has been identified as an important source of strain for widowed men. Widowed men reduce the time they spend doing housework as the years since widowhood pass, and they are more likely than widows to have help doing it as time goes on (Umberson, Wortman, and Kessler 1992). Of course, today's widows and widowers came of age when the gendered division of labor in households was much more segregated than it is today and when living independently before or between marriages was much less common. While we expect widowed men today to have entered widowhood with relatively little experience in certain kinds of household chores, this may not be true in the future.

Widowed women may share some characteristics with divorced women; they may actually feel some relief from the strain of doing the bulk of household tasks for two (Umberson et al. 1992). Like widowed men, however, current cohorts of widowed women may have little experience in certain kinds of chores, in this case traditionally male chores such as yard work, car care, or financial management.

Other Factors Influencing Time Doing Housework

Men and women in different marital statuses are likely to differ on a variety of factors that can influence the performance of housework, such as their health, employment status, presence of children and other adults, and home ownership. We would expect the performance of housework to vary by marital status both because of these factors and because of the ways in which the marital status itself (or experience in a previous status) influences housework behavior. Here, we describe a model of time spent in housework that can be applied to persons in all marital situations. This model will then guide us in choosing control variables for the analysis of housework.

A person is expected to spend more time in housework as the *total amount to be done* increases. (Berk [1985] calls this the total "pie" in her study of married couple households.) We would expect the amount of housework to increase as the number of children increases, particularly when children are young, but to some extent for older children as well (Bergen 1991; Berk 1985; Ishii-Kuntz and Coltrane 1992; Rexroat and Shehan 1987). The amount of work will also increase with the addition of adults to the household, although of course they may perform housework as well. Work may also increase with the size of house and the responsibilities that go with home ownership, car ownership, and presence of a yard (Bergen 1991; Berk 1985).[1]

Note that the total housework to be done is to some extent a subjective concept. Two households with the same composition and type of home may accomplish different amounts of housework for several reasons. The standards held by the adults in the household will vary (Berk 1985) and may even vary systematically along dimensions such as education and age. Also, some households purchase more services than others, due to available income (Bergen 1991) and time constraints.

A second factor influencing the amount of housework a person does is the number of *other people* there are in the household with whom to share the work. Other people are most helpful if they are adults, and women are likely to contribute more than men. Teenagers and even grade-school-age children may be helpful, and their contribution may also vary by gender. The way that household labor is divided, and thus the amount performed by a particular man or woman, may also relate to gender-role attitudes that may vary with education, age, race, and other factors.

Third, persons with more *time and energy* will do more housework. Available time would be limited by hours spent in paid work, school enrollment status, health and disability status, and age (Coltrane and Ishii-Kuntz 1992; Ishii-Kuntz and Coltrane 1992; Rexroat and Shehan 1987). Concurrent roles, in addition to that of homemaker, detract from the time available to be devoted to housework.

DATA AND METHODS

Data for this study are drawn from the National Survey of Families and Households (NSFH), a national probability sample of 13,017 adults interviewed between March of 1987 and May of 1988 (Sweet, Bumpass, and Call 1988). The NSFH includes a wide variety of questions on sociodemographic background, household composition, labor force behavior, and marital and cohabitation experiences, as well as items describing respondents' allocation of time to household tasks. The NSFH oversamples single-parent families and cohabiters (as well as minorities and recently married persons), thus facilitating comparisons of household labor among persons in different—and relatively rare—household situations. Sample weights are used throughout the

---

[1] While owning appliances would be expected to decrease time spent doing housework, it has had much less clear-cut effects than expected, both over time and in cross-sectional studies (Gershuny and Robinson 1988).

334   AMERICAN SOCIOLOGICAL REVIEW

analysis to achieve the proper representation of respondents in the U.S. population.

The dependent variable, hours devoted to housework in the typical week, is derived from a series of questions asking respondents how many hours household members spend on various tasks. Respondents were provided with a chart and instructed: "Write in the approximate number of hours per week that you, your spouse/partner, or others in the household normally spend doing the following things." Nine household tasks include "preparing meals," "washing dishes and cleaning up after meals," "cleaning house," "outdoor and other household maintenance tasks (lawn and yard work, household repair, painting, etc.)," "shopping for groceries and other household goods," "washing, ironing, mending," "paying bills and keeping financial records," "automobile maintenance and repair," and "driving other household members to work, school, or other activities." This analysis uses only the number of hours that the respondents report *themselves* as spending on these tasks. To construct the dependent variable, we sum the number of hours spent on each of the nine tasks.[2]

We make two adjustments to this dependent variable. First, because a few respondents reported spending inordinate numbers of hours on specific tasks, we recode values above the 95th percentile for each task to the value at that percentile. This adjustment reduces skewness in the individual items and therefore in the summed variable as well. Second, so we can include respondents who omit one or two of the nine questionnaire items, we impute values for the household tasks for these respondents.[3] In-

dividuals who failed to respond to more than two of the questions are excluded from the analysis. Omitting these respondents and excluding cases with missing values on the independent variables leaves 11,016 respondents available for analysis.

Given our focus on differences in housework between unmarried and married persons, it is essential that the dependent variable records the absolute number of hours devoted to housework rather than the proportional distribution of hours (or tasks) performed by various household members (e.g., Waite and Goldscheider 1992; Spitze 1986). Of course, estimates of time spent on household tasks made by respondents (as recorded in the NSFH) are likely to be less accurate than estimates from time diaries (for a review of validity studies dealing with time use, see Gershuny and Robinson 1988). Yet, estimates of the relative contribution of wives and husbands to household labor are generally comparable across different reporting methods (Warner 1986). Moreover, the effects of respondent characteristics on the time spent on housework shown here are quite similar to the effects observed in time diary studies. The size of the NSFH (approximately five times larger than the typical time-use survey), its oversampling of atypical marital statuses, and its breadth of coverage of respondent characteristics adequately compensate for the lack of time-diary data.

The key explanatory variable combines respondents' marital status' with aspects of their

---

[2] The research literature on housework is inconsistent regarding the inclusion of time spent in childcare. Many data sets commonly used to analyze household labor do not include childcare in their measure (e.g., Bergen 1991; Rexroat and Shehan 1987) or, as is the case here, childcare time is not included as a separate task (Coltrane and Ishii-Kuntz 1992), in part because respondents have difficulty separating time spent in childcare from leisure and from time spent in other tasks. Thus, we are not able to include childcare in our measure. This probably creates a downward bias in estimates of household labor time.

[3] The NSFH assigns four different codes to the household task items for respondents who did not give a numerical reply: some unspecified amount of time spent; inapplicable; don't know; and no answer. Our imputation procedure substitutes a value of 0 for

those who did not answer this question (but answered at least seven of the nine items) or who said the task was inapplicable. In the former case, skipping the item most likely indicates that the respondent spent no time on that task; in the latter case, the respondent most likely could not logically spend time on that task (e.g., persons without cars could not spend any time maintaining them). For respondents who indicated spending some unspecified amount of time on a task and for those who indicated they didn't know, our imputation procedure substitutes the mean value for that task. In both of these instances, respondents presumably spent at least some time on that task. Our explorations of alternative ways of handling missing data, including omitting respondents who failed to answer one or more of the questions, treating all nonnumerical responses as 0, and substituting all nonnumerical responses with the mean, showed quite clearly that our substantive conclusions are unaffected by the method used to handle missing data.

living arrangements. (For stylistic convenience, we refer to this variable simply as marital status.) We distinguish six mutually exclusive statuses: never married and living in the parental household, never married (not cohabiting) and living independently, cohabiting, currently married, divorced or separated (not cohabiting), and widowed (not cohabiting). Because we are interested in the impact of a spouse or partner on respondents' time doing housework, cohabiters include divorced, separated, and widowed cohabiters as well as never-married cohabiters.

The other explanatory variables measure respondents' demographic background, socioeconomic standing, household composition, concurrent roles, and disability status. As suggested above, several of these factors may help explain any differences that we observe in housework time by marital status and gender. *Age* is measured in years. Because housework demands are likely to peak during the middle adult years and to moderate at older ages, we also include *age squared* as an independent variable. *Education* is measured by years of school completed. *Household earnings* refers to the wage, salary, and self-employment income of all members of the household.[4] *Home ownership* is a dummy variable scored 1 for respondents who own their own home and 0 for those who do not.

Several variables reflect the presence in the household of persons who may create or perform housework. *Children* in the household are

divided into the number of children younger than 5 years old, the number age 5 through 11, and the number age 12 through 18. Among the latter group, girls might be expected to create less (or perform more) housework than boys (Goldscheider and Waite 1991), and thus we include separate counts of male and female teenagers. We use several dummy variables to indicate the presence in the household of an *adult male* or *adult female* other than the respondent's spouse or cohabiting partner. Adult females are expected to reduce respondent's time devoted to housework, while adult males are expected to increase it. We further distinguish between adult household members who are the children of the respondent and those who are not.

Respondents who invest their time in activities outside the home are anticipated to devote less time to domestic labor. Employment status is measured by the usual number of *hours worked per week* in the labor force. And, whether the respondent is currently *attending school* is indicated by a dummy variable scored 1 for currently enrolled respondents and 0 for those not attending school.

Finally, *disability status* is measured by the response to the question, do you "have a physical or mental condition that limits your ability to do day-to-day household tasks?" Individuals reporting such a condition are scored 1 on this dummy variable; unimpaired respondents are scored 0.[5]

Our primary analytic strategy is to estimate OLS regression equations that examine the impact of gender, marital status, and the other explanatory variables on the time spent doing housework. Of particular importance for our theoretical model is whether marital status differences in housework time vary by gender—that is, do gender and marital status interact in affecting time spent doing housework? The "gender perspective" implies that marital status differences in housework will be more pronounced for women than for men and that the gender differences in housework will be greatest for married persons. The regression models are also used to determine the extent to which marital status differences in time doing

---

[4] So as not to lose an inordinate number of cases to missing data, we substituted the mean for missing values on household earnings, and we included a dummy variable for these respondents in the regression models (coefficients not shown). One potential difficulty with this procedure is that all respondents who were not the householder or the spouse of the householder receive the mean value, because respondents were not asked the earnings of other household members. Equations estimated only with respondents who are householders revealed effects almost identical to those reported in the text, although never-married respondents living in the parental household are necessarily excluded from these equations. Given that households with adult children include more adults than other households, the household earnings of these latter respondents are likely to be higher than average, but any bias in the effect of earnings is apt to be slight. With one exception (see footnote 5), the amount of missing data on the other explanatory variables is small.

[5] To retain the 5 percent of respondents who did not reply to the question on disability status, the regression equations also include a dummy variable for these respondents (coefficients not shown).

336   AMERICAN SOCIOLOGICAL REVIEW

Table 1. Descriptive Statistics for Hours Spent in Housework per Week and for Explanatory Variables, by Gender: U.S. Men and Women, 1987 to 1988

Variable	Women		Men	
	Mean	Standard Deviation	Mean	Standard Deviation
Housework hours per week	32.62	18.18	18.14	12.88
Marital Status[a]				
Never married/living in parental home	.06	.23	.11	.32
Never married/living independently	.10	.30	.11	.32
Cohabiting	.04	.19	.04	.20
Married	.57	.50	.63	.48
Divorced/separated	.12	.33	.08	.26
Widowed	.12	.33	.03	.17
Number of children ages 0 to 4	.26	.59	.22	.55
Number of children ages 5 to 11	.33	.70	.29	.66
Number of girls ages 12 to 18	.16	.44	.15	.43
Number of boys ages 12 to 18	.17	.45	.15	.43
Adult male child present (0 = no; 1 = yes)	.10	.29	.07	.25
Adult male nonchild present (0 = no; 1 = yes)	.09	.29	.18	.38
Adult female child present (0 = no; 1 = yes)	.08	.27	.05	.22
Adult female nonchild present (0 = no; 1 = yes)	.14	.35	.17	.38
Home ownership (0 = no; 1 = yes)	.59	.49	.58	.49
Household earnings (in $1,000s)	28.72	37.69	31.64	36.51
Education	12.45	2.93	12.94	3.32
Age	44.30	17.99	42.24	17.07
Age squared (/100)	22.86	17.81	20.75	16.38
Hours employed per week	18.43	20.01	31.81	22.55
School enrollment (0 = no; 1 = yes)	.06	.24	.07	.26
Disabled (0 = no; 1 = yes)	.06	.24	.05	.22
Number of cases	6,764		4,252	

[a] May not add to 1.00 because of rounding.

housework can be explained by other respondent characteristics and to assess whether the gender-specific impact of the explanatory variables holds for the general population (including unmarried people) in ways previously shown for married persons.

RESULTS

Table 1 presents descriptive statistics for all variables in the analysis. Immediately apparent is the sharp but unsurprising difference between men and women in the amount of time spent doing housework. In this sample, women report spending almost 33 hours per week on household tasks, while men report spending slightly more than 18 hours. Both figures are roughly comparable to the findings of prior studies, although of course those studies did not include unmarried persons.

Gender differences in current marital status are relatively slight. Men are somewhat more likely than women to have never married, reflecting longstanding differences in age at marriage. And, among the never married, men are more likely than women to reside in the parental household. Women are more likely than men to be currently divorced or widowed, a probable consequence of their lower remarriage rates following divorce and men's higher mortality. Four percent of both sexes are co-habiters.

Differences between women and men on the other explanatory variables are also generally small. The sole exception is the number of hours worked outside the home, with women averaging approximately 18 hours per week and men 32 hours.

The regression analysis of time spent on housework is shown in Table 2. In our initial equations (not shown here), we pooled the male and female respondents and regressed housework hours on the explanatory variables, including dummy variables for gender and marital status. We then added to this equation product terms representing the interaction of gender and marital status. As predicted by the theoretical model, allowing marital status and gender to interact in their effects on housework significantly increases the variance explained $(F = 67.06; p < .001)$. And specifically, the difference in housework hours between married women and married men is significantly larger than the housework hours differences between women and men in each of the other marital statuses. Product terms representing the interaction of gender with the other explanatory variables also revealed that several of the effects varied significantly by gender; thus, we estimate and present the equations separately for women and for men.[6]

The first equation in Table 2 is based only on the women respondents and regresses weekly housework hours on dummy variables representing five of the six marital statuses, with married respondents serving as the reference category. Persons in all five marital statuses work significantly fewer hours around the house than do the married respondents; at the extreme, married women spend over 17 hours more per week on housework than do never-married women who reside in the parental household. As anticipated, the amount of time spent on housework by women who are never

---

[6] The distribution of some of the factors that explain variation in housework hours differs by age group. For example, enrollment in school and the presence of children in the household are most prevalent for younger respondents, while disability and widowhood are more common among the aged. Yet, the correlation matrices showed little evidence of multicollinearity, and disaggregating the equations by age revealed patterns and determinants quite similar to those for the sample as a whole.

married and living independently, cohabiting, divorced (including separated), or widowed falls between that of women who have not married (and remain in the parental home) and those who have married.

The third column of Table 2 presents the parallel equation for men. As reflected in the constant term, married men report spending almost 18 hours per week in housework, compared to almost 37 hours for their female counterparts (the constant term in column 1). More importantly, marital status differences in housework hours among men are relatively small compared to the analogous differences among women. Married men do significantly more housework than never-married men who still live with their parents and significantly less than divorced and widowed men, but most of these differences are modest. Moreover, the pattern of time spent doing housework across marital statuses differs substantially between men and women; it is greatest for men during widowhood and greatest for women during marriage.

Equation 2 in Table 2 re-estimates marital status differences in housework hours for men and women, controlling for the other explanatory variables. As shown in column 2, differences among women in these additional variables account for some, though by no means all, of the marital status differences in housework. Controlling for these variables reduces the differences between married women and other women by between 17 percent (for widows) and 66 percent (for cohabiters). Further, the difference between married women and cohabiting women is no longer statistically significant once these variables are controlled. Thus, among women a moderate proportion of the marital status differences in time spent doing housework is attributable to compositional differences. Particularly important in accounting for these marital status differences in housework hours are the number of hours the respondent works outside the home and the presence of children in the household; both variables vary significantly by marital status and are at least moderately related to time spent doing housework. We discuss these and the other effects of the explanatory variables in detail below.

For men, in contrast, controlling for the other explanatory variables does somewhat less to explain marital status differences in house-

338   AMERICAN SOCIOLOGICAL REVIEW

Table 2. OLS Coefficients for Regression of Hours Spent in Housework per Week on Marital Status and Other Explanatory
Variables, by Gender: U.S. Men and Women, 1987 to 1988

Independent Variable	Women		Men	
	(1)	(2)	(1)	(2)
Marital Status				
Never married/living in parental home	−17.41***†	−9.73***†	−2.90***†	−.52†
	(.93)	(1.34)	(.63)	(1.18)
Never married/living independently	−11.62***†	−6.45***†	1.09†	1.43†
	(.74)	(.84)	(.63)	(.80)
Cohabitating	−5.54***†	−1.86†	1.34†	1.73†
	(1.14)	(1.14)	(.98)	(1.03)
Married	Reference		Reference	
Divorced/separated	−5.30***†	−3.68***†	3.73***†	4.58***†
	(.66)	(.68)	(.75)	(.80)
Widowed	−9.08***†	−7.51***†	5.66***†	6.97***†
	(.67)	(.77)	(1.16)	(1.21)
Number of children ages 0 to 4	—	3.63***†	—	.67†
		(.38)		(.39)
Number of children ages 5 to 11	—	3.77***†	—	.85***†
		(.31)		(.32)
Number of girls ages 12 to 18	—	1.62***†	—	−.64†
		(.46)		(.46)
Number of boys ages 12 to 18	—	1.88**	—	.74
		(.47)		(.47)
Adult male child parent (0 = no; 1 = yes)	—	1.79*	—	.91
		(.74)		(.82)
Adult male nonchild present (0 = no; 1 = yes)	—	−.10	—	−.37
		(.97)		(.72)
Adult female child present (0 = no; 1 = yes)	—	−2.46**	—	−2.93**
		(.80)		(.92)
Adult female nonchild present (0 = no; 1 = yes)	—	−1.18	—	−1.40
		(.85)		(.84)
Home ownership (0 = no; 1 = yes)	—	2.24**	—	−1.22*
		(.52)		(.52)
Household earnings (in $1,000s)	—	−.03***†	—	−.02***†
		(.01)		(.01)
Education	—	−.44***†	—	.14**†
		(.08)		(.06)
Age	—	.40***†	—	.05†
		(.08)		(.08)
Age squared (/100)	—	−.44***†	—	−.15†
		(.08)		(.08)
Hours employed per week	—	−.17***†	—	−.08***†
		(.01)		(.01)
School enrollment (0 = no; 1 = yes)	—	−4.07**	—	−2.48**
		(.91)		(.82)
Disabled (0 = no; 1 = yes)	—	−5.34**	—	−2.96**
		(.86)		(.94)
Constant	36.67**	34.26**	17.83**	19.87**
	(.28)	(2.07)	(.25)	(2.08)
Root mean squared error	17.39	16.37	12.76	12.57
R^2	.08	.19	.02	.05
Number of cases	6,764	6,764	4,252	4,252

*$p < .05$ **$p < .01$ (two-tailed tests)

Note: Numbers in parentheses are standard errors. Equations in columns 2 and 4 include dummy variables for missing values
on household earnings and disabled.

†Difference in coefficients for women and men is statistically significant at $p < .05$.

work. Although the difference between never-married men living in the parental home and married men becomes statistically nonsignificant when these variables are controlled, the absolute size of the decline (about 2.5 hours per week) is small. More important, with these controls the initially larger differences between married men and both divorced and widowed men actually increase.

Most of the explanatory variables have significant effects on time spent doing housework for either the men *or* the women, and many have significant effects for both sexes. Several variables have stronger effects among one sex than the other. The presence of children in the household creates more housework, especially for women, with pre-teenagers creating slightly more work than older children. The impact of children on housework hours tends to be significantly stronger for women than for men, a finding also found in studies limited to married couples (Bergen 1991; Rexroat and Shehan 1987). The presence in the household of the respondent's adult children also significantly affects housework hours, but the direction of the effect depends on both the sex of the adult children and the respondent. For female respondents, the presence of an adult male child increases housework hours, while for both female and male respondents the presence of an adult female child significantly reduces time allocated to housework. These findings are consistent with the view that men create housework, while women perform work men would otherwise do themselves (Hartmann 1981). Adults who are *not* children of the respondent do not add or subtract significantly, on average, from the respondent's housework time. This may be because the household is a heterogeneous group, including some roommates, siblings and other relatives, and elderly parents. Some household members may be helpful and others may be a burden, and their effects may cancel out.[7]

As expected, home ownership significantly increases housework time, and it appears to do so about equally for men and women. This may

be due to larger amounts of living space to be cleaned and to the increase in yard work and maintenance and repair chores among home-owners. Total household earnings reduce housework significantly more for women than for men, suggesting that purchased household services substitute more for women's than for men's domestic labor.[8] Among women, education is inversely associated with housework, while for men the association is positive and significant. Educated women and men tend to hold egalitarian attitudes, which may lead to greater symmetry in their housework patterns (Huber and Spitze 1983). The hypothesized curvilinear (bell-shaped) association between age and housework emerges for women, but not for men.

As indicated by the significant effects of employment and school enrollment on time spent doing housework, investing time in nonhousehold activities significantly reduces household labor. The impact of hours employed is significantly greater for women than for men, a finding consistent with prior research (Gershuny and Robinson 1988; Rexroat and Shehan 1987). This suggests that women have less discretionary time than men, so that increased expenditures of time outside the home must necessarily divert time away from housework.[9]

---

[7] While it is possible to separate persons in heterogeneous households into a number of categories and attempt to sort out those who tend to help and those who create more work, the small number of respondents with *any* other adult present suggests that this would not be a useful refinement to the analysis.

---

[8] The gender difference in the effect of household earnings on housework is complicated by the fact that, for couple households, wife's (or female cohabiting partner's) hours employed per week is controlled for in the women's equation, but not in the men's equation. If hours employed are deleted from both equations, the gender difference in the effect of household earnings becomes statistically nonsignificant. Hence, this difference, which is barely significant to begin with, should be interpreted cautiously.

[9] From the perspective of the New Home Economics, the amount of time allocated to housework and to paid labor are frequently considered to be jointly determined, and thus the inclusion of employment hours as a predictor of housework has been questioned (Godwin 1991). We believe that for most persons, and particularly persons in nonmarital households, decisions regarding the allocation of time to the paid labor force are made prior to decisions about housework time (especially given that our measure of housework excludes childcare), and thus that the treatment of paid employment as an explanatory variable is justified. In any event, omitting respondent's hours employed per week from the equations does not

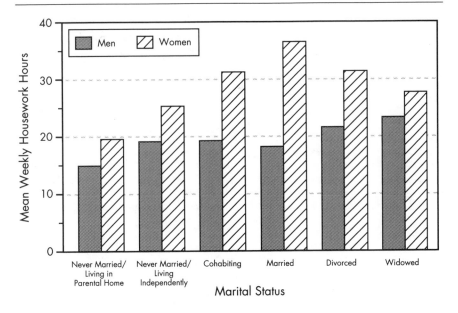

Figure 1. Mean Hours Spent Doing Housework Each Week, by Gender and Marital Status

Because the combined effects of gender and marital status are moderately complex, we present Figure 1 to help clarify the nature of their interaction. This figure graphs the (unadjusted) mean housework hours for men and women along the most common temporal sequence of marital statuses. In all marital statuses, women spend more hours than men on housework. The gender gap among never-married men and women living in the parental home is about 4 hours. Both never-married women and men who live independently do more housework than their counterparts who remain at home, but because the increase is slightly greater for women than for men (almost a 6-hour increase for women versus 4 hours for men), the gender difference in housework in this group grows to a little over 6 hours. Presumably, both men and women who live independently perform household tasks that previously had been done for them by their parents when the respondents resided in the parental homes.

The gender difference in housework hours widens dramatically as one moves to the couple households—cohabiters and married persons. Cohabiting women do more housework than never-married women (regardless of the latter's living arrangements), while cohabiting men work about the same hours around the house as never-married men living independently. The result of these discrepant trajectories is that the gender difference among cohabiters increases to approximately 12 hours per week. The gender gap in housework hours reaches its zenith among married women and men, at approximately 19 hours per week. This disparity is primarily a consequence of married women doing substantially more housework than never-married and cohabiting women, although these differences diminish with controls, as shown in Table 2. Rather than simply maintaining a behavioral pattern established prior to forming a conjugal union, married and, to a lesser extent, cohabiting women appear to increase substantially the time they devote to housework. In contrast, the amount of housework done by married men is fairly similar to that done by never-married and cohabiting men. Hence, as the "gender perspective" would suggest, it is in marital and cohabiting

_____

appreciably alter the effects of marital status and gender that are the crux of our analysis, nor does the omission modify the impact of the other explanatory variables.

HOUSEWORK IN MARITAL AND NONMARITAL HOUSEHOLDS   341

Table 3. Mean Hours Spent per Week in Various Household Tasks, by Marital Status and Gender: U.S. Men and Women, 1987 to 1988

Household Task[b]	Marital Status[a]					
	Never Married/ Living in Parental Home	Never Married/ Living Independently	Cohabiting	Married	Divorced	Widowed
Women						
Preparing meals	3.64	6.74	7.99	10.14	8.15	7.96
Washing dishes	3.92	4.38	5.51	6.11	5.14	4.73
Cleaning house	3.95	5.16	7.10	8.31	6.68	5.68
Washing/ironing	2.45	2.63	3.44	4.16	3.37	2.50
Outdoor maintenance	1.39	1.24	1.34	2.06	1.94	2.26
Shopping	1.72	2.28	2.69	2.86	2.67	2.40[ns]
Paying bills	.81[ns]	1.53	1.66	1.52	1.70	1.48[ns]
Car maintenance	.48	.42	.28	.16	.40	.20
Driving	.90[ns]	.65	1.10[ns]	1.34	1.30	.38[ns]
Total housework hours	19.26	25.04	31.12	36.67	31.37	27.59
Number of cases	383	649	248	3,838	829	817
Men						
Preparing meals	2.23	5.06	3.71	2.69	5.50	6.48
Washing dishes	1.92	2.77	2.63	2.15	3.24	3.87
Cleaning house	2.20	2.97	2.60	2.03	3.54	3.38
Washing/ironing	1.30	1.92	1.16	.70	1.75	1.67
Outdoor maintenance	3.56	1.56	3.18	4.94	2.60	3.38
Shopping	.83	1.92	1.73	1.58	1.93	2.14[ns]
Paying bills	.90[ns]	1.38	1.35	1.32	1.45	1.65[ns]
Car maintenance	1.23	.92	1.51	1.37	.99	.52
Driving	.75[ns]	.42	1.28[ns]	1.04	.57	.41[ns]
Total housework hours	14.93	18.92	19.16	17.83	21.56	23.49
Number of cases	477	476	181	2,668	323	127

[a]All associations between marital status and time spent on household tasks are significant at the $p < .05$ level.

[b]Within marital status and task type, all gender differences are significant at the $p < .05$ level with the following exceptions (marked ns): for never married in parental home—paying bills and driving; for cohabitors—driving; for widows—shopping, paying bills, and driving.

unions that gender differences in housework are most evident.

Among the formerly married, hours spent on housework by men and women begin to converge. Relative to their married counterparts, women who are divorced or widowed do less housework, while divorced or widowed men do more, with or without controlling for other variables. For women, this difference is perhaps best explained by a reduction in the total amount of housework required brought about by the absence of a husband in the household. For men, divorce and widowhood means doing household tasks previously done by a wife.

In general, then, patterns of time spent in housework across different marital statuses appear at least broadly consistent with the emerging "gender perspective." While there is a gender gap in housework in all marital statuses, this disparity varies dramatically and, as predicted, is widest for men and women in couple households (i.e., married or cohabiting relationships). However, to determine the extent to which these totals reflect behavior that becomes more gender-differentiated in couple households, we examine marital status differences in the completion of particular household tasks.

AMERICAN SOCIOLOGICAL REVIEW

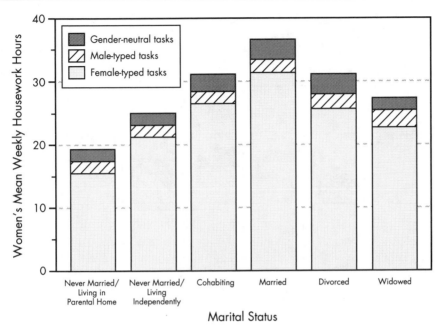

Figure 2. Mean Hours Spent by Women Doing Housework each Week, by Sex Type of Task and Marital Status

Accordingly, Table 3 presents the mean hours spent per week in each of the individual nine household tasks, disaggregated by gender and marital status. Figures 2 and 3 summarize the information in Table 3, graphing for women and men the (unadjusted) amounts of time spent in "female-typed" tasks (preparing meals, washing dishes, cleaning house, washing and ironing, and shopping), "male-typed" tasks (outdoor chores and automobile maintenance), and "gender-neutral" tasks (paying bills and driving other household members).[10] Among women, the marital status differences in *total* housework hours shown in Figure 1 are replicated for the female-typed tasks, which constitute in each marital status category the vast bulk of housework hours (see Figure 2). Of the female-typed tasks, the largest differences are in the number of hours spent preparing meals and cleaning house, although all five tasks consume more time for married women than for any of the other groups (Table 3). Because in each marital status the amount of time allocated to male-typed tasks is small, *differences* by marital status in these tasks are also slight. Married women do less car maintenance than do other women, but, with the exception of widows, spend slightly more time on outdoor maintenance. For women, then, marital status differences in total housework hours are largely a consequence of differences in hours spent on female-typed tasks.

Among men, however, marital status differences in gender-specific tasks do not always reflect those for housework as a whole. For example, as shown in Figure 3, although the difference in *total* housework hours between never-married men living independently and married men is small (about 1 hour), the difference is composed of several counterbalancing components. Never-married men living independently spend over 5 hours more per week than married men on female-typed tasks, but offset most of this difference by spending less time on male-typed tasks. Similarly, never-married men living independently spend al-

---

[10] This categorization is consistent with other analyses, including those by Ferree (1991b) and Aytac and Teachman (1992). Shelton (1992) shows shopping to be somewhat intermediate between female- and neutral-typed tasks, and others (e.g., Presser 1993) have treated it as a gender-neutral task.

HOUSEWORK IN MARITAL AND NONMARITAL HOUSEHOLDS   343

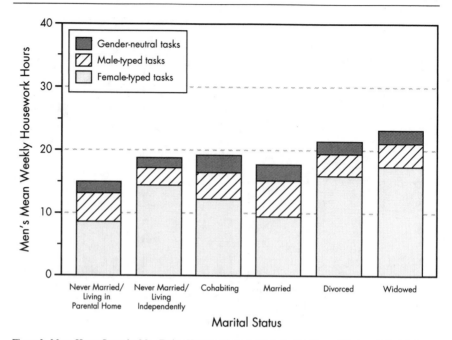

Figure 3. Mean Hours Spent by Men Doing Housework Each Week, by Sex Type of Task and Marital Status

most 3 hours per week more than cohabiting men in female-typed chores, but cohabiting men more than compensate for this difference by spending more time doing male-typed and gender-neutral tasks. Hence, to the extent that cohabiting men differ from never-married men living independently, they do so not by greater participation in female-typed chores, but by increasing their time doing stereotypically male tasks (e.g., automobile maintenance and outdoor chores) and gender-neutral tasks (e.g., driving other household members). On a smaller scale, the difference between cohabiting men and married men in total housework (about 1.3 hours per week) masks an important difference: Cohabiting men spend over 2.5 more hours per week than do married men on traditionally female chores, but married men make up over half of this difference by spending more time on outdoor maintenance. Like never-married men living independently, cohabiting men do more female-typed tasks than do married men, although they do not work on outdoor maintenance tasks to the same degree as their married counterparts.

The difference in total housework hours between married men and divorced men and be-

tween married men and widowed men is also composed of counterbalancing chores. Divorced and widowed men spend 6 to 8 hours more per week than married men on female-typed tasks, but the greater time expenditures by married men on outdoor and automobile maintenance partially offset this difference. In general, the distribution of housework hours by the sex-type of task appears consistent with the gender perspective: Married and cohabiting men spend less time on female-typed tasks and more time on male-typed tasks than do men in most other marital statuses.

DISCUSSION AND CONCLUSION

Doing housework is a significant part of many people's lives, yet few studies have explored housework patterns and determinants across household types. Indeed, because much prior research has been motivated by concerns about marital equity, the erroneous impression may exist that housework is performed only by members of married-couple families. Clearly, this is not the case.

Our results suggest that even never-married men, who might be expected to eschew housework, spend almost half as much time working around the home as they do in the paid labor force. Given prior studies suggesting little contribution by adult sons who live at home (Hartung and Moore 1992; Ward et al. 1992), the amount of housework reported being done by never-married men living in parental homes may seem surprisingly high — approximately 2 hours per day. However, the largest single component of this time (approximately one-quarter of it) is spent on outdoor maintenance, and outdoor and automobile maintenance together constitute one-third of the total time spent. Further, it is likely that much of the time spent in other chores, such as cooking, cleaning, or laundry, is directed more toward self-maintenance than to the well-being of the entire household (Hartung and Moore 1992). Thus, given this context, the amount of housework reported by never-married men living in the parental home appears reasonable.

The performance of housework by men is substantially similar across marital statuses. Differences in total housework hours among never-married, cohabiting, and married men are rather small and are partly attributable to differences in other social and economic characteristics. The most noteworthy differences among men in housework hours involve the appreciable differences between divorced and widowed men and the men in other marital statuses. The number of hours married women spend doing housework approaches a typical full-time work week and is termed the "second shift" by Hochschild (1989). But women in other living situations that do not include a male partner also spend 20 to 30 hours a week doing household chores. The gender gap in housework hours is highest in marriage, but is evident in other marital statuses as well. Although social and economic differences among women in various marital situations (especially the presence of children and hours spent in paid work) account for approximately half of these differences in housework hours, marital status differences in housework among women are generally greater than the corresponding differences among men.

From these patterns and from our detailed analysis of individual household tasks, we have concluded that there is suggestive evidence for the "gender perspective." Housework that women perform for and in the presence of men displays gender more so than the same work performed with no man present. We find that the gender gap in housework time is greatest in married couple households relative to other households, and that much of this difference *cannot* be explained by the fact that marriage often brings children and reduced hours of paid work for women. Thus, we conclude that men and women must be "doing gender" when they live together. Moreover, relative to their unmarried counterparts, married men spend very little time in the traditionally female tasks of cooking and cleaning.

Of course, there are also significant gender gaps among persons in nonmarital households, implying that the dynamics of doing gender are not entirely absent in other household situations. However, we view our analysis and the patterns displayed in couple and noncouple households to be suggestive evidence that these dynamics operate differentially across household types. Perhaps our analysis and tentative interpretation will encourage those theorists working in the new gender perspective to further specify the conditions under which these processes operate so that future empirical tests can be more precise.

Analysis across household type and marital status may also have implications for the application of equity theory to the allocation of household labor. While most analyses of equity in household labor have used a comparison between husbands and wives as the implicit or explicit base for judging fairness, several recent discussions have raised the possibility that other standards may be used as well. Thompson (1991) discusses the issue of comparison referents and points out that husbands may compare themselves with *other husbands* and wives with *other wives*, while both Ferree (1990) and Kollock, Blumstein, and Schwartz (1988) present empirical comparisons between the predictive value of intracouple and intragender standards. To our knowledge, however, the idea that spouses may compare themselves to *their own past or projected experiences in another marital status*, or even to others who are not currently married, has not been discussed in the empirical literature on housework equity, although fear of divorce was certainly a potent factor in the ideological and behavioral choices of Hochschild's (1989) female respondents. Although this is necessarily speculative, we suggest that married men might use their experience prior to marriage as a reference point for both negotiating and evaluating their own contribution to household labor within marriage. People are spending increasing amounts of time in nonmarital statuses, particularly never-married, cohabiting, and divorced. During their lives, they often go through transitions which include a sequence from being never married to cohabiting to married to divorced or widowed. By examining the time men and women spend doing housework in each of these living situations we may be better able to understand what occurs when people negotiate how housework will be divided within marriage.

SCOTT J. SOUTH *is Associate Professor of Sociology at the State University of New York at Albany. His recent research focuses on the social demography of American families, with particular emphasis given to contextual influences on patterns of family formation and dissolution. He is Co-Editor (with Stewart E. Tolnay) of* The Changing American Family: Sociological and Demographic Perspectives *(Westview Press, 1992).*

GLENNA SPITZE *is Professor of Sociology and Women's Studies at the State University of New York at Albany. In addition to her research on household labor, she is working on a book with John R. Logan based on their research on family structure and intergenerational relations.*

REFERENCES

Aytac, Isik A. and Jay D. Teachman. 1992. "Occupational Sex Segregation, Marital Power, and Household Division of Labor." Paper presented at the meetings of the American Sociological Association, 20–24 Aug., Pittsburgh, PA.

Becker, Gary. 1981. *A Treatise on the Family.* Chicago, IL: University of Chicago.

Benin, Mary H. and Joan Agostinelli. 1988. "Husbands' and Wives' Satisfaction with the Division of Labor." *Journal of Marriage and the Family* 50:349–61.

Benin, Mary Holland and Debra A. Edwards. 1990. "Adolescents' Chores: The Difference Between Dual and Single-Earner Families." *Journal of Marriage and the Family* 52:361–73.

Bergen, Elizabeth. 1991. "The Economic Context of Labor Allocation." *Journal of Family Issues* 12:140–57.

Berk, Sarah Fenstermaker. 1985. *The Gender Factory.* New York: Plenum.

Blair, Sampson Lee. 1991. "The Sex-Typing of Children's Household Labor: Parental Influence on Daughters' and Sons' Housework." Paper presented at the meeting of the American Sociological Association, 23–27 Aug., Cincinnati, OH.

Blair, Sampson Lee and Michael P. Johnson. 1992. "Wives' Perceptions of the Fairness of the Division of Household Labor: The Intersection of Housework and Ideology." *Journal of Marriage and the Family* 54:570–81.

Blair, Sampson Lee and Daniel T. Lichter. 1991. "Measuring the Division of Household Labor: Gender Segregation Among American Couples." *Journal of Family Issues* 12:91–113.

Blood, Robert O. and Donald M. Wolfe. 1960. *Husbands and Wives.* New York: Free Press.

Blumberg, Rae Lesser and Marion Tolbert Coleman. 1989. "A Theoretical Look at the Gender Balance of Power in the American Couple." *Journal of Family Issues* 10:255–50.

Blumstein, Philip and Pepper Schwartz. 1983. *American Couples.* New York: William Morrow.

Coltrane, Scott and Masako Ishii-Kuntz. 1992. "Men's Housework: A Life-Course Perspective." *Journal of Marriage and the Family* 54:43–57.

Coverman, Shelley. 1985. "Explaining Husbands' Participation in Domestic Labor." *Sociological Quarterly* 26:81–97.

Coverman, Shelley and Joseph F. Sheley. 1986. "Changes in Men's Housework and Child-Care Time, 1965–1975." *Journal of Marriage and the Family* 48:413–22.

DeVault, Marjorie L. 1991. *Feeding the Family: The Social Organization of Caring as Gendered Work.* Chicago, IL: University of Chicago.

Ferree, Myra Marx. 1990. "Gender and Grievances in the Division of Household Labor: How Husbands and Wives Perceive Fairness." Paper presented at the meeting of the American Sociological Association, 11–15 Aug., Washington, DC.

———. 1991a. "Feminism and Family Research." Pp. 103–21 in *Contemporary Families,* edited by A. Booth. Minneapolis, MN: National Council on Family Relations.

———. 1991b. "The Gender Division of Labor in Two-Earner Marriages: Dimensions of Variability and Change." *Journal of Family Issues* 12:158–80.

Gershuny, Jonathan and John P. Robinson. 1988. "Historical Changes in the Household Division of Labor." *Demography* 25:537–52.

Gillespie, Dair L. 1971. "Who Has the Power: The Marital Struggle." *Journal of Marriage and the Family* 33:445–58.

Glazer-Malbin, Nona. 1976. "Housework." *Signs* 1:905–22.

Godwin, Deborah D. 1991. "Spouses' Time Allocation to Household Work: A Review and Critique." *Lifestyles: Family and Economic Issues* 12:253–94.

Goldscheider, Frances K. and Linda J. Waite. 1991. *New Families, No Families? The Transformation of the American Home.* Berkeley, CA: University of California.

346   AMERICAN SOCIOLOGICAL REVIEW

Gove, Walter R. and Hee-Choon Shin. 1989. "The Psychological Well-Being of Divorced and Widowed Men and Women: An Empirical Analysis." *Journal of Family Issues* 10:122–44.

Grief, Geoffrey L. 1985. "Children and Housework in the Single Father Family." *Family Relations* 34:353–57.

Hartmann, Heidi I. 1981. "The Family as the Locus of Gender, Class, and Political Struggle: The Example of Housework." *Signs* 6:366–94.

Hartung, Beth and Helen A. Moore, 1992. "The Return of the 'Second Shift': Adult Children Who Return Home." Paper presented at the meeting of the American Sociological Association, 20–24 Aug., Pittsburgh, PA.

Hilton, Jeanne M. and Virginia A. Haldeman. 1991. "Gender Differences in the Performance of Household Tasks by Adults and Children in Single-Parent and Two-Parent, Two-Earner Families." *Journal of Family Issues* 12:114–30.

Hochschild, Arlie with Anne Machung. 1989. *The Second Shift: Working Parents and the Revolution at Home*. New York: Viking.

Huber, Joan and Glenna Spitze. 1983. *Sex Stratification: Children, Housework, and Jobs*. New York: Academic Press.

Ishii-Kuntz, Masako and Scott Coltrane. 1992. "Remarriage, Stepparenting, and Household Labor." *Journal of Family Issues* 13:215–33.

Kollock, Peter, Philip Blumstein, and Pepper Schwartz. 1988. "The Judgment of Equity in Intimate Relationships." Paper presented at the meeting of the American Sociological Association, 24–28 Aug., Atlanta, GA.

Oakley, Ann. 1974. *The Sociology of Housework*. New York: Pantheon.

Peterson, Larry R. and Judy L. Maynard. 1981. "Income, Equity, and Wives' Housekeeping Role Expectations." *Pacific Sociological Review* 24: 87–105.

Presser, Harriet B. 1993. "Gender, Work Schedules, and the Division of Family Labor." Paper presented at the meeting of the Population Association of American, 1–3 April, Cincinnati, OH.

Rexroat, Cynthia and Constance Shehan. 1987. "The Family Life Cycle and Spouses' Time in Housework." *Journal of Marriage and the Family* 49:737–50.

Rindfuss, Ronald R. and Audrey VandenHeuvel. 1992. "Cohabitation: A Precursor to Marriage or an Alternative to Being Single?" Pp. 118–42 in *The Changing American Family: Sociological and Demographic Perspectives*, edited by S. J. South and S. E. Tolnay. Boulder, CO: Westview Press.

Rodman, Hyman, 1967. "Marital Power in France, Greece, Yugoslavia, and the United States: A Cross-National Discussion." *Journal of Marriage and the Family* 29:320–24.

Ross, Catherine E. 1987. "The Division of Labor at Home." *Social Forces* 65:816–33.

Sanik, Margaret Mietus and Teresa Mauldin. 1986.

"Single Versus Two-Parent Families: A Comparison of Mothers' Time." *Family Relations* 35:53–56.

Shelton, Beth Anne. 1990. "The Distribution of Household Tasks: Does Wife's Employment Status Make a Difference?" *Journal of Family Issues* 11:115–35.

———. 1992. *Women, Men and Time*. New York: Greenwood Press.

Shelton, Beth Anne and Daphne John. 1993. "Does Marital Status Make a Difference? Housework Among Married and Cohabiting Men and Women." *Journal of Family Issues* 14:401–20.

Spitze, Glenna. 1986. "The Division of Task Responsibility in U.S. Households: Longitudinal Adjustments to Change." *Social Forces* 64:689–701.

———. 1988. "Women's Employment and Family Relations: A Review." *Journal of Marriage and the Family* 50:595–618.

Stafford, Rebecca, Elaine Backman, and Pamela Dibona. 1977. "The Division of Labor Among Cohabiting and Married Couples." *Journal of Marriage and the Family* 39:43–57.

Sweet, James, Larry Bumpass, and Vaughn Call. 1988. "The Design and Content of the National Survey of Families and Households." (Working Paper NSFH-1). Center for Demography and Ecology, University of Wisconsin, Madison, WI.

Sweet, James A. and Larry L. Bumpass. 1987. *American Families and Households*. New York: Russell Sage Foundation.

Thompson, Linda and Alexis J. Walker. 1991. "Gender in Families." Pp. 76–102 in *Contemporary Families*, edited by A. Booth. Minneapolis, MN: National Council on Family Relations.

Thompson, Linda. 1991. "Family Work: Women's Sense of Fairness." *Journal of Family Issues* 12: 181–96.

Timmer, Susan G., Jacquelynne Eccles, and Keith O'Brien. 1985. "How Children Use Time." Pp. 353–82 in *Time, Goods, and Well-Being*, edited by T. F. Juster and F. P. Stafford. Ann Arbor, MI: Institute for Social Research, University of Michigan.

Umberson, Debra, Camille B. Wortman, and Ronald C. Kessler. 1992. "Widowhood and Depression: Explaining Long-Term Gender Differences in Vulnerability." *Journal of Health and Social Behavior* 33:10–24.

Waite, Linda and Frances K. Goldscheider. 1992. "Work in the Home: The Productive Context of Family Relationships." Pp. 267–99 in *The Changing American Family: Sociological and Demographic Perspectives*, edited by S. J. South and S. E. Tolnay. Boulder, CO: Westview Press.

Walker, Kathryn E. and Margaret E. Woods. 1976. *Time Use: A Measure of Household Production of Goods and Services*. Washington, DC: American Home Economics Association.

Ward, Russell, John Logan, and Glenna Spitze. 1992. "The Influence of Parent and Child Needs on

Coresidence in Middle and Later Life." *Journal of Marriage and the Family* 54:209–21.

Warner, Rebecca A. 1986. "Alternative Strategies for Measuring Household Division of Labor: A Comparison." *Journal of Family Issues* 7:179–95.

Watkins, Susan Cotts, Jane A. Menken, and John Bongaarts. 1987. "Demographic Foundations of Family Change." *American Sociological Review* 52:346–58.

West, Candace and Don H. Zimmerman. 1981. "Doing Gender." *Gender and Society* 1:125–51.

White, Lynn K. and David B. Brinkerhoff. 1981a. "Children's Work in the Family: Its Significance and Meaning." *Journal of Marriage and the Family* 43:789–98.

———. 1981b. "The Sexual Division of Labor: Evidence from Childhood." *Social Forces* 60:170–81.

Appendix E
How to Use a Statistical Package (SPSS)

Thomas J. Linneman

"May you live in interesting times," so the ancient proverb says. This is certainly true enough today, as technological advances appear on a daily basis. Within the social sciences, powerful computers and sophisticated programs have made it easy to perform a wide array of statistical procedures with large sets of data. Tasks that previously took entire summers to perform can now be completed in mere seconds with the aid of a statistical program. The possibilities today are so great that it becomes a job in itself to master one of these programs. But the basics *are* simple enough, and it is the purpose of this appendix to help you become proficient with them.

A *statistical package* is a set of computer programs that work together so that you can calculate many different statistics and perform other related tasks. There are many statistical packages available for mainframe (multiuser) and personal computers. Once you have learned how to use one or two of them, you should find it easy to use others (if you have the right manual or guidebook). Here I will review the basic procedures for using the Statistical Package for the Social Sciences (SPSS), one of the most popular and best-documented comprehensive social science statistics packages. This appendix can be used with any SPSS Windows-based version, as all such versions operate in the same manner.

Getting Acquainted with the SPSS Environment

The Windows version of SPSS allows "regular" people to perform complex tasks through the use of a graphical interface. Instead of having to write elaborate lines of programming code to tell the computer what to do, the user need only know how to point and click with the mouse. If you are unfamiliar with the Windows environment (you have never touched a mouse), you may want someone to help you with your first Windows experience. Once you are comfortable with the environment, though, all the steps are similar to each other.

Communicating with SPSS is simply a matter of using drop-down menus, toolbars, and dialog boxes.

Drop-down menus appear at the top of the screen. This is the set of drop-down menus that appears at the top of the basic SPSS screen:

If you wanted to do something with a data file, you would click on *File,* and that would give you a set of options, including opening a new file, saving a file, and closing a file. If you wanted to make a graph, you would click on *Graphs.*

A second way to tell SPSS what to do is through the use of toolbars. Even though you could use the drop-down menus to perform certain tasks, sometimes it is easier to click a button in the toolbar. Here is the basic toolbar for SPSS:

Click this button to print a document.

Click this button to search for a particular element in your data.

The final way to communicate with SPSS is through the use of dialog boxes. You can get to a dialog box through the drop-down menus or through a button on a toolbar. For example, this dialog box lets you tell SPSS information about how you would like to sort your cases:

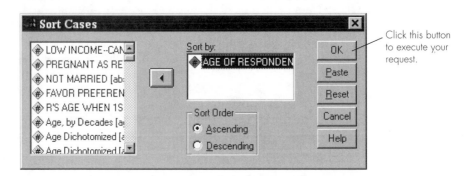

Click this button to execute your request.

As you can see, the SPSS Windows environment is highly intuitive. All you do is look for the correct button and click it. If this seems extremely simple, that's because it is. Let's get started on our guided tour of SPSS.

■ ■ ■ ■ **Getting In and Getting Data**

Getting into SPSS is simply a matter of clicking on the program icon: 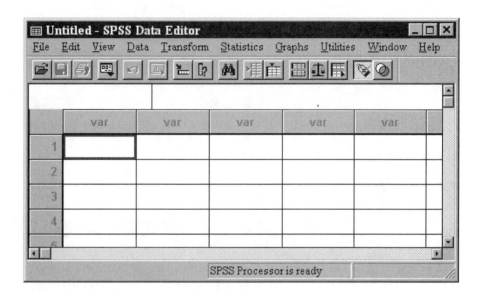 .
This may require a single-click or a double-click. Clicking is a skill that requires
a little bit of practice. Don't worry, you will get the hang of it. After clicking on
the icon, the following window will appear:

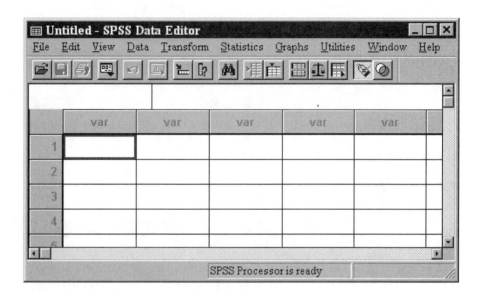

This is called the data window. As you can see, not a whole lot is going on in
the data window. This "Untitled" data window is like a playground without
any swings or slides: You can go there, but you can't do much. So the first thing
you need to do is get some data. If you have collected your own data, at this
point you would enter it. More likely, though, you will be working with a set of
data that already exists, such as a General Social Survey dataset or a dataset
from one of the other national surveys. Instead of creating a brand new dataset,
you will load a preexisting data file. Creating a dataset is easy enough, but we
won't go into it here. For this appendix, we will be using the 1996 GSS dataset
on the disk that accompanies this book.

To load a dataset, click on the *File* drop-down menu. From the *File* menu,
click on *Open*. Another menu pops up. From the *Open* menu, click on *Data*.
From now on, such a list of directions will appear as follows:

File → Open → Data

This takes you to the "Open Data File" dialog box, where you will tell SPSS
which file you want to open.

SPSS, having received its orders, retrieves your file and puts it into the data window. You will see something that looks like this:

The data window is divided up into rows and columns. Each row represents a person (a respondent to the survey, a "case"). This particular dataset has 979 rows, or 979 respondents. Each column represents a variable. At the top of the column, you will see the variable name (sometimes the names are quite amusing, because SPSS limits the length of the variable name to eight characters). Most datasets will have hundreds of variables and thus hundreds of columns. Our dataset has almost 400 variables. You can move around within the dataset by using the arrows you see on the borders of the window. Try it.

■ ■ ■ ■ **Looking at the Data**

So from this little pane of the data window, we see that Respondent 3 is 51 years old. The respondent was 20 years old when her first child was born. She scored a "2" on the variable abrape, a "2" on the variable absingle, and a "2" on the variable affrmact. What does all this mean? All of the responses to the GSS questions have been *coded*. That is, each possible response has been assigned a number. For some variables, such as AGE and AGEKDBRN, the numbers simply correspond to the number of years. For other variables (like ABRAPE, ABSINGLE, and AFFRMACT), each number corresponds to a particular response or category. For example, for the variable ABSINGLE ("Do you think it should be possible for a pregnant woman to obtain a legal abortion if she is not married and does not want to marry the man?"), "1" stands for "yes" and "2" stands for "no." Within SPSS, such labels are referred to as *value labels*: for a value of 1, the label is "yes," and so on.

How do I know this? There are three ways of locating the value labels for variables. The most common way is by referring to a *codebook*. A codebook is similar to a dictionary. It contains pertinent information about each variable in the dataset. So we could open up the GSS codebook (or look at the codebook on the GSS Web site) to the variable ABSINGLE and find out how it was coded by the GSS researchers. What if there is no codebook? Never fear. Within SPSS it is quite easy to find the value labels. The first way is through the use of a dialog box. To get to this dialog box, click:

Utilities → Variables

This will take you to the "Variables" dialog box, which looks like this:

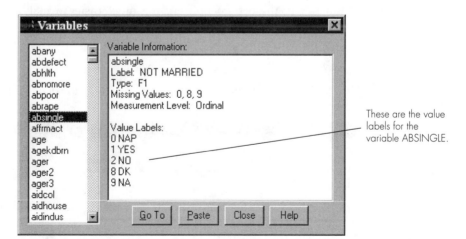

The third way to examine the value labels is to click the toolbar button that looks like a pricetag. When you click this, the numbers in the dataset will magically change to their respective labels. Or, if the labels are what you are seeing, clicking on this button will magically turn them back to numbers.

So, referring to the value labels, let's compare Respondents 1 and 2. They both support abortion rights when a woman has been raped or when she is single. However, their responses differ on the variable AFFRMACT ("Are you for or against preferential hiring and promotion of blacks?"). Respondent 1 answered "4," which means that he "strongly opposes preferential hiring." So since Respondent 2 was scored an "8," does that mean that she is *extremely* strongly opposed to preferential hiring?

The answer involves *missing values*. Missing values are values (or codes) determined by the researcher to refer to missing data. Let's face it, in a survey of 1,000 people, not everyone will be willing to answer everything. To deal with such a situation, the GSS interviewer can pencil in responses like "don't know" or "no answer," and for that one respondent, data on that variable will be considered "missing." If you call up the value labels for AFFRMACT, you will see that there are three missing values: 0, 8, and 9: "0" was the value given to people who weren't even asked the question (respondents to the GSS are asked only certain sets, or modules, of questions); "8" was the value given to people who didn't know the answer to the question; and "9" was the value given to people who did not want to answer the question. In calculations, such as calculating the median response of the respondents, SPSS takes those cases with missing values "out of the equation" and calculates the median based on the responses of the other respondents. Some variables have more missing data than others, particularly variables for questions that are of a sensitive nature or variables for questions that were not asked of the entire sample. So, to finally answer the question posed in the preceding paragraph, Respondent 2 said that she didn't know the answer to that question.

We could play around in the data window for hours without getting a good picture of who these 979 people are. It is much easier to analyze data by having SPSS make frequency distributions or graphs for your variables of interest, and such things are only a dialog box away. Click:

Statistics → Summarize → Frequencies

Now we're in the "Frequencies" dialog box, which looks like this:

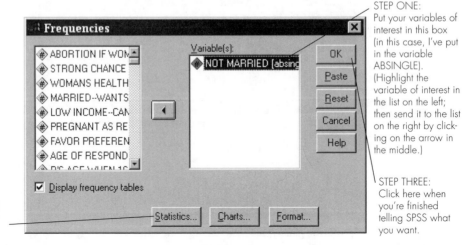

STEP ONE:
Put your variables of interest in this box (in this case, I've put in the variable ABSINGLE). (Highlight the variable of interest in the list on the left; then send it to the list on the right by clicking on the arrow in the middle.)

STEP TWO:
Click here to get statistics on your variables.

STEP THREE:
Click here when you're finished telling SPSS what you want.

Here is what happens when we click *OK*:

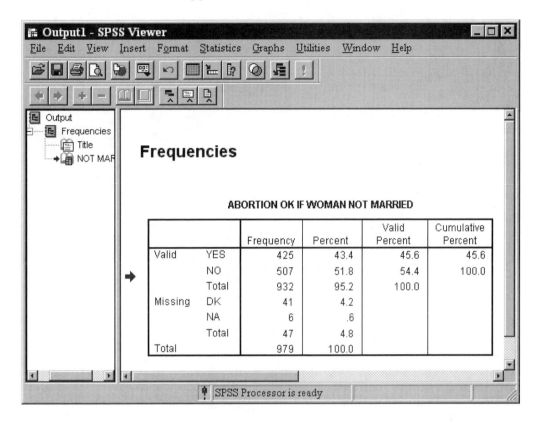

SPSS gives us a new window called "Output 1 - SPSS Viewer." Within this window, we look at all of the results of what we have asked SPSS to do. The viewer has two "panes." The left pane is called the Output Navigator.[1] This is simply a list of everything we have asked SPSS to do since we began our session. In this case, so far, we have asked it to do only one thing, but normally, this pane will be full of stuff. Why is this pane useful? Well, imagine you have been working on SPSS for a couple of hours (it could happen!), and you have asked it to do many many things. You have dozens of tables, graphs, and statistical models to pore over. The Output Navigator is aptly named because it helps you to navigate through your output. So, if you want to go to a specific graph, you find it in the Output Navigator, click on it, and SPSS takes you there. The right pane is the actual output. Here, we have a frequency distribution of the variable ABSINGLE.

We could also get the same results from a bar graph. To use the SPSS graphing capabilities, click:

Graphs → Bar → Simple → Define

[1]Note: If you are using SPSS 6.1 for Windows, you will not have an Output Navigator. So you will see only one pane.

We end up in a dialog box that looks like this:

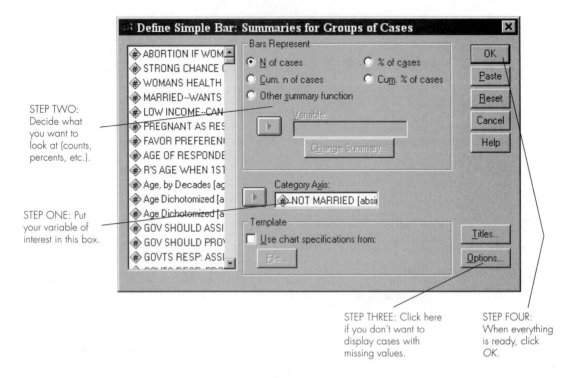

STEP TWO:
Decide what
you want to
look at (counts,
percents, etc.).

STEP ONE: Put
your variable of
interest in this box.

STEP THREE: Click here
if you don't want to
display cases with
missing values.

STEP FOUR:
When everything
is ready, click
OK.

Here is the graph that results from this request:

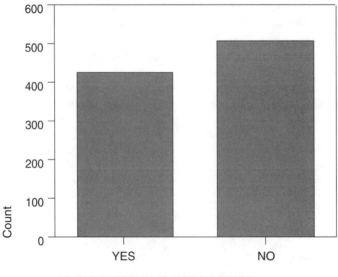

■ ■ ■ ■ Recoding Variables

Not all variables are coded exactly as you would like them to be coded. Most of the time, to do what you want to do, you will need to recode variables. Let's say we want to recode EDUC (highest year of education completed) so that:

■ Everyone with less than a high school diploma is put into a single group

■ Everyone with a high school diploma, but no more, is put into a second group

■ Everyone with some college, but not a college diploma, is put into a third group

■ Everyone with a college degree, but no more, is put into a fourth group

■ Everyone with postcollege education is put into a fifth group

Make sure you understand what we are doing here. We are taking the original 21 categories (years of education from 0 to 20) and collapsing them into 5 categories. We are going to accomplish this task by creating a new variable called EDUC1. Click:

Transform → Recode → Into different variables

This takes us to the first of two dialog boxes involved in recoding variables:

STEP TWO: Type the name of the new variable, give it a label, and click *Change*.

STEP ONE: Double-click the variable you want to recode.

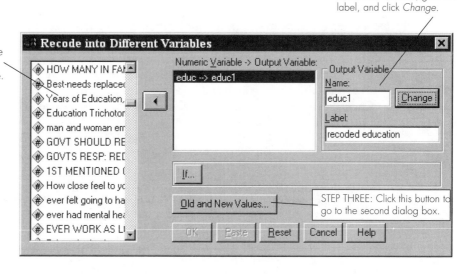

What we're doing in this first dialog box is telling SPSS which old variable we are recoding *from* and which new variable we are recoding *to*. After doing this, we go to the second dialog box:

STEP ONE: Tell SPSS which old values are to be recoded (e.g., 0 through 11)

STEP TWO: Tell SPSS the new value (e.g., 1).

STEP THREE: Click *Add* to add this specification to the Old → New box.

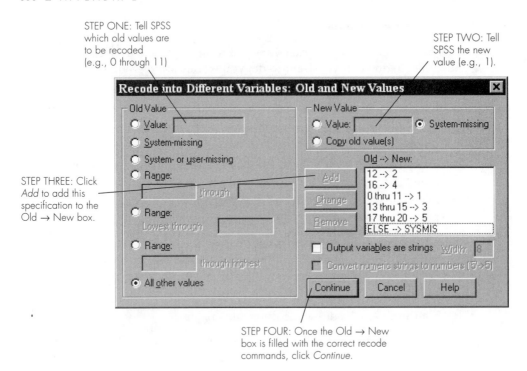

STEP FOUR: Once the Old → New box is filled with the correct recode commands, click *Continue*.

In this box, our goal is to fill the Old → New box with the appropriate recode specifications. For example, we want everyone with less than a high school diploma to be put into one group. On the left side of the dialog box, we tell SPSS to take a particular value or set of values, such as the values ranging from "0 through 11" (those people with less than high school). On the right side of the dialog box, we tell SPSS to collapse these values into a single value: "1." Look through the list of recodes to make sure you understand what is going on here. When you have the list as you like it, click *Continue* to exit the second dialog box, then click *OK* to exit the first dialog box.

SPSS now creates a new variable named EDUC1, giving all the respondents new values for their levels of education:

GSS96 Respondent #:	Old Value on Variable EDUC	New Value on Variable EDUC1
1	18	5
2	8	1
3	17	5
4	16	4
5	13	3

To give you more examples to peruse, here are possible recode commands for two basic variables from the GSS:

$1 \rightarrow 0$ $2 \rightarrow 1$ $3 \rightarrow 1$	This set of recodes will recode the RACE variable into a dichotomous variable, where whites (originally coded as 1's) are coded as 0's and nonwhites (previously coded as 2's and 3's) are coded as 1's.
1 through $2 \rightarrow 1$ 3 through $5 \rightarrow 2$ 6 through $7 \rightarrow 3$ ELSE $\rightarrow$ SYSMIS	This set of recodes will recode the POLVIEWS variable into three categories: liberals (originally coded as 1's and 2's) will be coded as 1's, moderates (originally coded as 3's, 4's, and 5's) will be coded as 2's, and conservatives (originally coded as 6's and 7's) will be coded as 3's. Everyone else will be coded as a missing value.

Now let's look at a frequency distribution for our new education variable:

recoded education

		Frequency	Percent	Valid Percent	Cumulative Percent
Valid	1.00	180	18.4	18.5	18.5
	2.00	267	27.3	27.4	45.8
	3.00	260	26.6	26.7	72.5
	4.00	139	14.2	14.3	86.8
	5.00	129	13.2	13.2	100.0
	Total	975	99.6	100.0	
Missing	System	4	.4		
Total		979	100.0		

As you can see, there are no value labels. If we handed someone this output, he or she would have no way of knowing what a "1" or "2" means. To make this output easier to read, we should attach labels to our values. This requires using another dialog box. In the data window, go to the right-most column (this is where SPSS puts all the new variables you create). Double-click on the name of the variable EDUC1. A dialog box pops up. In that dialog box, click *Labels*. Up pops the dialog box you need:

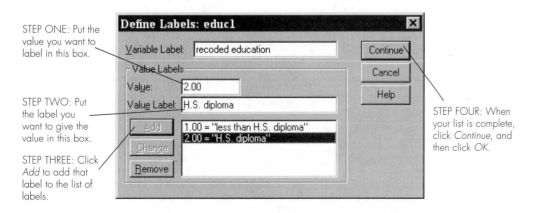

STEP ONE: Put the value you want to label in this box.

STEP TWO: Put the label you want to give the value in this box.

STEP THREE: Click *Add* to add that label to the list of labels.

STEP FOUR: When your list is complete, click *Continue*, and then click *OK*.

Notice that in the first dialog box (the one that takes you to the "Define Labels" dialog box), you can also tell SPSS what the missing values are for a variable and format the column in which the variable appears. Remember, telling SPSS what values are the missing values is a *very* important step! You don't want SPSS to consider, for example, that someone is 99 years old. Skipping this step can easily muddle any analysis you are performing. Haste truly does make waste.

After you've created new variables, you will most likely want to save your work. Otherwise, the next time you use SPSS, you will have to start all over. Call up the "Save Data" dialog box by clicking:

File → Save As...

Then tell it on what drive you want to save your file and in which directory you want to save it, give your file a name, and click *OK*. Please note that if you are using this book's disk, you cannot save a new version of the GSS96b3 dataset onto that disk since the disk is already quite full.

■ ■ ■ ■   Crosstabulation

Now that we've gone through the basics of how to manipulate data in SPSS, let's move on to some real statistics. You already know how to get descriptive statistics on single variables, but how about looking at the relationships between variables? This calls for tables.

Let's say we want to examine the relationship between education (EDUC1: categorized education) and attitudes about abortion (using the ABSINGLE variable). We will create a crosstab with these variables, using EDUC1 as our independent variable and ABSINGLE as our dependent variable. Click:

Statistics → Summarize → Crosstabs

Now we're in the "Crosstabs" window:

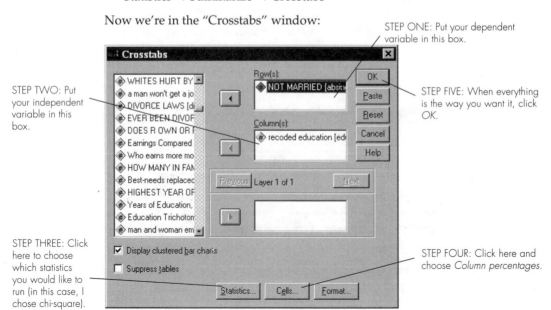

Here are our results:

NOT MARRIED * recoded education Crosstabulation

		recoded education					
		less than H.S. diploma	H.S. diploma	some college	college diploma	more than college	Total
ABORTION OK IF NOT MARRIED	YES	62	97	115	74	74	422
		36.7%	37.7%	46.9%	55.6%	59.2%	45.4%
	NO	107	160	130	59	51	507
		63.3%	62.3%	53.1%	44.4%	40.8%	54.6%
Total		169	257	245	133	125	929
		100.0%	100.0%	100.0%	100.0%	100.0%	100.0%

Chi-Square Tests

	Value	df	Asymp. Sig. (2-sided)
Pearson Chi-Square	26.714	4	.000

So, we see that there definitely *is* a relationship between education and attitudes about abortion. As educational level rises, people are more likely to support abortion. The chi-square test tells us that the relationship is highly significant. At this point, we could print our output. One caution about printing in a Windows environment: The computer will print whichever window is "active." Therefore, if you want to print your output, make sure the output window is the active window. If the data window is the active window, you will end up with only a paper copy of the data window.

■ ■ ■ ■ **Computing a New Variable**

Let's look at another procedure concerning data modification. What we are going to do now is compute a new variable using information from other variables. This will be an especially useful skill if you are going to be using an index. In fact, that's what we are going to do: create a simple index. Let's say we're interested in how people feel about the government's role in the economy. The 1996 GSS asked two questions that relate to this:

"Here are some things the government might do for the economy. Circle one number for each action to show whether you are in favor of it or against it":
    SETPRICE: Control of prices by legislation
    SETWAGE: Control of wages by legislation

Both of these questions were coded as follows:

0: Not asked question
1: Strongly in favor
2: In favor
3: Neither
4: Against
5: Strongly against
8: Don't know
9: No answer

We are going to compute a variable that is the average of these two variables. For example, if someone answered "strongly in favor" for both questions, her index score would be $(1 + 1)/2$, or 1. If someone answered "in favor" on the first question but "strongly against" on the second question, his index score would be $(2 + 5)/2$, or 3.5. A low score on the index will mean that the respondent supports government control of the economy, and a high score on the index will mean that the respondent does not support government control of the economy.

Click:

Transform → Compute

We get the "Compute Variable" dialog box:

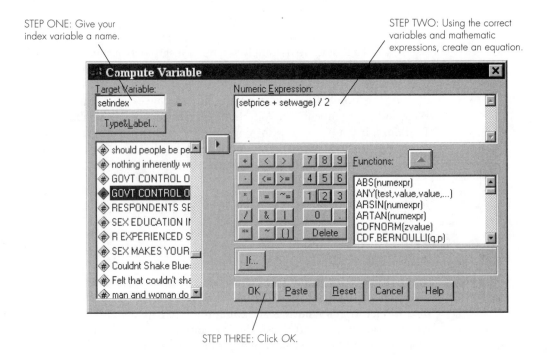

STEP ONE: Give your index variable a name.

STEP TWO: Using the correct variables and mathematic expressions, create an equation.

STEP THREE: Click OK.

SPSS whirs away and then puts the new computed variable SETINDEX over on the right (where all the new variables go). Here are more examples of scores on this index:

Response on SETPRICE:	Response on SETWAGE:	Score on SETINDEX:
4	2	3
3	5	4
4	5	4.5
9	1	.
0	0	.

As you can see, SPSS could compute index scores only for people who answered both questions. The fourth respondent above answered "No answer" to the first question, so we cannot compute an index score for that respondent. The fifth respondent above was not even asked the questions, so we obviously don't have an index score for that person.

Selecting Cases

In addition to recoding and computing, one other common procedure involves telling SPSS to look at only a certain group of cases. For example, perhaps we are especially concerned about how *women* feel about abortion. We would want to tell SPSS to temporarily set aside all of the men and involve only women in our analyses. To do this, we use a dialog box called "Select Cases":

We click:

Data → Select Cases

We get:

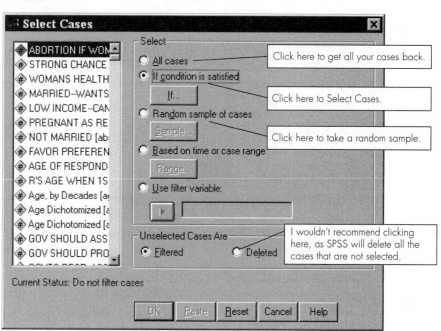

We want to click on *If condition is satisfied* and then click the *If* button. This brings us to the second dialog box:

Simply put your condition in this box. In this case, we are telling SPSS to select the cases if sex = 2 (if sex of respondent is female).

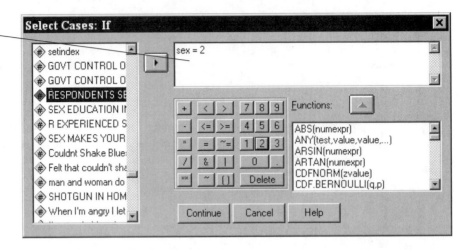

Once we click *Continue* and *OK*, SPSS searches through the dataset and finds all the cases that satisfy the condition that we gave it (find all females). The data window now looks like this:

Because Respondents 1 and 5 do *not* satisfy our condition (they are males), they have been crossed off.

Because Respondents 2, 3, and 4 *do* satisfy our condition (they are females), they remain in the mix.

Until we tell it differently (by going back to the "Select Cases" dialog box and clicking on *Select All Cases*), SPSS will include only the "uncrossed-off" cases. If you use this procedure, you will have to keep track of who is still in the mix and who has been left out of the mix, lest you forget and think you're looking at the entire dataset when SPSS is not. SPSS helps you a little here by telling you, at the bottom of the screen, whether the Filter is on or off. Also, keep in mind that you can give it more complicated "Select If" commands. For example, let's say we wanted to look at only women with college degrees or greater. Our "Select If" statement would be:

Select If: sex = 2 and educ > 15

which would give us a database of all women with more than 15 years of education.

Comparing Means

One last useful procedure is to compare the means of two groups on some variable of interest. Perhaps we are interested in whether whites make more money than nonwhites, or whether Protestants are more educated than Catholics. For example, let's say we want to investigate the question: Does the average woman have her first child at a younger age than the average man? We will use the variable AGEKDBRN, the age of the respondent at the time of first child. Click:

Statistics → Compare Means → Means

We get this dialog box:

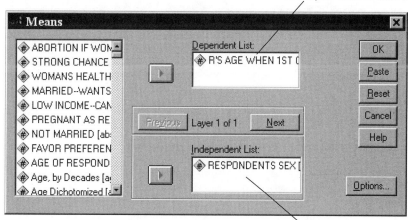

STEP ONE: Put the variable you want to compare values of in this box.

STEP TWO: Put the variable whose groups you want to compare in this box.

Once we click *OK*, we get the following output:

R'S AGE WHEN 1ST CHILD BORN

RESPONDENT'S SEX	Mean	N	Std. Deviation
MALE	24.88	280	5.35
FEMALE	22.67	426	4.97
Total	23.55	706	5.23

From looking at this output, we can see that the mean age of first birth for men is 24.88, and the mean age of first birth for women is 22.67, over 2 years younger. So, it does indeed seem that females are younger when they have children.

■ ■ ■ ■ Conclusion

If you've followed this appendix all the way through, you should have a good grasp of the basics of using a statistical package. It's just like any other skill: The more you practice, the better you'll be. If you get hung up on a procedure, just remember that there are many sources of assistance beyond this appendix: the Help drop-down menu in SPSS, the SPSS manual, your local computer lab consultant, and, of course, your instructor. Just don't be scared—the computer is not a monster or a nemesis; it is merely a tool to help you get your work done. Good luck!

Appendix F
Table of Random Numbers

A Table of 14,000 Random Units

Line/Col.	(1)	(2)	(3)	(4)	(5)	(6)	(7)	(8)	(9)	(10)	(11)	(12)	(13)	(14)
1	10480	15011	01536	02011	81647	91646	69179	14194	62590	36207	20969	99570	91291	90700
2	22368	46573	25595	85393	30995	89198	27982	53402	93965	34095	52666	19174	39615	99505
3	24130	48360	22527	97265	76393	64809	15179	24830	49340	32081	30680	19655	63348	58629
4	42167	93093	06243	61680	07856	16376	39440	53537	71341	57004	00849	74917	97758	16379
5	37570	39975	81837	16656	06121	91782	60468	81305	49684	60672	14110	06927	01263	54613
6	77921	06907	11008	42751	27756	53498	18602	70659	90655	15053	21916	81825	44394	42880
7	99562	72905	56420	69994	98872	31016	71194	18738	44013	48840	63213	21069	10634	12952
8	96301	91977	05463	07972	18876	20922	94595	56869	69014	60045	18425	84903	42508	32307
9	89579	14342	63661	10281	17453	18103	57740	84378	25331	12566	58678	44947	05585	56941
10	85475	36857	43342	53988	53060	59533	38867	62300	08158	17983	16439	11458	18593	64952
11	28918	69578	88231	33276	70997	79936	56865	05859	90106	31595	01547	85590	91610	78188
12	63553	40961	48235	03427	49626	69445	18663	72695	52180	20847	12234	90511	33703	90322
13	09429	93969	52636	92737	88974	33488	36320	17617	30015	08272	84115	27156	30613	74952
14	10365	61129	87529	85689	48237	52267	67689	93394	01511	26358	85104	20285	29975	89868
15	07119	97336	71048	08178	77233	13916	47564	81056	97735	85977	29372	74461	28551	90707
16	51085	12765	51821	51259	77452	16308	60756	92144	49442	53900	70960	63990	75601	40719
17	02368	21382	52404	60268	89368	19885	55322	44819	01188	65255	64835	44919	05944	55157
18	01011	54092	33362	94904	31273	04146	18594	29852	71585	85030	51132	01915	92747	64951
19	52162	53916	46369	58586	23216	14513	83149	98736	23495	64350	94738	17752	35156	35749
20	07056	97628	33787	09998	42698	06691	76988	13602	51851	46104	88916	19509	25625	58104
21	48663	91245	85828	14346	09172	30168	90229	04734	59193	22178	30421	61666	99904	32812
22	54164	58492	22421	74103	47070	25306	76468	26384	58151	06646	21524	15227	96909	44592
23	32639	32363	05597	24200	13363	38005	94342	28728	35806	06912	17012	64161	18296	22851
24	29334	27001	87637	87308	58731	00256	45834	15398	46557	41135	10367	07684	36188	18510
25	02488	33062	28834	07351	19731	92420	60952	61280	50001	67658	32586	86679	50720	94953
26	81525	72295	04839	96423	24878	82651	66566	14778	76797	14780	13300	87074	79666	95725
27	29676	20591	68086	26432	46901	20849	89768	81536	86645	12659	92259	57102	80428	25280
28	00742	57392	39064	66432	84673	40027	32832	61362	98947	96067	64760	64584	96096	98253
29	05366	04213	25669	26422	44407	44048	37937	63904	45766	66134	75470	66520	34693	90449
30	91921	26418	64117	94305	26766	25940	39972	22209	71500	64568	91402	42416	07844	69618

Line/Col.	(1)	(2)	(3)	(4)	(5)	(6)	(7)	(8)	(9)	(10)	(11)	(12)	(13)	(14)
31	00582	04711	87917	77341	42206	35126	74087	99547	81817	42607	43808	76655	62028	76630
32	00725	69884	62797	56170	86324	88072	76222	36086	84637	93161	76038	65855	77919	88006
33	69011	65797	95876	55293	18988	27354	26575	08625	40801	59920	29841	80150	12777	48501
34	25976	57948	29888	88604	67917	48708	18912	82271	65424	69774	33611	54262	85963	03547
35	09763	83473	73577	12908	30883	18317	28290	35797	05998	41688	34952	37888	38917	88050
36	91567	42595	27958	30134	04024	86385	29880	99730	55536	84855	29080	09250	79656	73211
37	17955	56349	90999	49127	20044	59931	06115	20542	18059	02008	73708	83317	36103	42791
38	46503	18584	18845	49618	02304	51038	20655	58727	28168	15475	56942	53389	20562	87338
39	92157	89634	94824	78171	84610	82834	09922	25417	44137	48413	25555	21246	35509	20468
40	14577	62765	35605	81263	39667	47358	56873	56307	61607	49518	89656	20103	77490	18062
41	98427	07523	33362	64270	01638	92477	66969	98420	04880	45585	46565	04102	46880	45709
42	34914	63976	88720	82765	34476	17032	87589	40836	32427	70002	70663	88863	77775	69348
43	70060	28277	39475	46473	23219	53416	94970	25832	69975	94884	19661	72828	00102	66794
44	53976	54914	06990	67245	68350	82948	11398	42878	80287	88267	47363	46634	06541	97809
45	76072	29515	40980	07391	58745	25774	22987	80059	39911	96189	41151	14222	60697	59583
46	90725	52210	83974	29992	65831	38857	50490	83765	55657	14361	31720	57375	56228	41546
47	64364	67412	33339	31926	14883	24413	59744	92351	97473	89286	35931	04110	23726	51900
48	08962	00358	31662	25388	61642	34072	81249	35648	56891	69352	48373	45578	78547	81788
49	95012	68379	93526	70765	10593	04542	76463	54328	02349	17247	28865	14777	62730	92277
50	15664	10493	20492	38391	91132	21999	59516	81652	27195	48223	46751	22923	32261	85653
51	16408	81899	04153	53381	79401	21438	83035	92350	36693	31238	59649	91754	72772	02338
52	18629	81953	05520	91962	04739	13092	97662	24822	94730	06496	35090	04822	86772	98289
53	73115	35101	47498	87637	99016	71060	88824	71013	18735	20286	23153	72924	35165	43040
54	57491	16703	23167	49323	45021	33132	12544	41035	80780	45393	44812	12515	98931	91202
55	30405	83946	23792	14422	15059	45799	22716	19792	09983	74353	68668	30429	70735	25499
56	16631	35006	85900	98275	32388	52390	16815	69298	82732	38480	73817	32523	41961	44437
57	96773	20206	42559	78985	05300	22164	24369	54224	35083	19687	11052	91491	60383	19746
58	38935	64202	14349	82674	66523	44133	00697	35552	35970	19124	63318	29686	03387	59846
59	31624	76384	17403	53363	44167	64486	64758	75366	76554	31601	12614	33072	60332	92325
60	78919	19474	23632	27889	47914	02584	37680	20801	72152	39339	34806	08930	85001	87820
61	03931	33309	57047	74211	63445	17361	62825	39908	05607	91284	68833	25570	38818	46920
62	74426	33278	43972	10119	89917	15665	52872	73823	73144	88662	88970	74492	51805	99378
63	09066	00903	20795	95452	92648	45454	09552	88815	16553	51125	79375	97596	16296	66092
64	42238	12426	87025	14267	20979	04508	64535	31355	86064	29472	47689	05974	52468	16834
65	16153	08002	26504	41744	81959	65642	74240	56302	00033	67107	77510	70625	28725	34191
66	21457	40742	29820	96783	29400	21840	15035	34537	33310	06116	95240	15957	16572	06004
67	21581	57802	02050	89728	17937	37621	47075	42080	97403	48626	68995	43805	33386	21597
68	55612	78095	83197	33732	05810	24813	86902	60397	16489	03264	88525	42786	05269	92532
69	44657	66999	99324	51281	84463	60563	79312	93454	68876	25471	93911	25650	12682	73572
70	91340	84979	46949	81973	37949	61023	43997	15263	80644	43942	89203	71795	99533	50501
71	91227	21199	31935	27022	84067	05462	35216	14486	29891	68607	41867	14951	91696	85065
72	50001	38140	66321	19924	72163	09538	12151	06878	91903	18749	34405	56087	82790	70925
73	65390	05224	72958	28609	81406	39147	25549	48542	42627	45233	57202	94617	23772	07896
74	27504	96131	83944	41575	10573	08619	64482	73923	36152	05184	94142	25299	84387	34925
75	37169	94851	39117	89632	00959	16487	65536	49071	39782	17095	02330	74301	00275	48280

Line/Col.	(1)	(2)	(3)	(4)	(5)	(6)	(7)	(8)	(9)	(10)	(11)	(12)	(13)	(14)
76	11508	70225	51111	38351	19444	66499	71945	05422	13442	78675	84081	66938	93654	59894
77	37449	30362	06694	54690	04052	53115	62757	95348	78662	11163	81651	50245	34971	52924
78	46515	70331	85922	38329	57015	15765	97161	17869	45349	61796	66345	81073	49106	79860
79	30986	81223	42416	58353	21532	30502	32305	86482	05174	07901	54339	58861	74818	46942
80	63798	64995	46583	09765	44160	78128	83991	42865	92520	83531	80377	35909	81250	54238
81	82486	84846	99254	67632	43218	50076	21361	64816	51202	88124	41870	52689	51275	83556
82	21885	32906	92431	09060	64297	51674	64126	62570	26123	05155	59194	52799	28225	85762
83	60336	98782	07408	53458	13564	59089	26445	29789	85205	41001	12535	12133	14645	23541
84	43937	46891	24010	25560	86355	33941	25786	54990	71899	15475	95434	98227	21824	19585
85	97656	63175	89303	16275	07100	92063	21942	18611	47348	20203	18534	03862	78095	50136
86	03299	01221	05418	38982	55758	92237	26759	86367	21216	98442	08303	56613	91511	75928
87	79626	06486	03574	17668	07785	76020	79924	25651	83325	88428	85076	72811	22717	50585
88	85636	68335	47539	03129	65651	11977	02510	26113	99447	68645	34327	15152	55230	93448
89	18039	14367	61337	06177	12143	46609	32989	74014	64708	00533	35398	58408	13261	47908
90	08362	15656	60627	36478	65648	16764	53412	09013	07832	41574	17639	82163	60859	75567
91	79556	29068	04142	16268	15387	12856	66227	38358	22478	73373	88732	09443	82558	05250
92	92608	82674	27072	32534	17075	27698	98204	63863	11951	34648	88022	56148	34925	57031
93	23982	25835	40055	67006	12293	02753	14827	22235	35071	99704	37543	11601	35503	85171
94	09915	96306	05908	97901	28395	14186	00821	80703	70426	75647	76310	88717	37890	40129
95	50937	33300	26695	62247	69927	76123	50842	43834	86654	70959	79725	93872	28117	19233
96	42488	78077	69882	61657	34136	79180	97526	43092	04098	73571	80799	76536	71255	64239
97	46764	86273	63003	93017	31204	36692	40202	35275	57306	55543	53203	18098	47625	88684
98	03237	45430	55417	63282	90816	17349	88298	90183	36600	78406	06216	95787	42579	90730
99	86591	81482	52667	61583	14972	90053	89534	76036	49199	43716	97548	04379	46370	28672
100	38534	01715	94964	87288	65680	43772	39560	12918	86537	62738	19636	51132	25739	56947

Source: Beyer, 1968.

Appendix G
How to Use QSR NUD*IST
for Qualitative Analysis

Lyn Richards

Overview

QSR NUD*IST is a software program for qualitative analysis. It provides ways of managing data and developing and exploring ideas that would not be possible if you were working on paper and index cards. It can be used for small or big projects.

As Chapter 8 showed, qualitative analysis usually requires that we explore and sensitively interpret messy data (interviews, documents, field notes, and so on). Researchers with this sort of *N*onnumerical, *U*nstructured *D*ata need ways of *I*ndexing, *S*earching, and *T*heorizing. Hence, NUD*IST. (The name appeared by accident, but nobody believes that.)

Using This Appendix

In this appendix you will learn what a project feels like in this software and then how the program can help with five major tasks of qualitative research: managing and exploring data, creating ideas, coding, searching and asking questions, constructing and testing theories. These are illustrated with a hypothetical project. In 1958—before qualitative computing—Howard Becker wrote the paper on medical students that was quoted in Chapter 8. How might you do that project now with QSR NUD*IST?

This appendix doesn't require that you use the software, but you will of course learn more if you are running it. Your college may have a site license; if so, you can set up a small project of your own data. If not, you can get free demonstration software from the Web site for Qualitative Solutions and Research, the development company in Australia (http://www.qsr.com.au). If you don't have Web access, contact Scolari Sage Publications, who distribute QSR's software.[1] The demo versions of the software have tutorials in them, so you can follow the instructions, put in the demonstration documents, and conduct small analyses.

[1]Scolari Sage Publications Software, Sage Publications, Inc., 2455 Teller Road, Thousand Oaks, CA 91320 USA. Phone: 805-499-1325; fax: 805-499-0871; e-mail: nudist@sagepub.com; Web site: http://www.sagepub.com/.

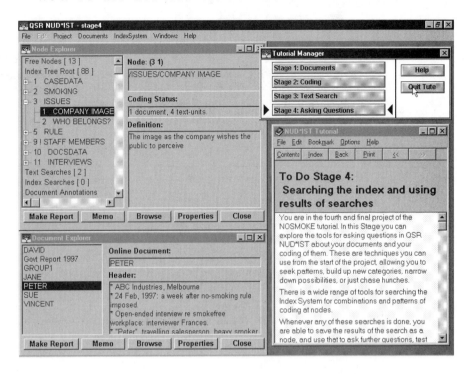

■ ■ ■ ■ **Following Developing Methods**

Qualitative software is evolving fast, with researcher demands driving software development. You can get a feel for the debates and demands in this fast-growing area by joining Internet discussion groups, including one on NUD*IST.[2] You can read about NUD*IST and about qualitative computing on

[2]Internet discussion groups and Web sites now reliably provide the latest information and sharing of user experience. The CAQDAS Project (Computer Assisted Qualitative Data Analysis Systems) in the UK is funded to run seminars and maintain a Web site including reference lists and links to Web pages and a discussion group (qual-software) on all software for qualitative analysis. You can visit the Web page and ask your questions on the list.

The CAQDAS WWW page is:

http://www.soc.surrey.ac.uk/caqdas/

The software demo version ftp address is:

ftp.soc.surrey.ac.uk

To join qual-software, send an untitled message to mailbase@mailbase.ac.uk. In text, enter: join qual-software *your first name your second name.*

QSR runs a Web site and a forum for discussion of NUD*IST and other qualitative software:

http://www.qsr.com.au

To send a message to the QSR-Forum, send e-mail to QSR- Forum@qsr.com.au. To subscribe to the QSR-Forum, send e-mail to mailing-list-request@qsr.com.au. In the main body of the text include the words SUBSCRIBE QSR-Forum.

the World Wide Web or in papers the development team members have written (see the bibliography at the end of this appendix).

Since software is changing fast, most books are out of date when they appear. This appendix is an exception. It describes QSR NUD*IST4 (known as N4), the package discussed in Chapter 8 and the most recent version as this book goes to press. It concludes by describing a completely new product, nearing completion, by the same development team, and tentatively named NVivo–NUD*IST alive.

■ ■ ■ ■ What Is a NUD*IST Project Like?

There is no typical qualitative project, and none is typical of this software. NUD*IST is designed to offer tools for a wide variety of qualitative work. But most researchers want to go directly into their data and the process of thinking aloud about the data. With a simple map of where things are in a project you can move between data and ideas.

A NUD*IST project has two parts, the Document System and the Index System. If you have started the tutorial with a new project, you will see a Document Explorer and a Node Explorer, both empty at first. As you work through the tutorial, documents you put in the project and the categories you create for thinking about them appear in the Explorers.

The Document System holds all your data. If the study of medical students were an N4 project, it might have a document system of interview transcripts, field notes, memos about them, photos, and videos.

The Index System is made up of *nodes*, places where you keep concepts and ideas. You code data by putting references to the passages at nodes. In the medical student study, there might early on be nodes for concepts about attitudes to patients (supporting, condescending) and for factors that seem relevant to images (networks, family) as well as things known about the hospital setting or behavior (bedside manner and clinical approach).

Many researchers also keep information about people, places, and so forth in the Index System, so they can ask questions using that information. (For example, you might store the gender and seniority of each student.) The software is designed to automate many of these more routine information-storing tasks, with a command file system and the ability to import from and export to statistical packages like SPSS and spreadsheets. (If a table of information about the students is typed and imported, NUD*IST will make the categories and do the coding for you.)

The Document and Index systems are linked by tools for searching and theorizing. As you start asking questions, you can use the coding and stored information to retrieve the material you want. (For example: Do the younger students view medical responsibility differently than do the older ones? What does this suggest about hierarchy and ways of moving through it?)

■ ■ ■ ■ **Managing Data**

Usually qualitative data is "rich," containing a lot of meanings, suggestions, new ideas. Such rich records as Chapter 8 describes are always challenging to handle.

Documents in a NUD*IST4 project can be imported from plain text files or external documents of any sort. If you have the software, type the record of your field notes or transcribe an interview in a word processor. Save it as plain text. To tell NUD*IST the units it will number, code, and retrieve, choose the word processor option that puts "hard returns" marking those units. (Most people use paragraphs, lines, or sentences.) From within NUD*IST, import that document. You can now browse the document, thinking about it, editing it, annotating, and coding as you wish. (You can code and analyze any type of "document" because even if it is not typed or scanned into the computer, it can be coded and annotated as an External Document. In the medical students' study, for example, you might have newspaper clippings, photographs, maps, music or videotapes, and books in the library.)

You can manage almost any kind of unstructured data this way. If your college has a site license for NUD*IST, try using the software for essay preparation, storing typed notes and scanned abstracts as imported documents, and making external documents for books in the library—coding and bringing them all together by topic.

■ ■ ■ ■ **Managing Ideas at Nodes**

In NUD*IST, you store categories, ideas about them, and coding for them at nodes. Nodes are created in many ways, every time you want to store a thought. You can move them around, adding or deleting nodes, shifting or merging them.

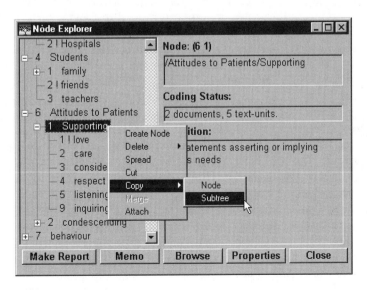

Nodes can be free or in a hierarchical "tree" (category/subcategory). As your ideas take shape, the tree-structured index of nodes helps you gather sets of ideas together, as you would sort index cards. But this is a very flexible index system. There is no limit to the number of nodes you can create or to resorting and combining them. You can cut, copy, attach, or merge nodes without losing the coding or memos at them. You can combine them, collect all coding stored hierarchically below them for recoding, and try different ways of organizing them.

Nodes do not have to be created in advance, but doing so often helps you identify the basic ideas about your research project. For example, make a list of the possible starting categories you might want for the medical students study and a list of things you would want to know about the attributes of students. The lists will be quite long and can be organized into small "trees" for easy access. If you have the software, creating the nodes is easier than writing them down!

■ ■ ■ ■ Coding

Most qualitative researchers want to code data to store their ideas of what the data are about and to link passages about the same thing. To view that text and think more about the topic, the researchers then retrieve all the data coded about it. Usually they also want to ask subtler questions, to create more specific categories. Without computers, it is hard to ask even for everything on a topic and sometimes impossible to think more subtly about new dimensions for the topic.

In NUD*IST4 you can code data in many different ways, but they all do essentially the same thing: You tell the software to put a reference to just *this* part of *this* document, *here*, at *this* node. If the document is imported, coding is usually done on the screen because it is more direct and swiftly done and because the program can take you to other contexts that might be relevant.

To code on the screen, select a document and click Browse. A palette of options appears. Highlight the text you are interested in, click Add Coding, and specify which node you want to code at. If you are making new, unconnected categories, click Free Node and just type the name you want to give the category (for example, "crocks"). If you want to code at an existing node, just select it. To see all the material on a topic ("What have I coded at 'crocks'?"), select that node in the Explorer and browse. All the text coded at the node will appear. The palette changes slightly, since now you can do different things, such as widening the spread of your coding, or jumping from any extract to the source document.

You can code on paper if you prefer. Print a document. (If you have the software, print a report, so the text units are numbered.) Sit under a tree and think about the report, scribbling in the margins. Then come back to NUD*IST and use the menu option under Index System (Add/Delete coding) to tell NUD*IST where to code the passage.

You can "auto-code" in several ways, by text search or by a command file.

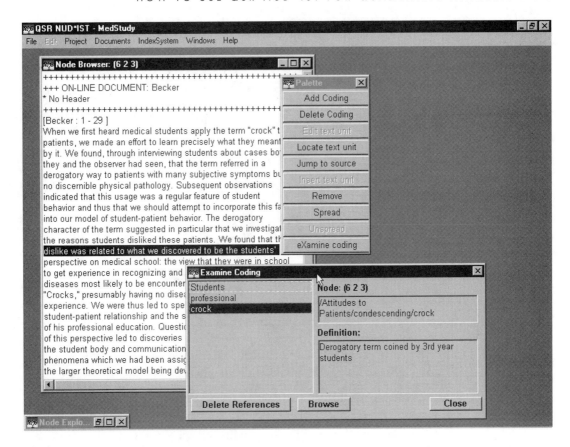

Searching and Asking Questions

Qualitative researchers spend a lot of time searching—for words or for patterns of ideas. As you work with data, you explore the ideas or concepts you create, seek patterns (do the younger students have different attitudes on this issue?), and build more questions on the answers. This way of building an analysis is crucial in qualitative work. It is called *system closure,* the process of entering results as more data so you can ask another question (Richards & Richards, 1994b).

You can separately search text or search the Index system for patterns of coding. The program will give you the answer from a text or index search by coding all the finds (with whatever context you want) at a new node it makes for storing the finds in appropriate index categories.

Searching Text

To search text, you specify what "string" of characters (or pattern) you want to find. (For example, a request might be to find every time the students say "crock" or "crocks" or "phony" or "complain," "complains," or "complaining.")

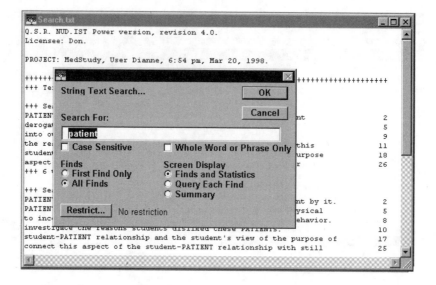

You can fine-tune the search by specifying details, including which documents to search (for instance, only the younger students' interviews) and which text (only when they are talking about patients). The answer is given to you as a new node, and you can browse and rethink that or spread it for a wider context.

This means that as long as the word or characters you enter will accurately find what you are seeking, you can "cheat" on at least some coding! You might search for "crock," and spread it to the whole of the students' statements in the group. You then have an instant node coding all speeches where the word was used. Be careful: Text search is a blunt instrument relying on a mechanical process. Even with the pattern searches, you can't be sure to find every time students showed the attitudes you're researching.

Searching for Patterns of Coding

You can also search for patterns of coding at nodes or for relationships between categories (index search). This sort of search looks for relationships between coding at two or more nodes. (For example, when medical students talk of hierarchy, what do they say about the student-patient relationship?)

NUD*IST4 provides a large number of ways of studying and building on the relationships between coding at different nodes. For the search just described, you would use the first of 17 choices, or Intersect. But a more interesting question might be about the proximity of these ideas. (When students in the same statement talk of those two topics, what do they say about their learning?) This needs a different search operator (called Near). There is a search operator, or a combination of them, to answer almost any question about coding patterns. You can combine them to gather a lot of material, to test a specific hypothesis, to make a matrix showing patterns, or to ask just which students showed these characteristics.

As with text search, this type of search can be restricted to certain documents or to text coded somewhere you specify. As with text search, NUD*IST gives you the result of an index search as a new node, coding all the material you want. You can browse, recode, spread the text you found so as to include more context, and of course rename the node or shift it elsewhere in the index tree.

■ ■ ■ ■ Creating and Testing Theories

The end of a qualitative project is always theory. The theory may be small, local explanations or "grounded theory" that offers new concepts or wider claims to new understanding. The theory may be quite simple, a general understanding or explanation of the data, a sense of what's going on. Or it may be a new, thorough theory of behavior in the area studied. In Becker's terms, "part-models" can build up a larger theoretical model. You may wish to take this theory on to another stage by exporting the results of your analysis to a statistics package or a mind-mapping tool. NUD*IST will export the concepts to other software or give you editable reports on any aspect of your documents (or show the patterns of your coding) so you can write and report on the project.

Theories can be tentatively expressed in Memos you write at documents or nodes. These can be edited and combined as firm ideas. Ideas can also be inserted in documents. Your field notes from observation of students discussing patients, for instance, would contain theories about their behavior, and these would be expressed as Annotations in the text. NUD*IST codes these at a node for annotations and you can retrieve them using the index search tools ("Give me all the annotations in interviews where students are speaking about professional status.") There is no limit to the amount of text you can store to contain your ideas and interpretations.

The expression and testing of theories and hypotheses is also done through the Index system. You can build up, merge, gather together, and ask questions about nodes that store new ideas. Using index searches, you can find patterns in those ideas or display them or, if appropriate, construct and test hypotheses. You can also use search procedures to show patterns and explore them. For instance, NUD*IST will draw up a matrix of all the attitudes to patients divided by age of student, including what Becker described as "quasi-statistics." Make a report on the matrix node, and you can read in turn what each group of students actually said on each of these topics—as long as you did the coding well!

```
Matrix.txt                                                    _ □ X
Matrix Node:  (I 5) //Index Searches/Index Search196
Operator:     INTERSECT
Definition:   Search for (MATRIX INTERSECT (1 1 2) (6)). No restriction
Rows:         (1 1 2) /base data/interviewees/age-group
Columns:      (6) /Attitudes to Patients
Data:         Number of text-units coded


+-----------+-----------+-----------+
| age-group | Supporting |condescendi~|
+-----------+-----------+-----------+
|    20s    |     5     |    14     |
+-----------+-----------+-----------+
|    30s    |     3     |     3     |
+-----------+-----------+-----------+
|    40s    |     5     |     3     |
+-----------+-----------+-----------+
```

NUD*IST Alive: Toward NVivo

This final section describes QSR's design for the next-generation software package, which will offer an upgrade from NUD*IST4. The description is of software still in the testing stage; when you see NVivo, it may not fit this description exactly.

If you are working in NVivo, a project might start looking similar to those already described (in fact, you can lift an N4 project straight into NVivo). Menu items for documents and nodes lead to Explorers. In NVivo, these show more information than in NUD*IST4 and give a first hint of the differences. For example, you can see a full outline of a document and select any subhead to go straight to that place. More differences appear when you start importing documents. They look alive because they can come now in rich text, with font, color, formatting, and so forth to show meaning. They can come from many more sources, and you can make proxy documents for summaries of, for example, your videotapes. They are linked to illustrations, to ideas, and to other documents.

NVivo is not just a pretty new interface; these changes are methodologically important. Take a plain text document (such as one from NUD*IST4) and alter it using a variety of fonts, colors, styles, and levels of headings to see how much more meaning can be conveyed. Put it in an NVivo project, and you can insert links to DataBites, which can be your text annotations or any other file you select (graphics, spreadsheet, video). A student's description of a patient as a "crock" can now be annotated and illustrated: Click DataBite to link this text to

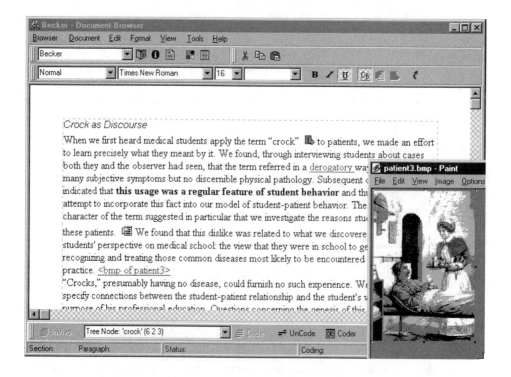

your comment that "crock" hardly fit your observation or to a picture of the elderly but sprightly "crock" in question. You might now link that document to others or to nodes (DocLinks and NodeLinks). Links to other documents take you straight to relevant data (in your field notes of student discussions, for example, you might insert a link to the interview when this student spoke in private quite differently about the patients). Links can take you to your memos, which are full-status documents in NVivo (code and link them like any other data). Links to nodes can take you to a concept or to special extracts you want to see here. (Insert a link to a node with the extract from another student's interview where he discussed this case.) So documents in NVivo are "live" in the sense that they can take you to other data and ideas—a goal qualitative researchers from all disciplines share.

Which software you use will inevitably affect your method. With NVivo, your field notes from hospital observations would contain direct links to film clips, photos, even the voices in the student discussions. Or you could use these links to create a dynamic report on the medical students project—a report that grows as the project does and contains the links to your emerging ideas and the evidence for them.

Coding in NVivo will feel very different from coding in N4. The rich text documents are not formatted in fixed text units, so you can code exactly the words or characters you wish. And you can do it in many different, very fast ways. "Drag and drop" takes the selected text to the node, or the node to the text. A speed coding bar lets you type the node below the text and simply click Code. Or name the code, from text you select, and create and code in it (what some methods call In Vivo coding) by simply selecting text and clicking the In Vivo button. Or use a Coder that shows you all your nodes, or just the ones you

recently used, or all the ones coding this section, or that lets you make working sets of nodes and code passages with the whole set. Coding is also easier because you can store information and filter inquiries in other ways. Tell the program (by simple import) the attributes of documents or nodes, to store things you know about people or places (student characteristics, demographic details, and so on).

Nodes can be used in different ways, and managed in Sets, so you can think about groups of issues or ideas. With NVivo, the different uses of nodes are separated into three areas: Free, Tree, and Case. Cases can be separately handled, with access to all the data about each case.

Searching also looks and feels very different in NVivo. Searching the text or the index is an integrated function. The program walks you through a search very much as you would naturally be asking a question. NVivo will do all of the searches available in N4 (and a few different ones), but it offers ways of combining and specifying them to bring you closer to what you want. You start not by asking which tool you want but "What do I want to ask?" Select the sort of search (from any of the text and index searches) and specify how it will be done. Now ask, "Where do I want to look?" and Scope the search by choosing to look at particular documents or material coded by a particular node or nodes or combinations of documents and coding, and then filtering the scope according to coding or attributes. At any stage, ask, "What have I got here?" and assay the data you are exploring: "Which sorts of students are represented here?" "Which of the many ideas about medical authority come up in the interviews where the derogatory attitudes to patients occurred?"

Thus theory making and testing in NVivo will be different. Researchers will draw on a wider range of ways to store the varieties of material that contain growing theory—from little hunches to significant reflections. Annotations and memos are accessible in new ways, embedded in the document in DataBites and DocLinks. The field notes from the hospital would in this program become a dynamic account of the emerging theory rather than a dead account of a past event. That account would also be visual because NVivo supports diagrams and models. The Modeller allows you to draw any number of models of how things link or what is going on. A node or a document in a model is "live": Click on it to go to the text and think about it. In the hospital study, the part-models that built up the theoretical model Becker describes could be drawn, changed, and linked to the documents and ideas. In the Model Explorer these and the items in them would be shown and be movable. So the theoretical models Becker describes not only can be sketched but also can directly call the data related to each of these parts of the model.

When both NUD*IST4 and NVivo are available, how would you choose which to use? You would first look at your equipment and your goals, since the programs run on different machines and they support different methods. Then for most researchers the best advice is to play with both programs and talk to those using them. The Internet makes demonstration software and discussions freely available. It also gives you a chance to take part in the next development of qualitative software. QSR has put on its Web site a discussion space for stu-

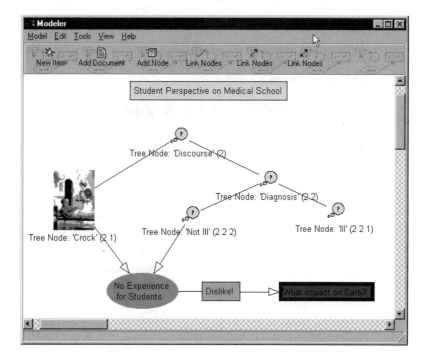

dents using this textbook. Visit it to read and contribute comments on the ways this software works and where qualitative methods and qualitative software are going. Visit us at **http://www.qsr.com.au.**

■ ■ ■ ■ ■ ## Bibliography

Richards, L. 1997a. "Computers and Qualitative Analysis." *The International Encyclopedia of Education*, 2nd ed. Oxford: Elsevier Science.

Richards, L. 1997b. "User's Mistake as Developer's Challenge." *Qualitative Health Research*, 7 (3): 406–416.

Richards, L. In press. "Closeness to Data: The Changing Goals of Qualitative Data Handling." *Qualitative Health Research*.

Richards, L., and T. Richards. 1994a. "From Filing Cabinet to Computer." Pp. 146–172 in *Analyzing Qualitative Data*, edited by Alan Bryman and Robert G. Burgess. London: Routledge.

Richards, L., and T. Richards. 1994b. "Using Computers in Qualitative Analysis." Pp. 445–462 in *Handbook of Qualitative Research*, edited by Norman K. Denzin and Yvonna S. Lincoln. Thousand Oaks, CA: Sage.

Weitzman, E., and M. B. Miles. 1995. *Computer Programs for Qualitative Data Analysis*. Thousand Oaks, CA: Sage.

Appendix H
Annotated List of Web Sites

http://www.abanet.org/domviol/mrdv/identify.html

The American Bar Association's Commission on Domestic Violence. It includes a definition of domestic violence, procedures for identifying a person as a victim of domestic violence, and a list of "basic warning signs."

http://www.asanet.org/

American Sociological Association. Includes lists of publications, Ethics Code, Employment Bulletin, and summaries of research funding opportunities.

http://www.annurev.org/ari

Follow the publications links to an on-line version of the *Annual Review of Sociology*. Abstracts from volumes can be searched by subject or by keywords. Offers downloads of complete text of articles for a fee.

http://www.ojp.usdoj.gov/

The Web site of the Bureau of Justice Statistics with an analysis of the adequacy of juvenile court records.

http://stats.bls.gov

Bureau of Labor Statistics, Department of Labor. A significant source of data on employment and earnings.

http://www.rci.rutgers.edu/~cas2/

Center of Alcohol Studies. Offers links to numerous sites related to alcohol, alcoholism, and so on. A comprehensive index of a wealth of information on the subject.

http://www.scpr.ac.uk/cass

Centre for Applied Social Surveys (CASS). Offers access to the Question Bank (a reference source for information on how questions are formatted and worded in major social surveys) and general knowledge about survey data collection methods, design, and measurement. Access to CASS newsletters and CASS courses as well as links to other research sites of interest such as Articles on Social Survey Methodology.

http://www.city.net

This Web site offers a huge volume of information on counties, cities, states, and countries throughout the world. A virtual encyclopedia of demographic, cultural, organizational, and political information plus much, much more. Offers links to each of the states in the United States as well as U.S. cities.

http://www.well.com/user/theory/

The Common Theory Project, an academic program to develop more integrated theorizing in the social sciences. Includes a description of the Common Theory Project, its purpose, and beliefs that motivate it.

http://www.c-s-i.org/

Crime Stoppers International, an organization devoted to fighting crime and violence around the world. Offers links to interesting sites related to the subjects of crime and violence.

http://www.sociology.org/

Electronic Journal of Sociology. Full text of articles published only on-line.

http://www.uark.edu/depts/plscinfo/pub/ethics/ethics.html

Ethics site maintained by the University of Arkansas. Cases are described that involve various ethical and moral dilemmas confronted in social science research, public administration, policy making, and so on. Each case offers a different example of an ethical issue. Lists of questions allow the reader to explore the complexity of the ethics issues involved and reflect on his or her own opinions regarding the cases.

http://www.fbi.gov/

Federal Bureau of Investigation. This site provides the FBI's descriptions of different types of gang activities.

http://thomas.loc.gov

Federal legislation, including pending and past legislation, and committee composition.

http://gilligan.prod.oclc.org:3057/

FirstSearch on-line bibliography and electronic journals. Available only through libraries.

http://www.gallup.com

Gallup poll. Election poll results back to 1936 and information from polls on current events.

http://www.icpsr.umich.edu/gss/

General Social Survey. Search all years of the GSS for variables of interest. Check wording of questions and response choices, see frequency distributions for variables in different sets of years, obtain lists of GSS publications, and download GSS datasets.

http://lib-www.ucr.edu

INFOMINE (Scholarly Internet Resource Collections). This is one example of a site that scholars can use to link to other sites containing a wide range of scholarly materials.

http://www.uakron.edu/hefe/lib1.html

Library of Congress, presidential libraries, database of academic research journals, academic libraries with Web servers.

http://www.fisk.edu/rri.org

The Fisk University Race Relations Institute site, with information about race in America and policy suggestions.

http://www.socsciresearch.com

Links to data archives, reference materials, case studies for sociology courses.

http://www.trinity.edu/~mkearl/index.html

Links to many resources, including government statistics, data sources, theory groups.

http://www.princeton.edu/~sociolog/links.html

Links to lists of professional associations, sociology departments, university catalogs, data archives.

http://osiris.colorado.edu/SOC/links.html

Links to sociology resources.

http://nch.ari.net/

The National Coalition for the Homeless. Current statistics, publications, legislative developments, links to other resources.

http://www.umich.edu/~nes

National Election Studies. Includes responses to questions asked since 1952, test of 1996 NES questionnaire, data for on-line analysis. Searchable by keyword.

http://www.nih.gov/

National Institutes of Health. Information about NIH programs and grants.

http://www.nsf.gov/sbe/sber/sociol/start.htm

National Science Foundation's Sociology Program Web site. Information regarding the Sociology Program, research funding, current and past supported projects, and so forth.

http://www.pirg.org/nscahh

The National Student Campaign Against Hunger and Homelessness. Information on projects and ways to volunteer.

http://www.fedworld.gov/index.html

National Technical Information Service for ordering government publications.

http://www.Nytimes.com

The New York Times Web edition, with regular news stories and other regular newspaper sections. Some pictures and audio files. Also, special news sections for Web users; on-line forums, allowing you to read comments on some issue—and to send a comment yourself; and search options.

http://ous.usa.net

Organizational Universe Systems. Specializes in organizational and management development. Offers information regarding methodology for surveys, focus groups, and so on that can be used to help assess organizations or help in creating surveys, etc. Offers "freebies" such as papers and presentations including one titled "Sensing with Focus Groups," which is a guide to the structure, design, and implementation of focus groups.

http://www.umich.edu/~psid

The Panel Study of Income Dynamics. Provides data and publications.

http://popindex.princeton.edu/

Population Index for 1986–1996.

http://www.erols.com/bainbri/qf.htm

The Question Factory. A laboratory for exploring survey instruments. Allows Web users to participate in interactive survey creation and gives access to survey results.

http://www.ropercenter.uconn.edu/

The Roper Center. General information on the center and poll results on presidential performance.

http://www.socabs.org

Sociological Abstracts. General information; search service available to subscribers only.

http://www.socresonline.org.uk/socresonline/

Sociological Research Online. Full text articles published only on-line.

http://www.geocities.com/~sociorealm/welcome5.htm

SocioRealm. Offers a comprehensive list of subjects related to sociology and other areas of social science with numerous links to related sites. A great source to start from for Web browsers interested in the social sciences.

http://sosig.esrc.bris.ac.uk/roads/cgi/search.pl

Social Science Information Gateway. An omnibus source offering a comprehensive index of links to multiple resources in sociology, including research methods sites, professional associations, and research centers. A good reference source for social science browsing on the Web.

http://www.pscw.uva.nl/sociosite

Sociosite-Going Dutch Sociology. Information system of the Sociological Institute of the University of Amsterdam. Offers links and access to a vast number of helpful sites on the Internet related to sociology. Can be used as a reference source for sociology on the Web.

http://www.samhsa.gov

The Substance Abuse and Mental Health Services Administration site offers summaries of publications, reports, and statistical information on SAMHSA research.

http://www.pathfinder.com

Time Warner's popular Web guide to the latest news and information from around the world. Updated throughout the day. Allows the reader to access cover stories, late-breaking news, and so forth from major newspapers, magazines, and other sources. Offers links to numerous sources of information on subjects of interest.

http://ftp.census.gov/

U.S. Census Bureau home page. Contains tables and graphs reporting detailed census data. Population data and economic indicators.

http://www.usps.gov/

ZIP codes corresponding to street addresses. Useful for survey mailings.

References

Abbott, Andrew. 1992. "From Causes to Events: Notes on Narrative Positivism." *Sociological Methods and Research,* 20 (May): 428–455.

Abbott, Andrew. 1994. "History and Sociology: The Lost Synthesis." Pp. 77–112 in *Engaging the Past: The Uses of History Across the Social Sciences.* Durham, NC: Duke University Press.

Abrams, Philip. 1982. *Historical Sociology.* Ithaca, NY: Cornell University Press.

Adair, G., T. W. Dushenko, and R. C. L. Lindsay. 1985. "Ethical Regulations and Their Impact on Research Practice." *American Psychologist,* 40: 59–72.

Alfred, Randall. 1976. "The Church of Satan." Pp. 180–202 in *The New Religious Consciousness,* edited by Charles Glock and Robert Bellah. Berkeley: University of California Press.

Altheide, David L. and John M. Johnson. 1994. "Criteria for Assessing Interpretive Validity in Qualitative Research." Pp. 485–499 in *Handbook of Qualitative Research,* edited by Norman K. Denzin and Yvonna S. Lincoln. Thousand Oaks, CA: Sage.

Altman, Drew, Ellen L. Bassuk, William R. Breakey, A. Alan Fischer, Charles R. Halpern, Gloria Smith, Louisa Stark, Nathan Stark, Bruce C. Vladeck, and Phyllis Wolfe. 1989. "Health Care for the Homeless." *Society,* 26 (May/June): 4–5.

Alvarez, Lizette. 1996. "Who Needs Emergency Family Shelter? Try Asking Mothers Who Are There." *The New York Times,* September 2, pp. 23, 25.

American Psychiatric Association. 1994. *Diagnostic and Statistical Manual of Mental Disorders,* 4th ed. (DSM IV). Washington, DC: American Psychiatric Association.

American Sociological Association. 1989. *Code of Ethics.* Washington, DC: American Sociological Association.

American Sociological Association. 1997. *Code of Ethics.* Washington, DC: American Sociological Association.

Aminzade, Ronald. 1992. "Historical Sociology and Time." *Sociological Methods & Research,* 20: 456–480.

Anderson, Elijah. 1990. *Streetwise: Race, Class, and Change in an Urban Community.* Chicago: University of Chicago Press.

Anderton, Douglas L., Richard E. Barrett, and Donald J. Bogue. 1997. *The Population of the United States.* New York: Free Press.

Anspach, Renee R. 1991. "Everyday Methods for Assessing Organizational Effectiveness." *Social Problems,* 38 (February): 1–19.

Aponte, Robert. 1990. "Definitions of the Underclass: A Critical Analysis." Pp. 117–137 in *Sociology in America,* edited by Herbert J. Gans. Newbury Park, CA: Sage.

Applebome, Peter. 1993. "Racial Divisions Persist 25 Years After King Killing." *The New York Times,* April 4, p. 16.

Arnold, David. 1994. "Manners Found, Good and Bad . . ." *Boston Globe,* July 7, pp. 1, 31.

Aronson, Elliot and Judson Mills. 1959. "The Effect of Severity of Initiation on Liking for a Group." *Journal of Abnormal and Social Psychology,* 59 (September): 177–181.

Aseltine, Robert H., Jr., and Ronald C. Kessler. 1993. "Marital Disruption and Depression in a Community Sample." *Journal of Health and Social Behavior,* 34 (September): 237–251.

Ashenfelter, Orley. 1973. "Discrimination and Trade Unions." Pp. 88–112 in *Discrimination in Labor Markets,* edited by Orley Ashenfelter and Albert Rees. Princeton, NJ: Princeton University Press.

Babbie, Earl and Fred Halley. 1994. *Adventures in Social Research: Data Analysis Using SPSS.* Thousand Oaks, CA: Pine Forge Press.

Babbie, Earl and Fred Halley. 1995. *Adventures in Social Research: Data Analysis Using SPSS for Windows.* Thousand Oaks, CA: Pine Forge Press.

Babor, Thomas F., Robert S. Stephens, and G. Alan Marlatt. 1987. "Verbal Report Methods in Clinical Research on Alcoholism: Response Bias and Its Minimization." *Journal of Studies on Alcohol,* 48(5): 410–424.

Bahr, Howard M. and Theodore Caplow. 1973. *Old Men Drunk and Sober.* New York: New York University Press.

Bailey, William C. 1990. "Murder, Capital Punishment, and Television: Execution Publicity and Homicide Rates." *American Sociological Review,* 55 (October): 628–633.

Bainbridge, William Sims. 1989. *Survey Research: A Computer-Assisted Introduction.* Belmont, CA: Wadsworth.

Bandura, Albert, Dorothea Ross, and Sheila A. Ross. 1963. "Imitation of Film-Mediated Aggressive Models." *Journal of Abnormal and Social Psychology*, 66: 3–11.

Banks, J. A. 1972. "Historical Sociology and the Study of Population." Pp. 55–70 in *Population and Social Change*, edited by D. V. Glass and Roger Revelle. London: Edward Arnold.

Barclay, George W. 1958. *Techniques of Population Analysis.* New York: Wiley.

Barrett A. Lee, Sue Hinze Jones, and David W. Lewis, 1990. "Public Beliefs About the Causes of Homelessness." *Social Forces,* 69:253–265.

Barringer, Felicity. 1993. "Majority in Poll Back Ban on Handguns." *The New York Times,* June 4, p. A14.

Baum, Samuel. 1993. "Sources of Demographic Data." Pp. 3-1–3-50 in *Readings in Population Research Methodology. Volume 1, Basic Tools*, edited by Donald J. Bogue, Eduardo E. Arriaga, and Douglas L. Anderton. Chicago: Social Development Center, for the United National Population Fund.

Baxter, Ellen and Kim Hopper. 1984. "Shelter and Housing for the Homeless Mentally Ill." Pp. 109–139 in *The Homeless Mentally Ill*, edited by H. Richard Lamb. Washington, DC: American Psychiatric Association.

Bean, Lee L., Geraldine P. Mineau, and Douglas L. Anderton. 1990. *Fertility Change on the American Frontier: Adaptation and Innovation.* Berkeley: University of California Press.

Becker, Gary S. 1971. *The Economics of Discrimination,* 2nd ed. Chicago: University of Chicago Press.

Becker, Howard S. 1958. "Problems of Inference and Proof in Participant Observation." *American Sociological Review,* 23: 652–660.

Becker, Howard S. 1963. *The Outsiders: Studies in the Sociology of Deviance.* New York: Free Press.

Becker, Howard S. 1986. *Writing for Social Scientists.* Chicago: University of Chicago Press. (This can be ordered directly from the American Sociological Association, 1722 N Street, NW, Washington, DC 20036, 202–833–3410.)

Bellah, Robert N., Richard Madsen, William M. Sullivan, Ann Swidler, and Steven M. Tipton. 1985. *Habits of the Heart: Individualism and Commitment in American Life.* New York: Harper & Row.

Bendix, Reinhard. 1962. *Max Weber: An Intellectual Portrait.* Garden City, NY: Doubleday/Anchor.

Berk, Richard A., Alec Campbell, Ruth Klap, and Bruce Western. 1992. "The Deterrent Effect of Arrest: A Bayesian Analysis of Four Field Experiments." *American Sociological Review,* 57 (October): 698–708.

Beyer, William H. (Ed.). 1968. *CRC Handbook of Tables for Probability and Statistics*, 2nd ed. Boca Raton, FL: CRC Press.

Binder, Arnold and James W. Meeker. 1993. "Implications of the Failure to Replicate the Minneapolis Experimental Findings." *American Sociological Review,* 58 (December): 886–888.

Black, Donald J. (Ed.). 1984. *Toward a General Theory of Social Control.* Orlando, FL: Academic Press.

Blair, Johnny E. 1989. Letter to Catherine E. Ross. April 10. Unpublished.

Blakely, Edward J., and Mary Gail Snyder. 1997. *Fortress America: Gated Communities in the United States.* Washington, DC, and Cambridge, MA: Brookings Institution Press and Lincoln Institute of Land Policy.

Blalock, Hubert M., Jr. 1967. *Toward a Theory of Minority-Group Relations.* New York: Wiley.

Blauner, Robert. 1964. *Alienation and Freedom: The Factory Worker and His Industry.* Chicago: University of Chicago Press.

Bogue, Donald J. 1969. *Principles of Demography.* New York: Wiley.

Bogue, Donald J., Eduardo E. Arriega, and Douglas L. Anderton. 1993. *Readings in Population Research Methodology. Vol. 1, Basic Tools.* Chicago: Social Development Center, for the United Nations Population Fund.

Bollen, Kenneth A., Barbara Entwisle, and Arthur S. Alderson. 1993. "Macrocomparative Research Methods." *Annual Review of Sociology,* 19: 321–351.

Booth, Wayne C., Gregory G. Colomb, and Joseph M. Williams. 1995. *The Craft of Research.* Chicago: University of Chicago Press.

Bourgois, Philippe, Mark Lettiere, and James Quesada. 1997. "Social Misery and the Sanctions of Substance Abuse: Confronting HIV Risk Among Homeless Heroin Addicts in San Francisco." *Social Problems,* 44: 155–173.

Bradshaw, York W. and Michael Wallace. 1996. *Global Inequalities.* Thousand Oaks, CA: Sage.

Brent, Edward and Alan Thompson. 1996. *Methodologist's Toolchest™ for Windows: User's Guide and Reference Manual.* Columbia, MO: Idea Works.

Bridges, George S. and Joseph G. Weis. 1989. "Measuring Violent Behavior: Effects of Study Design on Reported Correlates of Violence." Pp. 14–34 in *Violent Crime, Violent Criminals*, edited by Neil Alan Weiner and Marvin E. Wolfgang. Newbury Park, CA: Sage.

Burt, Martha R. 1996. "Homelessness: Definitions and Counts." Pp. 15–23 in *Homelessness in America*, edited by Jim Baumohl. Phoenix: Oryx Press.

Bushman, Brad J. 1995. "Moderating Role of Trait Aggressiveness in the Effects of Violent Media on Aggression." *Journal of Personality and Social Psychology*, 69(5): 950–960.

Butler, Dore and Florence Geis. 1990. "Nonverbal Affect Responses to Male and Female Leaders: Implications for Leadership Evaluations." *Journal of Personality and Social Psychology*, 58 (January): 48–59.

Butterfield, Fox. 1996a. "After 10 Years, Juvenile Crime Begins to Drop." *The New York Times*, August 9, pp. A1, A25.

Butterfield, Fox. 1996b. "Gun Violence May Be Subsiding, Studies Find." *The New York Times*, October 14, p. A10.

Butterfield, Fox. 1997. "Serious Crime Decreased for Fifth Year in a Row." *The New York Times*, January 5, p. 10.

Cain, Leonard D., Jr. 1967. "The AMA and the Gerontologists: Uses and Abuses of 'A Profile of the Aging: USA.' " Pp. 78–114 in *Ethics, Politics, and Social Research*, edited by Gideon Sjoberg. Cambridge, MA: Schenkman.

Campbell, Donald T. and Julian C. Stanley. 1966. *Experimental and Quasi-Experimental Designs for Research*. Chicago: Rand McNally.

Campbell, Richard T. 1992. "Longitudinal Research." Pp. 1146–1158 in *Encyclopedia of Sociology*, edited by Edgar F. Borgatta and Marie L. Borgatta. New York: Macmillan.

Center for Survey Research, University of Massachusetts at Boston. 1987. "Methodology: Designing Good Survey Questions." *Newsletter*, April, p. 3.

Chase-Dunn, Christopher and Thomas D. Hall. 1993. "Comparing World-Systems: Concepts and Working Hypotheses." *Social Forces*, 71: 851–886.

Chen, Xiangming. 1994. "The Changing Roles of Free Economic Zones in Development: A Comparative Analysis of Capitalist and Socialist Cases in East Asia." *Studies in Comparative International Development*, 29: 3–25.

Clements, Mark. 1994. "What Americans Say About the Homeless." *Parade Magazine*, January 9, pp. 4–6.

Coffey, Amanda and Paul Atkinson. 1996. *Making Sense of Qualitative Data: Complementary Research Strategies*. Thousand Oaks, CA: Sage.

Cohen, Sheldon. 1992. "Stress, Social Support, and Disorder." Pp. 109–124 in *The Meaning and Measurement of Social Support*, edited by Hans O. F. Veiel and Urs Baumann. New York: Hemisphere.

Cohen, Susan G. and Gerald E. Ledford, Jr. 1994. "The Effectiveness of Self-Managing Teams: A Quasi-Experiment." *Human Relations*, 47: 13–43.

Coleman, James S. and Thomas Hoffer. 1987. *Public and Private High Schools: The Impact of Communities*. New York: Basic Books.

Coleman, James S., Thomas Hoffer, and Sally Kilgore. 1982. *High School Achievement: Public, Catholic, and Private Schools Compared*. New York: Basic Books.

Converse, Jean M. 1984. "Attitude Measurement in Psychology and Sociology: The Early Years." Pp. 3–40 in *Surveying Subjective Phenomena*, vol. 2, edited by Charles F. Turner and Elizabeth Martin. New York: Russell Sage Foundation.

Cook, Thomas D. and Donald T. Campbell. 1979. *Quasi-Experimentation: Design and Analysis Issues for Field Settings*. Chicago: Rand McNally.

Cooper, Harris and Larry V. Hedges. 1994. "Research Synthesis as a Scientific Enterprise." Pp. 3–14 in *The Handbook of Research Synthesis*, edited by Harris Cooper and Larry V. Hedges. New York: Russell Sage Foundation.

Core Institute. 1994. "Core Alcohol and Drug Survey: Long Form." Carbondale, IL: FIPSE Core Analysis Grantee Group, Core Institute, Student Health Programs, Southern Illinois University.

Corse, Sara J., Nancy B. Hirschinger, and David Zanis. 1995. "The Use of the Addiction Severity Index with People with Severe Mental Illness." *Psychiatric Rehabilitation Journal*, 19(1): 9–18.

Costner, Herbert L. 1989. "The Validity of Conclusions in Evaluation Research: A Further Development of Chen and Rossi's Theory-Driven Approach." *Evaluation and Program Planning*, 12: 345–353.

Crenshaw, Edward M. 1995. "Democracy and Demographic Inheritance: The Influence of Modernity and Proto-Modernity on Political and Civil Rights, 1965 to 1980." *American Sociological Review*, 60: 702–718.

Crossen, Cynthia. 1994. "How 'Tactical Research' Muddied Diaper Debate." *The Wall Street Journal*, May 17, pp. B1, B9.

Czaja, Ronald and Bob Blair. 1995. *Survey Research*. Newbury Park, CA: Pine Forge Press.

Damasio, Antonio R. 1994. *Descartes' Error: Emotion, Reason, and the Human Brain*. New York: Grosset/Putnam.

Daniels, Arlene Kaplan. 1967. "The Low-Caste Stranger in Social Research." Pp. 267–296 in *Ethics, Politics, and Social Research*, edited by Gideon Sjoberg. Cambridge, MA: Schenkman.

Dannefer, W. Dale and Russell K. Schutt. 1982. "Race and Juvenile Justice Processing in Court and Police Agencies." *American Journal of Sociology*, 87 (March): 1113–1132.

Davies, Paul. 1993. "The Holy Grail of Physics." *The New York Times Book Review*, March 7, pp. 11–12.

Davis, James A. and Tom W. Smith. 1992. *The NORC General Social Survey: A User's Guide*. Newbury Park, CA: Sage.

Dawes, Robyn. 1995. "How Do You Formulate a Test-able Exciting Hypothesis?" Pp. 93–96 in *How to Write a Successful Research Grant Application: A Guide for Social and Behavioral Scientists*, edited by Willo Pequegnat and Ellen Stover. New York: Plenum Press.

Denzin, Norman K. and Yvonna S. Lincoln. 1994. "Introduction: Entering the Field of Qualitative Research." Pp. 1–17 in *Handbook of Qualitative Research*, edited by Norman K. Denzin and Yvonna S. Lincoln. Thousand Oaks, CA: Sage.

Devine, Joel A. and James D. Wright. 1993. *The Greatest of Evils: Urban Poverty and the American Underclass*. New York: Aldine de Gruyter.

Diamond, Jared. 1987. "Soft Sciences Are Often Harder Than Hard Sciences." *Discover* (August), pp. 34–39.

Diamond, Larry, Juan Linz, and Seymour Martin Lipset. 1990. *Politics in Developing Countries: Comparing Experiences with Democracy*. Boulder, CO: Lynne Rienner.

Diamond, Timothy. 1992. *Making Gray Gold: Narratives of Nursing Home Care*. Chicago: University of Chicago Press.

Dillman, Don A. 1978. *Mail and Telephone Surveys: The Total Design Method*. New York: Wiley.

Dillman, Don A. 1982. "Mail and Other Self-Administered Questionnaires." Chapter 12 in *Handbook of Survey Research*, edited by Peter Rossi, James Wright, and Andy Anderson. New York: Academic Press. As reprinted on pp. 637–638 in Delbert C. Miller, 1991. *Handbook of Research Design and Social Measurement*, 5th ed. Newbury Park, CA: Sage.

Dillman, Don A., James A. Christenson, Edwin H. Carpenter, and Ralph M. Brooks. 1974. "Increasing Mail Questionnaire Response: A Four-State Comparison." *American Sociological Review,* 39 (October): 744–756.

Dolnick, Edward. 1984. "Why Have the Pollsters Been Missing the Mark?" *The Boston Globe,* July 16, pp. 27–28.

Drake, Robert E., Gregory J. McHugo, Deborah R. Becker, William A. Anthony, and Robin E. Clark. 1996. "The New Hampshire Study of Supported Employment for People with Severe Mental Illness." *Journal of Consulting and Clinical Psychology,* 64: 391–399.

Drake, Robert E., Gregory J. McHugo, and Jeremy C. Biesanz. 1995. "The Test-Retest Reliability of Standardized Instruments Among Homeless Persons with Substance Use Disorders." *Journal of Studies on Alcohol,* 56(2): 161–167.

Duncan, Otis Dudley and Stanley Lieberson. 1959. "Ethnic Segregation and Assimilation." *American Journal of Sociology,* 64: 364–374.

Durkheim, Emile. 1951. *Suicide*. New York: Free Press.

Durkheim, Emile. 1956 [1906]. "The Evolution and the Role of Secondary Education in France." Pp. 135–154 in *Education and Sociology*, translated by Sherwood D. Fox. New York: Free Press.

Durkheim, Emile. 1964. *The Division of Labor in Society*. New York: Free Press.

Earley, P. Christopher. 1994. "Self or Group: Cultural Effects of Training on Self-Efficacy and Performance." *Administrative Science Quarterly*, 39: 89–117.

Egan, Timothy. 1995. "Many Seek Security in Private Communities." *The New York Times*, September 3, pp. 1, 22.

Emerson, Robert M. (Ed.). 1983. *Contemporary Field Research*. Prospect Heights, IL: Waveland Press.

Emerson, Robert M., Rachel I. Fretz, and Linda L. Shaw. 1995. *Writing Ethnographic Fieldnotes*. Chicago: University of Chicago Press.

Emirbayer, Mustafa. 1996. "Durkheim's Contribution to the Sociological Analysis of History." *Sociological Forum*, 11: 263–284.

Erikson, Kai T. 1966. *Wayward Puritans: A Study in the Sociology of Deviance*. New York: Wiley.

Erikson, Kai T. 1967. "A Comment on Disguised Observation in Sociology." *Social Problems*, 12: 366–373.

Farley, Reynolds. 1977. "Trends in Racial Inequalities: Have the Gains of the 1960s Disappeared in the 1970s?" *American Sociological Review*, 42: 189–208.

Fenno, Richard F., Jr. 1978. *Home Style: House Members in Their Districts*. Boston: Little, Brown.

Fine, Gary Alan. 1980. "Cracking Diamonds: Observer Role in Little League Baseball Settings and the Acquisition of Social Competence." Pp. 117–131 in *Fieldwork Experience: Qualitative Approaches to Social Research*, edited by William B. Shaffir, Robert A. Stebbins, and Allan Turowetz. New York: St. Martin's Press.

Fowler, Floyd J. 1988. *Survey Research Methods*, revised ed. Newbury Park, CA: Sage.

Fowler, Floyd J. 1995. *Improving Survey Questions: Design and Evaluation*. Thousand Oaks, CA: Sage.

Fraker, Thomas and Rebecca Maynard. 1987. "Evaluating Comparison Group Designs with Employment-Related Programs." *Journal of Human Resources*, 22(2): 194–227.

Franklin, Mark N. 1996. "Electoral Participation." Pp. 216–235 in *Comparing Democracies: Elections and Voting in Global Perspective*, edited by Lawrence LeDuc, Richard G. Niemi, and Pippa Norris. Thousand Oaks, CA: Sage.

Freedman, David A. 1991. "Statistical Models and Shoe Leather." Pp. 291–313 in *Sociological Methodology*, vol. 21, edited by Peter V. Marsden. Oxford: Basil Blackwell.

Freeman, Richard B. 1974. "Alternative Theories of Labor-Market Discrimination: Individual and Collective Behavior." Pp. 33–49 in *Patterns of Racial Discrimination*, vol. 2, edited by George von Furstenburg, Ann Horowitz, and Bennett Harrison. Lexington, MA: Heath.

Friedlander, Daniel, James Riccio, and Stephen Freedman. 1993. *GAIN: Two-Year Impacts in Six Counties.* New York: Manpower Demonstration Research Corporation.

Garrett, Gerald R. and Russell K. Schutt. 1990. "Homelessness in Massachusetts: Description and Analysis." Pp. 73–90 in *Homeless in the United States: State Surveys,* edited by Jamshid Momeni. New York: Greenwood.

Gill, Richard T., Nathan Glazer, and Stephan A. Thernstrom. 1992. *Our Changing Population.* Englewood Cliffs, NJ: Prentice Hall.

Glaser, Barney G. and Anselm L. Strauss. 1967. *The Discovery of Grounded Theory: Strategies for Qualitative Research.* London: Weidenfeld and Nicholson.

Glasgow, Douglas G. 1980. *The Black Underclass: Poverty, Unemployment, and Entrapment of Ghetto Youth.* San Francisco: Jossey-Bass.

Glashow, Sheldon. 1989. "We Believe That the World Is Knowable." *The New York Times,* October 22, p. E24.

Gleick, James. 1990. "The Census: Why We Can't Count." *The New York Times Magazine,* July 15, pp. 22–26, 54.

Glover, Robert W. and Ray Marshall. 1977. "The Response of Unions in the Construction Industry to Antidiscrimination Efforts." Pp. 121–140 in *Equal Rights and Industrial Relations,* edited by Leonard J. Hausman, Orley Ashenfelter, Bayard Rustin, R. F. Schubert, and D. Slaiman. Madison, WI: Industrial Relations Research Association.

Goffman, Erving. 1961. *Asylums: Essays on the Social Situation of Mental Patients and Other Inmates.* Garden City, NY: Doubleday.

Goldenberg, Sheldon. 1992. *Thinking Methodologically.* New York: HarperCollins.

Goldfinger, Stephen M., Russell K. Schutt, Larry J. Seidman, Winston M. Turner, Walter E. Penk, and George S. Tolomiczenko. 1996. "Self-Report and Observer Measures of Substance Abuse Among Homeless Mentally Ill Persons in the Cross-Section and Over Time." *The Journal of Nervous and Mental Disease,* 184(11): 667–672.

Goldfinger, Stephen M., Russell K. Schutt, George S. Tolomicenko, Winston M. Turner, Norma Ware, Walter E. Penk, et al. 1997. "Housing Persons Who Are Homeless and Mentally Ill: Independent Living or Evolving Consumer Households?" Pp. 29–49 in *Mentally Ill and Homeless: Special Programs for Special Needs,* edited by William R. Breakey and James W. Thompson. Amsterdam, The Netherlands: Harwood Academic Publishers.

Goleman, Daniel. 1993a. "Placebo Effect Is Shown to Be Twice as Powerful as Expected." *The New York Times,* August 17, p. C3.

Goleman, Daniel. 1993b. "Pollsters Enlist Psychologists in Quest for Unbiased Results." *The New York Times,* September 7, pp. C1, C11.

Goleman, Daniel. 1995. *Emotional Intelligence.* New York: Bantam Books.

Gordon, Raymond. 1992. *Basic Interviewing Skills.* Itasca, IL: Peacock.

Griffin, Larry J. 1992. "Temporality, Events, and Explanation in Historical Sociology: An Introduction." *Sociological Methods & Research,* 20: 403–427.

Griffin, Larry J. 1993. "Narrative, Event-Structure Analysis, and Causal Interpretation in Historical Sociology." *American Journal of Sociology,* 98 (March): 1094–1133.

Grimes, William. 1995. "Does Life Imitate Violence on Film?" *The New York Times,* November 30, p. B1.

Grinnell, Frederick. 1992. *The Scientific Attitude,* 2nd ed. New York: Guilford Press.

Gross, Jane. 1992. "Divorced, Middle-Aged and Happy: Women, Especially, Adjust to the 90s." *The New York Times,* December 7, p. A14.

Groves, Robert M. and Robert L. Kahn. 1979. *Surveys by Telephone: A National Comparison with Personal Interviews.* New York: Academic Press. As adapted in Delbert C. Miller, 1991. *Handbook of Research Design and Social Measurement,* 5th ed. Newbury Park, CA: Sage.

Gruenewald, Paul J., Andrew J. Treno, Gail Taff, and Michael Klitzner. 1997. *Measuring Community Indicators: A Systems Approach to Drug and Alcohol Problems.* Thousand Oaks, CA: Sage.

Grunwald, Michael. 1997. "Gateway to a New America: Illinois Community Defends Its Barricade to 'Unwelcome' Outsiders." *The Boston Globe,* August 25, pp. A1, A8.

Guba, Egon G. and Yvonna S. Lincoln. 1989. *Fourth Generation Evaluation.* Newbury Park, CA: Sage.

Guba, Egon G. and Yvonna S. Lincoln. 1994. "Competing Paradigms in Qualitative Research." Pp. 105–117 in *Handbook of Qualitative Research,* edited by Norman K. Denzin and Yvonna S. Lincoln. Thousand Oaks, CA: Sage.

Gubrium, Jaber F. and James A. Holstein. 1997. *The New Language of Qualitative Method.* New York: Oxford University Press.

Hadaway, C. Kirk, Penny Long Marler, and Mark Chaves. 1993. "What the Polls Don't Show: A Closer Look at U.S. Church Attendance." *American Sociological Review,* 58 (December): 741–752.

Hagan, John. 1994. *Crime and Disrepute.* Thousand Oaks, CA: Pine Forge Press.

Hage, Jerald and Barbara Foley Meeker. 1988. *Social Causality.* Boston: Unwin Hyman.

Hallinan, Maureen T. 1997. "The Sociological Study of Social Change." *American Sociological Review,* 62: 1–11.

Hamilton, V. Lee and Joseph Sanders. 1983. "Universals in Judging Wrongdoing: Japanese and Americans Compared." *American Sociological Review,* 48 (April): 199–211.

Haney, C., C. Banks, and Philip G. Zimbardo. 1973. "Interpersonal Dynamics in a Simulated Prison." *International Journal of Criminology and Penology*, 1: 69–97.

◆ Harding, Sandra. 1989. "Value-Free Research Is a Delusion." *The New York Times*, October 22, p. E24.

Heckathorn, Douglas D. 1997. "Respondent-Driven Sampling: A New Approach to the Study of Hidden Populations." *Social Problems*, 44: 174–199.

Herek, Gregory. 1995. "Developing a Theoretical Framework and Rationale for a Research Proposal." Pp. 85–91 in *How to Write a Successful Research Grant Application: A Guide for Social and Behavioral Scientists*, edited by Willo Pequegnat and Ellen Stover. New York: Plenum Press.

Hirsch, Eric L. 1990. "Sacrifice for the Cause: Group Processes, Recruitment, and Commitment in a Student Social Movement." *American Sociological Review*, 55 (April): 243–254.

Hirsch, Kathleen. 1989. *Songs from the Alley*. New York: Doubleday.

Hite, Shere. 1987. *Women and Love: A Cultural Revolution in Progress*. New York: Alfred A. Knopf.

Holden, Constance. 1986. "Homelessness: Experts Differ on Root Causes." *Science*, 232: 562–570.

Hollingsworth, T. H. 1972. "The Importance of the Quality of Data in Historical Demography." Pp. 71–86 in *Population and Social Change*, edited by D. V. Glass and Roger Revelle. London: Edward Arnold.

Holmes, Steven A. 1994. "Census Officials Plan Big Changes in Gathering Data." *The New York Times*, May 16, pp. A1, A13.

Holmes, Steven A. 1996. "In a First, 2000 Census Is to Use Sampling." *The New York Times*, February 29, p. A18.

Hoover, Kenneth R. 1980. *The Elements of Social Scientific Thinking*, 2nd ed. New York: St. Martin's Press.

Horney, Julie, D. Wayne Osgood, and Ineke Haen Marshall. 1995. "Criminal Careers in the Short-Term: Intra-Individual Variability in Crime and Its Relation to Local Life Circumstances." *American Sociological Review*, 60: 655–673.

Huberman, A. Michael and Matthew B. Miles. 1994. "Data Management and Analysis Methods." Pp. 428–444 in *Handbook of Qualitative Research*, edited by Norman K. Denzin and Yvonna S. Lincoln. Thousand Oaks, CA: Sage.

Huff, Darrell. 1954. *How to Lie with Statistics*. New York: W. W. Norton.

Humphrey, Nicholas. 1992. *A History of the Mind: Evolution and the Birth of Consciousness*. New York: Simon & Schuster.

Humphreys, Laud. 1970. *Tearoom Trade: Impersonal Sex in Public Places*. Chicago: Aldine.

Hunt, Morton. 1985. *Profiles of Social Research: The Scientific Study of Human Interactions*. New York: Russell Sage Foundation.

Inter-University Consortium for Political and Social Research. 1996. *Guide to Resources and Services 1995–1996*. Ann Arbor, MI: ICPSR.

Janesick, Valerie J. 1994. "The Dance of Qualitative Research Design: Metaphor, Methodolatry, and Meaning." Pp. 209–219 in *Handbook of Qualitative Research*, edited by Norman K. Denzin and Yvonna S. Lincoln. Thousand Oaks, CA: Sage.

Jencks, Christopher. 1992. *Rethinking Social Policy: Race, Poverty, and the Underclass*. New York: Harper-Perennial.

Jencks, Christopher. 1994. *The Homeless*. Cambridge, MA: Harvard University Press.

Jervis, Robert. 1996. "Counterfactuals, Causation, and Complexity." Pp. 309–316 in *Counterfactual Thought Experiments in World Politics: Logical, Methodological, and Psychological Perspectives*, edited by Philip E. Tetlock and Aaron Belkin. Princeton, NJ: Princeton University Press.

Johnson, Dirk. 1997. "Party Animals in Fraternities Face the Threat of Extinction." *The New York Times*, May 15, pp. A1, A29.

Kagay, Michael R. with Janet Elder. 1992. "Numbers Are No Problem for Pollsters. Words Are." *The New York Times*, October 9, p. E5.

Kahn, Ric. 1997. "A Last Drink on New Year's." *The Boston Globe*, January 3, pp. B1–B2.

Kamin, Leon. 1974. *The Science and Politics of IQ*. Potomac, MD: Erlbaum.

Kane, Emily W. and Howard Schuman. 1991. "Open Survey Questions as Measures of Personal Concern with Issues: A Reanalysis of Stouffer's *Communism, Conformity, and Civil Liberties*." Pp. 81–96 in *Sociological Methodology*, vol. 21, edited by Peter V. Marsden. Oxford: Basil Blackwell.

Kaufman, Sharon R. 1986. *The Ageless Self: Sources of Meaning in Late Life*. Madison: University of Wisconsin Press.

Kenney, Charles. 1987. "They've Got Your Number." *The Boston Globe Magazine*, August 30, pp. 12, 46–56, 60.

Kifner, John. 1994. "Pollster Finds Error on Holocaust Doubts." *The New York Times*, May 20, p. A12.

King, Gary, Robert O. Keohane, and Sidney Verba. 1994. *Scientific Inference in Qualitative Research*. Princeton, NJ: Princeton University Press.

King, Miriam L. and Diana L. Magnuson. 1995. "Perspectives on Historical U.S. Census Undercounts." *Social Science History*, 19: 455–466.

Knox, Richard A. 1997. "Time Running Out for Key Women's Study: Push Is on for Volunteers." *The Boston Globe*, September 8, pp. C1, C3.

Koegel, Paul. 1987. *Ethnographic Perspectives on Homeless and Homeless Mentally Ill Women*. Washington, DC: Alcohol, Drug Abuse, and Mental Health Administration, Public Health Service, U.S. Department of Health and Human Services.

Koegel, Paul and M. Audrey Burnam. 1992. "Problems in the Assessment of Mental Illness Among the Homeless: An Empirical Approach." Pp. 77–99 in *Homelessness: A National Perspective,* edited by Marjorie J. Robertson and Milton Greenblatt. New York: Plenum.

Kohn, Melvin L. 1987. "Cross-National Research as an Analytic Strategy." *American Sociological Review,* 52: 713–731.

Kohut, Andrew. 1988. "Polling: Does More Information Lead to Better Understanding?" *The Boston Globe,* November 7, p. 25.

Kolata, Gina. 1993. "Family Aid to Elderly Is Very Strong, Study Shows." *The New York Times,* May 3, p. A16.

Kolbert, Elizabeth. 1992. "Test-Marketing a President." *The New York Times Magazine,* August 30, pp. 18–21, 60, 68, 72.

Kotre, John. 1995. *White Gloves: How We Create Ourselves Through Memory.* New York: Free Press.

Kraemer, Helena Chmura and Sue Thiemann. 1987. *How Many Subjects? Statistical Power Analysis in Research.* Newbury Park, CA: Sage.

Krauss, Clifford. 1996. "New York Crime Rate Plummets to Levels Not Seen in 30 Years." *The New York Times,* December 20, pp. A1, B4.

Krippendorff, Klaus. 1980. *Content Analysis: An Introduction to Its Methodology.* Thousand Oaks, CA: Sage.

Krueger, Richard A. 1988. *Focus Groups: A Practical Guide for Applied Research.* Newbury Park, CA: Sage.

Kubey, Robert. 1990. "Television and the Quality of Family Life." *Communication Quarterly,* 38 (Fall): 312–324.

Kuhn, Thomas S. 1970. *The Structure of Scientific Revolutions,* 2nd ed. Chicago: University of Chicago Press.

Kvale, Steinar. 1996. *Interviews: An Introduction to Qualitative Research Interviewing.* Thousand Oaks, CA: Sage.

La Gory, Mark, Ferris J. Ritchey, and Jeff Mullis. 1990. "Depression Among the Homeless." *Journal of Health and Social Behavior,* 31 (March): 87–101.

Labaw, Patricia J. 1980. *Advanced Questionnaire Design.* Cambridge, MA: ABT Books.

Laireiter, Anton and Urs Baumann. 1992. "Network Structures and Support Functions—Theoretical and Empirical Analyses." Pp. 33–55 in *The Meaning and Measurement of Social Support,* edited by Hans O. F. Veiel and Urs Baumann. New York: Hemisphere Publishing Corp.

Lakshmanan, Indira A. R. 1993. "Do You Think Jurassic Park Is Too Scary for Children?" *The Boston Globe,* June 16, p. 28.

LaLonde, Robert J. 1986. "Evaluating the Econometric Evaluations of Training Programs with Experimental Data." *The American Economic Review,* 76: 604–620.

Larson, Calvin J. 1993. *Pure and Applied Sociological Theory: Problems and Issues.* New York: Harcourt Brace Jovanovich.

Larson, Calvin J. and Gerald R. Garrett. 1996. *Crime, Justice and Society,* 2d ed. Dix Hills, NY: General Hall.

Lathrop, Barnes F. 1968. "History from the Census Returns." Pp. 79–101 in *Sociology and History: Methods,* edited by Seymour Martin Lipset and Richard Hofstadter. New York: Basic Books.

Lavin, Michael R. 1994. *Understanding the 1990 Census: A Guide for Marketers, Planners, Grant Writers and Other Data Users.* Kenmore, NY: Epoch Books.

Lavrakas, Paul J. 1987. *Telephone Survey Methods: Sampling, Selection, and Supervision.* Newbury Park, CA: Sage.

Lazarsfeld, Paul F. and Anthony R. Oberschall. 1965. "Max Weber and Empirical Research." *American Sociological Review* (April): 185–199.

LeDuc, Lawrence, Richard G. Niemi, and Pippa Norris (Eds.). 1996. *Comparing Democracies: Elections and Voting in Global Perspective.* Thousand Oaks, CA: Sage.

Lee, Barrett A., Sue Hinze Jones, and David W. Lewis. 1990. "Public Beliefs About the Causes of Homelessness." *Social Forces,* 69: 253–265.

Lempert, Richard. 1989. "Humility Is a Virtue: On the Publicization of Policy-Relevant Research." *Law and Society Review,* 23: 146–161.

Lempert, Richard and Joseph Sanders. 1986. *An Invitation to Law and Social Science: Desert, Disputes, and Distribution.* New York: Longman.

Levi, Margaret. 1996. "The Institution of Conscription." *Social Science History,* 20: 133–167.

Levine, Robert V., Todd Simon Martinez, Gary Brase, et al. "Helping in 36 U.S. Cities." *Journal of Personality and Social Psychology,* 67 (July): 69–82.

Liang, Diane Wei, Richard Moreland, and Linda Argote. 1995. "Group Versus Individual Training and Group Performance: The Mediating Role of Transactive Memory." *Personality and Social Psychology Bulletin,* 21: 384–393.

Lieberson, Stanley. 1985. *Making It Count: The Improvement of Social Research and Theory.* Berkeley: University of California Press.

Lieberson, Stanley. 1991. "Small N's and Big Conclusions: An Examination of the Reasoning in Comparative Studies Based on a Small Number of Cases." *Social Forces,* 70: 307–320.

Lieberson, Stanley. 1992. "Einstein, Renoir, and Greeley: Some Thoughts About Evidence in Sociology." *American Sociological Review,* 57 (February): 1–15.

Liebow, Elliot. 1967. *Tally's Corner: A Study of Negro Streetcorner Men.* Boston: Little, Brown.

Link, Bruce G., Jo C. Phelan, Ann Stueve, Robert E. Moore, Michaeline Brenahan, and Elmer L. Struening. 1996. "Public Attitudes and Beliefs

About Homeless People." Pp. 143–148 in *Homelessness in America*, edited by Jim Baumohl. Phoenix: Oryx Press.

Lipset, Seymour Martin. 1968. *Revolution and Counterrevolution*. New York: Basic Books.

Lipset, Seymour Martin. 1990. *Continental Divide: The Values and Institutions of the United States and Canada*. New York: Routledge.

Lipset, Seymour Martin, Martin Trow, and James Coleman. 1956. *Union Democracy*. New York: Free Press.

Lipsky, Michael. 1980. *Street-Level Bureaucracy*. New York: Russell Sage Foundation.

Litwin, Mark S. 1995. *How to Measure Survey Reliability and Validity*. Thousand Oaks, CA: Sage.

Lofland, John and Lyn H. Lofland. 1984. *Analyzing Social Settings: A Guide to Qualitative Observation and Analysis*, 2nd ed. Belmont, CA: Wadsworth.

Loth, Renee. 1992. "Bush May Be Too Far Back, History of Polls Suggests." *The Boston Globe*, October 25, p. 19.

Lynch, Michael and David Bogen. 1997. "Sociology's Asociological 'Core': An Examination of Textbook Sociology in Light of the Sociology of Scientific Knowledge." *American Sociological Review*, 62: 481–493.

Mangione, Thomas W. 1995. *Mail Surveys: Improving the Quality*. Thousand Oaks, CA: Sage.

Marini, Margaret Mooney and Burton Singer. 1988. "Causality in the Social Sciences." Pp. 347–409 in *Sociological Methodology*, vol. 18, edited by Clifford C. Clogg. Washington, DC: American Sociological Association.

Marshall, Ray and Vernon V. Briggs, Jr. 1967. "Negro Participation in Apprenticeship Programs." *Journal of Human Resources*, 2: 51–59.

Martin, Linda G. and Kevin Kinsella. 1995. "Research on the Demography of Aging in Developing Countries." Pp. 356–403 in *Demography of Aging*, edited by Linda G. Martin and Samuel H. Preston. Washington, DC: National Academy Press.

Marx, Karl. 1967. *Capital: A Critique of Political Economy*. New York: International Publishers.

Maticka-Tyndale, Eleanor. 1992. "Social Construction of HIV Transmission and Prevention Among Heterosexual Young Adults." *Social Problems*, 39 (August): 238–252.

Matt, Georg E. and Thomas D. Cook. 1994. "Threats to the Validity of Research Syntheses." Pp. 503–520 in *The Handbook of Research Synthesis*, edited by Harris Cooper and Larry V. Hedges. New York: Russell Sage Foundation.

Maxwell, Joseph A. 1996. *Qualitative Research Design: An Interactive Approach*. Thousand Oaks, CA: Sage.

Mayr, Ernst. 1982. *The Growth of Biological Thought: Diversity, Evolution, and Inheritance*. Cambridge, MA: Harvard University Press.

McLellan, A. Thomas, Lester Luborsky, John Cacciola, Jeffrey Griffith, Frederick Evans, Harriet L. Barr, and Charles P. O'Brien. 1985. "New Data from the Addiction Severity Index: Reliability and Validity in Three Centers." *The Journal of Nervous and Mental Disease*, 173(7): 412–423.

Merton, Robert K., Marjorie Fiske, and Patricia L. Kendall. 1956. *The Focused Interview*. Glencoe, IL: Free Press.

Metro Social Services. 1987. *PATH Community Survey*. Nashville, TN: Metro Social Services, Nashville-Davidson County.

Meyer, John W., John Boli, George M. Thomas, and Francisco O. Ramirez. 1997. "World Society and the Nation-State." *American Journal of Sociology*, 103: 144–181.

Miczek, Klaus A., Joseph F. DeBold, Margaret Haney, Jennifer Tidey, Jeffrey Vivian, and Elise M. Weerts. 1994. "Alcohol, Drugs of Abuse, Aggression, and Violence." Pp. 377–570 in *Understanding and Preventing Violence. Volume 3, Social Influences*, edited by Albert J. Reiss, Jr., and Jeffrey A. Roth. Washington, DC: National Academy Press.

Milbrath, Lester and M. L. Goel. 1977. *Political Participation*, 2nd ed. Chicago: Rand McNally.

Milgram, Stanley. 1965. "Some Conditions of Obedience and Disobedience to Authority." *Human Relations*, 18: 57–75.

Mill, John Stuart. 1872. *A System of Logic: Ratiocinative and Inductive*, 8th ed., vol. 2. London: Longmans, Green, Reader, & Dyer.

Miller, Delbert C. 1991. *Handbook of Research Design and Social Measurement*, 5th ed. Newbury Park, CA: Sage.

Miller, Warren E. and Santa Traugott. 1989. *American National Election Data Sourcebook, 1952–1986*. Cambridge, MA: Harvard University Press.

Mills, C. Wright. 1959. *The Sociological Imagination*. New York: Oxford University Press.

Mirowsky, John. 1995. "Age and the Sense of Control." *Social Psychology Quarterly*, 58: 31–43.

Mirowsky, John and Paul Nongzhuang Hu. 1996. "Physical Impairment and the Diminishing Effects of Income." *Social Forces*, 74: 1073–1096.

Mirowsky, John and Catherine E. Ross. 1991. "Eliminating Defense and Agreement Bias from Measures of the Sense of Control: A 2 × 2 Index." *Social Psychology Quarterly*, 54: 127–145.

Mirowsky, John and Catherine E. Ross. 1992. "Age and Depression." *Journal of Health and Social Behavior*, 33: 187–205.

Mohr, Lawrence B. 1992. *Impact Analysis for Program Evaluation*. Newbury Park, CA: Sage.

Monkkonen, Eric H. 1994. "Introduction." Pp. 1–8 in *Engaging the Past: The Uses of History Across the Social Sciences*. Durham, NC: Duke University Press.

Moore, David W. 1992. "The Sure Thing That Got Away." *The New York Times*, October 25, p. E15.

Mueser, Kim T., Paul R. Yarnold, Douglas F. Levinson, Hardeep Singhy, Alan S. Bellack, Kimmy Kee, Randall L. Morrison, and Kashinath G. Yadalam. 1990. "Prevalence of Substance Abuse in Schizophrenia: Demographic and Clinical Correlates." *Schizophrenia Bulletin*, 16(1): 31—56.

Mullins, Carolyn J. 1977. *A Guide to Writing and Publishing in the Social and Behavioral Sciences*. New York: Wiley.

Munger, Frank. 1993. "From the Editor." *Law and Society Review*, 27 (2): 251–254.

National Institute of Alcohol Abuse and Alcoholism. 1994. "Alcohol-Related Impairment." *Alcohol Alert*, 25 (July): 1–5.

National Institute of Alcohol Abuse and Alcoholism. 1995. "College Students and Drinking." *Alcohol Alert*, 29 (July): 1–6.

National Institute of Alcohol Abuse and Alcoholism. 1997. "Alcohol Metabolism." *Alcohol Alert*, 35 (January): 1–4.

National Opinion Research Center (NORC). 1992. National Data Program for the Social Sciences. *The NORC General Social Survey: Questions and Answers*. Chicago: Mimeographed.

National Opinion Research Center (NORC). 1996. *General Social Survey*. Chicago: National Opinion Research Center, University of Chicago.

National Technical Information Service, U.S. Department of Commerce. 1993. *Directory of U.S. Government Datafiles for Mainframes and Microcomputers*. Washington, DC: Federal Computer Products Center, National Technical Information Service, U.S. Department of Commerce.

Navarro, Mireya. 1990. "Census Questionnaire: Link to Democracy and Source of Data." *The New York Times*, March 25, p. 36.

Needleman, Carolyn. 1981. "Discrepant Assumptions in Empirical Research: The Case of Juvenile Court Screening." *Social Problems*, 28 (February): 247–262.

Newport, Frank. 1992. "Look at Polls as a Fever Chart of the Electorate." Letter to the Editor, *The New York Times*, November 6, p. A28.

Norusis, Marija J. and SPSS Inc. 1993. *SPSS for Windows Base System User's Guide, Release 6.0*. Chicago: SPSS Inc.

Oberschall, Anthony. 1972. "The Institutionalization of American Sociology." Pp. 187–251 in *The Establishment of Empirical Sociology: Studies in Continuity, Discontinuity, and Institutionalization*, edited by Anthony Oberschall. New York: Harper & Row.

Olzak, Susan, Suzanne Shanahan, and Elizabeth H. McEneaney. 1996. "Poverty, Segregation, and Race Riots: 1960 to 1993." *American Sociological Review*, 61: 590–613.

Onishi, Norimitsu. 1997. "Life and Death Under the Highways." *The New York Times*, February 17, p. 29.

Orcutt, James D. and J. Blake Turner. 1993. "Shocking Numbers and Graphic Accounts: Quantified Images of Drug Problems in the Print Media." *Social Problems*, 49 (May): 190–206.

Oreskes, Michel and Robin Toner. 1989. "The Homeless at the Heart of Poverty and Policy." *The New York Times*, January 29, p. E5.

Orshansky, Mollie. 1977. "Memorandum for Daniel P. Moynihan. Subject: History of the Poverty Line." Pp. 232–237 in *The Measure of Poverty. Technical Paper I: Documentation of Background Information and Rationale for Current Poverty Matrix*, edited by Mollie Orshansky. Washington, DC: U.S. Department of Health, Education, and Welfare.

Pagnini, Deanna L. and S. Philip Morgan. 1996. "Racial Differences in Marriage and Childbearing: Oral History Evidence from the South in the Early Twentieth Century." *American Journal of Sociology*, 101: 1694–1715.

Papineau, David. 1978. *For Science in the Social Sciences*. London: Macmillan.

Passell, Peter. 1993. "Like a New Drug, Social Programs Are Put to the Test." *The New York Times*, March 9, pp. C1, C10.

Pate, Antony M. and Edwin E. Hamilton. 1992. "Formal and Informal Deterrents to Domestic Violence: The Dade County Spouse Assault Experiment." *American Sociological Review*, 57 (October): 691–697.

Paternoster, Raymond, Robert Brame, Ronet Bachman, and Lawrence W. Sherman. 1997. "Do Fair Procedures Matter? The Effect of Procedural Justice on Spouse Assault." *Law & Society Review*, 31(1): 163–204.

Pepinsky, Harold E. 1980. "A Sociologist on Police Patrol." Pp. 223–234 in *Fieldwork Experience: Qualitative Approaches to Social Research*, edited by William B. Shaffir, Robert A. Stebbins, and Allan Turowetz. New York: St. Martin's Press.

Phillips, David P. 1982. "The Impact of Fictional Television Stories on U.S. Adult Fatalities: New Evidence on the Effect of the Mass Media on Violence." *American Journal of Sociology*, 87 (May): 1340–1359.

Phillips, Derek L. 1971. *Knowledge from What? Theories and Methods in Social Research*. Chicago: Rand McNally.

Pollner, Melvin and Richard E. Adams. 1994. "The Interpersonal Context of Mental Health Interviews." *Journal of Health and Social Behavior*, 35: 283–290.

Presley, Cheryl A., Philip W. Meilman, and Rob Lyerla. 1994. "Development of the Core Alcohol and Drug Survey: Initial Findings and Future Directions." *Journal of American College Health*, 42:248–255.

Presser, Stanley. 1985. "The Use of Survey Data in Basic Research in the Social Sciences." Pp. 93–114 in *Surveying Subjective Phenomena*, vol. 2, edited by Charles F. Turner and Elizabeth Martin. New York: Russell Sage Foundation.

Price, Richard H., Michelle Van Ryn, and Amiram D. Vinokur. 1992. "Impact of a Preventive Job Search Intervention on the Likelihood of Depression Among the Unemployed." *Journal of Health and Social Behavior,* 33 (June): 158–167.

Punch, Maurice. 1994. "Politics and Ethics in Qualitative Research." Pp. 83–97 in *Handbook of Qualitative Research,* edited by Norman K. Denzin and Yvonna S. Lincoln. Thousand Oaks, CA: Sage.

Purdy, Matthew. 1994. "Bronx Mystery: 3d-Rate Service for 1st-Class Mail." *The New York Times,* March 12, pp. 1, 3.

Putnam, Israel. 1977. "Poverty Thresholds: Their History and Future Development." Pp. 272–283 in *The Measure of Poverty. Technical Paper I: Documentation of Background Information and Rationale for Current Poverty Matrix,* edited by Mollie Orshansky. Washington, DC: U.S. Department of Health, Education, and Welfare.

Radin, Charles A. 1997. "Partnerships, Awareness Behind Boston's Success." *The Boston Globe,* February 19, pp. A2, B7.

Radloff, Lenore. 1977. "The CES-D Scale: A Self-Report Depression Scale for Research in the General Population." *Applied Psychological Measurement,* 1: 385–401.

Ragin, Charles C. 1987. *The Comparative Method: Moving Beyond Qualitative and Quantitative Strategies.* Berkeley: University of California Press.

Ragin, Charles C. 1994. *Constructing Social Research.* Thousand Oaks, CA: Pine Forge Press.

Rand, Michael R., James P. Lynch, and David Cantor. 1997. *Criminal Victimization, 1973–95.* Washington, DC: Office of Justice Programs, U.S. Department of Justice.

Reed, Wornie L., Jodi Nudelman, Robert W. Adams, Jane Dockery, Nicol Nealeigh, and Rodney W. Thomas. 1997. *Infant Immunization Coverage Cluster Survey.* Cleveland: Urban Child Research Center, Cleveland State University.

Reiss, Albert J., Jr. 1971. *The Police and the Public.* New Haven, CT: Yale University Press.

Rele, J. R. 1993. "Demographic Rates: Birth, Death, Marital, and Migration." Pp. 2-1–2-26 in *Readings in Population Research Methodology. Volume 1, Basic Tools,* edited by Donald J. Bogue, Eduardo E. Arriaga, and Douglas L. Anderton. Chicago: Social Development Center, for the United National Population Fund.

Reynolds, Paul Davidson. 1979. *Ethical Dilemmas and Social Science Research.* San Francisco: Jossey-Bass.

Richards, Thomas J. and Lyn Richards. 1994. "Using Computers in Qualitative Research." Pp. 445–462 in *Handbook of Qualitative Research,* edited by Norman K. Denzin and Yvonna S. Lincoln. Thousand Oaks, CA: Sage.

Richardson, Laurel. 1995. "Narrative and Sociology." Pp. 198–221 in *Representation in Ethnography,* edited by John Van Maanen. Thousand Oaks, CA: Sage.

Ricketts, Erol R. and Isabel Sawhill. 1988. "Defining and Measuring the Underclass." *Journal of Policy Analysis and Management,* 7 (2): 316–325.

Rives, Norfleet W., Jr., and William J. Serow. 1988. *Introduction to Applied Demography: Data Sources and Estimation Techniques.* Sage University Paper Series on Quantitative Applications in the Social Sciences, series no. 07-039. Thousand Oaks, CA: Sage.

Robertson, David Brian. 1993. "The Return to History and the New Institutionalism in American Political Science." *Social Science History,* 17: 1–36.

Rosen, Lawrence. 1995. "The Creation of the Uniform Crime Report: The Role of Social Science." *Social Science History,* 19: 215–238.

Rosenberg, Morris. 1965. *Society and the Adolescent Self-Image.* Princeton, NJ: Princeton University Press.

Rosenberg, Morris. 1968. *The Logic of Survey Analysis.* New York: Basic Books.

Rosenthal, Rob. 1994. *Homeless in Paradise: A Map of the Terrain.* Philadelphia: Temple University Press.

Ross, Catherine E. 1989. "Work, Family, and the Sense of Control. SES-8916154." Final summary report submitted to the National Science Foundation. Columbus: The Ohio State University.

Ross, Catherine E. 1990. "Work, Family, and the Sense of Control: Implications for the Psychological Well-Being of Women and Men." Proposal submitted to the National Science Foundation. Urbana: University of Illinois.

Ross, Catherine E. and Chloe E. Bird. 1994. "Sex Stratification and Health Lifestyle: Consequences for Men's and Women's Perceived Health." *Journal of Health and Social Behavior,* 35: 161–178.

Ross, Catherine E. and Marieke Van Willigen. 1996. "Gender, Parenthood, and Anger." *Journal of Marriage and the Family,* 58: 572–584.

Ross, Catherine E. and Chia-ling Wu. 1995. "The Links Between Education and Health." *American Sociological Review,* 60: 719–745.

Ross, Catherine E. and Chia-ling Wu. 1996. "Education, Age, and the Cumulative Advantage in Health." *Journal of Health and Social Behavior,* 37:104–120.

Rossi, Peter H. 1989. *Down and Out in America: The Origins of Homelessness.* Chicago: University of Chicago Press.

Rossi, Peter H. and Howard E. Freeman. 1989. *Evaluation: A Systematic Approach,* 4th ed. Newbury Park, CA: Sage.

Roth, Dee. 1990. "Homelessness in Ohio: A Statewide Epidemiologial Study." Pp. 145–163 in *Homeless in the United States, Vol. I: State Surveys,* edited by Jamshid Momeni. New York: Greeenwood Press.

Roth, Dee, J. Bean, N. Lust, and T. Saveanu. 1985.

Homelessness in Ohio: A Study of People in Need. Columbus, OH: Department of Mental Health.

Rubin, Herbert J. and Irene S. Rubin. 1995. *Qualitative Interviewing: The Art of Hearing Data.* Thousand Oaks, CA: Sage.

Rueschemeyer, Dietrich, Evelyne Huber Stephens, and John D. Stephens. 1992. *Capitalist Development and Democracy.* Chicago: University of Chicago Press.

Ruggles, Patricia. 1990. *Drawing the Line: Alternative Poverty Measures and Their Implications for Public Policy.* Washington, DC: The Urban Institute Press.

Salisbury, Robert H. 1975. "Research on Political Participation." *American Journal of Political Science,* 19 (May): 323–341.

Sampson, Robert J. 1987. "Urban Black Violence: The Effect of Male Joblessness and Family Disruption." *American Journal of Sociology,* 93 (September): 348–382.

Sampson, Robert J. and John H. Laub. 1990. "Crime and Deviance over the Life Course: The Salience of Adult Social Bonds." *American Sociological Review,* 55 (October): 609–627.

Sampson, Robert J. and John H. Laub. 1993. "Structural Variations in Juvenile Court Processing: Inequality, the Underclass, and Social Control." *Law and Society Review,* 27 (2): 285–311.

Sampson, Robert J. and Janet L. Lauritsen. 1994. "Violent Victimization and Offending: Individual-, Situational-, and Community-Level Risk Factors." Pp. 1–114 in *Understanding and Preventing Violence. Volume 3, Social Influences,* edited by Albert J. Reiss, Jr., and Jeffrey A. Roth. Washington, DC: National Academy Press.

Sampson, Robert J., Stephen W. Raudenbush, and Felton Earls. 1997. "Neighborhoods and Violent Crime: A Multilevel Study of Collective Efficacy." *Science,* 277: 918–924.

Schuman, Howard and Otis Dudley Duncan. 1974. "Questions About Attitude Survey Questions." Pp. 232–251 in *Sociological Methodology 1973–1974,* edited by Herbert L. Costner. San Francisco: Jossey-Bass.

Schuman, Howard and Stanley Presser. 1981. *Questions and Answers in Attitude Surveys: Experiments on Question Form, Wording, and Context.* New York: Academic Press.

Schutt, Russell K. 1986. *Organization in a Changing Environment.* Albany, NY: State University of New York Press.

Schutt, Russell K. 1987a. "Craft Unions and Minorities: Determinants of Change in Admission Practices." *Social Problems,* 34 (October): 388–402.

Schutt, Russell K. 1987b. "Recent Research Methods Texts: Means for Achieving Course Goals?" *Teaching Sociology,* 15 (April): 203–213.

Schutt, Russell K. 1988. Shelter Staff Questionnaire. Unpublished questionnaire. Boston: Department of Sociology, University of Massachusetts, Boston.

Schutt, Russell K. 1989. "Objectivity Versus Outrage." *Society,* 26 (May/June): 14–16.

Schutt, Russell K. 1990. "The Quantity and Quality of Homelessness: Research Results and Policy Implications." *Sociological Practice Review,* 1 (2): 77–87.

Schutt, Russell K. 1992. "The Perspectives of DMH Shelter Staff: Their Clients, Their Jobs, Their Shelters and the Service System." A report to the Metro Boston Region of the Massachusetts Department of Mental Health. University of Massachusetts, Boston. Unpublished report.

Schutt, Russell K., Hubert M. Blalock, and Theodore C. Wagenaar. 1984. "Goals and Means for Research Methods Courses." *Teaching Sociology,* 11 (April): 235–258.

Schutt, Russell K., Robert Burke, Marsha Hogan, Patricia Ingraham, Richard Lyons, Tatjana Meschede, Richard Ryan, Joan Sinkiewicz, Helene Stern, and Andrew Walker. 1991. *The Shattuck Shelter Staff: Work Experience, Orientations to Work and AIDS Awareness.* Unpublished report to Shattuck Shelter. Boston: University of Massachusetts, Boston.

Schutt, Russell K. and Herbert L. Costner. 1993. "Another Edsel: The Collective Misperception of the Demand for the Certification of MA Sociologists." *The American Sociologist,* 23 (3): 57–71.

Schutt, Russell K. and W. Dale Dannefer. 1988. "Detention Decisions in Juvenile Cases: JINS, JDs and Gender." *Law and Society Review,* 22 (3): 509–520.

Schutt, Russell K. and M. L. Fennell. 1992. "Shelter Staff Satisfaction with Services, the Service Network and Their Jobs." *Current Research on Occupations and Professions,* 7: 177–200. JAI Press.

Schutt, Russell K. and Gerald R. Garrett. 1992. *Responding to the Homeless: Policy and Practice.* New York: Plenum.

Schutt, Russell K., Stephen M. Goldfinger, and Walter E. Penk, 1992. "The Structure and Sources of Residential Preferences Among Seriously Mentally Ill Homeless Adults." *Sociological Practice Review,* 3 (3): 148–156.

Schutt, Russell K., Stephen M. Goldfinger, and Walter E. Penk. 1997. "Satisfaction with Residence and with Life: When Homeless Mentally Ill Persons Are Housed." *Evaluation and Program Planning,* 20(2): 185–194.

Schutt, Russell K., Suzanne Gunston, and John O'Brien. 1992. "The Impact of AIDS Prevention Efforts on AIDS Knowledge and Behavior Among Sheltered Homeless Adults." *Sociological Practice Review,* 3 (1): 1–7.

Schutt, Russell K., with Tatjana Meschede. 1992. *The Perspectives of DMH Shelter Staff: Their Clients, Their Jobs, Their Shelters and the Service System.* Unpublished report to the Metro Boston Region of the Massachusetts Department of Mental Health. Boston: Department of Sociology, University of Massachusetts, Boston.

Schutt, Russell K., Tatjana Meschede, and Jill Rierdan. 1994. "Distress, Suicidality, and Social Support Among Homeless Adults." *Journal of Health and Social Behavior,* 35 (June): 134–142.

Schutt, Russell K., Alan Orenstein, and Theodore C. Wagenaar (Eds.). 1982. *Research Methods Courses: Syllabi, Assignments, and Projects.* Washington, DC: Teaching Resources Center, American Sociological Association.

Schutt, Russell K., Theodore C. Wagenaar, and Kevin P. Mulvey (Eds.). 1987. *Research Methods Courses: Syllabi, Assignments, and Projects,* 2nd ed. Washington, DC: American Sociological Association.

Schwandt, Thomas A. 1994. "Constructivist, Interpretivist Approaches to Human Inquiry." Pp. 118–137 in *Handbook of Qualitative Research,* edited by Norman K. Denzin and Yvonna S. Lincoln. Thousand Oaks, CA: Sage.

Schwartz, Mildred A. 1974. *Politics and Territory: The Sociology of Regional Persistence in Canada.* Montreal: McGill-Queen's University Press.

Scriven, Michael. 1972. "The Methodology of Evaluation." Pp. 123–136 in *Evaluating Action Programs: Readings in Social Action and Education,* edited by Carol H. Weiss. Boston: Allyn & Bacon.

Scull, Andrew T. 1988. "Deviance and Social Control." Pp. 667–693 in *Handbook of Sociology,* edited by Neil J. Smelser. Newbury Park, CA: Sage.

Sechrest, Lee and Souraya Sidani. 1995. "Quantitative and Qualitative Methods: Is There an Alternative?" *Evaluation and Program Planning,* 18: 77–87.

Seidman, Larry J. 1997. "Neuropsychological Testing." Pp. 498–508 in *Psychiatry, Volume 1,* edited by Allan Tasman, Jerald Kay, and Jeffrey Lieberman. Philadelphia: W. B. Saunders.

Seligman, Martin E. P. 1975. *Helplessness.* San Francisco: W. H. Freeman.

Sexton, Joe. 1994. "A Fatal Spiral to the Street: For Winter's First Exposure Victim, a Swift, Brutal Decline." *The New York Times,* January 2, pp. 19, 21.

Shadish, William R. 1995. "Philosophy of Science and the Quantitative-Qualitative Debates: Thirteen Common Errors." *Evaluation and Program Planning,* 18: 63–75.

Shepherd, Jane, David Hill, Joel Bristor, and Pat Montalvan. 1996. "Converting an Ongoing Health Study to CAPI: Findings from the National Health and Nutrition Study." Pp. 159–164 in *Health Survey Research Methods Conference Proceedings,* edited by Richard B. Warnecke. Hyattsville, MD: U.S. Department of Health and Human Services.

Sherman, Lawrence W. 1992. *Policing Domestic Violence: Experiments and Dilemmas.* New York: Free Press.

Sherman, Lawrence W. 1993. "Implications of a Failure to Read the Literature." *American Sociological Review,* 58: 888–889.

Sherman, Lawrence W. and Richard A. Berk. 1984. "The Specific Deterrent Effects of Arrest for Domestic Assault." *American Sociological Review,* 49: 261–272.

Sherman, Lawrence W. and Ellen G. Cohn. 1989. "The Impact of Research on Legal Policy: The Minneapolis Domestic Violence Experiment." *Law and Society Review,* 23: 117–144.

Sherman, Lawrence W. and Douglas A. Smith, with Janell D. Schmidt and Dennis P. Rogan. 1992. "Crime, Punishment, and Stake in Conformity." *American Sociological Review,* 57: 680–690.

Simon, Rita J. and Sandra Baxter. 1989. "Gender and Violent Crime." Pp. 171–197 in *Violent Crime, Violent Criminals,* edited by Neil Alan Weiner and Marvin E. Wolfgang. Newbury Park, CA: Sage.

Sjoberg, Gideon (Ed.). 1967. *Ethics, Politics, and Social Research.* Cambridge, MA: Schenkman.

Sjoberg, Gideon and Roger Nett. 1968. *A Methodology for Social Research.* New York: Harper & Row.

Skinner, Harvey A. and Wen-Jenn Sheu. 1982. "Reliability of Alcohol Use Indices: The Lifetime Drinking History and the MAST." *Journal of Studies on Alcohol,* 43(11): 1157–1170.

Skocpol, Theda. 1984. "Emerging Agendas and Recurrent Strategies in Historical Sociology." Pp. 356–391 in *Vision and Method in Historical Sociology,* edited by Theda Skocpol. New York: Cambridge University Press.

Smith, Tom W. 1984. "Nonattitudes: A Review and Evaluation." Pp. 215–255 in *Surveying Subjective Phenomena,* vol. 2, edited by Charles F. Turner and Elizabeth Martin. New York: Russell Sage Foundation.

Snow, David A. and Leon Anderson. 1987. "Identity Work Among the Homeless: The Verbal Construction and Avowal of Personal Identities." *American Journal of Sociology,* 92 (May): 1336–1371.

Sobell, Linda C., Mark B. Sobell, Diane M. Riley, Reinhard Schuller, D. Sigfrido Pavan, Anthony Cancilla, Felix Klajner, and Gloria I. Leo. 1988. "The Reliability of Alcohol Abusers' Self-Reports of Drinking and Life Events that Occurred in the Distant Past." *Journal of Studies on Alcohol,* 49(2): 225–232.

Sociological Abstracts, Inc. 1987. *Sociological Abstracts.* San Diego, CA: Sociological Abstracts, Inc.

Sosin, Michael R., Paul Colson, and Susan Grossman. 1988. *Homelessness in Chicago: Poverty and Pathology, Social Institutions and Social Change.* Chicago: Chicago Community Trust.

South, Scott J. and Glenna Spitze. 1994. "Housework in Marital and Nonmarital Households." *American Sociological Review,* 59: 327–347.

Specter, Michael. 1994. "Census-Takers Come Calling and Get a Scolding." *The New York Times*, March 3, p. A4.

Stake, Robert E. 1995. *The Art of Case Study Research.* Thousand Oaks, CA: Sage.

Stewart, David W. 1984. *Secondary Research: Information Sources and Methods.* Thousand Oaks, CA: Sage.

Stone, P. J., D. C. Dunphy, M. S. Smith, and D. M. Ogilvie. 1966. *The General Inquirer: A Computer Approach to Content Analysis.* Cambridge, MA: MIT Press.

Stout, David. 1997a. "Officials Are Starting Early in Their Defense of the 2000 Census." *The New York Times*, March 23, p. 37.

Stout, David. 1997b. "Senate Panel Opposes Use of Sampling in Next Census." *The New York Times*, May 4, p. 31.

Strunk, William, Jr., and E. B. White. 1979. *The Elements of Style*, 3rd ed. New York: Macmillan.

Sudman, Seymour. 1976. *Applied Sampling.* New York: Academic Press.

"Survey on Adultery: 'I Do' Means 'I Don't.' " 1993. *The New York Times*, October 19, p. A20.

Survey Research Laboratory. 1990. *Work, Family, and the Sense of Control.* Unpublished questionnaire. Urbana: University of Illinois. August.

Survey Research Laboratory. 1990. *SRL Study 688: Work, Family, and the Sense of Control. Interviewer Instructions.* Unpublished. Urbana: University of Illinois.

Swarns, Rachel L. 1996. "Moscow Sends Homeless to Faraway Hometowns." *The New York Times*, October 15, pp. A1, A12.

Tarnas, Richard. 1991. *The Passion of the Western Mind: Understanding the Ideas that Have Shaped Our World View.* New York: Ballantine.

Tetlock, Philip E. and Aaron Belkin. 1996. "Counterfactual Thought Experiments in World Politics: Logical, Methodological, and Psychological Perspectives." Pp. 3–38 in *Counterfactual Thought Experiments in World Politics: Logical, Methodological, and Psychological Perspectives*, edited by Philip E. Tetlock and Aaron Belkin. Princeton, NJ: Princeton University Press.

Thorne, Barrie. 1993. *Gender Play: Girls and Boys in School.* New Brunswick, NJ: Rutgers University Press.

Timmer, Doug A., D. Stanley Eitzen, and Kathryn D. Talley. 1993. *Paths to Homelessness: Extreme Poverty and the Urban Housing Crisis.* Boulder, CO: Westview Press.

Tobler, Nancy S. 1986. "Meta-Analysis of 143 Adolescent Drug Prevention Programs: Quantitative Outcome Results of Program Participants Compared to a Control or Comparison Group." *The Journal of Drug Issues*, 16 (4): 537–567.

Toby, Jackson. 1957. "Social Disorganization and Stake in Conformity: Complementary Factors in the Predatory Behavior of Hoodlums." *Journal of Criminal Law, Criminology and Police Science*, 48: 12–17.

Tufte, Edward R. 1983. *The Visual Display of Quantitative Information.* Cheshire, CT: Graphics Press.

Turabian, Kate L. 1967. *A Manual for Writers of Term Papers, Theses, and Dissertations*, 3rd ed., rev. Chicago: University of Chicago Press.

Turner, Charles F. and Elizabeth Martin (Eds.). 1984. *Surveying Subjective Phenomena*, vols. I & II. New York: Russell Sage Foundation.

Udry, J. Richard. 1988. "Biological Predispositions and Social Control in Adolescent Sexual Behavior." *American Sociological Review*, 53: 709–722.

U.S. Bureau of the Census. 1994. *Census Catalog and Guide, 1994.* Washington, DC: Department of Commerce, Bureau of the Census.

U.S. Bureau of the Census. 1996. *Census Catalog and Guide, 1996.* Washington, DC: Department of Commerce, Bureau of the Census.

U.S. Bureau of Labor Statistics, Department of Labor. 1991. *Major Programs of the Bureau of Labor Statistics.* Washington, DC: U.S. Bureau of Labor Statistics, Department of Labor.

U.S. Bureau of Labor Statistics, Department of Labor. 1997a. *Employment and Earnings.* Washington, DC: U.S. Bureau of Labor Statistics, Department of Labor.

U.S. Bureau of Labor Statistics, Department of Labor. 1997b. *Handbook of Methods.* Washington, DC: U.S. Bureau of Labor Statistics, Department of Labor.

U.S. Department of Health, Education, and Welfare. 1976. *The Measure of Poverty.* Washington, DC: U.S. Department of Health, Education, and Welfare.

U.S. Department of Health and Human Services, Substance Abuse and Mental Health Services Administration, Center for Mental Health Services. 1995, May. *Client-Level Evaluation Procedure Manual.* Washington DC: U.S. Department of Health and Human Services.

Vaessen, Martin. 1993. "Evaluation of Population Data: Errors and Deficiencies." Pp. 4-1–4-69 in *Readings in Population Research Methodology. Volume 1, Basic Tools*, edited by Donald J. Bogue, Eduardo E. Arriaga, and Douglas L. Anderton. Chicago: Social Development Center, for the United National Population Fund.

Vaillant, George E. 1995. *The Natural History of Alcoholism Revisited.* Cambridge, MA: Harvard University Press.

Valenzuela, Arturo. 1990. "Chile: Origins, Consolidation, and Breakdown of a Democratic Regime." Pp. 38–86 in *Politics in Developing Countries: Comparing Experiences with Democracy*, edited by Larry Diamond, Juan J. Linz, and Seymour Martin Lipset. Boulder, CO: Lynne Rienner Publishers.

Van Maanen, John. 1982. "Fieldwork on the Beat." Pp. 103–151 in *Varieties of Qualitative Research*, edited by

John Van Maanen, James M. Dabbs, Jr., and Robert R. Faulkner. Beverly Hills: Sage.

Verba, Sidney and Norman Nie. 1972. *Political Participation: Political Democracy and Social Equality.* New York: Harper & Row.

Verba, Sidney, Norman Nie, and Jae-On Kim. 1978. *Participation and Political Equality: A Seven-Nation Comparison.* New York: Cambridge University Press.

Vernez, Georges, M. Audrey Burnam, Elizabeth A. McGlynn, Sally Trude, and Brian S. Mittman. 1988. *Review of California's Program for the Homeless Mentally Disabled.* Santa Monica, CA: RAND.

Vidich, Arthur J. and Stanford M. Lyman. 1994. "Qualitative Methods: Their History in Sociology and Anthropology." Pp. 23–59 in *Handbook of Qualitative Research,* edited by Norman K. Denzin and Yvonna S. Lincoln. Thousand Oaks, CA: Sage.

Wallace, Walter L. 1971. *The Logic of Science in Sociology.* Chicago: Aldine.

Wallace, Walter L. 1983. *Principles of Scientific Sociology.* New York: Aldine.

Walters, Pamela Barnhouse, David R. James, and Holly J. McCammon. 1997. "Citizenship and Public Schools: Accounting for Racial Inequality in Education for the Pre- and Post-Disfranchisement South." *American Sociological Review,* 62:34–52.

Watson, Charles G., Curt Tilleskjor, E. A. Hoodecheck-Schow, John Pucel, and Lyle Jacobs. 1984. "Do Alcoholics Give Valid Self-Reports?" *Journal of Studies on Alcohol,* 45(4): 344–348.

Watson, Roy E. L. 1986. "The Effectiveness of Increased Police Enforcement as a General Deterrent." *Law and Society Review,* 20 (2): 293–299.

Weatherby, Norman L., Richard Needle, Helen Cesari, Robert Booth, Clyde B. McCoy, John K. Waters, Mark Williams, and Dale D. Chitwood. 1994. "Validity of Self-Reported Drug Use Among Injection Drug Users and Crack Cocaine Users Recruited Through Street Outreach." *Evaluation and Program Planning,* 17(4): 347–355.

Webb, Eugene, Donald T. Campbell, Richard D. Schwartz, and Lee Sechrest. 1966. *Unobtrusive Measures: Nonreactive Research in the Social Sciences.* Chicago: Rand McNally.

Weber, Max. 1947. *The Theory of Social and Economic Organization.* Translated by A. M. Henderson and Talcott Parsons. New York: Free Press.

Weber, Max. 1949. *The Methodology of the Social Sciences.* Translated and edited by Edward A. Shils and Henry A. Finch. New York: Free Press.

Weber, Robert Philip. 1985. *Basic Content Analysis.* Thousand Oaks, CA: Sage.

Wechsler, Henry, Andrea Davenport, George Dowdall, Barbara Moeykens, and Sonia Castillo. 1994. "Health and Behavioral Consequences of Binge Drinking in College: A National Survey of Students at 140 Campuses." *JAMA: The Journal of the American Medical Association,* 272(21): 1672–1677.

Wells, L. Edward and Joseph H. Rankin. 1991. "Families and Delinquency: A Meta-Analysis of the Impact of Broken Homes." *Social Problems,* 38 (February): 71–93.

Wheeler, Peter M. 1995. *Social Security Programs Throughout the World —1995.* Research Report #64, SSA Publication No. 13-11805. Washington, DC: Office of Research and Statistics, Social Security Administration.

Wheeler, Peter M. 1996. *Income of the Aged Chartbook, 1994.* Washington, DC: Office of Research, Evaluation, and Statistics, Social Security Administration.

White, Michael J. 1993. "Measurement of Population Size, Composition, and Distribution." Pp. 1-1–1-29 in *Readings in Population Research Methodology. Volume 1, Basic Tools,* edited by Donald J. Bogue, Eduardo E. Arriaga, and Douglas L. Anderton. Chicago: Social Development Center, for the United National Population Fund.

Whyte, William Foote. 1955. *Street Corner Society.* Chicago: University of Chicago Press.

Whyte, William Foote. 1991. *Social Theory for Social Action: How Individuals and Organizations Learn to Change.* Newbury Park, CA: Sage.

Wickham-Crowley, Timothy P. 1992. *Guerrillas and Revolution in Latin America: A Comparative Study of Insurgents and Regimes Since 1956.* Princeton, NJ: Princeton University Press.

Wilson, William Julius. 1987. *The Truly Disadvantaged: The Inner City, the Underclass, and Public Policy.* Chicago: University of Chicago Press.

Wolcott, Harry F. 1995. *The Art of Fieldwork.* Walnut Creek, CA: AltaMira Press.

Wright, James D. and Eleanor Weber. 1987. *Homelessness and Health.* New York: McGraw-Hill.

Wunsch, Guillaume J. and Marc G. Termote. 1978. *Introduction to Demographic Analysis: Principles and Methods.* New York: Plenum Press.

Zaret, David. 1996. "Petitions and the 'Invention' of Public Opinion in the English Revolution." *American Journal of Sociology,* 101: 1497–1555.

Zarozny, Sharon (Ed.). 1987. *The Federal Database Finder: A Directory of Free and Fee-Based Databases and Files Available from the Federal Government,* 2d ed. Chevy Chase, MD: Information US.

Glossary/Index

Tacit knowledge In field research, a credible sense of understanding of social processes that reflects the researcher's awareness of participants' actions as well as their words, and of what they fail to state, feel deeply, and take for granted, 317

Tactical research Research, sponsored by a client, that must yield findings that improve the market for a product or increase the acceptance of a policy, 464–465

Talley, Kathryn, 129

Target population A set of elements larger than or different from the population sampled and to which the researcher would like to generalize study findings, 110

Taylor, Charles, 351

Temporal A feature of narrative explanation, taking into account a related series of events that unfold over time, 335

Test-retest reliability A measurement showing that measures of a phenomenon at two points in time are highly correlated, if the phenomenon has not changed, or have changed only as much as the phenomenon itself, 87, 208

Theoretical perspectives on research design, 391–395

Theoretical sampling A sampling method recommended for field researchers by Glaser and Strauss (1967). A theoretical sample is drawn in a sequential fashion, with settings or individuals selected for study as earlier observations or interviews indicate that these settings or individuals are influential, 296–297

Theory A logically interrelated set of propositions about empirical reality
conflict, 35

described, 35
links between data and, 39
on Minneapolis Domestic Violence Experiment, 44
as part of research circle, 40
structural functionalism, 35, 395
See also Social theories

Thesis, 463–464
Thesis committee, 463–464
Thomas, Rodney W., 491
Thompson, James W., 486
Thorne, Barrie, 286–287, 295–296, 298, 312–313, 318, 319, 495

Time order A criterion for establishing a nomothetic causal relation between two variables; the variation (the dependent variable) indicating its effect
described, 155
identifying nomothetic cause and, 197
research designs to determine, 170–177

Time series design A quasi-experimental design consisting of many pretest and posttest observations of the same group, 202

Timmer, Doug, 129
Tipton, Steven, 304, 306–307
Tolomiczenko, George S., 486
Trajectory, 333
"Transactive memory," 195
Treating substance abuse case study, 448–454

Treatment The manipulation that exposes subjects in an experiment to a particular value of the independent variable, 188

Treatment misidentification A problem that occurs in an experiment when variation in the independent variable (the treatment) results in the observed outcome variation, but through an intervening process that the researcher has not identified, 206, 211–213

Trend study. *See* **Repeated cross-sectional design**

Triangulation The use of multiple methods to study one research question, 382–387

Trow, Martin, 489

Trude, Sally, 471

True experiment Experiment in which subjects are assigned randomly to an experimental group that receives a treatment or other manipulation of the independent variable and a comparison group that does not receive the treatment or receives some other manipulation. Outcomes are measured in a posttest
causality in, 197–198
control over conditions in, 196
critical social research roles of, 223
described, 187–188
experimental/comparison groups and, 188–190
identification of causal mechanism in, 194–196
pretest and posttest measures in, 190
randomization in, 190–194

True value of a statistic. *See* **Population parameter**

Truman, Harry S, 119
Trust, 294
Turabian, Kate L., 469
Turner, Charles, 249
Turner, Winston M., 486

Udry, J. Richard, 388
UnCover database, 502–505
Uncritical agreement with authority, 9
Ungrouped/grouped age distributions, 415

Unimodal A distribution of a variable in which there is only one value that is most frequent, 417

Union Democracy (Lipset, Trow, and Coleman), 169, 489
Union Literature Coding Form, 358–359

Units of analysis The level of social life on which a research question is focused, such as individuals, 176–180, 348

Units of observation The cases about which measures actually are obtained in a sample, 178

Univariate distributions
displaying, 406–415

Credits

Exhibit 12.3, from Edward Brent and Alan Thompson. 1996. *Methodologist's Tool-chest™ for Windows: User's Guide and Reference Manual.* Columbia, MO: Idea Works, pp. 3-8, 6-9, 6-10, 6-12, 6-14.

Exhibit 12.4, Egon G. Guba and Yvonna S. Lincoln. 1989. *Fourth Generation Evaluation,* p. 152. Copyright © 1989 by Sage Publications, Inc., Thousand Oaks, CA.

Exhibit 12.5, Robert H. Aseltine, Jr. and Ronald C. Kessler. 1993. "Marital Disruption and Depression in a Community Sample." *Journal of Health and Social Behavior,* 34 (September): 237–251.

Exhibit 12.6, Georges M. Vernez, Audrey Burnam, Elizabeth A. McGlynn, Sally Trude, and Brian S. Mittman, 1988. *Review of California's Program for the Homeless Mentally Disabled.* Santa Monica, CA: RAND, R-3631-CDMH.

Exhibit 12.9, Wornie L. Reed, Jodi Nudelman, Robert W. Adams, Jane Dockery, Nicol Nealeigh, and Rodney W. Thomas. 1997. *Infant Immunization Coverage Cluster Survey,* p. 19. Cleveland: Urban Child Research Center, Cleveland State University.

Exhibit B.1, from *Sociological Abstracts.* Copyright © 1993 Sociological Abstracts, Inc. All rights reserved.

Exhibit B.2, from *Sociological Abstracts.* Copyright © 1998 Sociological Abstracts, Inc. All rights reserved.

Exhibit B.3, from UnCover by the UnCover Company, Denver, CO.

Exhibit B.5 and *Exhibit B.6,* from Infoseek. Reprinted by permission. Infoseek and the Infoseek logo are trademarks of Infoseek Corporation which may be registered in certain jurisdictions. Other trademarks shown are trademarks of their respective owners. Copyright © 1994–1998 Infoseek Corporation. All rights reserved.